MOTION PICTURE PRODUCTION

IN

BRITISH COLUMBIA:

1898 – 1940

A Brief Historical Background and Catalogue

by

Colin Browne

British Columbia Provincial Museum

Heritage Record No. 6

1979

PROVINCE OF BRITISH COLUMBIA

MINISTRY OF THE PROVINCIAL SECRETARY AND GOVERNMENT SERVICES

Provincial Secretary

Published by the British Columbia Provincial Museum

Victoria

First Printing 1979

Canadian Cataloguing in Publication Data
Browne, Colin, 1946-
    Motion picture production in British Columbia,
1898-1940.

    (British Columbia Provincial Museum heritage
record ; no. 6 ISSN 0701-9556)

    Bibliography: p.
    ISBN 0-7718-8136-3

    1. Moving-pictures - British Columbia - Catalogs.
2. Moving-picture industry - British Columbia - History. I. Title. II. Series: British Columbia Provincial Museum. British Columbia Provincial Museum
heritage record ; no. 6.

PN1993.5.C3B76   010   C79-092045-X

FOREWORD

In this catalogue - the first of its kind in Canada - Colin Browne lists and describes over one thousand movie films made in or about British Columbia up to the time of World War II. Much of his inspiration for preparing this list stemmed from the wide variety of footage he discovered in researching British Columbia history for the British Columbia Provincial Museum, but mostly he was motivated by an urge to make the public aware of the existence, range, and often fragile state of these film materials. Museum curators and others agreed, and encouraged Colin Browne to press his survey as far as he could, though the credit for the massive task and its remarkable results must be given almost solely to him.

Of the two main parts to this publication, the catalogue entries are certain to be of most use to those interested in British Columbia's films. Producers, directors, researchers, writers, distributors, educators, and followers of the art generally cannot be anything but impressed by both the scope of Colin Browne's entries and the work he has done in finding and organizing his information. Like millions of Canadians who grew up believing it was mainly Hollywood where movies were made, it is more than surprising to realize now that countless thousands of films - long or short - were produced elsewhere, including hundreds in British Columbia, not the least of which were as commercially ambitious as many that originated in California. This province was the setting for several feature-length movies, and scores of British Columbians became producers, cameramen, actors, and distributors. Their story is outlined in Browne's lively though scholarly introduction which should be read by anyone seeking to understand the historical context in which early movies were made in British Columbia.

I do not believe it is widely known, for example, that the provincial government was active in the movie field as early as 1908. In that year the Province lent its support to short films aimed at promoting local industry in the hope of attracting settlers and foreign capital. In 1913 the first British Columbia censor was appointed with a mandate to curtail public viewing of films bearing unwanted political messages. Three years later, the federal government began its active participation in making films and otherwise supporting the movie industry. Among its goals was a determination to restrict the flow of American films to Canada, giving preference to British productions instead. Federal film bureaus, and other government agencies, also produced hundreds of short movies on British Columbia subjects, most of which might well have lain forgotten (some perhaps with good reason) had it not been for Colin Browne's research. There are several highly important revelations about film making in and about British Columbia in this book; the activities of government in the field are but one part.

With the publication of this film catalogue, the British Columbia Provincial Museum hopes that research into this highly significant but poorly known and little understood dimension of our social history will be both accelerated and strengthened. It appears that a British Columbia film tradition exists, and it is not unrealistic to believe that Colin Browne's catalogue will stimulate movie makers to build further on that tradition.

Daniel T. Gallacher
Curator of Modern History
British Columbia Provincial Museum

ACKNOWLEDGEMENTS

Much of the work compiling this catalogue was done by others. To the many archivists and researchers who have been before me and who have assisted me, I owe a large debt. Some have become friends, some I know only by signature, and many I will never meet, but together they did the lion's share of the work.

First I must thank the attentive and considerable staffs of both the British Columbia Provincial Library and the Provincial Archives of British Columbia who helped me find some of the skinniest pamphlets and catalogues in their collections, who kept their eyes open for something that might be of interest, and who assisted me in discovering all manner of obscure information I might otherwise never have found. In particular I would like to thank the Director of the Provincial Archives, Mr. Allan Turner, and the staff of Visual Records, Barb McLennan, Shane Mawson, and Jerry Davison, who made my long hours in the back corner pass quickly and happily.

At the British Columbia Provincial Museum the staffs of the Education and Extension Division, the Ethnology Division, and the Modern History Division gave freely of their time and knowledge and their sincere interest spurred me on. I received a great deal of encouragement from the Modern History Division where, in many ways, this project began. I would like to recognize the involvement of Dan Gallacher, Jim Wardrop, Monty Wright and Robin Patterson who never once told me I was phoning up with silly questions even though I was. As well, I would like to thank Harold Hosford for being such a patient editor, Chris Hall for her equally patient efforts in typing the final reproductions, and, finally, the Museum itself for undertaking the publication of this catalogue.

At the National Film Archives in Ottawa I am especially indebted to Director Sam Kula, Bill Galloway, Ken Larose, Jana Vosikovska, Micheline Morisset, J. Guenette, and particularly to D. John Turner who kept my trembling finger on the pulse. Joan Honeywell at the National Library in Ottawa was especially helpful in ferreting out the right documents. At the Department of Trade and Commerce I was given free access to the early files by Miss Mary O. Hill who also permitted me the opportunity to read the relevant chapters of her forthcoming history of the department.

In Montreal, Mr. Clyde Owen and his staff at the National Film Board Archives were both helpful and generous with their time and resources. And, in Toronto, I had the great pleasure of meeting and sharing an afternoon with both Jack Chisholm and Mary diTursi, who not only left no stone unturned in their excellent collection, but took time out to reminisce about the early days as well.

I owe a debt of thanks to Bill Murphy and Riley Sever at the United States National Archives in Washington, D.C., who made me feel very welcome, and to Paul Spehr, David Parker, and Patrick Sheehan at the Library of Congress without whose help a great deal of the early material contained herein would be missing. I cannot neglect to mention the work done by Eileen Bowser and Jon Gartenberg on my behalf at the Museum of Modern Art in New York, and the help I received from Elizabeth R. Albro at the Edison National Historic Site in Orange, New Jersey. I am also grateful to Ott H. Hyatt of the University of Washington Press in Seattle who provided me with information about the ethnographic film holdings in his care.

For the newsreel data I am indebted to Jack Muth and Nick Leary at Fox Movietonews, Dave and Bernard Chertok at Sherman Grinberg Film Libraries and Ted Troll at Hearst Metrotone, all in New York, and to Nancy Casey at Sherman Grinberg's west coast office in Hollywood. In England I was treated with great courtesy and generosity by Pam Turner at Visnews, H. C. Wynder at the Pathé Film Library, Pat Holder and John O'Kelly at the Movietone Film Library, and Elaine Burrows and Jeremy Boulton at the British Film Institute/National Film Archive in London, all of whom went out of their way to help me.

A great many others have contributed to the catalogue: Barbara Davies at the British Columbia Forest Service Photo Branch in Victoria; Mrs. Lorinda Daniels, who especially collated and interpreted the information about films in the University of British Columbia's Special Collections Library; Carole Harmon, who provided some clues about her grandfather Byron Harmon's activities in the Rockies during the first decades of this century; Ainslie Helmcken, City Archivist of Victoria and raconteur; E.G.W. Henn, who dug around in his marvellous basement for me; Greg Lowry, at the moviola console; Muriel Mixon at the Victoria Press Library; and all the private holders of motion picture film who took the time to write to me and invite me to their homes as if I was an old friend. I would especially like to thank Gordon Sparling, a pioneer of Canadian film-making whose long letters are a delight to read and whose contribution to all facets of this catalogue can only truly be assessed by those who know how much has been lost over the years. Mr. Sparling's keen memory has filled in so many gaping holes in the fabric that one may now wonder that it was ever torn.

Much specific information about film making in the early days is not included in the catalogue because there is not enough space. I learned most of it from the pioneers themselves. This catalogue is dedicated to those men who gave up a few minutes or hours to talk with a green young man about their adventures: Ivan Ackery, Alfred Booth, Ross Beesley, Don Carley, Stanley Carr, Dick Colby, Earl Dagliesh, Verne Edwards, Eduard Feuz, Howard Fletcher, Wally Hamilton, Mike Heppell, Martin Kroeger, Phil LeMare, Lew Parry, Russ Simpson, Gordon Sparling, Gerry Wellburn, and many others who left us such a rich legacy.

This project would have been impossible without the generous support of the Canada Council Explorations Programme, and the interest which they evinced in each stage of its progress. I would also like to thank those who so kindly put their faith in me and acted as referees: Bob Broadland, C.H. "Punch" Dickens (who also identified aircraft for me in the 1930 Trans Canada Air Pageant), Dan Gallacher, Ainslie Helmcken, Sam Kula, Dorothy Metcalfe, Allan Turner and Ken Williams. I am happy, too, to acknowledge Aisjah Lee's open-ended loan of film viewing and editing equipment, without which my job might have been much more difficult. Finally, for their support and uncompromising friendship I will always be grateful to Kateri and Karol Wenek who gave me succor in Ottawa, and to Ina and Karl Spreitz who never once thought I couldn't do it.

Colin Browne

CONTENTS

HISTORICAL BACKGROUND 1

    Illustrations 33

    Notes to Historical Background 64

    Bibliography 74

CATALOGUE 79

    How To Use This Catalogue 79

    Notes On Locating Film 79

    Addresses 80

    Abbreviations 81

    Catalogue Entries 83

    Index 348

HISTORICAL BACKGROUND

BEGINNINGS   In 1868, when Barkerville burned to the ground, Frederick Dally was there
with his camera to record the event and become British Columbia's first news photographer.
When the Canadian Pacific Railway (CPR) arrived twenty years later to establish a Pacific
terminus at Burrard Inlet, streetcar lines, telephone poles, and electric lights were
being installed as the trees were felled. Vancouver was an instant city. And cameras
were there from the beginning, documenting everything from oxen yarding timber, to the
construction of the first Hotel Vancouver on Granville Street.[1]

The city was only twelve years old when, in 1898, John Schuberg set up a projector in an
empty store on Cordova Street, near Cambie, to show what purported to be newsreels of
the Spanish-American War, most of which were faked in New Jersey by the enterprising
Edison Manufacturing Company. Four years later Schuberg established the first permanent
movie theatre in Vancouver, the Electric, also on Cordova. This was the first successful
movie house in Canada.[2]

The first movies to reach Victoria were shown in March 1897 at the Trilby Music Hall on
Broad Street. Less than two weeks after Bob Fitzsimmons pummelled Jim Corbett to the
mat in the fourteenth round of a grisly boxing match in Carson City, Nevada, Victorians
were thrilling to every moment of the action on film. The film of the Corbett-Fitz-
simmons fight eventually grossed three-quarters of a million dollars for the Rector's
Veriscope Company, and was so successful that it inspired a fraudulent recreation.[3]

Within two years, British Columbia itself was featured in the movies when an unknown
cameraman in Vancouver filmed horses boarding a steamship for the Klondike. The gold
rush was a big hit for the Edison Company which rushed one of its cameramen, Robert K.
Bonine, north for the event.[4] As a result, thousands of armchair miners panned their
gold in black tents and storefronts across North America and Europe unhampered by hard
work and frostbite. With luck a theatre patron of the day might even enjoy the illusion
of hurtling through the precipitous Fraser Canyon on the cowcatcher of a locomotive
enroute to the gold fields via the CPR, a favourite film subject at the turn of the century. All one needed was the price of admission - five cents - and the world appeared to
be one's oyster.

AUDIENCES   Motion pictures, which got their start as novelties in peep-show machines or
as travelling shows exhibited from town to town in black tents, quickly moved onto the
screen as supplements to the daily fare in vaudeville theatres across North America.
According to Maynard F. Macdonald, Victoria's first projectionist, the Searchlight
Theatre on Fort Street, built by Jim McConahy in 1899, was Victoria's first movie house

(See page 64 for enumerated notes)

to succeed in an established location. McConahy combined vaudeville with moving pictures of fire engines, trains, and other action shots, and was only forced to suspend operations when his selection of films was finally exhausted.

Inspired by McConahy's success, a cook at the Maryland Cafe in Victoria named Alexander Pantages established his own theatre, the Orpheum. Pantages combined vaudeville with movies, but his naive business practices prevented him from making money despite successful ticket sales. After three of four months of operation, an accident at the Orpheum involving one of the patrons forced him to close the theatre. Pantages' enthusiasm remained undiminished, however, and he moved his operation to Seattle, founding the Crystal Palace on Second Avenue. This theatre eventually grew into the impressive Pantages chain of vaudeville houses across the United States and Canada, and Pantages himself became one of the celebrated showbusiness entrepreneurs of the early twentieth century.[5]

As accommodating as vaudeville had been to the new form, however, the silver screen soon proved to be a ruthless competitor. Despite their obvious awkwardness, the first movies were popular and profitable, regardless of the fact that they rarely told a story or lasted more than one or two minutes. Even when films did begin to develop a dramatic line they remained patently thespian for years. Nonetheless, vaudeville quickly succumbed to the lure of new medium. Movies were able to provide the best talent and the greatest spectacles for the same price as live theatre. Audiences became more sophisticated and demanded better quality and more lavish productions. This in turn pushed the movie studios toward innovations they had never dreamed of. Actors gravitated to Hollywood and when the public wanted to know their names the star system was born. Movies centralized North American, in fact, planetary entertainment.[6]

FRONTIER MOVIE HOUSES   No place on earth seemed too small to receive the best entertainment America could provide. Enterprising businessmen in British Columbia acknowledged the amazing portability of the movies by losing no time in transporting a projector and several reels to the remotest, most lucrative, corners of the province. In his book _Moving Pictures, How They Are Made and Worked_, F.A. Talbot, a British popular science writer, tells of an encounter with one of these entrepreneurs on the banks of the Skeena River about 1909 or 1910:

> A cinematograph showman arrived in Hazelton, which at that time boasted a handful of white men, and several Indians. The operator took over an excavation on the side of a hill overlooking the town, which had been used for storing various goods, but which at that time was empty. In this cramped, unventilated cellar he rigged his screen and lantern. On the wooden door he nailed a large sheet of paper, on which was scrawled the name of the "theatre" and the programme of films now being shown.
>
> The preparations demanded only a few hours. Boxes, barrels, and logs sufficed for seats, while a good many patrons sat or sprawled upon the earthen floor. The little vault was packed to suffocation on the opening night. The Indians were amazed and whites were amused, though the films would not have been tolerated in London or New York, having long since passed their span of usefulness. The show was kept going day after day until the audience became too small to

defray the cost of the illuminant, when the "theatre" was closed, and the show-
man haunted the verandah of the hotel until he received some new subjects. His
supply of films was both uncertain and irregular. He had to order them by post
from Vancouver, whence they were brought up by boat. If the fates were kind he
received an entire change of programme in about a fortnight; if the river were
difficult to navigate, a month passed before they reached him, and often the boat
came up without his goods, owing to lack of space .... It was doubtful if he
would secure any films at all during the winter, as, the river being frozen,
communication between Hazelton and Prince Rupert had to be maintained by dog
trains, which carried letter-mail only.[7]

In fact, the *Hazelton Picture Palace* would have been a particularly impractical place to
exhibit movies during the winter considering the need for a place to store vegetables and
root crops during the cold weather. Talbot's personal reaction to the show, however,
must have been identical to that of most of the lonely men who paid their dime to be
transported elsewhere. In his words, he "saw it after being immured for several weeks
in the primeval bush; and though the pictures in the cellar danced and flickered on the
screen, they seemed to me like a welcome handshake with the great world".

It should be remembered, at this point, that no matter how critical or important the
arrival of the movies was to wilderness communities, British Columbia, in the eyes of
the great studios that soon came to control distribution, was no more important than
anywhere else; it was just another temperamental box-office. Movies, like all subsequent electronic media, are essentially a one-way street. Moreover, whenever motion
pictures were actually made in British Columbia they were almost always filmed by out-
siders and processed elsewhere, returning as finished products that interpreted the
province through either eastern Canadian or American or British eyes. In a sense this
was cultural colonization, but it is important to recall that there were fewer than
525,000 people living in British Columbia by 1921 and that more than ninety-five per
cent of these were not native born.[8] Nothing probably seemed more natural to these
people, at the far edge of the civilized world, than this reinforcement of their original preconceptions of the land of their choice.

EARLY PROMOTIONAL FILMS   While it would be pretentious therefore to find artistic
achievement in British Columbia's early films, there is merit in studying those that
remain since they provide insights into how our forefathers chose to present themselves
for posterity. A camera is highly selective, both in aiming and editing. It often shows
us less how we really are than how we want others to think we are. Much of the joy of
these early motion pictures is that they help us to understand the imagination of the
past. Swaggering, grinning, freezing, mugging -- all these pierce the armour and touch
the heart. Most early film is interesting because it deals with ordinary people, sometimes doing extraordinary things it is true, but usually attending to their daily business, enjoying themselves at a picnic, boarding an ocean liner, riding in a Model "T",
marching off to war, working at the bole of a spar tree, or along the bottom of a strawberry field. Whatever the original motive for making the film, it is the people in it
that tend to attract our attention most and stir our imaginations today.

Most of the early motion picture production in British Columbia was promotional or "educational", dealing with the province's industries and the technologies that made them possible. The world was fascinated by giant trees and mountains, and by the dark, steaming coastline where swart men in dugout double-enders hauled millions of salmon into their holds every year. Loggers and fishermen became titans in the public imagination, men who braved danger and hardship to provide a tiny can of pink salmon for our tables or the lumber used to frame our greenhouses. Descriptions of films in the first film catalogues refer to the trees as mighty "monarchs of the forest" and to their falling as an almost mystical rite, pitting industrial David against the Goliaths of nature. Forests were "conquered" in those days, "stripped" and carved-up by men proud to be part of "industry's endless war in the forests".[9] In truth, film descriptions in early catalogues were specifically designed to sell prints (films were not rented to theatres in the early days), and were always more exciting than the events they misrepresented.

Movies have always tended to be a hard-sell business, depending for their success on a greater degree of technical sophistication than their audiences possessed. Hand-cranked cameras, so heavy and cumbersome that they had to be bolted into a fixed position, both required, and suffered from, the producers' literary thirst for embellishment. Each new film about logging or fishing was made to portray greater struggle and present a greater triumph than its predecessors. If it did not, it would fail to attract an audience hungry for thrills. Perhaps the real illusion of the early "flicks" was the fusion between the memory of the promotional literature and the viewer's reaction to the film itself. Even today, trailers are seldom equalled by the pictures they represent, and advertisements have had to become parodies of themselves. Movies have always been, and probably always will be, show business first.[10]

TRAVELOGUE AND EDUCATIONAL FILMS   British Columbia, because of its scenery, was a favourite haunt for cinematographers in the early years. The province was a natural for travelogues. Apparently all one had to do was journey to Banff on the CPR, film in the Rockies for a week or so, and, with luck, obtain enough footage for a good scenic short, replete with wildlife, mountains, alpine lakes, titanic glaciers, and attractive young women hikers. Films of this type were popular during the 1920's and 1930's; dozens were made by professionals and amateurs alike.[11] In the meantime, if anything newsworthy came up, the photographer could run-off a hundred feet of film spiced with a few cute or sentimental captions and send it to a newsreel company in Montreal or New York, thus receiving money to pay at least some of the costs. Because the news was always a week late, and because newsreels tended to avoid anything controversial, there was always a market for the believe-it-or-not story, or the one about the family of ducklings brought up by a dog. A sure bet would be an all-girl ski class, as long as it was modest enough to pass the censor.[12]

It is not cynical to suggest that the formula for making a living as a filmaker in British

4

Columbia has not radically changed since the 1920's. Travelogues and educational films of the genre that have been putting students to sleep or at best into neutral for more than sixty years are still the main fare in schools and community centres, due largely to the funding sources available. The original trend of confusing "educational" films with pedantic, colourless statistics was the direct result of trying to convince sceptical authorities that the new medium was "good for you" and, if used "properly", need not promote vice and sin among weak-minded citizens. These long-winded, lifeless, "educational" films, designed to woo tough school boards, may have driven more young people to crime or desperation than they ever deterred. Their versions of the world were uniformly uninteresting. Today, however, these films are fascinating because they reveal to us some of what our towns, our jobs, our grandfathers, (and occasionally our grandmothers), were like.[13]

Usually confused with "educational" films were tourist promotion films, which were equally wooden and which glorified the obvious, glossing over ordinary life. Today, even these are irreplaceable documents. As for sin and vice, no early pornography has been unearthed although British Columbia surely must have had its share of dedicated enthusiasts. Given the style and content of early non-dramatic pictures shot in this province, it is not hard to realize why much of the early material was eventually recognized for the drab propaganda it was and thus discarded. Fortunately some remains for us to enjoy today, albeit not for reasons for which it was intended.

DRAMATIC FILMS As for dramatic pictures, British Columbia could most aptly be described as a "good set" if a stage manager was able to prove that it would cost less to shoot on location than in the studio. Photoplays about British Columbia were almost always instigated and funded outside the province, written according to romantic misconceptions that had little to do with life here, (or anywhere else for that matter) and attended with incredulity by locals who dug into their pockets to swell the coffers of foreign studios. Predictably, stories set in British Columbia were about lumberjacks, Mounties, or the CPR (preferably all three), the interpretation of which most Canadians felt should be treated with more reverence than British or American studios were willing to manifest.[14] Only in a few cases did original Canadian stories evolve into feature films and even these owe more to Hollywood than to British Columbia.[15]

Competition was fierce in the movie business and Hollywood had the skill, the money, the distributors and, more important, the theatres, in its thrall. Under such circumstances, local production never had a chance. Even when the British government, by imposing a quota on British distributors and exhibitors, essentially guaranteed that any film made in the Empire would be exhibited in England, Canada simply became a convenient loophole for American companies in their continuing domination of the market (see pg. 23). By producing cheap B-movies in British Columbia under a Canadian name, American studios were able to fill British theatres in off-hours with enough Empire-made padding to meet this quota and continue running their lucrative first-run hits in the evenings as they always had. The British quota, which by 1936 required that all British theatres exhibit Empire-made films at least twenty per cent of the time, was a compromise that failed from the beginning to legislate for quality. The legislation was in fact changed in 1938, making it almost impossible for Empire-made films to qualify for special status.[16] Why British Columbians essentially bit the hand that Britain extended may be more understandable in view of the province's relations with the movie industry throughout its history. It is a story of foreign domination and the quota legislation, as will be seen, was only one of the beckoning fingers that led to broken dreams.

II

MOVIEMAKER OBJECTIVES AND TECHNIQUES   The first movies made in British Columbia were like the first movies made anywhere; for a few cents they promised the illusion that a viewer, in a dark, smoky room, could duplicate a thrilling experience without leaving his chair -- an important factor for those in the slums and ghettos of the new industrial cities. Hence, news events and exotic journeys to foreign lands were understandably popular. The American Mutoscope and Biograph Company's views of the Rockies, shot in 1899 by Billy Bitzer, were so enthusiastically received that Thomas Edison sent his own camera-man out along the line the following year.[17]

In 1901 Edison released nine "Panoramic View" reels, which showed different stretches of tracks as the train raced around curves, across trestles, and through tunnels providing glimpses of scenery on either side. Occasionally a group of Chinese work-men were surprised around a bluff, fleeing for their lives as the train roared by. In reality there was nothing very panoramic about the views but they had a hypnotic effect on their audiences.[18] The method pioneered by Bitzer, with the full approval of the CPR, was to bolt his camera to a flatcar coupled ahead of the locomotive, which gave the illusion of sitting on the cowcatcher, a favourite method of travelling through the mountains in the early days. Edison's photographers employed the same method, not only in Canada but on all the interesting railways of the world, and early catalogues advertised panoramic railway views ranging from Borneo to California. Unfortunately, Bitzer, who went on to become D.W. Griffith's cameraman and one of the great innovators of the industry, does not remember much about the Panoramic Views in his autobiography. A young man of twenty-six at the time, his only recollection of the trip was that he learned what the hotel manager meant when asked whether or not he would like his hotel room "furnished".[19]

Due in part to the persuasive advertising of the CPR, the Rocky Mountains enjoyed an almost magical reputation in Europe and the United States. The Company itself, always looking for a new promotional angle, was suitably impressed by the publicity value of the new medium and decided to take advantage of its benefits. During the summer of 1899, for example, Winnipeg cinematographer James Freer was hired to shoot scenery along the tracks. These reels went on tour of the United Kingdom the following winter to encourage tourists and immigrants to what was being called the last great west.[20] They were obviously successful enough to warrant a further, heftier investment.

COMMERCIAL SPONSORS   Although details are, for the most part, no longer available, it appears that at some time during 1901 the CPR hired a cinematographer named Joseph Rosenthal, and two assistants, from the Warwick Trading Company of London, to prepare a film series for distribution abroad called *Living Canada*.   In 1903, the Warwick Trading Company, founded by an American named Charles Urban, changed its name to the Charles Urban Trading Company.   The Company's catalogue for that year lists twenty-one reels photographed in British Columbia.   Urban himself was enthusiastic about the possibilities of the motion picture film as an educational medium.   The films made and distributed by his company were mainly travel, natural history, and newsreel films.   One source states that the *Living Canada* reels were originally distributed in the United Kingdom by the CPR and that they were shown in town halls and theatres accompanied by a lecturer who extolled the beauties of the Canadian frontier.   According to the same source, the films took two years to complete because the CPR directed that no snow or ice appear in any of the scenes, any suggestion of which, it was felt, might dissuade rather than attract immigrants.

In fact, two of the films shot by Rosenthal during 1901 and 1902 specifically feature snow and ice, albeit in the depths of the Rocky Mountains along the frozen banks of the Columbia River.   That the novelty of head-on "panoramic" views of the world's railway tracks was wearing thin is evident by the note appended to the advertisement for THROUGH THE BEAVERMOUTH CANYON, SELKIRK MOUNTAINS, DURING A BLIZZARD: "NOTE - This picture and the following one differ from all other railway panoramas ever photographed, as it does not only show the approaching and passing scenery, but shows the entire train with the puffing engine drawing the coaches constantly in view."   Urban's first catalogue listed, not unexpectedly, twelve reels shot along the CPR tracks in British Columbia, all in typically mountainous regions.   The other reels are of salmon fishing on the Fraser River, the canneries at Steveston, logging near Vancouver, milling logs before loading them on ships for export, and the departure of the Canadian Pacific steamship *EMPRESS OF CHINA* for Japan.   These films mark the first time that British Columbia's industries and Vancouver's waterfront were recorded on motion picture film.   Unfortunately not a frame remains.[21]   It is certain that when the *Living Canada* series was shown in Europe it was to the great advantage of both Canada and the CPR.   Perhaps more important was the recognition of motion pictures as a vital and convincing medium for propaganda.

Not surprisingly, the subject matter of British Columbia propaganda has not radically altered from that day to this.   Indeed, few subjects appear to be more durable than the railway and the Rockies.   Panoramic railway footage was popular until World War I ended all such naive pursuits.   In 1907, a cameraman named W.H. Harbeck from the Hales Tourist Association of Portland, Oregon, arrived in Victoria on his way to film a trip up the Fraser Canyon via the CPR.   His intention was to crank backwards while holding his camera steady on the platform of the last carriage, thus creating, when projected normally, the illusion of moving forward. This film was apparently destined to be exhibited in fake railway carriages in Europe and the United States, accompanied by authentic noises and violent rocking to suggest the sensation of travel. Harbeck was responsible also for what may have been the first tourist promotion film ever made in Victoria, photographed prior to his Fraser Canyon trip. Unfortunately none of his work survives.[22]

Charles Urban's cameramen returned to the Rockies soon after Urban helped to develop and market an inexpensive, practical colour process called Kinemacolor. With the assistance of the CPR, (perhaps sponsored by the railway), the Kinemacolor crew, in 1911, travelled from coast to coast shooting scenic views, producing a finished film over 5000 feet long entitled CANADA - NOVA SCOTIA TO BRITISH COLUMBIA. The last reel deals entirely with the Rocky Mountains, concentrating on the Emerald Lake area of British Columbia, and represents the first time the Rockies were impressed onto colour motion picture film. To handle the delicate chemical requirements of Kinemacolor, the CPR provided the cameraman with a private locomotive and a darkroom on wheels for his convenience.

A Kinemacolor cameraman returned to the province in 1913 to film industrial, agricultural, and promotional reels for the provincial government, but the trip in 1911 is remarkable because it marks a shift away from the usual "panoramic" cowcatcher views, extolling instead the beauties of the destination.[23] With rail travel becoming more commonplace and the technology of film becoming more sophisticated, the CPR steered public interest away from the celebration of speed and steam to the pleasures of luxurious, restful holidays. Being there, not getting there, became all the fun. This was an important distinction for a company operating a new string of expensive hotels across a thinly populated wilderness nation.

More significant was a series sponsored by the railway company a year earlier, in 1910, which represents perhaps the most fascinating set of films ever made in this province.

The CPR hired the services of a dramatic troupe from the Edison Manufacturing Company, provided them with a private car for July and August, and asked them to travel across Canada developing fictional shorts which would glorify the new land and the opportunities for love and success it promised. Director J. Searle Dawley, cameraman Henry Cronjager, and six actors, worked out the plots and scripts as they went, inspired and assisted by the location in Alberta and British Columbia they found along the track. More than any other imaginative films made in British Columbia, these melodramatic two-reelers consciously fitted their stories into the landscape rather than cutting up scenery and cramming it into a plot. The locations and the extras were authentic and were used authentically. In fact, from the descriptions and the films that remain, it appears that, more often than not, the landscape actually determined the plot. It is frustrating, then, to contemplate that out of a dozen, or possibly fifteen, stories made by Dawley and Cronjager, only four remain and two of these are more properly regarded as travelogues.

We will never know how many were filmed wholly or partially in British Columbia but surviving shot-lists indicate that at least two of the stories contain locations shot in both Alberta and British Columbia, while another documents a trip from Montreal to Vancouver and beyond. These were romantic tales of love and marriage, danger and loneliness, with happy endings and titles like THE SONG THAT REACHED HIS HEART, THE LITTLE STATION AGENT, THE STOLEN CLAIM, THE UNSELFISH LOVE, and A WEDDING TRIP FROM MONTREAL THROUGH CANADA TO HONG KONG, one of the first comedies ever shot partially in British Columbia. Another was THE SHIP'S HUSBAND, filmed entirely in Victoria, about jealous spouses and a marital mix-up. No record of their exhibition or success exists although some, if not all, were released with Spanish captions and subtitles. It is impossible to determine what effect such films had on immigration for these years of the greatest influx of immigrants into Canada. The message however was loud and clear. Certainly no other company in Canada, or perhaps the world, realized the potential of film in selling its product as quickly and surely as the CPR. Through the years, and with great success, the company wasted no opportunity to depict its package of dreams through the newest dream medium of all.[24]

EARLY GOVERNMENT INVOLVEMENT   The Provincial Government of British Columbia appears to have become actively involved in promoting the province through film as early as 1908. That summer a British cameraman named James Ferens was brought out to record the region's industries and scenic beauty. He filmed scenes at the Hastings Sawmill near Vancouver, the loading of lumber onto ships, street scenes in downtown Vancouver, canning fish on the Fraser River, panoramic views of the Fraser Valley, and the beginnings of the large orchard plantings in the valleys of the Interior. Unfortunately none of this footage survives. Like almost all of the early provincially-funded promotional films, no records were kept and nothing is known today of how they were distributed or exhibited.[25]

Better luck attended some of the film shot for the province by Mr. H. Sintzenich, five years later. In 1913 the provincial government engaged the services of Sintzenich through Urban's Natural Color Kinematograph Company in London, England. He travelled British Columbia for the Department of Lands during September and October of that year, filming extensively in the woods and at sawmills, and documenting ranching and fruit farming in the Okanagan. In Victoria he shot two reels of what probably constitute the first colour travelogues of Victoria ever made. The logging and sawmilling footage that survives is unfortunately not in Kinemacolor because it was excerpted for a later monochromatic compilation called *Kineto Review*, an early British ciné-magazine which featured a wide assortment of national and international items derived from various sources. Kinemacolor, although a doomed novelty, was extremely popular for the first three or four years of its existence (1910-1914). Sintzenich's work was likely the first colour cinematography in the forests, cities, and farms of British Columbia.[26]

EXPERIMENTS WITH COLOUR AND SOUND   Kinemacolor employed a two-colour additive system to both film and project its "Animated Scenes and Moving Objects Bioscoped in the Actual Tints of Nature". Hence it was only capable of reproducing part of the colour spectrum. The resultant flickering hurt the eyes of the viewer, and the filters used to colour the film tended to shade the lens so much that the process of exposing the film was only really successful outside in bright sunlight. This effectively put an end to the use of Kinemacolor as a productive studio film at a time when audiences were spending almost all their money to see melodramas and dramatic films which were photographed almost entirely indoors. For a while, though, all the modern cities in the world, including Vancouver, had at least one Kinemacolor theatre and people flocked to see the new invention as long as it remained a novelty.[27]

The first Kinemacolor pictures were shown in Vancouver at the Opera House in September, 1911, and featured the coronation of King George V, an event that had taken place three months earlier. Almost everyone had seen the black and white version, so the real "news" was Kinemacolor.[28] Vancouver audiences were already accustomed to getting their news soon after it broke. Almost a year earlier, on July 27, 1910, they had had the opportunity to see what was probably the first instant replay in British Columbia. Hundreds of local lacrosse fans crushed into the Edison Theatre in New Westminster to watch their champions defeat the Montreal team in the first Minto Cup series played in western Canada, a game they had watched "live" four days earlier.[29]

But this was nothing compared to the gadget that arrived on the coast less than three years later. Billed as "the final twentieth-century touch", Edison's Kinetophone was unveiled at Victoria's Empress Theatre on May 26, 1913, and Victorians heard the word "talkies" for the first time. The Kinetophone was a one-man peepshow with a non-synchronous phonograph recording transmitted through stethoscopic tubes to the viewer's ears.[30] Needless to say, it was not exactly what the twentieth century was looking for. After a short life, Kinetophone passed into oblivion.

PRE-WAR TRENDS IN COMMERCIAL MOVIEMAKING AND PUBLIC TASTES   There were eight theatres exhibiting motion pictures in Vancouver in 1913 and no one seemed to mind that all the movies were silent. They were full of drama and passion, often very funny, and were accompanied by an organ or a piano which could send shivers up and down the rows of seats at a moment's notice. Mary Pickford and Charlie Chaplin were just beginning their careers and Billy Bitzer was helping his director David Wark Griffith plan one of the great classics of the cinema, *The Birth Of A Nation*. Motion pictures were beginning to recognize and experiment with their own vocabulary, and before long visual and literary artists would be turning to the cinema for structure and inspiration rather than vice versa. So would audiences. It was an exciting, seminal time, for no other medium would have greater influence on the social behaviour of the first half of the twentieth century.

Many British Columbians felt, however, that the motion picture was a medium with too much potential power to be allowed free and random entry into the province, particularly when virtually every film exhibited was a product of the United States. Consequently reformers, legislators, and countless clergymen expressed concern about the purely American vision being stuffed down eager Canadian gullets. They complained, too, about what they imagined to be the results of watching lewd, suggestive performances in dark rooms filled with cigar smoke. In response, and under the direction of attorney-general (later premier) W.J. Bowser, the British Columbia Motion Picture Act was passed in June, 1913, establishing a provincial censor who, in turn, created what quickly came to be known as the most rigid motion picture censorship on the continent.[31]

By October, 1913, regular complaints were being received from the United States regarding rejection of films displaying the Stars and Stripes. And although a compromise was sometimes made by cutting the offensive sections or substituting a Union Jack, rejections were still running between four and five per cent. Two years later the British Columbia Moving Picture Exhibitors Association was seeking public support for a campaign against a Censorship Board that in one sweep had rejected nine of twenty *Mutual Masterpieces* offered for consideration.[32] Despite a commendable desire for less United States propaganda on the screen there was an unwarranted moral superiority about the men and women who sat in judgement and operated on the false assumption that if Britons or Canadians made films they would contain far less violence and sexual innuendo. In the end, it can be argued, if audiences were offended they would not have been flocking to the theatres. The truth is that the provincial censor felt responsible for restricting the number of behaviour models available to the public.

Until very recently, censors have been concerned not only with sex, violence, and naughty words, but also with preventing audiences from watching what they considered to be anti-social behaviour. Eisenstein's films *Battleship Potemkin* and *October* were barred from the province for many years, and any film which treated authority with contempt, even when such contempt was deserved, was rejected. Censorship, more than anything else, was a political tool, especially during the 1930's when traditional belief in the free market economy was severely shaken. Films which suggested such radical solutions as people taking matters into their own hands were banned. Even the newsreels, which purported to tell the truth, were manipulated and tampered with at the provincial level.[33]

The instincts of the powerful, both in government and in commerce, were unerring regarding the potential of motion pictures. Although legislators and business leaders never attended the cinema, they were intuitively aware that motion pictures derived their inspiration from the masses and displayed, from their inception, an open distaste for authority and "culture". No matter how melodramatic, movies appealed to, and were interested solely in, the welfare of the man in the street who paid the price of admission. Movies took up the causes of mistreated children, oppressed workers, impoverished tenants, guiltless prisoners, and innocent soldiers being led to the slaughter. In a way that no other visual art at the time could, motion pictures angrily bared the lives of their audiences. No medium more accurately reflected the unrest and dissatisfaction of the common man and woman with industrial life in the western world on the eve of World War I. It is therefore not surprising that the hands which held the tiaras felt a little uneasy about permitting the new medium free rein over the populace, particularly when the news was so full of anarchists and communists trying to destroy established ways.[34]

RISE OF THE NEWSREEL By September, 1914, "the news" was an established part of every theatre programme. The first regular newsreels were introduced into North America in 1911 and, as early as 1912, one company, Universal Films Ltd., had correspondents, or stringers, in Canada "snapping events" of importance or interest for their *Animated Weekly*. Rather than providing an exciting opportunity for newsreel cameramen to dig out the truth, however, the advent of World War I had the effect of making all of Europe off-limits to the news camera. For the first two years, little <u>real</u> cinematic information about the war was available. Civilian cameramen were forbidden to take their camera to the continent from Britain and if they were caught returning with one it was confiscated. Most of the genuine footage now available was filmed by official military cinematographers, some of whom died in the line of duty when they were mistaken for operators of fearsome new weapons of destruction. Some resourceful companies faked their war news, using smoke bombs, spring-loaded bayonets, bladders full of gunpowder, and paying agricultural workers and villagers to charge each other across the British moors.[35]

In British Columbia the big news was mobilization. Newsreels were filled with scenes of soldiers signing-up and marching off to France. In Vancouver, an enterprising newsman named A.D. Kean made the most of hostilities by introducing a local newsreel called KEAN'S CANADA FILMS which were shown at Vancouver's Dominion Theatre and which consisted of troops marching through the streets, cheering crowds, departing soldiers, and other patriotic crowd-pleasers. In 1916 Kean assembled four reels from his military footage and, in conjunction with the Vancouver Red Cross, released a film called B.C. FOR THE EMPIRE.[36] Little else is known about Kean's newsreel, or its brief history, but Kean himself surfaced again after the war as official cameraman for the provincial government.

During the last two years of the war, official films of the Allied victories were widely circulated and were extremely popular, each one claiming to be better than the last. One of the earliest film companies established in Victoria, Superfluities Motion Pictures Ltd., hoped to raise money for its own productions by distributing these war films in association with the Victoria Red Cross and donating half its profits to the Red Cross for the duration of the war. This policy led to a howl of outrage and the company was forced to donate all its profits to the Red Cross, which quickly put an end to any hope its investors might have had regarding its survival. On February 26, 1917, Superfluities presented FIGHTING WITH THE ALLIES and a cartoon about a zeppelin attack called THE RAID ON LONDON (WHAT LONDON SAW ON SEPTEMBER 3), at the Royal Victoria Theatre, adding as well some of their own footage showing the departure of the Bantams (143rd Regiment) and the Yukon Regiment for Europe. The show ran for a week, but the company was never heard from again. Understandably so, for it would be another twenty-one months before they could expect to see any working capital coming their way.[37]

NATIONAL PROGRESS: PROMOTING TRADE AND INDUSTRY   In 1916 the Department of Trade and Commerce in Ottawa received a request from the United States Bureau of Economics for pictures of Canada's grain and hydroelectric industries. Intrigued by the possibilities, the department hired a crew from the Essanay Film Manufacturing Company of Chicago and, in the summer of 1916, four cameramen left Ottawa to see what they could find. They returned with enough footage to make six industrial films. One, WATER POWERS OF CANADA TRIBUTARY TO VANCOUVER, was a thirty-minute examination of the Fraser River and the hydroelectric sites on the lower mainland of British Columbia. A second film, three reels long and called HARVESTING, INSPECTION, AND TRANSPORTATION OF GRAIN IN CANADA, may have been partially shot on the west coast as well, possibly showing scenes of Vancouver's shipping facilities. Although primitive, the films were received with enthusiasm and proved the value of motion pictures to the department. Outside work was costly, however, and lead the Deputy Minister of Trade and Commerce to deduce that a centralized film unit could do the same job, or better, for less. B.E. Norrish, the Canadian in charge of the productions assigned to Essanay, was asked to head up the new film unit of what was to be called the Exhibits and Publicity Bureau (E & PB). He immediately began to lobby for full control over all motion pictures made for federal government departments, something that never actually happened.

Norrish became a man to contend with. By the time the E & PB was officially recognized by order-in-council on September 19, 1918, he had hired away Essanay's best cameraman, Athur Reeves, and had already completed a new series of travel and industrial reels. Among other subjects, one depicted a trip across Canada by train and four showed views of the new national park at Banff, the first of dozens that would be made by the E & PB and its successor the Canadian Government Motion Picture Bureau over the next twenty years.[38]

By the time Norrish left the Department in 1920 to join the Canadian office of Associated Screen News in Montreal, he had initiated fifty productions, thirteen and possibly seventeen of which were filmed partially or entirely in British Columbia. Predictably these dealt with logging, salmon fishing and processing, boat building, forest-fire prevention, camping in the Rockies, and Victoria's tourist attractions.[39] Canada was the first nation to set up a government film publicity unit and for years the E & PB was considered highly innovative in its field.[40] Before long films of the E & PB were being shown to encourage trade, immigration, tourism and mutual understanding throughout the Americas (with Spanish captions if necessary), in Europe (French captions), China, India, South Africa, and across the United States where, predictably, they were almost all exhibited non-theatrically to clubs and organizations. The films were well received and Canada quickly became a model for other countries seeking to publicize themselves through motion pictures.[41]

In addition to its role of promoting Canada overseas, the E & PB, which became the Canadian Government Motion Picture Bureau (CGMPB) in 1923, was also established to reveal Canada to Canadians. To this end a new SEEING CANADA short was released theatrically in Canada every three or four weeks. British Columbia was well served. Although exact figures are impossible to determine, it is certain that between 90 and 100 of the films made by the CGMPB from 1917 to 1940 were filmed, wholly or partially, in British Columbia. During the early years, the CGMPB also supervised the CANADIAN NEWS PICTORIAL, a news weekly made up "entirely of Canadian and a few British news events, together with a short industrial section to boost "made-in-Canada" goods and a number of quips from the Canadian press entitled *Sense and Nonsense*." Although none of the reels of the CANADIAN NEWS PICTORIAL remain, their brief presence indicates that a British Columbian who went to the movies once a week during the early 1920's was receiving, for the first time, an organized, intentional visual link-up with the rest of Canada, paid for with his own taxes.[42]

Interpretations, however, tended to be two-dimensional. British Columbia's image was that of rugged primary industries surrounded by "outdoor playlands" catering to tourists seeking wholesome, athletic vacations. Later the province itself took up the responsibility of keeping this vision intact.[43] Little effort was made to portray British Columbia's people or culture except as adjuncts to the province's raw materials and economic prosperity. Even the grim realities of a ten-year economic depression were rarely noticed and never questioned.

Most of the films of the CGMPB that exist today were made for National Parks Bureau or the highly successful SEEING CANADA series; the latter generally depicted industries and urban centres, the former were concerned with hikers and wildlife. While pedantic and often heavy-handed with ludicrous captions, these reels are invaluable today for their content if not their style. It would be wrong, however, to suggest that they were not popular in their own day. In 1933, for example, more than 5000 prints of films made by the CGMPB were in circulation theatrically and non-theatrically around the world; the Rockies must have looked good on a hot day in Malaya, even on silent film.[44]

GOVERNMENT INTERVENTION   Many of the early films of the CGMPB were no doubt shown to excess as a result of the amendment to the British Columbia Motion Picture Act in 1920 creating the British Columbia Patriotic and Educational Picture Service (BCP & EPS) under the Department of the Attorney-General. As well as setting up the machinery to produce films, the legislation also required each movie theatre in the province to exhibit up to fifteen minutes of government-made or government-ordained pictures with each programme. Films and slide shows were provided free by the department;[45] many of these were probably rented or purchased from the E & PB in Ottawa. No early records remain (the provincial Department of the Attorney-General has only been required to file an Annual Report since 1974), and little is known of the BCP & EPS motion picture production programme.

Only one of the government-initiated films, BEAUTIFUL OCEAN FALLS, has survived. Produced by the Pathéscope Company of Canada, it may have been photographed by A.D. Kean who seems to have been the official photographer for the BCP + EPS during the first four years of its existence. According to the Public Accounts for the Department of the Attorney-General, Pathéscope, a company heavily involved in the production and distribution of education films, received $1,821.65 from the BCP & EPS during the fiscal year 1922-23, and may well have received a share of the starting budget of $18,500 in 1920. Pathéscope's role was probably limited to post-production and laboratory services including titling; it is probably fair to say that the company was not involved after March, 1923.[46]

BEAUTIFUL OCEAN FALLS is not much different from any other tedious travelogue of the time except for the fact that Ocean Falls was singled out for ten minutes worth of film at all. The Victoria *Daily Colonist* , supporting the opposition Conservative Party in the provincial legislature, claimed that many of the appointed films and slides showed a high degree of political motivation and that occasionally films were faked to make the Liberal Government look more commendable.[47] This aggravation was particularly apparent during the first year and, as the provincial election of December, 1920, loomed closer, the propaganda became more blatant. The *Colonist* demanded that the BCP & EPS be eliminated and reported that theatre owners, under public pressure to desist from showing the offensive government-sponsored pictures, were determined not to exhibit them even if it meant losing their licences. Victoria theatre managers appear to have carried out their threat without being suspended.[48] The publicity did not affect the election much, however, for the Liberals won a conclusive victory and the issue disappeared.

The practise of renting, purchasing, and producing films for theatrical audiences appears to have continued on a less controversial scale until 1924 when, according to Public Accounts, and perhaps coinciding with the provincial election that year in which both premier John Oliver and opposition leader Bowser were defeated, money for the programme appears to have dried up.[49] Thus while the BCP & EPS remained on the statutes until 1970, its influence waned when the provincial government ceased to provide films.

The fifteen-minute rule was never again enforced. Many theatre managers, however, continued to exhibit regularly the popular SEEING CANADA shorts of the CGMPB until the introduction of sound in 1927-28. Due to financial parsimony on the part of the federal government, the CGMPB was unable to purchase sound equipment until 1934, by which time its hold on the market for short subjects had become tenuous. Furthermore, moviegoers were becoming used to a more commercial product. Although government-sponsored shorts continued to be shown occasionally, their theatrical days were numbered and British Columbia's cinematic connection with eastern Canada grew daily weaker.[50]

LARGE SCALE ENTREPRENEURIAL ATTEMPTS   The only large commercial film company in Canada
during the 1920's and 1930's was Associated Screen News (ASN) Ltd. of Montreal. The
Canadian operation began in 1920 as a subsidiary of ASN of New York to produce Canadian
stories for United States newsreels which were shown in Canada. The CPR invested heavily
in the Canadian subsidiary, called Associated Screen News of Canada, Ltd. During the
early 1920's, ASN controlled two newsreel companies in the United States, THE SELZNICK
NEWS and KINOGRAMS. The latter also specialized in short subjects and travelogues and
was responsible for a one-reeler about Victoria, called VICTORIA - "A KINOGRAM TRAVELOGUE",
which was probably filmed in 1923. Not surprisingly the film concentrates heavily on the
services offered by the CPR. In 1927, when the parent company went out of business, the
CPR secured a majority holding and moved the entire operation to Montreal. ASN continued to provide news stories for United States companies like Fox Movietonews but never
felt confident enough to produce its own Canadian newsreel. It set up a team of stringers
across the country to cover the news events and obtained sound equipment in 1928 to keep
abreast of the changing emphasis in film production.[51]

A story in the Victoria *Daily Times* on December 7, 1931, reports that ASN was about to
place the "first Canadian-owned portable sound motion picture equipment on the West
Coast for the purpose of shooting newsreels in Victoria by January 15, 1932", creating
the first movie news service in western Canada.[52] This equipment, which was intended to
cover the territory between Calgary and the sea, was the first Canadian-owned sound link
between eastern and western Canadian theatres, even though some of the glamour is un-
avoidably diminished by the fact that it had to go through a United States newsreel company to be exhibited from one coast to the other.

ASN also began to make theatrical shorts and films for private enterprise, advertisements, postcards, and anything else that was commercially profitable. The CPR made good
use of its investment and ASN turned out several travelogues each year (almost all now
lost), some of which catalogued British Columbia's vacation possibilities.[53] In 1932
ASN began its famous CANADIAN CAMEO series which was to fill the space between the news
and the feature in Canadian cinemas for the next 23 years. To make the distinction between the news service and the CANADIAN CAMEO more apparent, the ASN production department was called Associated Screen Studios and the shorts were released under the imprint:
An Associated Screen Picture. A new short was released every six weeks, except during
the war years. It was usually a travelogue, a sports film, or a selection of curiosi-
ties. In the hands of director Gordon Sparling these shorts were often original and
inventive.

In general the CANADIAN CAMEO shorts were livelier and more experimental and they covered more ground than the CGMPB films. But, in the end, their view of Canada and British Columbia was not much different from the governmental versions. In fact, at least

two CANADIAN CAMEOS, THE GAME IS UP and SEA ROVER'S SUMMER, were re-edited versions of
CGMPB footage photographed by Bill Oliver. ASN's contribution was a greater attention
to style and technique. The company was quick to appreciate an innovation in the interests
of creating a snappier, more sophisticated product. Of course ASN had to sell its films
and the theatres wanted entertainment, not instruction. ASN provided entertainment and
tempered it with a distinctly Canadian vision. Many of the CANADIAN CAMEOS were shown
abroad and, when the series ended in 1955, eighty-five had been produced. Of the fifty
CANADIAN CAMEOS PRODUCED up to 1942, twelve contain shots of British Columbia or deal
entirely with some part of the province.[54]

For years, except for CGMPB films, ASN processed almost all the 35mm motion picture film
exposed in Canada. Before the introduction of 16mm film this was an expensive process,
with the result that small-budget films for specialized audiences were almost impossible
to produce. This changed overnight with the introduction of cheaper 16mm film. Many of
the more interesting developments in British Columbia's film history result from the
opportunity to produce inexpensive "home-grown" films about regional subjects brought
about by 16mm film.

IMPACT OF 16mm FILMS   The Eastman Kodak Company introduced its first 16mm Ciné-Kodak
camera in 1923.[55] By 1928, amateur film-makers in British Columbia were showing off
their vacation movies to the neighbours. Cheaper to buy and process than 35mm film, the
new 16mm gauge enabled British Columbians for the first time to interpret their way of
life on motion picture film for a modest cost.

The economic factor interested a number of agencies of the provincial government, and
permitted the British Columbia Department of Agriculture to get into the business. The
driving inspiration for this seems to have been the then premier, Dr. Simon Fraser Tolmie,
a veterinarian and former federal minister of agriculture who dedicated his life to agricultural education and improvement. During Tolmie's five years as premier, from 1928
to 1933, many excellent agricultural films were produced by the department and shown to
farmers throughout the province to encourage modern methods of breeding and planting and
to demonstrate the benefits of exhibitions and youth programmes.[56] During the winter
of 1930, by arrangement with the Canadian National Railway, an Agricultural Demonstration Train travelled throughout the province visiting small communities for educational
purposes. The department filmed the whole journey and produced a fascinating document
about many parts of the province that may have not been photographed since.

Although the films were sometimes crudely edited and photographed, they depict the people
of British Columbia more honestly than any similar government attempts, before or since.
Because the cameramen knew their subject, being agriculturalists first, they treated it
with affection and candour. Unfortunately the department's involvement in film production seems to have ended the year Tolmie was defeated in the legislature and today not
even the department's old-timers remember the films being made. The last reel was ex-

posed on October 16, 1937, the day Dr. Tolmie was buried in the Royal Oak Cemetery near Victoria.[57]

The involvement of film production of both the British Columbia Forest Service and the provincial Bureau of Industrial and Tourist Development began during the 1930's and was also made possible by the development of 16mm film. Both these agencies (the latter under successively different names) are still actively involved in 16mm film production. Pioneer work in the Forest Service was done by George Melrose who made such films as THE COWICHAN LOG, THE GREAT FIRE (Courtenay, 1938), and BACK TO BACK, a short about making Cowichan sweaters.[58]

The history of what was to become the British Columbia Department of Travel Industry is more difficult to trace. According to the provincial Public Accounts there were two particularly active bursts of involvement by the provincial government in tourist-promotion films during the 1930's. The first occurred at the beginning of the decade when the Provincial Bureau of Information was still a part of the Department of Finance; the second coincided with the creation of the British Columbia Government Travel Bureau under the newly formed Department of Trade and Industry in 1938. Between 1930 and 1932 the Bureau paid out $6,735 to Motion Screen Adz Ltd., of Vancouver, for an unknown number of travelogues depicting the scenic beauties of Vancouver Island and the Interior.[59]

Motion Screen Adz was a commercial film production company connected with Vancouver Motion Pictures Ltd., for years the only film-processing lab in British Columbia. The company was founded by Harry Rosenbaum and J. Howard Boothe in 1928. Boothe appears to have been the cameraman, assisted when necessary by H. Cress, Wally Hamilton, and others. Boothe is known to have been involved in the making of two travelogues for the provincial government, one in 1930 and another in 1931, both on 35mm film. Motion Screen Adz was also responsible for at least three 35mm travelogues produced for the Victoria and Island Publicity Bureau during the 1930's. In 1935 Motion Screen Adz was purchased by Leon C. Shelley and the following year he bought out Vancouver Motion Pictures. The combined firm continued in Vancouver until 1945 when Shelley moved the operation to Toronto, changing the name to Shelley Films. Shelley was responsible for a number of promotional films for the provincial government during the early forties. Unfortunately little information is available about either Motion Screen Adz or Vancouver Motion Pictures. The company records have been lost. That they served an important function in maintaining some control over local production must be acknowledged; perhaps one day their story may be more fully told.[60]

As mentioned previously, 16mm film was beginning to cut into the business of commercial production houses. In 1937, Clarence Ferris and Dick Colby, of the provincial government, began touring the province with 16mm cameras for the Bureau of Industrial and Tourist Development, the reorganized Bureau of Information. This was the first year of primitive in-house production. The trend continued the next year when the bureau moved to the Department of Trade and Industry, and became known as the British Columbia Gov-

During preparation for publication, the following new information was found. It is provided here to make this book as up-to-date as possible.

Film No.

8. AFTER FIFTY YEARS. At the time of publication, a copy of this film existed only at the NFB Archives in Montreal.

91. BRITISH COLUMBIA ITEMS. The material in these reels is outfootage from film, shot in 1958, of the federal Progressive Conservative Party campaign.

303. FISHING FLEET STRIKE IN VANCOUVER, B.C., AFTER FINDING PRICE OFFER UNACCEPTABLE. The version of this news story at the NFA, Ottawa (NFA 9053), titled FISHERMEN GO ON STRIKE, is 80' on 35mm.

337. FROM SEA TO SEA - REEL 1. The entire film is five reels long (3,700' 35mm), and comprises a railway tour across Canada via the CNR. The NFA has a viewing copy.

531. LUMBERING IN BRITISH COLUMBIA. At the time of publication, copies of this film existed only at the BFI, London, England, and the BCPM.

634. PAGES FROM THE DIARY OF A ROCKY MOUNTAIN RANGER. The NFA has two gauges of this film: 28mm and 16mm.

696. PREMIER LAKE RANCH CAMP - REEL 24. This film was shot in 1929.

700. PREMIER TOLMIE OPENS CANADIAN PACIFIC EXHIBITION, VANCOUVER, B.C. A copy of this news story is now at the NFA, Ottawa, and is 88' on 35mm.

717. PROVINCIAL LEGISLATURE OPENS, VICTORIA, B.C. A copy of this news story is also held by the NFA, Ottawa, as part of a composite story titled ONTARIO AND BRITISH COLUMBIA LEGISLATURES OPEN. The date is January 22, 1929, and in both films it is Lieutenant Governor Randolph Bruce of British Columbia who arrives to inspect the guard of honour and take the salute, not Premier Tolmie. The NFA copy is 128' on 35mm.

723. QUEEN OF THE COAST. The NFA, Ottawa, also possesses 35mm copies of this film. Only NFA 7703 357, and 358 contain shots of the Vancouver Post Office, the Court House, and the corner of Georgia and Granville Streets.

758. THE ROYAL VISIT. It has recently come to light that the CGMPB also made a 16mm colour film of the Royal Visit in 1939. This film is 7,056 feet long (196 minutes), and is silent with English titles. A copy will eventually be deposited in the NFA, Ottawa. As in all films about the Royal Visit, there are shots of the King and Queen in Vancouver and Victoria.

The head titles are as follows.

TITLE: His Majesty's Government in Canada presents

                    THE ROYAL VISIT TO CANADA AND THE UNITED STATES OF AMERICA
                    May 17 - June 15, 1939.

PRODUCED BY: The Canadian Government Motion Picture Bureau

                    in association with

                    The National Film Board

                    with the cooperation of the

                    Eastman Kodak Company.

                    Photographed in Kodachrome film.

PRODUCTION AND DIRECTION: Frank C. Badgley

```
PHOTOGRAPHY:   J.B. Scott
               Norman Hull
               George Waters Jr.  (Courtesy Eastman Kodak Co.)

     EDITING AND TITLES:  J.B. Scott
                          Stuart Legg
```

909. TRAIL, B.C. - THE METALLURGICAL MECCA OF CANADA. Produced by ASN.

A-16. THE THOUSAND DAYS. The NFA, Ottawa, has a nitrate optical soundtrack only, from which a ¼" dub has been made.

ernment Travel Bureau. Ferris and Colby continued producing 16mm travelogues for the bureau for distribution in Canada and the United States. Inspired by the possibilities, the bureau spent $9,655.74 on travelogues and promotional films in 1939-40, although it is impossible to assess now which they prepared and which were done by commercial companies. With the exception of the footage of the Royal Visit in 1939, all these films have disappeared. This much is clear; for their services in 1939-40 Motion Screen Adz Ltd. received $5000 and Travel Films Ltd., a commercial travel film company, $2500.[61] The renewed economic vitality which accompanied World War II appears to have inspired the Travel Bureau, and from 1940 on there were few years when several promotional films were not made, either by or for the government. By 1952 the bureau was able to claim that thirty-one of the films listed in their catalogue were their own productions.[62]

III

FEATURE FILMS   So much then for travelogues and propaganda. The taxpayers of British Columbia were far more interested in seeing Rudolph Valentino, Jackie Coogan, Greta Garbo, Ronald Coleman, and Lon Chaney, and some British Columbians were becoming concerned with California's dominance over their movie screens. A letter from R.P. Matheson to the Victoria *Daily Colonist* in November 1925 expresses this concern with vigour:

> Americans have exploited the timber and other natural resources of Vancouver Island. Like savages our people receive wages for the labour of stripping their country of its wealth and the profits go to enrich the invaders. Our young people go south to serve those whose incomes are derived from their enterprises in Canada or stay home to wait upon them when they are on holiday. And when it is proposed that we show British ideals or romances in "Empire-made films", we telegraph to Los Angeles . . . Victoria's citizens cherish their servility."[63]

British Columbia's young people were leaving, some for successful film careers in the United States. It was not for lack of trying that feature films were seldom produced by British Columbians; profiteers and enthusiasts alike were disappointed by efforts to create a branch of the movie industry in Victoria or Vancouver. Few months went by when the papers did not print letters from sincere producers or syndicates seeking investment support, and editors and city councillors sought tirelessly to interest local businessmen.[64] Yet, despite the raving headlines and promised contracts, no money was forthcoming. Companies with names like Canadian Historic Features Ltd., British Canadian Pictures Ltd., Lion's Gate Cinema Studios, British-American Films Ltd., and Dominion Films Corporation Ltd. were created virtually overnight, but none lasted long enough to file their first annual report. A closer look at their founders reveals that, as often as not, they were not necessarily successful or patriotic men.

A few examples will be instructive. British Canadian Pictures Ltd. was a front for a Hollywood producer named Samuel Bischoff who saw incorporation in Vancouver as a way of taking advantage of the British quota legislation of 1927. The company was registered

19

on June 9, 1928, with Bischoff's wife in Hollywood holding ninety-six per cent of the shares. Bischoff had a binding agreement with Gaumont Company in England to supply them with six feature motion pictures starring the German Shepherd dog *Silverstreak*, already hot at the box office for his role in FANGS OF JUSTICE (1926). Bischoff never did make a *Silverstreak* movie in Vancouver, but he may have hired J.P. McGowan to direct a mysterious western starring William Cody and titled THE WILDERNESS PATROL, which may have been filmed in North Vancouver. THE WILDERNESS PATROL may have been released in the United States by Paramount Pictures. Two years later the company's name was stricken from the files of the Registrar of Companies for being in default of its second consecutive annual report.[65]

Dominion Films Corporation Limited was also the creation of an American producer, John Arthur Nelson of New York. Invited to Vancouver in 1916 to assist with the development of a company called Dominion Educational Films, Nelson advised them to open a photoplay studio in Victoria, assuring them that they would be well repaid for their effort. In 1917 Nelson created the Dominion Films Corporation (incorporated February 7th) and drew up agreements making himself president of the company and giving himself fifty-one per cent of the shares. Nelson also secured for himself full distribution rights in the United States, Mexico, South America, and Australia, leaving Canadian distribution under control of the company. He then tried to interest Victoria City Council in underwriting his purchase of land for a studio complex to be called Maple Leaf City, claiming that he would be paying at least $100,000 over the next three years to local employees as well as bringing in $516,000 in gross revenue over the same period. The City found him twenty-three acres in Saanich (outside the city limits) then declared it legally out of their hands. A group of business men in Victoria then rallied around Nelson but all they could raise was $2,800 toward the downpayment of $4,400 for the land. Many found it difficult to see how a man claiming to have two large contracts with North American distributors and tens of thousands of dollars to spend immediately on production, could be so badly in need of $4,400. Even after reading his charming twenty-four-page prospectus "The Industry Which is Making Millionaires" they remained sceptical. The money was never raised. Maple Leaf City was never built, and Nelson drifted out of view soon after being rejected by the Victoria businessmen. Dominion Films Corporation disappeared as quickly as it had arrived, without filing an annual report.[66]

In 1927, a company called The National Cinema Studios Syndicate of Hollywood, headed by Nils Olaf Chrisander, a former director for the German company UFA, decided to build a $750,000 studio on Vancouver's North Shore on the banks of the Capilano River. Here they intended to produce what they called "Clean Movies" to supply the guaranteed market created by the quota legislation in Great Britain. The studio was to encompass fifty acres with 350 acres around it being set aside for a Beverly Hills-type subdivision. Investors were expected to be found across Canada and in Great Britain. Chrisander announced that once underway the company would employ from 400-500 people. British actors and technical personnel would be brought from Hollywood. The syndicate stated that they had not yet decided on a name for the production company but that they were rather taken by "Lion's Gate Cinemas of Canada." Hye Bossin, in his brief history of the motion picture industry in Canada in the *Film Weekly Year Book of the Canadian Motion Picture Industry*, writes that, "The Lion's Gate venture provided an unhappy experience for those who heeded two Hollywood promoters with the idea of making films with British players. They bought the old Haddon property in West Vancouver in 1927. As the need for more money became apparent a battle for control began in which everyone was the loser, with the promoters sent to jail for false pretenses." The company, in fact, was never incorporated or registered.[67]

With the exception of the legal complications, British-American Films Ltd. suffered the same fate. Registered in Victoria on January 26, 1933, British-American planned a major studio in Victoria to produce feature films. British actors living in Hollywood were expected to own most of the stock in the company. The two driving forces behind the venture appear to have been Edwin Carewe, a veteran Hollywood producer who helped organize the MGM and First National Studios, and Major C. Fairbanks-Smith, builder of the RKO Studio in Hollywood. For unknown reasons the company disappeared without a whimper; no studio was ever built and no films were ever produced.[68] Obviously the British emigrés living in California were not interested in creating a Canadian version of the lame-duck British feature film industry they had left behind.

Many of the supposed investors in companies like Lion's Gate and British-American were expected to rally around the patriotic catchwords "British pictures" and "Clean Movies" which were considered to be one and the same thing, i.e. morally uplifting. Dreamers, perhaps, were lured into laying down a few dollars to this end, but hard-nosed business-men were well aware that "Clean movies" had a short life at the box office. Young people, moreover, looking for work in the movies, realized that British Columbia was too small to support a multi-million-dollar entertainment industry and, were thus drawn to Hollywood. Nor were investors fooled by extravagant claims that the climate was all any producer could desire. Southern California was the movie capital because of sunshine and no matter how much the promoters of British Columbia deluded themselves their financiers, who made money because of rain, remained unconvinced by the climatic arguments. What feature-length motion picture production there was in British Columbia before World War II was almost entirely the result of a decision made thousands of miles away in London, England, at the Imperial Conference of 1926. The Cinematograph Films Act, which was subsequently passed, guaranteed that a percentage of screen time in theatres of the United Kingdom would be devoted to films made in the British Empire (see p.). It did not, unfortunately, guarantee Canadian investors.

Several American features, with forgotten names like THE WINDS OF CHANCE and THE FLAMING FOREST, were made on location in British Columbia during the 1920's. In 1936, the Gaumont British Company spent the whole summer in Revelstoke filming their version of the construction of the CPR called THE GREAT BARRIER (U.S. and Canadian title: SILENT BARRIERS), starring Lilli Palmer and Richard Arlen.[69] However, the most interesting feature film ever made in the province, POLICING THE PLAINS, was never fully released and may well have been lost forever.

HISTORICAL THEMES   In 1922 a company called Canadian Historic Features was formed in Vancouver to produce "moving pictures portraying the historical life of the Dominion of Canada from its earliest inception". The first production was to be an authentic history of the North West Mounted Police called POLICING THE PLAINS, to be based on a book by the Reverend R.G. MacBeth of Vancouver. The company disappeared but in December, 1924, the Canadian Moving Picture Digest mentioned that cameraman A.D. (Cowboy) Kean (late of the British Columbia Patriotic and Educational Picture Service) had been in Alberta filming the historical romance POLICING THE PLAINS. Kean appears to have inherited, or taken over, the property. By 1925 he was fully involved in producing, writing, directing, and photographing the entire film himself. For at least three years he worked intermittently on this ambitious, documentary-like project, returning to his job as a newspaperman to pay for each successive stage. POLICING THE PLAINS apparently starred Dorothy Fowler, Cariboo rancher Jack Boyd, and a Calgary socialite known only as Miss Lougheed. It was filmed on location in Alberta and on Boyd's ranch, with the final exterior sequences being shot in Vancouver in 1927.[70]

According to the *Canadian Film Weekly* the picture cost more than $150,000 and the few people who remember seeing it, or part of it, were favourably impressed by Kean's treatment of the subject.[71] Where Kean seems to have failed was in the technical quality of his photography. Perhaps the extended shooting schedule in both summer and winter conditions was responsible for the uneven quality. Apparently the negative was developed at different stages in Vancouver, at ASN in Montreal, and at the laboratory of the Ontario Government Motion Picture Bureau in Toronto.[72] Perhaps Kean was not careful enough, or lacked the expertise and the skilled technicians a feature film requires. Whatever the case, the negative has since disappeared though occasionally it is rumoured that part of a print still exists. Kean said that the film was not fully released (it played for 6 days in Toronto at the Royal Alexander from Dec. 19, 1927) because of obstruction by the large distribution combines which controlled distribution and exhibition in Canada, which may be partially true. The fact remains that POLICING THE PLAINS, while filled with good intentions, was probably too primitive or lacked the usual show business cliches to interest American distribution chains or Canadian theatre managers.[73]

The loss of POLICING THE PLAINS is particularly unfortunate because, probably more than any other feature motion picture made in western Canada, it represented the possibility of exploring and interpreting a unique Canadian institution through Canadian eyes. It also underlines the loneliness and frustration that accompany a director when he tries to do the same thing today. Kean appears to have worked with singular vision and enthusiasm long before people thought of film as a director's medium. Though he reputedly went on to make another film called TOLD IN THE HILLS, the experience appears to have broken him. He returned to work as a newspaperman in Toronto and died in obscurity. Men now retired from the business can remember seeing film canisters lying around the vaults and on the floor at ASN, and Vancouver Motion Pictures Ltd., waiting for Cowboy Kean to pay his bills.[74]

DISTRIBUTOR MONOPOLIES   Kean's charges of obstruction at the hands of the foreign-owned combines apparently were not unfounded. By 1929 the tenacious hold over almost every motion picture theatre in Canada by a few distribution agencies in the United States was becoming obvious. In September of that year the federal government initiated an investigation of the motion picture industry, under the Combines Investigation Act, to look into a long list of charges and allegations against prominent men in the business.[75] Commissioner Peter White, reporting to the Federal Minister of Labour in July, 1931, confirmed what everyone suspected. The White Inquiry revealed that two American-controlled companies, Famous Players Canadian Corporation (controlled by Paramount Public Corporation) and Motion Picture Distributors and Exhibitors of Canada (controlled by the Motion Picture Distributors and Exhibitors of the U.S.A.) exercised complete control over ninety-five per cent of the film distribution in Canada as well as occupying a prominent or exclusive position in controlling theatres in towns of more than 10,000 people. Moreover, it appeared that both companies were working hard to discourage any British films from entering Canada, as well as lobbying vigorously against a Canadian quota system. Of 949 feature pictures released in Canada between 1928 and 1930, seventy-three were of British origin, or seven point five percent, a figure that infuriated provincial authorities.[76]

Attorney General Robert H. Pooley of British Columbia declared that he was going to look into the imposition of a quota system for his province which would require all theatres to show a much greater percentage of British films. In September 1931, the Province of Ontario decided to prosecute the motion picture distribution companies and the list of indictments went before a grand jury. Witnesses were sent from British Columbia to assist in the prosecution. It was during this trial that A.D. Kean testified that the corporations had conspired to keep his film out of the theatres.[77]

After six months of acrimonious testimony and eloquent defence, Justice Charles Garrow of the Ontario Supreme Court handed down a verdict that probably no one in the business found surprising. Not one of the fifteen motion picture distribution companies indicted was found guilty of combine activities or allegations laid under section of the Criminal Code or the Combines Investigation Act. Although the ruling adhered to the letter of the law, it was still a remarkable decision considering the evidence against the companies. The repercussions continue to be felt today in the movie theatres of Canada that are still under the thumb of the same companies.[78]

As a result of the decision, the provinces decided to take matters into their own hands. Ontario instituted a quota system for its theatres whereby seven point five per cent of all films shown each year had to originate in the British Empire. As well, the Ontario Board of Censors declared that all newsreels shown in theatres must have at least twenty-five per cent Canadian content. In British Columbia the Attorney General again announced plans for a quota system which drew heavy criticism from theatre lessees and managers as well as from several members of the legislative assembly who were opposed to the quota on principle. The Victoria *Daily Colonist* called for a stiff quota in British Columbia theatres running from twenty-five per cent British Empire films, the first year, to an eventual fifty per cent even though, as one member of the legislative assembly rightly pointed out, it was not unusual to see a British film that was just as unsavoury as any American film on the market.[79]

Opponents of the quota claimed that British films were still pushing class distinctions down the audience's throat. One Vancouver man had his remarks reprinted and praised by the London *Daily Express* for writing that, "the cast of British talkies is invariably divided into two distinct classes. One class is made to speak as if they had an apple lodged in their throats while the other class are all temporary members of the 'blimey' school of pronunciation."[80]

Although "British" obviously included Canadian productions, many opponents found the proposed legislation to be unfair, while representatives from the theatres claimed that they would be forced by law to exhibit second-rate material simply because it was British. The controversy was heated although it never made the headlines. The government finally compromised. An amendment to the Moving Pictures Act, on April 6, 1932, gave the Lieutenant Governor in Council special authority to regulate that:

> ...a proportion of the films available for distribution by film exchanges to the proprietors, lessees, managers, or employees of moving-picture theatres, and a proportion of the films exhibited in each moving-picture theatre, shall be of British manufacture and origin; and for fixing these proportions on a monthly or a yearly basis.

Although this special power remained on the statutes until the Moving Picture Act was revised in 1971, it was never implemented and a quota system was never imposed on the motion picture distributors or exhibitors of British Columbia.[81]

A quota in British Columbia would have been welcomed in England, where the motion picture industry was struggling to remain alive, but it probably would not have had much effect on the movie-goers at home. Perhaps a quota would have been like a foot in the door to Canadian investors, a sign that someone was interested in giving Canadian feature film production a chance. One can only speculate on the positive effect a British Columbia quota might have had. Certainly the quota imposed on British distributors and exhibitors in 1928 had an exhilarating effect on Victoria, lending credibility to that city's dream of becoming the movie capital of Canada.

MOVIES: QUOTA LEGISLATION AND POTENTIAL NEW INDUSTRY   Five years after Cowboy Kean completed work on POLICING THE PLAINS a man named Kenneth James (he often called himself John) Bishop arrived on Vancouver Island from California with a scheme he said would make Victoria the Hollywood of the British Empire. The time seemed ripe. In 1927 the British Government had passed a revised Cinematograph Films Act which prescribed a quota for British films which was to rise to twenty per cent for both exhibitor and distributor by 1936. That is, by 1936 every movie theatre in England was required to book at least one "British" film for every four foreign films. A "British" film was described as one made by a British subject or a British company in a studio within the British Empire from a scenario written by a British subject. With a margin of discretion allowed to the British Board of Trade, seventy-five per cent of the salaries and wages were to be paid to British subjects, exclusive of the renumeration paid to one foreign actor or director.[82]

The legislation was basically a compromise worked out at the Imperial Conference in London in 1926 where Canada had been instrumental in enlarging the provisions of the act-to-be to include overseas production within the Empire.[83]

Bishop was certain that he could make the act work to his advantage and began to look for financial support. Born in England, in 1893, Bishop arrived in Canada as a young man and claimed to have spent the next twenty-six years working between Hollywood and New York as an actor, a stage manager, a film distributor, and finally a small-time independent producer.[84] He managed to interest Kathleen Dunsmuir (Mrs. Seldon Humphries), heiress to part of the James Dunsmuir fortune, in the idea to establishing a feature film company in Victoria called Commonwealth Productions. Bishop would be producer and use local scenery and local actors, Kathleen foremost among them, importing only the director, and a few technicians and stars to get the pictures off the ground. Bishop felt that with distribution in Great Britain virtually guaranteed by the quota he would certainly be able to break even and maybe even turn a profit. Kathleen was very keen to become a movie actress and on July 30, 1932, Commonwealth Productions Ltd. was incorporated in British Columbia to make motion picture feature films.[85]

Bishop leased the main show building from the British Columbia Agricultural Association at the old Willows Park in Oak Bay and converted it into a primitive, drafty studio. Production began in February, 1933, on a revised radio script called THE MYSTERY OF HARLOW MANOR. By May, when shooting was scheduled to start, the story was found to be unmanageable and Bishop postponed the project.[86] The next production, begun in October, 1933, was a logging film called THE CRIMSON PARADISE, directed by the Canadian-born, Hollywood director, Robert Hill.

In the film, Nick Stuart plays a well-born young greenhorn from Boston who finds love (Lucille Browne) and meaning (hard work) in his life in the rough-and-ready lumber camps of Vancouver Island. THE CRIMSON PARADISE was in many ways a triumph of will. It premiered grandly at the Capitol Theatre in Victoria on December 14, 1933, to kind reviews from a home-town crowd. Few honestly thought it very good. In fact, the sound and the acting were not even close to the standard set by American pictures playing elsewhere; the only appeal was the local scenery and the faces of local actors. Everyone agreed though that this was only the beginning; things would surely improve.[87]

That THE CRIMSON PARADISE ever reached a theatre screen was a triumph for Ivan Ackery, the manager of the Capitol at that time. At first Famous Players Limited, which owned the theatre, refused permission to exhibit the film during regular hours because they did not want to lose money on it. They were probably not eager to encourage Canadian film production either, concerned as usual with protecting their market. Still, Ackery was able to convince them that the presentation would be profitable because, even if the picture was bad, the locals would flock to the theatre to see their friends and the familiar scenery. Finally he was allotted three days during what is traditionally the worst time of the year for movie theatres, the week before Christmas. THE CRIMSON PARADISE opened to the general public with an "Our Gang" comedy on December 20, 1933, and closed on Friday, December 22. Ackery still recalls with pride that he made more money that week than any other theatre manager in Canada during the same time.[88]

Bishop's next effort, SECRETS OF CHINATOWN, which was advertised and exhibited as THE BLACK ROBE in Victoria and Vancouver where the Chinese population was sensitive to the conspiratorial connotations of the title, was an improvement. It premiered, a year and three months after THE CRIMSON PARADISE, at Victoria's Empire Theatre.[89] It looks very crude today. The American trade paper *The Film Daily* called it a "lurid tale of a secret Oriental society headed by a mysterious hooded figure", and warned that it was "not made for the thinking element that may be found here and there in our picture theatres, but for the neighbourhood houses (where) this one should have 'em yelling from the balcony."[90] Despite the appearance of one of the actors on stage before each performance in Victoria to explain that the story was purely fictional, the portrayal of the Chinese as drug pedlars and criminals soon raised a complaint from the Chinese Consul in Vancouver and landed the film back on the Provincial Censor's desk.[91] Presumably the censor was not as sensitive to the racial issue as the consul for, when the film was re-released the only change was the elimination of "views of Chinaman with knife in back."[92]

Looking at the film now it is hard to imagine anyone taking it seriously even though it does exploit stereotypes almost to the exclusion of any real characterization. It appears as if director Fred Newmeyer set out to parody a boy's adventure story. The acting, markedly wooden, is not enhanced by the substandard sound recording. In the end, the quality of the film, not its content, led to its early demise. This was unfortunate for Bishop because, after the failure of THE CRIMSON PARADISE, he was hoping that SECRETS OF CHINATOWN would provide a handsome return.

Plucky, working on a shoestring, but lacking the professional skills required, Ken Bishop was in trouble. When THE CRIMSON PARADISE failed to become a box-office success, Commonwealth Productions went into receivership. Bankrupt, and faced with no way out, Bishop convinced Kathleen Dunsmuir to hold on.[93] He sold Commonwealth's assets to a Vancouver contrator named John F. Keen, for a dollar, and Keen, in return, transferred them to Bishop's new company, Northern Films Ltd., for fifty per cent of the shares in the company. It was Northern that finished work on and released SECRETS OF CHINATOWN. Northern tried to distribute both films more widely but neither were destined to recoup more than a slight percentage of their cost. In desperation Bishop left town, leaving Miss Dunsmuir as the victim of his dreams.[94]

Kathleen Dunsmuir took the company to court in an attempt to recover some of her losses. claiming that she had invested at least $28,000 (her lawyer later said she had spent something closer to $50,000), but in May 1934, the judge decreed that she was not entitled to receive possession of either of the two films, stating that they were required for distribution to earn back some of the losses and to satisfy the claims of the common creditors. Copies of THE CRIMSON PARADISE were at that time supposed to be in vaults in London and New York, while SECRETS OF CHINATOWN was still in Vancouver.[95] Northern Films went into receivership and was defunct by 1938. There is no record that either THE CRIMSON PARADISE or SECRETS OF CHINATOWN actually played in British theatres though it seems likely they did inasmuch as both were submitted to the British censor by Columbia Pictures. SECRETS OF CHINATOWN certainly played in the United States.[96] Of Bishop's two independent Canadian productions, it is the only one to survive.

Seemingly undaunted, Bishop returned to Hollywood and told Columbia Pictures about his studio, about the wonderful scenery, the cheap labour and the enthusiasm of the locals in Victoria. Since Columbia was looking for a place to produce inexpensive B-movies for the British quota market, they decided to take a look. Victoria seemed perfect. In 1935, Bishop established a new company called Central Films Limited, and, in a little over two years, twelve "quota quickies" were produced using Hollywood directors, stars and technicians, and a few local actors.[97]

Bishop oversaw the mechanics of the operation but never viewed the rushes or, for the most part, the finished films. Each night the exposed stock was flown to Hollywood for processing, the director receiving a numbered test strip the next day so that he could match exposures.[98] All the Central films were uncompromising B-movies. In England, they were shown in the morning, permitting the theatres to exhibit their first-run Columbia features at night when the paying public came out in force to see their favourite stars. Half of the Central productions suggested New York locations; the rest managed to locate their inevitable romantic triangles in logging camps, pitting their criminals against the Mounties. None cost more than $65,000 or took more than a month to shoot. Columbia overseer Jack Fier kept a strict shooting schedule and was tight on the purse, which accounts for some surprisingly swift denouements in several of the films, none of which was much more than an hour long. For Columbia, they were only means to a profitable end; they served this purpose admirably.[99]

27

British film companies, however, were not amused. The quota system was doing nothing for them, as many people, including George Bernard Shaw, had predicted. Without a quality clause, such legislation can never be very effective. The loopholes, which permitted Columbia to use Bishop so brazenly, were no help to the British or the Canadian film industries. In fact, Central Films became its own worst enemy. The kind of films turned out by Columbia in Victoria resulted directly in a revision of the Cinematograph Films Act in 1938 which eliminated films made in the Dominions and effectively shut down Central Films forever.[100]

The decisive new feature of the Act was the requirement that to qualify for the quota a film must cost at least £7,500 or £1 a foot for labour and that producers must pay technicians and employees according to a fair wage clause which meant pay scales set by trade union agreements.[101] Columbia was not willing to meet these requirements, which would have defeated their reason for being in Canada in the first place, so they packed up and left. Bishop continued to be optimistic about the possibility of making features and, as late as July, 1938, referred to a long-term contract with an unspecified Hollywood production company. Under the new contract the unfinished Central Films laboratory on Cadboro Bay Road in Victoria was to be completed. Bishop predicted that it would be able to do all its own processing instead of sending the film to Hollywood for developing and printing. This never came to pass. The Central Films studio was demolished in April, 1939, when hope of further support proved in vain.[102] Ken Bishop, who was responsible for the largest number of feature films ever made in Canada through the efforts of one man, died in Vancouver on September 6, 1941. The last three years of his life are a mystery.[103]

IV

LIMITS OF CANADIAN CONTENT It is interesting to speculate on the degree to which the success of talking pictures encouraged resentment against the foreign domination of British Empire movie screens at the beginning of the 1930's. Sound, of course, was what everyone had been waiting for, and when THE JAZZ SINGER finally proved, in 1927, that sound technology was ready to start providing the hits, the motion picture industry changed overnight.[104]

Voice and music reproduction did not necessarily mean better movies, but they did tend to identify the national origin of the film more readily. The "quota quickies" made in Victoria were filled with American voices and, despite the efforts of several expatriate British character actors who played supporting roles in several of the pictures, the immediate impression was not of a British film. Little wonder the quota was regarded as a joke. Sound gives film a greater sense of immediacy, but it also makes the viewer harder to fool.

Fox Movietonews, which once had an office in Toronto that compiled a semi-weekly Canadian news edition containing at least 300 feet of Canadian material, centralized all its operations in New York when sound was introduced to newsreels in 1927.[105] The exclusively Canadian edition disappeared in the scramble to fit narration and music to the week's disasters, and Pentictonites grew up as familiar as New Yorkers with the voice of Lowell Thomas. Yet, American news commentators appear not to have raised the nationalistic ire of Canadians until World War II. Paramount News, quick to equate profits with patriotism, led the way to change after the raid on Dieppe in 1942, by hiring a Canadian narrator for their Canadian edition.[106]

LIMITS OF ECONOMY   When ASN acquired sound equipment in 1928, it was able to produce news and short features in the new medium with great success. In 1935 ASN built Canada's first sound stage. The CGMPB, on the other hand, was not faring so well. In fact, from 1930 on, the government film unit lost so much ground that it finally had to be reorganized.

With expenses mounting and ever-decreasing depression budgets, the Bureau was unable to hire new staff and, most crucially, it could not afford to purchase sound equipment. The introduction of 16mm film created a wider but, per capita, less-lucrative audience, and much effort and expense went into providing prints in both 35mm and 16mm for the increasing public demand. Because they were borrowed and exhibited non-theatrically, 16mm prints were unable to pay their way, an unfortunate development for the Bureau's depression-ravaged finances. The result was that most of the CGMPB films shot in British Columbia during the 1930's are silent, decorated with captions, and somehow reminiscent of an earlier era. Once in great demand throughout the world, Bureau films, without sound, became old fashioned overnight. The situation was such that even when the Bureau was finally able to acquire audio equipment in 1934, it was forced to train its two projectionists as sound men. Despite the immediate initiation of several ambitious projects, however, the style of the CGMPB failed to change significantly with the addition of music and narration. Even more than money, the Bureau needed new blood, new ideas. Unfortunately all the bright young men had left for Montreal, Hollywood, or London. Although the small, overworked staff of the Bureau was too tired and too protective to realize it, there was something in the air that was about to revolutionize what the Exhibits and Publicity Bureau had started almost twenty years before.[107]

NEW IDEAS AND INNOVATIONS   The old guard was changing. For the first time, non-fiction films were feeling out their possibilities, recognizing themselves as a new medium and not just a loud magazine with a lot of pictures. A new genre, called the *documentary* by its fervent creator John Grierson, had appeared in England.

Grierson was a propagandist; he was also a thinker and a philosopher. He believed that there must be harmony between man and his works. He explored this relationship intimately and relentlessly on film, seeking unique and vital ways of doing so. In contrast, films of the CGMPB were silent and drab, somehow never coming to grips with more than a superficial, cosmetic depiction of their subject. They continued to work on what can be called the *eighth-wonder-of-the-world principle*. Content was supreme. If something unusual could be shown to an audience, the film was a success. The giant fir trees on the west coast, the towering Rockies, and the indescribably huge salmon catches, filled this bill and were supposed, as if by magic, to reflect the collective imagination of the citizens living nearby. Audiences in the 1930's, however, were becoming too sophisticated for this. More important, little of the prosperity depicted on the screen actually seemed to touch their lives. Machines, which had once inspired lofty thoughts, were becoming monsters in a new literary form called science fiction. Men and women began to remember that they were the real wealth of their nations, that if they suffered they laughed too, and that soon they would have to go to war again.

Certainly the hysteria that accompanied the royal visit of King George VI and Queen Elizabeth in 1939 was not so much simple joy as an eruption of relief in a mountain of terror. Germany, Italy, Spain, Ethiopia, China--these were realities demanding a personal response, and film was beginning to take notice. *Documentaries* were expressing this new spirit, rising to the new social consciousness.

Meanwhile, in Ottawa, the CGMPB was working overtime to maintain the status quo. With no sense of mission, nor the time or the money to respond to the changes around them, the CGMPB was becoming a Bureau of caretakers.[108] Finally, in an attempt to rectify the situation, Grierson himself was invited to Ottawa by the Bureau. He suggested sweeping reforms including the establishment of one national body to oversee the film production of all government departments. This he called the National Film Board. In 1939 he was appointed its first Commissioner.[109] By 1940, however, it became apparent that both the Board and the Bureau could not exist independently. Grierson insisted that they merge to present a more coherent front. The exigencies of war made this more convincing and, in 1940, the old CGMPB ceased to exist. The last films shot in British Columbia by the Bureau were about mobilization for another war and a visit by a King who would never see Canada again.[110]

END OF AN ERA   The Royal Visit of King George VI and Queen Elizabeth, in May 1939, was a fitting end to British Columbia's first four decades of motion picture activity. For Canadian film-makers it was the challenge of the decade – a month-long news story here at home. All the most recent cinematic developments were brought into play. Amateurs, who since 1937 had been able to buy colour film in both 16mm and 8mm gauges, came out in force to greet their sovereigns and take home souvenirs. The British Columbia Government Travel Bureau, the Forest Service, and the Department of Fisheries, each sent cameramen out with 16mm colour film to record the event in Vancouver and Victoria. ASN compiled the first theatrical colour short in Canada called ROYAL BANNERS OVER OTTAWA as well as covering the whole tour. And the CGMPB produced an ambitious eighty-five minute sound film called THE ROYAL VISIT which contained an entire reel of highlights from Victoria and Vancouver.[111]

THE ROYAL VISIT played in theatres across the country for several weeks at the beginning of the war and proceeds from the box office went to the Canadian Red Cross.[112] In the meantime, government cameramen and newsreel photographers were dispatched to army camps, naval yards, and air bases to cover training programmes. In Esquimalt, fishermen were being shown how to fire machine guns, aircraft were suddenly taking shape in Vancouver factories and, for the second time in twenty-five years, the Seaforth Highlanders were marching off to war.[113] As had been forseen, the royal tour, and the films it spawned (none of which can be compared to the skillfully orchestrated work of German propagandists such as Leni Riefenstahl), had a positive effect on the enthusiasm of both Canadians and Americans, making more immediate the struggles of a troubled European continent.[114] For some Canadians going overseas, THE ROYAL VISIT was the last motion picture they saw.

Thus, film became middle-aged in British Columbia.

In this introduction it has only been possible to indicate the main trends. Many who made important contributions must, due to limited space, be left out. A more detailed account would identify such men as Edward Curtis, the American photographer whose fascinating dramatic film, IN THE LAND OF THE HEAD HUNTERS, was a remarkable personal achievement for 1914, and Harlan I. Smith of the National Museum of Canada who, on his own initiative, made more than twenty films of great anthropological and ethnological interest in British Columbia during the 1920's. Because motion pictures were not considered to be a serious medium at that time, Smith's reels were shown mainly for entertainment at the museum's Saturday morning lectures for children.[115]

Men like Bill Oliver, the veteran wildlife photographer who worked so hard on the CGMPB's National Parks adventure travelogues, and Len Roos, who shot over a hundred stories in British Columbia for Fox Movietonews, are now almost forgotten. Roos was typical of the high-balling, hot-shot cameramen who hired themselves out during the early days of film. A revealing, humourous portrait is drawn by Lewis R. Freeman in his book Down the Columbia (1921) in which he describes Roos as claiming to be from New York, where he apparently lived at the time.

> It was his misfortune to have been born in Canada, he explained, but he had always had great admiration for Americans, and had taken out his first papers for citizenship. He could manage to get on with Canadians in a pinch, he averred further; but as for Britishers - no "Lime-juicers" for him, with their "G'bly'me's" and afternoon teas. ...he was naturally very frank and outspoken and a great believer in saying what he thought of people and things.

> He had also rather a glittering line of dogma on the finer things of life. Jazz was the highest form of music (he ought to know, for had he not played both jazz and grand opera when he was head drummer of the Galt, Ontario, home band?); the Mack Sennett bathing comedy was his belle ideal of kinematic art; and the newspapers of William Hearst were the supreme development of journalism. This latter he knew, because he had done camera work for a Hearst syndicate himself. I could manage to make a few degrees of allowance for jazz and the Mack Sennett knockabouts

under the circumstances, but the deification of Hearst created an unbridge-
able gulf.[116]

A man as energetic but of a different temperament was the inspired amateur cameramen
George R.B. Kinney. During the 1930's, Reverend Kinney photographed some of the most
candid and thoughtful documentary footage ever attempted in the province, editing most
of the film in his camera as he shot it and making his own reels out of galvanized steel
and wire. His records of Kootenay Lake and the west coast of Vancouver Island, where
he operated his United Church waterways missions, are revealing in a way that professional films could never be. What set Kinney apart was that he liked and was interested
in people, not machines. His construction and logging camp footage concentrates on the
faces of the boys and men out working in the bush during the late twenties and thirties,
and he never went anywhere without getting at least a few shots of the cookhouse crew,
the most important people in camp. With his little black ciné-Kodak camera he caught
the true spirit of his time.[117]

It would be satisfying to somehow look back on these humble beginnings having as our
reference point a current and thriving industry, but, in truth, conditions for film
making in British Columbia, considering the increase in population and wealth, have not
really improved. Local investors still seem to prefer to sink their money into international or American productions, and producers continue to labour under the misconcep-
tion that landscape makes a film.

Perhaps this catalogue will inspire an interest in preserving our cinematographic heritage, and generate interest in the future of film production in the province. If the
only cinematic versions we have of ourselves continue to come from outside, then we
have nobody to blame but ourselves.

Thomas Meighan snapped in a grimacing pose in a scene from THE
ALASKAN, filmed in British Columbia by the Famous Players-Lasky
Corporation in 1924. (Photo courtesy of the National Film Archives,
Ottawa.)

From l. to r. on a speeder somewhere along the CPR tracks, are F.
Guy Bradford, Cliff Denham, T. Bell, and, with the camera, Joseph
Rosenthal. Rosenthal was sent out by the Warwick Trading Company
between 1900-1902 to make promotional travelogues for the CPR and
was the first cameraman to film British Columbia's fishing and forest industries in detail. Bradford and Denham were his assistants;
Bell was a publicity man for the CPR. (Photo courtesy of the National Film Archives, Ottawa.)

The original caption under this photograph read: "CINEMATOGRAPHING AFRICA FROM A LOCOMOTIVE. In order to secure scenes along the Cape to Cairo Railway a special platform was erected over the cow-catcher of a railway engine for the convenience of Mr. Butcher and his cameras." Mr. Butcher worked for the Charles Urban Trading Company of London, a firm which also filmed several railway sequences in the Canadian Rockies along the CPR, probably employing a similar method. See ADDENDA 27-54. (Photo originally appeared in F.A. Talbot, Moving Pictures, How They Are Made and Worked, 1912.)

These two are very likely "Lovey" (on the left) and "Dearie",
stars of the Edison Manufacturing Company's CPR promotional
film A WEDDING TRIP FROM MONTREAL THROUGH CANADA TO HONG KONG,
filmed along the CPR between June 27 and July 28, 1910. Here
they pose at the bathing pool in Banff just before falling "head
foremost onto the water." A WEDDING TRIP was one of the first
comedies made in Canada. (Photo originally published in Man to
Man Magazine, vol. 6, no. 10, 1910.)

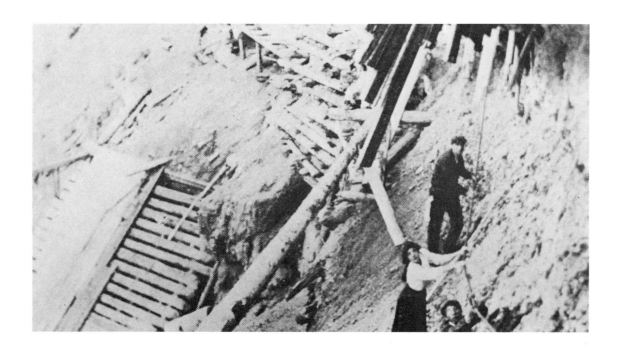

The original captions for this picture read: "Caught in a Land-slide. Thrilling Experience of Actors with Edison Moving Picture Company near Monarch, B.C." This may be a scene from the Edison Manufacturing Company's one-reel adventure A DAUGHTER OF THE MINES, begun on August 14, 1910, during the company's trip across Canada making promotional films for the CPR. (Photo originally published in Man to Man Magazine, vol. 6, no. 10, 1910.)

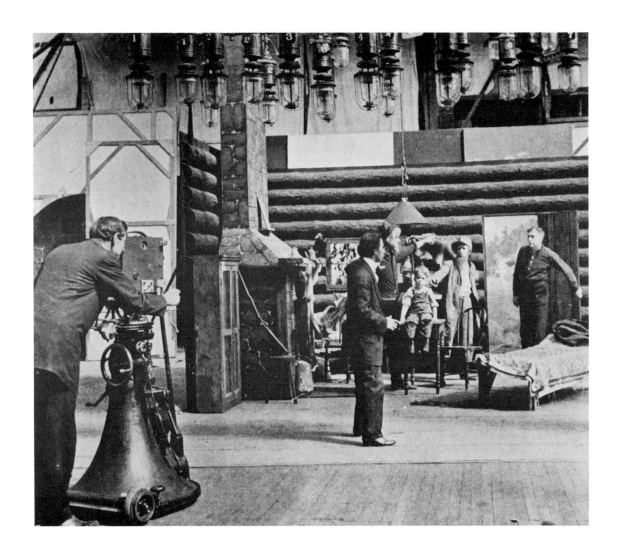

The original caption with this picture read: "THE FILM-PLAY PRO-
DUCER AT WORK. Rehearsing at the Edison Cinematograph Theatre.
This picture shows the stage setting, the powerful battery of
electric top-lights for illuminating the scene, and the electrically driven camera." It was most likely in this "theatre" that
the interior scenes for the Edison Company's promotional one-reel
melodramas for the CPR were filmed. If this is so, the studio
was located in the Bronx. Judging from the date it was printed
and the content, there is a slight possibility that this is in fact
a scene from one of the CPR promotional melodramas. (Photo originally appeared in F.A. Talbot, Moving Pictures, How They Are Made
and Worked, 1912.)

The man in the centre in the three-piece suit is George I. Warren, tireless Victoria promoter and head of the Victoria and Island Publicity Bureau. Warren was responsible for at least three travelogues made during the 1930's and was continually trying to get Victoria into the movies. Those with him are possibly members of the Lawrence A. Hughes Motion Picture Company of Hollywood, in Victoria to make a promotional film. The date is June 9, 1926. (Photo courtesy of the Victoria City Archives.)

Len H. Roos (left) and Byron Harmon on location at the Lake of the Hanging Glaciers, in the British Columbia Rockies, in September, 1920. See ADDENDA 56 & 57. (Photo originally appeared in Lewis Freeman, Down the Columbia, 1921. Print courtesy of Vancouver Public Library.)

A typical falling scene from the Canadian Government Motion Picture
Bureau one-reel industrial film BIG TIMBER, shot in British Columbia
in 1934. (Photo courtesy of the National Film Archives, Ottawa.)

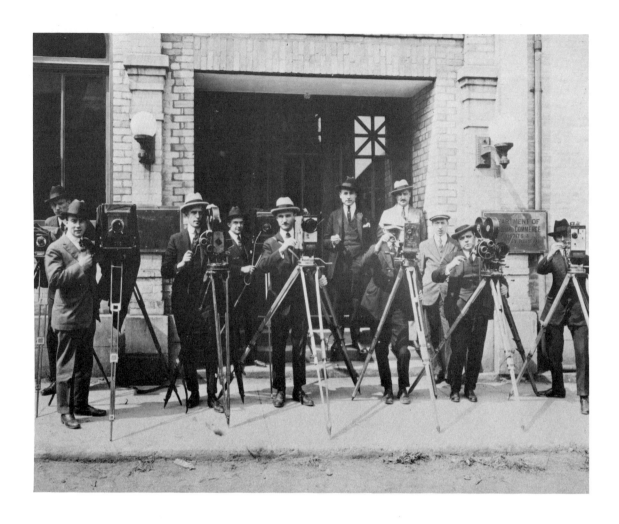

Camermamen of the Canadian Government Motion Picture Bureau outside the Department of Trade and Commerce building in Ottawa about 1925. The director of the Bureau, Raymond Peck, is standing on the steps wearing a black hat and a watch fob. (Photo courtesy of the National Film Archives, Ottawa.)

Victoria Hears "CAMERA"

By PERCY C. RICHARDS

With the announcement that Kenneth J. Bishop's Commonwealth Productions was about to start shooting its first feature, THE MYSTERY
OF HARLOW MANOR, Victoria got its first taste of movie fever.
Featured on the front page of this Sunday supplement are, from l.
to r., David Fair, carpenter and shareholder; Ken Bishop, producer;
and Evelyn Brent, the star. A weak script resulted in the cancell-
ation of the production, and Bishop began work the following September on THE CRIMSON PARADISE. (Photo courtesy of Victoria Press.)

The second floor of a ruined castle built in Victoria by David
Fair in 1933 for the Commonwealth Productions feature THE MYSTERY
OF HARLOW MANOR. The film was cancelled, and the set was never
used. (Photo originally appeared in the Victoria Daily Colonist,
April 23, 1933.)

Kenneth James Bishop, British-born film producer who sought to
make Victoria the film capital of Canada and who nearly succeeded.
His companies – Commonwealth Productions Ltd., Northern Films Ltd.,
and Central Films Ltd. – were responsible for 14 feature films
between 1933-1938. (Photo originally appeared in Victoria Daily
Colonist Magazine, August 29, 1937.)

The Exhibition Building at the Willows Exhibition Grounds
in Victoria where Kenneth Bishop built a motion picture
studio and where three successive motion picture companies,
COMMONWEALTH PRODUCTIONS, NORTHERN FILMS LTD., and CENTRAL
FILMS LTD., produced movies from 1932-1938. (Photo courtesy
of Victoria Press.)

The Capitol Theatre in Victoria, showing the queue for the midnight premiere of the first all-talking feature motion picture produced in Canada. Made by Kenenth Bishop's Commonwealth Productions in 1933, THE CRIMSON PARADISE opened on December 14th and was introduced by the Premier of British Columbia and the Mayor of Victoria. Although it was a great success, Famous Players, which owned the theatre, would only let the film run for three days before pulling it and substituting its usual American fare. The man in the dinner jacket under the "A" is theatre manager Ivan Ackery. (Photo courtesy of the Victoria City Archives.)

Celebrities pose outside the Capitol theatre before the premiere of THE CRIMSON PARADISE in Victoria, December 14, 1933. From l. to r. they are: Lucille Browne, Nick Stuart, Kathleen Dunsmuir (Mrs. Seldon Humphries), Kenneth J. Bishop, the producer, Premier T.D. Patullo, Mayor David Leeming of Victoria, Famous Players district manager Larry Bearg, and Ivan Ackery, manager of the Capitol. (Photo courtesy of the Victoria City Archives.)

Maxine Doyle and David Manners as the centre of attraction on
the gangway of a Canadian Pacific Princess ferry arriving in
Victoria during the filming of LUCKY FUGITIVES in the fall of
1935. The ferry, with life rings disguised by white paint, is
posing as an Atlantic liner. (Photo courtesy of the National
Films Archives, Ottawa.)

Finis Barton and Charles Starrett somewhere near Sidney on Vancouver
Island during the production of Central Films' only western, STAMPEDE,
in the spring of 1936. Note the technician kneeling in the foreground.
(Photo courtesy of the National Film Archives, Ottawa.)

Charles Starrett in Mountie uniform getting his man, J.P. McGowan,
in the Central Films production SECRET PATROL, filmed in and around
Victoria in the spring of 1936. The man looking on to the immediate
left of the Mountie being mauled is Arthur Kerr, and the man in the
hat on the extreme right is James McGrath. (Photo courtesy of the
National Film Archives, Ottawa.)

Some of the cast and crew of Central Films' SECRET PATROL in the
parking lot at Mount Douglas Park near Victoria in May, 1936.
Shown during their tea break are David Selman, director, with his
thumbs in his vest pockets, right-centre, and, standing to the immediate left of him in coat and hat, veteran actor, writer and director J.P. McGowan. The capless man in the center, wearing a scarf
and holding his cup aloft above the Mountie is assistant cameraman
Bill Beckway. Standing in the very centre in a long coat with a
cigarette in his mouth is actor James McGrath. (Photo couretsy of
the Victoria City Archives.)

Camp No. 6 at Youbou on Vancouver Island where the logging camp
sequences were shot for Central Films' "quota quickie" 'LUCKY CORRI-
GAN' during the summer of 1936. The man in the immediate foreground
is the star, William Gargan. (Photo courtesy of the National Film
Archives, Ottawa.)

A scene with Wally Albright, Wendy Barrie, and Lyle Talbot as a British Columbia Provincial Policeman in the Central Films production of VENGEANCE, the company's sixth "quota quickie", produced in Victoria in 1936. (Photo courtesy of the National Film Archives, Ottawa.)

Crew and some of the cast of Central Films' eighth "quota quickie"
shot in Victoria, DEATH GOES NORTH, posing at the base of Mt. Douglas
Park during April or May 1937. The man on the far left wearing a
heavy overcoat is cameraman Harry Forbes. His assistant Bill Beckway is a little to the left of and beneath the Mountie, wearing his
cap turned backwards. Standing to the immediate left of Beckway is
the ex-Mountie who worked as a consultant on the film. Squatting
in the centre of the group is riding instructor Don Carly wearing
the blonde wig he affected when doubling on horseback for Shelia
Bromley. To the left of him in black is director Frank MacDonald
and to the right and slightly above him in a raincoat with his hand
Carly's shoulder is Kenneth J. Bishop. The man with the dog is Lee
Duncan and the dog of course is Rin-Tin-Tin Jr. Standing behind
Bishop in a black coat and tipped fedora is actor James McGrath.
(Photo courtesy of Martin Kroeger.)

Colin Kenny and Iris Meredith with four unidentified policemen
and a corpse in Central Films' tenth "quota quickie" MURDER IS
NEWS, filmed in Victoria in 1937. (Photo courtesy of the National
Film Archives, Ottawa.)

Canadian smokes give away the scene of the action in this production still from Central Films' ACROSS THE BORDER, filmed in
Victoria for Columbia Pictures in 1937. The truck driver at the
left is Edgar Edwards. With him is Charles Quigley and Virginia
Coomb. (Photo courtesy of the National Film Archives, Ottawa.)

Directors of Columbia's "quota quickies" made in Victoria were not able to view "rushes" or "dailies" because exposed film was expressed to Hollywood for processing after each day of shooting. Instead, light-test strips like these were returned to permit the director to choose the density he wished for a given scene. These strips are from CONVICTED, Central's last film, made late in 1937, and show Charles Quigley on the left and Rita Hayworth on the right. (Photo sourtesy of Martin Kroeger.)

Promotional banner erected in Revelstoke during the summer of 1936 to advertise the forthcoming production of the Gaumont British version of the construction of the CPR. The film was released in Canada and the United States under the title SILENT BARRIERS. (Photo courtesy of Mrs. E. Dickey.)

Crew at work on the set of SILENT BARRIERS. (Photo courtesy of
Mrs. E. Bennison.)

Campbell Avenue, Revelstoke, on September 4, 1936, during the
filming of SILENT BARRIERS. In this fictional scene, CPR construction workers are being incited to riot because work on the tracks
has stopped. (Photo courtesy of Mrs. E. Dickey.)

Gaumont British Picture Corporation's version of Moodyville at
Three Valley Gap in the Monashee Mountains, about 250 miles northwest of the original Moodyville at the head of Burrard Inlet near
Vancouver. The extras are probably waiting for the first transcontinental train to arrive from Montreal in this version of the
construction of the CPR titled SILENT BARRIERS. The date is July
18, 1936. (Photo courtesy of Mrs. E. Dickey.)

Everybody's favourite Canadians pose on the cover of the sheet
music for "The Mounties", one of the hits from the 1936 version
of ROSE MARIE, partially filmed in North Vancouver.

(Page numbers refer to pages in the Historical Background)

Page 1

1. See Provincial Archives of British Columbia, Visual Records division (PABCVR) for Frederick Dally's photographs of Barkerville (1867-68) and for photos of Vancouver during that city's construction and the fire of 1886.

2. Information regarding John Schuberg gathered in interviews with his family; from *Canadian Film Weekly* (CFW), 24 Apr 1963, p. 4; and from "Pictures of the Past and Present" in *The History, Objects, By-Laws, and Roster of the Canadian Picture Pioneers*, Canadian Picture Pioneers, Toronto, 1955. The latter group is worthy of further attention by students of Canadian branch-plant mentality since the "Pioneers" were, and still are, the Canadian representatives of the United States distribution chains which have, since their creation, successfully throttled the exhibition and distribution of Canadian motion pictures.
Faking newsreels was common practice, particularly in the early days, and was carried out with skill and enthusiasm by the three United States companies then in competition: Edison, Biograph, and Vitagraph. Some of Edison's Cuban footage is genuine, but much of it was faked to provide "what the people wanted to see". Albert E. Smith, Vitagraph cameraman, quoted in R. Fielding, *The American Newsreel, 1911-1967*, Norman, Oklahoma, 1972, p. 29 ff.

3. Victoria *Daily Colonist*, 25 Mar 1930, p. 10. Also Fielding, *The American Newsreel, 1911-1967*, pp. 11-12, for more on the company, the fight, and the fraudulent recreation.

4. Fielding, *The American Newsreel*, p. 25. The U.S. Library of Congress Paper Print Collection cites Robert K. Bonine as Edison's Klondike Photographer.

Page 2

5. Victoria *Daily Colonist*, 1 July 1917, pp. 24-25, 27.

6. Most histories of film making chronicle the beginnings and development of Hollywood. See the Tantivy-Barnes *Hollywood* series, *Hollywood in the 20's, 30's, 40's, 50's, 60's, Today* for an ongoing idea of movie development (distributed in Canada by Smithers and Bonellie, Toronto).

Page 3

7. F.A. Talbot, *Motion Pictures, How They Are Made and Worked*, London, 1912, pp. 132-3.

8. Canada, Department of Trade and Commerce, *Sixth Census of Canada*, Vol. 1, Ottawa, 1921.

Page 4

9. See INDUSTRY'S ENDLESS WAR IN THE FORESTS, a Fox news story (1923); STRIPPING A FOREST IN WINTER, Urban-Eclipse (1909); CONQUEST OF THE FOREST, Canadian Government Motion Picture Bureau (CGMPB) (1936); SAGA OF THE SILVER HORDE, CGMPB (1935); SALMON FISHING ON THE SKEENA, CGMPB (1918).

10. Trailers are generally called previews by the public. Usually the most exciting and titillating scenes from a film are shown in the trailer to lure the customer into the movie house.

11. Some CGMPB and Associated Screen Studios films fitted this formula. Examples are SHE CLIMBS TO CONQUER, AMID ALPINE SNOWS, A BIT OF HIGH LIFE, YOHO, and THE GAME IS UP. The National Parks Bureau, for whom the CGMPB produced dozens of promotional films, was particularly disposed towards this kind of short.
See also Lewis R. Freeman, *Down the Columbia*. New York: Dodd, Mead and Company, 1921. This entertaining book chronicles the travels of an American adventurer down the Columbia River from Windermere, B.C., to the Pacific in September-November, 1920. With him were cameraman Len. H. Roos and, for a short time, Byron Harmon of Banff. Freeman's hilarious exposés of the cameramen's tricks are well worth reading, and provide a very accurate picture of how the popular nature films of the day were manipulated by imaginative photographers.

12. Such items were favourites of desperate newsreel photographers, some of whom often invented human-interest stories using their children as actors. Typical is KIDDIES HAVE A REAL PARTY AT ELKS PICNIC IN HASTINGS PARK, shot in Vancouver in the 1920's, and shipped to New York for hopeful inclusion in a Fox news story.

Page 5

13. One of the most interesting amateur reels is the Reverend G.R.B. Kinney's KOOTENAY LAKES SCENES which show an Old Timer's Picnic at Proctor, on Kootenay Lake, in 1933. This fascinating footage contains a wonderful sequence showing local pioneers in their sixties and seventies competing in energetic running and novelty races that few oldtimers would hazard today.

14. For more information see Pierre Berton, *Hollywood's Canada - The Americanization of Our National Image*, Toronto, 1975; and a Victoria *Daily Colonist* editorial for 11 Feb 1922, p. 4.

15. See POLICING THE PLAINS, THE CRIMSON PARADISE, SECRETS OF CHINATOWN, and THE GREAT BARRIER (in

Canada, SILENT BARRIERS). In other parts of Canada successful motion pictures were produced from the adventure novels of Ralph Connor, pseudonym of Major, the Reverend Charles W. Gordon. These include GOD'S CRUCIBLE (based on *The Foreigner*, 1920), CAMERON OF THE ROYAL MOUNTED (1920), THE MAN FROM GLENGARRY (1922), and GLENGARRY SCHOOL DAYS (1922).

Page 6

16. More information regarding Quota pictures follows in Part III of this introduction.

17. Three of Bitzer's reels for American Mutoscope and Biograph are still in existence: DOWN WESTERN SLOPE, FRAZER CANYON, and MOUNT STEPHEN. Two others are lost: FRAZER CANYON, EAST OF YALE, B.C., and UNDER SHADOW OF MOUNT STEPHEN.

18. The Edison reels are number 637-639 & 641-646 in the catalogue.

19. G.W. Bitzer, *Billy Bitzer, His Story*, New York, 1973, p. 6.

Page 7

20. Charles Backhouse, *Canadian Government Motion Picture Bureau, 1917-1941*, Ottawa, 1974, p. 3.

21. *Ibid.*, pp. 3-4; Canadian Picture Pioneers, *The History, Objects, By-Laws and Roster of the Canadian Picture Pioneers*, page seven of the "Pictures of the Past and Present" section; and, most importantly, the *Catalogue* of the Charles Urban Trading Company, 1903, pp. 27-31 & 39-46, and the *Supplement* to that catalogue of Jan 1904, pp. 5-8. The three members of the Warwick-Urban camera crew were Joseph Rosenthal, chief cameraman, and his two assistants F. Guy Bradford and Clifford Denham. The CPR advisor was T. Bell. The 21 Urban films appear in this catalogue as ADDENDA 27-54.

Page 8

22. Victoria *Daily Colonist*, 5 May 1907, p. 3.

23. Talbot, *Moving Pictures, How They Are Made and Worked*, p. 126, and Kinemacolor Limited, *Kinemacolor Catalogue of Films, 1912-13*, London, 1913, pp. 274-278. See also D.B. Thomas, *The First Colour Pictures*, London, 1969, pp. 13-34. Not to be outdone by the CPR, the Grand Trunk Pacific Railway and Steamship Company announced in May 1913, that it too was becoming involved in promotional film making. R.C.W. Lett, tourist and colonization agent for the railway, was preparing to escort a photographer along the line to Prince Rupert through northern British Columbia, promising at the same time to organize and film a grizzly bear hunt. Vancouver *Daily World*, 22 May 1913, p. 5. See *Moving Picture World Magazine (MPW)*, 1 Aug 1915, p. 1036, for details of a later expedition.

Page 9

24. Norman S. Rankin, "With the Edison Players Across the Continent", *Man to Man Magazine*, vol. 6, No. 10, 1910, pp. 934-40; Vancouver *Daily World*, 30 July 1910, p. 23; Victoria *Daily Times*, 3 Aug 1910, p. 3; *Colonist*, 5 Aug 1910, p. 3; *Colonist* "Magazine", 7 Aug 1910, p. 12; *ibid.*, 2 Jan 1911, p. 12; *MPW*, 1 Oct 1910, p. 942; *ibid.*, 29 Oct, p. 1004; *ibid.*, 5 Nov 1910, p. 1065; *ibid.*, 19 Nov 1910, p. 1178; *ibid.*, 31 Dec 1910, p. 1511. See also DREAMLAND: A HISTORY OF EARLY CANADIAN MOVIES 1895-1939, distributed by the National Film Board of Canada, for excerpts from the Edison two-reelers. The members of the cast were James P. Gordon, Richard R. Neill, Mr. and Mrs. Herbert Prior, Miss Laura Sawyer, and Charles Sutton. They were accompanied by J.S. Dennis, a vice-president of the CPR, J. Welsh of the *Columbia Magazine*, and part of the way by Norman S. Rankin representing *Man to Man Magazine*.
The four Edison films still in existence are AN UNSELFISH LOVE, THE SONG THAT REACHED HIS HEART, THE LIFE OF A SALMON, and about half of A TRIP OVER THE ROCKIES AND SELKIRK MOUNTAINS. The number of CPR promotional dramatic films made in 1910 is not known, but there were at least a dozen. According to the Edison Manufacturing Company's picture production log, a facsimile of which was furnished to the author by the Edison National Historic Site in Orange, New Jersey, the following twelve were made during the trip: THE SONG THAT REACHED HIS HEART, AN UNSELFISH LOVE, A WEDDING TRIP FROM MONTREAL THROUGH CANADA TO HONG KONG, RIDERS OF THE PLAINS, THE COWPUNCHER'S GLOVE, A TRIP OVER THE ROCKIES AND SELKIRK MOUNTAINS, THE SWISS GUIDE, THE LITTLE STATION AGENT, THE STOLEN CLAIM, THE LIFE OF A SALMON, THE SHIP'S HUSBAND, and A DAUGHTER OF THE MINES. A thirteenth film, MORE THAN HIS DUTY, is cited by Berton, *Hollywood's Canada*, p. 247, as made by Dawley and Cronjager during the western trip, while the following three may also have been filmed at the same time: OVER MOUNTAIN PASSES, THROUGH THE CLOUDS, and A MOUNTAIN MAID. See Howard Lamarr Walls, *Motion Pictures, 1894-1912*, Washington, D.C., 1953.
A copy of the Dramatic Synopsis of AN UNSELFISH LOVE exists today at the Museum of Modern Art in New York City, appended to which is the Spanish translation for each of the subtitles.

25. Vancouver *Daily Province*, 12 Mar 1908, p. 1; *ibid.*, 14 Aug 1908, p. 1.

26. *Ibid.*, 13 Sept 1913, p. 26; *Colonist*, 21 October 1913, p. 7; *ibid.*, 25 Apr 1914, p. 3 The surviving footage is listed as catalogue entry 891b.

Page 10

27. Thomas, *The First Colour Pictures*, pp. 29-30.

4

28. *Daily World*, 3rd Section, 9 Sept 1911, p. 1. For more information about the original corona-
     tion films and their disappointing effect on Vancouver audiences see *ibid.*, 10 July 1911, p. 11.

29. *Ibid.*, 28 July 1910, p. 8.

30. *Colonist*, 24 May 1913, p. 10; Fielding, *The American Newsreel*, p. 159.

Page 11

31. *Op. cit.*, 27 Feb 1913, p. 2; *Province*, 1 Oct 1913, p. 1. The opinion that British Columbia's
     censorship was the most rigid in the continent was widely held in the trade. Canadian motion
     picture trade magazines protested naturally enough because their very existence depended upon
     an unimpeded flow of American products.

32. *MPW*, 28 Aug 1915, p. 1503; *ibid.*, 9 Oct 1915, p. 305. The Victoria *Daily Times* reported on
     20 Feb 1914, p. 11, that the provincial censor, Mr. L.C. Gordon, had examined 4,500 films (av.
     length 1000' each) since the creation of his position in Apr 1913, and that he had rejected
     198, or 4.5%. He had, however, made excisions in 353, about 8% of the total, cutting 901 sec-
     tions totalling between 10,000 - 12,000 feet.
     Censorship of motion pictures is fascinating enough to study in depth, though space is limited
     here. Those interested should consult the Moving Pictures Act (1913) and the provincial cen-
     sor's recommendations for specific films requiring rejection or elimination. These documents,
     which today appear as bizarre as the films they deal with, are a particularly lucid guide to
     the official morality of the province from 1913 to the early 1960's. See Provincial Archives
     of British Columbia (PABC), Attorney General's Department, *Files of the Provincial Censor,
     1913-1960, passim.*

33. See PABC, Department of the Attorney General *Files of the Provincial Censor, 1913-1960.* The
     Motion Picture Censor's rejection and eliminations file reveals that Sergei Eisenstein's
     BATTLESHIP POTEMKIN (1925) was rejected on 9 Mar, 1935, as being "Quite unsuitable for public
     exhibition during present unrestful times." OCTOBER (TEN DAYS THAT SHOOK THE WORLD) (1927)
     was rejected on 29 Apr 1935, for much the same reason. It is a mark of their genius that these
     two masterpieces of the cinema were still found disturbing ten years after they were made.
     Sex and crime were usually dealt with much less severely by eliminating offensive sections.
     In a film called THE FATAL GLASS OF BEER the distributor was required to "Eliminate scene of
     Salvation Army girl kicking man in face, with accompanying dialogue." (1 Mar 1933). Often
     the only offense was suggestive language, in which case the phrase or sentence was eliminated,
     such as, "... when a gal's flat on her back." (PRIZEFIGHTER AND THE LADY), 2 Dec 1933), "Tell
     your boyfriend to keep his finger nails trimmed." (CHILD OF MANHATTAN, 25 Mar 1933), and an
     entire dialogue beginning with, "Do you think you can weekend me darling?" and ending with,
     "Of course if you want to change your meal tickets." (CALL HER SAVAGE, 13 Jan 1933).
     A film called NIGHT OF TERROR was totally rejected on 30 Oct 1933, for: "Too many murders".
     In NOTHING BUT THE TOOTH the censor directed that the sound of a toilet flushing be eliminated
     (30 Sept 1933). And in a one-reel short called STRANGE AS IT SEEMS, NO. 30, the censor made
     the following recommendation: "Eliminate entire scene of man being inflated by auto pump, and
     vulgar deflation. Dangerous example which might be followed by children." (2 Aug 1933). The
     author's favourite occurred on 14 June 1940, to a crime melodrama called MEN WITHOUT SOULS.
     In his reasons for rejecting, the censor penned the following remarkable paragraph with obvious
     conviction:

>   Even the title of the picture is out of keeping, as there are no men without souls,
>   and although this is a figurative title only, it would appear that they would have
>   the audience accept it as literally *(sic)*.

     Regarding newsreels, the censor's report on 4 Apr 1938, rejected scenes in a Fox Movietonews
     reel showing a May Day parade in Russia and, later, a spitting contest. On 12 Oct 1939, the
     following directive was issued on Fox newsreel no. 9: "Eliminate entire sequence of Hitler
     entering Poland, with demonstration - 150 feet." No further explanation is given or, presum-
     ably, required. And, in July 1940, a sequence showing two corpses was eliminated from Fox
     Movietone newsreel no. 79. These examples illustrate that the censor felt that some of the
     news was clearly not fit to print, especially if it was disturbing or contradictory to official
     propaganda.

Page 12

34. Charlie Chaplin's famous downtrodden tramp, representing the "little man" in industrial society,
     is the obvious example of the motion picture bias that Chaplin later clarified with film state-
     ments like CITY LIGHTS (1931), MODERN TIMES (1936), and THE GREAT DICTATOR (1940). See also
     D.W. Griffith's MUSKETEERS OF PIG ALLEY (1912), INTOLERANCE (1916), BROKEN BLOSSOMS (1919),
     Erich Von Stroheim's GREED (1923), Fritz Lang's METROPOLIS (1926), and the social revolutionary
     films of Sergei Eisenstein: STRIKE (1924), BATTLESHIP POTEMKIN (1925), OCTOBER (TEN DAYS THAT
     SHOOK THE WORLD) (1927), and QUE VIVA MEXICO! (1931), released under this title and also, be-
     cause he was not able to complete the film, released in sections titled THUNDER OVER MEXICO
     (1933) and TIME IN THE SUN (1939).

35. Fielding, *The American Newsreel*, pp. 115-122. Lt. D.J. Dwyer. an official Canadian Army cine-
     matographer, returning home to Victoria from the front during the war, related many of his

experiences, as an aerial photographer, to the *Colonist*. According to Dwyer, air pockets were responsible for a then extravagant shooting ratio of 1 to 4. *Colonist*, 20 Apr 1917, p. 5.

36. *MPW*, 28 Aug 1915, p. 1503; *ibid.*, 12 Feb 1916, p. 1000.

Page 13

37. *Colonist*, 27 Jan 1917, p. 9; *ibid.*, 2 Feb 1917, p. 8; *ibid.*, 22 Feb 1917, p. 8; *ibid.*, 27 Feb 1917, p. 7. See also Addendum 19 in this catalogue. One of the assignments of Superfluities' cameraman Rosedale was to film patrons as they entered the Royal Victoria Theatre to watch the Red Cross show. These films were developed, printed quickly, and shown later in the week to attract more customers.
A more profitable venture than Superfluities was the Sunset Film Company, established late in 1916. Sunset advertised as a training school for hopeful young screen actresses and asked the girls to deposit $5.00 towards their lessons when signing their contract. Apparently the applicants were never subsequently contacted and some of them complained to the police that the secretary had attempted to take liberties with them. Upon investigation the police discovered that the secretary had already left town and that his partner was in jail, having recently been convicted of molesting a twelve-year-old girl. The money, of course, had disappeared. *Ibid.*, 26 Jan 1917, p. 7.

38. Backhouse, *Canadian Government Motion Picture Bureau*, pp. 5-7; *Canadian Moving Picture Digest* (hereinafter *CMPD*), 15 Jan 1921, p. 21; Canada, Department of Trade and Commerce, *Annual Reports*, 1917-19; also an unpublished list of motion pictures produced by the Exhibits and Publicity Bureau, Department of Trade and Commerce up to Dec 1 1919, a copy of which was obtained from the archives of the Department of Trade and Commerce in Ottawa. See also *Report* of Privy Council Committee, 19 Sept 1918 re: the Bureau, and Mary O. Hill, *Manuscript of the Official History of the Department of Trade and Commerce*, Ottawa. The films mentioned are: THROUGH CANADA FROM COAST TO COAST, THRILLS APLENTY FOR THE ALPINE CLIMBER IN THE CANADIAN ROCKIES, VIRGIN FIELDS FOR EXPLORERS, and BANFF NATIONAL PARK.

39. Backhouse, *Canadian Government Motion Picture Bureau*, p. 8. As well as the films mentioned in the text and in n. 38, see THE GREAT NATURAL INDUSTRIES OF CANADA, MT. ASSINIBOINE, UNBLAZED TRAILS, WOODEN SHIP-BUILDING IN CANADA, A WORLD OF SCENIC WONDERS, BUILDING AEROPLANES IN CANADA, SALMON FISHING ON THE SKEENA, THE ENEMY OF THE FOREST, CAMPFIRES AMONG SNOW PEAKS, IN THE YOHO VALLEY, and A CITY OF SUNSHINE.

40. Backhouse, *ibid.*, p. 1. See also the chapter on "Cinema and the Empire" in *The Film in National Life*, London, 1932, pp. 126 ff. (Commission on Educational and Cultural Films into the service which the Cinematograph may Render Educational and Social Progress).

Page 14

41. Backhouse, *op cit.*, pp. 8 & 35; Canada, Department of Trade and Commerce, *Annual Reports*, 1921-22, *passim*.

42. Backhouse, *op cit.*, p. 11 and Canada, Department of Trade and Commerce, *Annual Reports*, 1921 and 1923, *passim*.

43. British Columbia, Department of Travel Industry, Photographic Branch, *Catalogue of Films 1975-76*. To this day, the Department is concerned almost entirely with promoting the province.

44. Canada, Department of Trade and Commerce, *Annual Report*, 1933.

45. "The Motion Picture Act Amendment Act, 1920", received Royal assent on 17 April 1920. The exact wording of the section which describes the type of films to be shown is laid down under the director's responsibilities as follows:

> "The Director, acting under instructions of the Attorney General, shall:
> (a) Provide for the taking, making, procuring, acquiring, and public exhibition of films and slides of a patriotic, instructive, educative, or entertaining nature; and in particular, without limiting the generality of the foregoing, films and slides depicting the natural, industrial, agricultural, or commercial resources, wealth, activities, development, and possibilities of the Dominion, and especcially of the Province, or which may tend to inform and educate the public as to the affairs, institutions, and people of the Dominion, and especially of the Province, or which may tend to inform or educate the public as to Imperial, Federal, or Provincial public events, and the men and women of note connected therewith; ..."

Page 15

46. *CMPD*, 1 June 1921, p. 10; British Columbia Legislature, *Public Accounts*, pp. A 75-76 (1922), p. A 74 (1923), p. O 74 (1924); and British Columbia, *Journal of the Legislative Assembly*, 29 Mar 1921. Because no information was available in the *Public Accounts* regarding the amount of money spent by the Patriotic and Educational Picture Service during its first year, the attorney general was questioned in the legislature on Tuesday, 29 Mar 1921. His answer was, that between 17 Apr 1920, and 1 Dec 1920, the total expenditure was "Approximately $18,500.00." According to the *Public Accounts*, far less was spent on the Service over the next three years:

$10,066.48 in 1921-22, $2,515.57 in 1922-23, and $3,298.34 in 1923-24. The large expenditure during the first year may have been for the purchase of the original inventory of slides and films for loan to the theatres. Kean is mentioned in the *Public Accounts* as a recipient for unspecified cinematographic services, earning over $3000.00 in 1923-24.

47. *Colonist*, 24 Nov 1920, p. 1; *ibid.*, 26 Nov 1920, p. 5; *ibid.*, 1 Dec 1920, p. 16. The edition of 24 Nov claimed that one of the films released to the theatres "depicts what is alleged to be oyster beds, alleged to be owned by Mr. W.J. Bowser (leader of the Conservative Party in opposition), with Hindus working thereon. The thing is a palpable fake!"

48. *Ibid.*, 26 Nov 1920, p. 5.

49. No mention of further expenditure under the authority of the Motion Picture Act Amendment Act (1920) occurs in the *Public Accounts* after 31 Mar 1924.

Page 16

50. Backhouse, *Canadian Government Motion Picture Bureau*, p. 22.

51. Gordon Sparling, Vankleek Hill, Ontario, correspondence with the author, 2 June 1977; Fielding, *The American Newsreel*, pp. 83-4. See also the NFB documentary DREAMLAND in which Mr. Sparling explains why Ben Norrish, president of ASN, was reluctant to enter the newsreel production business. His primary fear seems to have been retaliation by the large U.S. newsreel companies which were neither keen on more competition nor on losing the lucrative Canadian market.

52. *Daily Times*, 7 Dec 1931, p. 1.

53. See CANADIAN MOUNTAIN MAJESTY, FROM SEA TO SEA, MOUNTAIN SUMMER (Addendum 18). The CPR Archives have lost all track of promotional films made for the company in the early days.

Page 17

54. Sparling to author, 27 Sept 1976; 18 May 1977; and 2 June 1977. THE GAME IS UP is a re-edited version of the CGMPB's CLIMBING MOUNT TUPPER, and SEA ROVER'S SUMMER was put together with footage shot by Bill Oliver from the Bureau's SEA LIONS OF THE PACIFIC. The information about the CANADIAN CAMEOS is partially contained in a list, called "CANADIAN CAMEO SERIES - Releases from February 1932 to September 15 1953", in the ASN files at the National Film Archives in Ottawa. I am especially indebted, however, to Gordon Sparling who supplied many specific details not available elsewhere.

55. Eastman Kodak Company, *Ciné-Kodaks and Other Eastman Home Movie Equipment: The Catalogue of Eastman Home Movie Equipment*, Rochester, 1930, p. 4. The Ciné-Kodak was responsible for almost all amateur 16mm film shot in British Columbia before World War II because, despite its limitations, it was easy to use and reliable.

56. See PABCVR, Victoria, B.C., to view these films, which are available on a very restricted basis.

Page 18

57. Apparently British Columbia's Department of Agriculture produced no films after Tolmie's defeat in 1933. Moreover, the department, by 1976, was unable to shed any further light on this early film programme.

58. Information regarding films of the British Columbia Forest Service and George Melrose, thanks to Barbara Davies at the Service's Photo branch.

59. British Columbia Legislature, *Public Accounts*, Department of Finance, 1929-1938; *ibid.*, Department of Trade and Industry, 1938-1942; British Columbia, Department of Trade and Industry, *Annual Report*, 1938-1942.

60. See Registrar of Companies for files re: Vancouver Motion Pictures Ltd. The files on Motion Screen Adz Ltd. were unfortunately destroyed. I am indebted to Wally Hamilton for his insight into the history of these two firms. See also the *Colonist*, 17 Jan 1931, p. 7; *ibid.*, 5 Aug 1931, p. 3; and *CMPD*, 19 July 1930, p. 10, for more information about the involvement of Howard Boothe and Wally Hamilton in making travelogues for the provincial government.

Page 19

61. Information about early film making by the B.C. Government Travel Bureau thanks to Dick Colby, former deputy-minister of Travel Industry, who provided background information and an analysis unavailable elsewhere. See also British Columbia Legislature, *Public Accounts*, Department of Trade and Industry, 1938-1942; and Marjorie C. Holmes, *Publications of the Government of British Columbia, 1871-1947*, Victoria, 1950, p. 225 and *passim*. Holmes lists a 7-page *Catalogue of 16mm Motion Pictures* issued by the Provincial Bureau of Information in 1937 which would, if it had not been lost, assist greatly in detailing the early films made by the Bureau. See KAMLOOPS - WELLS GRAY PARK; SPA OF CANADA; PRO-RECS, VANCOUVER; THE RADIANT ROCKIES; NORTH OF THE BORDER and EVERGREEN PLAYLAND.

62. British Columbia Government Travel Bureau Photo Branch, *Catalogue of 16mm Motion Pictures*, Victoria, 1952.

63. *Colonist*, 17 Nov 1925, p. 18.

64. Interest in promoting either Victoria or Vancouver as the film capital of the British Empire increased with the first mention of a possible British quota in 1925. Alderman J.A. Shanks of Victoria was particularly voluble on the subject as seen in the *Colonist*, 5 July 1925; p. 29, *ibid.*, 18 Nov 1926, p. 4, while both the *Colonist*, 19 Nov 1926, p. 4, and the *Daily Times*, 19 Nov 1926, p. 4, carried editorials extolling the virtues of Victoria as the new Canadian Hollywood. Throughout December both papers received letters of support and proposals from various businessmen requesting financing. The sudden flurry of activity was apparently occasioned by questions being considered at the Imperial Conference in London. Canadians were lobbying hard for a place in the British quota legislation. When the "Cinematograph Films Act" was passed in London in December, 1927, and it was established that films produced in the British Empire with a large percentage of participation by British subjects would qualify for the quota.
   J.S.H. Matson, publisher of the *Colonist*, was particularly keen to acquire a piece of the movie business and arranged to seek support in Hollywood in May 1930. Matson told the Americans that there were plans afoot to build a great British Empire film studio in Victoria and that the first feature would be an "Indian story", using native Indians living on Vancouver Island. When he returned to Victoria he was forced to admit that the "Indian story" was not exactly accurate and that the studio was not really definite. All the same, the newspapers reported on June 17 that a Mr. Edwin Bower Hesser, a cameraman and art director from Hollywood, was visiting Mr. Matson and that he was most excited about Victoria's possibilities. On June 22 both newspapers lavished headlines on Hesser's visit and Matson's initiative. Hesser (*Colonist*, that date, p. 6) seems to have been the only realist. All Victoria needed, he said, was money. Which was not forthcoming. See *Colonist*, 1 June 1930, p. 5; *ibid.*, 8 June 1930, p. 5; *ibid.*, 17 June 1930, p. 3; *ibid.*, 22 June 1930, pp. 1 and 6; *Daily Times*, 22 June 1930, p. 1.
   It is interesting to reflect that twenty-four days later in London, England, "an historical event and scientific achievement" took place that would completely revolutionize the moving picture business thirty years later. Luigi Pirandello's *The Man With the Flower* was broadcast successfully over the Baird system of television. The new medium had assured its success by proving itself capable of handling theatrical events. *Daily Times*, 16 July 1930, p. 3.

Page 20

65. British Columbia Registrar of Companies, *Company file for British Canadian Pictures, Ltd.*; and Peter Morris, *Canadian Feature Films, 1913-69, Part I: 1913 - 1940*, Ottawa, 1970, p. 4.

66. British Columbia, Registrar of Companies, *Company file for Dominion Films Corporation, Limited*; *Colonist*, 17 Jan 1917, p. 8; *ibid.*, 21 Jan 1917, p. 7; *ibid.*, 1 Feb 1917, p. 8; *ibid.*, 13 Feb 1917, p. 11; and both the *Colonist*, p. 28 and the *Daily Times*, p. 7, 10 Feb 1917, for the company's large advertisement for its booklet "The Industry Which is Making Millionaires."

Page 21

67. Hye Bossin, *Film Weekly Year Book of the Canadian Motion Picture Industry*, Toronto, 1951, p. 36; Vancouver *Evening Sun*, 26 May 1927, pp. 1 and 16; and *ibid.*, 30 May 1927, p. 3, for the syndicate's advertisement entitled 'Clean Movies'.

68. *Colonist*, 27 Jan 1933, p. 1; *Daily Times*, 3 Feb 1933, p. 13, *ibid.*, 16 Feb 1933, p. 1; and *CMPD*, 18 Feb 1933 p. 5.

Page 22

69. See catalogue for these titles. Many more American films containing "Canadian" or "Northwestern" content were produced in the 1920's and 1930's, but all were photographed in California, Washington, Oregon, or Montana. The most famous American movie about Canada, MGM's version of Rudolph Friml's ROSE MARIE, made in 1936 and starring Jeanette MacDonald and Nelson Eddy, was supposed to be set in northern Quebec, but was actually filmed in North Vancouver, near Capilano Canyon, and at Lake Tahoe in California. See catalogue. Pierre Berton's *Hollywood's Canada* reveals the extent to which American studios have confused Canadians about their national image and provides a good introduction to the subject.

70. See *CMPD*, 8 July 1922, p. 5; *ibid.*, for 20 Dec 1922, p. 26; 24 Oct 1925, p. 2; 31 Oct 1925, p. 4; and 9 Apr 1927, p. 13.

71. *Canadian Film Weekly (CFW)*, 13 Mar 1963, p. 5. Gordon Sparling, who saw part of POLICING THE PLAINS, remembers seeing rolls of Kean's negative in the vault when he joined ASN in 1931. He writes: "One vivid shot showed a lonely Mountie wearing a pill-box cap, standing guard at the unfinished end of steel. (Probably Mr. Norrish was holding it as security for unpaid bills!) Whatever happened to the material I haven't a clue. In those days, expensive fireproof vault space was too valuable for storing current nitrate masterpieces or squandering it on sentimental archives." Sparling to author, 27 Sept 1976.

72. Wally Hamilton and Clifford Bourne remember seeing some of Kean's negative rolls at Vancouver Motion Pictures Ltd., in the 1930's. Information about the Ontario government lab is from *CMPD*, 9 Apr 1927, p. 13.

73. *CFW*, 13 Mar 1963, p. 5.

Page 23

74. *Ibid*. See fn. 71 and 72.

75. Vancouver *Daily Province*, 18 Sept 1929, p. 13. The original head of the investigation was Professor Kenneth W. Taylor of McMaster University.

76. *Ibid.*, 7 July 1931, p. 2.

77. Attorney-General Pooley's statement occured in *ibid.*, 7 July 1931, p. 1. Reference to the Province of Ontario action is from *ibid.* for 13 Sept (p.30), 23 Sept (p.4) and 9 Oct (p.13), 1931.

78. *Daily Province*, 7 Mar 1932, p. 1 and *Daily Times*, 29 Mar 1932, p. 13. See also the film DREAMLAND, distributed by the NFB, for more information about this remarkable case. A Canadian employee of an American newsreel company told the author that he was afraid to tell what he knew about inter-company practices when he was called as a witness before the inquiry. If his testimony had been discovered as having prejudiced his company he would have been fired, which meant he would also have been backlisted by the other newsreel companies. Since witnesses were questioned in secrecy and individually, he recalls that he was also very concerned about what those ahead of him had said, not wanting to compromise them either. As a consequence he divulged nothing of importance to the investigators.

Page 24

79. Information about the Ontario quota is from the *Daily Times*, 23 July 1932, p. 8, and André Pâquet (ed.), *How to Make or Not to Make a Canadian Film*, Montreal, 1967, 7th page. The Ontario Board of Censors ruling occured in 1932.
The *Colonist* editorial was written for the 9 July 1932 edition, p. 4. One year earlier the *Daily Times* of 8 July 1931, p. 4, had declared that the moving picture combine was the least detrimental combine in Canada, adding that the public determines the marketplace no matter who makes or distributes the pictures. The *Times* suggested that if the federal government really wanted to be useful it would look into the industrial combines that existed at that time. MLA George Walkem's statement appeared in the Vancouver *Sun*, 10 Mar 1932, p. 15.

80. Soloman Kean. *Daily Province*, 10 Apr 1932, p. 1.

81. British Columbia Legislature, "Moving Picture Act Amendment Act, 1932". The Act received Royal Assent on 13 April 1932.

Page 25

82. Parliament of Great Britain, "Cinematograph Films Act, 1927". See also the Report of the Commission on Educational and Cultural Films, *The Film in National Life*, pp. 45-6, and Rachel Low, *The History of the British Film, 1918-1929*, London, 1971, p. 97. The Cinematograph Films Act also made blind and block booking illegal in Great Britain. This prevented distributors from compelling an exhibitor to accept four or five pictures he had not seen as part of a package deal which included an obviously lucrative picture he had seen. It also eliminated the old lever of forcing an exhibitor to accept three or four inferior pictures as the price for booking a "hit". These booking practises are still fairly common in Canada today. The nine major American producer-distributors today split 80%-90% of the rental fees earned in Canada with the two largest theatre chains, Famous Players and Canadian Odeon. In 1978 these two chains owned or controlled 612 movie screens across Canada. Canada is the largest foreign market for American film and is the only film-producing country in the world with no form of protection for its own product. The result is an almost total lack of cash support generated at the box office for Canadian feature film production. Ninety-six per cent of the feature films shown in Canadian theatres originate in the United States. See Council of Canadian Film-makers, *Newsletter of the Council of Canadian Film-makers*, Toronto, Apr 1976, pp. 15-16 and 18-21.

83. Low, *The History of the British Film, 1918-1929*, p. 95. See also the Commission on Educational and Cultural Films, *The Film in National Life*, pp. 128-9, and the editorial in the *Colonist*, 19 Nov 1926, p. 4.

84. Information about Bishop's past is sketchy. He was born, the son of the Station Master, in the Station House at Sutton in Surrey, England, on the 20th of April, 1893. According to a newspaper interview, he came to Canada from his home in London, England, to work for the CPR c. 1907. He left for Hollywood in 1911, and worked as an actor for Colonel William Nicholas Selig for several years. Selig was a pioneer American film producer who reportedly made the first full-length feature film produced in Hollywood (IN THE SULTAN'S POWER, June 1909). Subsequently Bishop left for New York where he worked for a film distributing agency. A brief passage in *CMPD* (Apr 1937) tells how in 1923 Bishop became the owner of a dog called "*Lightning*", a famous canine star that apparently died in 1935. According to the article, Bishop took "*Lightning*" from Staten Island, N.Y., to make a movie in Hollywood with Eileen Sedgewick. He appears to have remained in Hollywood where he may have become an independent producer. Jack Chisholm recalled in a conversation with the author that he thought Bishop had been a promoter or "hustler" for Columbia during his later Hollywood days. Whatever the

truth may be, it is fair to say that Bishop's movie-making enterprises in Victoria were probably the most successful of his life. See *CMPD*, 9 Dec 1933, p. 10; *ibid.*, 3 Apr 1937, p. 5; and *Colonist* "Magazine", 29 Apr 1937, p. 1.

85. British Columbia, Registrar of Companies, *Company file for Commonwealth Productions, Ltd.* See also *Daily Times*, 24 Aug 1932, p. 1.

86. Information about the ill-fated THE MYSTERY OF HARLOW MANOR is from the *Colonist*, 5 Feb 1933, p. 1; *ibid.* "Magazine", 25 April 1933, p. 1; and *CMPD* for 18 Feb (p. 5), 13 May (p. 6), and 27 May (p. 6) 1933.

Page 26

87. Information re: THE CRIMSON PARADISE is from the *Colonist* "Magazine", 12 Nov 1933, p. 1, *Colonist*, 15 Dec 1933, pp. 1 and 14; *Daily Times*, 15 Dec 1933, p. 1 and 19; and *CMPD*, 4 Nov (p. 9 & 10) and 30 Dec (p. 6), 1933.

88. From a personal interview with Mr. Ackery, Vancouver, 1977. See also Ackery's memories of THE CRIMSON PARADISE in the *Daily Province* "Magazine", 14 Dec 1973, p. 4. In that article Ackery is quoted as saying: "We only played THE CRIMSON PARADISE a week, as I recall, but we did sensational business. It was a real turkey. So lousy it was good. Everyone wanted to see the local people and local scenes. I had 20,000 leaflets dropped from a plane. They said: 'Come to the premiere of the first all-Canadian talking picture made in Victoria.' People thought I was mad. But I wanted action."

89. *Daily Times*, 9 Mar 1935, p. 20.

90. *Film Daily (FD)*, 20 Feb 1935.

91. *Daily Province*, 15 Mar 1935 p. 4; and *Daily Times*, 15 Mar 1935, p. 1. The actor who introduced each performance in Victoria was Harry Hastings, who also portrayed Shan Tao Ling, the hooded leader of the smugglers. See also *Colonist*, 15 Mar 1935, p. 1, and *ibid.*, 16 Mar 1935, p. 2.

92. *Ibid.*, 19 Mar 1935, p. 6. The quote describing the eliminated scene is from the Provincial Censor's *Report*, 15 Mar 1935.

Page 27

93. *Daily Times*, 2 Feb 1934 (p. 13), 16 Feb 1934 (p. 15) and 5 Mar 1934 (p. 13); *Colonist* for 7 Feb (p. 3), 6 Mar (p. 3) 23 Aug (p. 5), 1934 and *CMPD*, 24 Feb (p. 4) and 7 Apr (p. 6), 1934.

94. Information about the transfer of assets from Commonwealth Productions Ltd., to Northern Films Ltd., is contained in documents held by the Registrar of Companies in Victoria. See also *Colonist*, 23 Aug 1934, p. 5.

95. The figure $28,000 was reported in a story in the *Daily Times*, 5 Mar 1934, p. 15. The figure of $50,000 was recalled by lawyer Patrick J. Sinnott in an article in the *Province* "Magazine", 14 Dec 1973, p. 4. Kathleen Dunsmuir's true investment in the enterprise probably was closer to the latter figure. Mr. Michael Heppell, a local actor who played in most of Bishop's films, recalls that when the Commonwealth Productions crew was shooting THE CRIMSON PARADISE at Hatley Park, Miss Dunsmuir's family estate, she fed everyone breakfast, lunch, and supper as it was needed. For many of the stagehands and extras these seemed like feasts; they were the first nutritious meals they had eaten in weeks. See also *CMPD*, 19 May 1934, p. 6.

96. Information courtesy National Film Archives (NFA), Ottawa.

97. See British Columbia, Registrar of Companies, Company File for Central Films, Ltd. Also, see *Daily Times*, 4 Dec 1935, p. 15; *ibid.*, 29 May 1936, p. 15; *Colonist*, 17 July 1937, p. 1; *Colonist* "Magazine", 29 Aug 1937, p. 1.
All the Central Films, with the exception of LUCKY FUGITIVES, are extant. The negatives have been entrusted to the NFA, Ottawa. A list of the Central films in order of completion is as follows: LUCKY FUGITIVES, TUGBOAT PRINCESS, SECRET PATROL, STAMPEDE, "LUCKY" CORRIGAN, VENGEANCE, WOMAN AGAINST THE WORLD, DEATH GOES NORTH, MANHATTAN SHAKEDOWN, MURDER IS NEWS, ACROSS THE BORDER, and CONVICTED. For dates and specifics see catalogue entries.
Not all the American stars were under contract to Columbia; some were free-lancers and others were loaned out from rival studios.
Nineteen year-old Rita Hayworth starred in ACROSS THE BORDER and CONVICTED. For more information about Miss Hayworth, see John Kobal's recent biography, *Rita Hayworth: The Time, the Place, and the Woman*, London, 1977.

98. I am indebted for this information to Martin Kroeger of Victoria, B.C., who worked continuity for each of the Central Films, and who began the adaptation of the radio script for THE MYSTERY OF HARLOW MANOR. Whenever the Columbia crew came up to Victoria from Hollywood, Columbia producer Jack Fier accompanied them. As the studio was interested in squeezing as much out of its Victoria venture as it could, two films were usually made together, often with the same actors and the same director and crew. Officially, Kenneth Bishop was listed as the producer of each film (he was still a British Subject) but it was really Fier who had the final word. Bishop might more correctly be called "local producer and location manager"

for the Central films.

99. The films which used a New York-type location were LUCKY FUGITIVES, VENGEANCE, MANHATTAN SHAKEDOWN, MURDER IS NEWS, WOMAN AGAINST THE WORLD, and CONVICTED. Logging camps were featured in "LUCKY" CORRIGAN, SECRET PATROL and DEATH GOES NORTH. Mounties appear in SECRET PATROL, DEATH GOES NORTH, and ACROSS THE BORDER.

Page 28

100. See Low, *The History of the British Film, 1918-1929*, pp. 102-106. Bernard Shaw's reaction to the 1927 quota legislation, reported by Ms. Low (p. 97) was: "My contempt for it deprives me of speech!", a remarkable admission for so eloquent a spokeman. The 1938 revision was titled "The Cinematograph Films Bill, 1938".

101. Lindgren et al., *20 Years of British Film, 1925-1945*, London, 1947, pp. 23-24. See also the *Colonist*, 24 Feb 1938, p. 1, and the *Daily Times*, 24 Feb 1938, pp. 1-2. The *Daily Times* article deduced that at the current rates the new "quality clause" required a British Empire producer to spend at least $37,500 on labour alone to have his picture qualify for the British quota. Going further and assuming that the labour costs represented usually fifty to sixty per cent of a film's cost, the producer would be faced with having to spend at least $77,500 for each picture, about half again as much as the average expenditure on each of the twelve Central films produced by Columbia.

102. Information about Bishop's optimistic hopes for a renewal of production is in *CMPD*, 19 Mar 1938, p. 11 and *ibid.*, 2 July 1938, p. 10. Demolition of the studios is mentioned in *ibid.*, 22 Apr 1939, p. 25. The *Colonist*, 7 Apr 1938, p. 2, reports that when Columbia Pictures deserted him, Bishop felt that they had broken their contract. He took the matter to court, but on 6 Apr 1938, was told that Central Films had no case since Columbia Pictures Corporation of N.Y. was out of the court's jurisdiction and because no provision had ever been made for them to be liable under any law of the province of British Columbia.

103. Information about Bishop's death is from Martin Kroeger and Don Carly, both of Victoria, B.C., and from the Division of Vital Statistics, Victoria. Bishop died on 6 Sept 1941, aged 48, and is buried in the Masonic Cemetery in Burnaby, B.C.

104. Fielding, *American Newsreel*, pp. 159-163. The famous Jolson film THE JAZZ SINGER used the Vitaphone system, a method whereby a phonograph record was synchronized to each reel of film as it was projected. Thoroughly impractical, it was soon replaced by a sound-on-film system pioneered by Lee De Forest during the early 1920's. At this time several films were made using the De Forest system but producers were not interested, probably because the system was still in its primitive stage of development. De Forest's design was improved upon, however, by Theodore Case, and was purchased by the Fox Film Corporation in July 1926. Soon after, the Fox Movietone Corporation was established and, more than eight months before THE JAZZ SINGER premiered, the first Movietone news films were being exhibited in New York. Five months later, on 20 May 1927, the world saw Lindbergh speaking on film for the first time. The first known Fox Movietone news film shot in British Columbia appears to have been a story about three old sea captains taking their tot of Silver Spring beer on an Esquimalt wharf on 31 Oct 1928. See OLD TIME MARINERS TAKE THEIR TOT, VICTORIA, B.C.

Page 29

105. From conversations with Mr. Russ Simpson who worked for Paramount News in Canada for many years, Sidney, B.C., 1976-77.

106. It is important to remember that there were no Canadian newsreels, merely Canadian editions of American newsreels. Russ Simpson claims from his own recollections that news prepared by Paramount and other companies was always checked by federal Liberal Party publicity flacks while Mackenzie King was prime minister to make sure that King's image was complimentary. An item which might compromise the leader in any way was followed by a demand that the sequence be withdrawn upon pain of the company having its licence to operate in Canada revoked. Paramount's decision to use Canadian news commentator Winston Barron after the Canadian raid on Dieppe in 1942 was, according to Mr. Simpson, a matter of expediency. Canadians felt that their contribution to World War II should be reported to them by Canadians, or at least appear that way. The war accentuated the differences between Canada and the United States, and with patriotism at its height after Dieppe (which the newsreels claimed was an American battle), the newsreel companies realized that Canadians wanted to feel as if their war effort was being channelled to them through Canadian sources. Using a Canadian voice in the Canadian edition was the surest way of creating the illusion.

107. Pâquet, *How to Make or Not to Make a Canadian Film*, p. 7; Backhouse, *Canadian Government Motion Picture Bureau 1917-1941*, pp. 20-27.

Page 30

108. See John Grierson, *Grierson on Documentary*, New York, 1947, *passim*. Grierson is quoted in Backhouse, *op. cit.*, p. 15, as reporting a friend's opinion on Canadian film in 1931 as follows:

"If life in the Dominion is as these films represent, we might expect Canadians to engage only in fishing, golf, and the observation of wild animals. There are practically no industries, very little work, and no working people."

Apparently nothing changes; a British Columbia travel film called IF I DIDN'T SEE IT I WOULDN'T BELIEVE IT (1976) has a traveller being exposed to a rapid montage of British Columbia scenery showing attractive people engaging in wholesome and costly sporting activities. In desperation he asks, "Doesn't anyone work here?"
The documentary form really flowered in Great Britain where Grierson produced such strong and memorable films as DRIFTERS (1929), a four-reeler about the herring fleet in the North Sea and, with the GPO film unit, THE SONG OF CEYLON (1934), COALFACE (1936) and NIGHT MAIL (1936), a flow of images and sound on the mail train from London to Scotland in counterpoint with verses by W.H. Auden and music by Benjamin Britten.

109. Backhouse, *ibid.*, pp. 26-31.

110. *Ibid.*, pp. 31-34. See THE ROYAL VISIT. Under Grierson's command Stuart Legg began the world-famous CANADA CARRIES ON series in 1939, a series so popular it was being distributed to nearly 700 theatres in Canada by 1941 and one which, in its early stages, showed scenes of mobilization and training from across the Dominion.

Page 31

111. Information about ROYAL BANNERS OVER OTTAWA is from Associated Screen Studios' CANADIAN CAMEO advertising pamphlet issued on the company's 20th anniversary in 1952, a copy of which was sent to the author by Gordon Sparling. Prints of the CGMPB film THE ROYAL VISIT and its French version, LA VISITE DE NOS SOUVERAINS, are at the NFA, Ottawa.

112. The opening titles and credits for THE ROYAL VISIT contain the following sentence: "All organizations associated with the production, presentation, and distribution of this film are donating their receipts to the Canadian Red Cross."

113. See FISHERMEN READIED FOR WAR, ESQUIMALT, B.C.; FISHING FLEET GETS NAVAL TRAINING, ESQUIMALT, B.C.; RCN TRAINING AT ESQUIMALT; RECRUITING, VANCOUVER, B.C.; and WOMEN'S MILITARY UNIT, VANCOUVER, B.C., in the catalogue.

114. See Riefenstahl's TRIUMPH OF THE WILL (1934) and OLYMPISCHE SPEILE (1936).

115. See references to each of these cinematographers in the catalogue cross-index. For more information about and stills from Edward S. Curtis's film, see his book-version of *In The Land of the Head-Hunters*, originally published in Yonkers-on-the-Hudson, New York. by The World Book Company, 1915. A reprint (1975) is available from Tamarack Press, Box 276, Stinson Beach, California.
Information regarding the exhibition of Harlan Smith's films is from David Zimmerly, *Museocinematography - Ethnographic Film Programs of the National Museum of Man. 1913-1972*, Ottawa, 1972, p. 2.

Page 32

116. Lewis R. Freeman, *Down the Columbia*, New York, 1921, pp. 23-24.

117. See references to Kinney's films, under his name in the index.

BIBLIOGRAPHY

ARCHIVES

British Columbia, Provincial Archives. *Annual Report of the Department of Trade and Industry*, in *Sessional Papers of the Parliament of British Columbia, 1939-42.* Victoria, King's Printer, 1939-1942.

British Columbia, Provincial Archives. Attorney-General's Department, *Report Files of the Provincial Film Censor* 1931-1942.

British Columbia, Provincial Archives. *Public Accounts*, in *Sessional Papers of the Parliament of British Columbia, 1921-40.* Victoria, King's Printer, 1921-40.

British Columbia, Provincial Library. *Journals of the Legislative Assembly, 1895-1940.* Victoria, King's Printer, 1895-1940.

Canada, Public Archives. *Annual Report of the Department of the Interior, 1917-1936.* Ottawa, King's Printer, 1917-36.

Canada, Public Archives. *Annual Report of the Department of Mines and Resources, 1937-1941.* Ottawa, King's Printer, 1937-41.

Canada, Public Archives. *Annual Report of the Department of Trade and Commerce, 1917-1941.* Ottawa, King's Printer, 1917-41.

Canada, Public Archives. *Certified copy of a Report of the Committee of the Privy Council, approved by His Excellency the Governor General on the 19th September, 1918, re the Exhibits and Publicity Bureau, Ottawa, Department of Trade and Commerce, 1918.*

PUBLISHED BOOKS

Backhouse, Charles. *Canadian Government Motion Picture Bureau 1917-1941.* Ottawa, Canadian Film Institute, 1974.

Beattie, Eleanor. *A Handbook of Canadian Film.* Toronto, Peter Martin Associates in association with *Take One* magazine, 1973.

Berton, Pierre. *Hollywood's Canada - The Americanization of Our National Image.* Toronto, McClelland and Stewart, 1975.

Bitzer, G.W. *Billy Bitzer, His Story.* New York, Farrar Straus and Giroux, 1973.

Bossin, Hye (ed.). *Film Weekly Year Book of the Canadian Motion Picture Industry.* Toronto, Film Publications of Canada, 1951.

Buchanan, Donald W. *Documentary and Educational Films in Canada (1935-1950).* Ottawa, Canadian Film Institute, 1952.

Buchanan, Donald W. *Educational and Cultural Films in Canada.* Ottawa, The National Film Society of Canada, 1936.

Canadian Picture Pioneers. *The History, Objects, By-Laws, and Roster of the Canadian Picture Pioneers.* Toronto, 1955-1958.

Cinema Commission of Inquiry instituted by the National Council of Public Morals. *The Cinema: Its Present Position and Future Possibilities*. London, Williams and Norgate, 1917.

Commission on Educational and Cultural Films into the service which the Cinematograph may render Educational and Social Progress. *The Film in National Life*. London, George Allen Unwin, 1932.

Eastman Kodak Company. *Storage and Preservation of Motion Picture Film*. Rochester, New York, n.d.

Fielding, Raymond. *The American Newsreel, 1911-1967*. Norman, University of Oklahoma Press, 1972.

Freeman, Lewis R. *Down the Columbia*. New York, Dodd Mead, 1921.

Grierson, John. *Grierson on Documentary*. London, Collins, 1946.

Lindgren, Balcon, Hardy and Marwell. *20 Years of British Film, 1925-1945*. London, The Falcon Press, 1947.

Low, Rachel. *The History of the British Film, 1918-1929*. London, George Allen and Unwin, 1971.

Morris, Peter (ed.). *The National Film Board of Canada: The War Years*. Ottawa, Canadian Film Institute, 1965.

Paquet, André (ed.). *How to Make or Not to Make a Canadian Film*. Montréal, la Cinémathèque Canadienne, 1967.

Talbot, F.A. *Moving Pictures: How They Are Made and Worked*. London, William Heinemann, 1912.

Thomas, D.B. *The First Colour Motion Pictures*. London, Her Majesty's Stationery Office, 1969.

Wood & Freeman. *Motion Pictures in the Classroom*. Boston, Houghton Mifflin, 1929.

UNPUBLISHED BOOKS

Hill, Mary O. *Manuscript of the official history of the Department of Trade and Commerce*. Ottawa, Department of Trade and Commerce, 1975.

CATALOGUES

British Columbia Forest Service. *A Catalog of the Educational Films Available From B.C. Forest Service*. Victoria, The King's Printer, 1947.

British Columbia Government Travel Bureau Photo Branch. *Catalogue of 16mm Motion Pictures*. Victoria, The King's Printer, 1952.

British Film Institute. *List of 16mm Geography Teaching and Travel Films*. London, The British Film Institute, 1939.

British Film Institute. *List of 16mm Science Films*. London, The British Film Institute, 1938.

Canadian Government Motion Picture Bureau. *Catalogue of Motion Pictures Produced by the Canadian Government Motion Picture Bureau*. Ottawa, The King's Printer, 1926.

Canadian Government Motion Picture Bureau. *Catalogue of Motion Pictures Produced by the Canadian Government Motion Picture Bureau.* Ottawa, The King's Printer, 1930.

Charles Urban Trading Co., Ltd. *Catalogue.* London, 1903.

Charles Urban Trading Co., Ltd. *Supplement to 1903 Catalogue.* London, 1904.

Charles Urban Trading Co., Ltd. *Catalogue.* London, 1909.

Chittock, John (ed.). *World Directory of Stockshot and Film Production Libraries.* Oxford, Pergamon Press, 1969.

Copyright Office, Library of Congress. *Motion Pictures, 1912-1939.* Washington, 1951.

Department of Trade and Commerce. *Unpublished mimeographed list of motion pictures produced by the Exhibits and Publicity Bureau of the Department of Trade and Commerce.* Ottawa, 1919.

Eastman Kodak Company. *Ciné-Kodaks and Other Eastman Home Movie Equipment: The Catalogue of Eastman Home Movie Equipment.* Rochester, New York, 1930.

Edison Manufacturing Company. *Catalogue of Motion Pictures.* Orange, New Jersey, 1902.

Kleine, George. *Catalogue of Educational Motion Picture Films.* Chicago, 1910.

Graphics Consultants, Ltd. *Early Films: A Catalogue of Films, 1907-1930.* Toronto, 1966.

Holmes, Marjorie C. *Publications of the Government of British Columbia, 1871-1947.* Victoria, The King's Printer, 1950.

Kinemacolor Catalogue of Films, 1912-13. London, 1913.

Kinemacolor Films 1915-16. London, 1916.

Kodascope Libraries of Canada, Ltd. *Descriptive Catalogue of Kodascope Library Motion Pictures.* Toronto, n.d. (late 1920's).

Kodascope Libraries of Canada, Ltd. *Descriptive Catalogue of Kodascope Library Motion Pictures.* Toronto, 1938.

Morris, Peter (ed.). *Canadian Feature Films: 1913-1969, Part I: 1913-1940.* Ottawa, Canadian Film Institute, 1970.

Munden, Kenneth W. *The American Film Institute Catalogue of Motion Pictures Produced in the United States - Feature Films, 1921-30.* New York, R.R. Bowker, 1971.

A National Encyclopaedia of Educational Films and 16mm Apparatus. London, 1935.

National Museum of Canada. *Catalogue of Motion Picture Films.* Ottawa, The King's Printer, 1933.

National Parks Bureau. *List of Films Available from the National Parks Bureau.* Ottawa, The King's Printer, 1943.

Niver, Kemp. *Motion Pictures from the Library of Congress Paper Print Collection. 1894-1912.* Berkeley, University of California Press, 1967.

Province of Ontario Film Bureau. *Catalogue of 28mm Slow-Burning Film.* Toronto, The King's Printer, 1927.

University of Washington Press. *University of Washington Press Books and Related Audio-visual Materials in Anthropology.* Seattle, University of Washington Press, 1976.

Walls, Howard Lamarr. *Motion Pictures, 1894-1912.* Washington, Copyright Office, Library of Congress, 1953.

Zimmerly, David W. *Museocinematography: Ethnographic Film Programs of the National Museum of Man, 1913-1972.* Ottawa, Ethnology Division, National Museum of Man, 1972.

MAGAZINE ARTICLES

Rankin, Norman S. *"With the Edison Players Across the Continent".* Vancouver, *Man to Man Magazine,* vol. 6, no. 10: 934-940, 1910.

MAGAZINES CONSULTED

Canadian Film Weekly. Toronto.

Canadian Moving Picture Digest. Toronto.

Film Daily. New York.

Monthly Film Bulletin of the British Film Institute. London.

Motion Picture World Magazine. New York.

NEWSPAPERS CONSULTED

The Daily News-Advertiser, Vancouver, 1895-1917.

The News-Herald, Vancouver, 1933-December 18, 1937.

The Vancouver News Herald, Vancouver, December 20, 1937-1941.

The Province, Vancouver, 1895-January 19, 1900.

The Vancouver Daily Province, Vancouver, January 20, 1900-1941.

The Sun, Vancouver, 1912-1916.

The Vancouver Daily Sun, Vancouver, 1917-May 1920.

The Vancouver Sun, Vancouver, June 1920 - May 1924.

The Vancouver Morning Sun, Vancouver, June 1924 - January 1926.

The Vancouver Daily World, Vancouver, 1895 - March 11, 1924.

The Vancouver Evening Sun, Vancouver, March 12, 1924 - September 1927.

The Vancouver Sun, Vancouver, October 1927 - 1941.

The Victoria Daily Colonist, Victoria, 1895-1941.

The Victoria Daily Times, Victoria, 1895-1941.

MOTION PICTURE FILMS

Dreamland: A History of Early Canadian Movies 1895-1939. Produced by The Great Canadian
Moving Picture Company with the assistance of the National Film Board of
Canada. 85 minutes 53 seconds, b+w, 16mm, sd. Available from the National
Film Board of Canada (106B 0174 112). 1974.

CATALOGUE

HOW TO USE THIS CATALOGUE

The entries in this catalogue are listed alphabetically by title. Each film is assigned a number. The index on p. |348| is an alphabetical arrangement of subjects and names, the numbers referring to the film numbers in this catalogue, not to page numbers.

Each entry is set out in a consistent format. A blank space indicates that information was not known at the date of publication. These spaces permit the researcher to complete the entry should missing data subsequently become available.

Line 1   Catalogue number, film title and year of production.
Line 2   Producing Company (p.c.)
Line 3   Length (l.), gauge (g.), tint (t.), and whether film is sound or silent (s.).
Line 4   Director (d.)
Line 5   Photographer (ph.)
Line 6   Current Status (c.s.) of film; e.g. if the film still exists, where it may be found. If the film is not known to exist an asterisk is shown.
Line 7   Description

Where more than one line is required to complete the information ascribed to that line, it will be completed on the next and subsequent lines. This will result in the remainder of the entry dropping one or more lines as space requires. The change required by this will not affect the order of the data.

Note - guage refers to the size of film (35mm or 16mm) on which the original was shot. Most 35mm films can be obtained on 16mm stock.

NOTES ON LOCATING FILM

When I began this project, it was my intention to view every piece of film that might qualify for inclusion. I was also guilty of throwing the word comprehensive around pretty loosely. Now, three years later, I wonder that I could ever have been so optimistic. The truth is that I only really had a chance to view a small portion of the films described and have therefore had to rely on the descriptions and shot lists of other archivists more than I had expected. Without disparaging their work, it is important to mention that description-writers who have never been to British Columbia are at the mercy of captions, titles, friends, co-workers, and extrapolations; there is a chance that they have been mislead or that they are not as aware of details as a native might be. With more time and greater resources this will eventually be remedied but, for now, this warning will have to suffice. I accept full responsibility for the information as it stands and any corrections or additions will be gratefully accepted. Every effort has been made to avoid mistakes and confusion.

The main problem with the catalogue is going to be access to films. While it may be enjoyable to dream about the films included, it will be difficult to actually view them and examine them closely because little of the footage is stored in British Columbia. The commercial film libraries will be pleased to show you anything they have but you must go to them. In the case of Fox Movietonews in New York, because there are 323 entries in their files dealing with British Columbia up to 1940, and because it is a long and costly procedure to check the vaults to see if the reels still exist, the entries listed do not guarantee that the film is available. Therefore, it would be wise to check with Fox for specific titles before going to see them. The National Film Archives in Ottawa can show you whatever they have available in their collection (many titles don't have viewing copies yet); so can the U.S. National Archives and the Library of Congress, both in Washington, D.C. The Provincial Archives of British Columbia have not catalogued their film holdings yet, nor do they have facilities for viewing the reels in their possession and access is severely limited. Most of the agencies charge a viewing fee, therefore it is a good idea to let them know beforehand exactly what you are looking for and why.

Royalty and reproduction fees vary and are subject to increases as the cost of processing rises. For this reason, none of the institutions listed are willing to guarantee a fixed price and all suggested that they can be contacted individually regarding fees. In most cases, price differs depending upon profit or non-profit use, so be sure to specify the reason for ordering at the beginning.

For obvious reasons, private holders of film were not anxious to have their names and addresses listed in the catalogue, so an arrangement has been made with the Pacific Cinémathèque in Vancouver whereby mail will be forwarded to the private holder who will then decide what steps he or she wishes to take regarding the request. The procedure is as follows: Write two letters - one to the Pacific Cinémathèque and one to the private holder. The letter to the private holder must be sealed in a stamped envelope, and enclosed in a second envelope which is addressed to the Pacific Cinémathèque.

Write a note to Cinématheque explaining which entry you wish to know more about, giving its number and title. They will then address your inside envelope and mail it to the appropriate holder who will then get in touch with you directly. Please add to the exterior of the envelope addressed to the Pacific Cinématheque the words: RE - B.C. EARLY FILM CATALOGUE. If this method works, it will save a great deal of frustration and trouble and will assure private holders of the seriousness of the request. A self-addressed, stamped return envelope with which to reply might also be appreciated by the private holder.

More information about the films listed in the Catalogue may be secured from the archive or film library possessing the material. The following addresses were correct at time of printing.

ADDRESSES

Archives of the Anglican Diocese of British Columbia
Synod Office
912 Vancouver Street
Victoria, B.C. V8V 3V7   (604) 386-7781

Astral Films
c/o Canfilm Screen Services
956 Richards Street
Vancouver, B.C. V6B 3C5   (604) 682-3646

Automobile Club of Southern California
PO Box 2890 Terminal Annex
Los Angeles, California 90051
USA   (213) 746-4410

Barry Casson Film Productions
895 Walfred Road
Victoria, B.C. V9C 2P1   (604) 478-7211

British Columbia Department of Highways
Attention: Senior Information Officer
Room 214, Douglas Building
Victoria, B.C. V8V 1X4   (604) 387-3182

British Columbia Department of Travel Industry
Photographic Branch
1117 Wharf Street
Victoria, B.C. V8W 2Z2   (604) 387-6419

British Columbia Forest Services Information
 Division
Photo Lab
527 Michigan Street
Victoria, B.C. V8V 1X5   (604) 387-5298

British Columbia Mines Library
Room 430, Douglas Building
Victoria, B.C. V8V 1X4   (604) 387-6407

British Film Institute
Information and Documentation Department
81 Dean Street
London W1V 6AA
England   01-437 4355

Canadian Film Institute
75 Albert Street
Suite 1105
Ottawa, Ontario K1P 5E7   (613) 238-7865

City of Vernon Board of Museum and Archives
3009-32nd Avenue
Vernon, B.C. V1T 2L8   (604) 542-3142

Fox Movietonews Library
c/o Movietonews, Inc.
1345 Avenue of the Americas
New York, N.Y. 10019
USA   (212) 397-8548

(Library address: 460 West 54th Street
                    New York, N.Y.)

Hearst Metrotone News
235 East 45th Street
New York, N.Y. 10017
USA   (212) 682-7690

Imperial War Museum
Lambeth Road
London SE1 6HZ
England   01-735 8922

Jack Chisholm Film Productions, Ltd.
277 Davenport Road
Toronto, Ontario M5R 1K4   (416) 925-2281

The Library of Congress
Reference Department
Prints and Photographs Division
Washington, D.C. 20540
USA   (202) 426-5000

Metro-Goldwyn-Mayer
c/o Bellevue Film Distributors, Ltd.
1644 West 75th Avenue
Vancouver, B.C. V6P 6G2   (604) 263-2494

Movietone Film Library (British Movietonews,
 Ltd.)
North Orbital Road
Denham, near Uxbridge
Middlesex
England   Denham 2323

The Museum of Modern Art
Department of Film
11 West 53rd Street
New York, NY 10019
USA   (212) 956-6100

National Archives and Records Service of the
  United States
Motion Picture Department
Pennsylvania Avenue and 8th N.W.
Washington, D.C.
USA   (202) 963-1110

National Film Archives
Public Archives Canada
344 Wellington Street
Ottawa, Ontario K1A 0N3   (613) 995-1311

National Film Board of Canada Archives
3155 Cote de Liesse
Saint-Laurent, Quebec H4N 2N4   (514) 333-3333

National Museum of Man
Communications Division
Ottawa, Ontario   (613) 996-9438

Pacific Cinematheque Pacifique
1616 West 3rd Avenue   (604) 732-6119
Vancouver, B.C. V6J 1K2   and   732-5322

Pathe Film Library
EMI Film Distributors, Ltd.
Film House, 142 Wardour Street
London X1V 4AE
England   01-437 0444

Provincial Archives of British Columbia
Visual Records
655 Belleville Street
Victoria, B.C. V8V 1X4   (604) 387-6505

British Columbia Provincial Museum
675 Belleville Street
Victoria, B.C. V8W 1A1

          Ethnology (604) 387-6514
     Modern History (604) 387-3648
          and 387-6001

Sherman Grinberg Film Libraries, Inc.
1040 North McCadden Place
Hollywood, California 90038
USA   (213) 464-7491

Sherman Grinberg Film Libraries, Inc.
630 Ninth Avenue
New York, NY 10036
USA   (604) 731-5288

University of British Columbia Library
Special Collections Divsiion
University of British Columbia
2075 Wesbrook Place
Vancouver, B.C. V6T 1W5   (604) 228-2521

University of Washington Press
Audiovisual Division
Seattle, Washington 98105
USA   (206) 543-4050

Visnews Film Library
Cumberland Avenue
London   NW10 7EH
England   01-965 7733

ADDENDUM

Direction Générale du Cinéma et de l'Audiovisuel
1601 Blvd. Hamel
Québec, Québec G1N 3Y7   (418) 643-2121

ABBREVIATIONS

ASN	Associated Screen News		HA	High angle shot
BCPM Eth	Ethnology Division, British Columbia		LHi's	low high shot
	Provincial Museum		LOC	Library of Congress
BCPM Hist.	History Division, British Columbia		l.p.	leading players
	Provincial Museum		LS	long shot
b.g.	background shot			
BFI	British Film Institute		MCU	medium close-up
BS	back shot		MGM	Metro-Goldwyn-Mayer
b+w	black & white		MLS	medium long shot
			mm	millimetres (refers to film guage)
CCF	Co-operative Commonwealth Federation		MS	medium shot
CFI	Canadian Film Institute			
CGMPB	Canadian Government Motion Picture Bureau		n.d.	no date
CNR	Canadian National Railway		NFA	National Film Archives (Canada)
col.	colour		NFB	Archives of National Film Board of Canada
c.s.	current status		NMM	National Museum of Man (Canada)
cu	close-up shot		NWMP	North West Mounted Police
d.	director		p	producer
elev.	elevated shot		PABC	Provincial Archives of British Columbia
EPB	Exhibits and Publicity Bureau, Department		pan	panoramic shot
	of Trade & Commerce		p.c.	production company
			PGE	Pacific Great Eastern Railway
f.g.	foreground		ph.	photographer
fol.	follow shot		PNE	Pacific National Exhibition

RCN	Royal Canadian Navy	UA	United Artists
red	stock tinted red for effect	UBC	University of British Columbia
		USNA	United States National Archives and Record Service
SCU	semi close-up		
sd.	sound		
si.	silent	vcs	very close shot
tit.	titling		

Director Gordon Sparling, on the left, and cameraman Ross Beesley shooting location material for several Associated Screen Pictures in Western Canada during the summer of 1937. The camera is a 35mm Bell & Howell silent, camera driven by a 100 v. motor powered by portable batteries. Beesley is using an Akeley gyro tripod. Mr. Sparling attributes their worried looks to the onslaught of a new batch of clouds covering the sun.

(Photo courtesy of Gordon Sparling.)

1. ACROBAT THRILLS SPECTATORS BY STANDING ON HIS HEAD ON TOP
   OF A HIGH BUILDING, VANCOUVER, B.C. (1923)
   p.c. Fox Movietonews (Fox #735.2-B1862)
   l.   g. 35mm   t. b+w   s. si.
   d.   *
   ph. Len H. Roos
   c.s. Fox Movietonews, N.Y.

   "He also eats meal upside down"

2. ACROSS CANADA (1925)
   p.c. CGMPB
   l. 1 reel   g. 35mm   t. b+w,   s. si. w/captions
   d.   *
   ph.   *
   c.s. Unknown

   "A one-reel journey from coast to coast, embracing many of the Dominion's scenic splendours and points of interest."

3. ACROSS CANADA BY CANOE AND PORTAGE IS LENGTHY TRIP
   ATTEMPTED BY PAUL PAQUIN AND DICK LESAGE, VANCOUVER,
   B.C. (1929)
   p.c. Fox Movietonews (Fox #731.53-D0163)
   l. 90'   g. 35mm   t. b+w   s. si.
   d.   *
   ph. Beesley
   c.s. Fox Movietonews, N.Y.

   "Mayor Malkin sees them off."

4. ACROSS CANADA BY CPR. (1934 ?)
   p.c. ASN
   l. approx. 400' g. 16mm   t. b+w   s. si.
   d.   *
   ph. ASN (?)
   c.s. Unknown

   Little is known of this film but presumably it shows scenes across Canada on the CPR mainline. It was made before 1935 and carries the following description: "From apple blossom time in Nova Scotia to the Canadian Pacific Rockies to Vancouver and Vancouver Island."

   The scenes shot in British Columbia show: Passing the Divide. Observation car on train. Mountain scenery - canyons, conifers and snow. Vancouver, views of the town with skyscrapers. Giant conifers near Vancouver. Crossing to Vancouver Island. Views of Victoria. C.P.R. steamer lying in harbour bound for Japan, etc.

5. ACROSS CANADA IN 15 MINUTES. (n.d.)
   p.c. *
   l. approx. 400' g. 16mm   t. b+w   s. si.
   d.   *
   ph.   *
   c.s. Unknown

   "A trip by rail and steamer up the St. Lawrence to Quebec, Ottawa, Toronto, Hamilton, Lake Superior, Ontario, Winnipeg, Vancouver."

5a. ACROSS THE BORDER. (1937)
   p.c. Central Films, Ltd.
   l. 54 min. 9 sec. g. 35mm   t. b+w   s. sound
   d.   Leon Barsha
   ph. George Meehan
   c.s. NFA (negative only, no sound track)

   Canadian p., Kenneth J. Bishop; sc. Edgar Edwards; ed. William Austin; asst.d., George Rhein; musical d. Moris Stoloff; art d. Lionel Banks; Columbia overseer, Jack Fier.

   l.p. Rita Hayworth, Charles Quigley, George McKay, Edgar Edwards, Eddie Laughton, Arthur Kerr, Bill Irving, Grant MacDonald, Robert Rideout, Virginia Coomb, Fred Bass, Vincent McKenna, Don Douglas.

Working title: THE DEVIL IN ERMINE. The eleventh Quota Quickie made by Central Films, Ltd., for Columbia Pictures in Victoria. It was begun in November 1937. ACROSS THE BORDER was copyrighted in the United States, with the title SPECIAL INSPECTOR, by Warwick Pictures, Ltd., on February 20, 1939. The story concerns a gang of fur thieves whose successful robberies are threatening the fortunes of a Canadian fur company called the Arctic Fur and Trading Company. It appears that the stolen furs are turning up in San Francisco so an agent from the United States Customs is brought in to investigate. He takes an undercover job as a truck driver for the Arctic Fur Company and during his first job he, and the driver showing him the ropes, pick up a girl seeking a ride to San Francisco. Farther along the road the robbers stop the truck and the two drivers are captured. The girl escapes. The truck is driven off to a secret hideout and the drivers are knocked out, tied up, and thrown out along the road. The girl reports the robbery to the police who search the highway and arrest the two drivers. The undercover agent is released and soon meets up with the girl again who is waiting for him near the fur company warehouse. There follows a romantic interlude after which we discover that the owner of the fur company is in league with a San Francisco businessman and that the two of them are using professional thieves to highjack the trucks as well as informers and operatives who work in the warehouse itself. To complicate matters, it also appears that the professional thieves are raking the best furs off the top and keeping them to turn to their own profit.

The customs officer returns to work and is given the job of driving the truck to San Francisco that night. The owner discovers this and sends word to the thieves to leave the truck alone. The thieves, however, fear that their own scheme is getting a little hot so they determine to highjack the truck and keep all the furs for themselves to sell to an American businessman who has not been involved before. They expect to make enough money to retire to the United States for life. A complication arises when the girl arrives to spy on them and, when they catch her, she tells them she's looking for the man who killed her brother, who was once a driver for the fur company. She is tied up and placed in a closet.

In the meantime the undercover customs agent has caught the previous night's stolen furs on their way across the border and has elicited a confession from the crooks who tell him where the hideout is.

The undercover officer takes his truck out onto the road at midnight and is stopped once again by the thieves. This time he is taken to the hideout and tied up pending a decision about what to do with him. In the meantime, the two masterminds of the fur robbers, the owner of the Arctic Fur Company and his associate from San Francisco, arrive at the hideout and one after the other surprise the gang selling the furs to the other American businessman. Since they're all crooks they each want everything for themselves. The U.S. Customs officer in the meanwhile has managed to escape and while the gang is bickering and re-asserting loyalties he arrives at the door with a gun and catches the whole bunch. The girl is freed from her bonds and 'phones the Canadian authorities. At the end, when all the crooks are behind bars, the Customs officer and the girl pledge their love and it looks like good old wedding bells. This was Rita Hayworth's first role for Central, as Patricia Lane. She subsequently went on to shoot CONVICTED with the company before it folded.

6. ADVENTURES IN TIBET TOLD BY EXPLORER HARRISON FORMAN,
    VICTORIA, B.C. (1936)
    p.c. Paramount (Lib. #5346)
    l.   g. 35mm   t. b+w   s. sound
    d.   *
    ph.   *
    c.s. Sherman Grinberg, N.Y.

    "Semi view & CU talking." Forman talks about his adventures.

7. AERIAL VIEWS IN THE KOOTENAYS, BRITISH COLUMBIA. (1930's)
    p.c. private
    l. approx. 270'   g. 16mm   t. b+w   s. si.
    d.   *
    ph. W.M. Archibald
    c.s. NFA, Ottawa

    Aerial views of the Cominco smelter at Trail. Unidentified dams and power plants on the Kootenay River. Other unidentified shots of the Kootenays.

8. AFTER FIFTY YEARS. (1936)
   p.c. CGMPB
   l. 1 reel   g. 35mm   t. b+w   s. sound
   d.   *
   ph. *
   c.s. NFA, NFB (1930 - FG - 220)

> "MS sign pointing to Gastown. Shot of Vancouver skyline from harbour. Various shots of Vancouver streets: Georgia Street with Hotel Vancouver, Granville Street with the old Post Office, the Orpheum Theatre, the Birks Building, the old Hotel Vancouver. Shot of Hastings Street looking down towards the Marine Building. HA of city towards Birks Building and the clock tower on the Vancouver Block, Hudson's Bay Company building on left and Hotel Vancouver on right, with auto, pedestrian & streetcar traffic throughout. Passenger liner at docks, Vancouver Harbour and freighters, a tug boat, etc. Stevedores loading a freighter, grain being loaded. Pan of Coal Harbour with fishing fleet moored in f.g. MLS three-stacked steamer moving out to sea. Good low level aerial of downtown Vancouver showing principally the Marine Building, the Birks Building, and the old Hotel Vancouver. Various shots of buildings: Marine Building, new Hotel Vancouver, HBCo. building at the corner of Georgia and Granville, Marine Bldg. in b.g. with Hastings Street in f.g., old Hotel Vancouver with clock, Georgia Hotel, Devonshire Hotel, Medical Arts Building, etc. Open air sightseeing street car passes by. Shot of conductor Teddy Lyons collecting tickets. Travelling shots of city streets, mostly Granville Street. Cenotaph on Hastings Street. HA shot of City looking north. Various shots of fine residences in rich residential district. Shot of trees in Capilano Canyon tilting up to suspension bridge way above. Level shots of suspension bridge with people walking across. Capilano River from suspension bridge. Cathedral Grove in Stanley Park, giant fir split down the middle, people walk in and out of the split. Open air concert at the Malkin Bowl, band shell, spectators and audience. Monument to President Harding. Var. shots of children playing in playground, of beach on English Bay, of pool at Second Beach, of bathers, bathing beauties posing, etc. People feeding animals at zoo. MS two grizzlies catching tidbits on the fly. Good MLS of CPR EMPRESS at dockside. Closer views of passengers at the rails with paper streamers spinning out across the wharf. LS Vancouver skyline across Coal Harbour. HA EMPRESS moving out."

9. AFTER TERRIFIC STRUGGLE AGAINST BATTLING SEA, SS BESSIE
   DOLLAR SUCCEEDS IN REACHING ESQUIMALT, ESQUIMALT, B.C.
   (1919)
   p.c. Fox Movietonews (Fox #090.1-C2567)
   l. 30'   g. 35mm   t. b+w   s. si.
   d.   *
   ph. Young's Studio
   c.s. Fox Movietonews, N.Y.

> "Some damage - ship looks like a coastal freighter."

10. AFTER 30,000 MILE WORLD CRUISE, EMPRESS OF CANADA ARRIVES
    WITH PARTY OF HAPPY TRAVELLERS, VANCOUVER, B.C. (1924)
    p.c. Fox Movietonews (Fox #463.11-A101)
    l.   g. 35mm   t. b+w   s. si.
    d.   *
    ph. Len H. Roos
    c.s. Fox Movietonews, N.Y.

11. AGRICULTURAL MISCELLANY - LAYRITZ NURSERIES, RABBITS, FOX
    FARMING, TURKEY FARMING, POTATO HARVESTING & B.C. AGRICUL-
    TURAL BOOTH AT CNE. (late 1920's)
    p.c. B.C. Dept. of Agriculture
    l. approx. 450' g. 16mm   t. b+w   s. si. w/some captions
    d.   *
    ph. *
    c.s. PABC

> Layritz Nurseries, Victoria, where Premier Tolmie and the Minister and Deputy Minister of Agriculture look on as shrubs are packed to be sent to the British Legation in Peiping.
>
> Rabbits in cages. Lady wearing fox fur in Victoria. B.C. Dept. of Agricul-

ture booth at CNE, Toronto. Fox farm pens & feeding. Catching foxes. Feeding turkeys and other turkey shots. A field of dug-up potatoes. Horse-drawn potato harvester working. Potatoes being sorted and bagged. Huge mounds of potatoes in trucks. Horse-drawn cutter cuts plants off at surface.

12. AIR VIEWS OF VANCOUVER, B.C. (1933)
    p.c. Paramount (Lib. #3872) NL 359
    1.   g. 35mm   t. b+w   s. si.
    d.   *
    ph.   *
    c.s. Sherman Grinberg, N.Y.

    "Good general air views of city showing buildings & air view of harbour."

13. AIR VIEWS OF VANCOUVER, B.C. (1934)
    p.c. Paramount (Lib. #4041) NL 382
    1.   g. 35mm   t. b+w   s. si.
    d.   *
    ph.   *
    c.s.Sherman Grinberg, N.Y.

    "Good general and close air views of city buildings and waterfront."

14. AIR VIEWS OF VANCOUVER, B.C. (1935)
    p.c. British Paramount (Lib. #4147)
    1. 50'   g. 35mm   t. b+w   s. si.
    d.   *
    ph.   *
    c.s. Visnews, London

15. ALAKSA. (1921)
    p.c. Grand Trunk Pacific R.R. (later CNR)
    1. 2 reels   g. 35mm   t. b+w   s. si. w/captions
    d.   *
    ph.   *
    c.s. NFB (1920 - N - 111 - 1)

    "Alaska is an Indian word meaning Great Country. Shot of mountains and rivers, excellent shot of main street of gold mining town with miners lounging around in front of hotel (taken during Gold Rush days). Miner removing sack of gold dust from dog's back and pouring out $10,000 worth of gold. CS of gold in pan. Good shot of miner's cabin at dusk. Boating shot past passenger ships in Vancouver Harbour and one LS Vancouver (1921). Shot of ships moving up coast, woman passenger aboard and two of crew. Shot of Ocean Falls, B.C. Main Street of Prince Rupert (1919) with early model cars along main street." From this point on, the film is about Alaska.

16. THE ALASKAN (1924)
    p.c. Famous Players - Lasky
    1. 6,736'   g. 35mm   t. b+w   s. si. w/captions
    d.   Herbert Brenon
    ph. James Howe
    c.s. Unknown

    p. Herbert Brenon; sc., Willis Goldbeck; from the novel by James Oliver Curwood.

    l.p. Thomas Meighan, Estelle Taylor, Anna May Wong, Maurice Cannon, John Sainpolis, Frank Campeau, Alphonz Ethier.

    Filmed in British Columbia and distributed by Paramount Pictures.

    Storyline: "Unable to obtain help from the government when his father is murdered by henchmen of a big business syndicate in Alaska headed by John Graham, Alan Holt decides to fight the combination alone. Returning home, he befriends Mary Standish who seeks refuge from the mistreatment of Graham. Eventually Graham is killed when he falls over a precipiece, and Alan and Mary are free to marry." (AFI Catalogue - Feature Films, 1921-1930)

17. ALASKAN INTERLUDE - PART 1. (1936)
    p.c. CNR
    1. 1 reel   g. 35mm   t. b+w   s. si. w/captions

d.   *
ph. *
c.s. NFA & NFB (1930 - FG - 21 - 1)

> "Memories of the Klondike Rush of 1898"
>
> A trip from Vancouver to Alaska via Prince Rupert. The film opens with shots
> of snow, ice, mountains, and the sternwheelers BONANZA KING and NASUTLIN.
> LS Vancouver waterfront, wharves & cruise ships. Good MCU of the CNR ship
> PRINCE ROBERT. LS ship at wharf, streamers hanging down, well-wishers wav-
> ing from the quay. Another cruise ship shown heading for the Strait of
> Georgia. Fol. of a seagull gliding past the camera aboard ship. Mountain-
> ous shoreline from ship. Ocean Falls from the ship, with fishboats, port
> installations, new dwellings on the hillside and the pulp mill on the water-
> front. Passengers playing deck games, looking at the scenery. Slow cruis-
> ing shots through Gardner Canal and Douglas Channel, high cliff-like shore-
> line. LS & closer shots of Prince Rupert. Pan of town from hillside. HA
> pier, cruise ship moored to it, CNR passenger train pulling in. This des-
> cription is taken from the NFB shot list for Part 1. Presumably Part II
> continues the trip to Alaska.

18. ALDERMAN G.H. WORTHINGTON AND W.C. SHELLY ARE MADE CHIEFS
    IN GYRO TRIBE FOR THE COMING POTLATCH, VANCOUVER, B.C.
    (1924)
    p.c. Fox Movietonews (Fox #047.9-A019)
    1. 60'   g. 35mm   t. b+w   s. si.
    d.   *
    ph. Len H. Roos
    c.s. Fox Movietonews, N.Y.

> "Smoking peace pipe, dancing braves, Chief Ketchiecum Kilum."

19. ALFALFA. (late 20's, early 30's)
    p.c. B.C. Dept. of Agriculture
    1. approx. 300'   g. 16mm   t. b+w   s. si. w/captions
    d.   *
    ph. *
    c.s. PABC

> A bulb digger "which will dig 5 tons of bulbs an hour with an average crop
> of 8 tons per acre" clears a field.
>
> Men harvesting alfalfa. Stacked alfalfa is heaped onto a wagon. Alfalfa is
> baled. A man in a test kitchen prepares something with milk & bacterial
> culture and a seed. View of farm and fields. This might be the Experimen-
> tal Farm at Sidney.

20. ALL ABOARD. (1937)
    p.c. ASN for CPR (?)
    1. 16 min.   g. 35mm   t. b+w   s. sound
    d.   *
    ph. *
    c.s. *

> Across Canada by train.

21. ALL-SOOKE DAY. (approx. 1939)
    p.c. B.C. Government Travel Bureau
    1. 1 x 400' reel g. 16mm   t. colour s. si.
    d.   *
    ph. R.L. Colby
    c.s. Unknown

> "Annual outing of the Sooke community, Vancouver Island, B.C."

22. AMATEUR SWIMMING CLUB CELEBRATES ARRIVAL OF 1923 WITH MID-
    WINTER SWIM IN ENGLISH BAY, VANCOUVER, B.C. (1923)
    p.c. Fox Movietonews (Fox #731.2-3539)
    1. 83'   g. 35mm   t. b+w   s. si.
    d.   *
    ph. Len H. Roos
    c.s. Fox Movietonews, N.Y.

23. AMERICAN BASKETBALL TEAM BEATS VICTORIA DOMINOES, VICTORIA,
    B.C. (1938)
    p.c. Fox Movietonews (Fox #33-884)
    1.   g. 35mm   t. b+w   s. sound
    d.   *
    ph.   ASN
    c.s. Fox Movietonews, N.Y.

        *"Interior shots of various scenes of the game. Elevation shots behind bas-
        kets. American team, 'Denver Safeways', with cup. CU pan of team. Jacob
        France Trophy, world's championship cup. Shot of the 'Dominoes' team.
        J. Adams congratulates Mr. Shelton, coach of the 'Denver Safeways'. Mr.
        Adams is acting-Mayor of Victoria. The score was 74 - 32 in favour of the
        American team."*

24. AMID ALPINE SNOWS. (1924)
    p.c. CGMPB
    1. 1 reel   g. 35mm   t. b+w   s. si. w/captions
    d.   *
    ph.   perhaps Byron Harmon
    c.s. Unknown

        *"A scenic film dealing with the 1924 meeting of the Canadian Alpine Club
        at Berg Lake near Mount Robson."*

25. AMONG THE CLOUDS. (n.d.)
    p.c. *
    1. approx. 700'   g. 35mm   t. b+w   s. sound
    d.   *
    ph.   *
    c.s. Unknown

        "Red Indians in the Canadian Rockies." This film may have been shot en-
        tirely in Alberta.

26. ANACORTES - VICTORIA FERRY PARADE, VICTORIA, B.C. (1921)
    p.c. *
    1.   g. 35mm   t. b+w   s. si.
    d.   *
    ph.   *
    c.s. NFA (Taylor reel 137)

        *"Giant floats, covered with flowers, parade through the streets of Victoria
        on the way to the waterfront where vacationers will board the PRINCESS
        LOUISE for an excursion to Bellingham. Floats. Large float with sign:
        ANACORTES-VICTORIA INTERNATIONAL FERRY. Many spectators lining the parade
        route. Good shots of huge crowd aboard PRINCESS LOUISE ferry boat, on
        their way to the USA for vacations."*

27. ANDY BAHR WITH REINDEER HERD IN VANCOUVER, B.C. (1935)
    p.c. Fox Movietonews (Fox #25 - 106)
    1. 400'   g. 35mm   t. b+w   s. sound
    d.   *
    ph.   ASN
    c.s. NFA & Fox Movietonews, N.Y.

        *"Daniel C. Crawley, legal advisor, & Andy Bahr, who has driven a large herd
        several thousand miles for Canadian Government and who has taken five years
        to do it. He speaks little English, but he says he is glad to be home. Re-
        porter asks Crawley questions. Rolf Lomens, contractor, congratulates Bahr
        and Crawley."*

        *(Cut negative includes library shots of herds crossing snow, water & moun-
        tains)*

28. ANGLING ACROSS CANADA. (before 1935)
    p.c. *
    1. 1 reel   g. 35mm   t. b+w   s. si.
    d.   *
    ph.   *
    c.s. Unknown

        "Salmon in Nova Scotia; trout in Quebec; bass, muskelunge, pike & pickerel

in Ontario; and trout in Jasper Park & British Columbia."

29. ANNUAL CELEBRATION IS FEATURED BY SCORES OF UNIQUE FLOATS
    SHOWING ACTIVITIES OF THE CITY, VANCOUVER, B.C. (1925)
    p.c. Fox Movietonews (Fox #751.15-B6642)
    l. 40'   g. 35mm   t. b+w   s. si.
    d.   *
    ph. Herron
    c.s. Fox Movietonews, N.Y.

> *"Lord Byng is in attendance - children with flowers - kids dancing folk*
> *dances - high shots of parade." Celebration is not identified.*

30. ANOTHER ADDITION TO THE FLEET OF CANADIAN NATIONAL SHIPS.
    (pre 1926)
    p.c. CGMPB
    l.   g. 35mm   t. b+w   s. si.
    d.   *
    ph. *
    c.s. Unknown

> *One of the HOW IT IS DONE IN CANADA series. The location is not given.*
> *May not be in British Columbia.*

31. ARCHAEOLOGY, NEAR COURTENAY AND CAMPBELL RIVER, AND BELLA
    COOLA, BRITISH COLUMBIA. (1923-1930)
    p.c. National Museum of Canada
    l. 1 reel   g. 35mm   t. b+w   s. si.
    d.   Harlan I. Smith
    ph. Harlan I. Smith
    c.s. Unknown

> *Little is known about this film but it is probably composed of footage taken*
> *by Harlan Smith during his trips through British Columbia.*

32. ARCHAEOLOGY OF BELLA COOLA AREA. (1923-1930)
    p.c. National Museum of Canada
    l. 1 reel   g. 35mm   t. b+w   s. si. w/captions
    d.   Harlan I. Smith
    ph. Harlan I. Smith
    c.s. Unknown

33. THE ARCHAEOLOGY OF SOUTHERN INTERIOR OF BRITISH COLUMBIA
    (1923-1930)
    p.c. National Museum of Canada
    l. 1 reel   g. 35mm   t. b+w   s. si.
    d.   Harlan I. Smith
    ph. Harlan I. Smith
    c.s. Unknown

34. ARRIVAL AT WESTERN LIMIT OF TOUR; THE ROYAL VISIT OF KING
    GEORGE VI & QUEEN ELIZABETH TO NORTH AMERICA, 1939.
    VANCOUVER AND VICTORIA, B.C. (1939)
    p.c. British Paramount (Lib. #8607)
    l. 327'   g. 35mm   t. b+w   s. sound
    d.   *
    ph. *
    c.s. Visnews, London

> *Vancouver welcomes King & Queen; Vancouver City Hall. King & Queen shake*
> *hands with Mayor. Crowd. King & Queen acknowledge cheering from balcony.*
> *CNR RR station & crowd. Banner; ITALIAN VETERANS WELCOME etc. Royal car*
> *drives through crowded street. CU Japanese WELCOME sign. Japanese kids*
> *wave flags & cheer, Royal car drives past them. CU Japanese kids waving*
> *flags. CPR ferry PRINCESS MARGUERITE leaving. CU King & Queen on board*
> *looking over rail. Shot from ferry of little boats in water. SCU King &*
> *Queen on board.*

> *Arrival at western limit of Tour: Coastline of Vancouver Island. Parlia-*

ment Buildings, Victoria. King inspects Guard of Honour. Steps of Parliament Buildings with dignataries, etc. Girl presenting bouquet to Queen. Ext. Empress Hotel. Premier introduces King, King standing at the table in Empress Hotel dining room. SCU King making a speech. At Beacon Hill Park the King presents new Colours to the RCN. Sailors in march-past. CU King saluting. During speech, the King says he is very grateful for the reception they have received in Canada.

35. ARRIVAL IN VANCOUVER OF HALIBUT CATCH.   (1921)
    p.c. Fox Movietonews (Fox #011-4052)
    l.   g. 35mm   t. b+w   s. si.
    d. *
    ph. D.C. Davey
    c.s. Fox Movietonews, N.Y. & NFB (1920 - 170 - FG - 4)

> *"Fishing boats and unloading halibut from ships. Record halibut catch helps ease food shortage. Fish being unloaded at wharf. Net swinging toward wharf. March 21, 1921."*

36. ARRIVAL OF FIRST GERMAN SHIP TO ARRIVE IN VANCOUVER, B.C.,
    SINCE 1914. (1919)
    p.c. Fox Movietonews (Fox #463.4-2315)
    l. 38'   g. 35mm   t. b+w   s. si.
    d. *
    ph. Brazill
    c.s. Fox Movietonews, N.Y.

> *"View of SS. WAIRUNA at dock and loading."*

37. AS FRASER RIVER FREEZES OVER FOR FIRST TIME IN 15 YEARS,
    SHIPPING IS COMPLETELY BLOCKED, NEW WESTMINSTER, B.C.
    (1929)
    p.c. Fox Movietonews (Fox #007.3602-C9006)
    l. 70'   g. 35mm   t. b+w   s. si.
    d. *
    ph. *
    c.s. NFB (1920 - 170 - FG - 4) and Fox Movietonews, N.Y.

> *"Various shots showing frozen river. Docks with goods on them. Steamer or ferry boat in mid-stream making little progress. Bridge in b.g., tug in ice."*

38. AS THEY TURN, TWIST AND PLUNGE, BUCKING BRONCOS AND UNTAMED
    STEERS MAKE STICKING ON A TOUGH JOB, VANCOUVER, B.C. (1929)
    p.c. Fox Movietonews (Fox #751.11-D2034)
    l. 80'   g. 35mm   t. b+w   s. si.
    d. *
    ph. *
    c.s. Fox Movietonews, N.Y.

> *Cowboys riding bucking broncos and wild steers.*

39. AS THOUGH SPEED BOATS WERE NOT FAST ENOUGH, THIS YOUNG
    LADY GETS BEHIND SEAPLANE, VANCOUVER, B.C. (1924)
    p.c. Fox Movietonews (Fox #731.3-A4118)
    l.   g. 35mm   t. b+w   s. si.
    d. *
    ph. Len H. Roos
    c.s. Fox Movietonews, N.Y.

> *Girl aquaplaning behind seaplane?*

40. 1. "AT HOME" - THE PREMIER ON HIS FARM   2. FUNERAL OF
    SIMON FRASER TOLMIE. (1. early 1930's; 2. 1937)
    p.c. B.C. Dept. of Agriculture
    1. approx. 400' g. 16mm   t. b+w   s. si. w/captions
    d. *
    ph. *
    c.s. PABC

> *1. A visit to Premier S.F. Tolmie's farm Cloverdale. Tolmie discussing his garden, inspecting his potatoes, working in the fields, prodding cows into*

barn for milking. Mrs. Tolmie and he posing several times, individually. Cloverdale consisted of 1300 acres, 400 under cultivation, and Tolmie took great interest in all agricultural pursuits. When he resigned in 1933 after five years as Premier of British Columbia, he dedicated himself to setting up a model farm on his land.

2. Simon Fraser Tolmie died at Cloverdale on October 14, 1937; his funeral was held on October 16, 1937 in Victoria with full honours. Scenes include flag at half mast. Coffin being carried down Parliament Buildings' steps and placed in hearse. Empress Hotel. Cars in the procession and the hearse in front of the Parliament Buildings. Entourage driving up Government Street with crowds lining the street. Procession continuing along Quadra Street. Procession on way to Royal Oak Burial Park. Removing the coffin from the hearse at the cemetery.

41. AUSSIE HOCKEY GIRL CHAMPIONS INVADE CANADA, VANCOUVER, B.C.
    (1936)
    p.c. Universale Newsreel V.8 R.501
    1. 99'   g. 35mm   t. b+w   s. si.
    d. *
    ph. ASN
    c.s. USNA

        "Aussies on boat, crowd looking on. Receiving corsages, leaving S.S. NIAGARA. In skirts, marching to field. Canadians. They start the game."

42. AVIATORS OF THE FUTURE BUILD THEIR OWN PLANES AND MEET IN
    COMPETITION FOR CITY CHAMPIONSHIP, VANCOUVER, B.C. (1929)
    p.c. Fox Movietonews (Fox #700.8-D2927)
    1. 100'   g. 35mm   t. b+w   s. si.
    d. *
    ph. *
    c.s. Fox Movietonews, N.Y.

        "Major D.R. MacLaren & Earl McLeod help the boys during the model plane contest."

43. AYRSHIRE CATTLE SALE AT ARMSTRONG AND KAMLOOPS. (1930)
    p.c. B.C. Dept. of Agriculture
    1. approx. 400'   g. 16mm   t. b+w   s. si. w/captions
    d. *
    ph. *
    c.s. PABC

        Excellent pan of Kamloops from height, looking down eventually into a street lined with cars. Indians in full regalia on apaloosa ponies. Bronco riding in a ring. Celery field and harvesting near Armstrong, B.C. Field of cabbage. Pan of fertile bottomlands. Salmon Arm farmers visit illustration station where Exhibition corn is grown. A combine in action drawn by a tractor. A two-horse team hauls the cart to collect the wheat. Stocks of grain in a field being loaded onto a horse-drawn wagon. Scenes of Ayrshire auction at Armstrong - Mat Hassen presents Percy French with winner's trophy. Ayrshire prizes awarded. Dunwaters, Davidson, Forest & Wells, outstanding at auction. Auction - $305.00 average for 30 two-year heifers. New owners parade their purchases. The Laird of Fintry. Pan of cattle. Fall fair at Lumby, crowded grounds & buildings. Veteran MLA J.H. Schofield of Trail. Donald Graham, a "veteran of the first Riel Rebellion, 1870", poses. He came to the Okanagan Valley in 1874.

44. BABE RUTH SAILS WITH OTHER MAJOR LEAGUE BASEBALL STARS TO
    PLAY IN JAPAN, VANCOUVER, B.C. (1934)
    p.c. Paramount (Lib. #4149) NL 1298
    1.   g. 35mm   t. b+w   s. sound
    d. *
    ph. *
    c.s. Sherman Grinberg, N.Y.

        Babe with wife & daughter walking down gangplank. CU pose together. CU Babe Ruth shaking hands with Connie Mack and exchanging hats. Ruth throwing streamers and taking pictures with a small movie camera as the boat leaves. Semi-side view ship away from pier & SCU Babe waving from deck.

45. BACK IN '22. (1932)
    p.c. ASN/ASS (#B-630)
    1. 1000'   g. 35mm   t. b+w   s. sound
    d.   Gordon Sparling
    ph. *
    c.s. NFA

> CANADIAN CAMEO NO. 9 - producer B.E. Norrish; music Vera Guilavoff; narration,
> Corey Thompson; script, Gordon Sparling.
>
> "As the years slip by we do not realize the changes time makes in things all
> around us. Priceless records from the vaults of Associated Screen News allow
> us to look way back into 1922 and see things as they really were those few
> short years ago. Many famous people and incidents flash across the screen,
> such as Baron (sic) and Lady Byng, Mary Pickford, Sir Henry Thornton, the
> great Haileybury Fire, the latest thing in bathing suits on Vancouver's
> beaches, even a glimpse of a Canadian feature movie released way back in '22."

46. BACK TO BACK. (1933)
    p.c. B.C. Forest Service
    1. 250'   g. 16mm   t. b+w   s. si. w/captions
    d.   George Melrose
    ph. George Melrose
    c.s. Unknown

> "Describes the making of the famous Indian sweaters by the Indians resident
> on the Koksilah Reserve at Duncan, British Columbia."

47. BADEN POWELL - BOY SCOUTS - GIRL GUIDES, VICTORIA, B.C.
    (1935)
    p.c. Fox Movietonews (Fox #25-333)
    1. 800'   g. 35mm   t. b+w   s. sound
    d.   *
    ph. ASN
    c.s. Fox Movietonews, N.Y.

> "Chief Guide Lady Baden-Powell addresses gathering of Girl Guides. Lord
> Baden Powell watches scout display. Review of Scouts and Guides. Lord &
> Lady B.-P. taking salute. B.-P speaks. Scouts giving salute."

48. BANFF NATIONAL PARK. (1917)
    p.c. Dept. of Trade and Commerce, Exhibits & Publicity
       Bureau, Ottawa
    1. 1 reel   g. 35mm   t. b+w   s. si. w/captions
    d.   *
    ph. *
    c.s. Unknown

> One of the first promotional films about Banff National Park; filmed in 1917
> in both Alberta and B.C. and described as follows: "This is a distinct scenic
> beauty film. It shows the wonders of glaciers, lakes and streams in Banff
> National Park, features Banff itself with relation to the sport life of Banff
> and vicinity. Finally it shows the magic beauty of Emerald Lake, B.C., jour-
> neys across Wapta Pass to Takakaw Falls, a cataract falling 1350 feet in the
> Valley of Yoho."

49. BANFF TO LAKE LOUISE. (1939)
    p.c. CGMPB
    1. approx. 400'   g. 16mm   t. colour s. si. w/captions
    d.   *
    ph. *
    c.s. NFB

> "A motor trip along the scenic highways of Banff National Park in the Cana-
> dian Rockies, with a side trip to Marble Canyon in Kootenay National Park.
> Fine views of Banff, Lake Louise, Castle Mountain and the Bow River Valley."
> Produced for the National Parks Bureau.

50. BARCLAY SOUND. (1930's)
p.c. Private
l. approx. 250'   g. 16mm   t. colour & b+w   s. si.
d.   *
ph.   Rev. George R.B. Kinney
c.s. NFA, Ottawa

> *b+w - Kildonan, B.C., in Uchucklesit Inlet. Kids swimming & diving off a wharf. A coastal freighter arrives. Brief glimpses of cannery. Freighter docks, people watching. Kids swimming again.*
>
> *Loggers at an unidentified camp roll/skid a bunkhouse into place using logs. Good CU's young kids watching as steam donkey pulls bunkhouse. Good CU man with long pipe working and smiling. Bulldozer in the woods scooping out a road. CU workers. Bulldozer in the woods scooping out a road. CU workers. Bulldozer working on roadbank.*
>
> *colour - Fishing boats. Group of men posing. Stream in the forest. Railroad tracks & camp. Men laying ties & track. Logging train comes through pushing flat-deck cars. Good CU men posing with locomotive. Steam donkey logging operations in the bush. Fine shots of donkey engine interspersed with shots of yarding, choking, etc. Group of loggers posing & waving. Yarding logs.*

51. BARKERVILLE, B.C., GOLD STRIKE. (1930)
p.c. ASN
l.   g. 35mm   t. b+w   s.
d.   *
ph.   *
c.s. NFB (1930 - FG - 274)

> *"Various shots of Barkerville - 1890 gold rush appearance. Sourdoughs working claims and panning gold as in 1890." The dates are incorrect for Barkerville's gold rush but the panning methods are no doubt the same as the 1860's.*

52. BARNEY OLSON MISCELLANEOUS. (1929-1932)
p.c. Private
l. several hundred feet   g. 16mm   t. b+w   s. si/
d.   *
ph.   Mr. Barney Olson
c.s. Barry Casson Film Productions

> *Mr. Casson was given all the 16mm footage shot by Barney Olson. It is on reels that are not separated into specific subjects so that family pictures occur with news events, etc. Subjects of interest are noted below. As well, two further reels by Olson are listed under specific titles. Mr. Casson may be contacted for further information.*
>
> *EMPRESS OF CANADA. Shots of the largest liner plying the Pacific aground in Homer Bay near Victoria - tugs working to free the ship - people watching - several good shots of the ship from various angles.*
>
> *Butchart Gardens. Includes shots of the sunken garden, Butchart's home, the Italian garden, the lawns, rose garden, and tourists. There is also some footage of the aviary which has since disappeared.*
>
> *Miscellaneous. Bus garage next to Public Library on Yates Street, Victoria. CPR princess ferry with passengers disembarking and coach drivers waiting for them on the causeway. Brentwood Bay ferry dock with ferry arriving and coach leaving the ferry. Street shots of Victoria with cars and buses. Buses at Strathcona Hotel. The Bastion in Nanaimo. Steam locomotive. Good shots of events at Calgary Stampede.*
>
> *Aircraft. Aeroplanes at Lansdowne Airfield at the Willows in Victoria. Passengers boarding aircraft G-CATX. Aerial views of Camosun College, Saanich, the Gulf Islands, and a brief shot of the interior of the plane.*
>
> *Miscellaneous. Barney Olson home life on Dallas Road, Victoria. Railway tunnel, Fraser Canyon. Shot from window of moving train along the Fraser River. Lake in the Interior. A small car ferry. The Malahat Drive. CU Dominion Astrophysical Observatory, passengers on tour bus. Looking down Saanich Mountain from the Observatory.*

53. BEACON HILL BIRDS, VICTORIA, B.C.   (1929)
    p.c. *
    l.   g. 35mm   t. b+w   s. si.
    d.   *
    ph. Young
    c.s. NFA (Taylor reel 134)

> *"Good shots of swans and birds in a park which has recently been set aside for a bird sanctuary. Ladies feeding birds, pigeons."*

54. BEAR HUNT IN THE ROCKIES. (1910)
    p.c. Edison Mfg. Co.
    l.   g. 35mm   t. b+w   s. si.
    d.   *
    ph. *
    c.s. Unknown

> *There is no evidence that this film was photographed in British Columbia although the title suggests that it may have been.*

55. BEAUTIFUL BLOSSOM TIME IN OKANAGAN VALLEY. BRITISH
    COLUMBIA FRUIT TREES - CHERRY, APPLE AND PEAR -
    PRESENT A PICTURE. (1926)
    p.c. Fox Movietonews (Fox #420.93-B2347)
    l. 55'   g. 35mm   t. b+w   s. si.
    d.   *
    ph. Herron
    c.s. Fox Movietonews, N.Y.

> *"SCU cherry tree in blossom. CU blossoms. Apple tree in blossom. SCU little boy on horse. CU boy on horse with blossoms in b.g. CU apple blossoms. Long shot of boy and horse in apple orchard."*

56. BEAUTIFUL BRITISH COLUMBIA. (1941)
    p.c. Shelley Films for the British Columbia Government
       Travel Bureau
    l. approx. 400'   g. 35mm & 16mm t. colour s. sound
    d.   *
    ph. *
    c.s. Unknown

> *This was apparently the first time the title BEAUTIFUL BRITISH COLUMBIA was ever used for a film. It was so popular that the film which up-dated and superceded this reel was given the same title, which has been with the Bureau ever since. The travelogue was released on Feb. 1, 1941, and was distributed successfully in large theatres in Canada and the United States.*

57. BEAUTIFUL OCEAN FALLS. (1926)
    p.c. Pathescope of Canada Ltd.
    l. 793'   g. 35mm   t. b+w   s. si. w/captions
    d.   *
    ph. A.D. Keen (?)
    c.s. NFA, Ottawa

> *Produced for: "British Columbia Patriotic and Educational Picture Service." Power dam with gate & wheelhouse at Ocean Falls. Link River Falls. New power house of Pacific Mills. Board walk at Link Falls. Bridal Veil Falls. Rocky canyon near Twin Lakes. Mountains near Ocean Falls. Beach at Bella Bella. Temple Mountain. Steamer sailing up coast. Lumber camp and new bungalow logging office. Dinner at the lumber camp. Twin Sister Mountains on Burk's Channel. Dean Channel. Wild flowers. Canyon Falls. New power house at Ocean Falls. Cave of the Winds. Fishing at Halfway Falls. Swinging footbridge over the Falls. Pleasure-craft at "the island". People swimming. Tour ship TILLICUMS and Mt. Baldy from tour ship. (This film was probably originally 810' long. Part of the end is missing but the figure 810 is on the can.)*

58. BEAUTIFUL VANCOUVER. (approx. 1939)
    p.c. *
    1. 1 x 400' reel g. 16mm   t. colour s. si.
    d.   *
    ph. *
    c.s. Unknown

> *"Vancouver to Chilliwack Lake." Produced for or by the British Columbia
> Government Travel Bureau.*

59. BEAUTY IN ROCKIES, B.C. AND ALBERTA AT THE GREAT DIVIDE.
    (1926)
    p.c. Fox Movietonews
    1.   g. 35mm   t. b+w   s. si.
    d.   *
    ph. ASN (?)
    c.s. NFB (1920 - 170 - FG - 4)

> *"First snowfall and beauty shows through. Shot of GREAT DIVIDE gate at foot-
> hills with snow around, and Pope's Peak in b.g. Hoar frost on trees and Mt.
> Fairview in b.g."*

60. BEHIND THE HEADLINES. (late 1930's)
    p.c. Vancouver Motion Pictures Ltd.
    1. 390'   g. 16mm   t. b+w   s. si. & sound
    d.   *
    ph. *
    c.s. NFB

> *"Various stages of producing a newspaper." Presumably this film deals with
> the production of a Vancouver newspaper, from the forest to the street cor-
> ner.*

61. THE BELLA COOLA INDIANS OF BRITISH COLUMBIA. (1923-24)
    p.c. National Museums of Canada
    1. approx. 450' g. 35mm   t. b+w   s. si. w/captions
                 (16mm available)
    d.   Harlan I. Smith
    ph. Harlan I. Smith
    c.s. National Museum of Man & NFA (# 3758)

> *"The beautiful fjords, mountains, glaciers and cataracts of Bella Coola region,
> halfway between Vancouver and Prince Rupert, on the Pacific coast, are the
> setting for this film. Here dwell the Bella Coola Indians, a branch of the
> Salish linguistic people who live in the interior of the province. The pic-
> tures of these Indians include a medicine man with his rattle, and the weird
> masked dance. Indians are shown drying salmon, picking berries, making bas-
> kets, back packing, carving and navigating a dugout cedar canoe. There are
> views of the mountain goat and black bear which furnished food and clothing,
> and the salmon - one of the chief foods."*
>
> *There are also shots of the weekly steamer to Bella Coola from Vancouver.
> Old totem poles outside abandoned lodges. Fish weirs. Indian fishermen men-
> ding & working nets. A dead man's belongings being burned. Monuments on a
> grave. Rock carving in the woods. New school and cgurch. Indians playing
> in a band. An old man in his headdress and blanket holding a rattle.*

62. BELLA COOLA VALLEY. (1923-1930)
    p.c. National Museum of Canada
    1. 1 reel   g. 35mm   t. b+w   s. si. w/captions
    d.   Harlan I. Smith
    ph. Harlan I. Smith
    c.s. Unknown

63. BELOW THE SURFACE IN ONE OF CANADA'S SUBMARINES.
    (pre 1922)
    p.c. CGMPB
    1.   g. 35mm   t. b+w   s. si.
    d.   *
    ph.   *
    c.s. Unknown

> One of the HOW IT IS DONE IN CANADA series. The location is not mentioned.
> Two H-Class submarines served on the West Coast and were disposed of in 1922
> when the RCN consolidated its fleet based at Esquimalt.

64. BEYOND THE SUNSET.   (1930's)
    p.c. ASN (#B708)
    1. (30 min) 2000' approx. g. 35mm t. b+w   s. sound
    d.   *
    ph.   *
    c.s. Unknown

> Produced for the Canadian Wheat Board; described in the BFI List of 16mm
> Geography Teaching and Travel Films of April 1939 as being about "The de-
> velopment of the Canadian West." There is no information about where the
> film was shot but it may contain scenes of the Port of Vancouver and grain
> shipments.

65. BIG CROWD ABOARD NEW COASTAL LINER SS ALEXANDRIA AS SHE
    SAILS ON MAIDEN VOYAGE, VANCOUVER, B.C.   (1924)
    p.c. Fox Movietonews (Fox #463.11-A3750)
    1.   g. 35mm   t. b+w   .s. si.
    d.   *
    ph. Len H. Roos
    c.s. Fox Movietonews, N.Y.

66. BIG GAME CAMERA HOLIDAY.   (1930's)
    p.c. *
    1. 511'   g. prob. 16mm t. colour s. sound
    d.   *
    ph.   *
    c.s. NFB

> Very likely a film about tracking bear, mountain goat, caribou, and other
> big game animals through the Rocky Mountains with a camera. In this case,
> some of the scenes probably were filmed in British Columbia.

67. BIG TIMBER.   (1935)
    p.c. CGMPB
    1. 844'   g. 35mm   t. b+w   s. sound
    d.   *
    ph.   *
    c.s. NFA, NFB Archives P.B. - 3 (1930 - L&DN - 19)

> Script, David Gwydyr; narration, Rupert Caplan.

> "Lumber in British Columbia is one of the main resources and, as such, equip-
> ment and transportation facilities are up to date: in this reel we see mass
> production in the forests of British Columbia and go through mills for a
> finished product. Machines used in this picture are cranes, lifters and
> power saws; also facilities for transporation by ships loading at the docks."

> Slow travel ahead on a rough woodland road. Tall trees. Men chopping
> at a large trunk. Tree falling. Several shots of men chopping at tree
> trunks, then sawing by hand, and trees falling. Man scaling a Douglas-
> fir and topping it. Several views of high riggers topping trees. Lum-
> berjacks sawing trunks into manageable lengths after falling. Drag-line
> in operation. Tree trunks being yarded, sliding down a chute, and hit-
> ting water with a splash. Log crane loading logs onto flatcars. Lumber
> train moving past camera, its cars loaded with huge logs. Large sawmill.
> Logs being dumped into mill pond, riding up jackladder and being sawn
> into equal lengths. Logs being sawn into boards by the carriage and
> buzz saw and by multiple band saws. High angle shot over grading ben-

ches, men grading lumber. Straddle-lifter lifting a huge stack of lumber and moving it. Overhead travelling crane picking up a stack of lumber and moving it onto huge piles. Cut to harbour. Various shots of freighter being loaded with lumber. There is no indication of where this sequence was shot or whether it is one operation on the same location by the same company.

68. BIGGEST PACIFIC LINER PILES UP ON ROCKS IN FOG, HOMER
    BAY NEAR VICTORIA, B.C. (1929)
    p.c. ASN and Pathé News (Pathé Sil .87, Neg #398)
    l. 100'   g. 35mm   t. b+w   s. si.
    d.   *
    ph. ASN
    c.s. NFB (1920 - FG - 182) Sherman Grinberg, Hollywood

    SS EMPRESS OF CANADA runs aground in fog in Homer Bay near Victoria; all passengers taken off safely.

    "High shot looking down from top of cliff to ship on rocks. CU pan on rocks. Shot from the air. Background shot of people on shore to bow of ship. Air and ground shots of tugs trying to pull her off."

69. BIRD LOVER HAS GARDEN OF EDEN FOR WINGED PETS, VANCOUVER,
    B.C. (1936)
    p.c. Universal Newsreel V.8 R.470
    l.   g. 35mm   t. b+w   s. si.
    d.   *
    ph. Sinkey
    c.s. USNA

    "Mr. Jones and family seated and birds atop each and every member of the family. Boy covered with birds. Pheasant eating from his mouth. Smaller birds eat from boy's mouth. CU birds on lady's hat, holding birds in her hand. Little girl sitting, birds around her. Man feeding birds. Bird flies to nest and CU feeding young, beaks open waiting for food and feeding. Cameraman Sinkey shooting pix covered with birds. Jones holding bird eating from mouth. Cameraman shooting. CU birds eating from man's mouth. Robin pecks Jones's ear, then eats from his mouth. Ditto, ditto, ditto, and again. LS Sinkey shooting." The Charles Jones family was a popular spectacle in Vancouver during the thirties, as well as being the subject of a number of news stories, they also went through their motions for a multitude of amateur cameramen and women.

70. BIRD SANCTUARY RUN BY CHARLES JONES, VANCOUVER, B.C.
    (1933)
    p.c. Fox Movietonews (Fox #19-734)
    l. 800'   g. 35mm   t. b+w   s. sound
    d.   *
    ph. ASN
    c.s. Fox Movietonews, N.Y.

    "Talk by Jones. Birds being fed by son. CU of bird feeding from Jones's mouth. Miss Marilyn Webster recites poems to kids. Children on grounds."

71. BIRDS AND BEASTS OF CANADA. (before 1935)
    p.c. *
    l. 1 reel   g. 35mm   t. b+w   s. si.
    d.   *
    ph.   *
    c.s. Unknown

    "A comprehensive survey of wild life in Canada."

72. BISHOP OF LONDON LAYS CORNERSTONE, VICTORIA, B.C.
    (1926)
    p.c. Fox Movietonews (?)
    l.   g. 35mm   t. b+w   s. si.
    d.   *
    ph.   *
    c.s. NFB (1920 - FG - 170 - 8)

    "Bishop of London, Rt. Rev. & Rt. Hon. A.F. Winnington-Ingram, D.D., lays cornerstone for new Anglican cathedral (Christ Church Cathedral). Shots

5

of group. Bishop laying stone, speaking, and CU plaque: THIS STONE LAID
1926 ETC. Group parading." See No. 85.

73. A BIT OF HIGH LIFE.   (1927)
    p.c. CGMPB
    l. 1 reel   g. 35mm   t. b+w   s. si. w/captions
    d.   *
    ph. *
    c.s. Unknown

> *"A scenic film following the journeys of alpinists on unblazed trails near
> Lake Louise, depicting the wonders of Bow Lake, and finally taking the trav-
> eller after many adventurous climbs into the Columbia ice area and back to
> Laggan." It is impossible to assess whether any of this film was shot in
> British Columbia but the view to the west from any mountain top will show
> the province, because much of the climbing takes place along the Alberta/
> B.C. boundary.*

74. BLACK BEAR MASCOT OF FIRE DEPARTMENT DRILLS WITH COMRADES
    AND DOES ALL THEIR TRICKS, VANCOUVER, B.C.   (1923)
    p.c. Fox Movietonews (Fox #411.344 - 7818)
    l. 42'   g. 35mm   t. b+w   s. si.
    d.   *
    ph. Len Roos
    c.s. Fox Movietonews, N.Y.

> *"Bear fools around with firemen & eats their smokes."*

75. THE BLACK ROBE.
    p.c. *
    l.   g.   t.   s.
    d.   *
    ph. *
    c.s. *

> *See SECRETS OF CHINATOWN - No. 799.*

76. BOBBY SIMPSON, THE HUMAN FLY, GIVES THRILLING EXHIBITION
    ON THE WINCH BUILDING, VANCOUVER, B.C.   (1921)
    p.c. Fox Movietonews (Fox #703.1 - 4412)
    l. 40'   g. 35mm   t. b+w   s. si.
    d.   *
    ph. D.C. Davey
    c.s. Fox Movietonews, N.Y.

> *"Ready to start. Climbing up the front of the building. Walking around
> ledge of building while blindfolded. Hi shot of crowd on street watching
> him perform. Balancing himself on chair on ledge of roof. Climbing on top
> of flag pole and sliding down head first."*

77. BONDS OF EMPIRE GROW STRONGER AS NEW DEEP SEA CABLE IS
    LANDED AND MADE READY, BAMFIELD, B.C.   (1926)
    p.c. Fox Movietonews (Fox #432.491 - B9732)
    l. 125'   g. 35mm   t. b+w   s. si.
    d.   *
    ph. *
    c.s. Fox Movietonews, N.Y.

> *"SCU cable ship coming into port. CU cable unwinding from hold of ship. CU
> cable running out from prow. CU landing the cable. CU interior of the cable
> station, a man at a desk." (Ship is either S.S. DOMINIA or S.S. RESTORER).*

78. BOY SCOUTS AND CUB PACKS PARADE AT GOVERNMENT HOUSE FOR
    INSPECTION AND PRESENTATION OF PRIZES, VICTORIA, B.C.
    (1921)
    p.c. Fox Movietonews (Fox #041.51 - 4415)
    l. 25'   g. 35mm   t. b+w   s. si.
    d.   *
    ph. Young's Studio
    c.s. Fox Movietonews, N.Y.   NFB (1920 - 170 - FG - 4)

> *"Lt. Gov. W.C. Nichol presents prizes. Long line of Cubs. Giving three
> cheers for Lt. Gov. Nichol. Marching."*

79. BOYS AND GIRLS AGRICULTURAL CLUBS. (1930's)
    p.c. B.C. Dept. of Agriculture (Reel 85)
    l. approx. 500'   g. 16mm   t. b+w   s. si.
    d.   *
    ph. *
    c.s. PABC

> *Saanich Boys & Girls Club at Sooke, looking at and wrestling with young heifers. Adults making presentations.*
>
> *Starting a Boys & Girls Club. Kids lined up on school steps. Teacher asks who'd like to join. Kids receive boxes of eggs for hatching. Young girl prepares her hen for laying. Potato and Calf Club. Field day at Sea Island. Calfs, picnic, spuds. Richmond and Delta Boys & Girls Club members in a field examining crops. Boys & Girls Club livestock judging in Vancouver: cows, horses & calves being judged outdoors and indoors.*

80. BOYS AND GIRLS IN ARMSTRONG, B.C. (1930's)
    p.c. B.C. Dept. of Agriculture
    l. approx. 400'   g. 16mm   t. colour s. si.
    d.   *
    ph. *
    c.s. PABC

> *Shots of kids grooming animals and parading them by the grandstand; cattle, swine, horses and poultry; no goats or sheep. Presumably taken at the Armstrong Fairgrounds.*

81. BRALORNE. (approx. 1932-33)
    p.c. prob. Bralorne Mine
    l. approx. 400'   g. 16mm   t. b+w   s. si. w/captions
    d.   *
    ph. *
    c.s. NFA

> *Appears to be a company film showing gold mining operations and an inspection trip by directors and officials through the mine and buildings. The operation was fairly new when the film was made, the store and hotel still under construction. Scenes include: the directors and officials leaving the main adit tunnel and touring buildings. Old stamp mill and some dumps and workings of the original Lorne gold mine. A miner walking out of mine shaft carrying a lamp. A visitor walking out of a disused shaft. Long pan back and forth across an old water wheel and arrasta. LS at the bottom of a grassy hill of camp buildings of the old Lorne Co. Pan down log-exterior chimney and across front of log house home of Mrs. D.C. Noel, a pioneer; Bradian Mines Ltd. cook house and office building. Pan from former across the new bunk house. Central powerhouse. Main tunnel site and dump at old Coronation Mine. LS Cadwallader Creek from Coronation. Man on road beside large pipe running alongside and under road. Residence of Mr. R. Bosustow, Manager of Bralorne Mine. Pan across Bralorne camp site, buildings and mine works at base of a logged hill with two men walking along road between buildings. Two children playing with a wagon. New store and hotel under construction. Excellent shots of sawmill used to cut mine timbers and some of the lumber. LS log on carriage being barked and cut into boards with circular saw, several very good shots of edger, circular saw and carriage again. Pan of mine dump, mill, power plant, and assay office. The complete operation of producing gold bricks is shown, with shots of ore cars leaving a shaft, ore being dumped into coarse ore bin and carried by conveyor belt to the crusher; Simons Cone Crusher in operation; conveyor belt transferring the crushed ore to the fine ore bin; the finely crushed ore going to the Ball Mill, Harding's Ball Mill operating in closed-circuit with classifier; overflow from classifier passing over corduroy blankets which picks up fine gold; tails from blanket tables being pumped to flotation cells, coarse gold from the traps held up to the camera by a worker who is washing it slightly; then flotation concentrates flaking off drying drum, sacked and weighed before shipment to the smelter. Two men shown at the smelter melting and pouring a gold brick. Various shots of $20,000 gold brick, steaming in its mold, cold, and free of the mold. Excellent shots follow of the cookhouse where the cooks are shown sampling and stirring the contents of great pots, making bread and rolls, and carving meat. Men lingering at the door of the messhall and trotting in for their meal. Officials leaving for home, talking, posing, getting into cars and driving away. LS sedan on rough mountain road.*

82. BRIDGE CHAT. (1933)
    p.c. ASN/ASS (#B-634)
    l. 1 reel   g. 35mm   t. b+w   s. sound
    d. Gordon Sparling
    ph. *
    c.s. United Artists

> *CANADIAN CAMEO No. 15. "The word bridge brings visions to many people of a card game. To others, it may mean part of a violin, or even a set of false teeth! The picture then goes on to the kind of bridge one uses to get to the other side, and finds an amazing variety of ways to do it, from the simple cable bridge to the huge cantilever span of the Quebec Bridge." One of the bridges shown is the Capilano suspension bridge in North Vancouver.*

83. BRIDGE RIVER - CARIBOO. (late 1930's?)
    p.c. *
    l. 1 reel   g. 16mm   t. colour s. si.
    d. *
    ph. *
    c.s. Unknown

> *"The famous Bridge River mining section of the Cariboo District." Distributed by B.C. Provincial Bureau of Information.*

84. BRIEF SHOTS - FREIGHT TRAIN IN THE ROCKIES. (1910-1920)
    p.c. *
    l. 6'   g. 16mm   t. b+w   s. si.
    d. *
    ph. *
    c.s. Jack Chisholm C743, B+W/roll 3

> *A freight train rounding a bend in the Rockies with a high cliff at the right and river on the left.*

85. BRILLIANT PAGEANT MARKS FOUNDATION STONE LAYING OF NEW
    ANGLICAN CATHEDRAL BY BISHOP OF LONDON, VICTORIA, B.C.
    (1926)
    p.c. Fox Movietonews (Fox #751.13 - B5213)
    l. 65'   g. 35mm   t. b+w   s. si.
    d. *
    ph. Herron
    c.s. Fox Movietonews, N.Y.

> *Laying cornerstone of Christ Church Cathedral. See No. 72.*

86. BRITAIN'S FUTURE KING. (1919)
    p.c. Pathéscope (?)
    l. approx. 400'   g. 28mm   t. b+w   s. si.
    d. *
    ph. *
    c.s. NFA

> *"The Prince of Wales landed in Canada on August 18, 1919 and left on November 29th. The interval was occupied in one triumphal popular tour to all the principal cities of the Dominion. The winsome personality of the Royal Visitor, his thoroughgoing good fellowship, his grace of manner and tact with people of all classes and his wholehearted, boyish enjoyment of everything he saw lifted the tour out of the category of patriotic ceremonials and made of it a brilliant holiday festival during which the Prince won the respect, admiration, and affection of the people of this Dominion. Our pictures are made up of incidents of the tour and initmate closeups taken by official cameramen who travelled with the Prince's party." - Pathéscope Catalogue.*

87. B.C. FIGHTS FOREST FIRES FROM THE AIR. (1924)
    p.c. Fox Movietonews, N.Y.
    l.   g. 35mm   t. b+w   s. si.
    d. *
    ph. probably Len H. Roos
    c.s. NFA, Ottawa

> *"Terrible fires necessitate drastic action and HS-2-L Flying Boats are used*

to drop pamphlets to appeal to smokers and arsonists. Excellent shots of HS-2-L taking off, airborne, dropping leaflets, people picking them up. Beautiful aerials over B.C. virgin forestland, log booms. HS-2-L landing."

88. B.C. FOR THE EMPIRE. (1914-1916)
    p.c. Kean's Canada Films
    1. 4 reels   g. 35mm   t. b+w   s. si.
    d.   *
    ph. A.D. "Cowboy" Kean
    c.s. Unknown

        In conjunction with the Vancouver Red Cross, Kean assembled 4 reels of patriotic films covering the period up to February, 1916. They showed the first troops leaving Vancouver and probably included scenes of the war effort at home, parades of departing soldiers. They were shown in the Dominion Theatre in Vancouver under the imprint Kean's Canada Films. During the war the Ford Motion Picture Laboratories used some of Kean's footage in their FORD CANADIAN MONTHLY scenes to help inspire recruits.

89. B.C. FORESTRY DEPARTMENT "BOMBS" LOGGING CAMPS AND COAST
    TOWNS WITH "SAVE THE FOREST" TRACTS, VANCOUVER, B.C.
    (1924)
    p.c. Fox Movietonews (Fox #544.8-A180)
    1.   g. 35mm   t. b+w   s. si.
    d.   *
    ph. Len Roos
    c.s. Fox Movietonews, N.Y.

        "Campbell River from plane. Pilot throws out literature. CU literature. Plane over river. Burned off timber land. Booming ground and logging camp at Menzies Bay; scene finishes with zoom at long raft. Shot of river." See No. 87.

90. B.C. GUN DOG CLUB RETRIEVER TRIALS, VANCOUVER, B.C.
    (1938)
    p.c. Fox Movietonews (Fox #34 - 122)
    1.   g. 35mm   t. b+w   s. sound
    d.   *
    ph. ASN
    c.s. Fox Movietonews, N.Y.

        "Parade of dogs. Line up of all the dogs in the competition. Dogs and owners marching toward camera. LS showing field and competition going on. Crowds watching. Man shooting gun. Bird being shot. Dog going after fallen bird in water. Various shots of the different dogs in the competition."

91. BRITISH COLUMBIA ITEMS. (n.d.)
    p.c. *
    1. approx. 1000' g. 16mm   t. b+w   s. si.
    d.   *
    ph. *
    c.s. NFA #5515

        Includes scenes, on nineteen 50-foot reels, of Victoria, Corner Brook Lakes (??? - Cranbrook?). Doukhobors, Sikhs, Prince George, entry into Vancouver, Clear Brook, Chinatown, Vancouver Riot, etc. The riot is not identified but it may be the unemployed march on the Post Office in 1938.

92. B.C. JERSEY BREEDERS SUMMER OUTING - 1931. (1931)
    p.c. B.C. Dept. of Agriculture (Reel 52)
    1. approx. 400' g. 16mm   t. b+w   s. si. w/captions
    d.   *
    ph. *
    c.s. PABC

        Oliver Evans, President of the B.C. Jersey Breeder's Association and A.J. Cameron, Secretary. "A Trip through Saanich (The Fair Land), The Home of the Jersey - May 26th". A file of automobiles travelling along the two-track dirt roads of the Saanich Peninsula visiting the various dairy farms of the district, looking over the premises and chatting with the owners. The trees grow right down to the road, and the whole vision is warm and bucolic. *Farms visited and shown are: Olympic Farm, W. Horsland; Babbacombe, H.E. Burbidge; Coleshill, Mr. Aldridge & Mrs. Clive; El Sereno, G.W. Malcolm; Dominion Experimental Farm at Sidney where lunch was served, courtesy of Mr. Straight, the Superintendant. The Hon. Dr. S.F. Tolmie, Premier of British Columbia, arrives to "grace the occasion" and speeches are made at a long table set up outside in the sun. Following lunch, more farms are visited: Blastree Farm, G. Hooper; Woodcote, Capt. F.C. Gibson; Easamo; Brackenhurst, A.W. Aylard; Duntulm Farm, Major & Mrs. MacDonald; Glamorgan Farm, S. Matson; Heather Farm, Capt. F.C. Wilson; and Sandy Gap, Geo. Clark. Home to the Parliament Buildings in Victoria. Other speakers at the Experimental Farm lunch included the Hon. Wm. Atkinson, Minister of Agriculture, and Hon. N. Lougheed. Also along for the trip were two members of the Agricultural Press: George Murray of the Vancouver Province, and H.B. Smith from the Nor'West Farmer.*

93. BRITISH COLUMBIA: LOGGING IN WINTER. (pre 1910)
    p.c. *
    1. 510'   g. 35mm   t. b+w   s. si.
    d. *
    ph. *
    c.s. Unknown

"(1) Winter in the forest. Trees and land snow covered. Huts of the lumbermen. A scene of great beauty. (2) A Far Western homestead. Rounding up the horses. Feeding the pigs. A washing day - men busy at the tubs. A horse-drawn sleigh, boy and girl passengers. (3) Felling the giant pine trees: CU preliminaries - chopping, wedging, sawing, a hasty retreat. (4) Marvellous snow effects are created as the noble trees gracefully decline. When the tree rushes to earth the displacement forms a scene of wonderful beauty and fascination, the fine snow rising in feathery, lace-like - almost vapoury - patterns to the very top of the screen. (5) Hauling logs through the forest. Raising and stacking logs by windlass. (6) A pause for dinner, well earned. (7) Loading a trolley with a score of huge logs. These pair-horse loads dash at a great pace down the slopes, gaining impetus in their descent for mounting the next incline. (8) The lumber yard. Chains of logs drawn by steam travelling cranes to the sides. (9) Scenes from the top of the chute, and from the opposite bank. The released logs with terrific force enter the river, dive under water and re-appear on the surface far away. Occasional log collisions cause great displacement and create weird effects." Also called LOGGING IN WINTER, BRITISH COLUMBIA. - George Kleine Catalogue, 1910. p.145.

94. B.C. LOGGING OPERATION PROVES INTERESTING TO CANADIAN
    PRESS DELEGATES IN CAPILANO VALLEY, VANCOUVER, B.C.
    (1924)
    p.c. Fox Movietonews (Fox #420.75 - A3690)
    1.   g. 35mm   t. b+w   s. si.
    d. *
    ph. Len H. Roos
    c.s. Fox Movietonews, N.Y.

"Delegates coming off ship. Various shots of crowd of delegates. Shot of high rigger cutting off top of tree for spar. Telephoto shot of high rigger cutting. CU high rigger talking to the ladies. LS of boat PRINCE GEORGE arriving in Vancouver Harbour."

95. B.C. MISCELLANY. (1930's)
    p.c. private
    1. approx. 470' g. 16mm   t. b+w & red s. si.
    d. *
    ph. Rev. George R.B. Kinney
    c.s. NFA, Ottawa

red: West coast islands & scenery. Two seiners at Klayoquot with men working on nets at the stern. Village of Ahousat from the water. Pan around harbour. Various shots of boats, buildings including church, oil tanks, etc. Nootka, with Nootka Packers building briefly visible and sign: NOOTKA PACKING CO. LTD., PACKERS & DISTRIBUTORS. FAMOUS SNOWCAP BRAND PILCHARDS & MINCED RAZOR CLAMS.

b+w: Sea Cadets on floats and boats in Victoria's Inner Harbour. Running up Causeway steps. Boats tied up to floats. Good CU's boys. Pan around Inner Harbour, CPR ships at berth. Sunset on West Coast. Kootenays. View across

Kootenay Lake. A cross mounted on a hill. Shots of Lake. Tent on snowy shore of the Lake, workers nearby. Various shots of the Lake in winter. Tents in snow, workers, man pounding something being held by another man on an anvil. A boat tied up near a work party. Many good shots of workers posing & working. Cook coming out of cook tent, men carrying supplies. This was probably shot before 1933 when the CPR was building its track around the shore of Kootenay Lake & Rev. Kinney ran a Mission for the workers.

Indians pushing a canoe out into a river. Sunday School class at Windsor United Church. Kids inside at desks, posing with teachers & adults outside. Others posing with the rector (probably Vancouver). Groups & couples strolling through Stanley Park, Vancouver. Large group on lawn outside pavillions. Crossing a bridge. Mobs about flower beds & lawns. Windsor United Church parishioners walking down steps out of church. Large group of kids posing with Rev. Kinney at foot of stairs. Many groups of kids posing by street & steps below church.

96. B.C. MOUNTAINEERING CLUB UNDERTAKES AN EXPEDITION THAT
    FOR THRILLING BEAUTY IS NOT SURPASSED ANYWHERE, LAKE
    O'HARA, B.C. (1928)
    p.c. Fox Movietonews (Fox #728-C7214)
    1. 100'   g. 35mm   t. b+w   s. si.
    d.   *
    ph. W.J. Oliver
    c.s. Fox Movietonews, N.Y.

        "Man walking across footbridge. Men climbing mountain. Seven Sisters Falls. Waterfalls. People climbing mountains. Valley scene. Dangerous crossing. Suspension bridge across gorge, river below. Climber on rocks. Sunset scene over lake."

97. B.C. PICTURESQUE HIGHWAYS. (1937)
    p.c. private
    1. 250'   g. 16mm   t. colour s. si.
    d.   *
    ph. H. Turner
    c.s. c/o Pacific Cinémathèque, Vancouver

        A trip up the Fraser Canyon, and points north, in an old Willis Knight. Scenes include: Hell's Gate. Old Alexandria suspension bridge. Alexandria Lodge. Log cabin in woods. Old tunnel on Fraser Canyon highway. Unfinished road. Sign on road reading Danger. DO NOT ROLL ROCKS - RAILROAD BELOW. LS CPR train crossing bridge. Scenic shots of river, sagebrush, etc. At the time the road between Lillooet and Bralorne had not been built and cars travelling that way were placed on a flatcar of the PGE, called the "Galloping Goose". There are several good shots of the "Galloping Goose" and cars and passengers being hauled by this gas-electric locomotive. Shots following include: Entrance to Seaton Lake Lodge. LS of Lodge. Good shot of car. Road into Gang Ranch. Sky Blue Water Camp on Marble Canyon. Trout in creek. Lone Butte Hotel. Old log building. Cowboy. Harrison's Ranch. Green Lake. Two days catch of trout. Good shot of 70-mile House. A, slightly-the-worse-for-the-weather, Vancouver-Ashcroft stagecoach at side of road. Bus at T.U. Auto camp.

98. B.C. PREMIER VOICES FAITH IN FUTURE, VICTORIA, B.C.
    (1933)
    p.c. Fox Movietonews (Fox #18-102)
    1.   g. 35mm   t. b+w   s. sound
    d.   *
    ph. ASN
    c.s. Fox Movietonews, N.Y.

        "Hon. S.F. Tolmie tells you why he expects early recovery from slump."

99. BRITISH COLUMBIA SCENES & MISCELLANEOUS & U.S.A. (1938)
    p.c. private
    1. approx. 400' g. 16mm   t. colour s. si.
    d.   *
    ph. Mr. & Mrs. T.G.S. Chambers
    c.s. NFA, Ottawa

        First Narrows Bridge, Vancouver, under construction. Vancouver shots. Mounted RCMP in front of Courthouse. Granville Street with Orpheum Theatre.

*Miniature Golf in Stanley Park. Shawnigan Lake. A.C. DesBrisay, Chief
Justice of B.C. Shovelling snow on Balfour Avenue. Qualicum Beach Hotel.
Jack Constantine & friend. T.G.S. Chambers. Vancouver at night. House &
garden. Ernest Gourlay fishing. River. Power dam at Bonnington Falls.
Wharf for ferry at Kootenay Lake. Trail. Osoyoos Lake taken from the old
highway. Looking down onto Christine Lake. Beach scene. St. Malo, France
& Carnac. Going into Belle Isle, Brittany. Welwyn Garden City (England?).
Weston. Southampton w/ EMPRESS OF BRITAIN. Snoqualmie Pass.*

100. BRITISH COLUMBIA TRAVEL SCENES.   (1936)
    p.c. private
    l. approx. 400'   g. 16mm   t. colour & b+w s. si.
    d.   *
    ph. Mr. & Mrs. T.G.S. Chambers
    c.s. NFA, Ottawa

*Mr. Chambers believes the first part of this reel was shot with some of the
first 16mm colour film to enter the Province.*

*colour: Victoria Harbour. Empress Hotel. View from Empress Hotel. Evening
in Esquimalt. University of British Columbia. A house in Shaughnessey.
Becky & Gore & her brother Bob. Vancouver skyline from Brockton Point.
Scottie Wilson. North Vancouver.*

*b+w: Osoyoos Lake, going up Anarchist Mountain. Looking S.W. through wind-
shield. Causeway between Osoyoos Lake and Skaha Lake. Penticton main
street. Looking at Okanagan Lake from Summerland. Kelowna Regatta. Aquatic
Club. Ferry from Westbank to Kelowna. Becky & Rob on ferry at Kelowna.
Black Mountain in distance. Looking north on Okanagan Lake. Kelowna main
street. Rutland Road, packing house. Dog on Edie Gay Ranch. T.G.S. Chamb-
ers & dog. House on Belgo. A.K. Lloyd, our next door neighbour. Apples.
Pixie Wilson with horse. Kelowna looking down Okanagan Lake. Paddy and
Patricia Acland. O.V. Maude Roxby & Mr. Hart. Looking over RLO Bench to
Kelowna. Looking at Black Mountain from ranch. House. Orchards on Belgo
Road., Kelowna. Pruning the orchard. Revelstoke - main ski jump. Nels
Nielson, champion jumper. Looking down the Columbia R. North shore road
at Agassiz. Harrison Lake with Mt. Douglas. Railway & road bridge across
the Fraser R. Patullo Bridge. Empress Hotel. Pier D, Vancouver, before
the fire. PRINCESS boat. View from Metropolitan Building. Marine Building
with Stanley Park. Top of Royal Bank Building, Vancouver, with representatives of Cockfield-Brown & both Chambers. Pan over Vancouver skyline. Cambie
Street Bridge. Advertising tea. Georgia Street. Old CPR Hotel. House on
Balfour St., Vancouver. Film star Lilian Chamber off to Chicago.*

101. BRITISH COLUMBIA TRAVEL SCENES.   (approx. 1936)
    p.c. private
    l. approx. 400'   g. 16mm   t. colour & b+w   s. si.
    d.   *
    ph. Mr. & Mrs. T.G.S. Chambers
    c.s. NFA, Ottawa

*b+w: HMS APOLLO in Vancouver Harbour. SS EMPRESS OF JAPAN in Vancouver
Harbour. Train at Seton Lake. Fraser Highway. Highlining in the woods.
Malahat Drive. Roses at Butchart Gardens. Thompson River. Oliver.
Kalamalka Lake. Hospital at Tranquille. Dr. Kingsley Terry.*

*colour: Bridge River. Mt. Halcyon. Upper Arrow Lake. Trail. Elk Falls.
Logging camp at Campbell R. in 1937.*

102. B.C. TRIBUTE TO OLD JOE FORTES.   (1925)
    p.c. Fox Movietonews, N.Y.
    l.   g. 35mm   t. b+w   s. si.
    d.   *
    ph. Bernard O. Dewey (?)
    c.s. NFA

*No other information given, but check Fox Movietone story #201 - 8937: THE
FUNERAL OF JOE FORTES, ENGLISH BAY LIFESAVER, MUCH BELOVED FRIEND OF
VANCOUVER CHILDREN, VANCOUVER, B.C., 2/7/22. (See No. 343)*

103. BRITISH COLUMBIA VIEWS. (n.d.)
     p.c. *
     1. 160'   g. 35mm   t. b&w   s. si.
     d.   *
     ph. *
     c.s. NFA #765

                    "Various news stories, untitled."

104. BRITISH COLUMBIA'S INVESTMENT IN YOUTH. (1936)
     p.c. British Columbia Forest Service (reel 64)
     1. approx. 400'   g. 16mm   t. b&w & colour   s. si. w/captions
     d.   *
     ph. *
     c.s. PABC

                    b+w: New Westminster celebrates her 66th May Day, May 2, 1936. Procession
                    of old Queen, Mary Doyle, and new Queen, Margaret Clark, and their court,
                    to park and grandstand.

                    colour: bandstand, crowds, band, various Queens from the Fraser Valley.
                    Ceremonial abdication and coronation. New Queen drives off in carriage to
                    greet subjects. Kids at 30 Maypoles perform Maypole Dance.

                    b+w: Dance continues; kids perform folk dances, physical education drill
                    and callisthenics.

105. B.C. WOMEN'S ASSOCIATION DECORATES GRAVES OF FALLEN
     HEROES, VANCOUVER, B.C. (1920)
     p.c. Fox Movietonews (Fox #095.6-2430)
     1. 24'   g. 35mm   t. b+w   s. si.
     d.   *
     ph. Brazill
     c.s. Fox Movietonews, N.Y. & NFA

106. BRITISH COLUMBIA'S 19TH LEGISLATURE IS OPENED BY
     LT. GOV. E.W. HAMBER, VICTORIA, B.C. (1937)
     p.c. Hearst Metrotone News Can no. 782 Roll no. 9
     1.   g. 35mm   t. b+w   s. sound
     d.   *
     ph. ASN
     c.s. Hearst Metrotone News, N.Y.

                    "Guard of Honour arrives at government buildings to perform at ceremonies.
                    Pipe band leading. CU soldiers. Hamber arrives. Band plays GOD SAVE THE
                    KING, then Lt. Gov. inspects Guard. Hamber leaves Parliament Buildings
                    after ceremonies. Prominent guests and members of the Legislature stand at
                    attention. Silent shots of the Lt. Gov. leaving."

107. BRITISH COLUMBIA'S PRO-REC. (1935)
     p.c. B.C. Provincial Bureau of Information
     1. 200'   g. 16mm   t. colour s. si. w/captions
     d.   *
     ph. B.C. Institute of Cinematography
     c.s. NFA

                    "Pro-Rec", or Provincial Recreation, was established in 1934 by the B.C.
                    Government to promote physical and moral well-being among the people of
                    British Columbia. This film shows a demonstration staged by Pro-Rec at
                    Brockton Point in Stanley Park, Vancouver.

                    Three films may have been produced, probably all by the B.C. Provincial Gov-
                    ernment, to publicize and promote the Provincial Recreation programme. All
                    were shown throughout the province, and one enjoyed an extended tour across
                    the country, probably BRITISH COLUMBIA'S PRO-REC.

108. BUILDING AEROPLANES IN CANADA. (1918)
    p.c. Dept. of Trade and Commerce, Exhibits and
        Publicity Bureau, Ottawa
    1. 1 reel   g. 35mm   t. b+w   s. si. w/captions
    d.   *
    ph. *
    c.s. Unknown

> *An early industrial film made by the Federal Government to show Canadian manufacturing. The entry from the first Catalogue of the EPB reads: "A film showing every process of the manufacture of aeroplanes in Canada. This picture was taken under the co-operation of the Imperial Munitions Board. The first part of the film shows the trees being cut down in British Columbia, to secure the excellent Canadian spruce for aeroplane building. Then we trace the spruce tree from the forest until it is being used to construct aeroplanes in Toronto. Finally we are shown Bishop, the noted Canadian ace, doing some stunts in a Canadian-made aeroplane. The entire film is very interesting and educational."*
>
> *Would that it were still with us!*

109. BULB GROWING IN BRITISH COLUMBIA. (1931 ?)
    p.c. B.C. Dept. of Agriculture (Reel 53)
    1. approx. 300'   g. 16mm   t. b+w   s. si. w/captions
    d.   *
    ph. *
    c.s. PABC

> *Vancouver Island bulb grower and his home and garden. October, planting time, bulbs being shaken from the back of the tractor into every second furrow, then placed by hand. Spring cultivation with a rototiller. Men in overcoats inspecting plants for disease and insect damage. Pan across field of daffodils. Pickers picking blooms to improve the bulb, then dumping them into a heap to be destroyed. Pickers playing in a pile of flowers. Men inspecting good blooms. Diseased or insect-smitten bulbs are rogued, or dug up and destroyed. Huge litter of cut blooms being carried away by pickers. Bulbs ploughed out of the ground by a tractor that once was a Ford car. Helpers collecting the bulbs from the top of the furrow. Bulbs in baskets, transported to drying sheds. Loose bulbs are unloaded into drying trays for storage. Stacking trays in storage shed, unloading truck.*

110. BURRO PACK TRAIN ON THE CHILCOOT PASS. (1899-1900)
    p.c. Edison Mfg. Co.
    1. 34'   g. 16mm   t. b+w   s. si.
    d.   *
    ph. Robert Bonine
    c.s. LOC Paper Print Collection

> *"The burro, or pack mule, is an almost indispensible adjunct to the miners in a new country. A long line of these sure-footed animals is seen in this view, loaded with supplies, wending their way toward the spectator. The expansive view of the snow-capped peaks of the distant mountains shows some of the difficulties these persistent animals encountered before reaching the present part of the trail." A single camera position discloses snow-covered mountainous terrain. From around a point of land a rider leads about 10 mules, each carrying a pack. The remainder of the film, from the same camera position, shows approx. 30 more mules, each with a pack. (The 35mm original print was 75' long and was copyrighted in May 1901 - Edison Catalogue, Sept. 1902. p.49)*

111. BUSH PLANES - SPORT PLANES. (1927-1929)
    p.c. *
    1.   g. 16mm   t. b+w   s. si.
    d.   *
    ph. *
    c.s. NFB (1920-P-198)

> *"Shots of an old Fairchild floatplane at dock. Low level aerial along lakeshore. Barge, tugboat, high and dry, trees. Indistinct aerials of Northern forest, one small townsite, lakes, etc. Aerial of lake as camera plane lands and shot of Fairchild on lake. Three men pushing a canoe up on the beach. Various shots of a small airshow at Vancouver Airport with CU of "Bluebird",*

one of the stunting biplanes to be featured. LS's of planes taking off.
Ground to air shots of planes." (Poor quality - reference only)

112. BUSY SEASON IN THE LOWER FRASER VALLEY. (late 1920's)
    p.c. B.C. Dept. of Agriculture
    1. approx. 500'   g. 16mm   t. b+w   s. si. w/captions
    d.   *
    ph. *
    c.s. PABC

> *Harvesting grain by tractor. Stooks. Threshing by "gas power" - thresher*
> *driven by a belt from the tractor. Sacking grain. Trucks taking it away.*
> *Sacks being loaded into CP boxcars. Train pulls out and passes acres of*
> *hops being picked. Hop pickers weighing their baskets. Two-horse load of*
> *hops. Scenes of workers' camp, nurse, community newspaper, kid's playground.*
> *Hops unloaded at processing plant. Hop-curing sheds. Dairy barn. Tobacco-*
> *drying sheds at Sumas. Tobacco harvesting, curing. Ploughing match at*
> *Chilliwack. Two-horse teams and tractors.*

113. BUTCHART'S GARDENS & UNITED CHURCH YOUNG PEOPLE'S PICNIC ON
    BOWEN ISLAND. (approx. 1934)
    p.c. private
    1. 300'   g. 16mm   t. b+w   s. si.
    d.   *
    ph. Rev. George R.B. Kinney
    c.s. NFA, Ottawa

> *Large crowds at Butchart Gardens. Shots of Italian Garden. Sunken Garden,*
> *house and one of the little gnomes. Summer camp on an unidentified beach*
> *with tent; people sitting about. United Church of Canada annual Young*
> *People's picnic to Bowen Island. Large crowd of young men and women board*
> *two steamships, the LADY ALEXANDER and the LADY CYNTHIA, sailing out of*
> *Vancouver Harbour. Scenery en route, shots of picnickers on deck. Arrival*
> *at Bowen Island, disembarking, running & walking up long wharf. Many shots*
> *of various sports: baseball, running races, gents carrying ladies races,*
> *wheelbarrow races, finding-your-shoe-in-the-pile races, swimming races and*
> *a diving competition.*

114. CALEDONIA GAMES, VANCOUVER, B.C. (1926)
    p.c. Fox Movietonews (?)
    1.   g. 35mm   t. b+w   s. si.
    d.   *
    ph. ASN (?)
    c.s. NFB (1920-FG-170-8)

> *"Massed Highland dancers. MS contestant tossing hammer, tossing the caber.*
> *Girl piper and Scottish lassies doing sword dance. MS: Pipe band leading*
> *the contestants onto the field."*

115. CALEDONIAN GAMES BRING MANY LOYAL SCOTCHMEN TO COMPETE AND
    AFTERWARDS ENJOY MUSICAL FESTIVAL, VANCOUVER, B.C. (1928)
    p.c. Fox Movietonews (Fox #751.13-C6681)
    1. 150'   g. 35mm   t. b+w   s. si.
    d.   *
    ph. Beesley
    c.s. Fox Movietonews, N.Y.

> *"Man throwing hammer, highland dancing & piper."*

116. CALEDONIAN SOCIETY'S ANNUAL DAY - 35TH CELEBRATION IN
    VANCOUVER, B.C. (1921)
    p.c. Fox Movietonews (Fox #751.13-A4834)
    1. 250'   g. 35mm   t. b+w   s. si.
    d.   *
    ph. *
    c.s. Fox Movietonews, N.Y.

> *"Visitors from U.S. battleship. Piping, dancing, kids, field sports, sailor's*
> *hornpipe, Punch & Judy Show."*

117. CAMERARING IN CANADA.   (before 1935)
    p.c. *
    1. 1 reel   g. 35mm   t. b+w   s. sound
    d.   *
    ph.   *
    c.s. Unknown

                    There is no indication that any of this film was photographed in British
                    Columbia.

118. CAMP FIRES AMONG SNOW PEAKS.   (1918 or 1919)
    p.c. Dept. of Trade and Commerce, Exhibits and Publicity
          Bureau, Ottawa
    1. 1 reel   g. 35mm   t. b+w   a. si. w/captions
    d.   *
    ph.   *
    c.s. Unknown

                    An early tourist promotion film made by the Federal Government.   The des-
                    cription in the original Catalogue reads: "This film is a scenic film show-
                    ing journeys up the Bow Valley into the Yoho and finally into Wilcox Pass,
                    showing how alpinists at the top of the world make this ascent into terri-
                    tory hitherto unexplored.   This film is produced in co-operation with the
                    Dominion Parks Branch of the Department of the Interior."   Released on
                    July 15, 1919.

119. CANADA - A TRAVELOGUE.   (n.d.)
    p.c. CGMPB
    1. 324'   g. 16mm   t. b+w   s. si.
    d.   *
    ph.   *
    c.s. LOC

                    A film journey across Canada, containing scenes of British Columbia.

120. CANADA CHEERS ROOSEVELT, VICTORIA, B.C.   (1930 and 1937)
    p.c. Hearst Metrotone News
    1.   g. 35mm   t. b+w   s. sound
    d.   *
    ph.   Mack-Bills and Paramount
    c.s. Hearst Metrotone News, N.Y.

                    Mack-Bills was responsible for photographing FDR at the Grand Coulee Dam in
                    1930.   The second part shows FDR and his wife in Victoria, escorted by Lt.
                    Gov. E.W. Hamber and Mrs. Hamber.   They are driven through the crowd-lined
                    streets to a wharf in the Inner Harbour where FDR, his wife and his son sail
                    away on a destroyer, the USS PHELPS.

121. CANADER ENTERS WAR, VANCOUVER, B.C.   (INCLUDES ALSO SHOTS FROM
     OTTAWA, TORONTO AND MONTREAL)   (1939)
    p.c. Paramount (Lib. #8890)
    1. 324'   g. 35mm   t. b+w   s. sound
    d.   *
    ph.   ASN
    c.s. Lost

                    IN VANCOUVER: "CU Highlanders signing up.   Recruits drilling, SCU & CU re-
                    cruits, SCU & CU recruits receiving medical examinations.   Recruits re-
                    ceiving uniforms.   Scrubbing belts, recruits drilling.   CU & SCU.   More
                    drilling & marching."

122. CANADA, FROM COAST TO COAST.   (1932-1933)
    p.c. CGMPB
    1. 7 reels   g. 35mm   t. b+w   s. si. w/captions
    d.   *
    ph.   *
    c.s. Unknown

                    The CGMPB was requested to produce a complete pictorial record of the Imperial
                    Economic Conference held in Ottawa in 1932, and as well as co-ordinating all
                    still photographs and newsreels, it produced this seven-reeler to mark the
                    occasion.   Locations photographed in British Columbia are not identified.

123. CANADA GOES OVER, VICTORIA, B.C. (1914 & 1915)
    p.c. *
    l.   g. 35mm   t. b+w   s. si.
    d.   *
    ph. Dwyer
    c.s. NFA (Taylor reel 132)

           "Hundreds of men of the Canadian Army parade through Victoria from Anscourt
           Military Camp along Government Street to board the PRINCESS MARY which will
           carry them overseas. Huge crowds gather to see them off.

           SECOND CONTINGENT LEAVES: Parades through streets to docks. MS band playing
           as ship pulls out. Tremendous crowds. Ship moving out with flags and
           cheering lads on all decks.

           88TH BATTALION LEAVING VICTORIA: Men of the 88th marching along Government
           St. Final inspection. Band and vehicles on way to board CPR ferry on way
           overseas.

           5TH REGIMENT UNDER CANVAS: (Sept. 1914) View of McCauley Plains & bell tents
           which house Regiment. Men around camp. Officers lined up, salute camera
           smartly."

124. CANADA LOOKS TO ELECTIONS, VANCOUVER, B.C. (1935)
    p.c. Paramount (Lib. #4938) NL 1454
    l.   g. 35mm   t. b+w   s. sound
    d.   *
    ph. *
    c.s. Sherman Grinberg, N.Y.

           "SCU pose H.H. Stevens of Reconstruction party. SCU Stevens talking. He
           explains why the new Reconstruction Party was formed and its purpose: 'A
           spontaneous Movement was born out of a deep-rooted sense of justice and a
           conviction that it is possible to take some practicable measures to allev-
           iate the suffering of the people and restore to them their power of self
           support & their self respect.'"

125. CANADA PAYS TRIBUTE TO ROGERS AND POST, VANCOUVER, B.C.
    (1935)
    p.c. Fox Movietonews (Fox #26-273)
    l. 500'   g. 35mm   t. b+w   s. sound
    d.   *
    ph. ASN
    c.s. Fox Movietonews, N.Y.

           "Alderman T. Wilkinson representing Mayor G. McGeer of Vancouver pays re-
           spects. Stanley McKeen, Member of Provincial Legislature, speaks. Shots
           of funeral plane. Taking off. John K. Davis, U.S. Consul General, acknow-
           ledges tribute."

126. CANADIAN-AUSTRALASIAN LINER MAKURA PRESENTS BEAUTIFUL SIGHT
    ON WAY TO SOUTH SEAS, VANCOUVER, B.C. (n.d.)
    p.c. Fox Movietonews (Fox #463.11-C1875)
    l. 20'   g. 35mm   t. b+w   s. si.
    d.   *
    ph. Len H. Roos
    c.s. Fox Movietonews, N.Y.

           "Ship leaving. Aerial shots of ship in harbour."

127. CANADIAN BRITISH EMPIRE TEAM FOR AUSTRALIA GAMES, VICTORIA, B.C.
    (1938)
    p.c. Fox Movietonews (Fox #33-887)
    l.   g. 35mm   t. b+w   s. sound
    d.   *
    ph. ASN
    c.s. Fox Movietonews, N.Y.

           "Interview with Manager Robinson. British Empire Team on deck. Rubens
           Higgins won javelin event. Tom Osbyrne, heavyweight boxing; Harold Brown,
           broad jump; Geo. Sutherland, hammer throw; John Loaring, hurdles; Eric Coy,
           discus; Bob Pirie, swimming; Noel Oxenbury, Florence Humble, Phyllis Dewar

& Dorothy Lyon comprise the girls relay team."

128. CANADIAN FRUIT. (pre 1938)
    p.c. possibly CGMPB
    l. 15 mins   g. 16mm   t. b+w   s. si.
    d.   *
    ph. *
    c.s. Unknown

> *The BFI Educational Catalogue entry reads: "Whilst mention is made of straw-berries, raspberries, cherries, peaches and celery, the bulk of the film is concerned with apples. Apple orchards are depicted in attractive styles, but the introduction of an occasional flippancy takes the attention from the essentials. The spraying (with what?) of the trees, and method of harvesting, is adequately shown, and the value of modern methods of transport stressed. Captions of photography uniformly good, but maps would convey more clearly than words the position of the regions under consideration." No mention of location but some of the apple orchards are likely in British Columbia.*

129. CANADIAN GIRLS IN BRISK DRILL, VANCOUVER, B.C. (1930's)
    p.c. ASN
    l.   g. 35mm   t. b+w   s.
    d.   *
    ph. *
    c.s. NFB (1930-FG-259)

> *"Dominion's best "Y" class at workout in Stanley Park, Vancouver, B.C."*

130. CANADIAN GOVERNMENT CONSTRUCTING ONE OF WORLD'S
    LARGEST DRYDOCKS, ESQUIMALT, B.C. (approx. 1923)
    p.c. Fox Movietonews (Fox #310.008-C2439)
    l. 50'   g. 35mm   t. b+w   s. si.
    d.   *
    ph. Young's Studios
    c.s. Fox Movietonews, N.Y.

> *"Hi pan excavating. Hi shot loading dirt and rocks on cars. Building the huge crib - LS & SCU. LS concrete pourer. LS & CU concrete crib moulder. SCU diver going down."*

131. CANADIAN HORSES ARE ROUNDED UP ON THE NORTHERN RANGES -
    WILL BE SENT TO RUSSIA, QUESNEL, B.C. (1919)
    p.c. Fox Movietonews, (Fox #411.58-C1323)
    l. 30'   g. 35mm   t. b+w   s. si.
    d.   *
    ph. Jos. Mandy
    c.s. NFA & NFB (1920-179-FG-1)

> *"LS herd of horses on plain. SCU herding a bunch on to the ferry. CU High shot same. SCU herding a bunch into a corral." Beautiful young horses are rounded up for shipment to Russia to alleviate meat shortage and to be used by Canadian Forces serving there.*

132. CANADIAN MOUNTAIN MAJESTY. (1935-1938)
    p.c. ASN (A679)
    l. approx. 400' g. 16mm   t. b+w   s. si.
    d.   *
    ph. *
    c.s. Unknown

> *Made for the CPR: depicting "A journey through the Rockies."*

133. CANADIAN NAVY, ESQUIMALT, B.C. (1921)
    p.c. Fox Movietonews (Fox #551.03-2962)
    l. 82'   g. 35mm   t. b+w   s. si.
    d.   *
    ph. D.C. Davey
    c.s. Fox Movietonews, N.Y.

> *"Long shot entering Esquimalt Harbour, B.C. Harbour - HMCS AURORA, HMCS PATRIOT & HMCS PATRICIAN. Wigwagging and flag signalling. Torpedo on deck of destroyer. Loading small gun. Loading torpedo on board. Loading 4"*

gun or torpedo destroyer."

134. CANADIAN PACIFIC EXHIBITION IS OPENED AND FEATURED BY A
     HOST OF FLAG-WAVING BOYS AND GIRLS, EVERYONE HAPPY.
     VANCOUVER, B.C. (1928)
     p.c. Fox Movietonews (Fox #751.14-C6038)
     l. 150'   g. 35mm   t. b+w   s. si.
     d.   *
     ph. Beesley
     c.s. Fox Movietonews, N.Y., & NFB (1920-FG-211)

> *"Dr. Tolmie, Premier-elect, declares big fair open. Freckle contest & SCU,*
> *CU of contestants. Crowds in grandstand." There are also scenes of a dance*
> *on a raised stage.*

135. CANADIAN PROFESSIONALS PLAY SENSATIONAL GOLF DEFEATING
     AMERICAN AND FRENCH STARS BY 3 TO 2, POINT GREY GOLF COURSE,
     VANCOUVER, B.C. (1929)
     p.c. Fox Movietonews (Fox #713-D2780)
     l. 125'   g. 35mm   t. b+w   s. si.
     d.   *
     ph. Beesley
     c.s. Fox Movietonews, N.Y. & NFB (1920-FG-147-Reel 1)

> *"Group shot, left to right: David Black, Duncan Sutherland, the referee,*
> *Horton Smith & Walter Hagen. Smith and Hagen, two of the world's most*
> *famous golfers in two SCU shots wearing plus fours and sweaters. David*
> *Black & Sutherland of Vancouver. Hagen driving off, Black driving off,*
> *scenes of gallery." The copy at the NFB is 85' long, and is an excerpt*
> *from the compilation: SPORTS EVENTS OF THE 1920's.*

136. CANADIAN RCAF AIRCRAFT, VANCOUVER, B.C. (1927)
     p.c. Fox Movietonews (?)
     l.   g. 35mm   t. b+w   s. si.
     d.   *
     ph. ASN (?)
     c.s. NFB (1920-FG-170-3)

> *"On west coast, an RCAF HS-2-L Amphibious aircraft is prepared for flight.*
> *Shots of men at work on plane. Plane anchored and two RCAF crewmen rowing*
> *boat ashore. HS-2-L being put in water and anchore being lowered. Crewmen*
> *preparing a SCHRECK FLYING BOAT (RCAF) for flight. Aerial shots over lake*
> *and bush. HS-2-L anchored offshore."*

137. THE CANADIAN ROCKIES IN WINTER. (pre 1906)
     p.c. Charles Urban (?)
     l. approx. 375' g. 35mm   t. b+w   s. si.
     d.   *
     ph. *
     c.s. Unknown

> *"Magnificent scenery, of which full advantage has been taken by the camera.*
> *Towering mountains, sky-piercing and snow covered. Frost and snow-bound*
> *rapids in the mighty solitudes. Interesting glimpses of big game: moose,*
> *bison, etc. Clearing a railway cutting of snow. Preparing the surface for*
> *the snow plough. A huge whirling wheel fixed on the front of a powerful*
> *locomotive is forced into the bank of snow, which is thrown from the track*
> *in a feathery stream on either side. The revolving wheel at close quarters;*
> *a marvellous invention." - George Kleine Catalogue, 1910. p.145.*

138. CANADIAN SHIPS GET SAILING ORDERS, VANCOUVER, B.C. (1939)
     p.c. MGM News of the Day
     l. 149'   g. 35mm   t. b+w   s. sound
     d.   *
     ph. *
     c.s. NFB (T-34-FG-58)

> *"HMCS FRASER (H-48) and HMCS ST. LAURENT (H-83) get orders to leave Vancouver*
> *for Halifax. Good shot of ST. LAURENT moving out of harbour and under bridge,*
> *of sailor preparing depth charge, civilians aboard watching man load gun.*
> *CU Captain of the ST. LAURENT, Lt. Cdr. A.M. Hope. Shot of H-48, HMCS FRASER,*
> *moving out of harbour under bridge. RCN sailors marching, crew of destroyers*
> *which will sail from Esquimalt to Halifax via Panama."*

139. THE CANADIAN VICTORY AT COURCELETTE AND ADVANCE OF THE TANKS.
    (1916)
    p.c. Canadian Government Official Films
    1. 4,483'   g. 35mm   t. b+w   s. si.
    d.   *
    ph. *
    c.s. Imperial War Museum (#466)

                    *Although these two films were photographed in Europe during WW 1, it is per-
                    haps of interest that one short sequence in Part 1, Section 2, shows: "A
                    battlefield Polling Station. The British Columbians record their vote for
                    their candidates at home, about 6,000 miles away." The excerpt is regret-
                    tably short, only 10 feet long.*

140. CANADIAN WARSHIPS, VANCOUVER, B.C. (1938)
    p.c. Paramount (Lib #7099)
    1. 102'   g. 35mm   t. b+w   s. sound
    d.   *
    ph. ASN
    c.s. Sherman Grinberg, N.Y.

                    *"Ships arriving, SCU ships arriving. Elevated views of H-48. Elevated view
                    of O-79. General view of H-83. CU HMCS SKEENA tied up. CU boats passing
                    flag. Back view of the docking. Acting Mayor Cornett and Col. J. Foster,
                    Vancouver Police Chief, going aboard one of the ships. Naval officers:
                    L-R - Lt. Cdr. A.M. Hope, Lt. Cdr. H.E. Reid, Lt. Cdr. W.J.R. Beach, and
                    Capt. V.G. Brodeur." H-48 was HMCS FRASER and H-83 was HMCS ST. LAURENT.*

141. CANADIAN WARSHIPS VISIT VANCOUVER. (1939)
    p.c. *
    1.   g. 35mm   t. b+w   s.
    d.   *
    ph. *
    c.s. NFB (1930-240-N-1)

                    *"Shots of RCN ships entering Vancouver Harbour. CS HMCS SKEENA, senior
                    Naval ship. Mayor Cornett of Vancouver going aboard SKEENA. Group of ratings
                    lined up on ship. Capt. V.G. Brodeur, Officer Commanding Pacific Defences,
                    leaving with Lt. Cdr. H.E. Reid (Capt.) (A note says Capt. H.E. Reid was
                    Officer Commanding Atlantic Defences.) Group poses on dock near immigration
                    shed." See also CANADIAN WARSHIPS, VANCOUVER, B.C., #140, which may be same
                    film.*

142. CANADIAN WHEAT STORY. (1939)
    p.c. British Paramount (Lib. #8888)
    1. 714'   g. 35mm   t. b+w   s. sound
    d.   *
    ph. *
    c.s. Visnews, London

                    *Map showing Churchill, Winnipeg & Vancouver. Dissolve to an air view of
                    Vancouver. View of Vancouver's buildings, from another building. Cargo
                    ship alongside. Two shots of the SS EMPRESS OF JAPAN being loaded. Cargo
                    ship SS GREGALIA of Glasgow being loaded. Vancouver Harbour. Giant grain
                    elevator. Shot through stacks of Grain Building. Ship alongside grain ele-
                    vator. CU grain filling hold. Stern shot of the GREGALIA. Vancouver sky-
                    scrapers with EMPRESS liner in b.g. Dissolve to map again, then to Winnipeg.*

143. CANADIAN YACHTSMEN WIN CHAMPIONSHIP OF NORTH PACIFIC AND
    LIPTON CUP IN THE INTERNATIONAL RACES, ENGLISH BAY, VANCOUVER,
    B.C. (1929)
    p.c. Fox Movietonews (Fox #755.8-D1047)
    1. 70'   g. 35mm   t. b+w   s. si.
    d.   *
    ph. *
    c.s. Fox Movietonews, N.Y.

                    *"LS of yachts under full sail in the bay, mountains in b.g. People on shore
                    watching races. Various CU's of the yachts under sail."*

144. CANADIANS FOR RUSSIA. (1918 & 1919)
    p.c. *
    l. approx. 400'   g. 35mm   t. b+w   s. si.
    d.   *
    ph. Angelo Accetti
    c.s. NFB (1910-FG-157)

> *In 1918, Great Britain asked Canada to join her in mounting an expeditionary force against the Bolsheviks in northern Russia and Siberia. The objectives were never clearly defined, and although Prime Minister Bordon hesitated, he eventually sent 500 men to Archangel and 4000 to Siberia via Vladivostock, the last contingent arriving in January, 1919, where they joined British, French, Italian, Czecho-Slovak, Rumanian, Polish, Serbian and Japanese contingents. The Canadians were forbidden to take part in any action which might have placed them in jeopardy, so they spent most of their time on guard duty and backing-up other troops. The Canadians in Archangel saw action but nothing on a major scale and all troops were embarked for home by the end of June, 1919. The expedition was not popular in Canada and some of the soldiers going to Siberia had to be put aboard ship at bayonet point; nearly all were draftees.*
>
> *Angelo Accetti, who later worked for Associated Screen News in Winnipeg, shot film of the second batch of 2,700 troops who left Vancouver for Vladivostock in January, 1919, spending time around their training camp before they left. Description: "Sequence on Canadian soldiers drilling, marching, drilling with bayonets, firing in rifle range, etc. Shots of horses being unloaded from Northern Railway cars in Vancouver. Shots of two men writing letters in tent, of other men playing cards. Shot of Cpl. Kennedy, of Calgary, with mascot, a cat. Shots of parades through Vancouver streets. Incidental view of two streetcars. Shots of horses being led to Docks and up loading ramp into ship. Shots of men boarding ship." One of the ships used to transport troops was the CPR liner EMPRESS OF JAPAN. The second half of this film was shot in Vladivostock and shows the troops on duty and relaxing.*

145. CANADIANS LEAVE VICTORIA FOR OVERSEAS, VICTORIA, B.C.
    (1914)
    p.c. *
    l.   g. 35mm   t. b+w   s. si.
    d.   *
    ph.   *
    c.s. NFA (Taylor reel 123)

> *"Autumn and Canadians board liner (ferry?) to go overseas as support for Canadian Regiments already there. Shots of huge crowd of civilians along quay as soldiers march smartly onto ship.*
>
> *Soldiers parade at race-track prior to going to Victoria dock to board liner for overseas. March past, inspection, troopships in harbour with decorations, flags, troops parading through Victoria on way to ships, pipe band following. Relatives marching alongside soldiers."*

146. CANADIANS MARCH TO SERVICE, VICTORIA, B.C. (1914-1917)
    p.c. *
    l.   g. 35mm   t. b+w   s. si.
    d.   *
    ph.   *
    c.s. NFA (Taylor reel 133)

> *"Very good shots from various news sources, and dates, of Canadians at various stages of preparation, preparatory to going overseas. Various regiments marching, inspections, parading around Victoria Race Track, marching to embarkation points in full marching order. Last story of Highland Regiment giving concert in downtown Victoria."*

147. CANADA'S AIRFORCE ON FOREST PATROL DUTY HAS WONDERFUL WINGED
    ALLIES TO AID FLYERS IN DISTRESS, VANCOUVER, B.C. (1924)
    p.c. Fox Movietonews (Fox #412.827-A153)
    l. 130'   g. 35mm   t. b+w   s. si.
    d.   *
    ph. Len H. Roos
    c.s. Fox Movietonews, N.Y.

"Pigeon man entering loft. CU man handling pigeon. Putting bird in box. Placing it in plane. Airplane taking off & in flight. Airplane forced to land. Sending message by pigeon. Pigeon entering loft. CU bell ringing. Man leaves orderly room. CU message. CU of pigeon held in man's hand."

148. CANADA'S DIAMOND JUBILEE. (1927)
    p.c. ASN
    l.   g. 35mm   t. b+w   s. si. w/captions
    d. *
    ph. *
    c.s. NFB (1920-DN-78-3)

    The film shows scenes from all over Canada of celebrations marking the country's 50th Anniversary as a nation. Scenes in Vancouver include: the 15th Artillery Battery firing a salute in Stanley Park. Various shots of float parade. A band marching through Confederation Arch and past the camera. HA Hastings Park 3000 children collectively forming words on park grounds.

149. CANADA'S EVERGREEN PLAYGROUND. (1934)
    p.c. Canadian Government Motion Picture Bureau
    l. approx. 800'   g. 35mm   t. b+w   s. si. w/captions
    d. Bill Oliver
    ph. Bill Oliver
    c.s. NFA (340' 16mm), BCPM History

    Produced for the National Parks Bureau, Ottawa.

    An animated curtain rises to reveal waves washing in on a sandy beach. LS Hatley Park castle from pond at bottom the garden, a rowboat passing by. PRINCESS KATHLEEN, CPR ferry, arrives in Victoria's Inner Harbour with visitors crowding the decks. CU passengers along the rails as ship passes. Empress Hotel over the after deck of the KATHLEEN. Passengers leave the ship, down gangways into a shed. Car driving along ramp out of a ferry named the OLYMPIC, under a sign reading: COME AGAIN, AU REVOIR. FOR INFORMATION APPLY VICTORIA PUBLICITY BUREAU. Several other cars disembark. Good aerial view of Inner Harbour, Customs House, CPR ferries and etc. from top of Parliament Buildings, pans across to Empress Hotel. Sign on a building reads: NEW ENGLAND CAFE - ? ? ? - ASK ANYBODY. Also good LS old Post Office, Belmont Building, streetcar passing on Causeway. A man & a girl examine a rose bush in the Empress garden. Ladies in Mayor Pendray's topiary garden look at a sitting bear, a fat bird, a bird's roost, etc. CPR ferry in b.g. Old codgers lawn bowling. Oak Bay golf course with golfers & CPR ferry sailing by in b.g. Swimming and diving in the Crystal Gardens. EMPRESS OF JAPAN in Esquimalt drydock. Shot down Moss Street (?) with Olympic Mountains in distance. Mt. Baker in far distance from Malahat overlooking Pat Bay. Car driving over Malahat Drive, several shots including one down Finlayson Arm. A car travelling through the forest over a dirt road; a man & woman walk through ferns beneath the trees. Two couples hold hands around the base of a large tree. Car continues through forest. A speedboat, perhaps on Cowichan Lake. A gracious tea being served outdoors by a maid dressed in black, somewhere on the Oak Bay Golf Course with the ocean & Olympic mountains in b.g. Curtain comes down over beach scene from beginning of film.

150. CANADA'S NATIONAL PARKS. (before 1930)
    p.c. Pathescope
    l. approx. 400'   g. 28mm   t. b+w   s. si.
    d. *
    ph. *
    c.s. NFA (from Graphics Consultants)

    The film probably includes shots of national parks in B.C.

151. CANADA'S PACIFIC GATEWAY. (1928-1929)
    p.c. CGMPB
    l. 1 reel   g. 35mm   t. b+w   s. si. w/captions
    d. *
    ph. *
    c.s. NFA & NFB Archives P.B. 50 (1930-DN-11)

    "Three score years ago, where Burrard Inlet dents the coastline of Canada, stood a tiny trading post. Today on this same site stands the Dominion's largest Pacific port and one of her greatest cities - Vancouver. With mountain

heights, ocean shores and forest realms as its borders, this western metropolis has many charms and attractions many of which are portrayed in this short travelogue of Vancouver and its scenic environs."

This film includes a high panoramic view of the city, and various busy street scenes include shots of sightseeing streetcars and buses. Also shots of Stanley Park, English Bay, Capilano Canyon and the suspension bridge, and Vancouver Harbour. There are also shots of Sunday at the beach, English Bay, giant trees in Stanley Park, and a CPR liner leaving the Harbour. (The print at the NFA is 625' long, 35mm.)

152. CANADA'S SHIPPING BOOMS AS STRIKE TIES UP U.S. COAST,
     VANCOUVER, B.C. (1936)
     p.c. Universal Newsreel V.8 R.521
     l. 55'   g. 35mm   t. b+w   s. si.
     d.   *
     ph. ASN
     c.s. USNA

> *"Japanese flag across bows of a British ship. Group of ships at terminal dock. LS ships at dock. Freight train passing dock. CU sling going aboard. Loading shots along dock, apples for Europe. Scenes of activity along dock. Ships mid-stream waiting for space. Loading shots. Canadian flour for Japan. Loading nickel. Loading frozen fish."*

153. CANADA'S THIRD LARGEST CITY IS ISOLATED BY FLOODS, VANCOUVER, B.C.
     (1935)
     p.c. Paramount (Lib. #4354) NL 1327
     l.   g. 35mm   t. b+w   s. sound
     d.   *
     ph. *
     c.s. Sherman Grinberg, N.Y. and Visnews (Lib. #4210)

> *"Pan rushing waters. SCU men walking toward washed out RR tracks. People along tracks. SCU girl getting out of marooned auto into rowboat. Highway under water. General & CU side of hill caving in. Pan villagers watching."*
> *The British Paramount story held by Visnews contains an aerial view of the city at the head, and shots of a tree caving in at the end.*

154. CAPTAIN WAARDE AND HIS CHINESE JUNK ARRIVE FROM SHANGHAI
     AFTER BEING 91 DAYS ON THE PACIFIC, VICTORIA, B.C. (1922)
     p.c. Fox Movietonews (Fox #463.4-2838)
     l. 18'   g. 35mm   t. b+w   s. si.
     d.   *
     ph. Young's Studio
     c.s. Fox Movietonews, N.Y.

> *"Shots of junk & Captain Waarde."*

155. CAR RACES, VANCOUVER. (1928)
     p.c. Fox Movietonews
     l.   g. 35mm   t. b+w   s. si.
     d.   *
     ph. *
     c.s. NFB (1920-DN-224)

> *"Racing cars compete for provincial honours. HA of race from top of stands. Level shots of cars negotiating turns in clouds of dust, racing by the camera. Shot of winning car & driver."*

156. CARIBOO DISTRICT. (late 1930's (?))
     p.c. *
     l. 1 reel   g. 16mm   t. b+w   s. si.
     d.   *
     ph. *
     c.s. Unknown

> *Depicts scenes in the Cariboo District of British Columbia.*

157. THE CARRIER INDIANS OF BRITISH COLUMBIA. (1923-27)
     p.c. National Museum of Canada
     1. 340'   g. 16mm   t. b+w   s. si. w/captions
     d.   Harlan Smith
     ph. Harlan Smith
     c.s. National Museum of Man & NFA (#3777)

                    *"The film shows scenes of the life of Carrier Indians, in the beautiful moun-
                    tains of British Columbia. Men are seen gaffing salmon during the annual run
                    of salmon and eels, children eating soapolalie or Indian ice cream, and there
                    is shown the making of fire by twirling one stick on another, the making of
                    kettles and dishes with birch bark, sewing of moccasins, use of moose and
                    buckskin, sewing with sinew for thread, the old and new methods of transpor-
                    tation (dogs, horses, & cars), and a glimpse at the weird old-time ceremonials.
                    These Indians speak a language of the Athapaskan stock which covers more of
                    North America than any other group of Indian languages." The "weird old-time
                    ceremonials" show men dancing in traditional costume & blankets, and some
                    women dancing. The end of the film shows old and new tombs in the graveyard,
                    Indian men who have become ranchers, women & children coming out of a church,
                    and an old man dancing in a field.*

158. CATTLE RANCHING AND POULTRY FARMING IN BRITISH COLUMBIA.
     (pre 1910)
     p.c. *
     1. 227'   g. 35mm   t. b+w   s. si.
     d.   *
     ph. *
     c.s. Unknown

                    *"A series of most instructive scenes of Canadian methods of ranching and farm-
                    ing in the great Northwest. An agricultural subject of great value to the
                    student and prospective farmer." George Kleine Catalogue, 1910. p.249.*

159. CENTENARY OF FOUNDING OF BRITISH COLUMBIA IS CELEBRATED BY
     COLOURFUL AND HISTORICAL PAGEANT, VANCOUVER, B.C. (1924).
     p.c. Fox Movietonews (Fox #095.92-B5638)
     1. 60'   g. 35mm   t. b+w   s. si.
     d.   *
     ph. R.E. Bourne
     c.s. Fox Movietonews, N.Y.

                    *"Parade of pioneers passing. LS crowd at ceremony. George Simpson and others
                    inspect Fort store. Hudson Bay men of 1924. Unveiling the marker of the
                    birthplace of B.C., a cairn."*

160. CHAMPION RETAINS LOG-BUCKER TITLE IN THRILLING TEST, VANCOUVER,
     B.C. (1937)
     p.c. Universal Newsreel V.9 R.593
     1. 80'   g. 35mm   t. b+w   s. si.
     d.   *
     ph. ASN
     c.s. USNA

                    *"Alan Heyd defending champ and Chris Bergdahl who seeks title. CU's sawing
                    individually. Various shots of the winner Heyd."*

161. CHAMPIONSHIP FIGHT. (1914)
     p.c. Capital Film Co., Victoria
     1.   g. 35mm   t. b+w   s. si.
     d.   *
     ph. *
     c.s. NFA (Taylor reel 140)

                    *Challenger Joe Bayley meets the Canadian Lightweight Champion, Johnnyie
                    O'Leary at the Big House Arena in Vancouver. Excellent shots of the fight
                    in progress, of various rounds and fighters hanging onto each other after set-
                    ting a torrid pace. Great shots of seconds fanning the fighters with capes
                    to cool them off and holding umbrellas over them to shade them from the sun.*

162. CHARMING MAY DAY FETE TO CELEBRATE ASCENSION OF POPULAR
     QUEEN TO THRONE - THE CORONATION, NEW WESTMINSTER, B.C.
     (1925)
     p.c. Fox Movietonews (Fox #095.7-B6219)
     1. 50'   g. 35mm   t. b+w   s. si.
     d.   *
     ph. Ball
     c.s. Fox Movietonews, N.Y.

              "SCU of procession. SCU crowning of Queen. CU Queen. Maypole dance."

163. CHECKING UP ON FARM LOAN PROSPECTS. (1930 ?)
     p.c. B.C. Dept. of Agriculture (reel 44)
     1. 50'   g. 16mm   t. b+w   s. si. w/captions
     d.   *
     ph. *
     c.s. PABC

              *Officials, including George Sangster, Chairman of the Farm Loan Board and Mat
              Hassen, local appraiser, looking over farm buildings and discussing loan with
              farmer. Obviously the loan is clinched because officials shake hands with
              the farmer at their car, smiling. This little film seems intended to assure
              farmers about receiving a fair shake when applying for a government loan.
              There are two other stories on this reel, following CHECKING UP..., and the
              three total approx. 450' 16mm.*

164. CHICK! CHICK! CHICKEN! 75,000 DAY OLD CHICKS ARE ANNUALLY
     SHIPPED FROM THIS MODEL FARM, WESTHOLME, B.C. (n.d.)
     p.c. Fox Movietonews (Fox #328-B8487)
     1. 25'   g. 35mm   t. b+w   s. si.
     d.   *
     ph. Jos. Mandy
     c.s. Fox Movietonews, N.Y.

              Shots of chicken farm & baby chicks.

165. CHICKEN LAYS 357 EGGS IN 365 DAYS, AGASSIZ, B.C. (1933)
     p.c. Pathé News Neg. no. 6073
     1. 38'   g. 35mm   t. b+w   s. sound
     d.   *
     ph. ASN
     c.s. Sherman Grinberg, Hollywood

              "CU Mr. Rutledge and his hen. Shot of the hen going into her hen-house, being
              taken out, and posing with one of her eggs on a scale."

166. THE CHIEF SCOUT IN CANADA, VANCOUVER, B.C. LORD BADEN-
     POWELL REVIEWS 2,500 BOYS AND GIRLS AND ADDRESSES THE
     RALLY. (1935)
     p.c. British Movietonews (No. 6523)
     1. 150'   g. 35mm   t. b+w   s. sound
     d.   *
     ph. *
     c.s. British Movietonews

              *At Point Grey (?), scouts on a large field marching past, drums rolling, scout
              band. Baden-Powell saluting from a dias in Scout uniform. Scout band plays,
              boys march past with staves in hand. More marching, wheeling, whistles blow-
              ing, drums playing. CU Baden Powell addressing Scouts through microphone,
              arms folded: "Canada is the finest country in the world..." LS B-P addressing
              Scouts. CU Scouts applauding. CU staves held high in the air with Scout hats
              atop, raised & dipped three times while Scouts cheer HIP HIP HOORAY!*

167. CHILDREN ATTEND COURT OF CARNIVAL QUEEN DURING MAY DAY
     CELEBRATIONS IN NEW WESTMINSTER, B.C. (1920's)
     p.c. Fox Movietonews (Fox #095.7-C2696)
     1. 25'   g. 35mm   t. b+w   s. si.
     d.   *
     ph. Thomson
     c.s. Fox Movietonews, N.Y.

              "High shot arrival of Carnival Queen at grounds. The Coronation. SCU Queen
              and attendants. LS children dancing, Maypole & folk."

168. CHILDREN ENJOY QUEEN OF THE MAY DAY, NEW WESTMINSTER,
     B.C. (1924)
     p.c. Fox Movietonews, N.Y.
     l.   g. 35mm   t. b+w   s. si.
     d.   *
     ph. *
     c.s. NFA

                    Scenes of May Day celebrations in New Westminster, B.C.

169. CHILDREN GIVE DEMONSTRATION OF ACTIVITIES ON PLAYGROUND,
     VANCOUVER, B.C. (1923)
     p.c. Fox Movietonews (Fox #322.6-B2241)
     l. 35'   g. 35mm   t. b+w   s. si.
     d.   *
     ph. Len H. Roos
     c.s. Fox Movietonews, N.Y.

                    Kids at play.

170. CHILLY THRILLS: BATHING BEAUTIES TAKE TO SKIIS, TO KEEP
     COOL, VANÇOUVER, B.C. (1933)
     p.c. Pathe News (Neg. #5678)
     l. 70'   g. 35mm   t. b+w   s. sound
     d.   *
     ph. *
     c.s. Sherman Grinberg, Hollywood

                    *"Long and close shots taken from various angles of party in bathing suits
                    climbing and skiing down hill. Shot of life of the party in a comic fall."*

171. CHINESE FUNERAL PARADE, VICTORIA, B.C.   (1918)
     p.c. *
     l.   g. 35mm   t. b+w   s. si.
     d.   *
     ph. *
     c.s. NFA (Taylor reel 105)

                    *Excellent shots of huge delegation of Chinese Canadians preceding hearse which
                    is horse drawn, followed by various dignitaries of Victoria as the Chinese
                    community parades to burial ground. Various shots as the cortege moves to-
                    ward and past camera along Yates St.*

172. CHINESE LION DANCE, VICTORIA, B.C. (1938)
     p.c. Hearst Metrotone News Can no. 816, Roll no. 6
     l.   g. 35mm   t. b+w   s. sound
     d.   *
     ph. Lucien Roy
     c.s. Hearst Metrotone News, N.Y.

                    Chinese lion dance through streets of Victoria.

173. CHURCH PICNIC AT CHERRY BAY ON KOOTENAY LAKE & MOUNTAIN
     CLIMBING. (1930-1933)
     p.c. private
     l. 200'   g. 16mm   t. b+w   s. si.
     d.   *
     ph. Rev. George R.B. Kinney
     c.s. NFA, Ottawa

                    *Church picnic at Cherry Bay on Kootenay Lake in 1931. Many children playing
                    on the beach, adults eating, drinking tea, etc. A sternwheeler, probably the
                    MOYIE, hoves into sight at the end, giving rise to a series of very lyrical
                    broadside shots as she sails by.*

                    *Mountain climbing party of young men & women, probably up at the Kokanee
                    Glacier where Rev. Kinney often took climbing groups. Good shots of snowy
                    peaks and alpine meadows. Boys & girls drinking from a creek, walking with
                    stout staves.*

174. CITIZENS GET TONSILS SUNBURNED WATCHING WORKMEN WASH FACE OF
     BIG CITY BLOCK AND CLOCK, VANCOUVER, B.C.   (1924)
     p.c. Fox Movietonews (Fox #011.1-A3952)
     l.   g. 35mm   t. b+w   s. si.
     d.   *
     ph. Len H. Roos
     c.s. Fox Movietonews, N.Y.

                 *"Cleaning building and clock." Probably the Vancouver Block at Georgia and
                 Granville.*

175. CITY HONOURS ITS HEROIC DEAD AND 7TH BATTALION TROOPS COLOURS
     IN PRESENCE OF HUGE CROWDS, VANCOUVER, B.C.   (1920's)
     p.c. Fox Movietonews (Fox #095.7-C1882)
     l. 60'   g. 35mm   t. b+w   s. si.
     d.   *
     ph. Len H. Roos
     c.s. Fox Movietonews, N.Y.

                 "Mayor Owen unveils Cenotaph on Armistice Day. Parade."

176. A CITY OF SUNSHINE.   (1919)
     p.c. Dept. of Trade and Commerce Exhibits and Publicity
          Bureau, Ottawa
     l. approx. 700'   g. 35mm   t. b+w & tinted s. si. w/captions
     d.   *
     ph.   *
     c.s. NFB (1920-FG-83), NFA (#327-332), BCPM History

                 *The first tourist promotion film about Victoria, B.C., made by the Federal
                 Government, and the first to use the title A CITY OF SUNSHINE. Scenes in-
                 clude shots of the Inner Harbour. Pan of Empress Hotel and the Causeway from
                 the old Post Office. Parliament Buildings. Passengers mobbing about on CPR
                 wharf after disembarking from CPR ferry. Four tourists get into an open 1915
                 McLaughlin touring car and proceed to drive about the city. Beacon Hill Park.
                 Beautiful homes on quiet streets. Butchart Gardens - sunken garden, roses
                 and gnomes. Brentwood Bay: LS ferry dock from Brentwood Hotel, the visitors
                 having tea on the porch and part of the front of the Hotel. Exterior shots
                 of the Dominion Astrophysical Observatory on Saanich Mountain. Boating and
                 swimming on the Gorge. Victoria Golf Club. Feeding swans and deer in Beacon
                 Hill Park. Good shots of new $6,000,000 breakwater built by Federal Govern-
                 ment. CN coastal steamer sails past. (The NFA has a 16mm copy 293' long).
                 See also #723.*

177. CITY OF SUNSHINE.   (1928/1929)
     p.c. CGMPB
     l. 1 reel   g. 35mm   t. b+w & tinted s. si. w/captions
     d.   *
     ph.   *
     c.s. NFA, NFB (1920-DN-20), BCPM History

                 *"Sunshine and flowers - thus it is that one thinks of Victoria, the capital of
                 British Columbia. Its enterprising business district is only overshadowed by
                 its beautiful gardens. Such places of interest as Beacon Hill Park, the
                 Mayor's Garden, the Dominion Observatory (which houses the second largest tele-
                 scope in the world) and the Butchart Gardens, are famed across the continent."*

                 *This is the second film made by the CGMPB with the title CITY OF SUNSHINE,
                 obviously meant to replace the former in the Catalogue in order to present a
                 more up-to-date view of the City. Scenes include a map of Victoria & Vancouver
                 with a line showing the ferry route, and an aerial view of Victoria, Inner
                 Harbour and CPR ferry entering. Parliament Buildings. Empress Gardens and
                 Hotel. Pan of cars driving along Causeway toward Belmont Building. Two shots
                 of busy street corner (Yates & Douglas ?). Beautiful homes and gardens along
                 Rockland Ave. (?). Mayor Pendray's topiary gardens with visitors. Exterior
                 shots of Dominion Observatory. At Butchart Gardens: Italian Garden, child
                 with clay rabbit and Sunken Gardens. Very picturesque shot of the Parliament
                 dome through the veranda portal of the Empress Hotel. (NFA holds a 16mm print
                 236' long.)*

178. CIRCUS VISITS CRIPPLED CHILDREN'S HOSPITAL IN
     VANCOUVER, B.C. (1938)
     p.c. Fox Movietonews (Fox #34-474)
     l.   g. 35mm   t. b+w   s. sound
     d.   *
     ph. ASN
     c.s. Fox Movietonews, N.Y.

                    *"Various shots showing children in bed, watching the circus performers. CU,
                    LS, etc. Clown talking to children. Pony & gos (? - sic) perform. Small
                    dog climbs long post and jumps. Girl climbs post held by men and does some
                    tricks. Jumbo goes through his routine for the kids. LS showing hospital &
                    crowds watching show."*

179. CLAM BAKE GIVEN TO CANADIAN WEEKLY NEWSPAPER ASSOCIA-
     TION JOURNALISTS AT JERICHO BEACH, VANCOUVER, B.C. (n.d.)
     p.c. Fox Movietonews (Fox #754.2-C1884)
     l. 25'   g. 35mm   t. b+w   s. si.
     d.   *
     ph. *
     c.s. Fox Movietonews, N.Y.

                    Journalists enjoying clam bake.

180. CLEANING UP STANLEY PARK, VANCOUVER, B.C. (1935)
     p.c. Fox Movietonews (Fox #24-838)
     l. 700'   g. 35mm   t. b+w   s. sound
     d.   *
     ph. ASN
     c.s. Fox Movietonews, N.Y.

                    *"Blowing up stumps. Tractor hauling out fallen trees. Gang of men going to
                    work. Sawing logs. Cleared portion of park. Park Commissioner Fred Crane
                    explains work. Topping a tree. High rigger climbing the tree. Brush fire.
                    Big tree falling. Pedestrians and equestrians among big trees."*

181. CLEARING THE SITE FOR GREEN TIMBERS NURSERY, NEW
     WESTMINSTER, B.C. (1929-30, 1939)
     p.c. B.C. Forest Service
     l. approx. 400' g. 16mm   t. b+w   s. si.
     d.   *
     ph. *
     c.s. B.C. Forest Service (Reel 59)

                    *The Green Timbers Nursery was set up by the British Columbia Forest Service
                    during the thirties to experiment with and develop better seeds for use in
                    reforestation, as well as preparing young trees for planting etc. The first
                    part of this film shows men blasting stumps, burning them, stacking them, and
                    yarding them out, when the land was being cleared to build the Nursery. Stumps
                    are hauled out with a high lead line and a small winch driven by a Caterpillar
                    tractor. Later shots show the Nursery about 1939-1940.*

182. CLIMBING IN THE YOHO. (1934-35)
     p.c. CGMPB
     l. 1 reel   g. 35mm   t. b+w   s. si. w/captions
     d.   *
     ph. *
     c.s. Unknown

                    *Produced for the National Parks Bureau. No further information is available,
                    but presumably the film shows scenes of climbing mountains in Yoho National
                    Park, British Columbia.*

183. CLIMBING MOUNT KOKANEE. (1928-1931)
     p.c. private
     l. approx. 400' g. 16mm   t. b+w   s. si.
     d.   *
     ph. Rev. George R.B. Kinney
     c.s. c/o Pacific Cinematheque, Vancouver

                    *United Church Young People's Group, led by Kinney, the first white man to
                    climb Mount Robson, and organized by Rev. Beverley Oaten, climb up to the*

Kokanee Glacier. Pan climbers. Line starting up from bottom. Climbers in truck getting a ride part way to the old Molly Gibson mine site. Views of old cars & climbers resting at Molly Gibson site. Climbing again. HS Gibson Lake. Kokanee Lake. Campfire and eating. Pans of mountains. Climbers on top looking down into valleys. Pans snow-capped peaks. Hut on the summit. A snowball fight on the glacier. Many shots climbing the glacier, clouds pouring over the mountain, sliding down the glacier, lines of climbers in snow, fun. Packhorse.

184. CLIMBING MOUNT TUPPER. (1934)
    p.c. CGMPB
    l. 1 reel   g. 35mm   t. b+w   s. si. w/captions
    d. Bill Oliver
    ph. Bill Oliver
    c.s. NFA & NFB Archives P.B. 58 (1930-N-54)

    "Mountaineering in Glacier National Park, British Columbia. A spectacular climb to the summit of Mount Tupper, which overlooks Roger's Pass in the Selkirk Mountains." Produced for the National Parks Bureau, Ottawa, this film concentrates on a climb up the sheer side of Mt. Tupper by renowned Alpine climber Eduard Feuz and his daughter. Feuz was hired by the CPR in 1903 to conduct mountain climbing expeditions from the hotels in the Banff area and accepted roles in so many movies portraying a guide, skiier or mountain climber that he has trouble remembering their titles, having first stood before the camera in 1909. He was still climbing mountains in the summer of 1976.

    The description of the film in the NFB files is as follows: "Mount Tupper in Glacier National Park tests the mettle of enthusiastic alpinists from all over the continent. Various shots of Mount Tupper and of other peaks of the Selkirk Range. Three alpinists leave base camp and tackle the mountain. Various shots of the men negotiating glaciers, snow fields, rocky ground, sliding down snowy slopes, climbing 45 degree slopes, resting and going on. Good shot of the summit of Mount Tupper, a vertical shaft of rock stabbing the heavens. Tilt down shot to two mountain climbers struggling up. CU climbers. Shot of men silhouetted against the sky on the highest pinnacle of Mount Tupper. Short pan of neighbouring mountains. Having reached the top, the men start the journey downwards. Various shots of men coming down mountain, reaching timber line, etc." (The copy at the NFA is 400' 16mm; at the NFB, 402' 16mm).

    Some of Oliver's CLIMBING MOUNT TUPPER footage was re-edited in 1935 by ASN to make CANADIAN CAMEO NO. 33, THE GAME IS UP. See Catalogue entry 346.

185. CLOSE FINISHES AT GORGE REGATTA KEEP BIG CROWD GREATLY EXCITED,
    WHILE THE NOVELTIES ARE MANY, VICTORIA, B.C. (1923)
    p.c. Fox Movietonews (Fox #755.8-B1704)
    l. 60'   g. 35mm   t. b+w   s. si.
    d. *
    ph. Len H. Roos
    c.s. Fox Movietonews, N.Y.

    Shots of war canoe and boat races at the Gorge in Victoria.

186. CLOUDBURST ALMOST WIPES OUT TOWN, BRITTANIA BEACH, B.C.
    (1921)
    p.c. Fox Movietonews (Fox #007.3628-8198)
    l. 59'   g. 35mm   t. b+w   s. si.
    d. *
    ph. D.C. Davey
    c.s. Fox Movietonews, N.Y.

    "General view. Pathway of turbulent waters. Searching for bodies and personal effects. LS of Miss Patterson who gave warning. Views of wrecked homes. Refugees on boats leaving for Vancouver."

187. CNR AGRICULTURAL DEMONSTRATION TRAIN. (1930)
    p.c. B.C. Dept. of Agriculture (Reels 49, 50 & 51)
    1. 3 reels/1050' g. 16mm   t. b+w   s. si. w/captions
    d. *
    ph. *
    c.s. PABC

> "The first Agricultural Demonstration train in British Columbia sponsored by
> the Canadian National Railways ... in conjunction with Dominion and Provincial
> Departments of Agriculture, left Vancouver March 6th, 1930 - made a short run
> through the Okanagan Valley - then followed the CNR line through the Northern
> Interior to Terrace, returning to Vancouver April 12th.
>
> Mr. H. Bowman, CNR Agricultural Representative for B.C., arranged 25 meetings
> with Farmer's Institutes. They showed their appreciation by turning out, men,
> women and children, 4,657 strong."
>
> REEL ONE: Kamloops, Tranquille Sanatorium. CNR Locomotive #2104, Lovington,
> Vernon, Armstrong, Falkland Station & gypsum mine, Birch Island, Foster
> Station, Mt. Robson, Croydon, McBride and Fort Fraser. At the stations local
> residents gather about and wander through the train. Agriculture experts
> demonstrate various skills, chief among them seeming to be poultry killing
> and plucking which is demonstrated in the open door of a freight car. Lots
> of school kids crowd around. (approx. 400').
>
> REEL TWO: Fort Fraser. Vanderhoof, poultry killing & plucking, Smithers,
> Telkwa, Houston, Hazelton, Woodstock, Skeena River seen from Cedarvale, Terrace,
> the terminus for the Agricultural train in the North. Many shots of staff and
> freight in the Terrace railyards. (approx 500').
>
> REEL THREE: Scenes between Fort Fraser and Vanderhoof, Vanderhoof and Prince
> George, Red Pass, snow plough in the mountains, Albreda Summit, Avola Station,
> train staff posing, Ashcroft, and staff members leaving the station after
> having disembarked in Chilliwack. (approx. 150')

188. THE COAST SALISH INDIANS OF BRITISH COLUMBIA. (1928)
    p.c. National Museum of Canada
    1. 1 reel   g. 35mm (16mm available) t. b+w s. si. w/captions
    d.   Harlan I. Smith
    ph. Harlan I. Smith
    c.s. NFA & National Museum of Man, Ottawa

> "Carving the cedar with ancient tools, canoeing in a cedar dugout, picking
> berries, spinning mountain goat wool and weaving it for blankets, weaving
> cedar bark for making hats, sewing rushes into mats, and making baskets are
> some of the phases of Coast Salish life shown in this film. Shoals of salmon,
> and the game animals - deer, goat, beaver - upon which these Indians depended
> for food are also shown. Drumming, rattling, and dancing in the old way wearing
> grotesque masks complete the story."
>
> Other sequences include: View of the coastline west of Becher Bay, B.C. The
> deer and the mountain goat in Victoria, the geese in Stanley Park. In Squamish
> an Indian is shown spearing salmon swimming upstream. Clams on a beach near
> Saanichton, B.C. Modern Indian village at Becher Bay. Indian kids play games.
> Men splitting cedar for boards and making boxes in North Vancouver. Carved
> tomb, showing animal figures, at Musquiam, B.C. Woman weaving basket at Chilli-
> wack, B.C. Women weaving mats at Musquiam, B.C. Women making hats at North
> Vancouver, B.C. Women weaving and wearing woven tump-lines at Squamish, B.C.
> Preparations for spinning & weaving of wool in Squamish, B.C. A famous blanket
> at Squamish, B.C. Dancing, singing & rattling at Musquiam, B.C. Man wearing
> Xoaexoal mask. (Copy at NFA is 360' 16mm)

189. COAST'S BIG SPLASH DRAWS BIG CROWD TO SEE JOHNNY BAYLEY FINISH
     FIRST IN BURRARD INLET SWIM EVENT, VANCOUVER, B.C. (1929)
    p.c. Fox Movietonews (Fox #755.91-D2296)
    1. 130'   g. 35mm   t. b+w   s. si.
    d.   *
    ph. Beesley
    c.s. Fox Movietonews, N.Y.

> "Also SCU of Gwen Clay, first girl to compete."

190. "COLONY" LIVESTOCK. (1930's)
     p.c. B.C. Dept. of Agriculture
     1. approx. 400'   g. 16mm   t. b+w   s. si.
     d.   *
     ph. *
     c.s. PABC

> *Totally concerned with a livestock parade of cattle being led past camera by various men.*

191. THE COLUMBIA COAST MISSION. (late 30's, early 40's)
     p.c. Columbia Coast Mission
     1. approx. 10,800' g. 16mm t. colour s. si.
     d.   *
     ph. Alfred Booth
     c.s. NFA

> *"The voyage of the hospital mission ship COLUMBIA along the B.C. coast, with calls at various coastal villages. Village Island, Alert Bay, Kingcome Inlet, etc." An account of the work of the mission personnel among the Indians and whites engaged in commercial fishing, logging, etc. As well, there is a portion dealing with the visit of the Duke and Duchess of Connaught to the coast; could this be the 1912 visit?*

> *Most of this footage was probably shot by Alfred Booth, a free-lance filmaker who shot thousands of feet for the Columbia Coast Mission, portraying all aspects of their valuable work during the thirties and forties. See ADDENDA.*

192. COLUMBIA COAST MISSION. (1930's)
     p.c. Columbia Coast Mission
     1. 345'   g. 16mm   t. red   s. si. w/captions
     d.   *
     ph. Alfred Booth
     c.s. Archives of the Anglican Diocese of B.C., Victoria.

> *The Columbia Coast Mission boat making its rounds near Alert Bay, Vancouver Island. A number of small settlements, with fishboats, are seen in the distance. They are visited, then left. Bones Bay is visited. Shots of fishermen working on wharf outside Bones Bay Cannery.*

> *Village Island is visited, as is Mrs. Kathleen O'Brien, M.B.E., who lives on the Reserve and works for the Anglican Church. Shots of the church and the main street.*

> *Logging show with steam donkey. Scenes of logs being felled, yarded with a spar tree and donkey and loaded onto rail cars pulled by small diesel locomotive. Logs being delivered to a long pier and dumped into salt-chuck. Ship, the VENTURE, at the end of the wharf, and leaving.*

> *Burial at sea, performed on the Mission boat with flag at half-mast and with red ensign covering body.*

> *Families up the coast living on floats in sheltered bays while the men are away logging. Kids going to school on motor launch.*

> *A long caption details how accidents are reported to the Hospital ship COLUMBIA from an isolated logging camp via the Dominion Government Radio Station at Alert Bay, and how the boat is despatched immediately to lend assistance. The exact story concerns a picnic during which a young boy hurts his foot badly. Probably the whole episode was dramatized, but only the opening sequences remain: the wounded boy in a launch with his family, a man running along rails to a logging camp where he makes use of the radio telephone, a man in Alert Bay on the other end sending an alert out to the COLUMBIA. See ADDENDA.*

193. COLUMBIA COAST MISSION MISCELLANY. (1939)
     p.c. Columbia Coast Mission
     1. approx. 1100' g. 16mm   t. colour s. si.
     d.   *
     ph. Alfred Booth
     c.s. Archives of the Anglican Diocese of B.C., Victoria

> *Probably members of the Columbia Coast Mission visiting the Mission boat in*

Vancouver harbour during the Royal Visit. Includes ladies and two nurses. Scenes up the coast taken from the Mission boat: blue sky & sea, islands, and an unidentified settlement and its residents. Lion's Gate Bridge LS, looking out Vancouver Harbour. Lighthouse up the coast. Scenery thru the islands, boats & settlements. Flowers in an unidentified garden and a little stone fountain in a pond with swans. Two women on deck of Mission boat look out over small village up the coast. Fishing boats, settlements. Man painting hull of Mission boat. Nurses. Boat at dock with other boats nearby, probably in Inner Harbour, Victoria. Empress Hotel. Ladies coming aboard. Fishermen picking fish out of hold, Mission boat nearby. Scenery & settlement with fish-boats up the coast. At a lighthouse (Pachena?) a small boat is transported across the top of the water by a cable, then lowered into the water when out of danger. The boat is then rowed out to the Mission boat. More scenery, settlements & islands. Scenery up the coast, islands, settlements, tugboat passing, destroyer passing. Point-No-Point Lodge and beach. Mission boat in Vancouver Harbour for King & Queen's visit. Many flags and pennants. Lion's Gate Bridge in b.g. Hundreds of boats in Harbour: fishboats with flags, cabin cruisers, motorboats, and RCN destroyer H 48, HMCS FRASER. Biplanes fly over Bridge very close to cables. PRINCESS MARGUERITE hoves into view then sails away under Bridge to Vancouver Island, carrying the King & Queen. Settlements, scenery and people up the coast. See ADDENDA.

194. COMEDY STUNT, VANCOUVER, B.C. (1924)
     p.c. Fox Movietonews (Fox #115.403-A6209)
     1. 60'   g. 35mm   t. b+w   s. si.
     d.   *
     ph. Len H. Roos
     c.s. Fox Movietonews, N.Y.

          "Couple of kiddies & some flypaper. A cat drinking milk. A dog, critically regarding cat. At this, the cat spits at the dog and beats retreat. Cat in difficulty with flypaper on its feet. Mother cleans children of flypaper while cat washes its own paws.

195. COMMISSIONER O'MALLEY VISITS ALASKA. (1929)
     p.c. U.S. Fish and Wildlife Service
     1. 53 min.   g. 35mm   t. b+w   s. si.
     d.   *
     ph. *
     c.s. USNA (22/.23 - Main Catalogue)

          Four reels record an inspection trip to Alaska made by Commissioner Henry O'Malley and party in 1929. REEL ONE contains scenic views and shots of the town of Campbell River, Vancouver Island, filmed while on their way north.

196. COMPANY "H", RNWMP, IS TRANSFERRED FROM REGINA TO RE-
     INFORCE VANCOUVER DETACHMENT, VANCOUVER, B.C. (1919)
     p.c. Fox Movietonews (Fox #560.4-2764)
     1. 39'   g. 35mm   t. b+w   s. si.
     d.   *
     ph. Len H. Roos
     c.s. Lost

          "Royal North West Mounted Police Co. "H" forming up on arrival outside the station. Marching to the new billets."

197. COMPLETE TRIP THROUGH THE ROCKY MOUNTAINS. (pre 1910)
     p.c. *
     1. 1220'   g. 35mm   t. b+w   s. si.
     d.   *
     ph. *
     c.s. Unknown

          Nothing is known about this film. It was probably photographed from a train travelling through the Canadian Rockies from Alberta to British Columbia. George Kleine Catalogue, 1910. p.63.

198. THE CONFLICT. (1921)
     p.c. Universal Film Mfg. Company
     l. 6,025'   g. 35mm   t. b+w   s. si. w/captions
     d.   Stuart Paton
     ph.   Harold Janes
     c.s. Unknown

Presented by Carl Laemmle; script
George C. Hull, from the novel
Conflict by Clarence Budington
Kelland, N.Y., 1922.

l.p. Priscilla Dean, Edward Connelly,
Hector Sarno, Matthew Mattox, Olah
Norman, and Herbert Rawlinson.

This feature film was shot partially on location on the Bull River above Cranbrook.

"Society girl Dorcas Remalie, to fulfill the dying request of her father, goes
to live in the Northwoods home of her Uncle John, a sinister and dictatorial
lumber baron whose household is managed by the forbidding Miss Labo. While
the Uncle is away, Miss Labo tries to poison Dorcas, and Dorcas seeks safety
with Jevons, a young man who is fighting her Uncle for land rights. Learning
that Jevons is in captivity and danger, Dorcas assumes his place and leads
his lumbermen to a fight with Remalie's men. She is forced to dynamite a dam,
thus creating a torrent that floods a dry streambed. Learning that Jevons is
trapped in the flood's path, she rescues him before he reaches the falls. The
Uncle repents, and Jevons and Dorcas become engaged." (AFI Catalogue, Feature
Films 1921 - 1930)

199. CONQUEST. (1930)
     p.c. Empire Marketing Board
     l. 2799'   g. 35mm   t. b+w   s. si. w/captions
     d.   John Grierson, asst. by Basil Wright
     ph.   CGMPB, CPR & CNR in Canada
     c.s. BFI

A dramatic documentary about the development of North America combining fictional cowboy-and-Indian material from Paramount Pictures with industrial
film footage supplied by the CGMPB and railroad companies. The description
reads as follows: "A story of the North American continent - of the pioneers
who opened up the country we now map as Canada and the United States. A film
for schools. The implements of man are the implements of his progress. Only
by the continual invention of more powerful tools and mechanisms has the conquest of the wilderness been made possible."

The fictionalized excerpts are from THE VANISHING AMERICAN (1926), THE
COVERED WAGON (1923) and THE PONY EXPRESS (1925) and are quite wonderful,
running throughout the first two reels and into the first 174' of Reel Three.
This reel contains 143' of material shot in British Columbia: CPR freight
train hauling grain to the Vancouver docks, grain being loaded onto a ship, a
tug towing the LOYAL BRITON out of Vancouver Harbour, and various shots of
trains and ships at dockside.

200. THE CONQUEST OF MOUNT LOGAN. (1925)
     p.c. National Museum of Canada & American Alpine Club
     l. 5 reels   g. 35mm   t. b+w   s. si. w/captions
     d.   *
     ph.   H.M. Laing & Allan Carpe
     c.s. Unknown

"Mount Logan, so named in honour of Sir William Logan, founder and first
Director of the Geological Survey of Canada, lies in the extreme southwestern
corner of the Yukon Territory. It is 19,850 feet above sea level and is the
second highest mountain in the British Empire, the Himalayas ranking first.
Around it is one of the largest ice-fields in the world.

The expedition that reached the summit of Mount Logan in June 1925 was organized under the auspices of the Alpine Club of Canada. The members of the expedition spent forty-four days under severe conditions of ice and snow, ex-
periencing a temperature of 33 degrees below zero in June and encountering
terrifying blizzards. They suffered from exposure for one night at an altitude of 19,000 feet and a camp made at 18,500 feet was the highest Alpine
camp made in North America.

Motion pictures taken on the expedition by H.M. Laing, representing the National Museum of Canada as naturalist, and Allan Carpe, American Alpine Club representative, have been assembled and edited under the title: CONQUEST OF MOUNT LOGAN. The film is an exceedingly interesting portrayal of the most hazardous mountaineering feat attempted in Canada."

201. CONSTRUCTION OF THE LION'S GATE BRIDGE, VANCOUVER.
     (1937-1939)
     p.c. Stuart Brown of Home Oil Dist. Ltd. & John
          Anderson of British-Pacific Properties Ltd.
     l. approx. 1250'   g. 16mm   t. colour   s. si. w/captions
     d.   *
     ph. The Whitefoot Studio, Vancouver
     c.s. B.C. Dept. of Highways, Victoria

> *Produced in conjunction with A.S. McLean and William F. Way of Stuart Cameron Ltd., and James Robertson and H.H. Minshall of Dominion Bridge Co.*
>
> *Opening shots praise and show Mr. A.J.T. Taylor who promoted the idea of the bridge and the residential settling of the North Shore. He discusses the plans with architect John Anderson. Shots of North Shore, Vancouver Harbour.*
>
> *The film covers virtually every aspect of construction of the First Narrows Bridge/Lion's Gate Bridge, from the clearing of the forest on the north shore right through to the opening of the structure. The captions go into very detailed descriptions of the processes being carried out and the parts being assembled, and in one case diagrams are used to explain how the suspension cables are constructed. On November 4th, 1938, the bridge was first crossed by a car, and Nov. 12th it was opened to the public. John Anderson receives the first toll ticket, #0001, 5¢. Shots of Charles Marega's two sculptured lions. The EMPRESS OF JAPAN sails underneath, her masts clearing the span by 30 feet. On May 29th, 1939, King George & Queen Elizabeth crossed the bridge, and later on, under naval escort, sailed under it on their way to Vancouver Island.*
>
> *The last part of this film deals with the construction of British-Pacific Properties on the North Shore, Capilano Estates. Men clearing bush, building country club house and golf links. Shows golfers teeing off on the course. LS view of bridge through the trees.*
>
> *At end: "Home Oil Distributors Ltd. is pleased to present this film in appreciation of the vision shown by the British investors in developing a Greater Vancouver. They also wish to thank their many customers for their confidence in supporting a B.C. company."*
>
> *Sunset over the mountains. Home Oil Distributor's flag.*

202. CONVICTED.   (1937)
     p.c. Central Films Ltd.
     l. 55 mins.   g. 35mm   t. b+w   s. sound
     d.   Leon Barsha
     ph. George Meehan
     c.s. NFA

> *Canadian prod. Kenneth J. Bishop; script Edgar Edwards, from the story Face Work by Cornel Woolrich; editor William Austin; asst. d. George Rhein; musical direction Morris Stoloff; Columbia overseer Jack Fier.*

> *l.p. Rita Hayworth, Charles Quigley, Marc Lawrence, George McKay, Edgar Edwards, Robert Rideout, Michael Heppell, Doreen MacGregor, Bill Irving, Eddie Laughton, Phyllis Clare, Noel Cusack, Grant MacDonald, Don Douglas, James McGrath.*

> *Working title: FACE WORK. The last Quota Quickie produced for Columbia Pictures by Central Films, Ltd., Victoria, in December 1937, is the only one still in circulation today, no doubt due to the presence of 19-year-old Rita Hayworth. The story is a typical B-grade American mystery thriller made in Canada to qualify for exhibition in Great Britain as an Empire-made film, and was copyrighted in the United States by Columbia Pictures of California on August 15, 1938.*
>
> *Story line: Jerry Wheeler (Rita Hayworth), a night club singer and dancer, learns*

that her younger brother Chick (Edgar Edwards) is about to run away with Ruby Rose (Phyllis Claire), a heartless gold digger. Jerry visits Ruby at her apartment but fails to persuade her to lay off Chick. Returning home she finds Chick on the point of leaving. He too refuses to listen to her and makes his way to Ruby's apartment only to find her dead. Ruby's maid Aggie (Noel Cusack), discovers him crouching over the dead body and calls the police. Chick is convicted of manslaughter. Burns (Charles Quigley), the detective in charge of the case, not convinced of Chick's guilt and not a little attracted to Jerry, helps her to pursue her own investigation. She learns that Ruby was formerly the girl friend of Milton Militis (Marc Lawrence), a crooked night club owner and finds a threatening note from Militis among Ruby's personal effects. Jerry now gets a job at the club owned by Militis and begins to get close to him, hoping to find some evidence which will prove him to be the murderer. Just when she discovers this evidence, Militis learns who she really is. He takes her to his country hideout where he plans to kill her at the exact moment her brother is electrocuted (the action is set in the U.S.). This delay permits Burns and his men to catch up with them and he arrives just in time to save Jerry, and of course Chick. (Storyline description courtesy of D. John Turner, NFA.)

203. A COOL DIP FOR KIDDIES WHO FLOCK TO ENGLISH BAY WHEN
     HEAT IS OPPRESSIVE, VANCOUVER, B.C. (n.d.)
     p.c. Fox Movietonews (Fox #757.4-C2765)
     1. 35'   g. 35mm   t. b+w   s. si.
     d.   *
     ph. Len H. Roos
     c.s. Fox Movietonews, N.Y.

204. CO-OPERATIVE POULTRY MARKETING IN WESTERN CANADA.
     (1927-1929)
     p.c. CGMPB
     1. 1 reel   g. 35mm   t. b+w   s. si. w/captions
     d.   *
     ph. *
     c.s. Unknown

          Made for the Dominion Live Stock Branch, Department of Agriculture, Ottawa, and described as: "An educational and informative film depicting the various details of co-operative poultry marketing in the winter months as carried on by the poultry "pools" of the Western Provinces." No indication is given as to which provinces take part, but presumably British Columbia will have been included.

205. CORA LYNN DAM CONSTRUCTION. (late 1930's)
     p.c. private
     1. 351½'   g. 16mm   t. b+w   s. si.
     d.   *
     ph. R.F. Mackenzie
     c.s. NFA

          Mr. Mackenzie worked for many years with the General Construction Co. of Vancouver.

          For the first 90 feet there are many poorly exposed scenic pans of flowing rivers, hills with snow, men walking, and one construction site. Other shots include: a steam train roaring by; a huge explosion in a river (blasting!); men inspecting results of blasting; shovel digging away at blasted rock; rail lines by side of river; a large speeder with rear car and operator; snow; buildings & boxcars along railroad tracks, man leaving (along tracks) for work; shovel working in snowy rock cut; large speeder with open car behind; rock fill being dumped into river in wooden-framed areas by open car pulled and pushed by large speeder; shovel chewing away at rock and loading it onto open car; worker playing with dog; shovel loading open car while another little diesel engine & car pass by; 2 cars roll up to be loaded by shovel, shovel responds; 2 men looking on; cars travel along rail & dump their rocks into the water; view of other side of the river, roads, a railway grade possibly, and back to shovel again; good C/U shovel loading cars, cars move off to unload; L/S worksite & river; man with jackhammer working in rock; L/S river with mountain above; another explosion - more blasting; looks like some of the railway rock transporting equipment has been damaged, men inspecting; scene of blasting; another series of blasts, debris falls into river; pan along results of blasting; men walking across narrow bridge; 2 more blasting scenes; a raft casts loose from the shore with rowboats attached, men aboard, and a piece of equipment; scenes along the river, then blasting, again; camera records changed landscape.

206. CORONATION DAY IN THE CITY OF VERNON AS RECORDED FOR
     THE CITY ARCHIVES. (1937)
     p.c. private
     l. approx. 200'   g. 16mm   t. b+w   s. si.
     d.   *
     ph. Douglas Kermode
     c.s. City of Vernon Museum

Dignitaries planting a tree beside Hickling Memorial in Polson Park. Crowds along the streets waving Union Jacks. Sea Cadets' band, Fire Department brass band and Vernon City Police on horseback parade along the street. A banner reads: WELCOME TO VERNON/CORONATION SHOPPING ?. Carriage with May Queen & Princesses, escorted by Boy Scouts, passes by. Also young children with Union Jacks, Sea Cadets, Boy Scouts. Kids from the "Indian School" parade down Barnard Avenue. "Vernon Chinese Community" members march past with dragon. Floats pass by, representing Brittania, Bulman's Ltd., Vernon Fruit Union, Orange Kist, Neil & Neil's Hillbillies (Fiddles, guitars, dancing, singing), followed by cowboys on horses, a kids' baseball team, then a float representing a stylized artillery piece with the words FOR EVER CANADA written on it - a Militia float. Then a float by Indians, then mothers & children parade.

Full grandstand at Polson Park. Boy Scouts parade into park. Blue Bird Brand apple float with words "Fit for A King". A speech. Girl Guides on parade. A speech by an older man. Very LS aircraft in sky. May Queen ceremonies: coronation, banquet & passing by in carriage escorted by Scouts. Watkins Motors Ltd. Float passes by grandstand. "Long May They Reign" - Neil & Neil (cartage & fuel) float passes by. Kids on decorated bicycles. Float with chef(?). Vernon Fruit Union float. Maypole dance before grandstand. CU crowd watching, City Policemen in f.g. Plane in sky. Running and bicycle races. Building lit up with many single light bulbs. (The second credit on the film reads: Cine Equipment Courtesy Mr. A. Garratt.)

207. CORONATION OF MAY QUEEN IN NEW WESTMINSTER. (1930's)
     p.c. B.C. Forest Service (Reel #47)
     l. approx. 300'   g. 16mm   t. colour s. si.
     d.   *
     ph. *
     c.s. PABC

Four girls in uniform spelling TECH. Girl's drum-and-bugle corps marching onto field & playing. Scarlet jacketed pipe band playing while marching past crowded grandstand. New & old Queen arriving with dignitaries. Abdication speech. Dancing about Maypoles in the field. Old Queen placing crown on head of new Queen, new Queen smiling. TECH marching squad marching by. Fancy drill by TECH girls. Folk dancing by kids - large crowds watching. Girl's drill team with staves. Boy's drill team doing semaphore. Making patterns on the field with shirt colours - boys. Mt. Baker Union High School banner preceding their Highland band, which marches past. Boy's drill team with red, white & blue flags performing field-wide precision marching.

208. COSTUME PLAY ACTORS IN STANLEY PARK TO MARK VANCOUVER'S 50TH
     ANNIVERSARY. (1936)
     p.c. private
     l. approx. 25'   g. 8mm   t. b+w   s. si.
     d.   *
     ph. J.W. Bowdery
     c.s. c/o Pacific Cinémathèque, Vancouver

There are no scenes of the costume pageant in this short piece of film but several of the cast are shown posing in frock coats and wigs and other costumes of Captain George Vancouver's day.

209. COWBOYS TRY THEIR SKILL IN SOME STRENUOUS RIDING FEATURED
     AT 59TH ANNUAL EXHIBITION IN ROYAL CITY, NEW WESTMINSTER,
     B.C. (1926)
     p.c. Fox Movietonews (Fox #751.11-B5212)
     l. 50'   g. 35mm   t. b+w   s. si.
     d.   *
     ph. Herron
     c.s. Fox Movietonews, N.Y.

              *"Parade of floats. Lt. Gov. Randolph Bruce speaking from porch. Bull-dogging
              and bronco riding."*

210. THE COWICHAN LOG (IS A FOREST CHRONICLE). (1938)
     p.c. B.C. Forest Service (Forestry reel 3)
     l. approx. 600'   g. 16mm   t. colour s. si. w/captions
     d.   George Melrose
     ph. George Melrose
     c.s. B.C. Dept. of Forests

              *"Logging at Cowichan, Vancouver Island. Many scenes of logging operations,
              natural forest reproduction, forest fires, and wild life. A lesson on
              forestry as recounted by an old-time logger." The old-time logger appears at
              the beginning and the end and is a white-bearded old fellow named John Newell
              Evans who smiles a lot, an MLA in the B.C. Legislature from 1903-1906. THE
              COWICHAN LOG was originally 800' long, but has been cut down to aid more re-
              cent productions (see FORESTRY REEL No. 326)*

211. THE COWPUNCHER'S GLOVE. (1910)
     p.c. Edison Mfg. Co. (Catalogue #6714)
     l. 1000'   g. 35mm   t. b+w   s. si.
     d.   J. Searle Dawley
     ph. Henry Cronjager
     c.s. Unknown

              *This film was shot in British Columbia and Alberta by the Edison Mfg. Company
              during a tour by its players across Canada to make promotional films for the
              CPR. It was started on July 2, 1910 and finished September 23, 1910.*

              *The story concerns two cowboys who fall in love with the same girl unbeknownst
              to each other, and who meet on a dangerous swinging bridge to settle the matter.
              The one discovers that the other has saved him from being lynched by angry
              settlers, and a resolution is reached although the Edison advertising blurb
              does not reveal exactly what happens. From the description of the "swinging
              bridge over a dangerous chasm", it might not be too extravagant to suggest
              that the climax of this short was filmed on the suspension bridge in Capilano
              Canyon where the Edison troupe spent a day shooting.*

212. CRANBROOK CORONATION FESTIVAL. (1937)
     p.c. private
     l. 2 reels, 250' & 350' approx. g. 16mm t. colour s. si.
     d.   *
     ph. A. Nichol
     c.s. c/o Pacific Cinémathèque, Vancouver

              *Mr. Nichol was a guide in the early days and most of his motion picture foot-
              age consists of game shots of moose, mountain goats, etc. He speaks of
              photographing a caribou migration of 50,000 animals about 100 miles west of
              Dawson in the Yukon, and of Billy Stork an old trapper.*

              *The Cranbrook Coronation Festival film shows parades and other festivities,
              bands, crowds, flags, school kids, etc., on the main street. The 350 foot
              reel may also contain shots of school children at the Fort Steele School,
              during the 30's.*

              *His game shots cover mainly the Fort Steele-Skookumchuck-White Swan Lake area
              near Cranbrook, B.C.*

6

213. CRESTON & KOOTENAYS, B.C., CALGARY STAMPEDE & 1000
ISLANDS & PORT ARTHUR, ONTARIO. (1930's)
p.c. private
l. approx. 300'   g. 16mm   t. colour & b+w   s. si.
d.   *
ph. W.M. Archibald
c.s. NFA, Ottawa

*The section filmed in British Columbia shows: School sports at the old park
in Creston, with large crowds milling around and watching events. Running
races, broad-jumping, pole vaulting, etc. Pan of the main street of Creston,
with crowds gathered along either side. Parade of American Legionnaires
through town with two flags and band. Many varied shots of the parade, people
watching, standing on rooftops, etc. (All B.C. material is b+w.)*

214. CRESTON and MISCELLANEOUS BRITISH COLUMBIA, with
brief QUEBEC CITY. (1930's)
p.c. private
l. approx. 375'   g. 16mm   t. colour & b+w   s. si.
d.   *
ph. W.M. Archibald
c.s. NFA, Ottawa

*b+w: Jockeys astride, and walking, their horses in the ring at Lansdowne
Racetrack (?).*

*colour: King's Birthday in Creston, B.C.: a huge picnic celebration at the
old park. Parade of children marching onto the grounds, followed by cars and
trucks decorated with flags and bunting, union jacks, red ensigns and the
stars & stripes. Boys riding decorated bikes. Sign on one old car, WW I
vintage, MAY HE LAST AS LONG AS I HAVE. A man in a scarlet devil's costume
on a decorated bike. A decorated flat-bed truck with a canopy on the back
decorated with crepe paper in which is a queen and her princesses. A sign
on the truck canopy reads LONG LIVE THE KING. An RCMP officer in scarlet on
his horse. Legionnaires and prayers, Boy Scouts standing by. Indians looking
on in ceremonial costume, and perform a dance. Little girls having a foot-
race. Man directing with a megaphone. The Militia lined up in front of a
store in the main street of Creston, in full uniform. An inspection begins.*

*b+w: Good long pan of the harbour of Prince Rupert from the water. Good
MCU's and a cabin cruiser. A large white hotel w/ a car full of passengers
approaching. Chateau Frontenac from promenade with people passing by. Pan
across/along St. Lawrence to Levis, pan along far shore. Chateau from promenade, pan across town, Chateau turret against sky. Scene at a small mine.*

*b+w: Mining scenes. A man wielding a sledge hammer at the side of a road,
mine buildings in b.g. Pan across hills to heaps of slag, then on to mine
shaft construction. Pan across other mine buildings. Salmon fishing on the
west coast of B.C. Camera pans across mouth of large bay; many small boats
are busy fishing - shot from an aeroplane. Aerial view of larger boats. A
commercial double-ender with men hauling in nets. Excellent pan of both sides
of the main street of Creston. A small mine. Views of buildings & shacks &
piles of slag.*

215. CRESTON, B.C. and KOOTENAY LAKE. (early 1930's)
p.c. private
l. approx. 500'   g. 16mm   t. b+w   s. si.
d.   *
ph. W.M. Archibald
c.s. NFA, Ottawa

*A placer mining outfit in the mountains near Creston. A huge claw, run on an
overhead cable, digging up gravel from a creek, dumping it into a huge hopper
affixed to a tower, then returning to the creek again, performing the same
operation several times.*

*Various good CU's of operation; tower, hopper, flumes, grids and men working.
Slag heaps. Aerial view over forest & above mining operations. Man beside
plane.*

Hooking up plough and ploughing behind an old tractor near Creston, c. 1937.

*Combining near Creston. Men digging into grain with a shovel. Combining at
Creston, many shots. Woman & child in field. LS Pan Creston and mountains
from field. CU cutters behind tractor. MCU grain pouring out spout. CU spout.
Continued combining shots. Men inspecting stooks. Grain running down conveyor.*

*Sports day at the old park in Creston. Pan of building & crowds. Baseball
game, broad jumping and high jumping. May Day Celebration at Creston. Girls
in white dresses performing drills around Maypole, then do the Maypole Dance.*

*Three-tiered steam sternwheeler, pulling into wharf on Kootenay Lake, letters
on side read CANADIAN PACIFIC. Excellent shots from LS on lake to CU at wharf.
Name of ship: SS MOYIE.*

216. CRESTON, B.C., AND OTHER SCENES IN B.C.   (1930's)
    p.c. private
    l. approx. 400'   g. 16mm   t. colour & b+w s. si.
    d.   *
    ph. W.M. Archibald
    c.s. NFA, Ottawa

        *b+w: A placer mining operation. Men working in the bottom of a huge ditch.
        Flumes. Water running into the ditch. Overhead cable carrying a load of sup-
        plies or equipment above ditch works. Views of a huge crater dug by hydraulic
        mining. Pan over sheds above ditches. Men working in the ditches. Hydraulic
        spray being levelled at ditch walls. Water sluicing down through ditches. CU
        water washing down ditches. Water racing through cuts in rock and dirt.*

        *1929. A family picnic on the shores of Kootenay Lake; everyone in a bathing
        suit. The sternwheeler SS MOYIE tied up at a nearby pier in the b.g. Univer-
        sity School boys boarding White Lines tour bus "Miss Victoria" at University
        School in Victoria. Good CU's of bus & driver.*

        *Faded Kodacolor - looks like b+w: Combining in a field near Creston, c. 1930.
        Good shots of machines. Young girl standing waist-high in a field of grain.
        Very good shots of harvesting silhouetted against mountains and the town of
        Creston in b.g. Mountain scenery. Good LS of a moose feeding in a pond.
        MAYDAY PARADE & celebration in the old park, Creston, with floats, marching,
        large crowds, Queen & Princesses on float, scenes down main street, many people
        milling about. May Pole dancing in b.g. Sign on float TURRET CIGARETTES. A
        very exuberant celebration. A Boy Scout parade in Creston. Scouts from U.S.A.
        & Canada staging a small parade. Kids straggling along behind on horses and
        on foot. Very good Barnes Circus signs behind them on the street.*

        *Colour: Buildings across a sheet of water. A pond. Men on road and a car. A
        ferry crossing a river. A man releasing grain from a hopper behind a tractor
        into a truck and shovelling it around to make room for more. Closing the
        hopper hatch and jumping to the ground. Colour - faded red. An air show, prob-
        ably at Grand Forks, B.C. A plane flying over; parachute opening and a man de-
        scending to earth. Plane landing. Large crowd along runway. Plane flying &
        landing. RCMP musical ride on runway; good manoeuvres with horses. Sign reading:
        BOXES - 25¢. Another parachute is following to the ground. A plane taxiing along
        the runway. Plane flying.*

        *Canadian destroyer in northern B.C. waters. A town on the edge of the forest
        at the base of a mountain with many white buildings, some very large, a can-
        nery (?), fishboats, and two huge flagpoles. (May be Alert Bay.)*

217. THE CRIMSON PARADISE.   (1933)
    p.c. Commonwealth Productions, Ltd.
    l. 7 reels   g. 35mm t. b+w   s. sound
    d. Robert F. Hill
    ph. James Brethertin, William Beckway & Clifford Bourne
    c.s. Unknown

        prod. Kenneth J. Bishop; script Arthur   *l.p. Nick Stuart, Lucille Browne,*
        Hoerl, from the novel THE CRIMSON WEST,   *Kathleen Dunsmuir, James McGrath,*
        by Alex Philip, published in 1925; sound   *Michael Heppell, Reginald Hincks,*
        Harry Rosenbaum, Wally Hamilton & Barrett   *Arthur Legge-Willis, C. Middleton*
        Webb; art dir. Ernest Ostman.   *Evans, Bob Webb, A. McNeil, Vivian*
                                                    Combe.

Billed as Canada's "First Full Length All-Talking Motion Picture", THE CRIMSON PARADISE was the first independent production to be released by Kenneth J. Bishop's Commonwealth Productions, Ltd. It premiered at the Capitol Theatre in Victoria, where it was made, on December 14, 1933, at eleven p.m. after the regular show. The "elite" of Victoria attended, sitting through an opening address by the Hon. T.D. Pattulo, the Premier of British Columbia, an introduction by the Mayor of Victoria, David Leeming, and a vocal solo by local basso Fred Wright, before the projectors were switched on and the picture got underway.

Reviews were kind and supportive when they stressed the photography, saying: "Everyone who attended agreed that few pictures have ever been shown here with more beautiful outdoor scenes." The film was processed and edited in Hollywood; the sound was poor, the editing rough, and the acting credible but often wooden, occasionally terrible. Ivan Ackery, the Resident Manager of the Capitol at the time, said in an interview forty years later: "We only played THE CRIMSON PARADISE a week, as I recall, but we did sensational business. It was a real turkey. So lousy it was good. Everyone wanted to see the local people and local scenes. I had a hell of a time to sell my home office (Famous Players) on it. They said they'd give me the week before Christmas - that's the worst week in the year in show business. I had 20,000 leaflets dropped from a plane. They said: COME TO THE PREMIERE OF THE FIRST ALL CANADIAN TALKING PICTURE MADE IN VICTORIA. People thought I was mad."

In fact, THE CRIMSON PARADISE ran for three days after its premiere, on December 20, 21 and 22, earning Mr. Ackery more money from box-office receipts than any other theatre in Canada during that week. It then moved to the Pantages Theatre in Vancouver for a week before leaving Canada entirely for England and the United States. No copies are known to exist today.

The locations chosen for THE CRIMSON PARADISE were Craigdarroch Castle and Beacon Hill Park in Victoria, and Hatley Park and the Butchart family gardens just outside the city.

Logging scenes were shot on location around Cowichan Lake, Chemainus and in Sooke. Many of the interiors were filmed in the old Industrial and Horse Show Buildings at the Willows Exhibition Grounds in Victoria, a huge barn Bishop outfitted as a studio and which was used for his successive motion picture ventures until the end of 1937. (See Introduction)

The story of THE CRIMSON PARADISE could readily be called a grab-bag of randomly placed, cliched confrontations ending in a predictable wedding clinch. A young ne'er-do-well named Donald McLean is disinherited by his father in Boston, Mass., and decides to come West in order to make his own way in the world. He arrives in British Columbia where, in the office of a local lumber company he meets a young man named Douglas, and Andy, a Cockney prize-fight promoter. Andy takes Donald under his wing and introduces him to the fight game while Douglas and his father Jack Gillis take an interest in his future with the lumber company, having in prospect for him a job on a timber cruise of some new territory they would like to log. Donald takes part in one fight under Andy's care and, after being saved from a knockout by the bell, he wins with a smashing right cross and wins $100. The night after the fight, Donald is entertained at the home of Douglas and his father and meets Janet who, when she hears he is a prize fighter, will have nothing to do with him.

Some days later, in the Cowichan Lake area, Donald, Douglas and a small party are riding horses through the forest, timber cruising. Donald meets Connie Wainright, a girl brought up in the woods by her father. Donald's company finally decides to log in the area and as he raises himself in the ranks through hard work, they establish a lumber mill (Chemainus) and begin turning out lumber for the market. Donald is confronted by a walkout of his lumberjacks, but after a fight with the leader they go back to work. The leader swears to get his revenge. Janet comes to stay at the camp with some friends and grows jealous of Connie and her relationship with Donald. During a Labour Day celebration in camp, Connie falls off a horse after winning a race. She wins a $500.00 purse and is thereby able to take her father on a trip to England. Soon after, they leave, but Donald is unable to see them off because an attempt has been made on his life by the leader of the lumberjacks while he is riding on an aerial tramway carrying logs. (Presumably Donald gets even somehow, but this is not explained.) Donald's father visits while Connie and her father are away, and having seen his son become a successful man of the

*world he reinstates him. Connie and her father return, and she and Donald
are happily reunited.*

218. CROSSING THE COAST RANGE. (before 1939)
   p.c. *
   1. 2000'   g. 16mm   t. b+w   s. si.
   d.   *
   ph. *
   c.s. Unknown

> *Only information available is: "Sir Norman Watson's expedition among coast
> range of B.C."*

219. CROWDED STREETCAR AND FREIGHT TRAIN CRASH CAUSING TWO
    DEATHS AND INJURY TO SCORES, VANCOUVER, B.C. (1923)
   p.c. Fox Movietonews (Fox #090.1-3384)
   1. 49'   g. 35mm   t. b+w   s. si.
   d.   *
   ph. Len H. Roos
   c.s. Fox Movietonews, N.Y. & NFB (1920-FG-157)

> *"Pan of wreckage. Shots of wrecked streetcar. Putting freight car back on
> track. Two die and many injured in weird crash. Shots of kids at crossing
> where accident happened, pan of debris, overturned box cars, men examining
> wreck, big crowd."*

220. CROWDS ENTHUSIASTICALLY GREET PRINCE OF WALES. (FROM
    CPR) (1919)
   p.c. Fox Movietonews (Fox #201-9735)
   1.   g. 35mm   t. b+w   s. si.
   d.   *
   ph. *
   c.s. Fox Movietonews, N.Y.

> *"Prince of Wales visits saw mill, reviews cadets. Leaves aboard the
> PRINCESS ALICE."*

221. CROWDS WELCOME MONSTER U.S. BATTLESHIP AND INSPECT NEW
    CANADIAN DESTROYER, VANCOUVER, B.C. (1928)
   p.c. Fox Movietonews (Fox #551.01-C4575)
   1. 45'   g. 35mm   t. b+w   s. si.
   d.   *
   ph. *
   c.s. Fox Movietonews, N.Y.

> *"People crowding about the two ships, the USS PENNSYLVANIA and the HMCS ?."*

222. CRUISE OF THE PRINCESS MAQUINNA. (before 1935)
   p.c. ASN (?)
   1. 1 reel   g. 35mm   t. b+w   s. si.
   d.   *
   ph. *
   c.s. Unknown

> *"Steamer trip up the West Coast of Vancouver Island."*

223. CRUISER SKIPPERS IN INTERNATIONAL BATTLE OF WITS,
    VANCOUVER, B.C. (1937)
   p.c. Universal Newsreel V.9 R.585
   1. 95'   g. 35mm   g. b+w   s. si.
   d.   *
   ph. ASN
   c.s. USNA

> *"General views of Canadian destroyers, mountains in b.g. Start of race, at
> wharf. Cruiser USS SEADOG of U.S. Coast Guard. U.S. competition yacht
> ELECTRA. The SYRENE. Destroyers. The race."*

224. DAD QUICK IS 109 YEARS OLD, VANCOUVER, B.C.   (1930)
    p.c. Fox Movietonews (Fox #6-894)
    l. 1320'   g. 35mm t. b+w   s. sound
    d.   *
    ph. Mayell & Foreman
    c.s. Fox Movietonews, N.Y.

> *"Although 109 years of age, Dad Quick is still active in his trade as a saddler. Children talking, mail carrier gives him a letter, and Dad gives his views on women, prohibition and a recipe for longevity. Dad Quick relates when Elias Howe invented the sewing machine in 1844 and his experience in the Chicago Fire."*

225. DAILY PROVINCE'S FOURTH ANNUAL BICYCLE RACE ATTRACTS BIG CROWDS
    OF FANS, VANCOUVER, B.C.   (1923)
    p.c. Fox Movietonews (Fox #755.4-B1718)
    l. 40'   g. 35mm t. b+w   s. si.
    d.   *
    ph. Len H. Roos
    c.s. Fox Movietonews, N.Y.

> *"CU Charles Staples, winner."*

226. DAIRY HERD IMPROVEMENT (DAIRY CATTLE IN BRITISH COLUMBIA)
    (1930 ?)
    p.c. B.C. Dept. of Agriculture (Reels 30, 31 & -)
         Dairy Branch
    l. 3 reels/1000' g. 16mm t. b+w   s. si. w/captions
    d.   *
    ph. *
    c.s. PABC

> *There are two prints of this three-reel film in the PABC; one contains, at the beginning of the first reel, a sequence missing in the other. This sequence consists of three captioned takes of (1) The Hon. S.F. Tolmie, Premier of British Columbia, (2) The Hon. Wm. Atkinson, Minister of Agriculture, and (3) Mr. J.B. Munro, the Deputy Minister of Agriculture. The copies are the same in all other respects.*

> *REEL ONE (400'): A day in the life of a Cow Testing Association Supervisor from Chilliwack. Cow testing shown in every detail and its results explained to the farmer being visited by the Supervisor. All the results are marked in a book for future reference, such as weight of milk given, butterfat content, etc. The Supervisor moves on to the next farm.*

> *REEL TWO (300'): This film is concerned with Jersey cows and shows how conformation and good looks don't necessarily make a good milker. It is impossible to tell butterfat content from looking at a cow. A little drama is staged: MR. BYER and MR. SELLAR do a little cow trading. SELLAR at first balks at the higher priced cow, not the one he fancies, but is convinced to take her, once he sees her Cow Testing Association records. Mr. G.H. Thornberry, Assistant-in-Charge of Cow Testing Association, standing talking to the two farmers.*

> *REEL THREE (300'): Cow Testing Association picnic at Coldstream Ranch near Vernon. President W.R. Powley speaks. W.F. Kennedy, M.L.A. for Vernon, speaks. Professor Boving of UBC speaks about Feed Evaluations. J.W. Berry, MLA, President of B.C. Dairyman's Association, tells jokes. Views of good sires the other important factor, besides testing, in Dairy Herd Improvement. Shot of Dairy Commissioner Mr. H. Rowe. This reel may not have been shown on occasion, the first two being the most important.*

227. DALE FRANZKA WINS OUTBOARD MOTOR CHAMPIONSHIP, HARRISON HOT
    SPRINGS, B.C.   (1938)
    p.c. Hearst Metrotone News (Can. No. 910 Roll No. 1)
    l.   g. 35mm t. b+w   s. sound
    d.   *
    ph. ASN
    c.s. Hearst Metrotone News, N.Y.

> *"Various scenes of the race and Franzka."*

228. DAMAGED BRIDGE SPAN FLOATED BY SCOWS INTO POSITION,
     VANCOUVER, B.C. (1934)
     p.c. Paramount (Lib. #4068) NL 386
     1.   g. 35mm   t. b+w   s. si.
     d.   *
     ph. *
     c.s. Lost

                    "Pan of bridge without span, view of missing span. CU scows in water nearing
                    span, tilt up from scows under span to top of span. SCU tilt up from tugboat
                    to fast pan of span being floated on scows. General view & CU span being
                    put into place. CU tilt up bridge & spans & view of three scows off in water."
                    The bridge is not identified.

229. DANCES AND CEREMONIES OF THE INDIANS OF BRITISH COLUMBIA.
     (1923-1930)
     p.c. National Museum of Canada
     1. 1 reel   g. 35mm   t. b+w   s. si.
     d.   Harlan I. Smith
     ph. Harlan I. Smith
     c.s. Unknown

                    This film is probably a compilation of the dancing and ceremonial film shot
                    by Harlan Smith over almost a decade of taking motion pictures among the
                    various Indian groups of British Columbia.

230. DARING RIDERS FROM THE CARIBOO RANGELANDS STAGE ANNUAL
     STAMPEDE, WILLIAMS LAKE, B.C. (1928)
     p.c. Fox Movietonews (Fox #751.11-C5037)
     1. 150'   g. 35mm   t. b+w   s. si.
     d.   *
     ph. Jos. Mandy
     c.s. Fox Movietonews, N.Y.

                    "Rodeo events, crowds, stagecoach races, wild horses."

231. A DAUGHTER OF THE MINES. (1910)
     p.c. Edison Mfg. Co. (catalogue #6710)
     1. 1000'   g. 35mm   t. b+w   s. si.
     d.   J. Searle Dawley
     ph. Henry Cronjager
     c.s. Unknown

                    This is one of the CPR promotional films photographed by the Edison troupe
                    during their tour of Western Canada in the summer of 1910. Unfortunately a
                    print does not exist and there is no information as to the location but it is
                    likely British Columbia. While in Victoria the troupe mentioned that mining
                    scenes had been filmed in British Columbia, and in an article in Man to Man
                    Magazine, Norman Rankin mentions that Cronjager had been photographing at
                    Monarch Mine in Field. This particular picture was begun on August 14, 1910
                    and finished on August 23, 1910.

232. DAWN TO DUSK FLIGHT FROM MONTREAL TO VANCOUVER. (1937)
     p.c. Fox Movietonews (Fox #32-262)
     1. 540'   g. 35mm   t. b+w   s. sound
     d.   *
     ph. ASN
     c.s. Fox Movietonews, N.Y.

                    "In Montréal, Minister of Transport, C.D. Howe, Chief of Air Services Comm.
                    C.P. Edwards and Director of Trans-Canada Airlines, H.J. Symington, are given
                    send off by officials. Howe boards plane and waves. Plane taxiing. At Van-
                    couver, plane in air, landing, taxiing. Howe welcomed by Mayor Miller who
                    speaks first. Howe congratulates pilot Tudhope and co-pilot Hunter. Crowd
                    around Howe." The plane was a Lockheed Electra, which could carry 10 passen-
                    gers in a non-pressurized cabin. The flight took 20 hours.

233. A DAY WITH THE OKANAGAN POULTRY INSPECTOR. (1928 ?)
   p.c. B.C. Dept. of Agriculture (reel 18)
   l. approx. 350'   g. 16mm   t. b+w   s. si. w/captions
   d.   *
   ph. *
   c.s. PABC

> The Poultry Inspector from the British Columbia Department of Agriculture
> visits Rose Comb Red Farm and inspects their hens, chicks, cows, pigs and
> bees. He also visits a Boy's and Girl's Poultry Club in Grindrod, where the
> school principal has been instrumental in establishing such clubs.   Later he
> visits another mixed farm and looks over 600 Barred Rock chicks. He marks
> and culls the "slow featherers" and looks over the pigs and cows. There is
> also an LS of the 40-acre orchard.

234. DAYS OF REEL SPORT. (late 1930's)
   p.c. B.C. Bureau of Industrial and Tourist Development
   l. 1 reel   g. 16mm   t. b+w   s. si. w/captions
   d.   *
   ph. Clarence Ferris (?)
   c.s. Unknown

> "Sport-fishing in Brentwood Bay, near Victoria, B.C."

235. DEATH GOES NORTH. (1937)
   p.c. Central Films, Ltd.
   l. 64 minutes (5742') g. 35mm t. b+w s. sound
   d.   Frank McDonald (and perhaps David Selman)
   ph. Harry Forbes and William Beckway .
   c.s. NFA

> Canadian prod. Kenneth J. Bishop;
> script, Edward R. Austin; editor,
> William Austin; sound, Herbert
> Eicke; Technical supervisor,
> Sergeant Walter Withers, RCMP,
> through the courtesy and co-
> operation of Major General Sir
> James MacBrian, K.C.B., C.M.G.,
> D.S.O., Commissioner, Royal Can-
> adian Mounted Police; Columbia
> overseer, Jack Fier.

> l.p. Edgar Edwards, Sheila Bromley,
> Rin Tin Tin Jr. (the second), Jameson
> Thomas, Dorothy Bradshaw, Walter
> Byron, Arthur Kerr, Michael Heppell,
> James McGrath, Vivian Combe, Reginald
> Hinks, Harry S. Hays.

> Working title: MURDER GOES NORTH.   The eighth Quota Quickie made by Central
> Films for Columbia Pictures in Victoria and the second produced in 1937.
> DEATH GOES NORTH was filmed around Victoria and Vancouver Island and was
> copyrighted in the United States by Warwick Pictures, Inc., on May 20, 1939.

> The plot is as follows: Elsie Barlow (Sheila Bromley) is anxiously awaiting
> the arrival of her uncle, Herbert Barlow - whom she has never seen, to take
> over the running of the Barlow Lumber Company. The company is in difficulty
> due to the activities of the Norton brothers, Bart (Arthur Kerr) and Albert
> (Walter Byron) who own the adjacent property and want Elsie to sell-out - to
> them. A stranger arrives at the local inn and is murdered.   Then the uncle
> arrives and identifies the dead man as his secretary, Robert Druid. Sus-
> picion falls on the Norton brothers who were in the bar at the time, Freddie
> (Reginald Hinks), a mildly demented vagabond, and Gordon Hayes, the repre-
> sentative of another company who just made Elsie an offer.

> Enter the Mounties. Sgt. Ken Strange (Edgar Edwards), who happens to have a
> romantic interest in Elsie, begins an investigation, aided by constable Dan
> MacKenzie (Michael Heppell).

> MacKenzie is killed and Strange arrests Albert Norton on suspicion, but the
> Norton men continue their harrassment - stealing cut timber and setting small
> fires - and an attempt is made to strangle Elsie while she sleeps.

> Eventually it turns out that the dead man was Elsie's uncle and the secretary,
> now posing as the uncle, is revealed as the murderer. Druid gets the death
> sentence, the Nortons get two years, and Strange gets official permission to
> marry Elsie. (Storyline description courtesy of D. John Turner, NFA.)

236. DEDICATION OF COLOURS BY BISHOP SEXTON OF VICTORIA
     ASSISTED BY J.H. WRIGHT, PADRE OF CANADIAN LEGION
     FOR NANAIMO, NANAIMO, B.C. (1938)
     p.c. Hearst Metrotone News (Can. No. 879 Roll No. 2)
     1.   g. 35mm t. b+w   s. sound
     d.   *
     ph. ASN
     c.s. Hearst Metrotone News, N.Y.

               "General salute. Lt. Gov. Hamber inspects regiment, 2nd Battalion of Canadian
               Scottish. General shot of officials watching the preceedings. Lt. Gov. in-
               spects the Veterans called the 416th. Dedication of Colours and consecration
               by Bishop Sexton. General marchpast, giving eyes right to Lt. Gov. taking
               salute. Feet & CU of men marching."

237. DELEGATES TO WESTERN LUMBERMEN"S CONVENTION ARE GIVEN
     A GLIMPSE OF ACTUAL LUMBERING OPERATIONS, NEAR VANCOUVER,
     B.C. (n.d.)
     p.c. Fox Movietonews (Fox #104-C1520)
     1. 50'   g. 35mm t. b+w   s. si.
     d.   *
     ph. Len H. Roos
     c.s. Fox Movietonews, N.Y.

               "Delegates in woods watch trees being felled. SCU train of logs going by.
               Convention officials: President Hendry; Mrs. Galbraith & Chas Garret.
               C.W. Steger is a 350 lb. lumberjack - "A big man in the business"."

238. DESTROYERS SAIL TO JOIN FLEET FOR WINTER TRAINING,
     VICTORIA, B.C. (1939)
     p.c. Universal Newsreel
     1. 99'   g. 35mm t. b+w   s. si.
     d.   *
     ph. ASN
     c.s. USNA

               "LS ships, people in f.g., sailor kissing daughter in mom's arms. Aboard
               ship, Captain George C. Jones talking to men. Final instructions, shot of
               the flag, pulling ropes, moving out stern first, pan over to another ship.
               CU top of superstructure, sailors at attention, boat poking nose from stern
               to bow (?). Ships steaming along, two ships. Three ships farewell." The
               cuts contain shots of the HMCS RESTIGOUCHE, HMCS OTTAWA, HMCS FRASER, and
               HMCS ST. LAURENT, and Lt. Cdr. A. Hope & Lt. Cdr. W. Holmes.

239. DEXTERITY OF LUMBERJACKS IS ILLUSTRATED BY A LIST OF
     UNIQUE SPORTING EVENTS SEEN ONLY IN LUMBER CAMPS, NEW
     WESTMINSTER, B.C. (1928)
     p.c. Fox Movietonews (Fox #731.93-C6810)
     1. 170'   g. 35mm t. b+w   s. si.
     d.   *
     ph. Beesley
     c.s. Fox Movietonews, N.Y.

               "Man chopping log. CU same. Log rolling has its peculiar attraction. Man
               rolling log, spectators watching. CU mens' legs, shoes."

240. DID YOU KNOW THAT? NO. 1. (1934)
     p.c. ASN/ASS (#B-659)
     1. 1000'   g. 35mm t. b+w   s. sound
     d.   Gordon Sparling
     ph. *
     c.s. NFA

               CANADIAN CAMEO NO. 26. "It's a queer old world we live in where very often
               things are not what they seem and the truth is stranger than fiction. When
               motorists drive down a certain hill in New Brunswick, they are forced to step
               on the gas, but going up they can coast to the top. There's a town in
               British Columbia with enough buildings to house four thousand people yet one
               man lives there alone. Ever hear of a religion which forbids its adherents
               to drive automobiles? There is one. Yes, indeed, there are strange things
               in this strange world and Canada has her share of odd facts. DID YOU KNOW
               THAT?"

241. DID YOU KNOW THAT? NO. 2. (1936)
    p.c. ASN/ASS (#B-673)
    1. 1 reel   g. 35mm   t. b+w   s. sound
    d.   Gordon Sparling
    ph. *
    c.s. United Artists, NFA

> *CANADIAN CAMEO NO. 35. "DID YOU KNOW THAT it takes an hour to score a hole-in-one on a certain golf course in Saskatchewan? DID YOU KNOW THAT there is a photograph in existence which shows a dog's ghost lying on his grave, or that a waterfall in New Brunswick flows both downstream and up? These are just a few of the unusual facts in DID YOU KNOW THAT? No. 2, which proves that Canada has her share of oddities in this queer old world we live in, where very often things are not what they seem." CANADIAN CAMEO NO. 35 also demonstrates how a train journey from Toronto to Vancouver is two miles shorter in the winter. See also entry numbers 240, 246, 247, and 248*

242. DISPLAY OF LOGGING MACHINERY TELLS STORY OF INVENTIONS
    TO LIGHTEN LABOURS OF MAN, VANCOUVER, B.C. (1926)
    p.c. Fox Movietonews (Fox #481.17-B6009)
    1. 20'   g. 35mm   t. b+w   s. si.
    d.   *
    ph. Herron
    c.s. Fox Movietonews, N.Y. & NFB (1920-FG-165)

> *"CU of a small tractor in operation. SCU of a machine that picks up pile of lumber and moves it away. CU of a saw cutting through an upright pole. Shots of cargo arch."*

243. DISTRICT FIRE CHIEFS TEST NEW FIRE FIGHTING MACHINE, VANCOUVER,
    B.C. (1922)
    p.c. Fox Movietonews (Fox #461.93-B8296)
    1. 25'   g. 35mm   t. b+w   s. si.
    d.   *
    ph. Len H. Roos
    c.s. Fox Movietonews, N.Y.

> *"SCU fire chief watching stream of water from nozzle into bay. SCU chiefs and underwriters inspecting new truck. SCU testing pressure from nozzle. LS officials and truck."*

244. DOLLARS AND SENSE. (late 30's, early 40's)
    p.c. B.C. Government Travel Bureau
    1. 1 x 800' reel g. 16mm   t. colour s. si.
    d.   *
    ph. C.R.D. Ferris
    c.s. Unknown

> *"Manufacturing in British Columbia."*

245. DOROTHY SIMPSON AND HER DOLL'S HOUSES, VANCOUVER, B.C. (1922)
    p.c. Fox Movietonews (Fox #201-3207)
    1. 52'   g. 35mm   t. b+w   s. si.
    d.   *
    ph. Len H. Roos
    c.s. Fox Movietonews, N.Y.

> *"CU Dorothy Simpson with 48 dolls and their houses."*

246. DID YOU KNOW THAT? NO. 3. (1937)
    p.c. ASN/ASS (#B-692)
    1. 1 reel   g. 35mm   t. b+w   s. sound
    d.   Gordon Sparling
    ph. *
    c.s. United Artists, NFA

> *CANADIAN CAMEO NO. 41. "Little known facts collected from all over the Dominion make this third edition of DID YOU KNOW THAT? a provocative compilation of true Canadian oddities. Can trains travel on air? Do eels swim to market? Can a ship keep afloat with her sides and bottom full of holes? These are samples of the many amazing and amusing questions discussed, and the answer is yes, but .... DID YOU KNOW THAT?" Although no specific British Columbia*

item is mentioned or recalled as being part of this CANADIAN CAMEO, the
Director, Mr. Sparling, suggests that each of the DID YOU KNOW THAT?'s had
a British Columbia item in them, so one may assume that NO.3 is of interest.

247. DID YOU KNOW THAT? NO 4. (1939)
    p.c. ASN/ASS (#B-712)
    l. 1 reel   g. 35mm   t. b+w   s. sound
    d.   Gordon Sparling
    ph. *
    c.s. United Artists, NFA, Jack Chisholm Film Prods. #C166

                CANADIAN CAMEO NO. 45. "DID YOU KNOW THAT you can stand in Canada and look
                straight north into the United States which lies south of Canada? DID YOU
                KNOW THAT Pelee Island has the most plentiful pheasant shooting in the whole
                world? DID YOU KNOW THAT some people still tell the time by the sun and
                right in the Nation's Capital? DID YOU KNOW THAT long before the ice age,
                Canada was the favourite hunting ground of the gigantic, terrifying dinosaurs?
                The truth is stranger than fiction." This CANADIAN CAMEO also shows scenes
                of the boundary between British Columbia and the United States where a road
                straddles the border and where a car travelling west will have its left
                wheels in the U.S.A. and its right wheels in Canada.

248. DID YOU KNOW THAT? NO. 5. (1940)
    p.c. ASN/ASS (#B-729)
    l. 1 reel   g. 35mm   t. b+w   s. sound
    d.   Gordon Sparling
    ph. *
    c.s. CFI

                CANADIAN CAMEO NO. 49. Although No. 5 was produced in 1940, it most likely
                contains scenes shot in Vancouver's Stanley Park during 1939. The ASN des-
                cription reads: "DID YOU KNOW THAT Canada has a desert every bit as real as
                the Sahara? DID YOU KNOW THAT a river can cut a tooth? DID YOU KNOW THAT a
                forest trail on a lonely Canadian hillside leads to a Scottish castle? DID
                YOU KNOW THAT there are two Stanley Parks in Canada? These and other little
                known facts prove that truth can be stranger than fiction."

249. Original entry deleted.

250. DOUKHOBOR CUSTOMS, GRAND FORKS, B.C. (1919 or 1924)
    p.c. Fox Movietonews, N.Y.
    l.   g. 35mm   t. b+w   s. si.
    d.   *
    ph. *
    c.s. NFA & NFE (1920-170-FG-7)

                "Excellent story showing women (Russian Immigrants) spinning and then ploughing
                gardens. One woman holds plough while others pull it along like horses.
                Good shot of family of Doukhobors leaving shack for field work. Women pick-·
                ing hops in field, three women spinning on wheel, women pulling a plough
                while man ploughs field. More excellent shots from various angles as women
                replace horses in tilling the soil."

251. DOUKHOBORS HOLD MEETING IN PROTEST, FULLY CLOTHED, AND
    CLAIM THE RIGHT TO OBEY THEIR OWN LAWS, NELSON, B.C.
    (1929)
    p.c. Fox Movietonews (Fox #003.15-D2300)
    l. 40'   g. 35mm   t. b+w   s. si.
    d.   *
    ph. *
    c.s. Fox Movietonews, N.Y.

                "Indian women & men congregate on town street." This description, probably
                written by a cataloguer in New York, is almost certainly erroneous. The
                "Indians" are no doubt Doukhobors.

252. DOWN WESTERN SLOPE. (1899)
    p.c. American Mutoscope and Biograph Company
    l. 39'   g. 16mm   t. b+w   s. si.
    d.   *
    ph. G.W. (Billy) Bitzer
    c.s. NFA

Also called: DOWN KICKING HORSE GRADE, CAN. R.R. and DOWN KICKING HORSE SLIDE, C.P.R. The film was shot from a flatcar ahead of a CPR locomotive, with the camera in a fixed position, and shows the tracks and surrounding countryside as the train passes through the Kicking Horse Pass. The film is very clear, and snow can be seen on the slopes of the mountains as the train travels along the river. (DOWN WESTERN SLOPE was copyrighted in January, 1903)

253. DUKE AND DUCHESS OF CONNAUGHT IN CANADA. (1912)
    p.c. Gaumont Graphic (142)
    l. 241'   g. 35mm   t. b+w   s. si.
    d. *
    ph. *
    c.s. Visnews (Video 31)

> *The Duke and Duchess of Connaught review highlanders. The troops march past. A quick glimpse of the Duke and Duchess on the reviewing stand. No specific location is mentioned but it may very likely have been Victoria, or Vancouver, where the Royal couple were escorted by a highland regiment.*

254. DUKE AND DUCHESS OF CONNAUGHT VISIT VANCOUVER AND
    KAMLOOPS, B.C. (1912)
    p.c. *
    l.   g. 35mm   t. b+w   s. si.
    d. *
    ph. *
    c.s. NFA (Taylor reel 110)

> *"VANCOUVER: Royal party in Royal Box located in front of Vancouver Court House. Mayor's wife presents Duchess with bouquet of flowers. Two autos pass in f.g. Still cameramen move in front of box to take photographs of the Duke and Duchess. D & D visit school children. Tracking shot along Granville St. decorated beyond belief. Highland regiment piping soldiers to Court House where reception will be held. Duke inspects Pipe Band.*
>
> *KAMLOOPS: Crowds waiting at the Kamloops Lacrosse field. Royal party arrives in horse drawn carriage. Shots of Main Street, Kamloops, with huge arch and sign: KAMLOOPS AGRICULTURAL ASSOCIATION. Excellent shots of procession: carriages, mounted military escort and several automobiles as they move past camera. Gigantic parade led by Knights of Columbus and representatives from lumbermen, firemen, City Council, horse-drawn vehicles and wagon pulled by two buffalo and driven by an Indian. Good shots of Duke and Duchess in box watching many floats passing."*

255. DUKE AND DUCHESS OF CONNAUGHT VISIT VICTORIA, B.C.
    (1912)
    p.c. *
    l.   g. 35mm   t. b+w   s. si.
    d. *
    ph. *
    c.s. NFA (Taylor reel 122)

> *"Gigantic parade with Duke and Duchess preceding procession in carriage, followed by carriages carrying Lt. Gov. and other officials. Many buggies and a couple of autos make up the procession. In front of the Westholme Grill & Ritz Hotel, huge crowds gather to see the Duke and Duchess who sit on platform with other dignitaries. Large crowd. Crowds of people, men, women & children and militiamen walking through Beacon Hill Park on way to view the Royal couple who will be appearing later in the day."*

256. DUKE OF DEVONSHIRE VISITS VANCOUVER TRAINING SCHOOL,
    VANCOUVER, B.C. (1920's)
    p.c. Fox Movietonews (Fox #201-9665)
    l.   g. 35mm   t. b+w   s. si.
    d. *
    ph. Len H. Roos
    c.s. Fox Movietonews, N.Y.

> *No further information given.*

257. EAST KOOTENAY HIGHWAY CONSTRUCTION. (late 1930's)
     p.c. private
     1. 225'   g. 16mm   t. colour s. si.
     d.   *
     ph. R.F. Mackenzie
     c.s. NFA

> Mr. Mackenzie was employed for many years by the General Construction Co. of
> Vancouver. Road sign SOURCE OF COLUMBIA RIVER. PREVENT FOREST FIRES. Pan
> across end of Columbia Lake & snow-capped hills. Columbia Lake in winter.
> Wild swans on Columbia Lake - summer - they take off and fly away. L/S
> Kimberley Mines. Crowsnest Mountain. Locomotive with several long ore cars
> & caboose passing by, with forest in b.g. Paving at Fernie. Men working with
> truck dumping gravel into a paving attachment moving slowly along the road.
> Different view of Crowsnest Mountain. Frank Slide, camera follows course of
> slide down mountain. Small rock bluff with vehicles beside it, paving at
> Michel. Crusher at Mud Creek. Mixers at Spring Brook. Mud Creek, a frog,
> a porcupine & a deer. Scenic shot of mountain in Fall. Moyie Lake. Reflec-
> tion of mountain on Moyie Lake. Crooked Tree Camp in mountains. Jack &
> Yorky. Shovel working at Windemere cut, with two trucks in attendance.
> Shovel working in a deep, sandy pit with trucks. Carryall in pit. Truck
> moving along road away from camera. Truck dumping fill onto road. Bulldozer,
> shovel, trucks assembled & working at pit. Several shots of bulldozer pushing
> fill around, shovel in f.g. CU shovel at work. CU cat at work. CU shovel at
> edge of Columbia River in preparation for crossing. Shovel ploughing through
> water across the river.

258. EDWARD SCOTT TALKS ON TECHNOCRACY, VANCOUVER, B.C.   (1935)
     p.c. Fox Movietonews (Fox #25-183)
     1.   g. 35mm   t. b+w   s. sound
     d.   *
     ph. ASN
     c.s. Fox Movietonews, N.Y.

> "Scott describes our choice between technocracy and price system."

259. EIGHTIETH ANNIVERSARY OF GOLD DISCOVERY AT BARKERVILLE, B.C.
     (1939)
     p.c. Fox Movietonews (Fox #38-473)
     1. 610'   g. 35mm   t. b+w   s. sound
     d.   *
     ph. ASN
     c.s. Fox Movietonews, N.Y.

> "At Lougheed Creek, two men working claim. Pan from water pipe to men. CU
> sluice box, man panning. CU same shot of outfit. 1862 shot of town. Bar-
> kerville with old church in b.g. Men cleaning claim. Claim operations. Pan
> of surrounding country. Caribou Gold Quartz mine visited by members. In-
> spect $38,000.00 gold brick. Brick being poured. Modern hydraulic nozzle
> spray."

260. EMORY CREEK PLACER MINING TRAINING SCHOOL. (1935-36)
     p.c. Government of B.C.
     1. approx. 400'   g. 16mm   t. b+w   s. si. w/captions
     d.   *
     ph. *
     c.s. B.C. Mines Library

> A detailed look at one of the government camps set up during the depression
> to keep young men occupied and teach them some skills and optimism. Instruc-
> tor Ben Barlow points out wing dam, comstock, flumes, pressure tank and sluice
> boxes with various riffles and grids. As well, young men are shown rocking
> and panning for gold in the black sand that gathers after sluicing. Each
> scene includes many shots of young men working on Emory Creek, pushing boul-
> ders around, staggering about in rushing water.
>
> Also shown are daily lectures in mining theory, held by Barlow, and various
> comic scenes about the cookhouse with chefs and methods of cooking in the
> woods. Good CU of Ben Barlow. Young men playing baseball alongside railway.

261. EMPIRE DAY AT BRACE BAY, B.C. (VICTORIA, B.C.) (1912)
    p.c. *
    l.   g. 35mm   t. b+w   s. si.
    d. *
    ph. *
    c.s. NFA (Taylor reel 108)

                    *"Procession to parade grounds and shots of line of Boy Scouts parading toward
                    Fair Grounds which can be seen in b.g. People milling about grounds and
                    several autos moving about as well. BEACON HILL PARK: Excellent shots of
                    Boy Scouts arriving at Beacon Hill Park to celebrate Empire Day. Autos pas-
                    sing. Children playing on swings. Swans swimming in lake. Beacon Hill
                    fountain. Family walking in park, little girl pushing a baby pram."*

262. EMPIRE OF THE WEST. (before 1935)
    p.c. *
    l. 4 reels   g. 35mm   t. b+w   s. si.
    d. *
    ph. *
    c.s. Unknown

                    About Canada; likely includes scenes of British Columbia.

263. EMPRESS OF CANADA ARRIVES, VANCOUVER, B.C. (1922)
    p.c. Fox Movietonews (Fox #463.1-3145)
    l. 26'   g. 35mm   t. b+w   s. si.
    d. *
    ph. R.J. Farrington
    c.s. Fox Movietonews, N.Y.

                    *"MS arrival of RMS EMPRESS OF CANADA, largest vessel to enter Port of Van-
                    couver, B.C."*

264. EMPRESS OF CANADA ARRIVES FROM ORIENT DECKED IN NEW COAT
    OF PRE-WAR COLOUR, VANCOUVER, B.C. (1927)
    p.c. Fox Movietonews (Fox #463.11-B8581)
    l. 20'   g. 35mm   t. b+w   s. si.
    d. *
    ph. Herron
    c.s. Fox Movietonews, N.Y.

                    *"Ship entering harbour, mountains in b.g. SCU ship. SCU ship at dock,
                    people waiting."*

265. EMPRESS OF CANADA LEAVES ON WORLD TOUR WITH SEVERAL CPR
    OFFICIALS, VANCOUVER, B.C. (1924)
    p.c. Fox Movietonews, (Fox #463.11-B3967)
    l. 35'   g. 35mm   t. b+w   s. si.
    d. *
    ph. Len H. Roos
    c.s. Fox Movietonews, N.Y.

                    *"Confetti, CU Superintendant W.F. Peters and his wife. Other departure
                    scenes."*

266. EMPRESS OF RUSSIA FIRST VESSEL TO LEAVE WITH FOOD FOR
    THE STRICKEN JAPANESE, VANCOUVER, B.C. (1923)
    p.c. Fox Movietonews (Fox #090.23-B2075)
    l. 35'   g. 35mm   t. b+w   s. si.
    d. *
    ph. Len H. Roos
    c.s. Fox Movietonews, N.Y.

                    *"Loading salmon. Good shot of ship. Miss I.M. Jeffares and Mr. A.M. Stabler
                    of the Red Cross. Ship leaving through the narrows."*

267. THE ENEMY OF THE FOREST. (1918)
    p.c. Dept. of Trade and Commerce, Exhibits and
         Publicity Bureau, Ottawa.
    l. 1 reel   g. 35mm   t. b+w   s. si. w/captions
    d. *
    ph. A.E. Reeves (?)
    c.s. Unknown

Canada's first fire prevention film, released by the Exhibits and Publicity Bureau on June 2nd, 1919. The description in the first Catalogue reads: "This film has been produced in co-operation with the Forestry Branch of the Department of the Interior. It has been admitted by foresters and fire protection organizations to be one of the best fire protection films produced. It shows the forest reserves with warden's cabin, and the equipment that he has, on high land, looking out over vast areas. It shows a camping party after a good time, leaving behind them campfire and cigarette stubs. A tiny blaze begins, the fire warden sees the first smoke, telephones to his brother wardens, then the rush to the fire, a real forest fire, and finally the fire wardens conquer and master the fire by means of equipment which the Government has placed at their disposal." There is evidence this this was filmed near Kamloops, British Columbia, and arranged by Inspector D. Roy Cameron of the Kamloops branch of the Forest Service. (See the Kamloops Telegram, Sept. 12, 1918).

268. ENGINEERS DEVELOP NEW LABOUR SAVING DEVICE. SELF-DUMPING
SCOWS SPEED CONSTRUCTION OF JETTY AT HEAD OF FRASER RIVER,
STEVESTON, B.C. (1929)
p.c. Fox Movietonews (Fox #463.23-   )
l. 130'   g. 35mm   t. b+w   s. si.
d.   *
ph. Beesley
c.s. Fox Movietonews, N.Y.

"Scow floods and drops 400 T. of rock to bottom in 40 seconds at Steveston and automatically rights itself."

269. EUCHARISTIC PILGRIMS SAIL, VANCOUVER, B.C. (1937)
p.c. Paramount (Lib. #4701);NL 489 silent; NL 1397 sound
l. 44'   g. 35mm   t. b+w   s. sound & si.
d.   *
ph. ASN
c.s. Sherman Grinberg, N.Y.

"General view SS EMPRESS OF JAPAN. SCU gangplank. SCU on deck. Special chapel erected aboard EMPRESS OF JAPAN for the 200 Catholics enroute to 33rd International Eucharistic Congress in Manila. SCU altar. CU altar. Papal ensign. Shot of SS WASHINGTON. CU name on bow of SS AORANGI. Shot of same at dock."

270. EVERGREEN PLAYLAND. (1938-39)
p.c. Shelley Films for B.C. Bureau of Industrial
     and Tourist Development
l. 400' reel   g. 16mm   t. colour s. sound
d.   *
ph. Shelley Films
c.s. Unknown

"Sport highlights in British Columbia."

271. THE EVERGREEN ISLAND. (n.d.)
p.c. ASN (probably)
l. approx. 400'   g. 16mm   t. b+w   s. si.
d.   *
ph. *
c.s. Unknown

Shot for the CPR, probably by ASN. A promotional film about Vancouver Island.

272. EXHIBITION PARADE, VANCOUVER, B.C. (1936)
p.c. Hearst Metrotone News; Can No. 751, Roll No. 5
l. 750'   g. 35mm   t. b+w   s. sound
d.   *
ph. ASN
c.s. Hearst Metrotone News, N.Y.

"Start of parade, entries from Portland, Oregon; Chinese; Playground Association of Vancouver; & Rotarians. Crowd shots. Junior Fire Rangers. Tea Association. Governor General of Canada, Lord Tweedsmuir. Band plays O CANADA."

273. EXPERT RIDERS TRY SKILL ON WILD STEERS, WITH A MEASURE
     OF SUCCESS, AT PROVINCIAL EXHIBITION, NEW WESTMINSTER,
     B.C. (1925)
     p.c. Fox Movietonews (Fox #410.621-B7064)
     l. 40'   g. 35mm   t. b+w   s. si.
     d. *
     ph. Herron
     c.s. Fox Movietonews, N.Y.

          "Wild steer riding. Bronco busting. All LS. Spills."

274. EXPLORATIONS OF GREAT ENGLISH NAVIGATORS COOK AND VANCOUVER
     COMMEMORATED BY A MONUMENT, NOOTKA SOUND, B.C. (1924)
     p.c. Fox Movietonews (Fox #095.8-A4052)
     l.   g. 35mm   t. b+w   s. si.
     d. *
     ph. Len H. Roos
     c.s. Fox Movietonews, N.Y.

          *"Indians in canoes coming to ship. Unveiling the monument, Lt. Gov. Nichol
          officiates. CU of tablet. Lt. Gov. shaking hands with Chief Maquinna of
          the Mowichit tribe. CU chief showing chief's head-dress. Indian totem poles
          in front of houses. Tilt shot of totem. Familiar scenes in this typical
          Indian village. Indians selling totems and baskets. CU of old Indian women."*

275. EXPORT OF CANADA'S WHEAT CROP. (1937)
     p.c. British Paramount (Lib. #6365)
     l. 95'   g. 35mm   t. b+w   s. sound
     d. *
     ph. *
     c.s. Visnews, London

          *"Shots of wheat fields. Cutting machine at work and grain being loaded onto
          ship."* Neither the ship nor the port is identified, so it may not be Van-
          couver.

276. EXTENSION OF LAPOINTE PIER, VANCOUVER, B.C. (1932)
     p.c. National Harbours Board
     l. 330'   g. 35mm   t. b+w   s. si.
     d. *
     ph. *
     c.s. NFB (N.H.B. - N - 2)

          *Workmen extending the Lapointe Pier, using square Douglas-fir timbers to con-
          struct cribs. Each crib containing five million feet of Douglas-fir, will
          measure 100' x 50' and weigh approximately 50 tons. President of Harbour
          Commission, Mr. S. McClay, and Mr. W. Fritch, Chief Engineer, look on as crib
          4 is pulled into position and later pose with foreman. Good shots of car-
          penters, tugboats, etc.*

277. FAMOUS AUSTRALIAN RUGBY TEAM OUTSCORES VANCOUVER "RIPS",
     BUT ONLY AFTER A GRUELLING STRUGGLE, VANCOUVER, B.C. (1928)
     p.c. Fox Movietonews (Fox #712-C3169)
     l. 75'   g. 35mm   t. b+w   s. si.
     d. *
     ph. Jos. Mandy
     c.s. Fox Movietonews, N.Y.

278. FAR HORIZON. (n.d.)
     p.c. Kodascope Library
     l. 850'   g. 16mm   t. b+w   s. si.
     d. *
     ph. *
     c.s. Unknown

          *"Daring mountaineers climb to dizzy heights amidst snow and ice in the Can-
          adian Rockies. Long vistas of snow-capped ranges, wooded valleys, waterfalls,
          and glaciers make this one of rare scenic beauty."*

279. FARM POULTRY IN BRITISH COLUMBIA/POULTRY POINTERS.
     (1931)
     p.c. B.C. Dept. of Agriculture (Reels 54 & 55)
     l. 2 reels/800'   g. 16mm   t. b+w   s. si. w/captions
     d.   *
     ph. *
     c.s. PABC

                    REEL ONE (16mm; 400'): Choosing a cockerel at a Fall Fair (looks like
                    Saanichton Fall Fair). A chickenyard. How to set eggs on the family farm.
                    Making a hatching nest. Three weeks later - hatched chicks. A successful
                    hawk trap from England. Four-week-old chicks drinking milk. Feeding greens
                    to chicks. Culling sick ones. An autopsy reveals congested lungs from chill-
                    ing. Cutting a tire in half lengthwise makes two watering rings. Feeding
                    water to chicks. Culling slow-feathering chicks. Cleaning out the poultry
                    shed. Poultry inspector visiting and helping farm wife select the best cock-
                    erels. The rest will be fattened. The correct feed explained for fattening.
                    A young boy on his wagon.

                    REEL TWO: Taking eggs to hatchery. Hatchery man inspects eggs then pays
                    farmer. Special incubator made in B.C. Toes punched on some little chicks.
                    Flocks of chicks & pullets in hatchery. Chicks drinking clabbered milk.
                    Smearing chicks with lard & snuff to prevent cannibalism. Pullets in a farm-
                    yard pen. Stages of growth for two young chicks, Jiggs & Maggie, from 1 week
                    to 12 weeks old, although Jiggs is not present for the last shot, having "got
                    the rolling pin." How to get roosting fowls down from a tree - make a long
                    stick with a "T" at the end. Mother hens with chicks on the free range.
                    Pullets in a pen. Marketing eggs at the Co-op, truck pulls up to COWICHAN
                    CREAMERY TRADERS. Man unloading and checking crates of eggs. How to skin a
                    chicken - better than dry-picking or scalding - a complete demonstration.
                    Show winners - cockerels and hens - Leghorn, Rhode Island Red, White Wyandottes,
                    Light Sussex, Barred Rocks.

280. FASTER THAN A MILE A MINUTE THEY SHOOT THROUGH THE AIR
     AT THE ANNUAL SKI TOURNAMENT, REVELSTOKE, B.C. (1924)
     p.c. Fox Movietonews (Fox #732-B3910)
     l. 65'   g. 35mm   t. b+w   s. si.
     d.   *
     ph. Len H. Roos
     c.s. Fox Movietonews, N.Y. & NFA

                    "LS and closer view ski jumping on hillside. Close view of jumpers taking
                    off. Back shot of a jump. Other shots of ski jumps. LS Ethel Granstrom
                    winning the ladies ski race. Head CU Ethel Granstrom. Several shots of
                    Arthur Needham of Seattle jumping."

281. FDR AT VICTORIA. (1937)
     p.c. Universal Newsreel V.9 R.603
     l. 79'   g. 35mm   t. b+w   s. sound
     d.   *
     ph. Fox Movietonews
     c.s. USNA

                    "Pan of group, in car, parade of FDR's car, natural sound of Star Spangled
                    Banner, on board ship, they're off - ". Cuts: Lt. Gov. Hamber & party: L to
                    R - Mrs. Hamber, Roosevelt, James, Mrs. Roosevelt, and Lt. Gov. Hamber. Lt.
                    Gov. rides with President. Roosevelt aboard destroyer (USS PHELPS).

282. FDR IN VICTORIA, B.C. (1937)
     p.c. Paramount (Lib. #6841)
     l. 91'   g. 35mm   t. b+w   s. sound
     d.   *
     ph. Hearst & Lowery
     c.s. Visnews (BPN Lib. #6835); Sherman Grinberg, N.Y.

                    "Lt. Gov. Hamber's home, Government House. SCU President's party on steps.
                    CU Mrs. Hamber & Mrs. Roosevelt. SCU Pres. Roosevelt & Lt. Gov. Hamber in
                    car. Car leaving Gov't. House. SCU President's car passing. SCU soldiers
                    presenting arms. Back view entering dock. SCU Pres., Mrs. & son James
                    Roosevelt on destroyer USS PHELPS. CU Pres. & party on destroyer. Semi-pan
                    destroyer. CU same. SCU pan away from destroyer. Destroyer leaving with
                    Roosevelts aboard, from Esquimalt."

283. FDR VISITS - VICTORIA - 1937.
    p.c. probably Fox Movietonews
    1.   g. 35mm   t. b+w   s. sound
    d.   *
    ph.   *
    c.s. NFB (1930-DN-321)

                    "Shots of FDR, Mrs. Roosevelt and son James posing from deck of warship, of
                    FDR and Lt. Gov. Hamber in convertible, of their car with secret service
                    agents on running board during drive. Two shots of the Roosevelts and Hambers
                    posing."

284. "FEATHERED FRIENDS", VANCOUVER, B.C.   (1937)
    p.c. Universal Newsreel #2149 X 1,2
    1. over 1000'   g. 35mm   t. b+w   s. si.
    d.   *
    ph.   *
    c.s. USNA

                    "Mr. and Mrs. Charlie Jones and their two young boys have created a bird para-
                    dise. Birds even perch on their heads and on Mr. Jones's nose. Birds eat
                    right from his mouth. Photographer even gets bird. All kinds of wild birds
                    have learned to trust this family." Part of GOING PLACES, NO. 32.

285. FIFTEEN MINUTES FROM SKYSCRAPERS.   (1927)
    p.c. CGMPB
    1. approx. 750'   g. 35mm   t. b+w   s. si. w/captions
    d.   *
    ph.   *
    c.s. NFA & NFB (1920-L-63)

                    "A scenic travelogue of Vancouver's famous forest playground, Stanley Park,
                    including views of the Harding Memorial, Pauline Johnson Monument, the park
                    zoo, the giant hollow tree, Siwash Rock, and English Bay."

                    Also included are street scenes in downtown Vancouver showing pedestrians,
                    autos, streetcars, stores. There are lots of trail & road shots throughout
                    the park with people driving, walking and riding horseback. During the sec-
                    tion on the Harding Memorial, there are news clips of U.S. Marines parading
                    and of President Harding speaking from a platform. Shots also of the giant
                    checker game with spectators watching. Animals in the zoo include bears,
                    both cubs and adults, young seal, monkeys, and a pelican. Cars drive through
                    the giant hollow tree. English Bay crowded with swimmers and sunbathers.

286. FIFTIETH ANNIVERSARY OF FIRST TRANSCONTINENTAL R.R.
    RUN AT PORT MOODY, B.C.   (1936)
    p.c. Fox Movietonews (Fox #29-193)
    1. 500'   g. 35mm   t. b+w   s. sound
    d.   *
    ph. ASN
    c.s. NFB (ASN 1930-FG-278); Fox Movietonews, N.Y.

                    "At Port Moody, the old train that made first run returns to old terminal.
                    Shots of original station with types of people of that time. Crowd in dress
                    of 50 years ago around train. July 3, 1936."

287. FIFTY-THIRD ANNUAL CELEBRATION ORGANIZED BY ST. ANDREW'S
    AND CALEDONIAN SOCIETY, VANCOUVER, B.C.   (1939)
    p.c. Hearst Metrotone News; Can 1112, Roll no. 4
    1.   g. 35mm   t. b+w   s. sound
    d.   *
    ph. ASN
    c.s. Hearst Metrotone News, N.Y.

                    Scottish games and dances in traditional costume attended by the Duke and
                    Duchess of Sutherland.

288. FIGHTING FOREST FIRES WITH HAND TOOLS (FIRE FIGHTING
     WITH HAND TOOLS). (1938-39)
     p.c. B.C. Forest Service
     l. approx. 400'   g. 16mm   t. B+w   s. si. w/captions
     d.   *
     ph. *
     c.s. PABC (Forestry reel 72)

> *A lookout spots a fire and radios the information to a dispatcher at the
> Ranger Station. He relays the message to the Forest Fire Suppression Crew
> who board a truck and drive to the scene of the blaze. Men use tools to con-
> fine the fire, which are explained in captions and shown in CU: machete,
> special small-bladed shovel, Pulaski tool (combination grub-hoe and axe),
> grub-hoe, steel broom, gasoline torches (flame throwers), hand-pumped fire
> extinguishers containing water in back tanks. A car drives through the forest,
> a cigarette is dropped out of a window and a fire starts. A tank truck
> arrives and puts the fire out.*

289. FILIPINOS ARRIVE TO DEMAND INDEPENDENCE, VICTORIA, B.C.
     (1923)
     p.c. Hearst Metrotone News   Roll no. 519
     l.   g. 35mm   t. b+w   s. si.
     d.   *
     ph. *
     c.s. Hearst Metrotone News, N.Y.

> *"Delegation planning appeal to U.S. Congress visits British Columbia Legisla-
> ture, Victoria. Ground shot of Filipino delegation walking to and fro past
> camera as they come down gangplank from ship after its arrival. Semi-close
> ground shot of delegation."*

290. FIRE BOAT ORION IN ACTION, VANCOUVER, B.C. (1932)
     p.c. National Harbours Board
     l. 570'   g. 35mm   t. b+w   s. si.
     d.   *
     ph. *
     c.s. NFB (N.H.B.-N-3)

> *"The fire boat ORION, completely built and designed in Canada, is shown demon-
> strating its power and ability to fight dock fires if and when they occur.
> Shots of fire boat arriving, of firemen assembling hoses, manning 2 main
> pumps and firing water stream 110 yards into the air as Harbour Commission
> President S. McClay and Trade Minister H.H. Stevens look on. CS water being
> fired to top of 260 foot high pier building. CS Stevens and McClay watching,
> some people with umbrellas.*
>
> *Good shots of passengers, including H.H. Stevens, boarding the EMPRESS OF ASIA
> passenger liner at CPR dock. Stevens arrives in car and boards liner. He is
> on his way to Honolulu to confer with delegates with regards to signing a new
> trade treaty. CS name on ship's bow: EMPRESS OF ASIA. Passengers cheering
> as streamers fly from ship."*

291. FIRE FIGHTING WITH HAND TOOLS.
     p.c. *
     l.   g.   t.   s.
     d.   *
     ph. *
     c.s. *

> *See FIGHTING FOREST FIRES WITH HAND TOOLS, No. 288.*

292. FIRST AID IN INDUSTRY. (1939-40)
     p.c. B.C. Government Travel Bureau
     l. 1 400' reel   g. 16mm   t. colour s. si.
     d.   *
     ph. C.R.D. Ferris
     c.s. Unknown

> *"Demonstration of mine rescue work and first aid at Nanaimo, B.C."*

293. FIRST AIR MAIL BY TRANS-CANADA AIRLINES TO WINNIPEG,
VANCOUVER, B.C. (1938)
p.c. Fox Movietonews (Fox #33-883)
l.   g. 35mm   t. b+w   s. sound
d.   *
ph. ASN
c.s. Fox Movietonews, N.Y.

        "Interior of station showing transmitter which operates radio beam. Operator checking equipment. Exterior showing towers and building housing radio range finding equipment. Air mail loaded. Mayor Miller of Vancouver, Mr. G.H. Clark, Pilots Barclay and Middleton, E.P.H. Wells. CU of both pilots. Plane landing. Mechanics. Plane interior. Taking off."

294. FIRST ANNUAL GYMKHANA OF LION'S GATE RIDING AND POLO CLUB,
VANCOUVER, B.C. (1938)
p.c. Hearst Metrotone News; Can no. 843, Roll no. 3
l.   g. 35mm   t. b+w   s. sound
d.   *
ph. ASN
c.s. Hearst

295. FIRST CAR RACES IN VANCOUVER, B.C. (n.d.)
p.c. *
l. 60'   g. 35mm   t. b+w   's. si.
d.   *
ph. *
c.s. NFA #4098

        "Jack Smith of Victoria wins three mile race."

296. FIRST SHIP TO REACH CANADA BRINGING EYE-WITNESSES OF JAPANESE
HORROR, VICTORIA, B.C. (1923)
p.c. Fox Movietonews (Fox #060.73-B2847)
l. 60'   g. 35mm   t. b+w   s. si.
d.   *
ph. Len H. Roos
c.s. Fox Movietonews, N.Y.

        "EMPRESS OF ASIA docking. Refugees. Officers of the EMPRESS OF ASIA. SCU Capt. Robinson & Ref, his dog. CU Robinson."

297. FIRST SNOWFALL ON GROUSE MOUNTAIN LURES A CROWD OF SKIIERS,
YOUNG AND OLD, WHO REVEL IN A DAY'S SPORT, VANCOUVER, B.C.
(1928)
p.c. Fox Movietonews (Fox #732.3-C8074)
l. 170'   g. 35mm   t. b+w   s. si.
d.   *
ph. Beesley
c.s. Fox Movietonews, NY..

        "Includes a team of dogs in a sleigh race, as well as skiiers, etc."

298. FISH AND MEDICINE MEN. (1928)
p.c. ASN
l. 650'   g. 35mm   t. b+w   s. si. w/captions
d.   Dr. J.S. Watson (?)
ph. Dr. J.S. Watson (?)
c.s. NFA, BCPM Eth.

        Produced by B.E. Norrish. CAPTION: "In the salmon season the Villages are left deserted." The Indians of northern British Columbia left their homes throughout the fishing season; the men to work upon the sea catching salmon, the women to work in the canneries up and down the inlets. This film appears to be about the Indians who lived north of Prince Rupert in the Nass River country around Kincolith. The description is as follows: "Various shots of villages by water. Shot of bay and sailing boat. Fish in hold of boat and Indian fisherman. Shots of ancient wooden machinery moving fish, a sort of wooden elevator/hopper. Indian boss in cannery gesticulating with his hands to the workers. Street of cannery village. Wooden huts, dogs, Indian women. Various shots of Indian children. Indian woman carrying large sack. Indian woman working in canning factory. Fish being pushed manually into cans. Indian fisherman in boat. Preparations for a fishing trip. Fishing fleet going out. More shots of Indian children in village. Women working at some kind of primitive machine. Indian fishermen talking. Sheets of music, a song called THANK YOU FOR THE BUGGY RIDE. MCU Indian father looking at his baby. CAPTION: Nearby is Kincolith. It means THE PLACE OF SKULLS, but it is a church town now. Shots of church, wooden, and of Indians standing outside. Indian child. Indians in traditional costumes walking up Village path. Various shots of Indians in traditional costumes. Indians getting costumes out of wooden box and dressing up. Various shots of Indians in the woods in their costumes."

The cannery scenes were filmed at Arrandale; the dancing and the shaman performing on a patient at Kincolith. It appears that this reel may be very similar or identical to reel 1 of NASS RIVER INDIANS.

299. FISHERMEN READIED FOR WAR, ESQUIMALT, B.C. (1939)
    p.c. *
    l.   g. 35mm t. b+w   s.
    d. *
    ph. *
    c.s. NFB (1930-240-N-1)

        "Shots of fishing boats in harbour, men lined up, receiving instruction on naval navigation, armament, etc. Fishermen learning semaphore practise, drilling with rifles. Men training at sea and firing at stationary object in water." Part of a collection of news stories called CANADA AT START OF WW II.

300. FISHERMEN'S LARDERS. (before 1935)
    p.c. *
    l. 1 reel   g. 35mm t. b+w   s. si.
    d. *
    ph. *
    c.s. Unknown

        "Salmon and whitebait hatcheries of Canada." No further information given, but the salmon hatcheries are probably in B.C.

301. FISHING ACROSS CANADA - PART 4. (1930's)
    p.c. *
    l. approx. 400' g. 16mm t. b+w   s. si.
    d.   *
    ph. *
    c.s. Unknown

        This title consists of four parts; 1. PICTON LODGE, NOVA SCOTIA (1 reel); 2. SALMON FISHING ON THE PETAWAWA RIVER, NEW BRUNSWICK (1 reel); 3. TROUT AT ALGONQUIN PARK AND NIPIGON (2 reels) and 4. LAKE AND RIVER IN BRITISH COLUMBIA (1 reel).

302. FISHING FLEET GETS NAVAL TRAINING, ESQUIMALT, B.C.
    (1939)
    p.c. Paramount (Lib. #7968)
    l. 91'   g. 35mm t. b+w   s. sound
    d.   *
    ph. ASN
    c.s. Lost

        "SCU PAN FISHING FLEET. Shots of fishermen. Fishermen being instructed in machine gunnery. SCU students exercising. Instructions on signal flags. Union Jack. Fishermen marching. Gun drill. Students with guns. Boats setting out. Student with machine gun. Target in water being hit."

303. FISHING FLEET STRIKE IN VANCOUVER, B.C., AFTER FINDING
    PRICE OFFER UNACCEPTABLE. (1938)
    p.c. Fox Movietonews (Fox #35-725)
    l. 550'   g. 35mm t. b+w   s. sound
    d. *
    ph. *
    c.s. Fox Movietonews, N.Y. & NFA

*"Elevated shots from Prospect Point at the entrance to Vancouver Harbour.
Arriving at Vancouver Harbour fish pier. Men throwing ropes and tying up
their boats. Boats tied up. Whole fleet tied up. Men leaving pier with
their baggage for home. Shots from boat, arriving at harbour entrance. At
pier and tying up."* (Negative cuts destroyed)

304. FISHING FOR TYEE. (1933-1934)
 p.c. Canadian Government Motion Picture Bureau.
 l. approx. 700'   g. 35mm   t. b+w   s. si. w/captions
 d.   Bill Oliver
 ph. Bill Oliver
 c.s. NFA (250' 16mm), NFB, & BCPM History (35mm)

Produced for the National Parks Bureau, Ottawa.

*"Members of the Campbell River Fishing Club in British Columbia stage their
annual outing during the tyee salmon season. Many fine catches of large
specimens are shown." OR "Tyee Club of British Columbia holds its annual
competition at Campbell River, V.I."*

*There are no particular landmarks in this film. The first scenes show small
boats out trolling on the ocean. CU fisherman polishing up a spoon. A 45-
pound tyee is hooked and brought aboard a small clinker-built boat. A lady
out fishing with a gent, after a long struggle, pulls in a 35-40 pounder.
Another tyee is landed aboard a small clinker boat. Caption: CLUB RULES DO
NOT PERMIT THE USE OF POWER BOATS OR HEAVY FISHING TACKLE? Two men and a
woman in a clinker boat pull in a tyee weighing about 35 pounds. They walk up
the beach smiling and carrying their catch. The fish is measured by club
officials. A display of five huge tyee with Tyee Club members gathered around.
The fish are weighed. The SILVER BUTTON, an indicator of fish caught in the
40-50 pound bracket, is awarded to the lady who caught the fish. Sunset and
some boats are still out on the sea fishing for a bigger one.*

305. FIVE HUNDRED PUBLIC SCHOOL BOYS UNDER CANVAS AT POINT GREY,
 VANCOUVER, B.C. (n.d.)
 p.c. Fox Movietonews (Fox #700.5-B8489)
 l. 20'   g. 35mm   t. b+w   s. si.
 d.   *
 ph. *
 c.s. Fox Movietonews, N.Y.

"L Pan the camp. LS boys lined up for inspection. SCU boys eating." (For
dope sheet see #B8448).

306. FISHING IN THE ROCKIES. (1930's)
 p.c. CGMPB
 l.   g. 35mm   t. b+w   s. si.
 d.   Bill Oliver
 ph. Bill Oliver
 c.s. NFB outs (1930-DN-302)

*Shots of a mountain lake. Woman casting from shore. Man and woman fishing
from raft in middle of lake. Groundhog near burrow. Man & woman ride horses
with mountains in b.g. A calf follows. Diagonally split screen shows, on
one side, a mountain, on the other, a man smoking. Fade out to woman in
sleeping bag. Mountains & hills at dusk.*

307. THE FLAMING FOREST. (1926)
 p.c. Cosmopolitan Productions (MGM)
 l. 6,567'   g. 35mm   t. colour & b+w s. si. w/captions
 d.   Reginald Barker
 ph. Percy Hillburn
 c.s. LOC

*Script, Waldemar Young from the novel   l.p. Antonio Moreno, Renée Adorée,
by James Oliver Curwood, THE FLAMING   Gardner James, William Austin, Tom
FOREST, A NOVEL OF THE CANADIAN NORTH-   O'Brien, Emile Chautard, Oscar
WEST; titling, Lotta Woods; editor   Beregi as Jules Lagarée.
Ben Lewis.*

*This amazing film claimed to tell the whole truth about the Riel Uprising of
1869, and hinged the creation of the Royal North West Mounted Police on it,*

an event that didn't happen until 1874 <u>and which in fact had nothing to do</u>
<u>with Riel or the Métis agitation</u>. It was filmed on location partly in Mon-
tana and partly in Canada, probably at Fort Steele in British Columbia. The
story is as follows: "Jules Lagarre, a halfbreed brigand, undertakes to dom-
inate the Canadian Northwest with the aid of Indians and cutthroats. André
Audemard, a trading post merchant, appeals to the Government for help and is
murdered by Lagarre's henchmen, Lupin and Francois, leaving his children,
Jeanne-Marie and Roger. Lagarre attempts to establish himself as head of a
provisional Government, but the Canadian Government forms the Northwest
Mounted Police to establish law and order. Jeanne-Marie persuades the sett-
lers to remain, and she falls in love with Sergeant Carrigan. Roger murders
Lupin and Francois in a rage, for the killing of his parents, and Carrigan
comes to arrest him. As a result Jeanne-Marie turns against him. Lagarre
organizes an Indian attack on the post and orders the forest set afire to
hem off the Mounted Police; however, the rescue is affected. Roger dies
protecting Jeanne, and she is reconciled with Carrigan." Pierre Berton re-
veals some of the backroom wrangling that went into the making of this pic-
ture in his HOLLYWOOD'S CANADA, pp. 125-127.

308. FLASHES OF ACTION: MIGHTY MONARCHS OF THE FOREST FALL
BEFORE THE AXE OF NORTHWEST LUMBERMEN, BRITISH COLUMBIA.
(1927)
p.c. Fox Movietonews (Fox #420.75-B7716 to B7719)
l. approx. 30'   g. 35mm   t. b+w   s. si.
d.   *
ph. J.T. Mandy
c.s. Fox Movietonews, N.Y.

       "SCU men cutting the tree. Back shot of tree falling. LS tree falling. LS
       man on a fallen tree. Another tree falling." (Carries on w/Montreal &
       Texas.)

309. FLASHY BALL PLAYERS OF FAMOUS HOUSE OF DAVID MAKE MERRY
PRIOR TO HARD GAME, VANCOUVER, B.C. (n.d.)
p.c. Fox Movietonews (Fox #711-B9726)
l. 50'   g. 35mm   t. b+w   s. si.
d.   *
ph. Jos. Mandy
c.s. Fox Movietonews, N.Y.

       "SCU pan of team. CU B.B. Faust, shortstop. LS warming up. L Hi's the
       game."

310. FLIERS ON "ROUND THE WORLD" TRIP STOP FOR MINOR REPAIRS
AND MORE FUEL, PRINCE RUPERT, B.C. (1924)
p.c. Fox Movietonews (Fox #663.02-B5725)
l. 20'   g. 35mm   t. b+w   s. si.
d.   *
ph. *
c.s. Fox Movietonews, N.Y.

       "LS plane landing. SCU hoisting plane from the water."

311. FLIGHT OVER CANADA'S CONTINENTAL DIVIDE - PILOTS ON FIRE
PATROL OVER VAST MOUNTAIN TERRITORY TAKE CAMERAMAN ALONG,
NEAR WATERTON LAKES NATIONAL PARK, ALBERTA. (1925)
p.c. Fox Movietonews (Fox #325.7-B206, B207)
l.   g. 35mm   t. b+w   s. si.
d.   *
ph. W.J. Oliver
c.s. Fox Movietonews, N.Y.

       "Shot of plane in air. Several good airplane shots of mountain & lake country.
       Mt. Sentinel in Waterton Lakes National Park. Frank Slide, where a town lies
       buried; shot of Frank Slide showing town at foot of mountain. The wonders of
       nature are all in a day's work for these fearless flyers."

312. FLOATING FORTRESS AS ROYAL ESCORT. (1919)
     p.c. Pathéscope
     1. approx. 400'   g. 28mm   t. b+w   s. si.
     d.   *
     ph. *
     c.s. NFA

> "This reel comprises scenes of the RENOWN, the warship which brought the
> Prince of Wales to Canada, and the pictures of other battleships that acted
> as escort in Atlantic and Pacific waters."

313. FLOOD AT BELLA COOLA. (1923-1930)
     p.c. National Museum of Canada
     1. 1 reel   g. 35mm   t. b+w   s. si. w/captions
     d.   Harlan I. Smith
     ph. Harlan I. Smith
     c.s. Unknown

314. THE FLYING POSTMAN. (before 1935)
     p.c. *
     1. 1 reel   g. 16mm   t. b+w   s. sound
     d.   *
     ph. *
     c.s. Unknown

> "The air mail in Canada." No further information but may contain scenes of
> British Columbia.

315. FOLLOW THE BIRDS THE VICTORIA, B.C. (actual title
     unknown) (early 1930's)
     p.c. Motion Skreen Adz Ltd., Vancouver, for the Victoria
          and Island Publicity Bureau.
     1. approx. 800'   g. 35mm   t. tinted b+w   s. si., no captions
     d.   *
     ph. *
     c.s. BCPM History

> FOLLOW THE BIRDS TO VICTORIA, B.C. may not be the title of this film. The
> titles at the beginning read:

>> Follow-the-Birds
>> to
>> VICTORIA, B.C.

> Where Summer Comes to Spend the Winter Months

> No Hot   No Cold
> Summers   Winters

>> write Geo. I. Warren, Publicity Commissioner, for Booklet.

> The titling was done by Motion Skreen Adz Limited in Vancouver. The head of
> the film with the actual title has been lost.

> Iris view of seagulls flying over the sea. Sunset view of Inner Harbour from
> top of Empress Hotel showing a CPR Princess ferry at the CPR wharf. Golfing
> at the Qualicum Beach Hotel Golf Course, showing several views of the club-
> house, the players and the ocean in the b.g. In Cathedral Grove, some men
> measure the girth of a large tree. A sign reads: THIS ACRE OF DOUGLAS FIR
> AND WESTERN HEMLOCK CONTAINS 73 TREES, 10 TO 69 D.B.M. & WITHOUT ALLOWING FOR
> ANY DEFECT IS CRUISED AT 188,000 BOARD FEET. AVERAGE HEIGHT OF DOMINANT TREES
> - 225'. A road through the forest - an open car drives through. A man beside
> a rushing stream. Three tourists stand at the brink of a roaring waterfall
> (Little Qualicum ?). Car with right-hand drive moves along road through
> forest toward camera. Two men on horses cross a log bridge in the forest. A
> deer in the forest at the side of the road. A small waterfall tumbling into
> a lake. Snow up high on Forbidden Plateau (?), a trail rider rides by. Trail-
> riders ride across a high snowfield. Riders dismount and walk their horses
> along rocky edge of a mountain. They ride up to the summit, culminating in
> a very LS of two riders on a stone bluff. Various shots of sheer stone cliffs.
> Trail riders ride across same snowy vista as before and along through snowy
> terrain with mountains in b.g. - they look out across snowy mountains and
> trees. Iris view of surf pounding on a west coach beach near Bamfield. Many

*shots of surf, beach, rocks, and birds. A nest off the beach in the rocks,
with three eggs. More shots of the beach and a little waterfall and river.
Bamfield Cable Station with a white steamer tied up at the wharf. A boat
chugs by. Surf on the rocks at Number 9 beach. The head on the pole at
Number 9 beach. CU head. Surf pounding in on jagged rocks. Sunset looking
out over the islands in Barclay Sound. Two trees silhouetted against the
sunset.*

316. FOLLOW THE BIRDS TO VICTORIA, B.C. - THE CITY OF SUNSHINE
     AND FLOWERS (actual title unknown) (early 1930's)
     p.c. Motion Skreen Adz, Ltd., for the Victoria and Island
          Publicity Bureau
     l. approx. 750'   g. 35mm   t. b+w on tinted stock   s. si. w/captions
     d.   *
     ph. *
     c.s. BCPM History

                         FOLLOW THE BIRDS TO VICTORIA, B.C.

                         "The City of Sunshine and Flowers"

                         "A Fairy Playground for Young and Old"

     *The titling was done by Motion Skreen Adz Limited in Vancouver. The head of
     the film with the actual title has been lost.*

     *LS destroyer in Esquimalt. Pan across buildings in Dockyard to other ships.
     Good shot of stern of the EMPRESS OF JAPAN in drydock. Shot down length of
     EMPRESS's hull. Front and back views of Dominion Astrophysical Observatory
     on Little Saanich Mountain. Interior of Observatory & shots of telescope.
     Fishermen unloading catch into a barge, many shots of salmon flashing in nets
     and fishermen working. A high-rigger starts up a tree, followed by his axe,
     and cuts the top off. He descends. At the landing a steam donkey loads
     logs onto a flatcar. Log being yarded through stumps. CU flatcars moving
     with logs. LS sunset over Vancouver Island.*

317. FOLLOWING A HAZARDOUS CLIMB, MEMBERS OF THE ALPINE CLUB
     OF CANADA CONQUER SUMMIT OF MOUNT PRESIDENT, YOHO VALLEY,
     B.C. (1920's)
     p.c. Fox Movietonews (Fox #728-C1207)
     l. 80'   g. 35mm   t. b+w   s. si.
     d.   *
     ph. *
     c.s. Fox Movietonews, N.Y.

                    Shots of mountain climbers climbing and at summit.

318. FOOD FOR THOUGHT. (1921)
     p.c. ASN
     l. 850'   g. 35mm   t. b+w tinted   s. si. w/captions
     d.   *
     ph. *
     c.s. NFA (#6733)

                    The story of salmon fisheries on the west coast.

319. FOR KING AND COUNTRY. (1939)
     p.c. B.C. Government Travel Bureau
     l. 1 reel   g. 16mm   t. colour s. si.
     d.   *
     ph. Clarence Ferris (?)
     c.s. Unknown

                    *"A detachment of Princess Patricia's Canadian Light Infantry leaves Victoria,
                    for active service, 1939."*

320. FORBIDDEN PLATEAU. (1923-1930)
     p.c. National Museum of Canada
     l. 1 reel 800'   g. 35mm   t. b+w   s. si.
     d.   Harlan I. Smith
     ph. Harlan I. Smith
     c.s. BCPM History

The print in the BCPM is not titled or captioned and does not appear to have been edited very closely. Some of the shots are quite dim and poorly exposed. The film band reads FORBIDDEN PLATEAU - HARLAN I. SMITH, and leads to the suspicion that this reel, still containing roll numbers and light flashes, is a workprint just back from the lab. The opening scenes are interesting and show an old bus marked COURTENAY pulling into the town of Courtenay on Vancouver Island and a CPR train, pulled by locomotive #461, arriving at the railway station. Out at sea a ferry hoves into view. In the ocean, some kind of animals are sporting about in the waves - seals perhaps, or sea otters. Two boys playing with a fawn. The remainder of the footage shows trailriders at an assembly point milling about and having their goods packed by an old guide, then setting off into the Forbidden Plateau. There are several shots of the camps made by the riders and many, scenic views of riders, mountains, lakes, flowers, etc. It appears that occasionally the riders are hunting for something on the ground; perhaps some of them are collecting plant specimens.

321. FORCE OF ROCKY BROOKS AND OTHER VICTORIA ITEMS. (1920's-1930's)
    p.c. private
    l.   g. 16mm   t. b+w   s. si.
    d.   *
    ph. J. Bradstock & others
    c.s. via Pacific Cinematheque, Vancouver

> *1930-35 Victoria strongman Rocky Brooks is seen picking up people with his teeth and tearing a pack of cards in half with his bare hands. He grins ferociously. Wonderful!*
>
> *1926 Elk Lake, near Victoria; frozen over. People skating, man picking up a swan, hockey games, crack-the-whip and figure skating.*
>
> *1937-39 Swan Lake, near Victoria, frozen over. People skating.*
>
> *1937-39 Scenes on Mackenzie Avenue, Victoria.*

322. FOREST ADVENTURES. (1930)
    p.c. British Pictures Producers, Ltd.
    l.   g. 35mm   t. b+w   s. sound
    d.   *
    ph. *
    c.s. Unknown

> *"The Canadian Government has been asked to sponsor a talking picture industry in the Dominion by Mrs. A. Carolyn Bayfield of Victoria, B.C., who has a financial interest in British Pictures Producers, Limited, which has a studio in Victoria. That Company has just turned out its first production, FOREST ADVENTURES." (Canadian Moving Picture Digest, 13 Sept., 1930. p.9)*

323. FOREST FIGHTERS OF THE SKIES. (1927-1929)
    p.c. CGMPB
    l. 2 reels   g. 35mm   t. b+w   s. si. w/captions
    d.   *
    ph. *
    c.s. Unknown

> *This film was produced for the Dominion Forest Service, The Department of the Interior, Ottawa, and the location of the various scenes is not given. The description is as follows: "An informative film depicting how Canada protects her forests from the ravages of fire by aerial patrol and service. The film shows the operations of air stations engaged in this work, views of the aerial patrol over our forest areas and how fire fighting equipment is transported to scenes of conflagrations by air and how fires are actually fought by the aerial forest protection forces." It's not known if any of this was filmed in British Columbia.*

324. FOREST FIRE AT COURTENAY, B.C.   (1938)
    p.c. Universal Newsreel (#3046x, Roll 3)
    l. 376'   g. 35mm   t. b+w   s. si.
    d.   *
    ph. ASN
    c.s. USNA

               "Radio operator at work. Sailors from HMCS FRASER at work on pump. Cat.
               Church service. Brush and logs burning. Men working in brush. Pan of
               burning area. Watering same. Navy on the job."

325. FOREST FIRES AT COURTENAY, V.I.   (1938)
    p.c. Fox Movietonews (Fox #35-417)
    l. 500'   g. 35mm   t. b+w   s. sound
    d.   *
    ph. ASN
    c.s. Fox Movietonews, N.Y.

               "Fires burning in forests, Men walking through forest, cutting snag. Pan
               of fires behind trees. Man at radio equipment keeping in touch with other
               station in fire area. Sailors from HMCS FRASER working pump. Cat at work
               making a fire trail. Snags burning."

326. FORESTRY REEL NO. 38.   (1938)
    p.c. B.C. Forest Service
    l. approx. 400'   g. 16mm   t. colour s. si.
    d.   *
    ph. George Melrose & others
    c.s. B.C. Dept. of Forests

               The B.C. Dept. of Forests has often selected footage from its earlier pro-
               ductions to include in later productions, and this reel contains extra bits
               from both THE GREAT FIRE OF 1938 and THE COWICHAN LOG. There is, on this
               reel, a good 2-foot long HA view of Duncan's main street circa 1938.

327. FOUR HUNDRED THOUSAND FEET OF DOUGLAS FIR IS LOADED ON
    SS VICTORY FOR GREAT BRITAIN, VANCOUVER, B.C. (1923)
    p.c. Fox Movietonews (Fox #463.14-3641)
    l. 25'   g. 35mm   t. b+w   s. si.
    d.   *
    ph. Len H. Roos
    c.s. Fox Movietonews, N.Y.

               "Pan of ship. Barge at side of ship. Loading ship. Putting lumber in hatch."

328. FOUR INCH SNOWFALL GIVES CITY SECOND SNOWIEST CHRISTMAS
    IN TWENTY-FIVE YEARS, VANCOUVER, B.C. (1934)
    p.c. Paramount (Lib. #4150) NL 399
    l.   g. 35mm   t. b+w   s. si.
    d.   *
    ph. *
    c.s. Sherman Grinberg, N.Y.

               "Moving shot down snow covered drive. Kids sleigh riding. Moving shot of
               kids throwing snowballs at cameraman. General & CU shots snow-laden trees.
               CU frozen robin in treetop. Kids rolling giant snowball. Frozen golfcourse.
               Two people feeding sea gulls on edge of shore."

329. FOX NEWS CAMERMAN INVADES NATURAL HAUNTS OF SEA LIONS
    BRINGING AN AMAZING PICTURE TO THE WORLD, NORTHERN
    BRITISH COLUMBIA. (n.d.)
    p.c. Fox Movietonews (Fox #411.3712-C1328)
    l. 125'   g. 35mm   t. b+w   s. si.
    d.   *
    ph. *
    c.s. Fox Movietonews, N.Y.

               "MLS rocky coast and sea lions. SCU sea lions on rocks and in water. CU
               same. LS herd. SCU bunch in water. CU bunch of baby sea lions on rock.
               LS sea-lions on rocks and in water."

330. FOX NEWS SECURES ONLY PICTURES OF KAIKYU MARU WRECK, 120
MILES NORTH OF VANCOUVER, WHEN JAP FREIGHTER STRIKES SHOAL,
HELMCKEN ISLAND, B.C. (1926)
p.c. Fox movietonews (Fox #090.1-B4999)
1. 100'   g. 35mm   t. b+w   s. si.
d.   *
ph. Jos. T. Mandy
c.s. Fox Movietonews, N.Y.

>"LS of wreck, mountains in b.g. Closer shot of same. LS of wreck, trees in
>f.g. LS wreck with the SALVAGE KING alongside. CU cable fastened to tree.
>CU SALVAGE KING and wreck. SCU Capt. Yhorii and officers on beach. Salvagers
>jettison the cargo. LS of wreck."

331. FRASER RIVER BREAKS THROUGH GOMLEY DYKE AND INUNDATES
DISTRICT, NICOMEN ISLAND, B.C. (1920's)
p.c. Fox Movietonews (Fox #090.1-C1880)
1. 25'   g. 35mm   t. b+w   s. si.
d.   *
ph.   *
c.s. Fox Movietonews, N.Y.

>"LS house in flooded field. The island is occupied by soldier settlers who
>fight the flood. Pan of the flooded district."

332. FRAZER CANYON (C.P.R.R.). (1899)
p.c. American Mutoscope and Biograph Co.
1. 63'   g. 35mm (16mm available) t. b+w   s. si.
d.   *
ph. G.W. (Billy) Bitzer
c.s. NFA

>Originally shot in 35mm, this film was taken by a stationary camera mounted
>ahead of a CPR locomotive travelling through the Fraser Canyon. It shows
>telegraph poles along the track, tunnels, bridges, and coolies scrambling
>out of the way as the train travels through, as well as mountain and river
>scenery and, of course, the tracks dead ahead. (FRAZER CANYON was copyrighted
>in May 1902).

333. FRAZER CANYON, EAST OF YALE, B.C. (1899)
p.c. American Mutoscope and Biograph Co.
1.   g. 35mm   t. b+w   s. si.
d.   *
ph. G.W. (Billy) Bitzer
c.s. Unknown

>Scenes of the Fraser Canyon near Yale, B.C., shot with a stationery camera,
>operated by Billy Bitzer, on a flatcar ahead of a locomotive. (Copyrighted
>in May 1902). No copy appears to have survived.

334. FRENCH CRUISER JEANNE D'ARC, TRAINING SHIP FOR YOUNG
OFFICERS, WELCOMED TO DOMINION, VANCOUVER, B.C. (1935)
p.c. Paramount (Lib. #4163) NL 401
1.   g. 35mm   t. b+w   s. si.
d.   *
ph.   *
c.s. Sherman Grinberg, N.Y.

>"SCU pan of cruiser at dock. SCU follow Captain & French Consul going aboard.
>Torpedo gun swings out for action. Back shot of crew handling 75 (?) gun.
>Ship at dock."

335. FRESH FROM THE DEEP. (1922)
p.c. Canadian Government Motion Picture Bureau (#73)
1. 746'   g. 35mm   t. b+w   s. si. w/captions
d.   *
ph.   *
c.s. NFA (28mm, 16mm), BCPM History (35mm)

>"This film treats of the various methods used in catching the British Columbia
>halibut. Over 200,000 lbs. of fresh fish are shipped daily from Prince Rupert.

This picture deals intimately with every phase of the work."

A man waving beside three stretched halibut skins. Map of B.C. showing coast to Kodiak Island in Alaska. Aboard a fishboat men clean and gut a halibut, dress it for packing and salt it away for shipment. Fishboats alongside a cannery or processor's wharf at Prince Rupert. Halibut being lifted out onto the wharf. Men in hold loading halibut into net. In more southerly waters, a small halibut boat at sea and description of how to catch the fish. Fisherman chucks a barrel-buoy overboard, followed by a coil of line, and he makes ready to feed out the long-line. The long-line is paid out slowly, with bundles of hooks, or "skates" being baited before they slip under the sea. LS and CU of halibut being pulled in over the side. Halibut in the hold. In northern waters, small boats are taken to the fishing ground by larger boats on their decks, then lowered into the sea where they hoist sail & row to their area. A large boat from Seattle arrives, lowers its boats onto the ocean, and they row away with two men in each. The line is let out by hand over the stern, then hauled in by hand. The mother ship picks up the small boats, their crews and their catch and sails away. LS Prince Rupert from the sea. Crowded wharfside scene with many fishboats. Halibut being lifted by net onto a wharf. Men on deck unloading the fish. Halibut being received in interior of packing shed, and being placed in fresh ice in crates. The lids are nailed securely and the crates are wheeled away to the Prince Rupert railway station where the crates are loaded into a refrigerator car. A fifteen car train, "The Fish Express", leaves Prince Rupert hauled by GRAND TRUNK PACIFIC locomotive #603. In immediate b.g. is a sign reading: KELLY DOUGLAS & CO. LTD. - PLAYER'S NAVY CUT CIGARETTES. The train approaches, then cut to caboose moving away.

336. FROM ALL OVER THE VAST CARIBOO COUNTRY COWBOYS, COWGIRLS,
RANCHERS AND INDIANS GATHER FOR THE BIG WILLIAMS LAKE STAMPEDE,
WILLIAMS LAKE, B.C. (1920's)
p.c. Fox Movietonews (Fox #751.11-C1199)
1. 100'   g. 35mm   t. b+w   s. si.
d.   *
ph. Jos. T. Mandy
c.s. Fox Movietonews, N.Y.

"Riding wild steers & unbroken ponies. Crowds. Rodeo events. Indians dance and make merry all through the night."

337. FROM SEA TO SEA - REEL 1. (1920's)
p.c. CNR
1. at Chisholm's, 206'(16mm) g. 35mm t. b+w s. si. wi/captions
d.   *
ph. *
c.s. Jack Chisholm (C 746 b+w roll 1); NFB (1920-N-11-1)

MS steamship with three funnels. MS steamship LADY NELSON. Ice fields from deck of boat, ice cliffs. Good shots of Canadian Steamships cruise ship LADY NELSON, and others, in port, being loaded, sailing, etc. from Vancouver. Shots of halibut and salmon fleet in port and at sea, of individual boats hauling in fish, of trawlers and small boats. Map of Vancouver Island. (at NFB, a shot of the Canadian Coat of Arms). Good, though bumpy, low level aerials of Victoria and Vancouver. In Victoria, there are shots of the Parliament buildings, street scenes, cars, people, golf course, parks and gardens. MS shipping, passenger liner and ferry. Scenes in Vancouver of Stanley Park, swimming pool and street scenes. Vancouver CNR Station. Various shots of passenger trains drawn by steam engines pulling past camera, engineers smiling, interior of a dining car. Travelling shot of coast from ship. Travelling shots of canyons and tunnel, from a train, and of Okanagan Valley. In NFB print only, there is an MS of an apple orchard, of lumberjacks felling a fir tree, of logs sliding down a chute and hitting the water, and logs being sawn up into planks. Good shots of lake, of fishermen, fish struggling, being scooped up with a net. Moose swimming away from camera. MS hunter with dead deer and CU dead grizzly bear. MS totem poles & medicine man in ceremonial attire.

338. FROM SEA TO SEA. (1936 and 1937 - two versions)
    p.c. ASN (#B-696) and, later, CGMPB
    1. 1 reel   g. 35mm   t. b+w   s. sound
    d.   John McDougall
    ph. *
    c.s. NFA

       A promotional film for the CPR with narration written by Margot Blaisdell
       and voiced by Corey Thompson. The description is as follows: "A travelogue
       across Canada from coast to coast by train, taking in most of the principal
       cities. In addition to scenes of Halifax, Saint John, Quebec, Montreal,
       Ottawa, Toronto, Winnipeg, Regina, Calgary, Edmonton, Vancouver and Victoria,
       there are fine views of Niagara Falls and of the Canadian Rockies at Banff
       and Lake Louise."

       This is not the same film as the one by the same name made for the CNR during
       the 1920's. In 1937 the CGMPB apparently re-edited, or at least acquired
       ASN's silent negative and added their own sound track, probably for the pur-
       pose of deleting the references to the CPR, and placed this new version, still
       called FROM SEA TO SEA, in their own catalogue.

339. FROM THE PRAIRIE TO THE SEA - TRAIN LOAD OF GRAIN SER-
    PENTINES THROUGH ROCKIES TO THE PACIFIC, KICKING HORSE PASS,
    B.C. & VANCOUVER, B.C. (1927)
    p.c. Fox Movietonews (Fox #462.8-B7400)
    1. 40'   g. 35mm   t. b+w   s. si.
    d.   *
    ph. *
    c.s. Fox Movietonews, N.Y.

       "Looking ahead from top of freight cars as train crosses bridge and goes
       through tunnels. LS of a freighter pulling out with a load of grain for
       Japan. (NOTE:- snow & mountains in train scene)."

340. FROM VANCOUVER, CANADA, TO SYDNEY, AUSTRALIA, IN SIXTY SECONDS,
    VANCOUVER, B.C. (1924)
    p.c. Fox Movietonews (Fox #663.1-A718, A719)
    1. 297'   g. 35mm   t. b+w   s. si.
    d.   *
    ph. Len H. Roos
    c.s. Fox Movietonews, N.Y.

       "LS RMS NIAGARA at dock in Vancouver. Shot of passengers going aboard. Pass-
       enger's car coming aboard. Crowds on dock. Ship leaving Vancouver. Van-
       couver's skyline." End of Vancouver part; the passengers eventually disem-
       bark in Sydney, Australia.

341. FRUIT AND ITS MARKETING. (1930's)
    p.c. probably CGMPB
    1. approx. 400'   g. 35mm   t. b+w   s. si.
    d.   *
    ph. *
    c.s. Unknown

       The film depicts the growing and marketing of peaches and strawberries in
       Canada, although a specific region is not identified. "Picking peaches, the
       cherry harvest, overhead irrigation, cultivating strawberries, machine grading
       fruit, Government cold storage system." Made before 1935.

342. FUNCTIONAL TRAINING CLASSES. DEMONSTRATIONS BY ARMLESS VETERANS
    OF THE CANADIAN ARMY SHOWING HOW THEY CAN CARRY ON BOTH AT WORK AND
    PLAY,VANCOUVER, B.C. (1920)
    p.c. Fox Movietonews (Fox #003.705-1714)
    1. 45'   g. 35mm   t. b+w   s. si.
    d.   *
    ph. British - American Film Co.
    c.s. Fox Movietonews, N.Y. & NFB (1920-FG-195)

       "In carpenter shop. Artificial limbs. Farming. Rowing. Using brooms. Play-
       ing pool."

343. THE FUNERAL OF JOE FORTES, ENGLISH BAY LIFESAVER, MUCH BELOVED
FRIEND OF VANCOUVER CHILDREN, VANCOUVER, B.C. (1922)
p.c. Fox Movietonews (Fox #201-8937)
l. 100'   g. 35mm   t. b+w   s. si.
d.   *
ph. Bernard O. Dewey
c.s. Fox Movietonews, N.Y.

> *"The procession coming down Main Street. Inspector of mounted Police, Hood, followed by Elks Band, Chief of Police and civic authorities. The rowboat which Joe used as a lifesaver follows hearse filled with flowers. At the ceremony many people add to the mass of flowers. Small child places wreath on Joe's grave." See No. 102.*

344. THE FUR TRAPPER. (1925-1926)
p.c. Fox Film Corporation, N.Y. (#729.25)
l. 6 rolls   g. 35mm   t. b+w   s. si.
d.   *
ph. Byron Harmon
c.s. 20th Century - Fox (?)

> *ROLLS 1 & 2: "Material in these two rolls was shot originally for THREE DOORS AWAY, and is marked so on the negative. It consists of scenery in Canadian mountains, of a dog team passing across snow fields, a cabin, a river, and sunset over pine trees.*
>
> *ROLLS 3 & 4: "Some additional THREE DOORS AWAY material, and men sitting on the porch of a store. Mountain seen through frame of trees, farm in a forest, valley. CU of a bear. Bringing furs to post. Scenes of trapping. Water scenes, with rowboat going downstream. Bear cub CU.*
>
> *ROLLS 5 & 6: "Deer CU. Log cabin. Stream. Making snowshoes (the trapper himself), canoeing. CU of animal in tree. Deer in forest. Trapper, settlement."*
>
> *No actual location is given for this footage. Most or all of it may have been shot in Alberta.*

345. FURTHERING CANADA'S TRADE IN THE ORIENT. (pre 1926)
p.c. CGMPB
l.   g. 35mm   t. b+w   s. si.
d.   *
ph. *
c.s. Unknown

> *Part of the HOW IT IS DONE IN CANADA series, and probably containing scenes of the port of Vancouver, etc.*

346. THE GAME IS UP. (1935)
p.c. ASN/ASS (#B-665)
l. 1 reel   g. 35mm   t. b+w   s. sound
d.   Gordon Sparling
ph. Bill Oliver
c.s. NFA, NFB

> *CANADIAN CAMEO NO. 33. "A sport of kings and mountain-goats is alpine climbing. But where even the goat refuses to trust his sure-footedness, man stubbornly clambers on. THE GAME IS UP is the screen story of a climb in which every moment makes you hold your breath. Thousands of feet below - a sheer drop - are the haunts of man. Away above is victory. And, hanging on by tooth and nail, crampon and ice-pack, the mountain climbers wriggle and claw their way cloudwards. Majestic Mount Tupper, in the Canadian Rockies, is the exciting conquest in THE GAME IS UP."*
>
> *THE GAME IS UP is a re-edited version of the CGMPB film CLIMBING MOUNT TUPPER produced in 1934. How this came to be was explained by the director, Gordon Sparling, in 1977: "CANADIAN CAMEO NO. 33 was made up from the multi-reel silent CLIMBING MOUNT TUPPER. Bill Oliver provided me with a lot of good atmospheric information for the narration. In the early days of the CANADIAN CAMEO Series we were glad to acquire spectacular items to keep up our promised monthly releases to theatres. B.E. Norrish (our president) made an informal deal with his great friend J.C. Campbell, Director of Publicity for the National Parks. Several of their silent non-theatrical films were lying around without much circulation. But they contained some terrific nature and wild life footage*

which needed tighter editing and presentation. The deal was that in exchange
for our laboratory processing Parks Branch negative, we could make blue prints
and combine any of it to make subjects for theatrical release as we saw fit.
The only stipulation was that J.C. Campbell had to approve our sound versions,
and our credit titles always carried the line: 'By special arrangement with
the National Parks of Canada'. We got some excellent subjects and they got
wide publicity."

347. GERMAN CRUISER KARLSRUHE AT VANCOUVER, B.C. (1935)
    p.c. Hearst Metrotone News; Can no. 277, Roll no. 4
    1. 600'   g. 35mm   t. b+w   s. sound
    d.   *
    ph. ASN
    c.s. Hearst Metrotone News, N.Y.

        "Thousands inspect the German cruiser KARLSRUHE. Police have difficulty in
        controlling crowd. Sailors live up to reputation of sweetheart in every
        port. The KARLSRUHE docks at the Ballantyne Pier. At six A.M. sailor's day
        starts with exercises, scrubbing and polishing."

348. GLACIERS OF BRITISH COLUMBIA. (1920's)
    p.c. Bray
    1.   g. 28mm   t. b+w   s. si.
    d.   *
    ph.   *
    c.s. Unknown

        "Beautiful scenic pictures of snow-capped mountain peaks, glaciers, and ice-
        choked rivers of British Columbia." (From a Province of Ontario Catalogue
        of 28mm films published in May, 1927)

349. GLADSTONE MURRAY, MANAGER OF CANADIAN BROADCASTING CORPORATION,
    SPEAKS IN VANCOUVER, B.C. (1937)
    p.c. Hearst Metrotone News; Can no. 632, Roll no. 3
    1. 770'   g. 35mm   t. b+w   s. sound
    d.   *
    ph. ASN
    c.s. Hearst Metrotone News, N.Y.

        "Interior of new 5000-watt transmitter. New tower and new building. Murray
        speaks."

350. GOBBLERS. (before 1935)
    p.c.   *
    1. 1 reel   g. 35mm   t. b+w   s. si.
    d.   *
    ph.   *
    c.s. Unknown

        "An account of the great turkey farms of Western Canada, and the co-operative
        collection of poultry for the winter market." No specific mention of British
        Columbia.

351. GOOD-BYE TO ALL THAT. (1930)
    p.c. CGMPB
    1. 967'   g. 35mm   t. b+w   s. si. w/captions
    d.   Bill Oliver
    ph. Bill Oliver
    c.s. NFA & NFB

        Produced for the National Parks Bureau. The film recounts a trip by pack
        train from Jasper National Park to Mount Robson in Mount Robson Provincial
        Park, B.C. (The NFB copy is 330' 16mm)

352. GOOD OLD FASHIONED PICNIC, VICTORIA, B.C. (1914)
    p.c.   *
    1.   g. 35mm   t. b+w   s. si.
    d.   *
    ph.   *
    c.s. NFA (Taylor reel 106)

        THE SIR RICHARD MCBRIDE PICNIC: Hundreds of Victorians in attendance. Shots
        of baby contest, three-legged race, barrel race, wheelbarrow race, tug-o-war
        with highland laddie straining everything for the cause. Good CU's of people
        attending.

353. GOVERNMENT AND FREIGHT OFFICIALS MAKE A TOUR OF THIS
     HARBOUR AND INSPECT ITS SHIPPING FACILITIES, VANCOUVER, B.C.
     (1924)
     p.c. Fox Movietonews (Fox #007.336-B4041)
     1. 40'   g. 35mm   t. b+w   s. si.
     d.   *
     ph. Len H. Roos
     c.s. Fox Movietonews, N.Y.

          *"Officials aboard PRINCESS LOUISE. Pan ships in harbour. SCU Sir James
          Lougheed and F.W. Peters with ship's captain." (Peters was CPR Superinten-
          dent at the time)*

354. GOVERNMENT BUILDS BIG ELEVATOR FROM BASEMENT TO ROOF
     IN RECORD TIME OF 16 DAYS, VANCOUVER, B.C. (1924)
     p.c. Fox Movietonews (Fox #313.6-B4686)
     1. 35'   g. 35mm   t. b+w   s. si.
     d.   *
     ph. Len H. Roos
     c.s. Fox Movietonews, N.Y.

          *"LS building with scaffolding on side. Taking down forms. Various shots of
          workmen finishing up, one showing harbour in b.g."*

355. GOVERNMENT, CITY AND HARBOUR OFFICIALS ATTEND FORMAL
     OPENING OF PROSPECT POINT SIGNAL STATION, VANCOUVER,
     B.C. (1923)
     p.c. Fox Movietonews (Fox #358.4-B1698)
     1. 35'   g. 35mm   t. b+w   s. si.
     d.   *
     ph. Len H. Roos
     c.s. Fox Movietonews, N.Y.

          *"LS PRINCESS PATRICIA coming through the Narrows. Dedication of Sailor's
          Home Contribution Box, formerly a German mine. H. McGowan, Inspector of
          Police, is shown signal shutter."*

356. GOVERNMENT STEAMER TAKES SUPPLIES TO LONELY PLACES WHERE
     LIGHTHOUSE KEEPERS GUARD VESSELS FROM THE ROCKS, ALONG
     THE BRITISH COLUMBIA COAST. (1925)
     p.c. Fox Movietonews (Fox #358.2-B6218)
     1. 60'   g. 35mm   t. b+w   s. si.
     d.   *
     ph. *
     c.s. Fox Movietonews, N.Y.

          *"Shot of deck of government boat. LS of lighthouse through rigging. Surf
          breaking on rocks. LS small boats en route to lighthouse. Crane hoists
          supplies from small boats. Pretty scene through rigging of clouds and sea-
          gulls flying. LS supply boat and hoist. High shot supply boat loading crane.
          Seagulls fly close past. Gulls dive for food. Good shot of the lighthouse.
          Surf and seagulls on rocks."*

357. GOV. GENERAL IS NEW CHIEF RAINBOW AFTER VERY COLOURFUL CEREMONY BY
     VANCOUVER ISLAND INDIANS, VICTORIA, B.C. (1927)
     p.c. Fox Movietonews (Fox #201-B7942)
     1. 120'   g. 35mm   t. b+w   s. si.
     d.   *
     ph. Jos. T. Mandy
     c.s. Fox Movietonews, N.Y.

          *"High shots of procession of canoes. High shots of canoes. SCU of the chiefs
          awaiting the arrival of Lord and Lady Willingdon. Names included are David,
          Saanich Chief; Michael, Saanich Chief; Lt. Gov. Bruce; Miss Mackenzie."*

358. GRADING AND PACKING APPLES - VANCOUVER WINTER FAIR. (1928)
     p.c. B.C. Dept. of Agriculture
     1. approx. 100'   g. 16mm   t. b+w   s. si.
     d.   *
     ph. *
     c.s. PABC

7

This film is a section of a 400' reel beginning with VARIOUS SHOTS OF BOUCHIE
LAKE FAIR - 1948. It contains shots of girls and conveyor belts, grading and
packing apples, lots of CU'S. Crates being sealed and labels stuck on. Shot
of a couple holding up two huge apples. Others come along and pose with the
apples.

359. GRAIN ELEVATORS WORKING TO CAPACITY CONTINUE TO CREATE NEW
     RECORDS FOR PACIFIC COAST SHIPMENTS, VANCOUVER, B.C. (1929)
     p.c. Fox Movietonews (Fox #313.6-C8530)
     1. 90'   g. 35mm   t. b+w   s. si.
     d.   *
     ph. Beesley
     c.s. Fox Movietonews, N.Y.

          Shots of docks, grain filling ships.

360. GRANVILLE STREET FIRE, VANCOUVER, B.C. (1919)
     p.c. *
     1. (125' 16mm)   g. 35mm   t. b+w   s. si.
     d.   *
     ph. *
     c.s. NFA (Taylor reel 138)

          "A disastrous fire rips through the downtown business section of the City,
          creating endless destruction and pouring clouds of dense smoke over the City.
          Shots of the firemen at work, pumping water onto the blaze, of spectators
          sitting aboard wall watching the smoke and flames, of destroyed section of
          the City and a view of the Albany Hotel which was damaged by the blaze."
          Research has failed to turn up a fire of this description in Vancouver in
          1919.

361. GRASS HOCKEY (REMINDS US OF LACROSSE) AS IT IS PLAYED
     IN WINTER ON THE WEST COAST, VANCOUVER, B.C. (1924)
     p.c. Fox Movietonews (Fox #726-B4694)
     1. 60'   g. 35mm   t. b+w   s. si.
     d.   *
     ph. Len H. Roos
     c.s. Fox Movietonews, N.Y.

          "Mounted Police team VS UBC team. Shots of the game."

362. GREAT CROWD ATTENDS EASTER SUNRISE SERVICE ON SUMMIT OF MOUNT
     TOLMIE, VICTORIA. B.C. (n.d.)
     p.c. Fox Movietonews (Fox #050.55-C1949)
     1. 25'   g. 35mm   t. b+w   s. si.
     d.   *
     ph. Len H. Roos
     c.s. Fox Movietonews, N.Y.

          Worshippers on Mt. Tolmie.

363. THE GREAT FIRE OF 1938. (1938)
     p.c. B.C. Forest Service
     1. approx. 400'   g. 16mm   t. colour s. si.
     d.   George Melrose
     ph. George Melrose
     c.s. B.C. Dept. of Forests

          "Showing the terrors of the fire at Campbell River, Vancouver Island, in 1938,
          the efforts of hundreds of men in fighting it, and the terrible damage done
          to homes, property, and thousands of acres of timber. This is the most ser-
          ious forest fire ever recorded on the Island." Originally THE GREAT FIRE
          was 800' long, but a number of pieces have been cut out of it to make other
          films. There are still excellent shots of fire-fighting operations, of the
          forest burning, men working with hand tools and bulldozers, and animals flee-
          ing the flames. Near the end there is a shot of the site of the burnt-down
          Forbes Landing Hotel. See FORESTRY REEL NO. 38 for additional scenes, No.
          326.

364. GREAT HERD OF CARIBOU SWIMMING YUKON RIVER, SELWYN,
     B.C. (1927)
     p.c. Paramount News (Lib. No. 383) NL 32
     1.   g. 35mm   t. b+w   s. si.
     d.   *
     ph.   *
     c.s. Lost

                    "Very fine picture."

365. GREAT INTEREST SURROUNDS RAISING OF ORPHAN COUGARS, A
     RECENT ADDITION TO THE STANLEY PARK ZOO, VANCOUVER,
     B.C. (1923)
     p.c. Fox Movietonews (Fox #411.317-3559)
     1. 30'   g. 35mm   t. b+w   s. si.
     d.   *
     ph. Len H. Roos
     c.s. Fox Movietonews, N.Y.

                    Shots of cubs at zoo.

366. GREAT INTERNATIONAL HIGHWAY - VANCOUVER TO MEXICO -
     OPENED WITH AN IMPOSING CEREMONY, CLOVERDALE, B.C.
     (1923)
     p.c. Fox Movietonews (Fox #321.5-B2072)
     1. 35'   g. 35mm   t. b+w   s. si.
     d.   *
     ph. Len H. Roos
     c.s. Fox Movietonews, N.Y.

          *"Crowd. John Oliver, B.C. Premier - CU - speaking. Dr. W.H. Sutherland,
          Minister of Public Works for B.C., cutting tape. Semi CU. Crowd and high-
          way."*

367. THE GREAT NATURAL INDUSTRIES OF CANADA. (1917)
     p.c. Dept. of Trade and Commerce, Exhibits and
          Publicity Bureau - Ottawa
     1. 1 reel   g. 35mm   t. b+w   s. si. w/captions
     d.   *
     ph. Essanay Film Mfg. Co., Chicago
     c.s. Unknown

          *One of the first films made by the newly created Exhibits and Publicity Bureau
          under B.E. Norrish. The film has been lost but this description remains:
          "An educational and industrial film showing many phases of the lumberman's
          life as it is in New Brunswick, Quebec, and British Columbia. A lumber drive
          is shown on the Nashwaak. Lumbering operators are shown on the St. Maurice
          River and in British Columbia. The journey of the big logs of the latter
          province from birthplace to mill is clearly depicted."*

          *It is interesting that the Essanay Film Mfg. Co. of Chicago copyrighted this
          film on December 11, 1917. Essanay was in fact hired to make six promotional
          films for the Department of Trade and Commerce one of which was THE GREAT
          NATURAL INDUSTRIES OF CANADA, and one would expect that full rights would
          remain with the Department. Perhaps Essanay was granted distribution rights
          in the U.S., or maybe they just pirated a copy. At any rate, the Dept. of
          Trade and Commerce was so pleased with the films that it decided to set up
          its own motion picture unit. Norrish was placed in charge and lured away
          Essanay's best cameraman, Arthur Reeves. This became the first government
          motion picture unit in the world.*

368. GREEN TIMBERS NURSERY SCENES. (late 1930's)
     p.c. B.C. Forest Service (Reels 18, 23, 25 & 8)
     1. approx. 1000' g. 16mm   t. colour s. si.
     d.   *
     ph.   *
     c.s. B.C. Dept. of Forests

          *Shots of Green Timbers tree nursery in New Westminster, built and run by the
          B.C. Forest Service, showing methods employed for extracting seeds, planting
          and growing the seedlings in seed beds, root pruning, lifting, baling and
          shipping to the planting site. Also shows planting crews in action and method*

of planting seedlings.

Some of this footage was probably shot in the early 1940's. The Forest Service later compiled a film titled FOREST FARMING, about Green Timbers, which is mentioned in their 1947 Catalogue.

369. GRENFELL MISSION SCHOOLS AND TOTEM POLES OF B.C.   (n.d.)
    p.c. *
    1. 100'   g. 35mm   t. b+w   s. si.
    d.   *
    ph. *
    c.s. NFA (#75-12-25)

370. GROWING CANADIAN APPLES.   (1926-1929)
    p.c. CGMPB
    1. 2 reels   g. 35mm   t. b+w   s. si. w/captions
    d.   *
    ph. *
    c.s. PABC and NFB (outs)

This film was made for the Fruit Branch of the Department of Agriculture, Ottawa, and filmed in Ottawa and at orchards in Quebec, Ontario and British Columbia. The two reels in the PABC are 16mm and each about 400' long. Part One deals with the initial stages of growing and training an apple tree, and shows the steps taken from cross-pollination to seed selection and on to budding, pruning and top working. Part Two begins with bridge grafting and then shows entomologists in the laboratory studying insects that attack fruit trees. The various life stages of the coddling moth are examined and explained. A horse-drawn spray unit moves through an orchard in British Columbia. The need for three and four applications of spray are explained and the stages at which it must be done. Scene of a spray and dust manufacturing plant. Blossom time in Quebec. Cultivating around the bottom of the trees to prevent the moisture being sapped by weeds. A grass mulch around the base of trees. Wire protectors around the trunk to discourage mice from eating the bark. Scenes of irrigation works in British Columbia, showing sluices, flumes, etc. costing about $14.00 per acre-foot. Thinning fruit in July, remaining apples left about six inches apart. Ripe apple in sunlight. Much of this film was shot on an experimental farm, probably in Ottawa.

371. GUIDED AND MISGUIDED.   (pre 1939)
    p.c. *
    1. approx. 400'   g. 16mm   t. b+w   s. si.
    d.   *
    ph. *
    c.s. Unknown

"Travelogue of Canadian Rockies, showing Mt. Assiniboine, Lake Louise."

372. GYPSY TOUR.   (1930)
    p.c. CGMPB
    1. 1 reel   g. 35mm   t. b+w   s. si. w/captions
    d.   *
    ph. *
    c.s. NFB Archives P.B. 89 (1920-DN-71)

"A modern caravan of "Seattle Mountaineers" arrives at the western gate of the Canadian Rockies, their happy hunting ground for the year. HA several cars moving through a canyon, crossing a wooden bridge. Shot of car entering gate leading to three Parks: KOOTENAY, YOHO and BANFF National Parks. Tilt down sheer rock wall to car speeding along highway. Shot of tourist on horseback at Lake Louise Lodge, of tourists advancing in single file through the trees. In a camp near Lake O'Hara, tourists eat, saw wood, relax, etc. Various shots of a party of mountaineers climbing. Excellent pan of mountains from mountain top. Shot of party returning to camp, gathering souvenirs, enjoying a last campfire. Shot of Takakkaw Falls and the Kicking Horse Canyon." (Filmed in 1929)

373. GYRO CLUB IS AT IT AGAIN! THIS TIME IT'S A PLAYGROUND
     DONATED TO HAPPY CHILDHOOD, VANCOUVER, B.C. (1923)
     p.c. Fox Movietonews (Fox #322.6-B2073)
     1. 35'   g. 35mm   t. b+w   s. si.
     d.   *
     ph. Len H. Roos
     c.s. Fox Movietonews, N.Y.

                    Kids playing on the new apparatus.

374. GYROCLUB SENDS NEWSBOYS OFF FOR A DAY'S OUTING AND SELL
     THE PAPERS WHILE THEY ARE GONE, VANCOUVER, B.C. (1924)
     p.c. Fox Movietonews (Fox #754-A4048)
     1.   g. 35mm   t. b+w   s. si.
     d.   *
     ph. Len H. Roos
     c.s. Fox Movietonews, N.Y.

          *"Gyros Charles "Hoop" Garrett and "Mickey" McKay selling papers. Ship leaves
          with newsies. Their picnic on Bowen Island."*

375. GYRO MEMBERS HUSTLE PAPERS TO GIVE NEWSIES A DAY OFF FOR PICNIC AT
     BOWEN ISLAND, VANCOUVER, B.C. (1923)
     p.c. Fox Movietonews (Fox #047.9-B2078)
     1. 65'   g. 35mm   t. b+w   s. si.
     d.   *
     ph. Len H. Roos
     c.s. Fox Movietonews, N.Y.

          *"Rev. Art Sovereign checking boys. Boys leaving aboard ferry CAPILANO for
          Bowen Island. Businessmen selling papers. Boys enjoying picnic."*

376. HAIR RAISING IS ATTAINED BY EXPERTS WHO NEGOTIATE WORLD'S
     LARGEST SKI JUMP, REVELSTOKE, B.C. (1920's)
     p.c. Fox Movietonews (Fox #732.3-C1540)
     1. 40'   g. 35mm   t. b+w   s. si.
     d.   *
     ph. Len H. Roos
     c.s. Fox Movietonews, N.Y.

          *"High BS man going off jump. CU same. Same high BS. Nels Nelson, world's
          amateur champion, jumping twice. "Now we'll all go down! Are you there?
          It's a spill!" - coming down the jump with a camera from the top to a spill
          at the bottom."*

377. HALIBUT FLEET LEAVES VANCOUVER, B.C. (1937)
     p.c. Hearst Metrotone News
     1.   g. 35mm   t. b+w   s. sound
     d.   *
     ph. ASN
     c.s. Hearst Metrotone News, N.Y.

          *"LS & SCU of fleet at pier. Two fishermen fixing gear. Al Hager wishing good
          luck to skipper. Boats getting ready to leave and coming out of harbour and
          heading out to sea. Fleet on way. CU Al Hager."*

378. HARVESTING, INSPECTION AND TRANSPORTATION OF GRAIN IN
     CANADA. (1916)
     p.c. Dept. of Trade and Commerce, Ottawa
     1. 3 reels/45 min. g. 35mm   t. b+w   s. si.
     d.   *
     ph. Essanay Film Mfg. Co., Chicago.
     c.s. Unknown

          *One of the films shot by the Essanay Company of Chicago for the Department of
          Trade and Commerce in 1916 which eventually led to the CGMPB being formed in
          1922. The film has long been lost but the original description reads: "A
          film of the grain fields of Western Canada depicting every step in the pro-
          gress of the grain, from the Western plains to ocean front and featuring grain
          inspection at Winnipeg, methods of transporting, handling, threshing and mill-
          ing of wheat. An interesting educational film." Inasmuch as Vancouver is a
          grain shipping port it can be assumed some of the scenes for this film were
          shot in B.C.*

379. HARVESTING PEAS. (late 1920's)
     p.c. B.C. Dept. of Agriculture
     l. approx. 225'   g. 16mm   t. b+w   s. si.
     d.   *
     ph. *
     c.s. PABC

> Depicts the harvesting of peas, almost all mechanically, from cutting to processing, showing automatic shucker and sorting by girls.

380. HAULING IN SALMON NETS AT VANCOUVER, B.C. (pre 1910)
     p.c. Charles Urban Trading Co., for CPR (?)
     l. 75'   g. 35mm   t. b+w   s. si.
     d.   *
     ph. *
     c.s. Unknown

> "A lively scene with the fishing fleet on the Fraser River, showing hundreds of salmon struggling in the nets as they are drawn to the surface and emptied of their contents." George Kleine Catalogue, 1910. p.72.

381. HEALTH SPRINGS ETERNAL. (prob. 1939)
     p.c. CGMPB
     l. 1 reel   g. 16mm   t. colour s. si. w/captions
     d.   *
     ph. *
     c.s. Unknown

> "Picturing the health-giving qualities of the hot mineral springs in Banff, Jasper, and Kootenay National Parks in the Canadian Rockies. Natural colour views of the bath-houses and swimming pools situated in attractive surroundings at Banff, Jasper and Radium Hot Springs. A mimeographed commentary for lecture purposes accompanies this film." Produced for the National Parks Bureau.

382. HEAPS OF LUMBER. (late 1930's)
     p.c. B.C. Bureau of Industrial and Tourist Development
     l. 2 reels   g. 16mm   t. b+w   s. si. w/captions
     d.   *
     ph. Clarence Ferris (?)
     c.s. Unknown

> "British Columbia's sawmilling industry; portable, semi-portable, stationary sawmills are depicted on location. British Columbia manufactured machinery is a feature of this important phase of our logging and lumber industry."

383. THE HEART OF THE OKANAGAN. (1929)
     p.c. B.C. Dept. of Agriculture (reel 19)
     l. approx. 475'   g. 16mm   t. b+w   s. si. w/captions
     d.   *
     ph. *
     c.s. PABC

> "A Birdseye View of our Okanagan Fruit Section."

> Long Lake, on way to Kelowna from Vernon by train. Storefront window (Kelowna ?) of Department of Agriculture, Horticultural Branch, office. A shipping point on Okanagan Lake - wharfs, buildings, ferry dock. Vineyards, irrigation systems. Orchard without irrigation, and with flume and furrow irrigating. Alfalfa growing in orchard to help crop. Horse-drawn spraying of fruit trees. Tank-truck with arsenate of lead and sprayers. Coddling moth traps pulled up into trees, buckets of poison. Banding trees against coddling moths. Thinning pears and plums. Wire screen protectors around base of tree to deter mice. Greenhouses. Family life - kids, mother, car and dog in the Okanagan.

384. 'HEART SMASHING" LIFEGUARDS FOUND ON B.C. COAST FORM
     SNAPPY DRILL SQUAD, VANCOUVER, B.C. (1925)
     p.c. Fox Movietonews, (Fox #099.41-B2065)
     l. 75'   g. 35mm   t. b+w   s. si.
     d.   *
     ph. Len H. Roos
     c.s. Fox Movietonews, N.Y.

"Boy CU blowing bugle - Robert Jewett. Girls sleeping, waking up, going back to sleep, are finally awakened by Jewett. Girls get rifles & form line. Girls drilling. Girls attack the boy. CU attack. All sitting together and singing."

385. HEAVY VESSEL IS LIFTED CLEAR OF WATER AS IF IT WERE A TOY BY
     NEW MILLION DOLLAR DRYDOCK, VANCOUVER, B.C.   (1924)
     p.c. Fox Movietonews (Fox #356.3-B4691)
     1. 60'   g. 35mm   t. b+w   s. si.
     d.   *
     ph. Len H. Roos
     c.s. Fox Movietonews, N.Y.

             "LS ship CAMOSUN entering drydock. Pan bilge blocks. Electric pumps. Men watching gauges. Stop motion depth gauges. SCU prop awash. SCU men examining props."

386. HENRY FORD'S NEW CAR DRIVES COAST TO COAST FROM HALIFAX TO
     VANCOUVER.   (1925)
     p.c. *
     1. 519'   g. 16mm, 35mm originally t. b+w   s. sound (added later) & captions
     d.   *
     ph. *
     c.s. Visnews (#4867/74) & NFA

             The British Columbia section of this film is 60'. The sound track is musical (piano and banjo); there are no spoken words.

             After reaching Calgary, the car, clearly marked FORD, drives into the foothills of the Rockies, lurching up rocky roads into the mountains. The car arrives at an arch reading: GATEWAY TO ROCKY MOUNTAIN NATIONAL PARK. The car continues through the mountains to another arch reading: KOOTENAY NATIONAL PARK, where a man smoking a pipe comes out and greets the driver of the car. The car continues along perilous canyon roads. At Donald, flanged wheels are placed on the car and it continues its journey on the CPR tracks through the mountains and two tunnels. A train roars past the car on parallel tracks, billowing smoke and cinders. At Greely the car returns to the road on wheels. Mayor Taylor of Vancouver offers congratulations and is presented with a letter from Mayor Kenny of Halifax. The car arrives in Vancouver, streetcars passing, traffic. The car drives down onto a sandy beach covered with driftwood. A big black dog looks on. A cloudy, maybe rainy, day. The car hesitates, then places front wheels in the ocean.

387. HENRY MACRAE AND PARTY SET SAIL FOR SIAM TO COLLECT
     DATA ON TRIBE OF CANNIBALS, VANCOUVER, B.C.   (1923)
     p.c. Fox Movietonews (Fox #201-B1522)
     1. 15'   g. 35mm   t. b+w   s. si.
     d.   *
     ph. Len H. Roos
     c.s. Fox Movietonews, N.Y.

388. HERE AND THERE WITH THE BIRDS OF CANADA.   (1932)
     p.c. CGMPB
     1. 1 reel   g. 35mm   t. b+w   s. si. w/captions
     d.   Bill Oliver
     ph. Bill Oliver
     c.s. NFA, NFB

             Produced for the National Parks Bureau, Ottawa. Depicts bird life in Canada. Included are swans, Blue Goose, Canada Goose, Lesser Snow Goose, Wood Duck, Great Blue Heron, flicker, Tree Swallow, mallard, Peregrine Falcon, and sandpipers. Some of these birds may have been photographed in British Columbia. (At NFA-320' 16mm; at NFB-338' 16mm)

389. HIGH LEAD LOGGING.   (1939)
     p.c. ASN (#B748)
     1.   g. 35mm   t. b+w   s.
     d.   *
     ph. *
     c.s. *

HIGH LEAD LOGGING was never completed or released. It was intended to show logging methods on Vancouver Island.

390. HIGHWAY BUILDING AT SALMON ARM. (late 1930's)
    p.c. private
    l. 465'   g. 16mm   t. colour s. si.
    d.   *
    ph. R.F. Mackenzie
    c.s. NFA

Mr. Mackenzie was employed for many years by the General Construction Co. of Vancouver.

A rock-crushing site; asphalt is loaded into a truck. At road-building site the truck dumps the asphalt. The road is graded and rolled.
MIXERS. The camera records the operation of 2 giant machines, fed by trucks. The trucks dump gravel from crusher into huge scoops which raise the rock, dumping it into the mixer which digests it until processed, at which time the asphalt is moved in buckets to a hopper under which sits a truck ready to receive the material. The truck, once filled, drives away and is replaced by another. There are several complete shots of this operation.

Scene of workyard in wild country where crushers and other machines are operating and filling trucks. Truck dumping fill with grader waiting. Grader grading. Shovel working. Blasting a sandy bluff. Huge machine moving dirt overhead, seems to be scraping it off the road then dumping it behind. Heavy dirt movers assemble on the road and drive by. Many shots of carryalls, from many angles. Forms and some already-poured cement posts for a large bridge across a gully. Many·good shots of a crane moving dirt.

391. HIKERS MARATHON AT GROUSE MOUNTAIN NEAR VANCOUVER. (1935)
    p.c. Fox Movietonews (Fox #26-83)
    l. 700'   g. 35mm   t. b+w   s. sound
    d.   *
    ph. ASN
    c.s. Fox Movietonews, N.Y.

"200 competitors start, shots along route, finish at Grouse Mountain Chalet. W.W. Kelley presents prizes to Mrs. Margaret Gale, Mrs. F. Wright, Mr. Mike Pasternick, Marcus McMillan and John Foster. Norman Pearson presents Junior Fire Wardens prize. Charles Wilkinson gets special silver Warden's badge."

392. HIMALAYAS OF THE GREAT NORTH WEST. (1935)
    p.c. Pathé
    l. 307'   g. 35mm   t. b+w   s. sound
    d.   *
    ph. *
    c.s. EMI Pathé Film Library

A film about climbing in the St. Elias Range in the Yukon. Scenes include: Map of Yukon with St. Elias marked. Shot of steam locomotive and train carrying explorers to Carcross over the White Pass & Yukon line. Map again. Aerials shots over snowy mountains and glaciers. Aerial view of glacier and mountains in b.g. Plane lands at a tent on one vast glacier. Dog teams carry explorers into the mountains, two disappearing on the left. Three men climb across the glacier. Men pushing sleds up a snowy cliff with dogs following through heavy drifts. A camp at the 5000' mark. Tents and skis and sleds outside; snow blowing. A blizzard; exterior shot of camp in blizzard. Weather clears and they mush on through the snow. A new camp is made at the base of a huge bluff. At over 8000' they reach the highest point on the glacier. The explorers proceed across the glacier toward the Alaskan boundary. They climb rock faces with packs on their backs. They cross "Hell's Half Mile" to the other side of the glacier. They finally succeed in traversing the entire icefield. Narrator and storm sounds.

393. HMS COLOMBO AND USS MISSISSIPPI VISIT VANCOUVER. (1929)
    p.c. Fox Movietonews (Fox #551.01-D0836)
    l. 180'   g. 35mm   t. b+w   s. si.
    d.   *
    ph. Beesley
    c.s. Fox Movietonews, N.Y.

"Sailors from the two warships engage in boat racing, log tilting & other contests

394. HOLIDAY SEEKERS HIKE TO FAMILIAR RETREATS WHEN OLD SOL
     BECOMES INVITING, NORTH VANCOUVER, B.C. (1923)
     p.c. Fox Movietonews (Fox #007.1361-B8304)
     1. 70'   g. 35mm   t. b+w   s. si.
     d.   *
     ph. Len H. Roos
     c.s. Fox Movietonews, N.Y.

               "Young men & girls boarding ferry to North Vancouver and visiting Capilano
               Canyon Suspension Bridge, Seymour Canyon & Lynn Creek Canyon and Falls."

395. HOLLY FARM, VICTORIA, B.C. (1936)
     p.c. Fox Movietonews (Fox #36-211)
     1. 500'   g. 35mm   t. b+w   s. sound
     d.   *
     ph. ASN
     c.s. Fox Movietonews, N.Y.

               "Pickers returning with baskets full to packing house. Pickers emptying bas-
               kets. Men packing. LS of farm. Farm men working in foreground. Working
               on trees. Trees of holly. CU of a branch. Samples inspected and explain (sic)
               to worker the various types of holly. Wagon loaded. Leaving farm with load
               for shipment."

396. HOLLYWOOD STARS VS VANCOUVER: CRICKET, VANCOUVER, B.C. (1936)
     p.c. Universal Newsreel #2979 X 5
     1. 93'   g. 35mm   t. b+w   s. si.
     d.   *
     ph. William Deighton
     c.s. USNA

               "LS field. Errol Flynn & C. Aubrey Smith watching. Frank Lawton returning
               from play. Nigel Bruce and Smith talking. Flynn playing. Shot of pitch,
               City and Harbour in distance with the EMPRESS OF CANADA tied up at the pier.
               No finish to game - camera jammed."

397. HON. J.H. KING, MINISTER OF PUBLIC WORKS, OPENS NEW
     $3,000,000.00 DRYDOCK FOR PACIFIC OCEAN SHIPS, VANCOUVER,
     B.C. (1925)
     p.c. Fox Movietonews (Fox #356.3-B6790)
     1. 40'   g. 35mm   t. b+w   s. si.
     d.   *
     ph. Herron
     c.s. Fox Movietonews, N.Y.

               "King speaking. Crowd. Sir Henry Thornton speaking. Ship in dock, KING
               CLOSINS."

398. HON. LO. CHONG, NEW CHINESE CONSUL GENERAL FOR CANADA,
     ON HIS ARRIVAL AT VICTORIA. B.C. (1920's)
     p.c. Fox Movietonews (Fox #201-C1524)
     1. 10'   g. 35mm   t. b+w   s. si.
     d.   *
     ph. Len H. Roos
     c.s. Fox Movietonews, N.Y.

               Shots of Lo Chong arriving.

399. HOP PICKERS HOP OFF FOR THE HOP FIELDS: HARVEST SCENES IN ONE
     OF THE LARGEST FARMS, SARDIS, B.C. (1924)
     p.c. Fox Movietonews (Fox #422.02-A4119)
     1.   g. 35mm   t. b+w   s. si.
     d.   *
     ph. Len H. Roos
     c.s. Fox Movietonews, N.Y.

               "Pan shot of hop fields. Shot down hop vineyards. 850 Indians are employed.
               CU of Indian flapper picker. CU baby in hammock. CU of old Indian woman
               picking. Baled and ready for the British market."

400. HORSE RACING SEASON OPENS AT BRIGHOUSE PARK, VANCOUVER,
     B.C. (1921)
     p.c. Fox Movietonews (Fox #755.11-3981)
     1. 20'   g. 35mm   t. b+w   s. si.
     d. *
     ph. D.C. Davey
     c.s. Fox Movietonews, N.Y.

              "Crowds. Horse racing."

401. HORSE LOADING FOR KLONDIKE, VANCOUVER, B.C. (1898)
     p.c. *
     1. 18'   g. 35mm (16mm available) t. b+w s. si.
     d. *
     ph. *
     c.s. NFB (1900-FG-3)

              "Crated horses are loaded from dock to steamship while crowd looks on."
              Quality of original 35mm print not good.

402. HOUSES FOR WIDOWS, VANCOUVER, B.C. (1919)
     p.c. Fox Movietonews, (Fox #090.2-4896)
     1. 25'   g. 35mm   t. b+w   s. si.
     d. *
     ph. Len H. Roos
     c.s. Fox Movietonews, N.Y., NFA, Chisolm, and NFB (1920-FG-196)

              "First house completed under Federal Soldier's Housing Scheme. Cosy interior,
              happy owner."

403. HOW AN ENTHUSIASTIC BALL FAN PAID HIS WAGER WHEN HE LOST HIS BET
     ON THE WORLD'S SERIES, VANCOUVER, B.C. (1923)
     p.c. Fox Movietonews (Fox #071.71-B2931)
     1. 60'   g. 35mm   t. b+w   s. si.
     d. *
     ph. Len H. Roos
     c.s. Fox Movietonews, N.Y., and NFB (1920-170-FG-4)

              "Rodger Imhof bet on N.Y. Giants (who lost series to Yankees). Shot of Imhof
              getting peanut at peanut stand. VCS: peanuts in hands, line drawn on side-
              walk and shots of Imhof rolling peanut along wet street (raining) with tooth-
              pick. Shot of winner Bill Alrem (R) and loser Rodger Imhof (L)."

404. HOW SALMON ARE CAUGHT. (1922)
     p.c. Dept. of Trade and Commerce Exhibits and
          Publicity Bureau, Ottawa
     1. 1 reel   g. 35mm   t. b+w   s. si. w/captions
     d. *
     ph. *
     c.s. NFA (28mm copy) & NFB (1920-DN-33)

              "Canada's fisheries are the most extensive in the world. The salmon industry
              on the British Columbia coast is replete with commercial romance. This film
              deals with four distinct methods of catching fish. The film was taken along
              the Pacific Coast from Vancouver to Prince Rupert and shows the beautiful
              scenery of the region."

              The NFB outs give an idea of the contents of this film, which shows how sal-
              mon are caught by gill-netting, purse-seining, fish weirs or traps, and trol-
              ling. The scenes include: LS small boats in the river. Pan along small boat,
              several men at oars, nets, etc. Follow shot of small boat moving in circle
              as men lower the nets from the stern. LS same. Men rowing strenuously to-
              ward beach, holding net up to show salmon flapping in shallow water. LS
              flotilla of small craft trolling. Boat trolling, man hauling salmon in. LS's
              weirs. Men unloading traps. HA of fish by the hundreds filling the frame,
              splashing in the water, pouring over the gunwales of boat as men empty trap.
              Boating shot of small seiner laying net. MS net sliding over stern. Men
              hauling in net, brailing fish into hold. Men sorting fish in full hold.
              Seiner on way home.

405. HRH PRINCE HENRY HERE AFTER CONFERRING HONOUR UPON
     EMPEROR OF JAPAN AS KING'S REPRESENTATIVE, VICTORIA,
     B.C. (n.d.)
     p.c. Fox Movietonews (Fox #201-D0643)
     l. 100'   g. 35mm   t. b+w   s. si.
     d.   *
     ph. *
     c.s. Fox Movietonews, N.Y.

               "Tour of city and Esquimalt dry dock."

406. HUDSON'S BAY COMPANY CELEBRATES ITS BIRTH. (1920)
     p.c. *
     l. approx. 400' g. 28mm   t. b+w   s. si.
     d.   *
     ph. *
     c.s. NFA

               "In 1670 King Charles the Second granted a charter to the Hudson's Bay Com-
               pany and 250 years later we see the same Company celebrating the event with
               pomp and pageant in the five great cities of the Canadian West: Winnipeg,
               Edmonton, Calgary, Vancouver and Victoria, a commercial record without para-
               llel in the history of the West."

407. HUDSON'S BAY SCHOONER LADY KINDERSLEY BRINGS FURS FROM HERSHELL
     ISLE, WORTH A QUARTER OF A MILLION DOLLARS, VANCOUVER, B.C. (1922)
     p.c. Fox Movietonews (Fox #463.46-3046)
     l. 23'   g. 35mm   t. b+w   s. si.
     d.   *
     ph. Len H. Roos
     c.s. Fox Movietonews, N.Y.

               "Shots of schooner coming into port. Schooner passing, showing crew in fore-
               ground."

408. HUGE PASSENGER LINER IS WRECKED ON ROCKS. THE PALATIAL
     EMPRESS OF CANADA RUNS ASHORE IN STRAITS NEAR VICTORIA, B.C.
     (1929)
     p.c. Fox Movietonews (Fox #090.1-D2650)
     l. 109'   g. 35mm   t. b+w   s. si.
     d.   *
     ph. Piper
     c.s. Fox Movietonews, N.Y.

               "Angular views of great three-stack steamer stranded on rocks. Salvage ships
               struggling to free her. Aerial shots."

409. HUNDREDS OF PHEASANTS RELEASED TO REPLENISH SUPPLY OF GAME BIRDS
     IN THE FRASER RIVER VALLEY, PORT COQUITLAM, B.C. (1929)
     p.c. Fox Movietonews (Fox #412.86-C9349)
     l. 120'   g. 35mm   t. b+w   s. si.
     d.   *
     ph. *
     c.s. Fox Movietonews, N.Y.

               "Men unloading crates from auto. CU man holding pheasant and lets it go.
               L & CU shots of men releasing pheasants."

410. HUNTER'S PARADISE. (1936)
     p.c. CGMPB
     l. 1 reel   g. 35mm   t. b+w   s. si. w/captions
     d.   Jack Brewster & Bill Oliver
     ph. Jack Brewster & Bill Oliver
     c.s. NFB (1930-FG&DN-310); NFB also has outs (1930-DN-302)

               A hunting trip in the Rocky Mountains, shot mostly in British Columbia. "Shot
               of Jack Brewster appearing from behind a rock, peering through binoculars.
               Various LS's of mountain goats, mountain sheep, a bull moose, a magnificent
               ram seen in MLS, and a black bear in a tree. Various closer views of sheep
               grazing, mountain sheep, mountain goats. Hunters and guides travelling trail
               on horseback, making camp in Eagle's Nest Pass. Shots of hunters with dead
               moose, men displaying large antlers of moose. Two men moving away with

antlers on a pack horse. LS's of herd of caribou. LS herd scattering as man in f.g. shoots bull. Men approach dead caribou, display antlers. Another sequence of a caribou being shot. Hunters arriving in camp with caribou antlers on pack horses. Hunters approaching dead grizzly, inspecting it. MCU dead bear. Two hunters and two dead mountain goats. Two hunters with two ram's heads. Hunters posing in group with their trophies, hunters around campfire. hunters on their way back to civilization. Med. front view of Jack Brewster."

The outs contain many shots of caribou, hunters, moose antlers, heads of moose, caribou, deer and mountain sheep, pack train on trail, hunters in camp, one with head of large ram, cow moose and calf running down an incline, waterfall, female campers fishing, displaying their catch, dead moose with man and woman looking on. There are also scenes of winding a 16mm movie camera, MLS of a dead moose, hunters heading for camp with moose head tied to pack animal, camp, hunters displaying moose head, mountain sheep on rocky slope, mountain scenery, hunter moving by and pausing, grizzly bear in death throes, dead bear.

411. HUNTERS SECURE RECORD BAG OF DUCKS AND GEESE ON CRUISE OF
     KNIGHT'S INLET, B.C. (1922)
     p.c. Fox Movietonews (Fox #729.21-3267)
     l. 92'   g. 35mm t. b+w   s. si.
     d.   *
     ph. Len H. Roos
     c.s. Fox Movietonews, N.Y.

"Running the Yuculta Rapids on board the RIO BONITA. Hunters hunting. Views of Mt. Gibson. Birds on deck of ship."

412. HUNTING THE WILD GOAT. (1920?)
     p.c. Byron Harmon
     l.   g. 35mm t. b+w   s. si.
     d.   *
     ph. Byron Harmon
     c.s. Unknown

Filmed near the Lake of the Hanging Glaciers in the Selkirk Mountains.

413. HUNTING WITHOUT A GUN. (1933)
     p.c. CGMPB
     l. 1 reel   g. 35mm t. b+w   s. si. w/captions
     d. Bill Oliver
     ph. Bill Oliver
     c.s. NFA

Contains scenes photographed in British Columbia. Likely a compilation of Rocky Mountain animal footage from Bill Oliver's many trips into the Rockies. The descriptions reads: "A wonderful wild animal picture, showing deer, moose, grizzly bear and other species in their natural surroundings in Canada's National Parks." Produced for the National Parks Bureau, Ottawa.

414. HYDRAULIC MINING, CANADIAN ROCKIES. (1922)
     p.c. Fox Movietonews (Fox #011-4601)
     l. 49'   g. 35mm t. b+w   s. si.
     d.   *
     ph. M. Nelson
     c.s. Fox Movietonews, N.Y.

"Hydraulic mining as it is carried on in the Canadian Rockies, various shots."

415. ICE SKATING AND HOCKEY PLAYING AT VANCOUVER, B.C. (1919)
     p.c. Fox Movietonews (Fox #732.1-2118)
     l. 28'   g. 35mm t. b+w   s. si.
     d.   *
     ph. Brazill
     c.s. Fox Movietonews, N.Y.

416. IMMENSE PONTOONS, TO BE USED IN NEW MILLION DOLLAR DRY-
     DOCK, SUCCESSFULLY LAUNCHED, VANCOUVER, B.C. (1923)
     p.c. Fox Movietonews (Fox #356.3-B3015)
     l. 50'   g. 35mm   t. b+w   s. si.
     d.   *
     ph. Len H. Roos
     c.s. Fox Movietonews, N.Y.

                    Location not identified.

417. IMPRESSIVE CEREMONY IS TRIBUTE TO CANADA'S SONS AS GOV.
     GEN. BYNG UNVEILS A NEW MEMORIAL, VANCOUVER, B.C. (1925)
     p.c. Fox Movietonews (Fox #095.8-A8125)
     l. 90'   g. 35mm   t. b+w   s. si.
     d.   *
     ph. Herron
     c.s. Fox Movietonews, N.Y.

                    *"Long shot of the memorial draped in flag. CU of the arch of memorial. BS
                    of the vets in line two deep, in uniform facing memorial. CU group of sol-
                    diers with wreath. Byng of Vimy greets man he led in France."*

418. IMPRESSIVE CEREMONY MARKS UNVEILING OF HANDSOME MEMORIAL
     ERECTED BY CANADIAN PACIFIC RAILROAD IN HONOUR OF ITS
     EMPLOYEES WHO FELL IN THE WAR, VANCOUVER, B.C. (1922)
     p.c. Fox Movietonews (Fox #095.8-4435)
     l. 28'   g. 35mm   t. b+w   s. si.
     d.   *
     ph. R.J. Errington
     c.s. Fox Movietonews, N.Y.

                    *"Unveiling the monument. Crowd standing bareheaded during ceremony. Hon.
                    W.C. Nichol, Lt. Gov., makes address. Places wreath on memorial."*

419. IN AND AROUND ATLIN, B.C. (1927)
     p.c. private
     l. 200'   g. 16mm   t. b+w   s. si.
     d.   *
     ph. *
     c.s. NFA (#2859)

                    *"Towns and inhabitants in and around the site of the famous Atlin gold rush
                    in northern B.C. and southern Yukon. Supply ships. Skiers. Hunters. Gold
                    mining."*

420. INAUGURATION OF NEW TCA ROUTE, VANCOUVER, B.C. (1937)
     p.c. *
     l.   g. 35mm   t. b+w   s. sound
     d.   *
     ph. *
     c.s. NFB (1930-DN-296) (1930-FG-295)

                    *"Shots of ground crew loading mail into a TCA Lockheed 14H in Vancouver.
                    Shots of dignitaries handing letter to the pilot, aircraft in b.g. TCA liner
                    taking off." Part of CANADIAN AIR NEWS. If, in fact, the date of this foot-
                    age is 1937, this plane is more likely a Lockheed Electra 10A, the first
                    passenger plane purchased by the newly formed airline, and the first TCA plane
                    to go into regular service - between Vancouver and Seattle on September 1,
                    1937. Lockheed Lodestars, which carried 14 passengers, four more than the
                    Electras, were purchased and put into trans-Canada service in 1941.*

421. IN CANADA'S FJORDS (or THE NORWAY OF CANADA) (1923-1930)
     p.c. National Museum of Canada
     l. 1 reel   g. 35mm   t. b+w   s. si. w/captions
     d.   Harlan I. Smith
     ph. Harlan I. Smith
     c.s. Unknown

                    *"The fjords, forest clad mountains, glaciers, and innumerable waterfalls of
                    Bella Coola region, midway between Vancouver and Prince Rupert, are so like
                    Norway that a colony of Norwegians have settled in this district so much
                    like their homeland. They live on farms, but also work at logging and fishing.*

Many of them have brought their gala native costumes with them and various handicrafts, and it is of interest that they have not lost their artistic skill in needlework, wood carving, and painting."

422. IN THE CANADIAN ROCKIES: FOX NEWS CAMERAMAN SCENES SOME
UNUSUAL PICTURES IN THE VICINITY OF THE GREAT ASULKAN
GLACIER, ASULKAN RIVER. (1926)
p.c. Fox Movietonews (Fox #007.325-B7457)
1. 200'   g. 35mm   t. b+w   s. si.
d.   *
ph. Bill Oliver
c.s. Fox Movietonews, N.Y.

> *"SCU of the Asulkan River and Glacier looking up the River. CU of the Asulkan Glacier. SCU of the fireweed. SCU of a girl on horseback riding through the woods. LS of the Ramparts, Mt. Dome and Asulkan River. SCU of a bear hunting for berries. LS of Mt. Swanzy and the Glacier, stream running past in f.g. The warden's cabin and his daughter in dog cart in the f.g."*

423. IN THE LAND OF THE HEAD HUNTERS. (1914)
p.c. Edward S. Curtis
1.   g. 35mm   t. b+w   s. si. w/captions
d.   Edward S. Curtis
ph.   Edward S. Curtis
c.s. original print lost

> *See: IN THE LAND OF THE WAR CANOES.*

424. IN THE LAND OF THE WAR CANOES. (1914, 1974)
p.c. originally by Edward S.Curtis, latterly the
     Burke Museum, University of Washington, Seattle.
1. 47 min.   g. 35mm (16mm available) t. b+w s. sound
d.   originally Edward S. Curtis
ph.   Edward S. Curtis
c.s. National Museum of Man, Ottawa; University of Washington
     Press and BCPM Eth.

> *As IN THE LAND OF THE HEAD HUNTERS, this film premiered at the Moore Theatre in Seattle on December 7, 1914. After playing both Seattle and New York for two years, the 35mm prints disappeared and were presumed lost. In 1947, George I. Quimby, a curator in the Anthropology Department of the Field Museum in Chicago, discovered some reels of original nitrate film shot by Curtis, which had been donated to the Museum, and took them with him when he went to the University of Washington. Twenty years later Professor Quimby and his colleague Bill Holm set to work examining and editing the original footage. It was transferred to 16mm stock and an authentic soundtrack added as a complement to Curtis' breathtaking photography. This re-editing has been as faithful to Curtis' notes as possible.*
>
> *IN THE LAND OF THE WAR CANOES is not really a documentary film. It is a dramatized tale of romance and magical power, using Kwakiutl Indians on the west coast of Vancouver Island as actors. The canoes, the weapons, the masks, everything is real, and village life is portrayed with accuracy. Curtis' genius is that he was able to <u>begin</u> at this point and transcend the usual travelogue style by revealing the knowledge that the hearts and minds of one race of men are not so very different from those of another. Already famous for his still photographs, which have recently enjoyed a revival, Curtis' reputation was favourably enhanced by his motion picture debut, although he did not make any further films on the west coast.*
>
> *I am grateful to the University of Washington Press for providing the original press release for the premiere:*
>
> *To gain power from the spirit forces, Motana, the son of a great chief, goes on a vigil journey. Through the fasting and hardships of the vigil he hopes to gain supernatural strength which will make him a chief not less powerful than his father, Kenada.*
>
> *First upon a mountain's peak he builds a prayer-fire to the gods. After long dancing about the sacred flames he drops from exhaustion, and in vision-sleep the face of a maid appears in the coiling smoke, thus breaking the divine law which forbids the thought of women during the fasting.*

*Now he must pass another stronger ordeal. Leaving his desecrated fire to go
to the Island of the Dead, he meets Naida, the maid of his dream, and woos
her. She tells him she is promised to the hideous Sorcerer. Motana bids
the maid return to her father and say that when this vigil is over he will
come with a wealth of presents and beg her hand in marriage. Now he renews
his quest of spirit power and tests his courage by spending the night in the
fearful "house of skulls". And to prove his prowess he goes in quest of sea-
lions and then achieves the greatest feat of all--the capture of a whale.*

*Then, for his final invocation to the gods, Motana again builds his sacred
fire upon the heights. While he fasts and dances there about his prayer
fire, the Sorcerer in a dark glade of the forest has gathered about him fellow
workers in evil magic and they sing "short time songs" to destroy him. The
Sorcerer sends his daughter to find Motana and in some way get a lock of his
hair, that they may destroy his life by incantation. This ever-treacherous
plotting woman, on seeing Motana asleep by his fire, becomes infatuated with
him and decides to risk even the wrath of her Sorcerer father and win the
love of Motana. When she awakens him with caressing words, he bids her begone,
as he is thinking not of women, but of the spirits. With angry threats she
departs, but in stealth watches the faster until he drops asleep; then creep-
ing up steals his necklace and a lock of hair, and disappears.*

*Motana, returning, asks his father to send messengers demanding the hand of
Naida. Her father, Waket, replies to the messengers: "My daughter is promised
to the fearful Sorcerer. We fear his magic. If your great chief, Kenada,
would have my daughter for his son's wife, bring the Sorcerer's head as a
marriage gift." With song and shout they start upon the journey and attack
the Sorcerer's village. With song triumphant they return with the Sorcerer's
head; and in great pomp of primitive pageantry, Naida and Motana are married.*

*Even while the wedding dancers make merry, a cloud of tragedy hangs above
them, for Yaklus, the fearful war-chief, returning from a fishing expedition,
learns of the attack and is preparing to avenge the death of his brother, the
Sorcerer.*

*In his magnificent high-prowed canoes he starts upon his war of vengeance.
It is a tribal law that the war party shall destroy all who are met, whether
friend or foe. While they are on their foray, fishing parties and travellers
are encountered.*

*Then they make their night attack upon the village of Motana. Kenada and his
tribesmen give way before the infuriated Yaklus, and amid the smoke and flames
of the burning village Motana is wounded and Naida carried away to captivity.
Yaklus, returning to his village, gives a great dance of victory.*

*In the sleeping hours Naida sends her fellow captive-slave with a token and
message to Motana, who has been revived by the surviving medicine men of his
village. When he receives the message from his bride-wife, Motana calls for
volunteers.*

*By stealth he rescues her. Yaklus in rage starts in pursuit. Motana, hard
pressed, dares the waters of the surging gorge of Hyal, through which he
passes in safety. Great was his "water magic". Yaklus attempts to follow,
but the raging waters of the gorge sweep upon him, and he and his followers
become the prey of the evil ones of the sea.*

425. IN THE SHADOW OF THE ASSINIBOINE. (1936)
     p.c. CGMPB
     1. 1 reel   g. 35mm   t. b+w   s. si. w/captions
     d.   Bill Oliver
     ph. Bill Oliver
     c.s. NFA; NFB (1920-L-15)

          *"A climbing expedition to the summit of Mount Wedgewood, one of Mount
          Assiniboine's neighbours."*

          *"Mounts Assiniboine and Wedgewood offer tempting inducement to mountain
          climbers. Here a girl and her guide attempt to scale these two formidable
          obstacles to man's courage and ingenuity."*

          *Shots include base camp of tents with Mount Assiniboine in b.g. The girl
          and her guide set out, walk toward camera, and move on up the side of Mount*

Wedgewood. Good shots of climbing in rock and snow, and of climbers on the summit. Some shots include Mount Assiniboine, glaciers, etc. Excellent pan of Mount Assiniboine and mountain scenery. MLS of Mount Assiniboine and slow tilt down to base camp. (The copy at the NFA is 345' on 16mm; at the NFB, 353' on 16mm). Produced for the National Parks Bureau.

426. IN THE VALLEY OF THE YOHO. (1919)
     p.c. *
     l.   g.   t.   s.
     d.   *
     ph. *
     c.s. *

                    See IN THE YOHO VALLEY.

427. IN THE WAKE OF CAPTAIN COOK. (1922)
     p.c. Dept. of Trade and Commerce Exhibits
          and Publicity Bureau, Ottawa
     l. 1 reel   g. 35mm   t. b+w   s. si. w/captions
     d.   *
     ph. *
     c.s. Unknown

                    "A unique travelogue film of an aeroplane trip to Nootka Sound, on the northern Pacific coast of Canada, made famous by the intrepid British navigator and explorer Captain Cook and showing its inhabitants, and the many queer features of life in this quaint Indian fishing village, including the Totem poles, images, etc." It is especially sad that this film is lost. It was not even included in the CGMPB catalogue of 1930.

428. IN THE YOHO VALLEY. (1919)
     p.c. Dept. of Trade and Commerce Exhibits and Publicity Bureau, Ottawa
     l. 1 reel   g. 35mm   t. b+w   s. si. w/captions
     d.   *
     ph. *
     c.s. Unknown

                    Also known as IN THE VALLEY OF THE YOHO. The Original description reads: "A scenic film showing the Yoho Valley and Emerald Lake region in Yoho Park. An interesting climb is made with the Alpine Club of Canada over Mount Vice President, across its great glacier, down into the Yoho Valley. Beautiful Twin Falls, Takakaw Falls, and Emerald Lake with its girdle of glorious mountains are featured as is also the camp of the Alpine Club. This film was produced in co-operation with the Dominion Parks Branch of the Department of the Interior."

429. INDIAN HANDICRAFTS OR ARTS AND CRAFTS OF THE COAST INDIANS
     OF BRITISH COLUMBIA. (1923-1930)
     p.c. National Museum of Canada
     l. 1 reel   g. 35mm   t. b+w   s. si.
     d.   Harlan I. Smith
     ph. Harlan I. Smith
     c.s. Unknown

                    Little more is known about this lost film, but presumably it depicts carving techniques, weaving with wool, cedar and spruce roots, and other work by Indians of the west coast.

430. INDIANS FROM ALL PARTS OF WESTERN AMERICA MEET HERE IN
     SPECTACULAR POW-WOW, CRANBROOK, B.C. (1922)
     p.c. Fox Movietonews (Fox #007.434-3365)
     l. 83'   g. 35mm   t. b+w   s. si.
     d.   *
     ph. M. Nelson
     c.s. Fox Movietonews, N.Y.

                    "The camp. CU of Indians. Visitors from 'across the line' wear $500.00 vest. CU of vest. The pow-wow. Riding bronchos."

431. INDIANS, SOUTH SEA ISLANDERS, PIRATES - ALL ARE SEEN AT
     BIG PLAYGROUND FESTIVAL IN BEAUTIFUL STANLEY PARK, B.C. (1925)
     p.c. Fox Movietonews (Fox #751.13-B4669)
     1. 60'   g. 35mm   t. b+w   s. si.
     d.   *
     ph. Herron
     c.s. Fox Movietonews, N.Y.

                    "Kids dressed up & dancing and playing in grass skirts, pirate costumes,
                    etc."

432. INDUSTRIAL BRITISH COLUMBIA. (pre 1910)
     p.c. *
     1. 365'   g. 35mm   t. b+w   s. si.
     d.   *
     ph. *
     c.s. Unknown

                    "Of great general interest and educational usefulness. Mechanical raising of
                    logs from river to saw mills. Panoramas of the workings of coal and copper
                    mines. Indian girls packing salmon, etc." George Kleine Catalogue, 1910.
                    p. 258.

433. INDUSTRY'S ENDLESS WAR IN THE FORESTS. BRITISH TIMBER
     EXPERTS SEE GIANTS FALL IN CANADIAN WOODS, VANCOUVER,
     B.C. (1923)
     p.c. Fox Movietonews (Fox #640.94-7704)
     1. 42'   g. 35mm   t. b+w   s. si.
     d.   *
     ph. Len H. Roos
     c.s. Fox Movietonews, N.Y.

                    "Party on logging train en route to logging operations. Logging train round-
                    ing curves. Party watching logs being loaded. Loading logs. A "high-
                    rigger" tops a master white pine."

434. THE INSIDE STORY. (1938)
     p.c. CGMPB
     1. 1 reel   g. 16mm & 35mm t. b+w   s. sound
     d.   *
     ph. *
     c.s. NFA, BCPM Eth., BFI

                    Propaganda for tinned salmon, showing how carefully the canning is done. The
                    films opens with this caption: "This is the inside story of an important
                    Canadian industry and of a domestic commodity that ranks among the chief pro-
                    ducts annually exported from the Dominion." There is a musical score which
                    is typical of many industrial or "progress" type films. Scenes include sal-
                    mon being brought up in a net and dumped into the hold of a boat. The fish
                    are later lifted into the hold of another boat. CU salmon squirming in the
                    hold. Boats leaving a large cannery town. Two fishermen jump into a large
                    holding area, where the salmon are being kept on ice, and pitch them through
                    a slot into the cannery. CU fish on ice. Interior of cannery - two rows
                    of girls with white aprons and hats processing the fish. CU cans rolling
                    down a wire framework during the processing. More processing. CU cans being
                    lifted by machines. CU cans being labelled. CU top of tin being embossed
                    CANADA. Back to first operation of cannery: a hatch is opened and fish spill
                    out into a trough of running water. MS trough with conveyor belt. LS fish
                    being carried up into plant. Interior of plant showing salmon being gutted,
                    cleaned, headed and tailed by machine. Salmon spill out after being cleaned
                    onto conveyor belts. CU fish being inspected. Shot of girls cleaning salmon
                    manually then placing them on the conveyor belt again. Salmon being inspected
                    by woman. Fish are placed in conveyor buckets which carry them to the slicer.
                    CU slicer. Slices exiting and being packed by girls into cans. Japanese
                    girl skillfully packing cans. CU cans and salmon being cut and packed by two
                    hands. LS girls packing. Open cans move along belts to be inspected, weighed,
                    etc. CU machines placing and clinching lids. CU sealing machine. Cans move
                    along belt to sorting department where Japanese workers place them on large
                    trays and wheel them into huge ovens. Men close the hatches of the ovens.
                    CU valve turning on the steam. CU thermometer at 240°. Back of ovens with
                    man checking machinery. Serious-looking men in inspection laboratory, weigh
                    tins while others are wheeled in. CU tins being weighed. Man puncturing tin

for a vacuum reading. CU vacuum meter showing 11 inches as man punches test cans. CU machines testing texture and men inspecting colour etc. with microscope. Man totals figures on old Marchant adding machine: i.e., a greater volume of sales this year. Shipping room - girls pack tins from trays into cardboard boxes and men wheel boxes to storeroom. A woman in a modern kitchen opens a tin of salmon. She breaks the chunk of salmon apart on a china plate. A salmon casserole revolves on a silver dish. A salmon aspic (?) decorated with asparagus does the same. More shots of cooked salmon in several combinations. The narrator suggests that tinned salmon is better than fresh salmon.

435. THE INSIDE STORY OF YOUR TELEPHONE. (1928)
    p.c. Western Electric Co. for A.T. & T.
    l. 34 minutes   g. 35mm   t. b+w   s. si. w/captions
    d.   *
    ph. *
    c.s. USNA (Main Catalogue #111/M/228)

> *A film about how materials for telephones are secured and processed, from raw material to finished product. Contains scenes of a gold mine in British Columbia, and shows gold being smelted and poured into moulds.*

436. INSPECTION AT VICTORIA BY HUGHES AND MCBRIDE. (1918)
    p.c. *
    l. 850'   g. 35mm   t. b+w   s. si.
    d.   *
    ph. *
    c.s. NFA (McMartin footage reel 4)

> *"Soldiers in kilts on parade. Inspection. Officers talking, etc. Endless parades. Officers on horseback. More parades. Army ambulances lined up. Numerous shots of soldiers parading. MCU of important officer. Officer sitting at desk writing." This film seems suspiciously similar to INSPECTION BY BORDEN, HUGHES AND MCBRIDE, held by the NFB. If they are the same, then the later sections of this film were photographed in England.*

437. INSPECTION BY BORDEN, HUGHES AND MCBRIDE. (1914-1918)
    p.c. In Victoria - ? British Army for latter half
    l.   g. 35mm   t. b+w   s. si.
    d.   *
    ph. in England, British Army
    c.s. NFB (1910-FG-14-18)

> *The scene in Victoria shows Premier Richard McBride and Lt. Gen. Sir Sam Hughes on the steps of the Parliament Buildings. Shots of highlanders parading past the camera, of highlanders and other officers passing by camera, shaking hands with Hughes. Several shots of soldiers parading. This is followed by an inspection by Prime Minister Borden at Shorncliffe, England.*

438. INSPECTION DAY IN ESQUIMALT, B.C. (before 1927)
    p.c. Pathéscope
    l.   g. 28mm   t. b+w   s. si.
    d.   *
    ph. *
    c.s. Unknown

> *"The Lieutenant Governor of British Columbia pays an official visit to Canada's fleet in Pacific waters." (from Province of Ontario Film Catalogue, May 1927)*

439. INTERIOR PROVINCIAL EXHIBITION, ARMSTRONG, B.C. PART 1.
    (1935)
    p.c. B.C. Dept. of Agriculture
    l. approx. 400'   g. 16mm   t. b+w   s. si. w/captions
    d.   *
    ph. *
    c.s. PABC

> *Part II of this film is lost. PART I contains the following: Pan of Armstrong from hill. A celery field at picking time; fields of cabbage and lettuce. Pan of onion field, onions on edges of furrows. President F.B. Cossitt and party in grandstand. Secretary Mat Hassen walking across racetrack. Dr. K.C. MacDonald, Minister of Agriculture, with the Fair Directors. Judging Ayrshires*

and Hereford steers. The famous "Salmon Arm Red Polls" - judging steers.
"A Farmer's Hazard" - one of the Red Polls gets away. More judging and live-
stock processions, Percy French and Sam Shannon judging. The Laird of Fintry,
Captain J.C. Dun-Waters, meets Mgr. Hassen and others. Ayrshire Procession.
Pan of Fairgrounds. Jerseys, Clydesdales. Jim Turner, Cadboro Bay. Clerks
for Judge Hicks of Agassiz. More horses. Kids showing calves. Morris Mid-
dleton judging calves. B.C. Provincial Policeman. Junior Shorthorn Club.
Horse events - riding and jumping. Hon. F.M. MacPherson, Minister of Public
Works, awarding horse prizes.

440. INTERNATIONAL PEACE MEMORIAL TO LATE PRESIDENT HARDING UNVEILED
IN CANADA WITH IMPRESSIVE CEREMONIES, VANCOUVER, BRITISH COLUM-
BIA. (1925)
p.c. Gaumont Graphic (9492)
1. 41'   g. 35mm   t. b+w   s. si.
d.   *
ph. Allison
c.s. Visnews (Video roll 69)

"Crowd scene at monument. CU monument covered in Stars and Stripes and Red
Ensign. Flags raised up to reveal monument. CU bust of Harding's head.
President Moss of the Kiwanis International extols Mr. Harding's ideals of
International friendship, symbolized in the friendly flags raised together -
CU Moss on the podium gesticulating. Cut to both flags being raised up flag-
poles at the same time, side by side."

441. INTERVIEW WITH HON. RANDOLPH BRUCE, CANADIAN MINISTER TO
JAPAN, VANCOUVER, B.C. (1937)
p.c. Hearst Metrotone News; Can no. 938, Roll no. 4
1. 325'   g. 35mm   t. b+w   s. sound
d.   *
ph. ASN
c.s. Hearst Metrotone News, N.Y.

442. INTERVIEW WITH S.F. TOLMIE. (1932)
p.c. Fox Movietonews (Fox #16-210)
1. 375'   g. 35mm   t. b+w   s. sound
d.   *
ph. Roy Hague
c.s. Fox Movietonews, N.Y.

"LS and SCU and CU of S.F. Tolmie of Victoria, British Columbia." Dr. Tolmie
was Premier and leader of the Conservative Party of British Columbia at the
time.

443. INTREPID BRITISH WORLD FLIERS ARRIVE ON HMCS THEIPVAL. CITY
TENDERS HEARTY WELCOME, VANCOUVER, B.C. (1924)
p.c. Fox Movietonews (Fox #544.8-A3955)
1.   g. 35mm   t. b+w   s. si.
d.   *
ph. Len H. Roos
c.s. Fox Movietonews, N.Y.

"CU Major Godfrey & Squadron Leader MacLaren. L-R: Chief Long, MacLaren,
Miss Margaret Stewart, Major A.D. Bell-Irving, and Major Godfrey. Shots of
remains of McLaren's plane, wrecked motor, etc."

444. INVINCIBLE NEW ZEALANDERS SWAMP LOCAL RUGBY TEAM IN THRILLING GAME
BEFORE RECORD CROWD OF 15,000 FANS, VANCOUVER, B.C. (1925)
p.c. Fox Movietonews (Fox #712-B6639)
1. 30'   g. 35mm   t. b+w   s. si.
d.   *
ph. Errington
c.s. Fox Movietonews, N.Y.

"Game, teams & crowd."

445. ISLAND OF ENCHANTMENT. (1930)
    p.c. CGMPB
    1. 883'   g. 35mm   t. b+w. tinted stock   s. si. w/captions
    d.   Bill Oliver
    ph. Bill Oliver
    c.s. NFA (360' 16mm); NFB and BCPM Hist. (two 35mm prints)

            Produced for National Parks of Canada, Department of the Interior, Ottawa.

            *LS pan of Victoria from Mt. Douglas (?). The PRINCESS KATHLEEN, CPR ferry,
            draws into Victoria's Inner Harbour. Crowds leave the ship, crowding down
            the gangways, Captain looking on from bridge, Empress Hotel in b.g. LS
            Empress Hotel, visitors milling about in f.g. Shot from verandah of Empress
            out onto causeway. Parliament Buildings from Empress Hotel. LS two ships
            in drydock in Esquimalt. One of the ships is the PRINCESS ELAINE, the other
            cannot be identified. Salmon being turned out of the hold of a fishing boat;
            fishermen, nets, rain gear; salmon being dumped into a scow. Fishing boat
            at sea, the crew wash down the deck. A huge flora display in a window. A
            woman collecting flowers in a garden. Tropical conservatory in the Empress
            Hotel. Woman in different part of previous garden, possibly at Hatley Park.
            Man and woman in a garden; woman offers man a rose to sniff. Italian and
            Sunken Gardens at Butchart Gardens, with glimpses of house and little gnome
            fishing. Pond and stone bridge in Beacon Hill Park; kids feeding swans.
            Deer browsing on a forest road; a car drives along a paved road through trees.
            a deer in the bush looks up intently. A canoe trip down the Cowichan River;
            four passengers - two white and two Indians, the whites fishing and the In-
            dians navigating with paddles. CU stern Indian with paddle. Many shots of
            canoe on the river and a portage around a waterfall and rapids. They course
            through some rapids and end up in the ocean at the mouth of the river. Shot
            of the beach and waves. In one of the two prints at the BCPM there is a sun-
            set shot over the beach.*

446. JACK BOWDERY 1935-1937. (1935-1937)
    p.c. private
    1. 50'   g. 8mm   t. b+w   s. si.
    d.   *
    ph. J.W. Bowdery
    c.s. contact Pacific Cinémathèque, Vancouver

            *This reel shows Mr. Bowdery and his friends in the 1930's. Of particular
            interest is a scene of Mr. Bowdery and two friends, a young man and young
            woman, at the CPR wharf on the passenger ramp beside the EMPRESS OF CANADA,
            as well as shots of the bow and down the side of the EMPRESS with the harbour
            of Vancouver in the b.g.*

447. JAMES SEED FARM, BALING AT PROCTER, HIKING ON KOKANEE
    GLACIER. (1930's)
    p.c. private
    1. approx. 338'   g. 16mm   t. colour & b+w s. si.
    d.   *
    ph. Rev. George R.B. Kinney
    c.s. NFA, Ottawa

            *colour: James Seed Farm. Fields of daffodils, narcissi, hyacinth, tulips,
            men picking and packing tulips. Summer flowers in field, asters, mums, etc.
            Seed shed with sign: JAMES CANADIAN SEEDS LTD. / RETAIL SEED GROWERS / CATA-
            LOGUES ON REQUEST. Many more seedflower fields. Baling hay at Proctor on
            Kootenay Lake.*

            *b+w: Kids swimming at Proctor. View from Kokanee Glacier, pan mountains.
            (not so good). Goldfish pond. Unidentified people at Proctor. (Camera
            seems to be acting up). Hikers on Kokanee Glacier. Long row of boys and
            girls in sleeping bags and blankets waking up in the morning and smiling.
            Group posing for camera by log huts.*

448. JAPANESE CRUISERS VISIT CANADA, VANCOUVER, B.C. (1933)
    p.c. British Paramount (BPNews Lib. #1880)
    l. 118'   g. 35mm   t. b+w   s. sound
    d.   *
    ph. *
    c.s. Visnews, London

> "Long view of cruiser passing. General view of SS IWATE & sailor at atten-
> tion. Shot from IWATE of cruiser. Canadian officers going aboard. Japanese
> and Canadian officers shaking hands. Canadian sailors leaving pier. Cere-
> mony around memorial. Japanese officer inspecting Canadian soldiers. Jap-
> anese Admiral saluting at memorial."

449. JAPANESE ON WEST COAST, KOOTENAYS, CADETS IN VANCOUVER,
    PETROGLYPHS ON HORNBY ISLAND. (1930's)
    p.c. private
    l. approx. 375' g. 16mm   t. colour & b+w s. si.
    d.   *
    ph. Rev. George R.B. Kinney
    c.s. NFA, Ottawa

> colour: Brady's Beach, near Bamfield, surf rolling in, people swimming.
> People visiting the blow hole. Shots of blow hole. (faded) Trawler (faded).
> Group of Japanese adults and kids all dressed up, western style. Japanese
> girls dressed in traditional costume perform a lovely dance (faded). Bull-
> dozers and other heavy machines work on the Coulee Dam site. Good shot of
> dam. Scenic views near Nelson. Old car perched on a hill overlooking a
> valley. Man feeding bear. Mountains. Many good shots of a chipmunk run-
> ning on road. Kids posing in f.g., young men posing in b.g. They move to
> a tree and measure it with a yardstick. Beautiful old maroon car with second
> car body hitched behind; both fitted with train wheels, moving toward camera
> on railway track. On side of car is painted: M. 600. Young men at Lake
> Kaslo. Youth group from University Hill Church, Vancouver, on beach collec-
> ting rocks and shells. Cook and staff of Cadet camp pose. Cadets in plain
> clothes line up before huts. Cook rings gong, boys come running. Group on
> beach again. Cadets in uniform. Four trucks driving around camp.
>
> b+w: Petroglyphs, outlined in chalk, on Hornby Island - human shapes, birds,
> fish, sun, etc. Very lyrical shots of these wonderful carvings.

450. JAPANESE STEAMER RETURNS TO PORT WITHOUT AID AFTER BATTLING
    TERRIBLE STORMS THAT RAGED 900 MILES OUT, ESQUIMALT, B.C. (1928)
    p.c. Fox Movietonews (Fox #463.14-C7913)
    l. 110'   g. 35mm   t. b+w   s. si.
    d.   *
    ph. Ross Beesley
    c.s. Fox Movietonews, N.Y.

> "Part of gallant crew that brought the crippled ship CHOYO MARU in for re-
> pairs. Various land shots and shots made on board steamer showing broken
> rails. Shots of crew working about, lumber in water."

451. JAPANESE STOWAWAYS ARE SHIPPED BACK TO JAPAN BY RCMP,
    VANCOUVER, B.C. (1923)
    p.c. Fox Movietonews (Fox #610.1-3491)
    l. 26'   g. 35mm   t. b+w   s. si.
    d.   *
    ph. Len H. Roos
    c.s. Fox Movietonews, N.Y.

> "Stowaways and police in front of Canadian immigration detention prison."

452. JAPANESE VISIT VICTORIA & OTHER VICTORIA STORIES. (1913-1917)
    p.c. *
    l. about 715'   g. 35mm   t. b+w   s. si.
    d.   *
    ph. *
    c.s. NFA (#4557-4560)

> 1915 - Japanese fleet in Victoria. Delegates and exhibitions.
> N/D - Parade through Victoria, featuring the band of the 5th Regiment.
> 1913 - Spencer's picnic. Ferry with crowd leaving for ?

1916 - Fire prevention display. Mayor of Victoria.
1917 - Firemen display Hibben building fire and truck pumper.
1917 - Parade and races at picnic of Victoria Park Jockey Club.

453. J.C. PENDRAY IN HIS UNIQUE GARDEN OF STREETS TRIMMED TO RESEMBLE
     BIRDS AND ANIMALS, B.C. (1924)
     p.c. Fox Movietonews (Fox #325.1-B4040)
     l. 50'   g. 35mm   t. b+w   s. si.
     d.   *
     ph. Len H. Roos
     c.s. Fox Movietonews, N.Y.

     Topiary work in Pendray's garden on Belleville St., Victoria.

454. JERSEY BREEDERS OF VANCOUVER ISLAND.   (1936)
     p.c. B.C. Dept. of Agriculture
     l. 250'   g. 16mm   t. b+w   s. si.
     d.   *
     ph. *
     c.s. PABC

     Jersey breeders convene for a day trip to the Cowichan Valley to meet with
     other breeders and visit a Jersey farm in the Valley. There are good shots
     of cars on the Brentwood-Mill Bay ferry, driving on and off. A group of
     breeders and a barn full of Jersey cows. Cloth banner: WELCOME FROM COWICHAN
     JERSEY CATTLE CLUB. Pan across farm, perhaps just south of Duncan, to banner
     over the driveway. Shots of Jersey bulls. Breeders having a glass of beer.
     Shots of Jersey cows and breeders. Ladies at farmhouse - a long buffet table.
     Breeders eating. A little girl with a big cake.

455. JERSEY, LOWER FRASER VALLEY.   (1934 or 1935)
     p.c. B.C. Dept. of Agriculture (Reel 75)
     l. approx. 250'   g. 16mm   t. b+w   s. si.
     d.   *
     ph. *
     c.s. PABC

     A large group of agriculturalists visit the FRASEA DAIRY FARM to inspect the
     cattle, grounds, barns, etc., and to have lunch.

456. JIM BARNES, AMERICAN OPEN GOLF CHAMPION, AND JOCK HUTCHISON,
     BRITISH OPEN GOLF CHAMPION, LOSE FIRST GAME ON CONTINENTAL
     TOUR WHEN DAVE BLACK, SHAUGHNESSY CLUB, AND PHIL TAYLOR, VIC-
     TORIA CLUB, BEAT THEM 2 UP AND ONE TO PLAY, VICTORIA, B.C. (n.d.)
     p.c. Fox Movietonews (Fox #713-C2698)
     l. 60'   g. 35mm   t. b+w   s. si.
     d.   *
     ph. Young's Studio, Victoria
     c.s. Fox Movietonews, N.Y.

     "Eleventh green, seventeenth green, houses & gallery in b.g."

457. JIMMIE MCLARNIN TRAINS FOR LIGHTWEIGHT FIGHT, VANCOUVER, B.C.   (1928)
     p.c. Fox Movietonews (?)
     l.   g. 35mm   t. b+w   s. si.
     d.   *
     ph. ASN (?)
     c.s. NFB (1920-FG-152)

     Several good shots of McLarnin training, punching speedbag, and running
     through Central Park, N.Y. This excerpt is part of Canada Capsule No: 5.

458. A JOB FOR YOU - "TWO FOREST SERVICE CAMPS ON VANCOUVER ISLAND". (1938?)
     p.c. B.C. Forest Service (Forestry reel 70)
     l. approx. 400'   g. 16mm   t. colour s. si. w/captions
     d.   *
     ph. *
     c.s. B.C. Dept. of Forests

     Young men building huts in a nearly completed camp. Fire fighting practice.
     Building a bridge abutment. Splitting shakes with a froe. Snag falling.

Bucking firewood. Men fighting a fire with hand tools and a bulldozer. After fire, men showering, having haircuts and washing up. CU grub - meal on plate. Pay parade. LS scenery on Vancouver Island. This short film was intended to interest young men in a career with the Forest Service, or a summer's employment.

459. JOHN HENRY MEARS AND CHARLES G.D. COLLYER ARRIVE AT NIGHT
AND HOP OFF BEFORE DAYBREAK FOR NEW YORK ON RECORD GLOBE
CIRCLING TOUR, VICTORIA, B.C. (1928)
p.c. Fox Movietonews (Fox #201-C4990)
l. 100'   g. 35mm   t. b+w   s. si.
d.   *
ph. Ross Beesley
c.s. Fox Movietonews, N.Y.

"Shots of the EMPRESS OF RUSSIA and their aeroplane the CITY OF NEW YORK, as well as shots of Mears & Collyer."

460. JOURNALISTS OF B.C. ARE SHOWN SOME RARE SIGHTS AT CHEAKAMUS CANYON AND
BRANDYWINE FALLS. (1925)
p.c. Fox Movietonews (Fox #249.8-B6736)
l. 35'   g. 35mm   t. b+w   s. si.
d.   *
ph. Balts
c.s. Fox Movietonews, N.Y.

Scenic shots.

461. KAMLOOPS - WELLS GRAY PARK. (late 1930's)
p.c. B.C. Bureau of Industrial and Tourist Development,
     later B.C. Government Travel Bureau
l. 1 reel   g. 16mm   t. colour   s. si.
d.   *
ph. C.R.D. Ferris
c.s. Unknown

"The Clearwater District north of Kamloops, B.C."

462. KENNEDY LAKE & WEST COAST, V.I. with INDIANS FISHING
FROM DUGOUTS. (1930's)
p.c. private
l. approx. 350' g. 16mm   r. red & b+w s. si.
d.   *
ph. Rev. George R.B. Kinney
c.s. NFA, Ottawa

b+w: Kennedy Lake. CU logger, A.P.L. Camp 5. Shovel working in forest. Two men and two women visiting, standing on railway tracks near trestle. Scenes with men and women at logging site watching, some CU's. Tree being fallen. Man topping a tree. Loggers near railway tracks. Donkey engine. Men working, posing for camera, mugging it up during break. Highrigger rigging a spar, lady watching. Boom on spar tree operating. Donkey engine steaming. Logs being lifted onto flat car.

red: Kennedy Lake, A.P.L. Camp 6. Good shots of steam donkey and men working. Logs being yarded and lifted onto flat cars. Good shot of steam donkey. Donkey being skidded down a steep hill on railway wheels. Logging locie moving through woods with logs. CU loggers, visitors.

b+w: Tofino. View of town from boat. Seaplane lands, CF-ADP. CU plane, pilot, kids, passengers. Fish boat. Men in canoes, dugouts, netting and gutting Coho; stripping eggs and milt; squirting it into a bucket. Indian village, men casting nets from canoes.

red (slightly faded): Large freighter wrecked on reef. Men in dugouts bringing salmon ashore, stripping eggs and milt, squirting same into bucket, gutting and cleaning fish. Cove with house. Good CU's old Indian sitting, another old woman working at a low table. Dugouts in the bay. Two old women preparing fish. Man and dugout at beach, piking fish ashore. Old woman posing, laughing. Old woman on beach. Beach and dugouts. CU Indian man. Dugouts, laying nets for fish. Young boy posing. Bringing fish ashore. Going out again. White people on shore. CU net.

463. THE KICKING HORSE TRAIL. (1929)
    p.c. CGMPB
    1. 1 reel   g. 35mm t. b+w   s. si. w/captions
    d. *
    ph. *
    c.s. Unknown

> *"Opening with the incident which gave the Kicking Horse Pass its name in 1858, the picture follows the new motor road from Lake Louise to Golden. Winding up and down, around and across it is a succession of sudden glories, among which are the Natural Bridge, Snowpeak Avenue, the Great Divide and Wapta Falls. It is a tribute to the triumph of courage and engineering which forced a passage through the very backbone of the continent."*

464. KIDDIES CARNIVAL, VANCOUVER, B.C. (1938)
    p.c. Fox Movietonews (Fox #35-11)
    1. 500'   g. 35mm t. b+w   s. sound
    d. *
    ph. ASN
    c.s. Fox Movietonews, N.Y.

> *"Parade led by Vancouver City mounted police and band. Girls carrying Union Jack. Floats and Children in various costumes. Mayor Miller opens carnival. Last year's King & Queen crown the present King & Queen. CU same. Crowd. Floats, wagons, kids dressed up in various costumes. Little girls getting ready for parade. Kids watching show. (Cuts destroyed)"*

465. KIDDIES ENJOYING THEMSELVES IN STANLEY PARK, VANCOUVER,
    B.C. (1921)
    p.c. Fox Movietonews (Fox #421-2978)
    1. 40'   g. 35mm t. b+w   s. si.
    d. *
    ph. D.C. Davey
    c.s. Fox Movietonews, N.Y.

466. KIDDIES HAVE A REAL PARTY AT ELKS PICNIC IN HASTINGS
    PARK, VANCOUVER, B.C. (1920)
    p.c. Fox Movietonews (Fox #754-1205)
    1. 26'   g. 35mm t. b+w   s. si.
    d. *
    ph. *
    c.s. Fox Movietonews, N.Y.

> *"CU of a boy called Freckles. Watermelon eating contest."*

467. KIDDIES STAGE EXCITING KITE FLYING CONTESTS AT MOODY PARK AS
    GUESTS OF LOCAL KIWANIS CLUB, NEW WESTMINISTER, B.C. (1929)
    p.c. Fox Movietonews (Fox #759.23-C9928)
    1. 90'   g. 35mm t. b+w   s. si.
    d. *
    ph. Ross Beesley
    c.s. Fox Movietonews, N.Y.

> *"Group of children on lawn sending up kites. Kites in flight. Crowd of kiddies watching the contest. Group of winners."*

468. THE KING AND QUEEN ON THEIR CANADIAN TOUR. (1939)
    p.c. Pathé Gazette Newsreel #47
    1. 260'   g. 35mm t. b+w   s. sound
    d. *
    ph. *
    c.s. EMI Pathé Film Library

> *This reel, showing the western end of the visit by King George VI and Queen Elizabeth to Canada in May of 1939, also contains shots taken in Calgary and Banff, Alberta.*
>
> *Establishing shot of CNR station, Vancouver. Crowds along the streets. Banner reading THE ITALIAN VETERAN'S ASSOCIATION EXTEND THEIR MAJESTIES A ROYAL*

WELCOME. Open car bearing King and Queen moves between cheering crowd. Banner reading: WELCOME TO OUR SOVEREIGNS - JAPANESE CANADIANS. Cheering Japanese children in kimonos wave Union Jacks. Shot of car again, King and Queen wave. Japanese children wave flags again. King and Queen enter Vancouver City Hall and are greeted by the Mayor of Vancouver. King and Queen aboard the PRINCESS MARGUERITE. Crowds line seawall. Ships, little boats, in the First Narrows, escort the MARGUERITE. Escort of RCN destroyers, one moves past the camera with sailors standing at attention along the guardrails. CU King and Queen on bridge of ferry looking at Vancouver Island. An Indian canoe paddles by. King and Queen on bridge, Vancouver Island in distance. Night falls, destroyers form up in line, silhouetted by dusk. Beacon fires burn along the shore. The RCN destroyers participating were HMCS FRASER and HMCS ST. LAURENT.

King and Queen arrive Victoria next morning. Establishing shot of Empress Hotel in Inner Harbour. King and Queen alight from car. They walk among a cheering mob waving flags. Shot of front balcony Empress Hotel. Soldiers and sailors in Beacon Hill Park, in parade formation. Band plays. King presents Colours to the RCN - first time colours ever presented by a sovereign outside England. CU King saluting as the sailors march past and band plays. King and Queen leave reviewing stand, children scream: "We want/love the Queen." King and Queen leave in open car surrounded by cheering crowds. Narrator and actuality sound.

469. KING AND QUEEN WILDLY HAILED IN CANADA'S WEST, VANCOUVER,
     B.C. (1939)
     p.c. Universal Newsreel (#11-777)
     l. 346'   g. 35mm   t. b+w   s. si. & sound
     d.   *
     ph. ASN
     c.s. USNA

"Arrival at City Hall, Guards. Mayor Telford greets the King and Queen. They walk up into City Hall with crowds cheering. LS 2000-voice choir singing National Anthem. King on balcony. Girl with flowers, King and Queen smiling. Royal Coat of Arms. King and Queen shake hands with girl. King and Queen pass by in open car. Japanese kids waving flags and cheering. Margaret Robertson presents flowers. Boarding the PRINCESS MARGUERITE for Victoria. Ships of the RCN and airplanes attending. (The RCN destroyers participating were HMCS FRASER and HMCS ST. LAURENT.) King and Queen aboard ferry at sunset. Silhouette of ship and destroyers against Vancouver Island. Dawn. LS Parliament Buildings, Victoria. King reviews Guard, Queen looks on. King walks up Parliament Building steps with Premier Patullo. On the steps he receives a charter and flowers. At Beacon Hill Park the King walks to the saluting stand, presents colours and new drums. The King salutes while walking to field, flag, etc. King salutes, inspects sailors." The remainder deals with Edmonton, Alberta. The CUTS list the following: SS PRINCESS MARGUERITE sails. Choir singing. Wide angle CNR station. Park, formation of Indian War canoes. Flags bedeck Royal Scot. They wave goodbye on bridge. Various shots of scenic beauty enroute to Victoria. Bonfires along shoreline of V.I. Empress Hotel. Arrival. Beacon Hill Park. Colours. Marching. Royal Car pulls away. Premier's address (sound). Presenting King's colours. Scenes of luncheon at Empress Hotel. Premier & Mrs. Patullo of B.C. The King speaks (sound).

470. KING OF SIAM ARRIVES WITH QUEEN, VANCOUVER, B.C. (1931)
     p.c. Fox Movietonews (Fox #10-194)
     l.   g. 35mm   t. b+w   s. si.
     d.   *
     ph. Ross Beesley
     c.s. Fox Movietonews, N.Y.

"King of Siam and party arrive in Canada. Party led by King Prajadhipok and Queen Rambaibarni. CU of King & Queen of Siam."

471. KIWANIANS SPONSOR COURTESY WEEK. (1921-1928)
     p.c. *
     l. 160'   g. 35mm   t. b+w   s. si.
     d.   *
     ph.   *
     c.s. Jack Chisholm Film Productions #C746/B+W/roll 2

There is nothing to indicate where this footage was photographed but it may have been in Vancouver. Shots include MS Kiwanians. MS women crossing street; a car nearly knocks them over, then backs up. MS passengers boarding streetcar; one man pushes past others and sits down. Another man gets up to give his seat to a lady. MS two little girls curtseying to each other.

472. KIWANIANS START AMBITIOUS PLAN TO LINE BOTH SIDES OF PACIFIC
HIGHWAY WITH MAPLE TREES TO BOUNDARY, VANCOUVER, B.C. (1926)
    p.c. Fox Movietonews (Fox #047.9-B5895)
    1. 25'   g. 35mm   t. b+w   s. si.
    d. *
    ph. Herron
    c.s. Fox Movietonews, N.Y.

           "Scenes of Kiwanians with shovels, planting trees. Officials include: C.D. Bruce, J. Stables, and Dr. Burnett."

473. KIWANIS CLUB, NEW WESTMINSTER, HOLD POST HOLE DIGGING BEE
FOR FENCE TO ENCLOSE CHILDREN'S PLAYGROUND, NEW WESTMINSTER,
B.C. (1922)
    p.c. Fox Movietonews (Fox #047.9-3176)
    1. 60'   g. 35mm   t. b+w   s. si.
    d. *
    ph. Len Roos
    c.s. Fox Movietonews, N.Y.

           "Unloading auto of tools. Mayor J.J. Johnston, Pres. of club, digging a hole. Digging holes."

474. KIWANIS CONVENTION, VANCOUVER, B.C. (1935)
    p.c. Hearst Metrotone News, Can no. 328; Roll no. 2
    1. 600'   g. 35mm   t. b+w   s. sound
    d. *
    ph. ASN
    c.s. Hearst Metrotone News, N.Y.

           "Bands. Crowd shots. Bands playing. Harper Gatton, President International, CU."

475. KLONDIKE DAYS RECALLED IN NEW GOLD STAMPEDE. SCORES OF
POSPECTORS THRONG RIVER BOAT IN BIG RUSH FOR RICH DIGGING
REPORTED AT CASSIAR CREEK, B.C. WRANGELL, ALASKA. (1925)
    p.c. Pathé News (Pathé Sil. .45. Neg. no. 2115)
    1.   g. 35mm   t. b+w   s. si.
    d. *
    ph. *
    c.s. Lost

           Includes scenes of Cassiar Creek and Telegraph Creek.

476. KLONDIKE GOLD RUSH LURES THOUSANDS TO SEEK FORTUNES.
(1898)
    p.c. Edison Film Mfg. Co. (?)
    1. 20'   g. 35mm (16mm available) t. b+w s. si.
    d. *
    ph. *
    c.s. NFA (#3150)

           Shots of miners, etc.

477. THE KOOTENAY INDIANS OF BRITISH COLUMBIA. (1928)
    p.c. National Museum of Canada
    1. approx. 300' g. 35mm   t. b+w   s. si. w/captions
    d. Harlan I. Smith
    ph. Harlan I. Smith
    c.s. National Museum of Man & NFA (#3772, 3773)

           "This film shows the Kootenay Indians, who dwell on the lakes and rivers of southeastern British Columbia in the shadow of the Rocky Mountains. They obtained horses from the south before the tribes of the plains, and formerly rode across the Rocky Mountains every summer to hunt buffaloes on the Alberta prairie. So long as they could obtain buffaloes they made their tents of hide

Now they use canvas tents (tipis), but paint pictures of buffaloes on some of them.

There are pictures of the camp, the people, a Kootenay infant carried on its mother's back, a woman embroidering a moccasin with silk, earrings worn by both men and women, bead work, two men engaged in a ceremonial smoke, buffaloes, the Kootenay drum, the ceremonial costume of the children, and ceremonial dress."

A man named Chief Paul appears briefly, and there are shots of the whole band in ceremonial dress, dancing.

478. KOOTENAY LAKE CONSTRUCTION AND LOG CABIN IN SNOW. (c. 1931)
    p.c. private
    1. 350'   g. 16mm   t. b+w   s. si.
    d.   *
    ph. Rev. George R.B. Kinney
    c.s. NFA, Ottawa

Snow and ice on Kootenay Lake. Men walk out onto a snow-covered wharf. Digging a tunnel in the rock for the railway. Tamping before blasting. Waterfall covered in ice. Man bringing a horse out of a crude stable in the snow. A barge on the lake. Kids throwing snowballs. Men at snowy campsite clowning about with a dog. Men climbing up a hill from the lake with laundry, to the campsite, having washed clothes in lake. Snowy campsite; pan out across lake, clothes drying in trees. Men climbing snowy bluffs. A horse hauls a boom line pulling supplies up onto the bluff near the campsite above the beach. Workers grabbing supplies, pulling them in, working the boom.

LS sternwheeler out on the snowy lake, probably the MOYIE. The ship comes closer and glides beautifully by, snow-clad trees in f.g. LS sternwheeler stopping at snowy wharf, docking broadside on. Sternwheeler pulls out into the lake again.

Girl walks along snowy road by shore of lake. A large snow-covered chalet, men returning with horse-drawn sleigh. View over the lake and cemetery (?). A snowy log cabin, a man leaves with a rifle. Views of lake and mountains covered in snow. Two men in a snowy woodshed chopping wood and sharpening an axe. A woman comes out of a house wearing a long headdress, perhaps a shawl, and walks past the two men, looking at them briefly. Woman in f.g. while men work in b.g., house behind. A small boy comes to her then runs away. She walks a few paces then stands still. Dark shot of a man with a lantern on a trail. (This latter is excellent and has a dramatic quality about it.)

479. KOOTENAY LAKE CONSTRUCTION CAMPS & STANLEY PARK. (c. 1933)
    p.c. private
    1. 300'   g. 16mm   t. b+w   s. si.
    d.   *
    ph. Rev. George R.B. Kinney
    c.s. NFA, Ottawa

Reverend George R.B. Kinney worked for the United Church in the Kootenays during the late twenties and early thirties. His parish included all the CPR work camps during the construction of the track along the west side of Kootenay Lake in 1928. He served on the lake until 1933 when he and his family came to the coast. During this time he shot film of the construction workers which he showed, along with cartoons, shorts, and trailers for features, on his return visits.

Camp Lockhart. Small boats tied up to a wharf on Kootenay Lake. Shots of the lake. Men working on the railbed. Bulldozer and trucks working on a road near an unidentified town. Two men playing with a bear in the Kootenays. The bear climbs a pole; they all play. CPR construction gang working on the railbed beside Kootenay Lake, then relaxing, singing, dancing. A home-made rowboat. Laying track. Working on a wharf. Many shots of lake and buildings.

A sunny day in Stanley Park, Vancouver. Gents playing a game with huge checkers. People strolling about, pavillion with people on the lawns, duck pond, crowded children's playground, playing at bowls.

187

480. KOOTENAY LAKE PICNIC AND CONSTRUCTION WORK, & HORNBY
    ISLAND PETROGLYPHS. (1930's)
    p.c. private
    1. 360'   g. 16mm   t. b+w   s. si.
    d. *
    ph. Rev. George R.B. Kinney
    c.s. NFA, Ottawa

        Kootenay Lake. Children on a farm. Views of shoreline, towns and houses.
        Picnic.

        Group of well-dressed men meeting and examining petroglyphs on the shores of
        Hornby Island. The Petroglyphs have all been outlined with chalk and the
        camera work is very good, showing all manner of whimsical and familiar fish,
        birds and animals.

        Scenes, probably from the United Church boat, along the shore of Kootenay
        Lake, revealing clusters of tents, men sitting on logs, construction camps.
        A barge with men working. A tunnel carved out of the rock along the shore,
        for the railway.

481. KOOTENAY LAKE RAILWAY CONSTRUCTION & VANCOUVER ISLAND
    WORK CAMPS. (1930's)
    p.c. Private
    1. 300'   g. 16mm   t. b+w & colour s. si.
    d. *
    ph. Rev. George R.B. Kinney
    c.s. NFA, Ottawa

        b+w: Rainy construction site on the CPR line along the shore of Kootenay Lake,
        before 1933. Men building railbed by hand. Grader, a truck and some cars,
        but mostly the men are digging and hacking through the stone by hand. Some
        blasting and burning, chopping with axes.

        colour: Thetis Lake, Vancouver Island. Young men working on maps. Large
        group of young men relaxing, playing ping-pong, one young man playing piano
        while others listen. Dissolve to inside of a mess hall, the Oyster River
        Dining Hall, with men entering, sitting down and beginning to eat.

        colour: Elk Falls, Vancouver Island. Scenes from a tree planting camp during
        the depression years. These camps were set up by the Provincial Government
        to occupy young men & others who were out of work. At this camp the men
        board trucks outside their huts and leave for their work area. Bundles of
        trees are wrapped up. Tents in an area to be reforested. Two young men saw
        down a dead tree. MS & CU's planting trees. Meal served outside at long
        tables. Englishmen's River. Young men making rustic furniture out of peeled
        logs. Waterfalls.

482. KOOTENAY LAKE RAILWAY CONSTRUCTION, CAMP KOKANEE &
    PROCTOR, B.C. (early 1930's)
    p.c. private
    1. 350'   g. 16mm   t. b+w   s. si.
    d. *
    ph. Rev. George R.B. Kinney
    c.s. NFA, Ottawa

        Railway construction on shores of Kootenay Lake. Steam shovel working. Last
        scene shows tents construction workers lived in.

        Camp Kokanee, United Church Camp in the Kootenays. Many shots of young men
        and women talking, sunning, taking snaps of one another, swimming, boating,
        playing volleyball, and mugging it up for the camera.

        Proctor, on Kootenay Lake, in the winter. Kids playing on front steps, making
        a snowman. Scenes down by the lake, ships by the mill, trains coming in,
        steam in the air.

483. KOOTENAY LAKE SCENES. (pre 1933)
    p.c. private
    1. 225'   g. 16mm   t. b+w   s. si.
    d.   *
    ph. Rev. George R.B. Kinney
    c.s. NFA, Ottawa

> *Small mining settlement near Kootenay Lake. Men with wheelbarrow full of ore,*
> *one man pounding ore. Children in forest at camp. A little settlement in*
> *snowy mountains. Ladies pose, man saws a log, babies, shots of buildings.*
> *Scenic views from Mission boat, the PAT passing down Kootenay Lake. Good*
> *shots of train moving along CPR tracks on shore of Kootenay Lake taken from*
> *passing Mission boat.*
>
> *Miners at Riondel Mine ham it up for camera outside shacks and shaft building.*
> *Good CU miners. Excellent CU Rev. Kinney with hat full of ore, hamming it*
> *up.*
>
> *Nelson Old-Timers' Picnic at Proctor on Kootenay Lake, 1933. Oldtimers*
> *arrive aboard the MOYIE which comes alongside, ties up at the wharf with old-*
> *timers at the rails. Oldtimers go ashore. Oldtimers play sports; races for*
> *old men, race with large balls for ladies and men, apple-peeling contest,*
> *lots of observers, two pipers march by. Indian in what looks like a hand*
> *made canoe - excellent. (Chief John Alexander?)*

484. KOOTENAY WATER-WAYS MISSION OF THE UNITED CHURCH OF
    CANADA. (c. 1930)
    p.c. private
    1. 423'   g. 16mm   t. b+w   s. si. w/captions
    d.   *
    ph. Rev. George R.B. Kinney
    c.s. NFA, Ottawa

> *TITLE: KOOTENAY WATER-WAYS MISSION OF THE UNITED CHURCH OF CANADA*
> *   Pastor - Rev. Geo. Kinney, B.A., F.R.C.S. Proctor, B.C.*
>
> *Shows a number of CPR construction camps on Kootenay Lake between 1928-1933.*
> *Rev. Kinney travelled to the camps aboard a Mission boat called the PAT and*
> *often took movies of the men.*
>
> *Kootenay Lake. Ten Mile Point. Near the Ellis-Cotton Camp. Merz Camp in*
> *the snow. Men working and packing dynamite up from the wharf. Camp 4 at*
> *Wilson Creek receives supplies. Men of Camp 4 outside their tents in the*
> *snow and unloading supplies into a small jetty from the PAT. Captain, En-*
> *gineer and Crew of the PAT - 2 men pose on the frosty deck. Men chopping*
> *the landing clear of ice. Two men unwrapping a side of beef. The cook.*
> *Scenic shots of the bluffs near the camp. The cook rings the triangular*
> *bell for lunch. Two other cooks appear in the doorway and come out into the*
> *sun. Men pour out of the tents to eat, some have snowball fights on the way.*
> *Pan out across the lake.*
>
> *Kootenay Lake CPR construction site. Snow is gone. Men working with hoses*
> *in a heap of rocks. Men sitting about drinking coffee. A shovel at work by*
> *the lake. Men pose, smiling, for camera. Broadside view of a sternwheeler,*
> *probably the MOYIE. A trip by small open boat out onto the lake one choppy*
> *day. A dinghy behind carries supplies.*
>
> *Exterior of a tunnel on the railway line. A man walks in with 2 culverts*
> *under his arms. Three men push a cart out of the tunnel. Three men inside*
> *tunnel, illuminated. An unfinished tunnel on the line. Two men with a horse-*
> *drawn cart enter and return with cart full of soil and rock. Cart travels*
> *down hill toward camp. Pan across camp. Engineer's camp, men in front of*
> *buildings. Boat leaves, camp seen astern as dinghy bobs behind.*
>
> *New tent camp on the beach below forest. Larger camp with snowy hills behind.*
> *Two cooks ring gong, men run up slope to dining hall. Men posing for camera.*
> *Two have a boxing match for fun. Camp in the woods near Kootenay Lake. A*
> *man walks by, hills in b.g. Snowy hill (above Boswell??). Four men walking*
> *in single file through the woods above a large camp (Camp Wasookinat?).*

485. THE KWAKIUTL INDIANS OF BRITISH COLUMBIA. (1923-1930)
    p.c. National Museum of Canada
    1. 1 reel   g. 35mm   t. b+w   s. si.
    d.   Harlan I Smith
    ph.   Harlan I. Smith
    c.s. Unknown

> *This film, now lost, likely demonstrates the skills and home life of the Kwakiutl Indians living on the east coast of Vancouver Island, with scenes of their daily existence, preparing food, sewing, carving, and many forms of their art.*

486. THE KWAKIUTL OF BRITISH COLUMBIA. (1930-1931)
    p.c. Franz Boas
    1. 55 minutes   g. 15mm   t. b+w   s. si.
    d.   Franz Boas
    ph.   Franz Boas
    c.s. University of Washington Press & BCPM Eth.

> *Edited and available with copious excellent notes by Bill Holm of the University of Washington. The film is in two parts.*
>
> *PART I: Technology and Games. View of Fort Rupert on Vancouver Island where Boas made this film. View of the house and the main street, followed by a shot of Beaver Harbour and the islands. Mrs. George Hunt demonstrates the Kwakiutl cradle and eats from an alderwood dish to show how the hands were left free while feet rocked the baby. George Hunt demonstrates the principle techniques of woodworking, employing an elbow adze, a D-adze or hand adze and a crooked knife. George Hunt demonstrates the native drill and shows how it is capable of boring at any angle with great control. The manufacture of cedar-bark rope is demonstrated. Mrs. Hunt demonstrates methods of weaving cedar-bark mats. She makes a small square basket. The method of shredding cedar bark is shown, and the spinning of mountain goat wool and nettle fibres is demonstrated, using a maple spindle 2' long and a disk-shaped whorl made of whalebone. Sam Hunt and Frank Walker demonstrate how the Kwakiutl ring game is played, and also play a game of throwing sticks. Two children's games are shown: Ball, using a ball made of skunk cabbage leaves wrapped with cedar bark, and Throwing Stones, which uses a target rock. Sarah (Hunt) Omhid plays a game of Counting, where small sticks are picked up while the player holds his or her breath. Also shown are Hitting a Ring in which thin cedar sticks are dropped through a small ring; Guessing, in which the players are required to guess the number of sticks in various arrangements as they are removed from the field of play; Kicking, which consists of two teams of boys who kick each other while riding piggyback; carrying and Hair-pulling which has team members carrying each other across a field, dropping the one being carried who is finally transported to the rest of the team who pull the carried one's hair; and Pretending to Sleep, in which a ring of boys pretend to be sleeping on a given command, and wake up again when signalled. A long sequence of the Bone Game or lehal is shown with three members on each team.*
>
> *PART II: Dances and ceremonial activities. Two chiefs, portrayed by Charley Wilson and Sam Hunt, boasting about their wealth and their noble accomplishments are shown. This was a public ritual, and both men wear handkerchiefs tied around their heads and trade blankets, and punctuate their gestures with bouncing, deep knee bends and long poles which are jabbed into the ground. Charley Wilson next portrays a chief presenting his prince to the people, and uses his copper (copper plates, often patched together, symbolizing wealth) to indictae the wealth and power of the prince and, of course, himself. The following winter ceremonial dances at Fort Rupert are shown: Cannibal Dance, the Woman's Cannibal Dance, the Healing Dance, the Woman's Winter Dance, the Toogwid Dance, the Bird Dance, the Dance of the Trees, the Salmon Dance, the Paddle Dance, the Woman's Grizzly Bear Dance, the Weather Dance, the Begging Dance, the Newettee Shaman's Dance, the Shaman's Dance, the Feather Dance, the Mitla Dance, the Nonum, Summer Dance and the Nootka Dance. Mrs. George Hunt demonstrates the movements used by a Shaman to cure a patient.*

487. LAND OF MAKE BELIEVE BECOMES INTENSE REALITY FOR THE
CHILDREN ENJOYING PLAYGROUND FESTIVAL, VANCOUVER, B.C.
(1924)
p.c. Fox Movietonews (Fox #751.13-A4047)
l.   g. 35mm   t. b+w   s. si.
d.   *
ph. Len H. Roos
c.s. Fox Movietonews, N.Y.

"Playground, kids, Mayor Owen. Two of the kids: Ella Rennie & Lillian Claver."

488. LAND OF TOTEMS. (1930?)
p.c. ASN (B629?)
l. 1 reel   g. 35mm   t. b+w & tinted s. si. w/captions
d.   *
ph. J.B. Scott (?)
c.s. Unknown

See TOTEM LAND.

489. LANDING, SORTING AND GUTTING FISH. (1902)
p.c. Edison Mfg. Co.
l. 200'   g. 35mm   t. b+w   s. si.
d.   *
ph.   *
c.s. Unknown

This film is probably lost for all time. It was almost certain to be a companion-piece to SPEARING SALMON, the catalogue numbers being consecutive, so that if SPEARING SALMON is about British Columbia, then this is too. It is in three sections: LANDING FISH (75'), SORTING FISH (75'), and GUTTING FISH (50'). Edison Catalogue, 1902.

490. LANSDOWNE RACE TRACK OPENS SEASON. (1924)
p.c. Fox Movietonews (?)
l.   g. 35mm   t. b+w   s. si.
d.   *
ph.   *
c.s. NFB (1920-FG-105 or 135)

"Horses parade to post, start and action during race. Crowd & winner gets wreath at finish. Victoria."

491. LARGE SPAN OF NEW BRIDGE TO NORTH VANCOUVER IS FLOATED
TO POSITION ON SCOWS, VANCOUVER, B.C. (1920's)
p.c. Fox Movietonews (Fox #011-B8472)
l.   g. 35mm   t. b+w   s. si.
d.   *
ph.   *
c.s. Fox Movietonews, N.Y.

492. LARGE TURTLE CAUGHT ON LULU ISLAND IS PRESENTED TO
THE ZOO, VANCOUVER, B.C. (1923)
p.c. Fox Movietonews (Fox #413.33-B1850)
l. 18'   g. 35mm   t. b+w   s. si.
d.   *
ph. Len H. Roos
c.s. Fox Movietonews, N.Y.

Zoo accepting turtle, shots of turtle.

493. LARGEST SINGLE UNIT LUMBER FLUME IN THE WORLD IS 13½ MILES
LONG, CRANBROOK, B.C. (1920's)
p.c. Fox Movietonews (Fox #420.75-B3189)
l. 40'   g. 35mm   t. b+w   s. si.
d.   *
ph. Herron
c.s. Fox Movietonews, N.Y.

"Flume on trestle 125 feet high. Logs running down flume. Logs coming out of tunnel. Log pond."

494. THE LAST GREAT WEST. (1925)
    p.c. CGMPB
    1. 1 reel   g. 35mm   t. b+w   s. si. w/captions
    d.   *
    ph. *
    c.s. Unknown

         "Third of the (CGMPB) series of three films entitled CANADA FROM COAST TO COAST, and containing views of many of the outstanding features of the Provinces of Manitoba, Saskatchewan, Alberta and British Columbia. Included are glimpses of the cities of Winnipeg, Regina, Edmonton, Vancouver, Victoria and Prince Rupert, as well as the great grain growing areas of Western Canada, the scenic beauties of the Canadian Rockies, Jasper National Park, Wainright National Park and the Pacific coast of British Columbia." The first two titles in the series were: THE MARITIME PROVINCES and THE HEART OF CANADA.

495. LAUNCHING OF PRINCESS ELAINE AT YARROWS SHIPYARD.
    (late 1920's)
    p.c. private
    1. 100'   g. 16mm   t. b+w   s. si.
    d.   *
    ph. Barney Olson
    c.s. Barry Casson Film Productions, Victoria

         The CPR ferry PRINCESS ELAINE being launched at Yarrows shipyard in Esquimalt on a rainy day, and crowds watching.

         NOTE: This is not the maiden launching of the PRINCESS ELAINE. She was built in Glasgow in 1928 and sailed to Victoria where she was registered. Perhaps this scene is the result of a check or a refit the CPR undertook after she arrived and before she went into service.

496. LEON MOREL, SEATTLE SCULPTOR, WORKING ON THE HEROIC
    STATUE OF A CANADIAN SOLDIER WHICH IS BEING CAST FOR
    VANCOUVER, VANCOUVER, B.C. (1922)
    p.c. Fox Movietonews (Fox #201-3238)
    1. 164'   g. 35mm   t. b+w   s. si.
    d.   *
    ph. Singelow
    c.s. Fox Movietonews, N.Y.

         Shots of sculptor working.

497. LIFE ABOARD THE EMPRESS. (1934)
    p.c. ASN (A 657)
    1. 1 reel   g. 35mm   t. b+w   s.
    d.   *
    ph. *
    c.s. Unknown

         Produced for the CPR as a promotional film. No other information is available. The CPR EMPRESS ships served on both the Atlantic and the Pacific coasts, so without viewing the film it cannot be determined whether any scenes of British Columbia appear in it.

498. LIFE IN THE YUKON AND NORTHWEST TERRITORIES. (1927-1929)
    p.c. private
    1. 200'   g. 8mm   t. b+w   s. si.
    d.   *
    ph. Corporal Betts, RCMP
    c.s. NFA (# 7388)

         Various scenes around Atlin, the Yukon, and the Northwest Territories.

499. THE LIFE OF A SALMON. (1910)
    p.c. Edison Mfg. Co. (Catalogue # 6716)
    1. 381'   g. 35mm   t. b+w   s. si. w/captions
    d.   J. Searle Dawley
    ph. Henry Cronjager
    c.s. NFA & BFI (Location # 3147A (a))

One of the films made by the Edison Mfg. Co. on its summer tour of Western Canada for the CPR. It was filmed entirely on the west coast and has little dramatic content, being almost entirely a documentary on salmon fishing. The film opens with a shot of the Capilano Canyon, followed by fish jumping the falls. Spawn in test tubes shows the development of salmon fry from 1-20 days. LS fishing fleet at the mouth of the Fraser River. Lifting the trap on the river. CU fish caught in the nets. A spring salmon weighing 55 lbs. held by a man. A barge, containing fish, landing. CU of the landing of the fish. Fish arriving at the cannery. The film ends with shots of a Regatta on the Gorge, showing canoe races with both Indians and whites racing, and spectators. There is also a shot of the Empress Hotel. This film was begun on July 31, 1910, and finished on August 5, 1910, and was originally 435' long. The Edison Log mentions some work having been done in their Bronx Studio, presumably with actors. The synopsis seems to indicate that this was omitted from the final version.

Edison's advertising synopsis reads as follows:

"Mr. & Mrs. Salmon are very interesting individuals of the inhabitants of the sea. Their life has many strange facts, interesting features, and gives one food for thought. That the maternal instinct is deeply rooted in their nature is only too plainly exemplified in the opening picture of this very interesting film by the Edison Company.

We are first shown the picturesque canyon of Capilano near Vancouver, B.C. As the camera descends down this rocky cliff showing its height and grandeur, we pause for a moment to give the spectator a passing glimpse of a roaring mountain stream which is exceedingly swift and icy cold. A moment more and we are shown a water fall between two huge jagged rocks, the drop being about six and a half feet. A boiling mass of water is hurled with terrific force downward and here we catch the first glimpse of Mr. Salmon and his wife and their life's struggle for the continuation of the species. We are shown the salmon frantically endeavouring to leap the falls. Time and time again they hurl their bodies into the air only to be caught by the swift current of water and dashed against the rocks but again they try and so keep trying until either they succeed in jumping the falls or are dashed to death and all for what - so that they may reach the place of their birth and lay their spawn and then they have completed their life's work. We are then shown the spawn in its various stages of evolution until it takes the form of a tiny salmon. These small fish remain in fresh water until a certain age, then drift down the mountain streams until they reach the salt sea and there remain for three years then they go back to their birthplace, lay their spawn, and so the operation continues age after age or would do so but for the invention of man who drops his nets at the mouth of these rivers and Mr. and Mrs. Salmon are soon transported to the cans and ready for the world's markets.

This picture shows the operation of catching the silver horde, the setting of the trap, the drawing in of the net in the cold grey of the dawn with a catch of fifteen thousand salmon and finally their delivery to the salmon cannery. We are also shown in this picture an Indian canoe race participated in by Indians who worked in the cannery, eleven men in each crew and three crews, in their long slim craft hewed out of solid trees. This is an exceedingly interesting sight and one that holds the attention and interest.

The entire picture was taken at Victoria and Vancouver in British Columbia and is one that is novel, interesting, instructive and pleasing in every detail."

500. LIFE ON A NORTHWEST INDIAN RESERVATION, CANADA. (pre 1910)
    p.c. *
    1. 275'   g. 35mm   t. b+w   s. si.
    d.   *
    ph.   *
    c.s. Unknown

    "An enlightening subject of great general and anthropological interest. Scenes on the prairie and in camp; parade of the tribe; war dance in full native costume." It is almost certain that this film was not shot in British Columbia, but it is in this catalogue on the outside chance that it might have been. George Kleine Catalogue, 1910, p. 280.

8

501. THE LILLOOET INDIANS OF BRITISH COLUMBIA. (1923-1930)
    p.c. National Museum of Canada
    1. 1 reel   g. 35mm   t. b+w   s. si. w/captions
    d.   Harlan I. Smith
    ph. Harlan I. Smith
    c.s. Unknown

            This film has been lost and no description remains. Presumably it showed
            the customs and work habits of the Lillooet Indians and examined their art
            and handicrafts.

502. LILLOOET RACES, LILLOOET, B.C. (1910)
    p.c. *
    1.   g. 35mm   t. b+w   s. si.
    d.   *
    ph. *
    c.s. NFA (Taylor reel 113)

            "Huge crowd in little town of Lillooet waiting for results of endurance horse
            race. Shots of riders coming in, as much as 5 minutes apart, due to great
            mileage and rough country. They report to judges' stand and walk their horses
            to cool them down. A cowboy is challenged to ride a "Real wild one", and
            after accepting the challenge, he has trouble mounting the horse. Once in
            the saddle, he delights the crowd by hanging on well."

503. LINER EMPRESS OF CANADA ON ROCKS. HOMER BAY, B.C.,
     NEAR VICTORIA. (1929)
    p.c. Paramount (Lib. # 3169)
    1.   g. 35mm   t. b+w   s. si.
    d.   *
    ph. *
    c.s. Lost. Sherman Grinberg, N.Y.

            General view and pan through trees of liner on rocks. Three good air views
            of liner held fast.

504. LION'S GATE BRIDGE BEING BUILT ACROSS ENTRANCE TO VANCOUVER'S
     HARBOUR, VANCOUVER, B.C. (1938)
    p.c. Hearst Metrotone News; Can no. 832 or 833, Roll no. 10
    1.   g. 35mm   t. b+w   s. sound
    d.   *
    ph. ASN
    c.s. Hearst Metrotone News, N.Y.

            Shots of Lion's Gate Bridge under construction.

505. LION'S GATE BRIDGE, SPANNING THE FIRST NARROWS OR LION'S
     GATE, ENTRANCE TO VANCOUVER'S HARBOUR, VANCOUVER, B.C.
     (1938)
    p.c. Hearst Metrotone News; Can no. 952, Roll no. 4
    1.   g. 35mm   t. b+w   s. sound
    d.   *
    ph. ASN
    c.s. Hearst Metrotone News, N.Y.

            "Various shots of the bridge and the SS EMPRESS OF JAPAN."

506. THE LITTLE STATION AGENT. (1910)
    p.c. Edison Mfg. Co. (Catalogue # 6700)
    1. 1000'   g. 35mm   t. b+w   s. si.
    d.   J. Searle Dawley
    ph. Henry Cronjager
    c.s. Unknown

            Filmed by the Edison Co. during its tour through western Canada making pro-
            motional films for the CPR. It was begun on July 13 and finished on August
            10 with some finishing touches added at Edison's Bronx Studio. The location
            is not known, nor is the story, but the chances are good that it was photo-
            graphed in British Columbia in the Rockies.

507. LIVESTOCK GRAND PARADE, VANCOUVER, B.C.   (1938)
     p.c. Fox Movietonews (Fox # 35-933)
     l. 639'   g. 35mm   t. b+w   s. sound
     d.   *
     ph. ASN
     c.s. Fox Movietonews, N.Y.

> "Canadian Pacific Exhibition stages a grand parade of all livestock which
> took part in the competition. Elevation, pan before parade. Horse team,
> young boy in Indian suit and riding pony leading parade. Other teams foll-
> owing. Cattle various shots. Shot from grandstand of livestock lined up
> forming C.P.E. Various shots of different champions of the exhibition.
> Pres. Leek, V.P. Dunsmuir, Pete More, animal champions."

508. LIVEWIRES OF LOCAL GYRO CLUB ARE JUST BACK FROM MILWAUKEE
     CONVENTION AFTER WINNING ALL THE PRIZES, VANCOUVER, B.C.
     (1923)
     p.c. Fox Movietonews (Fox #095.5-B1622)
     l. 35'   g. 35mm   t. b+w   s. si.
     d.   *
     ph. Len H. Roos
     c.s. Fox Movietonews, N.Y.

> Shots of Gyros, including Charles Garrett, vice-president.

509. LOADING THE TOYOOKA MARU WITH GRAIN AT VANCOUVER, B.C.
     (1923)
     p.c. Fox Movietonews (Fox #463.11-2833)
     l. 35'   g. 35mm   t. b+w   s. si.
     d.   *
     ph. Len H. Roos
     c.s. Fox Movietonews, N.Y.

> The SS TOYOOKA MARU is loaded with grain.

510. LOGGING CAMPS, VANCOUVER ISLAND, SS MALAHAT IN VICTORIA,
     KOOTENAY LAKE CONSTRUCTION, AND CANNERY AT "SEACHART"(?).
     (1930's)
     p.c. private
     l. approx. 458' g. 16mm   t. b+w   s. si.
     d.   *
     ph. Rev. George R.B. Kinney
     c.s. NFA, Ottawa

> A.P.L. Camp 3. Loggers operating steam donkey near a camp or town. A.P.L.
> Camp 6. Logging train. CU loggers. Yarding logs by high-lead method. Man
> and truck. Sharpening an axe on a big foot-operated grindstone. Bloedel's
> Franklin River Camp 4. LS Camp in woods. Men falling tree with a swedish
> fiddle. Bucking tree with hand-saw, donkey puffing away in b.g. Man split-
> ting cedar. Dumping log from carriage into pond.

> Kootenay Lake CPR construction site. Steam shovel digging into bank, dumping
> soil into a car being pushed by a steam locomotive. Men pounding ties. Good
> CU workers.

> Excellent shots of the SS MALAHAT unloading logs at Gibson Bros. mill in
> Victoria. Good CU's of East Indians looking on. Scenes aboard ship as logs
> are carefully hooked up and unloaded. Good broadside shots of ship and deck.
> General shots of logs being unloaded, pan of mills and Victoria in b.g., CU
> workers unloading.

> West Coast cannery (at Seachart?). Gulls playing in harbour. Fish boat
> MAPLE LEAF. Cannery roof covered with gulls. Fishing boats lined up, thous-
> ands of gulls flocking about cannery. Fish in hold. CU fishermen. Load of
> fish at cannery. Wharf with large freighter unloading goods. Men on wharf,
> thousands of gulls. Gulls ravage fish, fighting and flapping. Steam pile-
> driver operating.

> A.P.L. Camp 5. Large camp in the forest. Men falling trees. Men working
> on the railroad, laying ties and using hoses. Good shot of a uniformed man
> watching train enter populated area. Locie passes, CU engineer. A pike
> pushes logs off flat cars into a pond. Locie steaming along toward camera.

Men on rails between rows of bunkhouses. Men working donkey engine. Timbers being pulled through camp. Camp scenes. Yarding scenes with steam donkey and spar tree. Locie passes by, CU pistons and wheels. Yarding, loading logs onto flat cars. Shot from locie back to rear of moving logging train. Logs dumped into pond from flat cars. Locie. Spar tree, boom and rigging. Yarding, falling and loading onto train.

A.P.L. Mill at Port Alberni. LS mill. Large freighter passing, good shots. Deer swimming. Pan of Port Alberni. A British destroyer in the roads - good shots. Fishing boat at jetty. Boat from destroyer arrives at wharf. Many good shots of destroyer and Port Alberni shoreline. (Whole reel is excellent, clear, material)

511. LOGGING IN BRITISH COLUMBIA. (before 1927)
   p.c. Pathéscope
   l.   g. 28mm   t. b+w   s. si.
   d.   *
   ph. *
   c.s. Unknown

   "Cutting giant trees on the mountain side and the wild rush as they slide down the steep decline and plunge end on in the river; such scenes graphically portray something of the thrill that accompanies the lumbering industry in the Pacific province." (Province of Ontario Film Catalogue, May 1927)

512. LOGGING IN WINTER, BRITISH COLUMBIA.
   p.c. *
   l.   g.   t.   s.
   d.   *
   ph. *
   c.s. *

   See BRITISH COLUMBIA: LOGGING IN WINTER

513. LOOK BEFORE YOU LIGHT. (late 1930's)
   p.c. B.C. Forest Service (Reel 44)
   l. approx. 250'   g. 16mm   t. colour & b+w s. si. w/captions
   d.   *
   ph. *
   c.s. PABC

   "A short account of the Smith family's picnic at the sea shore and the Forest Ranger who showed them how to build a campfire safely."

514. LORD AND LADY WILLINGDON VIEW OVER 2,000 CHILDREN IN
   SPECTACULAR MAY DAY PARADE AND CELEBRATION, NEW WEST-
   MINSTER, B.C. (1927)
   p.c. Fox Movietonews (Fox #201-C4335)
   l. 100'   g. 35mm   t. b+w   s. si.
   d.   *
   ph. Jos. T. Mandy
   c.s. Fox Movietonews, N.Y.

   "High shot parade, crowds & floats. Margaret Gould crowned Queen of the May. SCU. High shot crowd at field and people forming word WILLINGDON."

515. LORD BYNG AT WAR MEMORIAL, VICTORIA, B.C. (1921)
   p.c. Fox Movietonews (?)
   l. 28'   g. 35mm   t. b+w   s. si.
   d.   *
   ph. Young's Studio (?)
   c.s. NFA (#2710-2712)

   "Lord Byng of Vimy, Governor General of Canada, attends a ceremony at Soldier's Memorial Cenotaph in Victoria, B.C."

516. LORD BYNG IN VICTORIA. (1921)
    p.c. Fox Movietonews (?)
    1. 42'   g. 35mm   t. b+w   s. si.
    d.   *
    ph. Young's Studio (?)
    c.s. NFA (#2713-2715)

                        "Lord Byng, Governor General of Canada, decorates General Clark during a
                        ceremony in Victoria, attends a Scout reception in his honour, and visits
                        the Victoria Memorial Cemetery."

517. LORD BYNG, GOV. GENERAL OF CANADA, PAYS VISIT TO VICTORIA, B.C.
    (1922)
    p.c. Fox Movietonews (Fox #201-3317)
    1. 52'   g. 35mm   t. b+w   s. si.
    d.   *
    ph. Young's Studio
    c.s. Fox Movietonews, N.Y.

                        "His arrival. Inspecting Scottish Battalion and presenting colours. Plan-
                        ting tree. Unveiling memorial cross. Inspecting Boy Scouts. Decorating
                        Brig. Gen. R.P. Clark and Lt. Col. Lorne Cross."

518. LORD BYNG UNVEILS MONUMENT, VANCOUVER. (1925)
    p.c. Fox Movietonews (?)
    1.   g. 35mm   t. b+w   s. si.
    d.   *
    ph. ASN (?)
    c.s. NFB (1920-170-FG-4)

                        "Lord Byng unveils monument to Canada's soldiers. Shot of flag draped arch,
                        erected by Most Noble Order of Crusaders, with officials in f.g. Union Jack
                        is removed from Arch, Chaplain Bishop dePencier officiating. Lord Byng meet-
                        ing Canadian WW I vets." Lord Byng was at this time Governor General of
                        Canada.

519. LORD TWEEDSMUIR ARRIVES ON HMS APOLLO, VANCOUVER, B.C. (1939)
    p.c. Fox Movietonews (Fox #29-516)
    1. 490'   g. 35mm   t. b+w   s. sound
    d.   *
    ph. ASN
    c.s. Fox Movietonews, N.Y.

                        "HMS APOLLO arriving. Gov. Gen. Lord Tweedsmuir with party at the Cenotaph.
                        Lord Tweedsmuir places wreath. Seaforth Highlanders parade for Tweedsmuir
                        on official opening of new armoury. Tweedsmuir taking salute, Seaforth High-
                        landers trooping the colours."

520. LORD TWEEDSMUIR PAYS A VISIT TO VANCOUVER, B.C. (1939)
    p.c. Hearst Metrotone News; Can no. 1008, Roll no. 4
    1.   g. 35mm   t. b+w   s. sound
    d.   *
    ph. ASN
    c.s. Hearst Metrotone News, N.Y.

                        "Lord Tweedsmuir, Governor General of Canada, visits Vancouver. It is his
                        second visit to the west coast. This is his first official appearance. Lady
                        Tweedsmuir is travelling with him."

521. LORD TWEEDSMUIR PRESENTED WITH DOCTOR OF LAW DEGREE,
    VANCOUVER, B.C. (1939)
    p.c. British Movietonews (No. 36027)
    1. 88'   g. 35mm   t. b+w   s. sound
    d.   *
    ph. *
    c.s. British Movietonews

                        Lord Tweedsmuir, Governor General of Canada, is presented with a Doctor of
                        Law degree at the University of British Columbia in Vancouver. Lady Tweeds-
                        muir was also present.

522. LORD TWEEDSMUIR RECEIVES HONOURARY DEGREE, VANCOUVER,
B.C. (1939)
p.c. Fox Movietonews (Fox #37-66)
l. 490'   g. 35mm   t. b+w   s. sound
d.   *
ph. ASN
c.s. Fox Movietonews, N.Y.

"C.O.T.C. Guard of Honour present arms. Lord Tweedsmuir arrives. Salute,
inspection. Rides to UBC Theatre. Procession. Students lined up. Leaving
University Theatre with H.E. McKechnie and Lady Tweedsmuir. At City Hall
Tweedsmuir arrives. On steps. At University line-up. Applauding students
at arrival. Procession to University Theatre. Inside shot of ceremony.
Shots at City Hall. Group L - R: Lord & Lady Tweedsmuir, Mayor & Mrs. Telford.
Party leaves City Hall."

523. LORD WILLINGDON STARTS HOME FROM WEST COAST TOUR,
VANCOUVER, B.C. (1927)
p.c. Fox Movietonews (?)
l.   g. 35mm   t. b+w   s. si.
d.   *
ph. ASN (?)
c.s. NFB (1920-170-FG-5)

"Shot of Governor General Lord Willingdon's boat being escorted by HMCS
PATRICIAN. Good shot of HMCS PATRICIAN under full steam. Shot of CPR ferry
PRINCESS ALICE and PATRICIAN near bridge. Lord and Lady Willingdon greeting
Canadian soldiers near monument in Stanley Park. Greeting Hindu deputation
and Governor of Bombay."

524. LORD WILLINGDON STARTS 600 WALKERS ON 7 MILE MARATHON
THROUGH STANLEY PARK, VANCOUVER, B.C. (1929)
p.c. Fox Movietonews (Fox #733.11-D0074)
l. 200'   g. 35mm   t. b+w   s. si.
d.   *
ph. Ross Beesley
c.s. Fox Movietonews, N.Y.

"Governor General Lord Willingdon starts race. David Bolton is the winner."

525. LOWER SKEENA VALLEY (THE TSIMSHIAN PEOPLE) (1925-27)
p.c. National Museum of Canada
l. 1 reel   g. 35mm   t. b+w   s. si. w/captions
d.   Harlan I. Smith
ph. Harlan I. Smith
c.s. Unknown

Presumably this film shows Indian people and their way of life in the Lower
Skeena Valley. Harlan Smith seems to have had enough footage from his travels
on the Skeena to put together three films, only one of which, THE TSIMSHIAN
INDIANS OF THE SKEENA RIVER OF BRITISH COLUMBIA, is known to exist.

526. LT. GOV. AND MRS. HAMBER PREPARE FOR VISIT OF THE KING
AND QUEEN IN MAY, VICTORIA, B.C. (1939)
p.c. Hearst Metrotone News; Can no. 993, Roll no. 4
l.   g. 35mm   t. b+w   s. sound
d.   *
ph. ASN
c.s. Hearst Metrotone News, N.Y.

"Government House at Victoria, residence of Lt. Gov. and Mrs. Hamber, prepares for visit of King and Queen in May. Gardeners and decorators plan to
make a good showing for the 37 hour visit of the Royal couple. Scenes of
the house and Lt. Gov. and Mrs. Hamber."

527.'LUCKY' CORRIGAN. (1936)
p.c. Central Films, Ltd.
l. 66 min. (5940') g. 35mm   t. b+w   s. sound
d.   Lewis D. Collins
ph. Harry Forbes and William Beckway
c.s. NFA

Canadian producer, Kenneth J. Bishop;
script, Philip Conway; editor, William
Austin; sound, Herbert Eicke; 2nd asst.
dir., Harry Calahan; asst. sound, Jack
Haynes; Columbia overseer, Jack Fier.

l.p. William Gargan, Molly Lamont,
Libby Taylor, James McGrath, J.P.
McGowan, David Clyde, Reginald
Hincks, Harry Hastings, Ernie Impett,
Arthur Kerr, and Robert Rideout.

Working title: VENGEANCE OF THE FOREST. The fifth Quota Quickie made by
Central Films in Victoria and the third of four shot in June and July, 1936.
These were all quota films, costing no more than $50,000, processed and edited
in Hollywood by Columbia Pictures, and sent to England to appease the British
government while still permitting Columbia to exhibit its big costly productions without interruption. Central Films was organized by Kenneth J. Bishop
whose two previous film companies had failed due to a lack of Canadian financing. 'LUCKY' CORRIGAN was released in the United States by Rialto Productions
Corp. with the title FURY AND THE WOMAN.

The plot is as follows: Bruce Corrigan (William Gargan) declines to join the
Carson lumber camp though it is offering ten cents more than the Hamilton
camp with which he has just signed and, after a scuffle with the man doing
the hiring, makes his way alone to the Hamilton camp. On the way he meets
camp boss' wilful daughter June (Molly Lamont) who takes a pot shot at him.
This is the beginning of a love-hate relationship which will only be resolved
at the fade-out. The camp is in difficulty, unable to meet its commitments
due to a shortage of men, some enticed away by higher wages at the Carson
camp, others dismissed by Anderson (J.P. McGowan) the camp foreman, who is
in the pay of the rival camp. Corrigan, mistakenly accused by camp boss
McRae (David Clyde) of sowing dissention among the men, is dismissed and
makes his way to the rival camp pretending to have been in their pay all
along. He persuades the Carson camp to move its men onto the Hamilton territory and cut lumber there, prior to an eventual takeover. Then he learns of
other sabotage plans, including a fire, which he is too late to prevent, and
he rushes back to help McRae and his men fight the blaze. Anderson gets his
just desserts, the company is able to fulfill its contracts with the lumber
already cut by the Carson men, and Corrigan, who is revealed to be Old Hamilton's son, gets the girl.

One of the best of the Central productions, the pace is fast and furious
though it skips over many unlikely moments - nobody makes any attempt to explain to McRae the misunderstanding for which he dismisses Corrigan - and
there are some spectacular action scenes, particularly a head-on collision
high on a trestle bridge between a train hauled by an ancient steam locomotive and a rake of runaway freight cars loaded with logs. A curious item,
given the Canadian setting, is the presence of a black maid (played by Libby
Taylor, who played Mae West's maid in BELLE OF THE NINETIES in 1934). The
traditional Chinese cook was played by Harry Hastings, last seen in SECRETS
OF CHINATOWN. (Storyline description courtesy of D. John Turner, NFA.)

528. LUCKY FUGITIVES. (1935)
p.c. Central Films Ltd.
1. 68 min.   g. 35mm   t. b+w   s. sound
d.   Nick Grinde
ph.   William C. Thompson and William Beckway
c.s. Unknown

Canadian producer, Kenneth J. Bishop;
sound, Herbert Eicke; asst. sound,
Jack Haynes.

l.p. David Manners, Maxine Doyle,
Bob Rideout, James McGrath, Michael
Heppell, Reginald Hincks and J.P.
McGowan.

Working title: STOP, LOOK, AND LOVE. The first feature film produced by Central Films Ltd., the company organized by Kenneth Bishop to make Quota Quickies
for Columbia Pictures of Hollywood. The picture was begun in November 1935
and completed by early 1936. The reviews, while not praising the picture,
did appreciate the "workmanlike" and "efficient" qualities of the direction
and the acting.

LUCKY FUGITIVES is apparently the story of a famous author who gets into
trouble when a man who is his double escapes from prison. From an examination
of the production stills that remain, it appears that the author is for some
reason handcuffed to a young woman and that the two of them become fugitives,
probably from the police and the crooks. The film presumably chronicles their
adventures and, one can imagine, the onset of an unintentional romance. Loca-

tions included the old Crystal Pool, made to resemble an ocean liner's swimming tank, and parts of the E & N Railway line near Langford on Vancouver Island where Doyle and Manners jumped handcuffed from a train. Scenes were also filmed on the RMSS EMPRESS OF RUSSIA and on the CPR wharfs in Victoria.

According to the Monthly Film Bulletin (March 1936, p.44) the plot of LUCKY FUGITIVES is as follows:

"The story is of a young and successful author who has a double who is a gangster and escaped convict. On board ship the author, Jack, meets a bogus prince engaged to Aileen, a rich man's daughter, and Aileen falls in love with Jack. The "prince" frames Jack, who is arrested on his arrival in America, and has considerable difficulty in proving that he is himself and not his double, whose name is King. Jack is next abducted by King who, in return for help he once gave Jack, demands that Jack should help him and his wife to escape. This involves the temporary disappearance of Jack, who disguises himself as a waiter to be near Aileen. Meanwhile, Aileen's father has discovered that the "prince" is a fraud and a cardsharper, and has him arrested. Aileen goes off indignant. Jack escapes in her car. They are pursued by detectives who again think Jack is King. A hectic chase leads up to explanations all round, and the expected happy ending. Allowing for the inherent improbabilities of the plot, the film provides excitement and romance and an abundance of incident. The direction is workmanlike, and the acting efficient rather than outstanding."

529. THE LUMBER TRAIN, CANADA. (1922)
    p.c. Pathé News
    1. 99'   g. 35mm   t. b+w   s. si. w/captions
    d. *
    ph. *
    c.s. EMI Pathé Archives

"Aerial tramway across a heavily treed gulch - "American canyon" - camera mounted on top of gondola piled with heavy boards. Shots of tram crossing canyon with boards and cameramen on top. Finally reaching other side." Caption reads: MOVING 9 TONS OF TIMBER EACH JOURNEY." This may have been near Campbell River on Vancouver Island.

530. LUMBER TRANSPORTATION REMARKABLY FACILITATED BY AERIAL
    TRAMWAYS. (1928)
    p.c. Pathé
    1.   g. 35mm   t. b+w   s. si.
    d. *
    ph. *
    c.s. NFB (1920-FG-187)

"LS of trailer trucks hauling giant logs, passing by camera. LS Pathé cameraman boarding "Skyline". Aerial shots of wooded ravines as seen from aerial tramline." This may have been near Campbell River on Vancouver Island.

531. LUMBERING IN BRITISH COLUMBIA. (1925)
    p.c. CGMPB (#97)
    1. 751'   g. 35mm   t. b+w   s. si. w/captions
    d. *
    ph. *
    c.s. NFA, BFI & BCPM (35mm)

"British Columbia produces many million feet of lumber annually and one-third of the total output of Canada. Her immense forests contain probably the finest timber in the world today and in this educational film, replete with scenic beauties, is depicted, in graphic manner, the lumbering operations, from the felling of the giant trees to the export shipping of the finished product."

View up a tall Douglas-fir. At the base two men are examining the trunk. Two notches are cut and springboards placed in them. The two men test the springboards, then make an undercut with saw and axe, both men chopping. The men test the direction of the falling tree by putting the head of the axe into the notched undercut and sighting down the handle. They begin to saw through from the other side with a swedish fiddle. The tree falls, five men stand on the stump. View of the end of the tree, shot of the length of the tree. *Two buckers arrive and begin to saw the tree into manageable lengths. LS high rigger at the top of a spar after topping. A log is lifted off the ground by a steel cable. Good view of a donkey engine working. Log moving down skid-way. Head-on shot of log plunging into a pond with spectacular spray. Logs are formed into Davis rafts in the bay. LS large boom of logs. Logs piled at the mill, a donkey working, sheds, etc. Good shot of a heap of logs with red ensign on a boat in the f.g. Logs being loaded onto a B.C. ELECTRIC flatcar. Train moves out on way to mill, passing a little station, etc. LS HASTINGS SAW MILL with rafts and booms of logs spread out before it. Log being drawn up endless chain into the saws. Shot of booms. Good shots of log on carriage being squared by saw with operator in f.g. Men receiving lumber on green chain. Scene in the lumber yard where lumber is being sorted, graded and piled. Big timbers being pushed down a ramp into a pile. Long timbers on a speeder on the RR tracks in the mill. Long timbers being loaded onto a chute where they slide down onto a pile of lumber.*

532. LUMBERING IN CANADA. (before 1935)
    p.c. *
    1. 17 minutes   g. 16mm   t. b+w   s. si.
    d.   *
    ph. *
    c.s. Unknown

        "A pictorial visit to the forests of British Columbia. Lumberjacks at work. The skill of felling. Liquid refreshment for the cross cut saw. Cutting the tree into lengths. Snaking out. Loading on rail cars. Dumping into storage ponds. The circular saw and the result."

533. MACKENZIE PARK. (1923-1930)
    p.c. National Museum of Canada
    1. 1 reel   g. 35mm   t. b+w   s. si.
    d.   Harlan I. Smith
    ph. Harlan I. Smith
    c.s. Unknown

534. MAGIC METAL. (before 1935)
    p.c. *
    1. 1 reel   g. 35mm   t. b+w   s. sound
    d.   *
    ph. *
    c.s. Unknown

        "Gold mining in British Columbia."

535. MAINTAINING THE QUALITY OF CANADIAN GROWN SEED THROUGH THE
     PRODUCTION AND USE OF REGISTERED SEED. (1930 or 1931)
    p.c. CGMPB
    1. 3 reels/1100'   g. 35mm   t. b+w   s. si. w/captions
    d.   *
    ph. *
    c.s. PABC (Agriculture reels 60, 61 & 62)

        Produced under the direction of the Seed Division, Dominion Seed Branch, in co-operation with the Cereal Division, Experimental Farms Branch, Dept. of Agriculture, Ottawa.

        The first two reels establish the importance of crossing different strains of wheat to create hardier and better strains, but there is nothing about British Columbia. REEL THREE however, after showing the harvesting and threshing of grain on the prairies, moves to scenes of grain handling and shipping at the Port of Vancouver. LS grain elevator, Vancouver and closer shots of same. Pan across harbour to ship being loaded. Many good shots of terminal loading and storage facilities. Ship at wharf: DALVEEN. Excellent shots of ship being loaded, the facilities, and men working on the ship and docks.

536. MAINTAINING THE SALMON SUPPLY. (1922)
    p.c. Dept. of Trade and Commerce Exhibits
         and Publicity Bureau, Ottawa
    l. 1 reel   g. 35mm   t. b+w   s. si. w/captions
    d. *
    ph. *
    c.s. Unknown

                    "The story of Lakelse Fish Hatchery, where male and female salmon, bound up-
                    river to spawn, are trapped, and the eggs removed and hatched by scientific
                    methods. Later the young fry and fingerlings are released to restock the
                    rivers and provide the fishing industry with its annual harvest." The fish
                    are Sockeye salmon.

537. MAJOR GENERAL A.G.L. MCNAUGHTON INSPECTS SEAFORTH HIGH-
    LANDERS IN VANCOUVER, B.C. (1939)
    p.c. Paramount (Lib. #8954)
    l.   g. 35mm   t. b+w   s. sound
    d. *
    ph. ASN
    c.s. Sherman Grinberg, N.Y.

                    Seaforth Highlanders marching out of barracks. Gen. McNaughton, Commander
                    of the First Canadian Division, walking with General Victor W. Odlum, in
                    civilian clothes. McNaughton comes forward, the soldiers present arms.
                    McNaughton inspects the recruits. They march across the field. March past.
                    McNaughton.

538. MALAHAT HIGHWAY TOUR, VANCOUVER ISLAND, B.C. - 1911
    p.c. *
    l.   g. 35mm   t. b+w   s. si.
    d. *
    ph. *
    c.s. NFA (Taylor reel 118)

                    "Excellent tracking shot along gravelled highway through virgin stand of
                    Douglas-firs, rear view of cars bouncing along road, over small bridge,
                    through newly slashed stand of coniferous trees. Group picnicking along
                    riverbank as people paddle past in pointer-style boat & punt. High angle
                    shot of autos passing through newly slashed area near Port Alberni, of cars
                    passing through narrow cut in a forest of huge firs. Good shot of Malahat
                    Highway, several autos speeding past camera along gravelled highway, autos
                    raising dust as they pass through downtown section of city of Victoria. Car
                    speeding along the Malahat drive, just two ruts in a narrow track. Various
                    shots autos on the Malahat, tilt up to train on way East on an upper level
                    of Malahat Mountain (?). Shots of road as seen from front of auto speeding
                    through forest area & over bridges. Fuzzy shot at end of Port Alberni folks
                    gathered for a picnic."

539. MAMMA COYOTE PRESENTS STANLEY PARK ZOO WITH TWO BABIES,
    VANCOUVER, B.C. (early 1920's)
    p.c. Fox Movietonews (Fox #411.339-B8389)
    l. 20'   g. 35mm   t. b+w   s. si.
    d. *
    ph. Len H. Roos
    c.s. Fox Movietonews, N.Y.

                    "Coyote, 2 cubs, one of them in keeper's arms."

540. MANHATTAN SHAKEDOWN. (1937)
    p.c. Central Films Ltd.
    l. 57 min.(5114') g. 35mm   t. b+w   s. sound
    d. Leon Barsha
    ph. George Meehan
    c.s. NFA

            Canadian prod., Kenneth J. Bishop;   l.p. Rosalind Keith, John Gallaudet,
            script, Edgard Edwards from a story   George McKay, Reginald Hincks, Robert
            by Theodore Tinsley; editor, William   Rideout, Phyllis Clare, Donald Douglas,
            Austin; asst. dir., George Rhein;   Michael Heppell, and Grant MacDonald.
            sound, Herbert Eicke; asst. sound,
            Jack Haynes; Columbia overseer, Jack
            Fier.

Working title: MANHATTAN WHIRLWIND. Quota Quickie number nine by Central Films, the cover-up company for Columbia Pictures in Victoria. MANHATTAN SHAKEDOWN, produced in August 1937, apparently had little to recommend it, one review calling it "wildly improbable". It was shot entirely in Victoria with sets and shots arranged to suggest a New York locale. This film, a companion piece to MURDER IS NEWS, was copyrighted in the United States by Warwick Pictures on March 17, 1939.

The plot is as follows: Jerry Tracey (John Gallaudet), a newspaper reporter, suspects that a psychiatrist, Dr. Stoner (Reginald Hicks), is blackmailing his patients. When Tracey's friend Al Redman (Michael Heppell), a bank employee, is blackmailed Tracey denounces Stoner publicly and sets out to prove his accusations. Mike Orell (Robert Rideout), a small time hood, is hired to kill Tracey but fails, and when his sister (Phyllis Claire) is also threatened Orell agrees to collaborate with Tracey. The denouement comes in an old brownstone house in Greenwich Village where the blackmail victims come to make their payments to a hooded man. Tracy, his assistant "Brains" (George McKay), Orell, his sister and Dr. Stroner's daughter, Gloria (Rosalind Keith), are present; Orell and the masked man are both killed and the black-mailer is revealed to be Hadley Brown (Donald Douglas), Gloria's finacée and Stoner's partner. (Storyline description courtesy of D. John Turner, NFA.)

541. MANY A YOUNG LADY THROUGHOUT CANADA WOULD CHANGE PLACES
     WITH THIS GIRL AND HER "MUMS", VANCOUVER, B.C. (1923)
     p.c. Fox Movietonews (Fox #423 - B3028)
     1. 30'   g. 35mm   t. b+w   s. si.
     d.   *
     ph. Len H. Roos
     c.s. Fox Movietonews, N.Y.

> *"Christmas scenes. Girl picking flowers in hot house. CU girl with chrysan-themums, making holly wreath."*

542. MARBLES AND JACKS CONTEST SPREADS TO THE WEST COAST UNDER THE
     AUSPICES OF THE SUN, VANCOUVER, B.C. (1924)
     p.c. Fox Movietonews (Fox #740.16-B5724)
     1. 25'   g. 35mm   t. b+w   s. si.
     d.   *
     ph. *
     c.s. Fox Movietonews, N.Y.

> *"Kids playing at jacks and marbles."*

543. MARKETING CANADIAN APPLES. (1927-1929)
     p.c. CGMPB
     1. 3 reels   g. 35mm   t. b+w   s. si. w/captions
     d.   *
     ph. *
     c.s. NFB Archives has a copy of Part 1, Archives P.B. 92/(1930-L-103-1)

> *Made for the Fruit Branch of the Department of Agriculture, Ottawa, and also known under the title MARKETING THE CANADIAN APPLE. The description in the Catalogue for 1930 reads: "That Canada's apple harvest amounts to more than three million barrels a year, gives some idea of the size of this great in-dustry. How the apples are picked and packed - by box in British Columbia, (where girls pack as many as a hundred and fifty a day!); by barrel in the East - how they are carefully graded according to size and quality, and guar-anteed through government inspection; their journey to the terminal markets; and the export trade, are highlights in a film which gives in popular style the story of marketing Canadian apples."*

> *REEL ONE: "The commercial apple harvest is a gigantic industry that stretches across Canada. Pan over what presumably is apple growing country from van-tage point. Shot of B.C. saw mill where boxes for packaging apples are made. CU apple tree and of three apples. A man picks apples rapidly then empties his bag into a barrel. Shot of boxes of apples being loaded onto a wagon, of wagon being pulled to packaging plant, of boxes being unloaded and carried into plant by an automatic carrier. In the plant, several persons sit at a table inspecting the fruits. The apples are graded by hand according to colour and by machines according to size. Then they are hand-wrapped and packed. Shot of Government inspector checking grading of boxes of apples. Some of the boxes are placed in cold storage plant for late shipping, others*

*are slated for export and must be wired. The boxes are carefully stacked
in box cars and brought to markets." (781')*

*REELS TWO & THREE presumably deal with the Ontario crop and further marketing,
perhaps in B.C. and abroad.*

544. MARKETING THE CANADIAN APPLE. (1927-1929)
    p.c. *
    l.   g.   t.   s.
    d.   *
    ph.   *
    c.s. *

                  See MARKETING THE CANADIAN APPLES.

545. MARSHALL JOFFRE, HERO OF THE MARNE, RECEIVES ENTHUSIASTIC WELCOME ON
    ARRIVAL HERE. VICTORIA, VANCOUVER, AND BLAINE PEACE ARCH, B.C. (1922)
    p.c. Fox Movietonews (Fox #201-B8399)
    l. 40'   g. 35mm   t. b+w   s. si.
    d.   *
    ph.   D.C. Davey
    c.s. Fox Movietonews, N.Y.

            *"LS SS SILVER STATE docking and passengers leaving. SCU Marshall Joffre with
            Alderman Andros and Mr. Samuel Hill leaving customs house. LBS Joffre plan-
            ting a tree. LS Joffre and party at Vancouver. LS Joffre & party at Blaine
            Peace Arch."*

546. MARSHALL JOFFRE VISITS VICTORIA, B.C. (1922)
    p.c. Pathé News (Pathé Sil .28, Neg. #3601)
    l.   g. 35mm   t. b+w   s. si.
    d.   *
    ph.   *
    c.s. Lost

                  Various shots of Joffre's visit.

547. MASS PHYSICAL DISPLAY, VANCOUVER, B.C. (1939)
    p.c. Fox Movietonews (Fox #37-433)
    l. 600'   g. 35mm   t. b+w   s. sound
    d.   *
    ph.   ASN
    c.s. Fox Movietonews, N.Y.

            *"Participants marching. Led into Provincial Recreational Centre by flag
            carrying group and all participants singing O CANADA. Swedish Weaving Dance
            by women. LS & Semi CU Barbell drill by men. Rythmic gymnastics by women.
            Participants march. Fundamental gymnastics by women. March. T. Patullo
            arrives. Ian Eisenhardt speech. Parade, dancing, gymnastics."*

548. MAMMOTH PARADE INTRODUCES SUMMER SPORTS ON THE COAST,
    VICTORIA, B.C. (1924)
    p.c. Fox Movietonews (Fox 751.15-A102)
    l.   g. 35mm   t. b+w   s. si.
    d.   *
    ph.   Len H. Roos
    c.s. Fox Movietonews, N.Y.

                  Includes shots of war canoe races and floats.

549. MAY DAY ANNIVERSARY AT GUELPH, ONTARIO, AND NEW WESTMINSTER,
    B.C. (1922)
    p.c. Fox Movietonews (Fox #095.7-4772)
    l. 55'   g. 35mm   t. b+w   s. si.
    d.   *
    ph.   in New Westminster: Errington
    c.s. Fox Movietonews, N.Y.

550. MAY DAY PARADE, VANCOUVER. (1938)
    p.c. private
    l. 50'   g. 8mm   t. b+w   s. si.
    d.   *
    ph. J.W. Bowdery
    c.s. via Pacific Cinémathèque, Vancouver

            *Parade marching along Hastings Street. American band (?). Highland band.
            Shriners. Pageant in Stanley Park (colour). Ladies in crinolines. This
            may have been a PNE parade, but is not identified.*

            *MAY DAY PARADE: This is quite exciting, and contains groups of men and women
            marching under several different banners. The banners read, in order: STOP
            HITLER - SAVE PEACE, ????? SUPPORT DEMOCRACY, MACKENZIE PAPINEAU BATTALION,
            WHITE LUNCH - EDEN - WALDORF - ON UNFAIR LIST, COMMUNIST PARTY CANADA - B.C.
            DISTRICT - Jobs - Recovery - Democracy and Peace, RELIEF PROJECT WORKERS
            UNION WORKERS DEMANDING JOBS, SPAIN VETS - WELCOME HOME, WE ARE AGAINST MIL-
            ITARISATION - THE YOUTH, DEMAND HANDS OFF YUGOSLAVIA - YUGOSLAVIAN PROGRES-
            SIVE MOVEMENT, DOWN WITH IMPERIALIST WAR, and BREAD NOT BULLETS. The film
            also shows a newsboy selling the PEOPLE'S ADVOCATE newspaper, and a group
            from the baker's union, as well as several bands.*

551. MEMBERS OF PORTLAND LODGE OF ELKS STOP OFF FOR SHORT
    VISIT ON THEIR WAY HOME, VANCOUVER, B.C. (1920)
    p.c. Fox Movietonews (Fox #042.04-1407)
    l. 27'   g. 35mm   t. b+w   s. si.
    d.   *
    ph. British - American Film Co.
    c.s. Fox Movietonews, N.Y.

552. MEMORY OF NELSON HONOURED IN CANADA, VICTORIA, B.C.
    (1932)
    p.c. Fox Movietonews (Fox #16-317)
    l.   g. 35mm   t. b+w   s. sound
    d.   *
    ph. ASN
    c.s. Fox Movietonews, N.Y.

            *"Anniversary of Trafalgar celebrated at ceremonies in Victoria, British
            Columbia, led by Lt. Gov. Johnson."*

553. MEN OF A CANADIAN INDIAN TRIBE PUT ON A RODEO IN VANCOUVER
    FEATURING BUCKING BRONCOS AND THRILLS AND SPILLS. (1930)
    p.c. *
    l.   g. 35mm   t. b+w   s. si.
    d.   *
    ph. *
    c.s. NFB (1930-FG-194)

            *Part of a news collection called NEWS FROM THE WILDS, 1930. The description
            reads: "Shots of riders being thrown from broncos, thrown from steers. One
            rider sticking with bronco."*

554. METHODS OF TRANSPORTING LOGS IN BRITISH COLUMBIA. (1909)
    p.c. *
    l. 450'   g. 35mm   t. b+w   s. si.
    d.   *
    ph. *
    c.s. Unknown

            *"Illustrated by pictures secured during the last season, these means of cut-
            ting down and hauling the giant trees of the great Northwest form a brilliant
            and wonderful subject fascinating every beholder. Chute scenes - mighty logs
            handled as though they were toys. Hauling logs by mechanical means through
            the primeval forests. A log train. Logs shot into the river from a trestle
            pier. Still waters disturbed and lashed into fury by the massive trunks. A
            raft of thousands of pine logs. Bracing together the individual logs. Logs
            brought down the river by chute from the heights. A weird spectacle. Per-
            fectly photographed in stereoscopic scenes of great beauty." George Kleine
            Catalogue, 1910. p.262.*

555. MICHIGAN SPRINTER SETS WORLD MARK, VANCOUVER, B.C.   (1930)
    p.c. Pathé News
    l.   g. 35mm   t. b+w   s. sound
    d.   *
    ph.   *
    c.s. NFB (1920-FG-273)

> *"LS six sprinters, Tolan winning, being congratulated, being awarded trophy, making a speech. Eddie Tolan, negro sprinter from Michigan."*

556. MID MAJESTIC SPLENDOUR OF TOWERING MOUNTAINS SKIING CHAMPIONS VIE FOR
    CANADA'S PREMIER HONOURS, REVELSTOKE, B.C.   (1920's)
    p.c. Fox Movietonews (Fox #732.3-B8725)
    l. 35'   g. 35mm   t. b+w   s. si.
    d.   *
    ph.   *
    c.s. Fox Movietonews, N.Y.

> *"LS jump & crowds. LBS & CBS jumper taking off."*

557. MIDWINTER SWIMMING IN ENGLISH BAY IS SPECIAL SPORT OF
    SEVERAL ROYAL LIFESAVING SOCIETY MEMBERS, VANCOUVER, B.C.
    (1925)
    p.c. Fox Movietonews (Fox #731.2-B6838)
    l. 40'   g. 35mm   t. b+w   s. si.
    d.   *
    ph.   Herron
    c.s. Fox Movietonews, N.Y.

> *"Swimming in ocean, running in quickly."*

558. MIKADO'S BROTHER IS FIRST ROYAL VISITOR FOR THE CORONATION,
    VANCOUVER, B.C. and other centres.   (1937)
    p.c. British Movietonews (No. 5300 or 5301)
    l. B.C.: 35'   g. 35mm   t. b+w   s. sound
    d.   *
    ph.   *
    c.s. British Movietonews

> *IN VANCOUVER: Japanese children waving Japanese flags and Union Jacks as Prince and Princess Chichibou are driven along the street, wet and rainy, with motorcycle behind. Prince and Princess stroll with dignitary, crowd in b.g. Japanese children waving flags again. CU Prince and wife from waist up, standing in doorway. Commentator: Eric Dunstan.*

559. MILES CANNON TRAMWAY.   (1899-1900)
    p.c. Edison Mfg. Co.
    l. 34'   g. 35mm (16mm available) t. b+w s. si.
    d.   *
    ph.   Robert Bonine (?)
    c.s. LOC Paper Print Collection

> *"This primitive railway made of rough logs show one of the means adopted by the miners in conveying supplies in a new country (the Klondike). Each car, as it approaches, can be seen as it passes to be loaded with all sorts of supplies, which are being transferred by this method from the steamer seen in the distance to another at a point above the rapids. The activity shown in handling these supplies at this point shows htat time is an important item in the Klondike." The print is not in good condition, and it is difficult ascertain what the miners in the film are doing. The only buildings to be seen are canvas-covered, tent-like structures. Some farm wagons, mounted on railroad train wheels and drawn by horses, are driven toward the camera. (The original 35mm print was 75' long and copyrighted in May 1901).*

560. MILL MAGIC, Part I.   (1930's)
    p.c. A.E.F. (A.F. Films?)
    l. approx. 300'   g. 16mm   t. b+w   s. si. w/captions
    d.   *
    ph.   A.E. Rutherford
    c.s. Via Pacific Cinémathèque, Vancouver

*An educational film showing how trees are taken from the forests of Vancouver
Island and sawn into lumber. Filmed almost entirely at VICTORIA LUMBER &
MFG. CO. LTD. in Chemainus.*

*Brief scenes of tree being felled, piled with other logs onto a flat car and
delivered by rail to the sawmill. The scenes inside the mill are extremely
detailed, each part of the sawing equipment being named and shown in CU. The
process ends at the sorting table. MILL MAGIC Part II has not been located.*

561. MILLION DOLLAR VIADUCT OPENED BY MAYOR HAYWARD WILL
    CONNECT OAK BAY TO ESQUIMALT HARBOUR, VICTORIA, B.C.
    (n.d.)
    p.c. Fox Movietonews (Fox #095.83-C2752)
    l. 45'   g. 35mm   t. b+w   s. si.
    d.   *
    ph. *
    c.s. Fox Movietonews, N.Y.

        "People, traffic."

562. THE MINE ON THE YUKON. (1912)
    p.c. Thomas A. Edison, Inc.
    l.   g. 35mm   t. b+w   s. si.
    d.   *
    ph. *
    c.s. Unknown

        *Little is known of this film. The title indicates that it might have been
        shot in the Yukon. It was released on April 2 1912.*

563. MINING IN CANADA. (1925)
    p.c. Ontario Government
    l. 1 reel   g. 35mm   t. b+w   s. si.
    d.   *
    ph. *
    c.s. NFB (1920-N-112)

        *There are three stories on this reel. The first two deal with asbestos
        mining in Quebec and nickle mining in Ontario. The third concerns gold
        mining in British Columbia and is described as follows: "Shot of miners at
        work underground. CU of main vein and nugget. Sequence showing gold being
        melted. Close shots of slabs being cast in foundry."*

564. MISS DORIS O. MCCLEAVE, 12 YEAR OLD GIRL OF VANCOUVER,
    B.C., CHAMPION AT HURDLES, VANCOUVER, B.C. (1920)
    p.c. Fox Movietonews (Fox #201-2353)
    l. 134'   g. 35mm   t. b+w   s. si.
    d.   *
    ph. Singelow
    c.s. Fox Movietonews, N.Y.

        Shots of Miss McCleave hurdling.

565. MISSION BOAT PURCHASED BY UNITED CHURCH OF CANADA, VANCOUVER,
    (1938)
    p.c. Fox Movietonews (Fox #33-886)
    l.   g. 35mm   t. b+w   s. sound
    d.   *
    ph. ASN
    c.s. Fox Movietonews, N.Y.

        *"Rev. Osterhaut turns boat THOMAS CROSBY 4TH over to Rev. Kelly. Kelly &
        wife reply to Osterhaut. LS showing old THOMAS CROSBY 3RD at left and
        THOMAS CROSBY 4TH at right. Boat on trial trip. This boat is used to visit
        Indian villages, lighthouses, and any remote spot where people may live. It
        covers an average of 1000 miles per month. It also takes care of the sick."*

566. MODEL YACHT RACING AS IT IS DONE BY THE INDEPENDENT
     CLUB DURING ITS MID-WINTER REGATTA, VANCOUVER, B.C.
     (1924)
     p.c. Fox Movietonews (Fox #755.8-B3900)
     1. 50'   g. 35mm t. b+w   s. si.
     d.   *
     ph. Len H. Roos
     c.s. Fox Movietonews, N.Y.

               Model yacht races.

567. A MODERN EDEN. (1930's)
     p.c. *
     1. approx. 400' g. 16mm t. b+w   s. sound
     d.   *
     ph. *
     c.s. Unknown

               *"Blossom and harvest times in the fruit belt." This film may not be about
               British Columbia.*

568. MONSTER LOGS SPEED DOWN ROARING FLUME AT 60 MPH
     FROM INTERIOR LAKE TO WAITING SEA, SCOTT COVE, B.C.
     (1928)
     p.c. Fox Movietonews (Fox #420.75-C7799)
     1. 100'   g. 35mm t. b+w   s. si.
     d.   *
     ph. Jos. T. Mandy
     c.s. Fox Movietonews, N.Y.

               *"Various shots of the logs going down the flume. A crooked, kinky pathway -
               close shot & LS logs going down flume."*

569. MONUMENT PERPETUATING MEMORY OF PAULINE JOHNSON, INDIAN
     SINGER, POETESS AND AUTHORESS, IS UNVEILED IN STANLEY
     PARK, VANCOUVER, B.C. (1922)
     p.c. Fox Movietonews (Fox #095.8-C2754)
     1. 20'   g. 35mm t. b+w   s. si.
     d.   *
     ph. Errington
     c.s. Fox Movietonews, N.Y.

570. MORE THAN HIS DUTY. (1910)
     p.c. Edison Mfg. Co.
     1. 1000'   g. 35mm t. b+w   s. si.
     d.   J. Searle Dawley (?)
     ph. Henry Cronjager (?)
     c.s. Unknown

               *This film is not mentioned in the Edison Co.'s Production Log, but may have
               been made during the Western tour of Edison's troupe in the summer of 1910,
               a trip underwritten by the CPR. There is no record of location, or content,
               but the film was probably made in B.C., or Alberta, if it was part of the
               CPR promotional series.*

571. MOST SPECTACULAR PROCESSION EVER HELD ON COAST USHERS IN A
     NEW SEASON OF SUMMER FROLIC, VICTORIA, B.C. (1923)
     p.c. Fox Moveitonews (Fox #751.15-C2175)
     1. 100'   g. 35mm t. b+w   s. si.
     d.   *
     ph. Len H. Roos
     c.s. Fox Movietonews, N.Y.

               *"Parade. Lt. Gov. Nichol crowns Queen of the May Dora Rolls. CU float
               SPIRIT OF VICTORIA."*

572. MOTORING IN CLOUDLAND. (1923)
   p.c. CGMPB
   1. 1 reel   g. 35mm   t. b+w   s. si. w/captions
   d.   *
   ph.   *
   c.s. Unknown

                    "A scenic travelogue of the new Banff-Windermere highway through the central
                    Canadian Rockies and the completing link of the world's most spectacular
                    motor route - the 4,200 mile Grand Circle Tour of Canada and the United
                    States. Interspersed with views of the magnificent scenery along the route
                    are unique glimpses of the wild life of the National Parks in the vicinity
                    of the famous resort, Banff, Alberta."

573. MOTORING IN CLOUDLAND. (1939-40)
   p.c. CGMPB
   1. 1 reel   g. 35mm   t. colour s. sound
   d.   *
   ph.   *
   c.s. Unknown

                    No further information available on this film. It presumably shows an auto-
                    mobile trip through part of the Rocky Mountains in either Alberta or British
                    Columbia or both. The title is taken from an earlier CGMPB film of the same
                    name.

574. MOUNT ASSINIBOINE (MOUNTAINEERING MEMORIES) (1917)
   p.c. Dept. of Trade and Commerce Exhibits and
        Publicity Bureau, Ottawa
   1. 1 reel   g. 35mm   t. b+w   s. si. w/captions
   d.   *
   ph.   *
   c.s. NFB (1920-DN-57)

                    MOUNT ASSINIBOINE was later issued under the title MOUNTAINEERING MEMORIES,
                    its original subtitle. The film was intended to promote tourism in Canada,
                    particularly from the United States. The original description reads: "A
                    scenic film of the rarest beauty. One that has been favourably commented on
                    by both American and Canadian journalists, depicting a trip from Banff, 35
                    miles out along a glorious trail to Mt. Assiniboine. It shows the party
                    camping at the foot of the mountain, story time around the campfire, prep-
                    aration for ascent on Mt. Assiniboine's tremendous glacier. A panorama of
                    glory around and about 8,500 feet altitude is reached, and then a storm
                    arising with a gale upon the mountain peak at 70 miles an hour forcing the
                    party to descend. This film depicts nature in many moods."

                    The footage held by the NFB Archives is out-footage but of a very interesting
                    nature. Much of it shows scenes of mountains and climbers, but there is a
                    comical meal sequence: "Cook making flap-jacks, tickles the bare feet of
                    sleeper which protrude from under the side of the tent. Sleeper wakes up
                    in a frenzy, grabs his trusty six-gun and promptly shoots a hole in the flap-
                    jack pot, thus letting all the batter flow into the fire." The NFB footage
                    is 824'.

575. A MOUNTAIN BLIZZARD. (1910)
   p.c. Edison Mfg. Co.
   1.   g. 35mm   t. b+w   s. si.
   d.   *
   ph.   *
   c.s. Unknown

                    There is no other information on this film. It may have nothing to do with
                    British Columbia.

576. MOUNTAIN CLIMBING IN BRITISH COLUMBIA. (1916)
   p.c. Ford Motion Picture Laboratories
   1. 244'   g. 35mm   t. b+w   s. si. w/captions
   d.   *
   ph.   *
   c.s. USNA Ford Film Collection (200FC-1022)

"A party of men and women go mountain climbing in the Rockies. Shot of Mt. Victoria. Snow-capped mountain peaks all around. Climbers approaching the snow line. Various climbing shots. One of the party disappeared into a crevasse and repeated it again for the camera. More climbing until they reach the Lake in the Clouds. Towering above the lake is Mt. Whyte. More climbing until they reach the Bridge on the Edge of the Earth. Here they traverse the narrow causeway very carefully. They stop for a rest and refreshments at a mountain lodge. A man and a woman sit on the porch. Views of mountain lake & forest. The climbers arrive at the vast Lefroy and Victoria Glaciers and are dwarfed by the 250' thick ice mass. They continue climbing, ever upward."

577. MOUNTAIN CLIMBING IN CANADA. (1916)
    p.c. Ford Motion Picture Laboratories. (1916)
    1. 102'   g. 35mm   t. b+w   s. si. w/captions
    d.   *
    ph. *
    c.s. USNA Ford Film Collection (200FC-1017c)

        Two men having a snowball fight. Canadian flag flying from a dead tree on summit of a mountain. Climbers come up over the rocks to the top, women in long skirts included in group of climbers. View of snow-capped mountain. (film very light). Group on top of mountain. View of mountains. Group at top of mountain, flag. Although the ground the climbers are standing on may not be in British Columbia, the mountain ranges in the b.g. will be. There are 17 unrelated feet at the beginning showing cattle and cowboys, unidentified. This reel may be the final section of LAGGAN TO LAKE LOUISE AND A CLIMB TO THE TOP OF THE WORLD, shot at the same time and available from the USNA.

578. MOUNTAIN INDIANS HOLD BIG SPORTS DAY, CRANBROOK, B.C.
    (1922)
    p.c. Fox Movietonews (Fox #007.434-3098)
    1. 59'   g. 35mm   t. b+w   s. si.
    d.   *
    ph. M. Nelson
    c.s. Fox Movietonews, N.Y.

        "Indians parading in fancy costumes. Indians at sport grounds. Best dressed Indian and squaw win prizes."

579. A MOUNTAIN MAID. (1910)
    p.c. Edison Mfg. Co. (Catalogue #6720)
    1. 755'   g. 35mm   t. b+w   s. si.
    d.   J. Searle Dawley (?)
    ph. Henry Cronjager (?)
    c.s. Unknown

        There is little information on this film. It is not in the Edison Mfg. Co.'s Production Log. No location given. There is a chance, however, that it is one of the shorts made by the Edison Co. during its tour of western Canada for the CPR to make promotional pictures.

580. MOUNTAIN OBSTACLES ARE GRADUALLY OBLITERATED AS CON-
    STRUCTION PROGRESSES ON TRANSCONTINENTAL HIGHWAY,
    CROW'S NEST PASS, B.C. (1926)
    p.c. Fox Movietonews (Fox #321.5-B3170)
    1. 38'   g. 35mm   t. b+w   s. si.
    d.   *
    ph. W.J. Oliver
    c.s. Fox Movietonews, N.Y.

        "LS of mountain. LS of road. Blasting. Gang at work. Steam shovel at work. Removing surface boulders."

581. MOUNTAINEERING BY CANOE. (before 1935)
    p.c. *
    1. 1 reel   g. 35mm   t. b+w   s. si.
    d.   *
    ph. *
    c.s. Unknown

"By pack and paddle down the Kootenay River, through the Vermillion Range, on the Banff-Windermere road, and other scenes of Western Canada."

582. MOUNTAINEERING MEMORIES. (1917)
    p.c. EPB
    l. 1 reel   g. 35mm   t. b+w   s. si. w/captions
    d.   *
    ph. *
    c.s. unknown

                    See MOUNT ASSINIBOINE.

583. MOUNTAINEERS PREPARE TO SCALE MOUNT LOGAN, 19,350 FEET
    HIGH, AND SEND OUT A GUIDE TO SELECT THE BEST ROUTE,
    YUKON. (1925)
    p.c. Fox Movietonews (Fox #007.341-A5578)
    l. 125'   g. 35mm   t. b+w   s. si.
    d.   *
    ph. Surratt
    c.s. Fox Movietonews, N.Y.

            "Guide ascending with dogs. Various shots of the guide covering a snowfield.
            Dogs are relieved of their packs and frolic in the snow. Forward over the
            vast icefields with the granite crags of the St. Elias Mountains looming near.
            CU of dog team."

584. MR. & MRS. JOHN DILL, AFTER WALKING ACROSS CANADA FROM
    HALIFAX, ARE WELCOMED BY ACTING MAYOR OWEN, VANCOUVER, B.C.
    (1924)
    p.c. Fox Movietonews (Fox #201-C1947)
    l. 20'   g. 35mm   t. b+w   s. si.
    d.   *
    ph. *
    c.s. Fox Movietonews, N.Y. & NFB (1920-FG-170-1)

            "SCU. 'They covered 3700 miles in 134 days. Some hikers!!."

            "Shots of Mr. & Mrs. John Dill meeting Acting Mayor Owen on City Hall steps.
            Owen hands flowers to Mrs. Dill. Group poses with flowers."

585. MT. STEPHEN. (1902)
    p.c. American Mutoscope and Biograph Co.
    l. 29'   g. 35mm (16mm available) t. b+w s. si.
    d.   *
    ph. G.W. (Billy) Bitzer (?)
    c.s. LOC Paper Print Collection

            The camera was mounted ahead of a locomotive travelling over a single track
            winding around points in the British Columbia Rockies. The camera photo-
            graphed the side areas of the tracks, showing trees, telegraph poles, and
            some running water by the roadbed. The film was originally shot in 35mm
            and was probably made in 1899, although not copyrighted until 1902.

586. MURDER IS NEWS. (1937)
    p.c. Central Films, Ltd.
    l. 55 mins (4979') g. 35mm   t. b+w   s. sound
    d.   Leon Barsha
    ph. George Meehan
    c.s. NFA

            Canadian prod., Kenneth J. Bishop;   l.p. Iris Meredith, John Gallaudet,
            script, Edgar Edwards; from a story   George McKay, Doris Lloyd, John Hamil-
            by Theodore A. Tinsley; editor,   ton, John G. Spacey, Frank C. Wilson,
            William Austin; Columbia overseer   Colin Kenny, William McIntyre, Fred
            Jack Fier.   Bass.

            The tenth Quota Quickie made by Central Films for Columbia in Victoria and
            a sequel to MANHATTAN SHAKEDOWN, completed immediately before. Made in
            August and September 1937, it seems to have been dramatically more success-
            ful than MANHATTAN SHAKEDOWN. Leon Barsha was destined to return and direct
            two more films for Central before the studio closed forever. MURDER IS NEWS

was copyrighted in the United States by Warwick Pictures, Inc., on May 3, 1939.

The plot is as follows: Wealthy industrialist Edgar Drake invites Jerry Tracey to join him at his Manhattan town house where he says he has been told he will find his wife with Corning, his company's lawyer. Tracey arrives in time to discover Drake's dead body. He is hit over the head and when he recovers the body has vanished. The only clue is an ear plug found where the body had been. Suspicion falls on a number of people. First in line are Drake's wife (Doris Lloyd) and Corning (John Hamilton) who are having an affair. Then there is Tony Peyden (Frank C. Wilson), Drake's step-son. On bad terms with Drake, Tony is making a living playing in the band at the Sarratoga Club; a nite spot owned by Fred Hammer (John G. Spacey) and frequented by Tracy. Hammer is also a suspect for, like Tony and Corning, he also uses ear plugs. A dubious note is also struck by Ann Leslie (Iris Meredith), Mrs. Drake's young and attractive secretary. Tracy eventually exposes Hammer as the murderer. Hammer is involved in a stock manipulation and has murdered Drake purely to depress the price of shares in Drake Utilities. (Storyline description courtesy of D. John Turner, NFA.)

587. THE MYSTERY OF HARLOW MANOR. (1933)
    p.c. Commonwealth Productions, Ltd.
    l. not completed g. 35mm t. b+w   s. sound
    d.   Clifford S. Smith
    ph. William Beckway
    c.s. *

Producer, Kenneth J. Bishop; editor, Arthur Hamilton; continuity, Martin Kroeger and Arthur Hoerl, from a radio play of the same name by Kolin Hager; sets, David Fair; sound engineer, Clifford Deaville; original story, Irving Smith.

l.p. Evelyn Brent, William Devan, Jameson Thomas, Kathleen Dunsmuir, James McGrath, Reginald Hincks, Arthur Legge-Willis, Edith Scott Burritt, Rene Lendegren, and Cicele Nicholas.

THE MYSTERY OF HARLOW MANOR was the first feature attempted by Kenneth J. Bishop after the establishment of Commonwealth Production in Victoria in July, 1932. Although some of the sets were constructed and the cast and production crew apparently signed, little, if any, film was shot and the film was never completed. This may have been because it possessed little cinematic or visually dramatic action. Interiors were planned for Hatley Park, the family home of Kathleen Dunsmuir, (who later financed Commonwealth Productions) the Butchart residence and the Butchart Gardens near Victoria, and the Commonwealth Productions studio in the Victoria Exhibition Grounds at the Willows, a remodelled horse show building. Carpenter David Fair, who apparently owned some shares in the company, constructed a castle facade which unfortunately was never used for this or any of Bishop's subsequent productions.

Martin Kroeger, who worked on adapting the script, recalls that he never did find out why THE MYSTERY OF HARLOW MANOR was dropped. He suggests that Kathleen Dusnmuir was not involved financially with Commonwealth at this stage, but that when she did offer some of her family fortune it was decided to drop MYSTERY in favour of something more extravagant and adventurous, which would include a substantial role for Miss Dusnmuir. This was the CRIMSON PARADISE, a logging western from a book by British Columbia author Alex Philip.

588. NASS RIVER INDIANS. (1927)
    p.c. National Museum of Canada
    l. 3 reels   g. 35mm t. b+w   s. si. w/captions
    d. Dr. J.S. Watson
    ph. Dr. J.S. Watson and C.M. Barbeau
    c.s. Unknown

"The fishing industry provides the chief occupation of the Indians of the Nass River region in British Columbia. In the first reel we are taken to a native village, which is one of the centres of the salmon industry, and the operations from the "catch" through the stages of canning are shown. There are also views of the cannery bungalows for the native families and life at the cannery during the summer. An Indian chief is seen dancing in his old-time regalia. Reel 2 opens with a peace dance. Several totem-pole villages of the former days are shown, and there are excellent views of totem poles of *the wolf, eagle and other clans. An Indian is seen carving a mask, and one of the old potlatch dances is depicted. On this expedition Mr. Marius Barbeau, of the National Museum, and Dr. Ernest MacMillan, of the Toronto Conservatory of Music, collected native songs, and a series of views show them in the act of recording the songs and music. Reel three shows pictures of the games and many other favourite pastimes of these Indians, and a medicine-man performing a cure." There is a strong similarity between Reel 2 and an ASN film called Saving the Sagas, and between Reel 1 and FISH AND MEDICINE MEN, also produced by ASN. Perhaps Dr. Watson sold the footage to ASN before presenting the original to the National Museum.*

589. NATURE'S ECHO, WITH THE CANADIAN ROCKIES AS HOST. (1919)
    p.c. Ford Motor Company
    l. 472'   g. 35mm   t. b+w   s. si. w/captions
    d.   *
    ph. *
    c.s. USNA Ford Film Collection (200FC-226a)

> *There is no indication that this film was photographed exclusively in either Alberta or British Columbia - presumably it covers parts of both provinces. It is a scenic film, punctuated with sentimental verse extolling the wonders of nature. Shots include waterfalls, tourists watching. Stream at base of falls. Wild flowers. Large hotel in the mountains. Lake with mountains rising above it. Mountain stream. Lake and mountains. Rugged snow-covered mountains and clear lakes. Streams, waterfalls. Car on mountain road. Tourists look at mountains. Lakes. Snow covered mountains. Cows crossing a stream. Bridge, waterfall below it. Train running along a mountain stream.*

590. NEAR FIELD, B.C. ON MT. STEPHEN, 6000 FEET HIGH, IS WORLD'S
    HIGHEST, RICHEST AND LOFTIEST LEAD MINE. (1924)
    p.c. Fox Movietonews (Fox #007.315-A4589, A4590)
    l. 134'   g. 35mm   t. b+w   s. si.
    d.   *
    ph. Len H. Roos
    c.s. Fox Movietonews, N.Y.

> *"Steep side of mountain & LS mountain. Men ascending mountainside. Mounting top of mountain. SCU "Jacob's Ladder" ascent to mouth of mine. SCU miners drilling the ore. Silhouette of four men at entrance to mine. Breaking ore with hammers. Ore in tripping buckets on the mine tramway. Buckets on cable over Kicking Horse Valley carrying ore to base of mountain. Mountain valley scene."*

591. NEARLY 300 YEARS OF AGE AND 196 FEET IN LENGTH, GIANT
    FLAGPOLE SHIPPED TO TORONTO EXHIBITION, NORTH VANCOUVER,
    B.C. (1929)
    p.c. Fox Movietonews (Fox #431.1-D0758)
    l. 45'   g. 35mm   t. b+w   s. si.
    d.   *
    ph. Ross Beesley
    c.s. Fox Movietonews, N.Y.

> *"Looking along length of huge spar, men standing on it. SS CANADIAN RANGER coming along end of wharf, pole in foreground."*

592. NEGRO SPRINTER BREAKS RECORD IN VANCOUVER, B.C. (1930)
    p.c. Fox Movietonews (Fox #6-853)
    l. 630'   g. 35mm   t. b+w   s. sound
    d.   *
    ph. Mayell & Foreman
    c.s. Fox Movietonews, N.Y.

> *"Eddie Tolan, Michigan U., runs 100 metres in 10 and 1/5 seconds at Dominion Day Meet in Vancouver, B.C."*

> *"Crowd shot. 100 metre race, Tolan winning. CU Eddie Tolan. 120 yard hurdles. 220 yard race. George Simpson, Ohio State U., equals world record. Eddie Tolan second. CU George Simpson. 220 yard hurdles. Eddie Tolan receiving cup."*

593. NET PROFITS, CATCHING SALMON IN THE SKEENA RIVER,
BRITISH COLUMBIA. (1919)
p.c. Ford Motor Company
1. 673'   g. 35mm   t. b+w   s. si. w/captions
d.   *
ph. *
c.s. USNA; Ford Film Collection (200FC-2473)

*The first shots show a little girl winding twine onto a shuttle preparatory
to mending nets, then men repairing nets and spreading them on sawhorse-like
structures. A man holds a salmon and a net up to the camera and shows how
a fish is caught by its gills when it swims into the net. The fishing boats
in the harbour begin to line up across the mouth of the river. CU one boat.
A man in the rear drops a buoy over the stern, with net attached, reeling the
net out. The other man is rowing the boat. The stern man leans over the
side to adjust the net. At the end of the drift the net is hauled back into
the boat and the fish removed. The method of trolling is shown next. View
from boat of sunset over river. Fisherman on troller dropping trolling poles
from side of boat. View from the boat of other trollers heading to sea.
Fisherman baiting hooks on boat. Men on other boats dropping lines over-
boards, with spoon-hooks attached, then hauling in the lines with the fish,
displaying fish, throwing them into the hold, and rebaiting hooks. Boats
returning to the cannery to unload. At the cannery dock, the men on the
boats chuck the salmon onto the dock in piles. Men loading net in stern of
rowboat moored beside larger boat, boat moving away dragging net off stern,
boat circling and setting net. View of fish jumping inside circle of net.
Men in boat in circle of net drawing net into boat. Fish being scooped from
net by net on larger boat - purse seining. Fishermen with large hand-nets,
and net on crane, scooping fish from water. Dumping fish into hold of a
larger boat. Man gaffing fish from deck to hold.*

594. NEW NOVELTY IN AN OUTDOOR CHECKER GAME NOW CLAIMING
THE ATTENTION OF B.C. FANS, VANCOUVER, B.C.   (early 1920's)
p.c. Fox Movietonews (Fox #740.13-B8298)
1. 25'   g. 35mm   t. b+w   s. si.
d.   *
ph. Len H. Roos
c.s. Fox Movietonews, N.Y.

"Stanley Park - various shots of the game."

595. NEW SKYSCRAPERS FOR OLD.   (1931)
p.c. CGMPB
1. approx 800'   g. 35mm   t. b+w   s. si. w/captions
d.   W.J. (Bill) Oliver
ph. W.J. (Bill) Oliver
c.s. NFA (330' 16mm), NFB (300' 16mm) and BCPM (35mm)

Produced for the National Parks Bureau, Ottawa.

*Mountain climbing with all its thrills near Lake O'Hara in Yoho National
Park, British Columbia."*

*The film begins on a busy street in Toronto with cars and a Yonge Street
streetcar contending with traffic, and pedestrians during rush hour. It
then cuts to a mountain in the Rockies and Lake O'Hara. A man is looking
over the rear platform of a train. Lake O'Hara with a mountain at the end.
A party of four have decided to take a mountain holiday and they set off
for some climbing, passing across alpine meadows, through creeks, and up and
down all manner of very lovely mountainous terrain with snowy peaks in the
b.g. They climb past the "Seven Sisters" waterfalls. Coming to an alpine
lake, they begin the ascent to the summit, using ropes and picks and traversing some tricky rock faces. They reach snow and use their ropes to cross
an abyss. Near the top they reach the "Devil's Window" and, finally, the
summit. Going back down is just as treacherous. They slide or "glissade"
down a mile-long snow bank. The last scene shows Lake O'Hara with a rowboat moving toward the camera across a still surface.*

596. NEW WESTMINSTER CELEBRATES ITS 50TH MAY DAY. (1920)
    p.c. Fox Movietonews (Fox #050.54-1821)
    1. 48'   g. 35mm   t. b+w   s. si.
    d.   *
    ph. (Len H. Roos?)
    c.s. Fox Movietonews, N.Y.

        *"View of the parade. Mrs. Spence. Queen of the May fifty years ago. Eileen
        Brooks being crowned today. CU Eileen Brooks."*

597. NEW WESTMINSTER FAIR - 1928. (1928)
    p.c. B.C. Department of Agriculture (reel 15)
    1. approx. 350' g. 16mm   t. b+w   s. si. w/captions
    d.   *
    ph. *
    c.s. PABC

        *Scenes include Manager and office staff of the New Westminster Fair. A
        young boy travelling to the fair on a toy horse and sulky. Decorated teams
        of six horses each hauling large wooden carts with proud drivers to the fair-
        grounds. Two of the carts are: RUBY STOCK FARMS - PORTLAND, OREGON and
        MAINLAND TRANSFER CO. LTD. Scenes of Clydesdale horses, an Ayrshire bull, a
        Guernsey bull, a Jersey bull, a Holstein cow, an Ayrshire bull and a small
        model bull-pen. A prize-winning Tamworth boar among several other boars and
        sows. Winners of best sheep breeds shown and named. Sheep dog demonstration.
        Mountain lambs, controlled by dog. B.C. honey display - stacks of bottles
        in display booth, First Prize shown.*

598. NEW WESTMINSTER MAY DAY CELEBRATION. (1924)
    p.c. *
    1.   g. 35mm   t. b+w   s. si.
    d.   *
    ph. ASN (?)
    c.s. NFB (1920-FG-150)

        *Part of Canada Capsule No. 3. "Pan shot of huge crowds in stadium. CS
        little Frances Schnoter being crowned Queen of the May. Children dancing
        and Maypole dance by children."*

599. NEWLYWED TOM HEENY LEAVES FOR NEW ZEALAND, VANCOUVER,
    B.C. (1928)
    p.c. Pathé Gazette #1536
    1. 20'   g. 35mm   t. b+w   s. si. w/captions
    d.   *
    ph. *
    c.s. EMI Pathé Collection

        *"JUMPS OUT OF PRIZE INTO WEDDING RING"
        "VANCOUVER, B.C. - FIGHTER WHO LOST TO GENE TUNNEY SAILS TO AUSTRALIA A
        NEWLYWED." CU Tom and bride. MS Tom and bride aboard ship, smiling. Others
        smiling around them. Shoulders and railing obscure until end.*

600. NEWS AROUND VICTORIA, B.C. (1918)
    p.c. *
    1.   g. 35mm   t. b+w   s. si.
    d.   *
    ph. *
    c.s. NFA (Taylor reel 121)

        *GIANT HOWITZER FIRING: Good shots of artillery unit of the Canadian Army load-
        ing and firing a howitzer at a military (tent) camp near Victoria. EMPRESS
        OF CANADA ARRIVES: The EMPRESS OF CANADA approaches Victoria docks. Good
        head-on shot, and closer view as she berths. MRS. BOWSER'S PARTY: Mrs. Bowser,
        the Premier's wife, and close friends, posing for camera during garden party.
        Children playing ring-around-the rosie in garden as Mrs. Bowser and guests
        look on. GOLF TOURNAMENT: Trophy is presented at Gorge Vale Golf Club. Re-
        cipients include Mrs. Bowser, Mr. Nichol and Mrs. Olag who takes a few prac-
        tise swings for the camera. CU shelf of trophies for golf tournament.*

601. NEWSREEL. (1896-1905)
    p.c. *
    l.   g. 35mm   t. b+w   s. si.
    d.   *
    ph. *
    c.s. Jack Chisholm C467 b+w roll 1

                    *Scenes from British Columbia include one certain, one uncertain: "Trees being
                    felled in B.C." and "logs in river, pulled by tugs".*

602. NINETEEN YEAR OLD BOY WINS BICYCLE RACE IN VANCOUVER,
    B.C. (1934)
    p.c. Fox Movietonews (Fox #22-685)
    l.   g. 35mm   t. b+w   s. sound
    d.   *
    ph. ASN
    c.s. Fox Movietonews, N.Y.

                    "Wilson Vannan beats Ken Manguall in bike race in British Columbia."

603. NO BABY MIX-UPS, NEW YORK, N.Y. AND VANCOUVER, B.C.
    (1937)
    p.c. Paramount (Lib. #6839)
    l. 74'   g. 35mm   t. b+w   s. sound
    d.   *
    ph. DeSions, ASN in Vancouver
    c.s. Sherman Grinberg, N.Y., & Visnews (BPN Lib. #6904)

                    *"NY: Hospital nursery. Nurse hold baby's arm and puts bracelet on baby.   CU
                    bracelet. VANCOUVER: SCU new machine for marking babies by suntanning. Baby's
                    name is placed on slide in machine. CU name in machine. Nurse holds baby's
                    back to machine. CU baby's back marked. Showing baby to mother."*

604. THE NOOTKA INDIANS OF BRITISH COLUMBIA. (1928-1929)
    p.c. National Museum of Canada
    l. 1 reel   g. 35mm (16mm available) t. b+w s. si. w/captions
    d.   Harlan I. Smith
    ph. Harlan I. Smith
    c.s. National Museum of Man, Ottawa, & NFA (3766, 3767)

                    *"The western side of Vancouver Island is the homeland of the Nootka Indians
                    and the opening pictures are scenes of the surf-dashed rocky shore and the
                    land with its heavy growth of cedar trees. There are views of the women
                    digging clams, picking berries, gathering cedar bark and weaving it into hats,
                    mats, and raincoats, and basket and fish trap making. Games and masked dan-
                    cing, the cedar canoe in use, and the silversmith at work are also shown."*

                    *The opening scenes were shot around Ucluelet, on the beaches and at the edge
                    of the forest. There is a shot of pilchards being caught in nets, and CU's
                    of various Indians at Ucluelet. Shots on the beach with men using primitive
                    tools. A man, Tyee Bob, makes a fire by twirling cedar sticks at Alberni.
                    Women weaving hats, mats, and preparing the cedar bark to do so, are in Ucluelet
                    good CU's. A woman weaves a clamming basket out of spruce root, Ucluelet.
                    The final scenes show women and children playing a bone gambling game (prob-
                    ably a women's beaver-teeth gambling game, and not lahal) around a mat in
                    their village at Ucluelet. A man whirling a bull roarer, a painted blanket,
                    a man carving a totem pole, a girl drumming on the door steps, a girl shaking
                    a rattle and singing, and an old woman dancing in front of a house with
                    shredded cedar bark on her head, Ucluelet.*

605. NORQUAY SKIIERS ON SNOWY HIKE. (1930's)
    p.c. Pathé News
    l.   g. 35mm   t. b+w   s. sound
    d.   *
    ph. *
    c.s. NFB (#1930-FG-243)

                    *"Various shots of skiiers of the Norquay camp pushing past the camera, skiing
                    down slope, of Rockies in b.g., and other scenic shots of skiiers and mount-
                    ains."*

606. NORTH OF THE BORDER. (1938)
     p.c. Shelley Films for the B.C. Bureau of Industrial
          and Tourist Development
     l. 1x400' reel   g. 16mm   t. colour   s. sound
     d.   *
     ph. Shelley Films
     c.s. Unknown

                    "A travelogue of British Columbia."

607. NORTH POLE FLYERS REACH CANADA FROM MOSCOW, VANCOUVER,
     B.C. (1937)
     p.c. British Paramount (Lib. #6473)
     l. 99'   g. 35mm   t. b+w   s. sound
     d.   *
     ph. *
     c.s. Visnews, London

                    *"General view of plane at Vancouver. CU three flyers: Baidukoff, Chekaloff &
                    Beliakof. Pan up one flyer in heavy clothes. View of map of a previous
                    arctic flight on tail of plane."*

608. NOVEL AERIAL TRAMWAY IS USED TO TAKE SUPPLIES TO
     WORKMEN CONSTRUCTING NEW UNIVERSITY, VANCOUVER, B.C.
     (1923)
     p.c. Fox Movietonews (Fox #433.264-B3033)
     l. 80'   g. 35mm   t. b+w   s. si.
     d.   *
     ph. Len H. Roos
     c.s. Fox Movietonews, N.Y.

                    *Filmed at the start of construction of the University of British Columbia at
                    Point Grey near Vancouver.*

609. OARSMEN LIMBER UP FOR 1934 ROWING SEASON, VANCOUVER,
     B.C. (1934)
     p.c. Fox Movietonews (Fox #22-276)
     l.   g. 35mm   t. b+w   s. sound
     d.   *
     ph. ASN
     c.s. Fox Movietonews, N.Y.

                    *"Coach Doug Forin gives crew workout. Various shots of crew rowing with
                    Forin giving instructions from launch."*

610. OKANAGAN ESTABLISHING INTERIOR PROVINCIAL EXHIBITION,
     ARMSTRONG, B.C. (1930)
     p.c. B.C. Dept. of Agriculture (reel 33)
     l. approx. 250'   g. 16mm   t. b+w   s. si. w/captions
     d.   *
     ph. *
     c.s. PABC

                    *"His Honour, Lieutenant-Governor Bruce, opened Armstrong's first exhibition,
                    1930."* No shots of Lieutenant-Governor, however. *Various shots of exhibition
                    grounds - ferris wheel, many cars, trucks, people, tents, stands. Carnival
                    Queen and attendants on racetrack at opening ceremony. New buildings and
                    improvements by the municipality. More than 500 head of farm animals assem-
                    bled - Ayrshire and Jersey cows predominate. March past of cattle. 600
                    schoolchildren on fire drill. "Boys and Girls of Armstrong District are
                    well-behaved, healthy, clean and intelligent." Mayor T. Aldworth and princi-
                    pal dismiss kids. Buses transport kids to the fair. Livestock parade past
                    grandstand. Highschool teachers pose. Hon. Wm. Atkinson, Minister of Agri-
                    culture, confers with principals of Armstrong and Salmon Arm highschools.*

611. THE OKANAGAN INDIANS OF BRITISH COLUMBIA. (1923-1930)
    p.c. National Museum of Canada
    l. 1 reel   g. 35mm   t. b+w   s. si. w/captions
    d.   Harlan I. Smith
    ph. Harlan I. Smith
    c.s. Unknown

              This film depicted the habits and customs of the Okanagan Indians in the
              Interior of B.C. and the various elements that made them unique to their en-
              vironment. It also examined their arts and handicrafts using local materials.

612. OLD HBC BUILDING, VICTORIA, B.C. (1930's)
    p.c. private
    l. 100'   g. 16mm   t. colour & b+w s. si.
    d.   *
    ph. *
    c.s. PABC

              This is the second item on a reel beginning with part of a bee-keeping film.
              The colour is faded and includes a long, lingering shot of the old HBC build-
              ing in Victoria and a CPR PRINCESS boat moving in the harbour.   The b+w seg-
              ment shows a warehouse in Victoria with a sign, painted on the side, reading
              FORT GARRY TEA & COFFEE, and two ocean-going salvage tugs, one of them per-
              haps called the SALVAGE QUEEN.   There is also a b+w pan over the CPR wharves
              and two PRINCESS boats tied up alongside. (Length of full reel, 300')

613. OLD TIME MARINERS TAKE THEIR TOT, VICTORIA, B.C. (1928)
    p.c. Fox Movietonews
    l.   g. 35mm   t. b+w   s. sound
    d.   *
    ph. Eric Mayell & Paul Heisy
    c.s. Unknown

              "Through the assistance of the Chamber of Commerce, Esquimalt Police Force,
              and officials of the Silver Spring Brewery, the Fox Movietone operators,
              Eric Mayell and Paul Heisy here yesterday secured a "talkie" scene of Vic-
              toria, romantically portraying the city as a seaport.

              Three old-time mariners, Captain Jacobson, 72, Captain Johnson, 88, and
              Captain McIntosh, 97, were the principal actors in the little drama, which
              took place on a wharf at the foot of Head Street with the harbour as a back-
              ground.

              While the Captains sat at the end of the dock and gossiped about seafaring
              adventures and "quaffed the foaming ale", the movietone recorded the scene
              pictorially and by sound. One of the sea veterans was a teetotaler, however,
              and took his "pot of tea" instead. (Victoria Times, Nov. 1, 1928).

614. ON BOARD HMCS AURORA. (pre 1922)
    p.c. CGMPB
    l.   g. 35mm   t. b+w   s. si.
    d.   *
    ph. *
    c.s. Unknown

              Part of the HOW IT IS DONE IN CANADA series. The HMCS AURORA was originally
              a British cruiser which Canada bought at the end of World War I. She served
              on the Pacific coast until 1922.

615. "ON THE ROCKS" - EMPRESS OF CANADA, LARGEST PASSENGER
    LINER IN THE PACIFIC - CARRYING 450 PASSENGERS - RUNS
    ASHORE IN DENSE FOG. SHE WAS REFLOATED TWO DAYS LATER,
    HOMER BAY, B.C. (1929)
    p.c. Pathé Gazette (#1654)
    l. 92'   g. 35mm   t. b+w   s. si.
    d.   *
    ph. *
    c.s. EMI Pathé Collection

              "Aerial view liner on rocks. Port side at low tide. Aerial view of tugs
              and barges refloating ship. People on the rocks looking at the EMPRESS.
              Aerial view starboard side. CU tugs from boat at side of EMPRESS. Aerial

218

view above deck, water being pumped out of ship. Bow shot from waterline of EMPRESS refloated with men working about the hull on barges & boats."

616. ON THE SKEENA/ON THE SKEENA RIVER/SALMON FISHING ON
     THE SKEENA. (1922)
     p.c. CGMPB (#75)
     l. 736'   g. 35mm   t. b+w   s. si. w/captions
     d.   *
     ph. *
     c.s. BCPM (35mm) (an excellent print)

> *"A film dealing with the salmon fisheries on the world's greatest salmon
> stream, showing the methods of catching and the preparation of fish in the
> canneries. This is one of the series of subjects on Canada's extensive fish-
> eries." The film had three different titles. See No. 782.*

> *Map of Canada, pointing to the Skeena, then a map of British Columbia with
> the Skeena being pointed out. Fish boats strung across the mouth of the
> Skeena on a cloudy day, engaged in drift-netting. Broadside shot of fishing
> trawler JEDWAY with many smaller sailboats in tow. Long line of small boats
> from astern, good CU's of boats in tow. Once at the fishing ground the
> small boats break away, hoist their sails and head for a likely spot. Gill-
> netting only is allowed so boats let out nets, one man rowing, the other
> tending net. The men pull their nets in to reveal their catch. LS cannery
> from the river. Nets drying at a cannery, a boy on the wharf mending his net,
> an old timer with beard in an iris shot. The salmon, still alive, are placed
> aboard a trawler and taken to the cannery. Crates of salmon being lifted off
> trawler onto the wharf and then moved into the cannery shed. Fish being gut-
> ted in the cannery. The backbone is removed. Rows of girls washing the fil-
> lets. The salmon are packed in bulk and mildly cured, with a little salt, in
> barrels. A barrel is sealed. The barrels are rolled out onto the wharf and
> loaded onto a steamer for "eastern canneries" or "foreign countries". LS
> the steamer sailing away in an iris.*

617. ON THIS BIG FOX FARM THE KEEPERS MAKE PETS OF THEIR CHARGES
     AND TREAT THEM TO RAISINS, CLOVERDALE, B.C. (1920's)
     p.c. Fox Movietonews (Fox #328-B9745)
     l. 60'   g. 35mm   t. b+w   s. si.
     d.   *
     ph. Jos. T. Mandy
     c.s. Fox Movietonews, N.Y.

> *"SCU of climbing up wire fence to be fed by a lady. SCU fox eating from a
> man's hand. SCU fox cubs in girl's arm. CU fox cubs on girl's lap. High
> pan of pens. LS foxes eating from bowls. CU fox peering out of runway, and
> coming out. SCU man showing baby fox to a large dog."*

618. ONE HUNDRED AND TWENTY FIFTH ANNIVERSARY CELEBRATION,
     KAMLOOPS, B.C. (1937)
     p.c. Hearst Metrotone News; Can no. 784, Roll no. 6
     l.   g. 35mm   t. b+w   s. sound
     d.   *
     ph. ASN
     c.s. Hearst Metrotone News, N.Y.

> *Parade, anniversary celebrations.*

619. ONE THOUSAND MILES THROUGH THE ROCKIES. (1912)
     p.c. Edison Mfg. Co. (Catalogue #6979)
     l. 350'   g. 35mm   t. b+w   s. si.
     d.   *
     ph. *
     c.s. Unknown

> *Little is known about this film. It may be that parts of it contain scenes
> of British Columbia, especially through the Rockies, a favourite subject in
> the early days of motion pictures.*

620. OPEN SKYWAYS IN THE ROCKIES. (1931)
     p.c. CGMPB
     l. 1 reel   g 35mm   t. b+w   s. si. w/captions
     d.   W.J. (Bill) Oliver
     ph. W.J. (Bill) Oliver
     c.s. NFA & NFB Archives P.B. 11 (NFB-N-122)

     A motor trip through the central Rockies from Banff to Golden, along the Kicking Horse Trail. "Modern motor highway provides open skyways through the glories of the Canadian Rockies. HA of highway with automobiles speeding along. Shot of car stopping at Banff National Park Guard House for information. Various shots of mountain scenery seen from the road, of deer, streams, etc. Shot of tourists walking over wooden foot bridge over Johnston Canyon. Shot of falls, of mountains, of steep falls, of Lake Louise and finally of the mountains of the Great Divide. Shot of automobile speeding along the road while train speeds in opposite direction on track. Shot of moose in water, of a family of moose on the shore. Shot of Kicking Horse River, of Emerald Lake with mountains reflected in it. Shot of Kicking Horse River squeezing into "Needle Eye" rock, jumping off cliff at Wapta Falls and finally emerging in the Columbia Valley along with road and railroad. Shot of the Selkirk Mountains in the setting sun, of an Indian in ceremonial dress on his pony against the sky." (Copy at NFA is 330' on 16mm; at NFB - 800' on 35mm)

621. THE ORIGIN OF THE FAMILY TREE. (n.d.)
     p.c. Bray
     l. 200'   g. 16mm   t. b+w   s. si.
     d.   *
     ph. *
     c.s. Unknown

     "Eagle Hawks, 113 years old. An Indian living in B.C. has 14 wives. Shows customs of Indians - trading, fishing, and trees carved to represent faces." Kodascope Library, Catalogue, n.d.

622. ORIGINALITY AND SKILL DISPLAYED BY KIDDIES WHO BUILD SAND
     CASTLES FOR CITY CHAMPIONSHIP, VANCOUVER, B.C.   (1929)
     p.c. Fox Movietonews (Fox #000.61-D1333)
     l. 105'   g. 35mm   t. b+w   s.
     d.   *
     ph. Ross Beesley
     c.s. Fox Movietonews, N.Y.

623. OUR NEW CANADIAN NAVY. (pre 1926)
     p.c. CGMPB
     l.   g. 35mm   t. b+w   s. si.
     d.   *
     ph. *
     c.s. Unknown

     Part of the HOW IT IS DONE IN CANADA series.

624. OUTDOOR SPORTS START OFF WITH A BANG WHEN CLUBS BEGIN
     SHOOTING HOLES IN THE AIR, VANCOUVER, B.C. (n.d.)
     p.c. Fox Moveitonews (Fox #729.241-C1513)
     l.   g. 35mm   t. b+w   s. si.
     d.   *
     ph. *
     c.s. Fox Movietonews, N.Y.

     "Shots of Terminal City Gun Club and Stanley Park Lawn Bowling Club in action."

625. OVER MOUNTAIN PASSES. (1910)
     p.c. Edison Mfg. Co. (Catalogue #6684)
     l.   g. 35mm   t. b+w   s. si.
     d.   J. Searle Dawley (?)
     ph. Henry Cronjager (?)
     c.s. Unknown

     This may have been filmed during Edison's tour of western Canada in the summer of 1910, as part of a series of promotional films put together for the CPR. It is not listed in Edison's Production Log however, and no location or storyline is known. It could have been made in either Alberta or British Columbia. It was released on Sept. 27, 1910.

626. PACIFIC COAST CHAMPIONS, OUR OAR CREW REPRESENTING CANADA
     AT OLYMPIC GAMES, PARIS IN JULY. TRAIN DAILY TO BRING OAR
     CHAMPIONSHIP OF WORLD BACK TO VANCOUVER, VANCOUVER, B.C.
     (1924)
     p.c. Fox Movietonews (Fox #718-A3680)
     l. 125'   g. 35mm   t. b+w   s. si.
     d.   *
     ph. Len H. Roos
     c.s. Fox Movietonews, N.Y.

          Shots of unidentified oarsmen training.

627. PACIFIC COAST CITIES EN FETE - ROYAL WELCOME EXTENDED
     TO VICE REGAL PARTY ON OFFICIAL VISIT, VICTORIA, B.C.
     (1927)
     p.c. Fox Movietonews (Fox #201-B8696)
     l. 100'   g. 35mm   t. b+w   s. si.
     d.   *
     ph. *
     c.s. Fox Movietonews, N.Y.

          "High shot of crowd waiting to greet Royal party. SCU of boat arriving at
          dock. LS of the party arriving on dock and inspecting the soldiers. SCU
          of Lord and Lady Willingdon in group. CU of Ernest Lapointe at Ottawa who
          is to represent Canada at next Australian Parliament."

628. PACIFIC COAST SALMON. (1934)
     p.c. Eastman Teaching Films Inc.
     l. approx. 400'   g. 16mm   t. b+w   s. si.
     d.   *
     ph. *
     c.s. Unknown

          The entry in the BFI Educational Catalogue reads: "View of Fraser River at
          or near the mouth, salmon shown leaping. Salmon ascending the river. Views
          of upper river with falls and rapids - salmon ascending these. Natural spawn-
          ing bed - salmon spawning. Artificial spawning bed - method of catching fish
          to stock this by means of nets. Method of squeezing eggs from female and
          milt from male to fertilize these - fish, of course, first killed. Hatching
          eggs in cold running water. Salmon fry feeding on yolk. Salmon in next
          stage of growth. Fishing for salmon as they come up the river. Fishing
          boats with nets at mouth of inlets into river. Boats shown filled with salmon.
          Conveying salmon ashore. Salmon traps near coast. Conveying salmon caught
          in these traps to the shore. Packing fresh salmon in boxes. At the Cannery:
          Cutting up, packing into tins, conveyor for filled tins, labelling. Loading
          on to ship for export."

629. PACIFIC INTERNATIONAL YACHTING REGATTA, VANCOUVER, B.C.   (1938)
     p.c. Hearst Metrotone News; Can no. 873, Roll no. 4
     l.   g. 35mm   t. b+w   s. sound
     d.   *
     ph. ASN
     c.s. Hearst Metrotone News, N.Y.

630. PACIFIC NORTHWEST GOLF CHAMPIONSHIP, VICTORIA, B.C. (1939)
     p.c. Fox Movietonews (Fox #38-165)
     l. 750'   g. 35mm   t. b+w   s. sound
     d.   *
     ph. ASN
     c.s. Fox Movietonews, N.Y.

          "Ken Black of Vancouver putts. Westland putts. Various shots of game.
          Crowd. Jack Westland of Seattle wins."

631. PACK TRAIN COMING OVER TRAIL AND FORDING STREAM. (pre 1910)
    p.c. *
    l. 80'   g. 35mm   t. b+w   s. si.
    d.   *
    ph. *
    c.s. Unknown

                    *Little is known of this film. It may not contain scenes of British Columbia,
                    but it is typical of films of this era. George Kleine Catalogue, 1910. p.63.*

632. PACK TRAIN IN THE ROCKIES. (1910-1920)
    p.c. *
    l.   g. 35mm   t. b+w   s. si.
    d.   *
    ph. *
    c.s. NFB (#1910-FG-145)

                    *Long level shot of pack-train moving along a narrow path against a sheer
                    cliff. H.A. of train snaking up trail as it proceeds up slope. Closer side
                    view of pack horses toting lumber and small crates. H.A. pans down slope
                    to horses and men resting during the trip. H.A.'s pack-train moving slowly
                    past large evergreens. Various scenic shots of mountains, valley and pack-
                    train. Shots of tents in trees, men loading horses, tree-trunks lying on
                    ground. More shots of pack-train leaving and on its way through mountain
                    country. This may not have been shot in British Columbia.*

633. PACKERS ON THE TRAIL. (1899-1900)
    p.c. Edison Mfg. Co.
    l. 35'   g. 35mm (16mm available) t. b+w s. si.
    d.   *
    ph. Robert Bonine
    c.s. NFA

                    *"A snow covered slope with a narrow trail is seen in the foreground of this
                    picture. In the distance, some figures are seen approaching. As they draw
                    nearer we recognize a dog team and sledge (sic) loaded with supplies, and
                    followed by miners loaded with tools and materials, trudging their way over
                    the well-run trail into the heart of the Klondike. This picture gives the
                    observer some idea of the hardships of the miners in the Alaskan Gold Field."
                    In fact, a dog sled followed by 12 men carrying digging implements passes a
                    camera in a fixed position, and then the same people return back down the
                    same trail past the camera. (The original 35mm print was 75' long and copy-
                    righted in 1901)*

634. PAGES FROM THE DIARY OF A ROCKY MOUNTAIN RANGER. (1920?)
    p.c. Pathéscope (?)
    l. approx. 400'   g. 28mm   t. b+w   s. si.
    d.   *
    ph. *
    c.s. NFA

                    *"We follow the Government Ranger on a tour of inspection of Mount Robson,
                    the Tumbling Glacier, Berg Lake and Emperor Falls. Wonderfully clear and
                    vivid pictures of the highest peak in the Canadian Rockies."*

635. PALATIAL NEW MOTORSHIP OF THE CANADIAN/AUSTRALIAN ROYAL
    MAIL LINE GIVEN GREAT RECEPTION HERE, VANCOUVER, B.C.
    (1925)
    p.c. Fox Movietonews (Fox #463.11-B6599)
    l. 30'   g. 35mm   t. b+w   s. si.
    d.   *
    ph. Errington
    c.s. Fox Movietonews, N.Y.

                    *"Mayor Taylor meets Commander Crawford of ARMS AVIANGE. Mrs. J.R. MacRae
                    gives Mrs. Holdsworth bouquet of flowers. Shots of ship."*

636. PANORAMA PASSING THROUGH VAN HORNE RANGE. (pre 1910)
   p.c. *
   1. 192'   g. 35mm   t. b+w   s. si.
   d. *
   ph. *
   c.s. Unknown

>   *If this film is like the other "Panorama" train films, it will show the view
>   from a locomotive's cowcatcher as it speeds along the tracks through the
>   Rockies. George Kleine Catalogue, 1910. p.63.*

637. PANORAMIC VIEW BETWEEN PALLISER AND FIELD, B.C. (1901)
   p.c. Edison Mfg. Co.
   1. 185'   g. 35mm (16mm available) t. b+w s. si.
   d. *
   ph. *
   c.s. LOC Paper Print Collection

>   *"We present in this picture numerous picturesque scenes taken in the most
>   mountainous portion of the entire Canadian Pacific R.R. system. In passing
>   between these two points the sharpest curves and the most diversified scenes
>   on the entire system are encountered, and this with the striking scenery
>   makes a most entertaining subject." The camera platform was located on one
>   end of a train travelling over a single track. Mostly scrub brush and foot-
>   hill countryside are seen. (The original was copyrighted in January 1902. A
>   16mm print is available and is 82' long.)*

638. PANORAMIC VIEW FROM THE WHITE PASS RAILROAD. (1899)
   p.c. Edison Mfg. Co.
   1. 32'   g. 35mm (16mm available) t. b+w s. si.
   d. *
   ph. Robert Bonine (?)
   c.s. Unknown

>   *"This scene was taken shortly after the completion of this railroad in 1899.
>   The impression received by the audience is that of riding on the pilot of
>   an engine. Shortly after starting, you plunge into the darkness of the tun-
>   nel, afterwards to emerge, and crossing a high trestle skirting the edge of
>   a deep chasm, you continue to wind about among the mountains and gorges.
>   The ice-covered peaks of the distant mountains form an ever changing back-
>   ground." Shot from the cow-catcher of a locomotive. (Copyrighted in 1901 -
>   original print was 75' long.)*

639. PANORAMIC VIEW NEAR MT. GOLDEN ON THE CANADIAN PACIFIC
   R.R. (1901)
   p.c. Edison Mfg. Co.
   1. 170'   g. 35mm (16mm available) t. b+w s. si.
   d. *
   ph. *
   c.s. NFA & LOC Paper Print Collection

>   *"Here we present to the audience a subject taken near Mt. Golden, one which
>   will thoroughly please all who are lovers of scenery. One minute you are
>   running straight to the mountain of rock, and then when you can expect to be
>   dashed into it, suddenly turn and skirt the very side of this mountain over
>   trestles, bridges, and finally stop where in front of you can be seen Mt.
>   Hector at a distance of about twelve miles. In this film we present a most
>   exciting ride on the engine of a Canadian Pacific R.R. train, and also afford
>   the audience a most beautiful panoramic view." Workmen, probably Chinese,
>   are seen running along the tracks. (Original was copyrighted in January
>   1902. A 16mm print, 80' long, is available.)*

640. PANORAMIC VIEW OF THE ROCKIES. (pre 1910)
   p.c. *
   1. 290'   g. 35mm   t. b+w   s. si.
   d. *
   ph. *
   c.s. Unknown

>   *Little is known about this film. Some of the scenes may show British Columbia.
>   George Kleine Catalogue, 1910. p.63.*

641. PANORAMIC VIEW OF ALBERT CAÑON. (1901)
     p.c. Edison Mfg. Co.
     1/ 175'   g. 35mm (16mm available) t. b+w   s. si.
     d.   *
     ph. *
     c.s. LOC Paper Print Collection

                    "This piece of scenery was taken in the Albert Cañon on the line of the Can-
                    adian Pacific R.R., and is considered to be one of the finest view in the
                    Rocky Mountains. The chief big features of these pictures are the towering
                    cliffs which rise straight up thousands of feet on either side, and between
                    which runs a river, adding materially to the interest of the view, and passing
                    through a tunnel hewn out of solid rock which can be seen from a distance of
                    nearly a mile during the time of approach of the train, forms a very inter-
                    esting climax to this picture." Mountain peaks, stands of timber and tele-
                    phone poles alongside the tracks are all visible from the camera mounted on
                    the front of the train. (The original print was copyrighted in 1901 and a
                    16mm print is available that is 76' long)

642. PANORAMIC VIEW OF KICKING HORSE CAÑON. (1901)
     p.c. Edison Mfg. Co.
     1. 200'   g. 35mm (16mm available) t. b+w   s. si.
     d.   *
     ph. *
     c.s. NFA & LOC Paper Print Collection

                    "We show here one of the grandest pieces of scenery in the West, namely,
                    "Kicking Horse Cañon" on the line of the Canadian Pacific R.R. This vast
                    cañon is fourteen miles long, running through the Rocky Mountains at an al-
                    titude of 5000' above sea level. The train from which our picture was made
                    ran along the very brink of the mountain with the valley thousands of feet
                    below, making the picture most thrilling. The train is going at a high rate
                    of speed, thus giving a long and diversified view as it rushes through the
                    cañon and rounds the sharp curves at breakneck speed." The train goes
                    through two tunnels and across two cantilever bridges, as well as scattering
                    a group of Chinese workmen who are working on the tracks. (The original was
                    copyrighted in December 1901. A 16mm print is available, and is 87' long.)

643. PANORAMIC VIEW OF LOWER KICKING HORSE CAÑON. (1901)
     p.c. Edison Mfg. Co.
     1. 185'   g. 35mm (16mm available) t. b+w   s. si.
     d.   *
     ph. *
     c.s. NFA & LOC Paper Print Collection

                    "In this picture we show the ending of this cañon, taken from the front of a
                    locomotive on the Canadian Pacific R.R., running through this marvellous
                    piece of scenery at a high rate of speed. The train seems to be running
                    into the mountains of rock as each curve is reached and rounded, making the
                    scene exciting from start to finish." (The original was copyrighted in Dec-
                    ember 1901. A 16mm print, 83' long, is available.)

644. PANORAMIC VIEW OF LOWER KICKING HORSE VALLEY. (1901)
     p.c. Edison Mfg. Co.
     1. 200'   g. 35mm (16mm available) t. b+w   s. si.
     d.   *
     ph. *
     c.s. NFA & LOC Paper Print Collection

                    "This charming piece of scenery commences at Mt. Hector on the Canadian Pac-
                    ific R.R. and runs through the Valley of the Kicking Horse, showing the huge
                    mountains covered with snow. It is among the most interesting of our Rocky
                    Mountain panoramic series. As the train runs along the Kicking Horse River,
                    we see in the distance Mt. Field and Mt. Stephen, both 10,000 feet above the
                    level, and passing through a tunnel cut through a mountain of solid rock we
                    finally enter the town of Field, which is in the heart of the Ottertail
                    group. As a panoramic mountain picture this is the most thrilling, as the
                    audience imagines while they are being carried along with the picture, the
                    train will be toppled over thousands of feet into the valley below." Some-
                    times streams can be seen, and telegraph poles. A group of Chinese workmen
                    is scattered by the train. The camera mounted on the cowcatcher records the
                    slow entrance into Field and passes a railroad siding with several boxcars,

a water tower and a few one-story buildings, but the film ends before a good view of the town is possible." (Original was copyrighted in December 1901. A 16mm print, 82' long, is available.)

645. PANORAMIC VIEW OF THE CANADIAN PACIFIC R.R. NEAR
     LEANCHOIL, B.C. (1901)
     p.c. Edison Mfg. Co.
     l. 185'   g. 35mm (16mm available) t. b+w s. si.
     d.   *
     ph. *
     c.s. LOC Paper Print Collection

> *"This scene was taken from the front end of a locomotive running through Leanchoil, B.C., in the heart of the Rockies, and presents a most beautiful picture. We are continually running along the very brink of the mountains which are thousands of feet high, and far below can be seen the Kicking Horse River as it flows toward the Grand Cañon of the Kicking Horse." There are no buildings to be seen but many telegraph poles along the single track. (The original print was copyrighted in January 1902. A 16mm print is available and is 79' long.)*

646. PANORAMIC VIEW OF UPPER KICKING HORSE CAÑON. (1901)
     p.c. Edison Mfg. Co.
     l. 200'   g. 35mm (16mm available) t. b+w s. si.
     d.   *
     ph. *
     c.s. NFA and LOC Paper Print Collection

> *"This charming piece of scenery was taken at Glenochole and Golden which is the commencing point of the picturesque part of the Ottertail Group of mountains on the Canadian Pacific Railroad. In the distance we see the huge mountains towering thousands of feet above the railroad tracks, the peaks of the mountains being covered with snow. The picture being taken from the front of an engine while the train is running a distance of several miles gives an excellent view of this beautiful section of the country." The train also crosses bridges. (The original was copyrighted in December 1901. A 16mm print, 81' long, may be obtained.)*

647. PAN-PACIFIC WOMEN'S ASSOCIATION GARDEN PARTY, VANCOUVER,
     B.C. (1937)
     p.c. Hearst Metrotone News, Can no. 697; Roll no. 4
     l.   g. 35mm   t. b+w   s. sound
     d.   *
     ph. ASN
     c.s. Hearst Metrotone News, N.Y.

> *Women's Association members attending garden party.*

648. PARADISE RE-DISCOVERED. (1921)
     p.c. Dept. of Trade and Commerce
          Exhibits and Publicity Bureau, Ottawa
     l. 1 reel   g/ 35mm   t. b+w   s. si. w/captions
     d.   *
     ph. *
     c.s. Unknown

> *"A beautiful scenic-industrial film illustrative of the famous Okanagan Valley and its apple industry." Unfortunately nothing else is known about this film.*

649. PARK RANGER BREAKS TRAIL FOR SUMMER VISITORS, B.C.
     (1934)
     p.c. Pathé News (Neg. no 7317)
     l. 55'   g. 35mm   t. b+w   s. sound
     d.   *
     ph. *
     c.s. Sherman Grinberg, Hollywood

> *"Good long and close shots of Ranger on skis breaking trail as he walks along snow-covered mountain. Beautiful shot of the Laughing Twin Falls, which he finds at the end of his patrol."*

9

650. PARLIAMENT OPENS, VICTORIA, B.C. (1939)
    p.c. Fox Movietonews (Fox #39-200)
    1. 700'   g. 35mm   t. b+w   s. sound
    d. *
    ph. ASN
    c.s. Fox Movietonews, N.Y.

              *"Princess Patricia's Canadian Light Infantry arrive at Parliament Buildings.
              Lt. Gov. Hamber arrives, salutes. Inspects Guard of Honour. Premier Pat-
              ullo interview. Soldiers march past. Hamber inspects troops. Governor's
              party entering Parliament Buildings. Presenting arms. LS Parliament Build-
              ings. Soldiers march past. LS Parliament Buildings."*

651. PASSENGER SERVICE IS INAUGURATED BY CANADIAN NATIONAL
    SHIPS. (1922-1926)
    p.c. CGMBP
    1.   g. 35mm   t. b+w   s. si.
    d. *
    ph. *
    c.s. Unknown

              *Part of the HOW IT IS DONE IN CANADA series. Nothing else is known about it.
              Some of the CNR ships depicted may be on the west coast.*

652. THE PATHFINDER. (1932)
    p.c. ASN/ASS (#B-589)
    1. 700'   g. 35mm   t. b+w   s. sound
    d. Gordon Sparling
    ph. *
    c.s. NFA & United Artists

              *CANADIAN CAMEO NO. 8. "Highlights in the career of Tom Wilson - pathfinder,
              explorer, adventurer. In 1882 he was the first white man to look at the
              Blue Lake of the Little Fishes, now known as Lake Louise. On the 50th
              anniversary of his discoveries, he visits many of the old landmarks and sees
              the amazing change since he first challenged the Great Barrier." Wilson was
              sent out to look for Major Rogers's son after the latter became lost. He
              found him. Filmed near Banff, Alberta.*

653. PATHWAYS OF THE ROCKIES. (before 1935)
    p.c. *
    1. 1 reel   g. 35mm   t. b+w s. si.
    d. *
    ph. *
    c.s. Unknown

              "The conquest of the Rockies Barrier by road, rail and water."

654. PATULLO BRIDGE OFFICIALLY OPENED IN NEW WESTMINSTER, B.C.
    (1937)
    p.c. Fox Movietonews (Fox #33-107)
    1. 750'   g. 35mm   t. b+w   s. sound
    d. *
    ph. ASN
    c.s. NFA & Fox Movietonews, N.Y.

              *"Boats in New Westminster harbour in an impressive parade just before the
              opening. Official parade arrives with guests and prominent people. Premier
              T.D. Patullo of B.C. cuts the chain officially opening the bridge. Soldiers,
              mounted police, bands and cars are the first to cross the bridge." (Negative
              cuts destroyed)*

655. PEACE CEREMONY, BLAINE, WASHINGTON. (1921)
    p.c. Pathé News
    1.   g. 35mm   t. b+w   s. si.
    d. *
    ph. *
    c.s. NFB (1920-FG-210)

              *"Shots of Peace Arch at Blaine, Washington. Crowd in f.g. Two girls dressed
              up to represent Brittania and Liberty. Men hoisting Stars and Stripes and*

Union Jack. LA top of Arch, flags flying. Scouts from both countries cross boundary to shake hands. MS of freckle-faced little tough holding small Stars & Stripes & Union Jack."

656. PERSONAL APPEARANCE. (1939)
     p.c. prob. UBC Summer School of the Theatre
     1. 100'   g. 16mm   t. b+w   s.
     d.   *
     ph. *
     c.s. Special Collection Division, The Library, UBC

          Property of the UBC Alumni Player's Club. No other information available.

657. PEAS- FRASER VALLEY, B.C.   (late 1920's-early 1930's)
     p.c. B.C. Dept. of Agriculture
     1. approx. 400'   g. 16mm   t. b+w   s. si.
     d.   *
     ph. *
     c.s. PABC

          *The film examines pea production from rolling, cultivating, disking and fert-
          ilizing the field to crop dusting with a biplane, seeding and harvesting.
          Much of the field work is done with horses, some with a tractor. Peas are
          dumped onto a conveyor belt at a barn, mechanically shucked, poured into
          wooden boxes and sorted by girls in white caps.*

          *Cows in a field and being milked in a barn, probably at Frasea Farms. Men
          (Agriculture inspectors?) drink milk from bottles beside a car. A sign on
          the roof of the car reads Frasea Farms.*

658. PEOPLE OF THE SEA. (before 1935)
     p.c. *
     1. 1 reel   g. 35mm   t. b+w   s. si.
     d.   *
     ph. *
     c.s. Unknown

          *"Denizens of the oceans of the Empire. Deep-sea fishing in the North Sea,
          whaling off South African coasts, salmon fishing in Canada." No other in-
          formation available but likely contains sequences from B.C.*

659. "THE PERFECT VIEW". (1924)
     p.c. Fox Movietonews (Fox #007.321-B943)
     1. 750'   g. 35mm   t. b+w   s. si.
     d.   *
     ph. Len H. Roos
     c.s. Fox Movietonews, N.Y.

          *"Story is that of two young men who notice a sign in a drug store offering
          $1000.00 for the best photograph of a perfect view. They go out for a per-
          fect view in their automobile and wander over some Canadian mountains and
          lake country in the course of their search. Scenes; camp in forest; sunset
          through forest; auto and motorists; forest with deer: porch of farm house;
          sign in drug store window; mountains, pine trees, rocks and boulders."*

660. PET SHOW AT PNE, VANCOUVER HARBOUR & WATER SPORT REGATTA AT
     KASLO, B.C. (1930's)
     p.c. private
     1. 420'   g. 16mm   t. b+w   s. si.
     d.   *
     ph. Rev. George R.B. Kinney
     c.s. NFA, Ottawa

          *Huge pet show at PNE Grandstand in Vancouver - mostly dogs, but one bird and
          a rabbit too. Long parade of people with dogs, marching with their animals
          walking beside them or in baby carriages. Judge examining a wild little dog.
          People posing with their animals. Pan of Vancouver Harbour (not good) on a
          cloudy day, showing a few ships. Water Sports Regatta at Kaslo. Swimming,
          diving, jousting in canoes, and water-skiing with a single sled or, aqua-
          planing.*

661. PHANTOM RIDE ON THE CANADIAN PACIFIC R.R.   (1901 or 1902)
    p.c. Edison Mfg. Co. #5656A
    1. 100'   g. 35mm   t. b+w   s. si.
    d.   *
    ph. *
    c.s. Unknown

662. PHANTOM RIDE ON THE CANADIAN PACIFIC R.R.   (1901 or 1902)
    p.c. Edison Mfg. Co. #5656
    1. 200'   g. 35mm   t. b+w   s. si.
    d.   *
    ph. *
    c.s. Unknown

663. P.H. ROUTLEDGE BUILDS PERFECT MODEL OF PRAIRIE TYPE
    LOCOMOTIVE, MISSION, B.C. (1923)
    p.c. Fox Movietonews (Fox #460.0001-B1863)
    1. 30'   g. 35mm   t. b+w   s. si.
    d.   *
    ph. Len H. Roos
    c.s. Fox Movietonews, N.Y.

        "CU of locomotive head on. Inventor behind model. CU of model. Various
        shots."

664. PHYSICAL DISPLAY, VANCOUVER, B.C. (1938)
    p.c. Hearst Metrotone News; Can no. 836, Roll no. 8
    1.   g. 35mm   t. b+w   s. sound
    d.   *
    ph. *
    c.s. Hearst Metrotone News, N.Y.

        Calisthenics.

665. PICNIC - DOMINION EXPERIMENTAL FARM, SUMMERLAND,
    OKANAGAN - JUNE 3RD 1930.
    p.c. B.C. Dept. of Agriculture (reel 44)
    1. 225'   g. 16mm   t. b+w   s. si. w/captions
    d.   *
    ph. *
    c.s. PABC

        Trucks and cars arriving. Kids running races, sack races and wheelbarrow
        races. Carpenter's competition - ladies' nail-hammering contest (into a
        thick beam). Mr. Leek, President of the Vancouver Exhibition Association,
        and Mrs. Leek, Mr. Matheson, Manager and Secretary, and Mrs. Matheson,
        posing. Crowds. An old timer, John Treffry of Summerland, with a long white
        beard. Pan of countryside from railway bridge. People walking across
        trestle, long drop to the bottom of the chasm. Pan across Experimental Farm
        grounds. Farmers try their hand at gold. Small group watches as train crosses
        trestle. Mr. Hunter, Superintendent of the Experimental Farm, poses with a
        cow. Stock judging demonstrations. $2000.00 cow owned by a man in the dis-
        trict. Poses with Dr. Knight, Livestock Commissioner. Pan of lake with cars
        in f.g. across the fields. This is the central story on Reel 44. The three
        stories add up to approx. 450' 16mm.

666. PICTURESQUE CELEBRATION OF ARRIVAL 100 YEARS AGO OF
    SIR GEORGE SIMPSON WHO HELD PROVINCE FOR CANADA, FORT
    ST. JAMES, B.C. (1926)
    p.c. Fox Movietonews (Fox #095.97-C7225)
    1. 100'   g. 35mm   t. b+w   s. si.
    d.   *
    ph. W.J. Oliver
    c.s. Fox Movietonews, N.Y. & NFA

        "People on beach. Men on beach, arrival. Crowd on beach. Scene of pageant.
        MLS stockade. Men passing gate. Indians carrying packs. CU Indians by
        stockade. Factor Connolly greeting friends. Lt. Gov. Randolph Bruce speak-
        ing. Indians having tom-tom dance."

667. PIER FIRE, VANCOUVER, B.C. (1938)
    p.c. Universal Newsreel V.10 R.689
    l.   g. 35mm   t. b+w   s. si.
    d.   *
    ph.   *
    c.s. USNA

        Scenes of the $2-million fire that destroyed CPR Pier D in 45 minutes.

668. PINES OF ROCKIES. (c. 1903)
    p.c. Warwick Trading Co.
    l. 100'   g. 35mm   t. b+w   s. si.
    d.   *
    ph.   *
    c.s. Unknown

        Location not identified, but may be British Columbia.

669. PLAYGROUND APPARATUS IS GIVEN CHILDREN'S AID SOCIETY
    BY GYRO CLUB, VANCOUVER, B.C. (1924)
    p.c. Fox Movietonews (Fox #759.4-A016)
    l. 100'   g. 35mm   t. b+w   s. si.
    d.   *
    ph.   Len H. Roos
    c.s. Fox Movietonews, N.Y.

        "Kids playing on apparatus. Shots of H.R. Glass & Dr. J.D. MacLean."

670. PLAYING CHECKERS IN VANCOUVER, B.C.   (1932)
    p.c. Fox Movietonews (Fox #15-440)
    l. 700'   g. 35mm   t. b+w   s. sound
    d.   *
    ph.   ASN
    c.s. Fox Movietonews, N.Y.

        *"Two men playing the Arnaut Brothers step in and show them how to play the
        game correctly. Playing checkers in Stanley Park. Leaving board for beer.
        Bawling each other out for faulty playing. CU of the checkers."*

671. POLICE OF SEATTLE, VICTORIA AND VANCOUVER MATCH THEIR
    SKILL IN ANNUAL TRACK AND FIELD SPORTS, VANCOUVER, B.C.
    (1923)
    p.c. Fox Movietonews (Fox #733-B1963)
    l. 75'   g. 35mm   t. b+w   s. si.
    d.   *
    ph.   Len H. Roos
    c.s. Fox Movietonews, N.Y.

        *"Bands, racing. E.C. Cox - 100 yard dash winner. Police wives race.   Tug
        of war. Pillow fight. George Goulding, world's champion walker."*

672. POLICING THE PLAINS. (1927)
    p.c. Canadian Historic Features Ltd., initially; later Western Pictures Canadian Co.
    l.   g. 35mm   t. b+w   s. si. w/captions
    d.   A.D. (Cowboy) Kean
    ph.   A.D. (Cowboy) Kean
    c.s. Unknown

        Script: A.D. (Cowboy) Kean from the   l.p. Dorothy Fowler, Jack Boyd,
        book POLICING THE PLAINS by Rev. R.G.·   Miss Lougheed, and Bill Feron.
        MacBeth.

        *The loss of this documentary-style feature by the indefatigable "Cowboy"
        Kean is immeasurable. He began work in 1922 with a production company called
        Canadian Historic Features (we assume), and appears to have taken over full
        production himself when the company collapsed under the name Western Pictures
        Canadian Co. For five years, as money and time permitted, he worked on the film,
        having most of it processed at ASN labs in Montreal. There is evidence that
        the photography was not very homogeneous, there being a problem with density
        changes, developing, etc. Locations were shot at Wainright and Fort MacLeod
        (an original NWMP post) in Alberta, and on Jack Boyd's ranch in the Cariboo.*

Final scenes were shot in Vancouver in the spring of 1927, the final cost of production amounting to over $100,000 according to the CANADIAN MOTION PICTURE DIGEST. POLICING THE PLAINS was only released for six days in Toronto in December 1927, and has since disappeared. Kean blamed the huge American distribution chains for obstructing his efforts to have it shown.

We may never know how Kean decided to handle his subject matter, but may presume that there was a romantic interest between Mr. Boyd and Miss Lougheed. POLICING THE PLAINS was meant to be a history of and tribute to the RCMP, and one man who saw part of it claimed that the film had a very strong documentary look about it. Kean was a newsreel photographer and was committed to providing an authentic version of RCMP history with Rev. MacBeth's book as a guide. MacBeth himself was a Vancouver man; how he figures after 1922 is not known.

673. POLO CHAMPIONSHIP OF B.C. RETAINED BY LOCAL CLUB WHO WIN HARD
     GAME FROM KAMLOOPS TEAM, VANCOUVER, B.C. (1929)
     p.c. Fox Movietonews (Fox #714-D0929)
     l. 100'   g. 35mm   t. b+w   s. si.
     d.   *
     ph. Ross Beesley
     c.s. Fox Movietonews, N.Y.

          "HRH Prince Henry presents cup, his arm in a sling."

674. POULTRY IN THE LAND OF THE MAPLE LEAF. (1927-29)
     p.c. CGMPB
     l. approx. 250'   g. 16mm   t. b+w   s. si. w/captions
     d.   *
     ph. *
     c.s. BCPM (Agriculture reel 24)

          Made for the Dominion Livestock Branch of the Department of Agriculture in Ottawa. There is no record of the film in the CGMPB Catalogue of 1926, but the 1930 edition lists a film called POULTRY RAISING IN BRITISH COLUMBIA. It might not be too far-fetched to suggest that these are one and the same film, POULTRY RAISING IN BRITISH COLUMBIA being a later and more specific title.

          POULTRY IN THE LAND OF THE MAPLE LEAF shows scenes on a large professional poultry farm in British Columbia with many views of the barns, sheds, pullets, feeding and ranging hens. There are shots of champion layers contributing over 300 eggs per year. The finale is an idyllic porch scene with the poultry farmer's family sitting in the warm evening surrounded by lovely gardens and neighbours and watching a sunset over the sea.

675. POULTRY POINTERS.
     p.c. *
     l.   g.   t.   s.
     d.   *
     ph. *
     c.s. *

          See FARM POULTRY IN BRITISH COLUMBIA.

676. POULTRY RAISING IN BRITISH COLUMBIA. (1926-1929)
     p.c. CGMPB
     l. 1 reel   g. 35mm   t. b+w   s. si. w/captions
     d.   *
     ph. *
     c.s. Unknown or PABC (See No. 674)

          Made for the Dominion Livestock Branch of the Department of Agriculture in Ottawa. The description: "A scenic and educational film depicting various phases of the Poultry Industry in the Province of British Columbia." See: POULTRY IN THE LAND OF THE MAPLE LEAF,

677. THE POWER OF WATER. (1923-1930)
     p.c. National Museum of Canada
     l. 1 reel   g. 35mm   t. b+w   s. si.
     d.   Harlan I. Smith
     ph. Harlan I. Smith
     c.s. Unknown

Apparently this film was put together from Smith's BELLA COOLA footage. Nothing else is known about it.

678. PREMIER LAKE RANCH-CAMP-REEL L. (1926-1929)
    p.c. private
    l. approx. 400'   g. 16mm   t. b+w   s. si. w/captions
    d. *
    ph. Mr. Elmore Staples.
    c.s. NFA, Ottawa

Camp Skookumchuck-in-the-Rockies, Premier Lake, B.C.

Elmore Staples conceived the idea of building a girl's ranch camp on Premier Lake near Skookumchuck and, over a period, from the construction in 1926 to a local rodeo in 1939, he shot film of its progress. He captioned some of his films which were distributed as advertisements for the camp. Many of the films, now owned by his daughter, show the period from 1926-1929, and contain many duplicate shots. During this time the camp took great pride in its expert riding instruction, its tennis courts and, especially, its trail riding into the Rocky Mountains. The camp eventually evolved into a dude ranch, the first of its kind in B.C. Certainly the location is nothing short of Paradise. Shots include: Pack trip over Saddleback Mountain, above Premier Lake, showing the climb to the summit and the view at the top. The girls have a meal at the top, as well as a snowball fight. Girls swimming in Premier Lake, temperature 72°. View of all the lodges, named after wild animals such as cougar and goat, where the campers sleep, and the boathouse with the art-room on top. The girls go on an autombile tour from Premier Lake to Banff through the National Parks, a 500-mile trip showing Sinclair Mountain, Banff Highway with old open cars, Lake Louise, mountain sheep, camping in an aspen grove, swimming at Banff Springs Hotel, the Prince of Wales at Lake Louise, and swimming at Chateau Lake Louise. The final shots show Charlie Johnson, Claire Staples, and a guide (Phillips?) on a fishing trip to Fish Lake.

679. PREMIER LAKE RANCH-CAMP-REEL 2. (1926-29)
    p.c. private
    l. approx. 400'   g. 16mm   t. b+w   s. si. w/captions
    d. *
    ph. Elmore Staples
    c.s. NFA, Ottawa

Camp Skookumchuck-in-the-Rockies, Premier Lake, B.C.

Hot pool, Banff Springs. Mountains near Banff. Open cars on Banff Highway. Lake Louise pool. Girls having lunch and pole jumping. Storm Mountain (now Mt. Eisenhower). Black bears in Park. These shots taken during an auto trip the campers made through Banff National Park.

Captioned shots follow: Lake Louise. Commander Booth, one of the guides, in CU. White Swan Lake, back in the mountains behind Premier Lake. Mrs. Staples and her faithful horse "Sunny", a good CU. Good CU of Mr. Staples and "Jim", his horse. CU Captain Arthur Innocent, riding instructor at the ranch. A group of young girls out trail riding. Various shots of interior of one of the lodges where the girls sleep. Group of girls around a fireplace. Group of counselors. Swimming race and diving from the tower into Premier Lake, swimming lessons. Kids resting on bed inside lodge. Aquaplaning behind Chriscraft motorboat. Art class with kids working inside, windows providing light, and some of the craft objects made by the campers. Interior of the dining hall, group of kids waiting to eat, the gong being rung, and girls leaping up and running inside dining hall. Junior girls off on a trail ride, leaving camp. Campers pitching a tipi. Man stretching hides on a log wall being watched by a group of campers. Camp scenes along the lakeshore, tennis game.

680. PREMIER LAKE RANCH-CAMP - REEL 4. (1926-29)
    p.c. private
    l. approx. 400'   g. 16mm   t. b+w   s. si. w/captions
    d. *
    ph. Elmore Staples
    c.s. NFA, Ottawa

Camp Skookumchuck-in-the-Rockies, Premier Lake, B.C.

Campers on a trail ride up Saddleback Mountain, playing in the snow. Excellent shots of a rodeo held at Premier Lake, including bucking horses, steer riding, wild cow milking (filling a beer-bottle with milk), and other events (approx. 200').

Captioned shots follow: Interior of one of the lodges where the campers sleep. Group of girls around a fireplace. Group of counselors. Swimming race and diving from the tower into Premier Lake. Aquaplaning behind Chriscract motorboat. Kids resting on beds inside lodge. Art class with kids working inside, windows providing light, and some of the craft objects made by the campers.

Campers cooking their breakfast outside. Rolling bedrolls. Repeat sequence above: "Interior of one of the lodges..." to "...craft objects made by campers." Swimming race. CU smiling camper with bathing cap. Swimming with umbrella. Diving, swimming and canoes. Girls wearing jodphurs and ties, riding sedately about the riding ring in a line. Canoe jousting. Swimming, CU two swimmers. Girls on tour through the Rockies in open autos, throwing snowballs, looking into a valley, two open cars on the road filled with girls.

681. PREMIER LAKE RANCH-CAMP - REEL 5 (DAWN OF ANOTHER DAY OF ADVENTURE) (1926-29)
p.c. private
l. approx. 400'   g. 16mm   t. b+w . s. si. w/captions
d.   *
ph. Elmore Staples
c.s. NFA, Ottawa

Camp Skookumchuck-in-the-Rockies, Premier Lake, B.C.

Campers arrive at the corral early with their bed rolls, ready to begin the trail ride up into the mountains. George West, Captain Arthur Innocent and others help pack the horses and prepare for the trip. They leave in a cloud of dust. Fording Sheep Creek. Drinking from a mountain stream. Views on the trail: Moose Lake, Columbia Lake, Madeline the camp cook preparing breakfast and campers digging in. Rolling up the bedrolls. Camp at Upper Columbia Lake, showing a tipi and some tents. Campers up early for another day on the trail. Fording Sheep Creek near the hot springs. Moose Lake. A dusty stretch near Sheep Creek. Swimming in an icy stream and in hot springs. Horses and riders crossing outlet at White Swan Lake. Camping at White Swan Lake. Billy Stork, guide. Turning in at the end of a perfect day. Rolling out early next morning. Fishing in White River. Climbing and view from Home Basin. Swimmers at Lake of Hanging Glaciers (iceburgs!) Snowballs in summer. Columbia Lake. Riders at Moose Lake. Single file of campers riding up a rocky valley. Glacier, mountain top, waterfalls, ice caves. Good shot of large group of riders climbing over Saddleback mountain.

682. PREMIER LAKE RANCH-CAMP - REEL 6 (SKOOKUMCHUCK-IN-THE-ROCKIES). (1926-29)
p.c. private
l. approx. 400'   g. 16mm   t. b+w   s. si. w/captions
d.   *
ph. Elmore Staples
c.s. NFA, Ottawa

Camp Skookumchuck-in-the-Rockies, Premier Lake, B.C.
SKOOKUMCHUCK-IN-THE-ROCKIES
    Unique Ranch-Camp
On the Beautiful Premier Lake in
    British Columbia

LS view of lake from top of Saddleback Mountain. LS Selkirk Range, campers on horses in f.g. Views of the log buildings in camp. LS camp from across the bay at the end of the lake. Main lodge. A small mountain lake on the 3000 acre ranch. Group of girls around the fireplace in their lodge. Group of counselors. Swimming race and diving from the tower into Premier Lake. Swimming lessons. Aquaplaning behind a Chriscraft motorboat. Kids resting on beds inside lodge. Art class with kids working inside, windows providing light, and some of the craft objects made by the campers. "The Wanagan Post

*Office and Camp Store": kids receiving and opening mail. Interior of dining
hall, group of kids waiting to eat, the gong being rung, and girls leaping
up and running inside to eat. Junior girls off on a trail ride, leaving
camp. Campers pitching a tipi. Man stretching hides on a log wall being
watched and listened to by a group of campers. Mrs. Staples and her horse
"Sunny". Mr. Staples and his horse "Jim". (CU's). Group of young trail
riders. Playing tennis. Boats and canoes near diving tower. Scenes on the
auto trip through Banff: kids on a bridge looking into a creek, mountain
scenery. Sunset on Premier Lake.*

683. PREMIER LAKE RANCH-CAMP - REEL 7. (1926-29)
        p.c. private
        l. approx. 300'   g. 16mm   t. b+w   s. si. w/captions
        d.   *
        ph. Elmore Staples
        c.s. NFA, Ottawa

        Camp Skookumchuck-in-the-Rockies, Premier Lake, B.C.

        *A camp at Horse Thief Creek showing campers cooking over a fire, then Made-
        line, the camp cook, preparing breakfast. From this point, on this reel is
        the same as Reel 5, with extra shots of the girls in bathing suits and moun-
        tain scenery at the camp on Columbia Lake, and longer takes of the guide
        Billy Stork. The reel finishes with "End of a Perfect Day".*

684. PREMIER LAKE RANCH-CAMP - REEL 8. (1926-29)
        p.c. private
        l. 300'   g. 16mm   t. b+w   s. si. w/captions
        d.   *
        ph. Elmore Staples
        c.s. NFA, Ottawa

        Camp Skookumchuck-in-the-Rockies, Premier Lake, B.C.

        *Lake of Hanging Glaciers, at the head of Horse Thief Creek, showing campers
        inspecting ice caves since collapsed, and the beginning of the creek itself,
        starting as streams and waterfalls. Many good shots of the annual rodeo
        held at the ranch, with cow milking, steer wrestling, etc. and riders arri-
        ving. Good shots of Kootenay Indians arriving and parading, and their tipi
        encampment on the ranch. CU Indian woman with child. Good shot of a Bennett
        Buggy. Many good shots of bronc-busting, steer-roping and crowds watching,
        and Indians in the camp.*

685. PREMIER LAKE RANCH-CAMP - REEL 9. (1927)
        p.c. private
        l. approx. 150'   g. 16mm   t. b+w   s. si. w/captions
        d.   *
        ph. Elmore Staples
        c.s. NFA, Ottawa

        Camp Skookumchuck-in-the-Rockies, Premier Lake, B.C.

        *Same as the beginning of Reel 5, DAWN OF ANOTHER DAY OF ADVENTURE, starting
        at the same point, and closing with the shots of "Views on the trail: Moose
        Lake, Columbia Lake". There are extra shots of the trail riders at the end.*

686. PREMIER LAKE RANCH-CAMP - REEL 10. (1926-29)
        p.c. private
        l. approx. 300'   g. 16mm   t. b+w   s. si. w/captions
        d.   *
        ph. Elmore Staples
        c.s. NFA, Ottawa

        *Camp Skookumchuck-in-the-Rockies, Premier Lake, B.C.
        SKOOKUMCHUCK-IN-THE-ROCKIES
        A Ranch-Camp in British Columbia*

        *Girls leaving for a 500-mile camping trip through the National Parks. Two
        truckloads of campers arriving at Fairmont Hot Springs, and swimming and
        sporting in the pool with its radium waters. They return to the trucks
        again. Excellent shots of cars along the highway. Tent camp pitched, girls
        in trucks. Campers at Lake Louise. Prince of Wales at Lake Louise. Girls*

*swimming in pools at Lake Louise. Shots of Chateau Lake Louise. Mountain
scenery, girls speeding past camera in cars. Girls at Takakkaw Falls. Castle
Mountain. Girls with mother bear and cubs. LS mountain sheep. CU elk feeding. Mountain scenery. Sinclair Canyon, girls on bridge over creek. Pole-
jumping back at Camp. Sinclair Canyon shots.*

687. PREMIER LAKE RANCH-CAMP - REEL 11. (1926-29)
    p.c. private
    l. approx. 400'   g. 16mm   t. b+w   s. si.
    d.   *
    ph. Elmore Staples
    c.s. NFA, Ottawa

Camp Skookumchuck-in-the-Rockies, Premier Lake, B.C.

*Girls at camp (out of focus) and walking across a bridge (also out of focus).
Girls stepping down from train, being met on platform and posing against
train at Banff(?). Cars on the road. Rider in corral at ranch (light flashes).
Tennis player on upper and lower courts. Swimming in Premier Lake. Pan of
lake. Riders in corral during a riding class with Capt. Arthur Innocent.
Aquaplaning on Premier Lake behind Chriscraft inboard motorboat. Swimming
at Fairmont Hot Springs. Chriscraft and aquaplaners. Swimming and canoe
jousting, campers engaged in various aquatic sports, tennis, diving, etc.
Riding lessons.*

688. PREMIER LAKE RANCH-CAMP - REEL 12. (1926-29)
    p.c. private
    l. approx. 350'   g. 16mm   t. b+w   's. si. w/captions
    d.   *
    ph. Elmore Staples
    c.s. NFA, Ottawa

Camp Skookumchuck-in-the-Rockies, Premier Lake, B,C.

*Mountain scenery. Lake of the Hanging Glaciers, campers looking into ice
caves. Camp on Columbia Lake, showing tents and campers, horses fording
Horse Thief Creek. Campers on horses climbing to the summit of a mountain.
An old timer, Paul Stevens, the guide, points out some game: mountain sheep,
elk and bear. Lots of trail riding, mountain scenery and glaciers. On the
top of a mountain the campers gaze out over the peaks and down into the
valleys. Snowballing in August on a glacier on top of Teepee Mountain.
Sliding down on the seat of their pants in Diorite Basin. Rodeo at the ranch,
showing Indians, rodeo events, Indian encampment, and Bennett Buggy, same as
in Reel 8.*

689. PREMIER LAKE RANCH-CAMP - REEL 13. (about 1926)
    p.c. private
    l. approx. 300'   g. 16mm   t. b+w   s. si. w/captions
    d.   *
    ph. Elmore Staples
    c.s. NFA, Ottawa

Camp Skookumchuck-in-the-Rockies, Premier Lake, B.C.

*A view of the lodges comprising the Camp from the Lake. Shots of construction
of the camp buildings with logs. Swimming in Premier Lake, floats, swimming
race, diving tower, Chriscraft inboard motorboat, pan along shore showing
lodges, the boat house, the second floor of which is the "Arts & Crafts Room".
Girls playing tennis on one of the cement courts. Group of girls on
horses waving. Horses being prepared for a week's trip into the Rockies.
Paul Stevens, an old time guide, packing one of the horses. showing the
'Barrel Hitch' and the 'Double Diamond'. Good shot of Aloysius Birdstone,
and Indian horse wrangler in a tall hat.*

690. PREMIER LAKE RANCH-CAMP - REEL 14. (1926-29)
    p.c. private
    l. approx. 400'   g. 16mm   t. b+w   s. si. w/captions
    d.   *
    ph. Elmore Staples
    c.s. NFA, Ottawa

Camp Skookumchuck-in-the-Rockies, Premier Lake, B.C.

Pan across Premier Lake. Lodges at the ranch, many shots with campers here and there. Mr. Staples with horse "Jim" and Mrs. Staples with horse "Sunny". Campers swimming, diving, aquaplaning, canoe-jousting, and having a swimming race with umbrellas. Tennis game with CU's girls playing. Well-dressed girls taking riding lessons from Captain Arthur Innocent, performing manoeuvres on horses. Preparing horses for a trail ride. Juniors off for a trail ride. A trail on the ranch with riders. Sunset, Premier Lake.

691. PREMIER LAKE RANCH-CAMP - REEL 18. (1926-29)
     p.c. private
     l. approx. 100'   g. 16mm   t. b+w   s. si. w/captions
     d.   *
     ph. Elmore Staples
     c.s. NFA, Ottawa

     Camp Skookumchuck-in-the-Rockies, Premier Lake, B.C.

     Truck at camp. Snow sliding in Diorite Basin. Building the camp, logs being readied for erection of Wolf Lodge. Campers arriving by train. Fairmont Hot Springs, swimming in pool. Swimming in Premier Lake. Truckload of girls on way to Fairmont Hot Springs. Brief shot of camp.

692. PREMIER LAKE RANCH-CAMP - REEL 19. (1926-29)
     p.c. private
     l. approx. 10'   g. 16mm   t. b+w   s. si.
     d.   *
     ph. Elmore Staples
     c.s. NFA, Ottawa

     Camp Skookumchuck-in-the-Rockies, Premier Lake, B.C.

     Aquaplaning on Premier Lake behind Chriscraft speedboat. Fishing. Staples family. Winter at ranch. Stallion CRYSTAL LORD. Campers lunching on a trail ride. Riders on Top of the World, mountain peak. Good CU's campers and horses.

693. PREMIER LAKE RANCH-CAMP - REEL 21. (1926-29)
     p.c. private
     l. 100'   g. 16mm   t. b+w   s. si. w/captions
     d.   *
     ph. Elmore Staples
     c.s. NFA, Ottawa

     Camp Skookumchuck-in-the-Rockies, Premier Lake, B.C.

     Horse riding in the corral. Trail riding through a creek. Horses and campers at the summit of Top of the World. Black Bear. Lake of Hanging Glaciers. Waterfall, mountain scenery. Sunset & Dawn shots. Campers learning to pack a horse, swimming, trail riding. Mountain scenery. Camp.

694. PREMIER LAKE RANCH-CAMP - REEL 22. (1926-29)
     p.c. private
     l. 100'   g. 16mm   t. b+w   s. si.
     d.   *
     ph. Elmore Staples
     c.s. NFA, Ottawa

     Camp Skookumchuck-in-the-Rockies, Premier Lake, B.C.

     Two little kids at camp. Diving tower shots. Pack horses and campers readying to leave on a trail ride, and leaving.

695. PREMIER LAKE RANCH-CAMP - REEL 23. (1929-26)
     p.c. private
     l. approx. 75'   g. 16mm   t. b+w   s. si.
     d.   *
     ph. Elmore Staples
     c.s. NFA, Ottawa

     Camp Skookumchuck-in-the-Rockies, Premier Lake, B.C.

     Playing tennis at the ranch. Scenery from ranch.

696. PREMIER LAKE RANCH-CAMP - REEL 24. (1939)
    p.c. private
    1. 100'   g. 16mm   t. colour s. si.
    d.   *
    ph. Elmore Staples
    c.s. NFA, Ottawa

        Camp Skookumchuck-in-the-Rockies, Premier Lake, B.C.

        *Excellent shots of the annual rodeo at the ranch. Billy Stork, Indians and
        squaws, children, corral. Mary Bills. Playing poker and bridge inside
        (dark). Lunch buffet table: Mary, Claire, Mrs. Bills, Elmore, Madeline
        Turnor, Jack MacBeth and Jeff Hotham. Lee Soon, the cook, in the kitchen.*

697. PREMIER LAKE RANCH-CAMP - REEL 25. (1926-29)
    p.c. private
    1. 100'   g. 16mm   t. b+w   s. si.
    d.   *
    ph. Elmore Staples
    c.s. NFA, Ottawa

        Camp Skookumchuck-in-the-Rockies, Premier Lake, B.C.

        Shots of campers on auto trip to Banff, swimming in the pool at Lake Louise.

698. PREMIER LAKE RANCH-CAMP - UNNUMBERED REEL. (1926-29)
    p.c. private
    1. 100'   g. 16mm   t. b+w   s. si. w/captions
    d.   *
    ph. Elmore Staples
    c.s. NFA, Ottawa

        Camp Skookumchuck-in-the-Rockies, Premier Lake, B.C.

        *Rodeo scenes at annual rodeo on ranch. Sliding down glacier in Diorite
        Basin. View from summit of mountain. Trail riding. Pam Staples on waterwings
        swimming in lake. Rodeo. Mountain scenery. Billy Stork, old trapper, with
        a hide on his wall. Bear. (Most of these are duplicates of shots on ear-
        lier reels)*

699. PREMIER LAKE RANCH-CAMP - UNNUMBERED REEL. (1926-29)
    p.c. private
    1. approx. 300' g. 16mm   t. b+w   s. si. w/captions
    d.   *
    ph. Elmore Staples
    c.s. NFA, Ottawa

        Camp Skookumchuck-in-the-Rockies, Premier Lake, B.C.

        *Three cars full of girls on a trip to Banff. Swimming and diving in the
        pool at Lake Louise. Swimming and diving off tower at Premier Lake. Tennis.
        Riding lessons. Mountain scenery. Swimming in a creek. Girls in the back
        of trucks. Trail riding and overnight camping. Views of Camp Skookumchuck.
        Trial riding, fording stream. Campers returning exhausted from their trail
        ride. Tennis players. Trail riding. Misc. swimming, diving, tennis, etc,
        at ranch. Trail riding. (most of this reel is made up of duplicates from
        earlier reels)*

700. PREMIER TOLMIE OPENS CANADIAN PACIFIC EXHIBITION,
    VANCOUVER, B.C. (1929)
    p.c. Fox Movietonews (?)
    1.   g. 35mm   t. b+w   s. si.
    d.   *
    ph. ASN (?)
    c.s. NFB (1920-FG-163)

        *"Premier Tolmie at microphone, Union Jack being built in front of grandstand.
        Pan of children in race. Crowds. Freckle contest and "longhair" contest.
        The Union Jack may be the creation of marchers in different coloured sweaters
        forming patterns, or ?."*

701. PRESENTING B.C., NANAIMO AND VANCOUVER ISLAND, B.C.
     (1912-1914)
     p.c. *
     l.   g. 35mm   t. b+w   s. si.
     d.   *
     ph. *
     c.s. NFB (1910-DN-29)

> "Soccer game in progress in an unidentified town, with various shots of spec-
> tators, grandstands, etc. Various travel shots along the shore of Cameron
> Lake, with some of picknickers. Elk River Falls in Strathcona Park. Travel
> shots along the Malahat Drive, showing the rough dirt road, trees, etc. Two
> stationary shots of 1910 autos driving past the camera. Boating shots of
> Nanaimo, of fishing boats in cove. Fishermen preparing to unload, etc. LS
> of a Great Northern freight train being pulled by an early locomotive. Short
> pan along train and LS imposing farm house when train moves out. A herd of
> cows waiting for the train to pass are driven over the crossing and toward
> the camera."

702. PRESIDENT ROOSEVELT IN CANADA, VICTORIA, B.C. (1937)
     p.c. British Movietonews (No. 5761/421 & 31330)
     l. 34'   g. 35mm   t. b+w   s. sound
     d.   *
     ph. *
     c.s. British Movietonews

> Roosevelt and wife and son aboard destroyer USS PHELPS, waving. Brief scene
> in drill hall with troops in Victoria. CU Roosevelt in open car with Lt.
> Gov. Hamber, chatting. Open car. with secret servicemen and police motor-
> cycle escort, moving along rainy street lined with throngs of people. CU
> standing in group with dignitaries, wife and son. Commentator: Leslie Mitch-
> ell.

703. PRESIDENT ROOSEVELT VISITS BRITISH COLUMBIA, VICTORIA,
     B.C. (1937)
     p.c. Fox Movietonews (Fox #32-356)
     l.   g. 35mm   t. b+w   s. sound
     d.   *
     ph. Paramount
     c.s. NFA, Fox Movietonews, N.Y. and NFB (1930-FG-333,339)

> "Destroyer bringing President arrives. Sailors throwing ropes. Roosevelt
> with Lt. Gov. Hamber in open car driving through city. Crowds along route.
> Gov't House group includes Pres. & Mrs. Roosevelt & Mrs. Hamber. Mrs.
> Roosevelt. Pipe band. Mounted police. Roosevelt passing school children,
> kids waving flags. Roosevelt arriving at dock. Honour guard. Pres. waving."

704. PRESIDENT ROOSEVELT'S VISIT, VICTORIA, B.C. (1937)
     p.c. Fox Movietonews (Fox #32-367)
     l. 200'   g. 35mm   t. b+w   s. sound
     d.   *
     ph. Tondra
     c.s. Fox Moveitonews, N.Y. & NFB (1930-FG-333,339)

> "President on pier in car. Car leaving pier. Canadian soldiers at attention.
> President with Lt.-Gov. Hamber and party. L-R: Mrs. Hamber, Pres. Roosevelt
> and Lt. Gov. Hamber. President & Lt.-Gov. Hamber ride through streets.
> Pres. Roosevelt aboard destroyer USS PHELPS."

705. PRINCE ALEXIS MDIVANI, EVADING A CALIFORNIA SUBPOENA,
     SAILS TO MEET BRIDE IN JAPAN. VANCOUVER, B.C. (1934)
     p.c. Paramount (Lib. #3548) NL 1174
     l.   g. 35mm   t. b+w   s. sound
     d.   *
     ph. *
     c.s. Sherman Grinberg, N.Y. & Visnews (BPN Lib. #2404)

> Prince Mdivani, husband of Barbara Hutton, Woolworth heiress, leaves auto
> and walks up gangplank onto ship.

706. PRINCE CHICHIBU ARRIVES IN VANCOUVER, CANADA, & GOES
     TO OTTAWA. (1937)
     p.c. Fox Movietonews (Fox #30-913,914)
     l. 985' & 530' g. 35mm & 16mm t. b+w s. sound
     d. *
     ph. ASN
     c.s. Fox Movietonews, N.Y.

> "VANCOUVER. HEIAN MARU entering harbour. Price & Princess arrive at Language Hall in Japanese quarter. Children wave flags and cheer. At U. of British Columbia, welcomed by President Dr. L.S. Klinck. At memorial of Inazo Nitobe, Statesman. Atop Vancouver Hotel. Procession through Japanese quarters. Japanese bow in reverence. Kids wave flags, cheer." (985' on 35mm)

707. PRINCE EDWARD, THE PRINCE OF WALES, REVIEWS SEAFORTH
     HIGHLANDERS IN BRITISH COLUMBIA (PROBABLY VANCOUVER).
     (1927)
     p.c. Gaumont Graphic 18028
     l. 42'   g. 35mm   t. b+w   s. si.
     d. *
     ph. *
     c.s. Visnews (Video roll 156)

> "Prince of Wales in uniform inspects Highlander troops. No establishing shot, could be anywhere. CU Prince of Wales. LS troops & inspection. CU inspection. Trees blowing in the b.g."

708. PRINCE OF WALES AND ROYAL PARTY ARE GREETED BY CROWDS/
     PRINCE OF WALES ARRIVES AT VANCOUVER ON HIS TOUR OF THE
     DOMINION, VANCOUVER, B.C. (1927)
     p.c. Paramount
     l. 145'   g. 35mm   t. b+w   s. si.
     d. *
     ph. *
     c.s. Visnews (BPN Lib. #189) Video roll 503

> Pan from crowds to cars arriving. Elev. follow shot of Prince's car. Canadian troops parade past crowd. Prince in uniform inspecting Guards. Guards on field at attention. Side view and SCU. Prince shakes hands with veterans. Various moving shots of landscapes taken from train, various moving shots of mountains and trees, some near Banff.

709. THE PRINCE OF WALES IN CANADA. (1919)
     p.c. Pathéscope
     l. approx. 400' g. 28mm   t. b+w   s. si.
     d. *
     ph. Tracy Mathewson (?)
     c.s. NFA

> "Authoritative pictures of the Prince's visit to the principal cities of the Dominion. CU scenes of our future King winning his way into the hearts of the people. These pictures are from official Canadian Government negatives." The Prince visited Vancouver, therefore, it is probably safe to assume that scenes of British Columbia are included.

710. PRINCE OF WALES INTERESTED IN FISH MIGRATING UP RIVER
     TO SPAWN, VANCOUVER. (1919)
     p.c. Gaumont Graphic (903(6))
     l. 35'   g. 35mm   t. b+w   s. si.
     d. *
     ph. *
     c.s. Visnews

> Shots of salmon swimming, almost hovering in a large school, in an unidentified stretch of water. No jumping. CU Prince of Wales and other men in civilian suits watching fish. Prince of Wales walks toward camera. Much activity about the Prince. An indistinct shot of fish in water.

711. PRINCE OF WALES ON TOUR OF CANADA. (1919)
     p.c. *
     l.   g. 35mm   t. b+w   s. si.
     d.   *
     ph.   *
     c.s. NFA

> "Arrives Montreal, HRH Prince Edward crosses to his ship in Vancouver. Prince
> meets Lord Willingdon, the Governor General, and Mackenzie King. Prince en-
> joys golf at the Jericho course in Vancouver. Prince visits Montreal Hunt
> Club and follows hounds, then leaves for U.K."

712. PRINCESS DONA BEATRICE, PRINCE ALFONSO, A COUSIN OF THE
     KING OF SPAIN, AND SIR AUSTEN CHAMBERLAIN, ENROUTE FROM
     THE U.S.A., STOP AT VANCOUVER, B.C.,(OR, PERHAPS IT SHOULD
     BE VICTORIA, B.C) (1928)
     p.c. Fox Movietonews (Fox #201-C7939 or C7942)
     l.   g. 35mm   t. b+w   s. si.
     d.   *
     ph.   Ross Beesley
     c.s. Fox Movietonews, N.Y.

> "As guests of Lt. Gov. Randolph Bruce, Chamberlain and others leave house.
> SCU Sir Austen Chamberlain, Miss Mackenzie & Randolph Bruce."

713. PRINCESS MARGUERITE AND PRINCESS LOUISE COLLIDE IN
     FOG, BUT COMPLETE JOURNIES, VICTORIA, B.C. (1929)
     p.c. Fox Movietonews (Fox #090.1-D2782)
     l. 30'   g. 35mm   t. b+w   s. si.
     d.   *
     ph.   Ross Beesley
     c.s. Fox Movietonews, N.Y.

> Shots of the two damaged CPR ferries.

714. PRIZE GOATS AT EL BAR RANCH, VALUED AT $40,000.00, SUPPLY
     MILK FOR BABIES AND HOSPITALS, NEW WESTMINSTER, B.C. (1923)
     p.c. Fox Movietonews (Fox #411.516-3622)
     l. 30'   g. 35mm   t. b+w   s. si.
     d.   *
     ph.   Len H. Roos
     c.s. Fox Movietonews, N.Y.

> "Flock of goats. Goats playing. Puppy feeding from goat."

715. PROFESSIONAL SKI JUMPERS HOLD MEET, REVELSTOKE, B.C.
     (1920)
     p.c. Fox Movietonews (Fox #732.5-1532)
     l. 39'   g. 35mm   t. b+w   s. si.
     d.   *
     ph.   British-American Films
     c.s. Fox Movietonews, N.Y.

> "Various shots of take-off and after contestants have made jump."

716. "THE PRIVATE SECRETARY" PLAYS AT THE CAPITOL THEATRE,
     VICTORIA, B.C. (1914)
     p.c. *
     l.   g. 35mm   t. b+w   s. si.
     d.   *
     ph.   Oldfield
     c.s. NFA (Taylor reel 109)

> "The film, THE PRIVATE SECRETARY, was filmed in 1913, edited in Hollywood,
> Calif., and released on May 9, 1914. It was produced, written and directed
> by Leonard Grover and one of the first theatres to receive a print was the
> Capitol in Victoria. Excellent shots of lineup in front of theatre with
> sign to the left reading: 10 - 20 - 30 THE GREAT COMEDY SUCCESS - THE PRIVATE
> SECRETARY - PRICES 10 - 20 - 30." Part of the comedy continues from this
> point.

717. PROVINCIAL LEGISLATURE OPENS, VICTORIA, B.C. (1929)
    p.c. Fox Movietonews (?)
    l.   g. 35mm   t. b+w   s. si.
    d.   *
    ph. ASN (?)
    c.s. NFB (1920-FG-155)

            "Guard of Honour lines up. Premier of B.C., S.F. Tolmie, arrives in auto,
            gun salute being fired. Tolmie inspects Honour Guard. Highland regiment
            parading and LS Parliament Buildings." Part of CANADA CAPSULE NO: 8.

718. PROVINCIAL RECREATION CENTRES RACE, VANCOUVER, B.C.
    (1938)
    p.c. Fox Movietonews (Fox #34-471)
    l.   g. 35mm   t. b+w   s. sound
    d.   *
    ph. ASN
    c.s. Fox Movietonews, N.Y.

            "At the entrance to Stanley Park. Start of race. Finish with Gerald Sankey
            the winner. Presentation of trophy to Sankey from Hugo Meilicke. After
            start, runners grouped together. Running shot. Entering trail. Various
            shots of the race showing Sankey leading. Near end of course various runners
            coming in. Crowd."

719. PULP MAKING. (1930's)
    p.c. *
    l. approx. 700'   g. 35mm   t. b+w   a. si.
    d.   *
    ph. *
    c.s. NFB (#1930-N-153)

            This film is called TOP OF THE WORLD in the NFB files, but it seems to be
            mistitled. TOP OF THE WORLD is an ASN film made for the CPR, probably about
            the Rockies. The description of this film is:"HA pan of small town near a
            large body of water. Shot of docks, high buildings, etc. Automatic saw
            cutting logs that travel on a conveyor. Carriage in saw mill rushing to
            and fro with logs that are gradually chopped to pieces. Edger at work. In
            a pulp mill, men prepare the digesters for cooking the wood chips. Shots of
            the wet end of dryer machine, of the dry end, and men picking up slabs of
            sulphite and piling them on a small cart. The finished product being loaded
            into the hold of a cargo ship. Various pans of shore installations, build-
            ings, paper mill, from offshore." This film was likely shot on the west
            coast, perhaps in Ocean Falls, but the location is not identified.

720. PUPPET SHOW FOR KIDS, VANCOUVER, B.C. (ONE OF FOUR
    INTERNATIONAL STORIES) (1939)
    p.c. Paramount (Lib #7618)
    l. total 248'   g. 35mm   t. b+w   s. sound
    d.   *
    ph. ASN
    c.s. Sherman Grinberg, N.Y. (Lost)

            VANCOUVER: SCU kids looking at puppet. SCU man gets puppets ready for show.
            Pan kids in the hospital, waiting. Various performances by the puppets. At
            the end of the show, the hospital kids applaud, look pleased. The show likely
            took place during Christmas, 1938.

721. QUAINT CUSTOM IS OBSERVED BY DOUKHOBORS WHO ATTEND
    FUNERAL OF LATE LEADER PETER VEREGIN, BRILLIANT, B.C.
    (1924)
    p.c. Fox Movietonews (Fox #095.6-A6651)
    l.   g. 35mm   t. b+w   s. si.
    d.   *
    ph. CPR
    c.s. Lost

            "At the grave and returning. Paul Czar proclaims himself Czar of the Earth.
            Paul Czar with crown of oranges proclaims self Czar of Earth. Crowd at the
            graveside. Bread, fruit & water on table. Vice President Kazakoff adresses
            mourners."

722. QUEEN OF MAY CROWNED IN NEW WESTMINSTER, B.C. (1938)
    p.c. Fox Movietonews (Fox #34-476)
    1.   g. 35mm   t. b+w   s. sound
    d.   *
    ph. ASN
    c.s. Fox Movietonews, N.Y.

            "New Westminster main street where parade starts. Lt. Gov. & Mrs. Hamber,
            Mayor Hume, Mayor Miller, Hon Wells Gray among the dignitaries. Pan of
            Queen & her attendants. Folk dancing by 1000 children. CU crowd. Maypole
            dancing. Band leader. Musicians, crowds. Elevated shots showing the entire
            show. CU Lt. Gov. & Mrs. Hamber."

723. QUEEN OF THE COAST. (1920)
    p.c. Dept. of Trade and Commerce
         Exhibits and Publicity Bureau, Ottawa
    1. 1 reel   g. 35mm   t. b+w   s. si. w/captions
    d.   *
    ph. *
    c.s. NFA (28mm); NFB outs (1920-FG-30A,30B)

            "A straight scenic picture of Vancouver, B.C. and its environs. This is one
            of the most beautiful scenics that the Bureau has made." - from the CGMPB
            Catalogue, 1926. The NFA possesses a 28mm copy, and the NFB holds 287' of
            out takes which give a fairly good idea of the contents of the finished
            print: A Grand Trunk passenger train pulls into Vancouver station and passen-
            gers disembark. Exterior of station. Pan Vancouver. Various views of a
            highschool, the Courthouse, Hastings and Granville streets with streetcars,
            autos and pedestrians. Post Office. Stately homes (30A). Shot of an art-
            istic archway with touring car driving through and past the camera. HA shot
            of beach at English Bay, hundreds of bathers. Two cars driving through
            Stanley Park. Two shots of Lumbermen's Arch. Cathedral Grove: towering
            firs, tourists strolling through. A girl writes on one of the huge trunks.
            Shots of the park and pavillion. (Note: the large trees are not on V.I. but
            in Stanley Park in an area also named Cathedral Grove.) A large open bus
            takes tourists to Capilano Canyon where they gaze into the chasm and walk
            across the 400' suspension bridge. Canyon View Hotel and two of the open
            tour buses leaving.

            There are also shots from Victoria at the end of the NFB roll: Pan from
            Empress Hotel to LS Parliament Bldgs. Closer shot of Parliament Bldgs.
            Tourists, 3 women and a man getting into a touring car. Two shots down city
            streets, moderate traffic. Beacon Hill Park and posh residences. The Vic-
            toria footage is from the Exhibits and Publicity Bureau's 1919 travelogue
            about Victoria called THE CITY OF SUNSHINE.

724. THE RADIANT ROCKIES. (late 1930's)
    p.c. *
    1. 1x400' reel   g. 16mm   t. colour s. sound
    d.   *
    ph. *
    c.s. Unknown

            "From Banff in the Canadian Rockies to Victoria, B.C."

725. RAISING THE DUST IN THE DIRT TRACK RACES FORMS PART OF THE
    THRILL FOR THE DRIVERS AND SPECTATORS, VANCOUVER, B.C. (1924)
    p.c. Fox Movietonews (Fox #755.2-A3979)
    1.   g. 35mm   t. b+w   s. si.
    d.   *
    ph. Len H. Roos
    c.s. Fox Movietonews, N.Y.

            Race, drivers, or machines not identified. Shots include "Jacob Smith,
            winner of 3-mile city championship race."

726a. RAY WOODS DIVING, VANCOUVER, B.C. (1935)
    p.c. Hearst Metrotone News; Can no. 289, Roll no. 6
    1. 480'   g. 35mm   t. b+w   s. sound
    d.   *
    ph. ASN
    c.s. Hearst Metrotone News, N.Y.

"Woods explaining how he makes his dives. Kissing his wife. Diving off Burrard Bridge. Mayor G. McGeer of Vancouver congratulates Woods. Various shots from bridge."

726b. RCAF ACTIVITIES AT VANCOUVER STATION. (1928)
    p.c. RCAF
    1.   g. 35mm   t. b+w   s. si.
    d.   *
    ph. RCAF Photo Unit
    c.s. NFB (1920-N-117)

"Slow pan shot from water to hangar of AVRO 504 LYNX trainers (with single pontoon moored to the shore or high and dry on land. RCAF personnel at work and hangars in medium distance. Sequence showing launching operation of AVRO seaplane. Motor is started, plane on trolley is pushed to slipway and allowed to slide free into the water. Good MS of AVRO LYNX motor starting and of plane taxiing away in front of camera. MLS of same plane taking off in heavy seas. Aerials along coastline showing Vancouver Air Force base and part of the City of Vancouver. MLS's of pilot getting a piggy-back ride on mechanic's shoulders from land to seaplane moored a few feet offshore. Two AVRO LYNX seaplanes taxiing in, in rough water. Men beaching AVRO LYNX seaplane with tractor, using same slipway as used for launching. Rough blurry aerials of mountains near Hazelton, B.C. Uninspiring shots of sub-Base at Fraser Lake with RCAF aircraft being towed by men in rowboats."

727. RCAF STAFF AT STATION ARE INSPECTED/ROYAL CANADIAN AIR
     FORCE TRAINING, VANCOUVER, B.C. (1938)
    p.c. Fox Movietonews (Fox #35-9)
    1. 800'   g. 35mm   t. b+w   s. sound
    d.   *
    ph. ASN
    c.s. NFA & Fox Movietonews, N.Y.

"Brigadier J.C. Stewart, DSO, arrives to inspect No. 3 Coast Artillery Co-op Squadron, RCAF. Pan beautiful old airplanes lined up. RCAF mechanics at work on Moths. Pilots polishing planes. Last minute inspection. Shots during inspection. Men winding propellor, motor started, plane warming up. Officers and men forming for parade. March past. Two-seater biplanes taking off. Three biplanes taxiing, taking off, airborne in formation."

728. RCAF TRAINS FOR WAR, VANCOUVER, 1938.
    p.c. *
    1.   g. 35mm   t. b+w   s. sound
    d.   *
    ph. *
    c.s. NFB (1930-DN-321)

"Soldiers parade towards and past camera on airfield. Shots of training planes - Avro 626, Moths, a Siskin, etc. A high-ranking Army officer inspects the troops. Two shots of Avro 626 taking off, and airborne."

729. RCMP, AMONG THEIR OTHER DUTIES, GUARD SEAGULL SANCTUARY
     ON MITLENATCH ISLAND, B.C. (1924)
    p.c. Fox Movietonews (Fox #412.911-A4145,4146 & 4147)
    1. 124'   g. 35mm   t. b+w   s. si.
    d.   *
    ph. Len H. Roos, Mayell
    c.s. Fox Movietonews, N.Y.

"Long shots of Island from highest point of Island. LS of constable on daily rounds coming over rocks. Shot from Island looking to sea, seagulls flying about. The constable makes a daily round of the Island to inspect the nests and eggs. CU of constable at breakfast feeding his pet crows. CU of crows being fed. PLUS add cuts of same."

730. RCN TRAINING AT ESQUIMALT. (1939)
    p.c. ASN
    1.   g. 35mm   t. b+w   s.
    d.   *
    ph. ASN
    c.s. NFB (1940-WW II-144-DN)

"Various shipboard shots of bow of camera ship slicing water, of officers on bridge below camera position, of other ships accompanying camera ship, etc. Sequence on sailors carrying out various tasks under the watchful eyes of instructors: firing deck guns, firing dummy torpedoes, dropping depth charges, launching life boats, retrieving dummy torpedoes, etc. Sequence on shore based training: sailors drilling, practising various routines. Shipboard shot of bridge, Aldis lamp glowing during transmission of message. Esquimalt base, men practising loading a deck gun in a hangar, studying the innards of a torpedo as an instructor stands by. Two final shots of a destroyer moving slowly past the camera in the harbour."

731. REAL CHILD OF NATURE IS EDITH MUNDAY WHO CLIMBS MOUNTAINS
AND MAKES FRIENDS OF BIRDS, VANCOUVER, B.C. (1926)
p.c. Fox Movietonews (Fox 728-B5888)
l. 50'   g. 35mm   t. b+w   s. si.
d.   *
ph. Herron
c.s. Fox Movietonews, N.Y.

"Edith Munday climbs Grouse Mountain near Vancouver and feeds birds."

732. RECENT GALES ON THE PACIFIC COAST HAVE TAKEN THEIR TOLL OF CANADIAN
SHIPPING, VICTORIA, B.C. (1919)
p.c. British-Canadian Pathé News
l.   g. 35mm   t. b+w, tinted s. si.
d.   *
ph. *
c.s. NFA (Taylor reel 100A)

Louis E. Ouimet issued the British-Canadian Pathé News twice weekly from Montreal with a selection of stories on each reel. They were released through Specialty Import Ltd. This story was the 7th of 8 on Release #17A. The description is: "S.S. BESSIE DOLLAR struggles into Victoria after bout with high gales and rough seas. The ship was badly battered by the force of the gale." See No. 9.

733. RECONSTRUCTION OF YOKOHAMA CALLS FOR LARGEST SHIPMENT
OF LUMBER FROM A B.C. PORT, VANCOUVER, B.C. (1924)
p.c. Fox Movietonews (Fox #431.1-B4038)
l. 55'   g. 35mm   t. b+w   s. si.
d.   *
ph. Len H. Roos
c.s. Fox Movietonews, N.Y.

"Several shots of loading SS VOREDA with lumber."

734. RECORD FLOOD WRECKS BRIDGE, VANCOUVER, B.C. (n.d.)
p.c. Fox Movietonews (Fox #090.1-A613)
l.   g. 35mm   t. b+w   s. si.
d.   *
ph. *
c.s. Fox Movietonews, N.Y.

735. RECRUITING, VANCOUVER, B.C. (1935)
p.c. Fox Movietonews (Fox #38-639)
l. 650'   g. 35mm   t. b+w   s. sound
d.   *
ph. ASN
c.s. Fox Movietonews, N.Y.

"Officers talking over drill plans. Platoon drilling. Handling gun instructions. Gun exercise and march. Col. Leslie. Drilling recruits. Type of recruits. Joining up. Details of each. Medical examinations. Interior same. Getting outfits. Drummer going through practice. Cleaning equipment. Marching. This is the Seaforth Highlanders Regiment."

736. REDISCOVER THE P.G.E. (1939)
     p.c. private
     l. 100'   g. 16mm   t. colour   s. si.
     d.   *
     ph. H. Turner
     c.s. via Pacific Cinémathèque

                    *Views from a boat on its way up Howe Sound. Locomotive #53 at station in
                    Squamish. Cheakamus River. Train going downhill to Garibaldi Station. A
                    horse-drawn cart comes to pick up passengers who disembark from train, taking
                    them back to Lamb's Ranch at Garibaldi. Shadow Lake at Garibaldi, lovely
                    scenics. LS Brandywine Falls. At the foot of Brandywine Falls. Train arri-
                    ving at Garibaldi Station. Views from boat sailing down Howe Sound. Aboard
                    PRINCESS MARGUERITE to Victoria, sunset from shipboard.*

737. REGIONS OF CANADA. (1930's)
     p.c. probably CGMPB
     l. approx. 400' g. 35mm & 16mm t. b+w   s. si.
     d.   *
     ph. *
     c.s. Unknown

                    *Little else is known of this film. Presumably it shows all regions of Canada,
                    including British Columbia.*

738. RIGHT HONOURABLE G.W. FORBES, PRIME MINISTER OF NEW ZEALAND,
     ON WAY TO ENGLAND FOR HIS MAJESTY'S JUBILEE CELEBRATION, TALKS,
     VANCOUVER, B.C. (1935)
     p.c. Hearst Metrotone News; Can no. 308, Roll no. 3
     l. 330'   g. 35mm   t. b+w   s. sound
     d.   *
     ph. ASN
     c.s. Hearst Metrotone News, N.Y.

                    Shots of Forbes talking.

739. RIVER FRASER IN FLOOD, NEAR VANCOUVER, B.C. (1937)
     p.c. British Paramount (Lib. #5947)
     l.   g. 35mm   t. b+w   s. sound
     d.   *
     ph. *
     c.s. Visnews, London

                    *Elevated view of flood water and scaffold. CU scaffold. View of spray hit-
                    ting bridge. Cat-walk on bridge. Spray hitting bridge. Long view of rush-
                    ing water.*

740. THE ROBSON TRAIL. (1920)
     p.c. Dept. of Trade and Commerce
          Exhibits and Publicity Bureau, Ottawa
     l. 1 reel   g. 35mm   t. b+w   s. si. w/captions
     d.   *
     ph. *
     c.s. NFA (28mm copy in 2 parts)

                    *"We commence our journey in this film at Winnipeg, Manitoba. Our first step
                    is Wainwright National Park and Wild Life Refuge. In Jasper Park we meet
                    the members of the Imperial Press Conference and show their activities at
                    this National Park. We continue our journey westward along the famous
                    Skeena River to Prince Rupert, B.C., with glimpses of outstanding scenic
                    features en route."*

741. ROCKING GOLD IN THE KLONDIKE. (1899-1900)
     p.c. Edison Mfg. Co.
     l. 31'   g. 35mm (16mm available) t. b+w s. si.
     d.   *
     ph. Robert Bonine
     c.s. NFA

                    *"Here we see one of the methods employed in the search for gold, where water
                    is scarce. We see the workmen using water over and over again in the rocker*

until it becomes too thick with earth for further use. The scene is one of action, as the valuable character of the ground enables many to work profitably in close quarters. An interesting and instructive subject." (original 35mm print was 65' long and copyrighted in May, 1901).

742. ROCKY MOUNTAIN GRANDEUR. (1937)
    p.c. MGM
    l. 731'   g. 35mm   t. colour s. sound
    d.   J.H. Smith
    ph. Winton G. Hoch
    c.s. *

    A Fitzpatrick Traveltalk with musical score by Nathaniel and Jack Shilkret. No further information is available. It is not known whether the Rocky Mountains referred to are in the U.S.A. or Canada and, if they are in Canada, whether any scenes of British Columbia appear.

743. ROCKY MOUNTAIN PANORAMA. (pre 1910)
    p.c. *
    l. 150'   g. 35mm   t. b+w   s. si.
    d. *
    ph. *
    c.s. Unknown

    Little is known of this film, mentioned in George Kleine's Catalogue, 1910, page 64.

744. THE ROCKY MOUNTAINS. (1921)
    p.c. Society for Visual Education
    l. 1 reel   g. 35mm   t. b+w   s. si. w/captions
    d.   *
    ph. *
    c.s. Unknown

    No specific location is given for the scenes photographed in the Rocky Mountains. The author was M.E. Goodenough.

745. THE ROCKY MOUNTAINS. (1921)
    p.c. Ford Motion Picture Laboratories
    l. 2 reels g. 35mm   t. b+w   s. si. w/captions
    d.   *
    ph. *
    c.s. USNA Ford Film Collection (?)

    Part of the Ford Educational Library, Regional Geography, Vol. 5, Parts 1&2. Contain various scenes of the Rockies, although it is not known whether in Canada or the U.S.

746. THE ROCKY MOUNTAINS. (1922)
    p.c. Ford Motion Picture Laboratories
    l. 1 reel   g. 35mm   t. b+w   s. si. w/captions
    d.   *
    ph. *
    c.s. USNA Ford Film Collection (?)

    Part of the Ford Educational Library, Regional Geography series. No further information is given. May be an amalgamation of Parts 1 and 2 of a film called THE ROCKY MOUNTAINS produced and released by Ford Educational Library in 1921. There is no indication whether it was photographed in Canada or the U.S.

747. ROCKY MOUNTAINS. (1938)
    p.c. ASN (#B-717)
    l.   g. 35mm   t.   s.
    d.   *
    ph. *
    c.s. *

    ROCKY MOUNTAINS was not completed or released.

748. ROCKY MOUNTAINS IN WINTER. (1912-1912)
    p.c. Thomas A. Edison, Inc.
    1.   g. 35mm   t. b+w   s. si.
    d.   *
    ph. *
    c.s. Unknown

> *This film was released on May 28, 1913, but nothing else is known about its content or location. Chances are fair that it was filmed in British Columbia.*

749. ROSE MARIE. (1936)
    p.c. MGM
    1. 110 min. g. 35mm   t. b+w   s. sound
    d. S.S. Van Dyke
    ph. William H. Daniels
    c.s. MGM

> *Script, Frances Goodrich and Albert Hackett from the musical of the same name by Rudolph Friml.*
>
> *l.p. Jeanette MacDonald, Nelson Eddy, James Stewart and David Niven.*
>
> *This most famous version of ROSE MARIE was one of three completed by MGM, each a little different from the musical stage play and each other. The first attempt starred Ralph Forbes and René Adorée but was scrapped redone entirely with Joan Crawford and James Murray, and released in 1928. The success of this silent version inspired a sound version eight years later, which has remained the favourite to this day. Another try was made in 1954 starring Howard Keel and Ann Blyth, but the memory of Jeanette MacDonald and Nelson Eddy was too powerful to permit a rival, and the later version was not well received.*
>
> *The story is simple. In the 1936 ROSE MARIE a Montreal opera star, Marie de Fleur, moves to the Canadian northwoods to help her brother who has escaped from a Quebec prison after killing a Mountie. To earn money she gets a job singing in a saloon and the local RCMP officer, Sergeant Bruce, falls in love with her. When he realizes who Marie is, he is torn between bringing-in her brother or helping him escape and winning Marie's love. He chooses to do his job and brings the escaped prisoner back to jail again. In the end he is forgiven by Marie. Of interest to this catalogue is the fact that many of the outdoor locations were photographed in British Columbia near Vancouver, on the North Shore around Capilano Canyon. These were taken back to Hollywood and used as transparencies for backgrounds. The film has recently been re-titled. It is now called INDIAN LOVE CALL.*

750. ROTARY ICE CARNIVAL, VANCOUVER, B.C.   (1938)
    p.c. Fox Movietonews (Fox #36-574)
    1. 1100'   g. 35mm   t. b+w   s. sound
    d.   *
    ph. ASN
    c.s. Fox Movietonews, N.Y.

> *"Elevation shot. Pageant of the Empire opening ceremony. Kinney from Seattle Skating Club. Huddy Stenuf of Vienna. Vancouver fancy skaters. Barbara Ann Oingg and Lloyd Baxter. Betty Lee and John Kinney. Seattle skating club. Lloyd Baxter. Heddy Stenuf. Ice shots."*

751. ROTARY ICE CARNIVAL, VANCOUVER, B.C.   (1939)
    p.c. Fox Movietonews (Fox #39-558)
    1. 700'   g. 35mm   t. b+w   s. sound
    d.   *
    ph. ASN
    c.s. Fox Movietonews, N.Y.

> *"Elevated shot of opening by Kitsilano Boy's Band. Dorothy and Hazel Caley of Granite Club. Erma Anderson in exhibitions. Vancouver Skating Club: "A Sailor's Dream". Seattle Club skating trio. Phyllis Thompson, 8 years old from California. Red McCarthy. Erma. V.S.C. Phyllis, Britta Lundequist. Eugene Turner. Erma. Caley Sisters."*

752. A ROTARY SNOWPLOW IN THE GREAT NORTHWEST. (1903)
   p.c. *
   l. 113'   g. 35mm   t. b+w   s. si.
   d.   *
   ph.   *
   c.s. Unknown

                    Probably photographed in 1902. No further information known. (See THE
                    CANADIAN ROCKIES IN WINTER)

753. ROWING CLUB TRIES PAINTING BEE WITH MORE OR LESS
     SUCCESS AS YOU WILL SEE, VANCOUVER, B.C. (1924)
   p.c. Fox Movietonews (Fox #000.54-A3621)
   l.   g. 35mm   t. b+w   s. si.
   d.   *
   ph. Len H. Roos
   c.s. Fox Movietonews, N.Y.

                    All the members of the Rowing Club try to paint, but there aren't enough
                    ladders. Includes shot of Colin Finlayson.

754. ROYAL CANADIAN MOUNTED POLICE, FORMERLY NORTHWEST
     MOUNTED POLICE, GO THROUGH CEREMONY OF KING'S BIRTH-
     DAY PARADE AT DAWSON, IN THE YUKON. (1931)
   p.c. Fox Movietonews (Fox #11-705)
   l. 1000'   g. 35mm   t. b+w   s. sound
   d.   *
   ph. Mayell & Darling
   c.s. Fox Movietonews, N.Y.

                    "Men lining up and coming to Present Arms. The Slope Arms. Various phases
                    of drill."

755. ROYAL NORTH WEST MOUNTED POLICE MUSICAL RIDE, VICTORIA,
     B.C. (1913)
   p.c. *
   l.   g. 35mm   t. b+w   s. si.
   d.   *
   ph.   *
   c.s. NFA (Taylor reel 130)

                    "The RNWMP Musical Ride visits Victoria and puts on a most dazzling display
                    of precision riding and horsemanship. Excellent shots of horses performing
                    actual dance with erect flagbearing Mounties in total command."

756. THE ROYAL TOUR OF CANADA. (1939)
   p.c. ASN (#739)
   l.   g. 35mm   t. b+w   s. sound
   d.   *
   ph. ASN
   c.s. Unknown

                    About the Royal Visit of King George VI and Queen Elizabeth to Canada in May,
                    1939. This film may never have been produced. ASN made a film to commem-
                    orate the Royal Visit in 1951 called THE ROYAL TOUR OF CANADA.

757. ROYAL TRAIN WITH DUKE AND DUCHESS OF YORK CLIMBING
     MOUNT HECTOR. (1901)
   p.c. Edison Mfg. Co.
   l. 80'   g. 35mm   t. b+w   s. si.
   d.   *
   ph.   *
   c.s. LOC Paper Print Collection

                    "It is a special train equippped by the Canadian Pacific Railroad for carry-
                    ing the Duke and Duchess of York and the Royal party from Montreal to Van-
                    couver. It is made up of ten coaches and five heavy mountain climbing
                    engines. The road which goes over Mt. Hector has the steepest grade in any
                    of North America. The engines suddenly come into view around a bend at a
                    distance of about one-half mile, sending up huge volumes of smoke from each
                    of the stacks. On the front of the first locomotive can be plainly seen the
                    lookout who travelled the entire distance from coast to coast keeping sharp

watch for obstructions which might be placed on the tracks by miscreants. This picture, besides being of great historical interest, gives the audience the most novel and stirring train scene." From a single camera position, a train, presumably carrying the Duke and Duchess, climbs a steep slope. Only two Pullman cars, hauled by three locomotives, are visible, and no people can be seen. The CPR tracks do not run up or around the side of Mt. Hector, but soon after reaching the summit at Stephen the train passes a station called Hector, eight miles west of Field. It would be reasonable to assume that the film was probably photographed in this area. (Original print was copyrighted in November 1901 and a 16mm print, 38' long, may be obtained.)

758. THE ROYAL VISIT.   (1939)
     p.c. CGMPB
     l. 7,700'   g. 35mm   t. b+w   s. sound
     d.   *
     ph. CGMPB
     c.s. NFA, BFI

Compiled and edited by Frank Badgley, J.B. Scott and R. Collyer, with music by Howard Fogg and commentary by Rupert Lucas. THE ROYAL VISIT was one of the largest undertakings by the CGMPB and filled ten reels. The sound recording was not good but the film was popular when released to theatres across Canada, even though it tended to be nothing more than a long compilation of typical news shorts, i.e., it caught the patriotic imagination of the Canadian public at the beginning of a dreadful war and had successful runs everywhere. The money that was made was donated to the Canadian Red Cross. A French version, LA VISITE DE NOS SOUVERAINS, was also produced.

British Columbia footage is all on REEL 9, and includes the following: shots of the Rocky Mountains. Their Majesties arrive at Vancouver. A Guard of Honour is provided by the Seaforth Highlanders, the King takes the salute, the Queen watches with the Mayor of Vancouver. The King inspects the Guard of Honour. Drive to Vancouver City Hall. As their Majesties enter the Hall a 2000-voice choir sings the National Anthem. The King and Queen step out onto the balcony and the crowds below cheer them. Street procession to West Vancouver. King and Queen cross bridge by automobile into Stanley Park. The PRINCESS MARGUERITE with the King and Queen aboard steams out of Vancouver Harbour. They arrive at Victoria where a Guard of Honour of the 5th British Columbia Coast Brigade is waiting at the Legislative Buildings. An address of welcome is read by the Premier (Patullo). A bouquet is presented to the Queen by his granddaughter. The King presents new colours to the Western Command of the RCN in Beacon Hill Park, Victoria. The steamship PRINCE ROBERT is boarded by the King and Queen, crowds wave goodbye. The steamship makes the journey across the Straits to Vancouver again. (REEL 9 is 909' long)

759. ROYAL VISIT, 1939, and BOUNDARY BAY, 1932.
     p.c. private
     l. approx. 150'   g. 16mm   t. b+w & colour   s. si.
     d.   *
     ph. I.J. Garrod
     c.s. via Pacific Cinémathèque

Colour: ROYAL VISIT, 1939. Hotel Vancouver draped with scarlet banners at the front door. View down Georgia Street, each lamp post decorated with scarlet banners. Unidentified city street decorated. Burrard Street Bridge decorated. City Hall decorated. Group atop a building waiting for King and Queen with little Union Jacks. Crowds at Kingsway and Knight Streets shot from top of building. Royal car passes, enthusiastic crowds line street, Sweet Caporal billboard in b.g. Crowds, CU car passing. Three planes in flight for occasion. Good LS CPR ferry PRINCESS MARGUERITE in Vancouver Harbour with lights at twilight and Lion's Gate Bridge in b.g. Three planes perform flypast with LS ferry moving out under bridge. CN locomotive near Patullo Bridge waiting for King and Queen to arrive to begin their homeward journey, large crowds and flags. Royal car arrives, King and Queen get out and bid farewell. They move toward train. Train pulls away as King and Queen wave from rear platform, sternwheeler in b.g. Train passing by on other side of river. Cabin cruiser and paddles of sternwheeler. (57')

b+w: BOUNDARY BAY, 1932. Shows summer cottages and cabins at Boundary Bay with various holidayers in residence. There are lots of trees, family scenes, and shots of the cabins. (44')

Colour: DOUBLE EXPOSURE consisting of the CPR Pier D fire in Vancouver in 1938, showing fire and charred ruins later (blended with) the July 1st parade through Vancouver streets by the Seaforth Highlanders in the same year. (50')

760. ROYAL VISIT - 1939 - IN VANCOUVER.
    p.c. private
    1. 33½'   g. 16mm   t. colour s. si.
    d.   *
    ph. R.F. Mackenzie
    c.s. NFA

King George VI and Queen Elizabeth in an open car. King and Queen behind a flag-bedecked wooden wall in Empire Stadium, masses of people on the field in sports gear. Crowds along the street as King and Queen pass in open car. CU Royal car. Two following cars, crowds along the route. Interior of sta- dium, a huge parade of boys and girls marches onto the field. White-clad athletes perform choreographed exercises. Bicycle teams perform precision riding. Guards in scarlet uniforms. Group of Army officers. Guards in scarlet march past. Scene down a decorated Vancouver street. Roses on the side of a house and a lady in a broadbrimmed hat. A view over Vancouver rooftops out over English Bay (?). A float plane flies overhead. Scene over roofs again.

761. ROYAL VISIT RAW FOOTAGE. (1939)
    p.c. British Columbia Government Travel Bureau
    1.   g. 16mm   t. colour s. si.
    d.   *
    ph. C.R.D. Ferris, R.L. Colby, & Cy Whiteman
    c.s. B.C. Dept. of Travel Industry

The B.C. Government Travel Bureau filmed the Royal Visit of King George VI and Queen Elizabeth to Victoria in May, 1939, but the footage was never edited or made into a finished production. It remains in the vaults to this day.

762. ROYAL VISIT SCENES - I. (1939)
    p.c. B.C. Forestry Service (Forestry reel 42)
    1. approx. 150' g. 16mm   t. colour s. si.
    d.   *
    ph. *
    c.s. PABC

There exist five reels of different lengths containing miscellaneous and often duplicated shots of the Royal Visit of King George VI and Queen Eliza- beth to Vancouver and Victoria in May of 1939, photographed by the B.C. Forest Service. This reel contains: King and Queen passing in open car. Fleet of small sports cars driving by. A huge paper crown. Billboard of the King and Queen reading WELCOME. Garden at the Empress Hotel, Victoria. Tumultuous parade down Government Street, Victoria. Masts of CPR ferry PRINCESS MARGUERITE flying pennants, entering harbour, Victoria. Soldiers marching up to Parliament Buildings, Victoria. King arrives and inspects troops. King begins to ascend red carpet onto steps of Parliament Buildings. Beacon Hill Park, decorated evergreen archways, crowds in stands, Naval band marching onto the field, little girls in dresses performing dance. Good CU of Queen and King arriving at Beacon Hill Park. Naval band marching past. King and Queen arrive at reviewing stand.

763. ROYAL VISIT SCENES - II. (1939)
    p.c. B.C. Forest Service (Forestry reel 51)
    1. approx. 200' g. 16mm   t. colour s. si.
    d.   *
    ph. *
    c.s. PABC

The second of five reels of Royal Visit shot by the B.C. Forest Service. Scenes include: A shed with Union Jacks strung along clothesline. Parliament Buildings decorated. Decorated hedges and fence. Welcome sign on the old Victoria Post Office. Belmont Building decorated, Victoria. Streetcars, bicycles, cars, all stores decorated - excellent shots of busy Victoria

*streets just prior to arrival of King and Queen. Ships decorated in Inner
Harbour, Victoria. LS Government House. MS Union Jack rippling in the wind.
Royal motorcade descends Government Street then passes by Empress Hotel.
Decorated ships in Victoria's Inner Harbour. LS Belmont Building and Gov-
ernment Street, Victoria, with crowds, from the Parliament Buildings. Pan
up Parliament Buildings from front steps. Crowds and cedar arches in Beacon
Hill Park. Naval band. Children dancing in Beacon Hill Park. King and
Queen arriving at Beacon Hill Park, driving through cedar arches. Rolling
up the red carpet on the reviewing stand, after the King and Queen have left,
Beacon Hill Park, Victoria.*

764. ROYAL VISIT SCENES - III. (1939)
    p.c. B.C. Forest Service (Forestry reel 55)
    l. approx. 300' g. 16mm t. colour s. si.
    d. *
    ph. *
    c.s. PABC

*Third reel of outs and duplications from the B.C. Forest Service's documen-
tation of the Royal Visit of King George VI and Queen Elizabeth to Vancouver
and Victoria in May 1939. Scenes include: The ceremonies at Parliament
Buildings, Victoria. Soldiers marching on Belleville Street, Victoria. King
and Queen leaving Parliament Buildings, getting into limousine. Highlanders
marching past Empress Hotel. King and Queen arriving at Empress Hotel,
Victoria. King and Queen leaving Beacon Hill Park, Victoria. Fireworks.
Duplication of King and Queen leaving the Parliament Buildings and arriving
at the Empress Hotel. B.C. Provincial Police lined up for inspection. Welcome sign on old Post Office, Victoria. Decorations in the streets of Victoria. Parliament Buildings, decorated. Fireworks.*

765. ROYAL VISIT SCENES - IV. (1939)
    p.c. B.C. Forest Service (Forestry reel 58)
    l. approx. 150' g. 16mm t. colour s. si.
    d. *
    ph. *
    c.s. PABC

*Fourth reel of duplications and out-footage from the B.C. Forest Service's
documentation of the Royal Visit of 1939. Scenes include: Huge parade of
veterans with crowds near Patullo Bridge in New Westminster, a building across
the street called PACIFIC MOTORS. PRINCE ROBERT leaving Victoria. WILL YE
NO COME BACK AGAIN captioned across the sky. People on the breakwater,
Victoria, watching the ship carry the Royal Couple back to Vancouver. Planes
fly over Lion's Gate Bridge, Vancouver. Children dance around the Maypole
to honour the King and Queen. Crowds of people. Parade of veterans. King
and Queen, preceded and followed by many cars, drive around a curve in the
road. A ceremonial WELCOME arch in Saanich. A sign reading SAANICH SCHOOL
CHILDREN, kids waving flags. King and Queen drive over a wooden bridge under
Saanich arch, throngs of people cheering and waving flags. Lunch at a picnic
table for a family. Street in Esquimalt (?) with cars and buildings decorated. Highland band marches past.*

766. ROYAL VISIT SCENES - V. (1939)
    p.c. B.C. Forest Service (Forestry reel 71)
    l. approx. 200' g. 16mm t. colour s. si.
    d. *
    ph. *
    c.s. PABC

*Fifth of five reels of B.C. Forest Service out-footage and duplicates from
their filming of the Royal Visit of King George VI and Queen Elizabeth to
Vancouver and Victoria in May 1939. Scenes include: Motorcade to the front
steps of the Parliament Buildings, Victoria. Bunting on Victoria City Hall.
Bunting and flags in Oak Bay. Black cars in clogged street, bunting on
buildings, one says C.C BROWN MOTORS - Esquimalt? Pipe band marches down
crowded street. In Vancouver, a series of welcoming banners stretched
across the streets from THE SONS AND DAUGHTERS OF ENGLAND, ISRAEL'S THRONE,
SONS OF NORWAY, MUNICIPALITY OF MAPLE RIDGE and PORT COQUITLAM. At Beacon
Hill Park in Victoria, the King and Queen leave the reviewing stand with Premier Patullo and other VIP's. The King inspects the Guard of Honour. Sailors
march past. Vets march through crowds. Men roll up the red carpet after
the King and Queen have departed. New scenes, possibly at Oakalla: B.C.*

*Provincial Police grooming and saddling their horses. BCPP insignia on
saddle blanket. BCPP sign on building. Parade of B.C. Provincial policemen,
mounted, leaving their stables and riding past. Large squad of B.C. Provincial policemen ride toward camera. (Oakalla was the mainland HQ for the
mounted troop of the BCPP.)*

767. ROYAL VISIT TO B.C. (1939)
     p.c. B.C. Forest Service
     1. 1200'   g. 16mm   t. colour s. si. w/captions
     d.   *
     ph. *
     c.s. Unknown

          *"A complete pictorial record of the visit of Their Majesties King George VI
          and Queen Elizabeth to the cities of Victoria, Vancouver and New Westminster
          in 1939, showing the preparations, decorations, and parades which were held
          in their honour in these three cities." Unfortunately this complete version
          of the B.C. Forest Service film of the Royal visit has been lost, but several
          reels remain that contain much of the same footage. See ROYAL VISIT SCENES -
          REELS I - V, SCENES OF THE ROYAL VISIT, and ROYAL VISIT TO VICTORIA.*

768. ROYAL VISIT TO VICTORIA. (1939)
     p.c. B.C. Provincial Fisheries Department
     1. approx. 400'   g. 16mm   t. colour s. si. w/captions
     d.   *
     ph. *
     c.s. PABC Agriculture Collection

          *Hand spliced. Exterior of Government House and gardens with Royal Standard
          flying. Interior of Royal Suite where King and Queen will stay at Government
          House. King and Queen arrive at Parliament Buildings, King George inspects
          guard. Premier presents the address. King and Queen leave, move up Govern-
          ment Street by open car to Empress Hotel. King and Queen arrive at Empress
          Hotel for "luncheon". King present colours to RCN Honour Guard in Beacon
          Hill Park. Sailors march past, King George takes salute. May 31, shots of
          the PRINCE ROBERT. On the wharf, hundreds of veterans. King inspects Honour
          Guard. King and Queen board the PRINCE ROBERT, crowds wave and cheer, King
          and Queen wave from bridge. The PRINCE ROBERT sails to Vancouver. The
          PRINCE ROBERT seen silhouetted in the Straits of Juan de Fuca. Two girls
          wave as the ship sails by, accompanied by two destroyers. A written farewell.
          Pen sketch of the two young Princesses on a Union Jack b.g.*

769. ROYAL VISIT TO VICTORIA, 1939.
     p.c. Fox Movietonews (Fox #37-755)
     1.   g. 35mm   t. b+w   s. sound
     d.   *
     ph. ASN
     c.s. Fox Movietonews, N.Y.

          "Various crowd shots, royalty (King George VI & Queen Elizabeth) In Victoria."

771. ROYAL VISIT, VANCOUVER, B.C. 1939.
     p.c. Fox Movietonews (Fox #35-753)
     1.   g. 35mm   t. b+w   s. sound
     d.   *
     ph. ASN
     c.s. Fox Movietonews, N.Y.

          *"Various shots of crowd & royalty in Vancouver during Royal Visit of King
          George VI and Queen Elizabeth to North America in 1939."*

772. RT. HON W.F. MASSEY, PREMIER OF NEW ZEALAND, POSES FOR
     FOX NEWS BEFORE LEAVING, VANCOUVER, B.C. (1924)
     p.c. Fox Movietonews (Fox #201-B3966)
     1. 25'   g. 35mm   t. b+w   s. si.
     d.   *
     ph. Len H. Roos
     c.s. Fox Movietonews, N.Y.

          *"Also in group: Fyfe Smith, J.R.V. Dunlop, Miss Bell-Irving, Blake Wilson
          and F.D. Thomson."*

773. RUGBY GAME FOR TROPHY CUP, VANCOUVER, B.C. (1938)
    p.c. Fox Movietonews (Fox #33-401)
    1. 825'   g. 35mm   t. b+w   s. sound
    d.   *
    ph. ASN
    c.s. Fox Movietonews, N.Y.

            "University of California & University of British Columbia play for World
            Rugby Trophy. British Columbia wins by a score of 8 - 5. R.E. McKechnie
            starts game with a kick. Reggie Woodward & Geo. Hodge are old timers who
            never miss a goal. Spectators yelling."

774. RUNNING SLOWLY IN DENSE FOG, EMPRESS OF CANADA IS DRIVEN
    ASHORE AT ALBERT HEAD AND BADLY DAMAGED, NEAR VICTORIA,
    B.C. (1929)
    p.c. Fox Movietonews (Fox 090.1-D2548)
    1. 150'   g. 35mm   t. b+w   s. si.
    d.   *
    ph. Ross Beesley
    c.s. Fox Movietonews, N.Y.

            "Various shots of the ship, crowds watching. Great liner in drydock for ex-
            tensive repairs. EMPRESS OF FRANCE takes sister ship's run to East - con-
            fetti dangling from the ship thrown by people on dock. CU people throwing
            confetti. Shots of liner pulling out of dock."

775. SADDLE JOURNEY TO THE CLOUDS. (1928-1930)
    p.c. Eastman Teaching Films (?)
    1. 284'   g. 16mm   t. b+w   s. si.
    d.   *
    ph. *
    c.s. Unknown

            No location given for this film, but likely shot near Mt. Robson in British
            Columbia. The BFI Educational Catalogue description reads: "This film
            shows a climb with ponies up a mountain side. After the ponies have been
            loaded with their packs, they are seen fording a stream, proceeding along a
            mountain path among the rocks, and passing by basaltic columns. A sportsman
            fishes with rod in a mountain stream; sheep graze among the trees. We see
            a tarn among the hills and the first sign of snow. After camping among the
            trees, the climb begins again past a waterfall and up over a bare, rocky
            plateau. Amongst the snow, ponies have to struggle to keep their footing.
            We see views of mountains, rocks, and pine trees, and a stream crossing over
            slanting beds of rocks. After some views of Minaret Lake, the party is seen
            to arrive at the summit from which a view of the surrounding country is shown."
            U.S. production.

776. SAGA OF THE SILVER HORDE. (1935)
    p.c. CGMPB
    1. 1 reel   g. 35mm & 16mm   t. b+w   s. sound
    d.   *
    ph. *
    c.s. BFI, NFA, NFB Archives B.B. 91 (1930-L&DN-9) & BCPM Eth.

            Narration written by David Gwydyr and spoken by Rupert Caplan. No indication
            of location, but some of the film was probably shot in or near the Fraser
            River and the rest near the Skeena River and Prince Rupert. The film begins
            with shots of snow-capped mountains and an inlet with trees down to the water.
            Small fish boats sailing off the coast. A large boat tows a chain of little
            gill-netters out of the river to the fishing grounds. They are released and
            row out from the boat into position for casting their nets. The gill-nets
            are let out across the current. A large salmon is brought in. CU fisherman
            and salmon. Moonlit or dawn scene with boats all offshore, drifting with
            nets in water. Double-ended trollers let out their hooked lines and haul in
            salmon. CU aboard trolling boat, 2 fishermen, one steering, the other bring-
            ing in a fish, holding it up, and grinning. Evening scene of troller sailing
            away with lines out. Indian drag-seiners in a bay, waiting. A man points,
            and they take off across the water, six oarsmen rowing in a very beamy boat.
            A man tosses the seine net over the stern and the oarsmen row very hard,
            turning the boat in a circle and closing the net, the man in the bow steering.
            The Indians finally close the circle and jump ashore, pulling the catch into

shallow water and showing the salmon splashing about near the beach. Large purse seiners close to a rocky bluff ready their nets. One of them heads toward the camera; a man in a small boat astern holds the net while it is played out over the stern of the seiner. A circle is made, net played out, LS seiner, CU fishermen slapping and splashing the water to keep the salmon from swimming out of the purse. CU winch pulling in net, men gathering and folding it neatly on the deck as it comes in. The salmon break the surface and a brailer is lowered, picks up the fish, and lifts them up to be dumped into the hold. The purse seiner is named the CAPE CALVERT. LS & CU salmon traps, salmon in the traps, winches raising the nets, men pulling nets in on a small barge inside the trap. Salmon splash about near the surface and a tender comes alongside, dipping a basket into the fish and brailing them into its hold. CU salmon in hold. A different method of brailing is shown; a large net called a spiller dumps fish into barge holds. After loading, salmon are separated, counted by men with pike poles. Man holds up 40-pound Tyee salmon. Holds are covered. Tender HARRIET E. sails to the cannery in the rain and mist. (NOTE: The scenes of the Indians purse-seining near the beach in their large rowboat and the fish trap sequences at the end appear to be from the Dept. of Trade and Commerce Exhibits and Publicity Bureau film HOW SALMON ARE CAUGHT, produced in 1922.)

777. SALMON CANNING, B.C. COAST. (late 1930's)
    p.c. *
    1. 975' & 700'   g. 35mm   t. b+w   s. si.
    d.   *
    ph. *
    c.s. NFB (1930-N-160-1) 700'
              (1930-N-160-2) 975'

> *Freighter unloading. Cannery shots, salmon being loaded onto a conveyor. Cases of salmon being loaded into ship's hold. Canning plant. Cases with destinations stamped on them. Trawler fleet, various shots. Hauling in fish and nets. Loading freighter. Cannery shots. (This may be Prince Rupert). May be out-footage, or two identical damaged reels.*

778. SALMON FISHING. (1936)
    p.c. ASN (#B-678)
    1.   g. 35mm   t. b+w   s. sound
    d.   Gordon Sparling
    ph. *
    c.s. *

> *The production was cancelled and the film never made.*

779. SALMON FISHING IN CANADA. (1910)
    p.c. Solax
    1.   g. 35mm   t. b+w   s. si.
    d.   *
    ph. *
    c.s. Unknown

> *"A film shot in Canada with lots of scenery, salmon fishing industry, shooting the rapids in a canoe, & salmon leaping the cascade." It's not known whether this film was shot in British Columbia or not, but there is a good chance it was. It was released on Dec. 10, 1910. (Description from Motion Picture World, Jan. 21, 1911)*

770. ROYAL VISIT TO WESTERN CANADA, VANCOUVER AND VICTORIA, B.C., OF KING GEORGE VI AND QUEEN ELIZABETH. (1939)
    p.c. British Movietonews (No. 36848)
    1. 246'   g. 35mm   t. b+w   s. sound
    d.   *
    ph. *
    c.s. British Movietonews

> *CNR Station, Vancouver. Italian veteran's sign. Japanese Canadian sign. King and Queen being driven along streets in open car. Japanese children in kimonos waving Union Jacks. Man carrying mace down steps of City Hall with veterans in berets standing by. King and Queen follow with Mayor of Vancouver, etc. They visit and pose by statue of George Vancouver. Excellent LS of PRINCESS MARGUERITE sailing through Vancouver Harbour, flanking shots of Canadian destroyers, one is good of H-83, HMCS ST. LAURENT. King and*

Queen on bridge looking at destroyers, King in naval uniform. Moody evening shot of destroyer off coast of Vancouver Island.

Next day in Victoria, King and Queen drive down Government Street in open car through huge crowds, past Empress Hotel. They walk up steps into Empress Hotel. The King escorts Mrs. Patullo, the Premier's wife, and the Premier escorts the Queen into lunch. Long tables are set in Empress Hotel dining room. King George VI reads a speech, and as he continues to read, flashback scenes of earlier shots of the cross-Canada tour play on the screen, winding up with the King and Queen entering the flag-bedecked Empress to make the speech. Later, the King inspects soldiers at the bottom of the Parliament Building steps. The King presents his colours to the RCN on the lawn at Beacon Hill Park. King takes salute for marchpast, CU King saluting, although no sailors are seen marching. Commentator: Leslie Mitchell.

780. SALMON FISHING IN CANADA. (pre 1927)
    p.c. Pathéscope
    l. 1 reel   g. 28mm t. b+w   s. si.
    d.   *
    ph. *
    c.s. Unknown

       "Salmon fishing, one of the chief industries of the Pacific Coast, is here shown from the time the fleet of small boats leaves the harbour until they return laden with the finny harvest. The process of cleaning and packing follows." (Province of Ontario Film Catalogue, 1927)

781. SALMON FISHING ON THE FRASER RIVER, BRITISH COLUMBIA.
    (pre 1910)
    p.c. *
    l. 420'   g. 35mm t. b+w   s. si.
    d.   *
    ph. *
    c.s. Unknown

       "Original, novel and instructive scenes, not only of the fishing fleet, the methods of capture and hoisting of salmon into the scows, where thousands of fishes lash the water into foam, but also of the subsequent methods of dealing with the delicacy in the canning factories. Every detail is shown - cleaning, cooking, packing - fully illustrated. A gigantic undertaking, efficiently worked and controlled. A picture for every class and every country." George Kleine Catalogue, 1910, p.260.

782. SALMON FISHING ON THE SKEENA. (1918)
    p.c. Dept. of Trade and Commerce
        Exhibits and Publicity Bureau (EPB), Ottawa
    l. 1 reel   g. 35mm t. b+w   s. si.
    d.   *
    ph. *
    c.s. outs at NFB

       This film, the first shot on the Skeena by the EPB, was released on May 18, 1919, and described as: "An educational and industrial film showing in detail different methods used in catching salmon, and disclosing the vastness of this industry in the vicinity of Prince Rupert, B.C. Beautiful views of the Pacific are here disclosed. Each party obtains a full catch and then the journey is made back to the canneries where fish are sold by count." Presumably gill-netting, trolling and purse-seining are shown and described. The NFB outs contain: MS fisherman preparing long lines. Fishing boat. Indian fisherman on boat paying out long line. Two men trolling, one man pulling in salmon. Several gill-netting boats coming in. Cut to HA of Indian fisherman unloading his boat one fish at a time. Fishermen setting purses from a dory, closing purse & pulling in net until batch of fish are brought to surface. Shots of men brailing salmon from purse seine into hold of fishing boat. HA's of operation, of hold alive with wiggling fish. Shots of man guiding full brail from seine to hold, of man cleaning loose fish from deck afterwards.
       NOTE: This title, SALMON FISHING ON THE SKEENA, was later applied to a similar film produced by the EPB (later the CGMPB) in 1922. The later film was originally called ON THE SKEENA, and, occasionally, ON THE SKEENA RIVER, but seems to have taken the title SALMON FISHING ON THE SKEENA by the 1930's.

783. SANCTUARY. (1930)
    p.c. CGMPB
    l. approx. 750'   g. 35mm   t. tinted & b+w   s. si. w/captions
    d.   Bill Oliver
    ph. Bill Oliver
    c.s. NFA (350' 16mm), NFB (358' 16mm), BCPM (35mm)

        "Various species of the wild life of Canada, including several varieties of game birds."

        The film at the BCPM has no title and there is probably no way of finding out whether portions of the film were shot in B.C. Therefore, we must assume that since Oliver spent much of his time shooting in British Columbia, and since some of the animals make their homes here, it is likely that some of the province is depicted. Animals shown are the white-tailed deer; swans; "Wa-Wa", the wild goose and mate nesting; "Quoskh" or the "Night's Question", probably a loon; beavers; "Kakh", the quill-pig or porcupine; a black bear; elk; bighorn sheep; mountain goats and moose. (Produced for the National Parks Bureau, Ottawa).

784. SASQUATCH INDIAN DAYS AT HARRISON HOT SPRINGS, B.C. (1939)
    p.c. Hearst Metrotone News; Can no. 986, Roll no. 3
    l. 950'   g. 35mm   t. b+w   s. sound
    d.   *
    ph. ASN
    c.s. Hearst Metrotone News, N.Y.

        Shots of Indians, Sasquatch ceremony, and canoe race.

785. SAVING THE SAGAS. (1927)
    p.c. ASN (An ASN Screenogram)
    l. 1 reel   g. 35mm   t. b+w   s. si. w/captions
    d.   Dr. J.S. Watson
    ph. Dr. J.S. Watson (?)
    c.s. NFA & National Museum of Man

        Produced by B.E. Norrish. This remarkable film records the culture, rites, and dances of the "Wolf" (?) Indians along the British Columbia coast, somewhat sentimentalized by the producer. Included are scenes of C. Marius Barbeau of the National Museum in Ottawa and Dr. Ernest MacMillan of the Toronto Conservatory of Music, recording the songs and speech of the Indians.

        Scenes include shots of the coast and boats. Three men in a canoe. Fishing troller. CU man in boat. Group of Indians listening to jazz on a short-wave radio. Men in a canoe going toward shore, totem poles in b.g. View of totem poles on shore. Deep in the bush we see a totem pole; CU's pole, men clearing brush. CU man sharpening knife. CU man carving; perhaps a mask. CU man adzing a pole. Chief in costume next to a totem pole. CU drum beating. Chief dances with rattle on site of his grave-to-be. Two women dance while a third drums. Woman dancing, man drumming. Mr. Barbeau and Dr. Mac-Millan sitting at a table writing down the songs, dances, and chants as given to them by the Indians. CU transcriptions of the songs as written down note by note by Dr. MacMillan. A portable recording phonograph records the songs of various singers and drummers. Two men play lahal. Members of a Christian congregation sing hymns directed by preacher. There follows a peculiar little story about a Chief who had three wives before being baptized, and his trouble in deciding which one he will keep now that he must become a monogamous Christian. He finally chooses a new young girl and discards all three former wives. For more Barbeau and MacMillan, see film called NASS RIVER INDIANS, Reel 2 of which appears to be almost identical to SAVING THE SAGAS.

786. SAWMILL FIRE, SAPPERTON, B.C. (1920's)
    p.c. Fox Movietonews
    l.   g. 35mm   t. b+w   s. si.
    d.   *
    ph. *
    c.s. NFB (Canadian News 1920-FG-204)

        Pan of ruins of sawmill after fire.

787. SCENES ALONG THE C.P.R.R. (1911)
     p.c. Edison Mfg. Co. (Catalogue # 6737)
     l. 70'   g. 35mm   t. b+w   s. si.
     d.   *
     ph. Henry Cronjager (?)
     c.s. Unknown

                    *There may be scenes in British Columbia in this film, because the most photo-
                    genic part of the CPR in those days seemed to be the Rockies, the British
                    Columbia side of the Rockies in particular. Henry Cronjager was the camera-
                    man for Edison during a summer trip through the Rockies in 1910 and it seems
                    reasonable that this film was put together with extra takes.*

788. SCENES AROUND THE PARLIAMENT BUILDINGS OF BRITISH COLUMBIA.
     (1929)
     p.c. B.C. Dept. of Agriculture (reel 13)
     l. approx. 400'   g. 16mm   t. b+w   s. si. w/captions
     d.   *
     ph. *
     c.s. PABC

                    *Opening ceremony of the Seventeenth Parliament of British Columbia. Shot of
                    War Memorial and Empress Hotel from west wing. Highlanders march past, band,
                    soldiers in front of buildings. Dignitaries arriving. Lieutenant Governor
                    inspects Guard of Honour. Group of Cabinet Ministers in top hats. The
                    Premier, Dr. S.F. Tolmie. Minister of Agriculture, Hon. Wm. Atkinson. Child-
                    ren celebrate 24th of May at Parliament Buildings. Parliament Buildings
                    greenhouse. Head gardner checking plants in greenhouse. Plants in cold
                    frames. Bedding summer plants. Grooming beds. Sprinklers on lawns. Mowing
                    back lawns of Parliament Buildings. Correct way of packing tulips for market
                    demonstrated.*

789. SCENES AT SALVAGING KAIKYU MARU WRECK ON HELMCKEN ISLE
     IN THE NORTHERN PACIFIC, HELMCKEN ISLAND, B.C. (1926)
     p.c. Fox Movietonews (Fox #090.12-B5635)
     l. 30'   g. 35mm   t. b+w   s. si.
     d.   *
     ph. Jos. T. Mandy
     c.s. Fox Movietonews, N.Y.

                    "High shots of the salvagers at work on decks."

790. SCENES OF THE ROYAL VISIT. (1939)
     p.c. B.C. Dept. of Agriculture
     l.   g. 16mm   t. colour s. si.
     d.   *
     ph. B.C. Dept. of Fisheries & B.C. Forest Service
     c.s. PABC Agriculture Collection

                    *Arrival of PRINCESS MARGUERITE off Victoria, carrying King George VI and
                    Queen Elizabeth. Fireworks. Good shot of B.C. Provincial Police lined up
                    on their horses. Small boats milling about under Lion's Gate Bridge. Stern
                    of the PRINCE ROBERT at wharf. Soldiers in scarlets and busbies parade on
                    wharf. King and Queen arrive, inspect Guard and leave aboard the PRINCE
                    ROBERT. In the sky, words read: WILL YE NO COME BACK AGAIN? Three planes
                    fly in formation overhead. King and Queen drive through stone gates. Girls
                    perform Maypole dance. Kids with Union Jack wave and cheer. Vets look on.
                    Banner over arch: WELCOME TO MUNICIPALITY OF MAPLE RIDGE. Another banner:
                    COQUITLAM WELCOMES OUR KING AND QUEEN. More banners. Train entering Van-
                    couver. Parliament Buildings, Empress Hotel and Beacon Hill Park, Victoria,
                    PRINCE ROBERT and two destroyers sail under the Lion's Gate Bridge. This
                    reel does not tell a coherent story but is rather a collection of various
                    scenes around Vancouver and Victoria in no particular order.*

791. SCENES ON THE CANADIAN PACIFIC RAILROAD, BRITISH
     COLUMBIA. (pre 1910)
     p.c. *
     l. 500'   g. 35mm   t. b+w   s. si.
     d.   *
     ph. *
     c.s. Unknown

"The Vancouver Express leaving Montreal. Houses of Parliament, Ottawa, including some fine river scenery. Champlain's ship on the St. Lawrence River (?). Montmorency Falls and Rapids. Railway construction work at Roger's Pass amid towering mountain scenery. Views of the Fraser River and Rocky Mountains. Passenger boat on Lake Okanagan and a great number of other most interesting views, making of this subject an exceptionally good travelogue."
George Kleine Catalogue, 1910, p.255.

792. SCENES ON THE WAY FROM PENTICTON TO PRINCETON. (1930)
    p.c. B.C. Dept. of Agriculture (reel 44)
    l. 175'   g. 16mm   t. b+w   s. si. w/captions
    d.   *
    ph. *
    c.s. PABC

This footage was possibly shot while returning from a picnic at Summerland Experimental Farm in June 1930. Keremeos passes by the window. Concentrator at Hedly Gold Mine and cable. Young shepherd from Inverness, Scotland, and his dog. The dog rounds up sheep. Shorthorn herd of Mr. Taylor, Princeton. His irrigation ditch and flume. Gold hunters in dry creekbed - one holds up fake gold. Beaver dam. Scenes on William Thompson's sheep farm near Merritt, sheep being driven into pens for shearing. From L to R: Mr. Munro, Deputy Minister of Agriculture; Mr. Davie; Dr. Knight, Livestock Commissioner; Mr. Patterson and Mr. Challenger; Mr. Halmer, manager of Nicola Lake Ranching Co.; Mr. Brodie, a prospective settler from Australia. This is the last of three stories on this reel, the total footage being about 450' on 16mm.

793. SCHOOL CHILDREN UNDER CANVAS AT POINT GREY, B.C.
    (1929)
    p.c. Fox Movietonews (?)
    l.   g. 35mm   t. b+w   s. si.
    d.   *
    ph. ASN (?)
    c.s. NFB (1920-FG-215)

"Shots of tents, army type. Boys drilling with rifles under supervision of soldier, having chow." There is no indication of what group these boys belong to; presumably they are cadets.

794. SEA BIRDS. (approx. 1939)
    p.c. B.C. Government Travel Bureau
    l. 1x400' reel   g. 16mm   t. colour s. si.
    d.   *
    ph. *
    c.s. Unknown

"Cormorants and sea-gulls in the Pacific."

795. SEA LIONS OF THE PACIFIC. (1936)
    p.c. CGMPB
    l. 1 reel   g. 35mm   t. b+w   s. si. w/captions
    d. Bill Oliver
    ph. Bill Oliver
    c.s. NFA & NFB (1930-FG-3)

"An excellent natural history reel of these great mammals of the sea taken in the vicinity of the Scott Island Group, north of Vancouver Island." Produced for the National Parks Bureau.

"MLS of small coastal freighter sailing by precipitous cliff. LS coastal mountains, with part of camera ship in lower f.g. Forecastle of camera ship. Ship's officers on flying bridge pointing off camera and looking through a spyglass. Five men get into a rowboat with equipment and shove off. Men stepping ashore from heaving boat. Threatening sea lion races for the water and slides down into it. MS several of the beasts jumping off the rocks. Several shots of sea lions, individually and in groups, sitting on the rocks and jumping off into the water. Two young sea lions in a mock fight. Mother and pup having a mock battle. A dozen young pups with an adult sea lion keeping guard. Water splashing against rocks in the b.g. MCU of pup, and two men petting him. Several shots of sea lions bobbing in the water. Vertical shot down from rocks to sea lions in the water near rocks. Sea lions

clambering up onto the rocks. Ship's officer looking through a telescope,
setting sun behind shore in distance." (The print at the NFA is 350' on
16mm, and at the NFB, 362' on 16mm).

796. SEA ROVER'S SUMMER (working title SEA LIONS) (1949)
      p.c. ASN/ASS (#B-686)
      1. 1 reel   g. 35mm   t.   s. sound
      d.   Gordon Sparling
      ph. Bill Oliver
      c.s. United Artists

                CANADIAN CAMEO NO. 60. Sea-lions on the Queen Charlotte Islands, British
                Columbia. "Most people have heard of sea lions. A few have seen one in a
                zoo. But the rest of us probably aren't even sure what a sea lion looks
                like! The strange instinct that brings them back each summer to the very
                rooks where they were born provides a fascinating insight into the Private
                Life of the Sea Lion." SEA ROVER'S SUMMER was filmed by Bill Oliver in 1935
                while he was shooting a film for the CGMPB called SEA LIONS OF THE PACIFIC
                which was released in 1936. It is likely that a deal was made between Ben
                Norrish of ASN and the publicity branch of the Parks Bureau whereby ASN would
                take the best of the CGMPB material and re-edit it into a commercially viable
                short for theatrical release. Why this took fourteen years is not known.

797. THE SEASONS OF CANADA. (1930)
      p.c. CGMPB
      1. 1 reel   g. 35mm   t. b+w   s. si. w/captions
      d.   *
      ph. *
      c.s. NFA

                A film about the changing seasons throughout Canada, edited by D.F. Taylor
                of the CGMPB from footage shot for other films. Presumably contains scenes
                photographed in British Columbia. (NFA copy is 653' long on 35mm)

798. SECRET PATROL. (1936)
      p.c. Central Films, Ltd.
      1. 59 min. (5353') g. 35mm t. b+w   s. sound
      d.   David Selman, after Ford Beebe
      ph. George Meehan and William Beckway
      c.s. NFA

                Canadian prod., Kenneth J. Bishop;   *l.p. Charles Starrett, Finis Barton,*
                script, Robert Watson and J.P. Mc-   *Henry Mollison, J.P. McGowan, James*
                Gowan; editor, William Austin; and   *McGrath, LeStrange Millman, Arthur*
                Columbia overseer, Jack Fier.   *Kerr, and Reginald Hincks.*

                SECRET PATROL was the third Quota Quickie completed by Central Films in
                Victoria although it was the fourth to be started (see STAMPEDE). SECRET
                PATROL was made during Feb. and March 1936 and copyrighted in the United
                States by Columbia Pictures, Inc., on May 11, 1936. According to an excerpt
                from SCREEN FACTS, "Ford Beebe began directing on this film but was taken
                off by Columbia executives as incompetent and replaced by David Selman.
                Script was officially credited to J.P. McGowan (who didn't write it) from a
                (non-existent) original story by Peter B. Kyne." The credits at the begin-
                ning of the film state that SECRET PATROL is "A Peter B. Kyne Production".
                Kyne's part in SECRET PATROL remains a mystery, however, and his name is
                probably linked with Charles Starrett through an undisclosed contractual
                agreement.

                The film opens with the following written introduction, betraying the actual
                location of southern Vancouver Island: "In the far reaches of the northwoods -
                FORT CHAPELLE - an outpost of the Royal Canadian Mounted Police..." The
                story continues as follows:
                Two Mounties, Alan Craig and Gene Barkley, are in love with the same girl,
                Ann. Gene happens to be the son of the post Superintendant and Ann the
                Superintendent's ward. The film opens with Ann (Finis Barton) announcing to
                the Superintendent (Reginald Hincks) her intention of marrying Gene (Henry
                Mollison) and the Superintendent breaking the news to Alan (Charles Starrett).
                Gene is sent to investigate a series of highly suspicious accidents at the
                Arnold and McCord lumber camp. When an Indian brings Gene's horse into the
                post Alan is sent off to look for him. The accidents are being masterminded
                by the blacksmith Barstow, who wishes to ruin the lumber company. One of the

*partners, Arnold (James McGrath), is really a front, secretly backed by
Barstow (J.P. McGowan). Alan puts a handcuff on his wrist and pretends to
be on the run. Barstow removes the handcuff then 'blackmails' him into
'masquerading' as a Mountie so that McCord (LeStrange Williams) will not
send for the real Mounties. Alan then finds Gene hiding in a cabin in the
woods stripped of his uniform and his dignity and planning to run away to
the far north with Ann. (The uniform provided Alan by the villains was originally Gene's). Alan persuades him to change his mind and together they
bring the villains to justice, but in the final showdown Gene is killed.
This leaves the way clear for Alan to marry Ann - Gene having confided to
Alan that she really preferred him all along. (Storyline description courtesy of D. John Turner, NFA.)*

799. SECRETS OF CHINATOWN (THE BLACK ROBE) (1934)
    p.c. Commonwealth Productions, Ltd. Completed by Northern
        Films, Ltd.
    l. 53 min. (4714') g. 35mm   t. b+w   s. sound
    d. Fred Newmeyer
    ph. James Brethertin and William Beckway
    c.s. NFA (copy not complete - 10 min. missing)

*Producer, Kenneth J. Bishop; technical
director, Li-Young; editor, William
Austin; script, Guy Morton, from his
novel THE BLACK ROBE; sound, Wally
Hamilton.*

*l.p. Nick Stuart, Lucille Browne,
Raymond Lawrence, James Flavin,
Harry Hastings, James McGrath,
Reginald Hincks, John Barnard, and
Arthur Legge-Willis.*

*SECRETS OF CHINATOWN was begun in 1934 by Kenneth Bishop's Commonwealth Pro-
ductions Ltd. with the same leading players as THE CRIMSON PARADISE. It was
completed in the fall of 1933. Unfortunately, the financial problems which
were beginning to hamper THE CRIMSON PARADISE finally paralyzed SECRETS OF
CHINATOWN and before the film could be assembled for distribution Bishop
was forced to declare bankruptcy. The leading shareholder, Kathleen Dunsmuir agreed not to collect her investment, however. Bishop probably
convinced other supporters that if SECRETS was completed they would still
be able to turn a profit, or at least break even. A new company, Northern
Films, Ltd., was created, and managed to complete SECRETS, which premiered
at the Empire Theatre in Victoria on March 8, 1934.*

*Northern Films distributed both THE CRIMSON PARADISE and SECRETS OF CHINATOWN
for four more years until it ceased to exist as a company. SECRETS probably
fared better in the United States than THE CRIMSON PARADISE. It seems to
have been a slightly better picture. A reviewer the THE FILM DAILY wrote in
the Feb, 20, 1935, issue that it was "Not made for the thinking element that
may be found here and there in our picture theatres, but for the neighbor-
hood houses this one should have 'em yelling from the balcony." The cry was
not loud enough, however, and Northern disappeared when it defaulted on its
bond repayments and went into receivership, virtually penniless, with its
only assets, its films, scattered around the world.*

*SECRETS OF CHINATOWN, which was called THE BLACK ROBE in Victoria and Vancouver
so as not to offend members of the Chinese community, was not even able to
draw large crowds after it provoked a scandal. The original version was
seized by the British Columbia Provincial Police after the Chinese Consul in
Vancouver requested that the Provincial Censor, J.A. Smith, withdraw it from
circulation because of racist slurs. The Consul charged that the film portrayed Sun Yat-sen as the head of a large smuggling operation and Chinatowns
as the repositories of dark, sinister secrets. Although Harry Hastings, the
actor who played the head of the smuggling gang Chan Tow Ling, prefaced each
showing in Victoria with the reminder that the story was purely fictional,
the picture was not released again until one section showing a "Chinaman with
knife in back" was cut. Apparently no material which might be considered
offensive to the Chinese community was discovered or eliminated by the censor.
The Consul's reaction to this is not known. The film returned to the Columbia theatre in Victoira, but only ran for three days on a double bill before
it disappeared forever.*

*The original version contained sequences of "Victoria's patrol wagon screeching
across part of the Hillside-Burnside district, and part of the Victoria's
police force attacking the gang's hideout with regulation equipment of clubs
and helmets." Most of the film was shot in the Willows studio built by*

Bishop in the Exhibition Horse Barn. The gang's hideout was a huge papier-mâché cave. The sound is poor, and the storyline incapable of creating much dramatic tension. The negative was developed in the Commonwealth Productions lab on Cadboro Bay road in Victoria, however, which represents an attempt at real independence which should not go unnoticed.

Storyline: THE BLACK ROBE dealt with a murderous gang of opium smugglers operating in Victoria's Chinatown and the efforts of the local police to track them down. Two men disappear - Doverscourt (John Barnard) a detective investigating a murder in Chinatown, and Brandham (James Flavin), a ship's chandler involved in the drug trafficking who has offered to tell the police all he knows because things are going too far. Completely baffled by the disappearance, Police Commissioner Parkins (James McGrath) reluctantly turns for assistance to Donegal Dawn (Raymond Lawrence), a Sherlock Holmes style private detective. Meanwhile Robert Rande (Nick Stuart), a young friend of Dawn, has been threatened by the Chinese after he has shown an interest in Zenobia (Lucille Brown), a pretty blonde girl working in a Chinese curio shop, and has discussed the matter with Dawn. The Chinese villains, who invariably wear hoods and long robes, are operating from a temple and Rande now goes to this temple where Zenobia is taking part in a religious ceremony, believing herself to be 'the Eye of Lao-Tsee', and attempts to rescue her. Just as Rande is about to be knifed Dawn appears and shoots the hooded attacker. Rande soon returns for another try, only to be attacked by the missing Brandham who is acting under the influence of drugs. Dawn appears yet again and saves his life but rescues only Brandham, leaving Rande behind. Brandham quickly recovers from the effects of the drug but can remember nothing and so a visit to a yogi (Arthur Legge-Willis) is arranged - to unlock the 'subjective' half of the poor fellow's mind. Brandham reveals another hideout further up the coast of Vancouver Island. Dawn rapidly penetrates this new stronghold, hoping now to extricate both Rande and Zenobia, but this time he is captured. Fortunately Victoria's finest are not far behind and arrive in the nick of time. When the leader's hood is removed he is revealed to be Chan Tow Ling (Harry Hastings), the owner of the curio shop and a secret police operative to boot. Chan Tow Ling takes poison and Rande gets Zenobia.

For implausibility THE BLACK ROBE takes some beating. Donegal Dawn seems to enter the Chinese hideouts at will. The fact that all the Chinese wear hoods could have helped him slip in unnoticed had he chosen to dress similarly but for some inexplicable reason he runs around disguised as a Hindu. The mind-numbing, character-bending drug used by the Chinese (Dawn just happens to know both what it is, and the antidote) affects, or fails to affect, their victims according to the requirements of the so-called plot. (Storyline description courtesy of D. John Turner, NFA.)

800. SECTION OF HISTORICAL FILM, UBC. (1916-1917)
    p.c. Dept. of University Extension, UBC
    l.   g. 16mm   t. b+w   s. si.
    d.   *
    ph. *
    c.s. UBC Film No. 10, UBC Library, Special Collections Division

    Contains scenes of the 196th Battalion, 1916-1917. (Orig. 35mm)

801. SEED FARM ON VANCOUVER ISLAND (SEED GROWING - VANCOUVER
    ISLAND) (1928)
    p.c. B.C. Dept. of Agriculture
    l. approx. 500' g. 16mm   t. b+w   s. si. w/captions
    d.   *
    ph. *
    c.s. PABC

    Cleaning up, burning and ploughing land in readiness for planting. Levelling soil before sowing with one-horse drag. Sowing fine seed with hand sower. CU demonstration of sowing. Planting lettuce sets for seed. Sowing sweet peas. A month later - plants up. Flailing garden peas with a hand flail after they've been brought in by a horse-drawn wagon. Dwarf beans, lettuce and radish. Pan across flower-seed farm. Picking, screening and drying. Dahlia seeds. Picking sweet pea seed. Turning, fanning, screening and sacking seed. Rows of onions lying on the ground and being picked. Several pans across field and out over ocean. There is no indication of where this was photographed, but the Saanich Peninsula seems likely.

802. SEED GROWING IN BRITISH COLUMBIA - EXTRACT PART II
(early 1930's)
p.c. B.C. Dept. of Agriculture (Reel 67)
1. approx. 200'   g. 16mm   t. b+w   s. si. w/captions
d.   *
ph.   *
c.s. PABC

> This is perhaps a discard from the end of Seed film #67. It shows people
> working in a field. Rows of blooms. Workers pulling garden peas. Men in-
> specting seed crops. Pan across a row of beans. Men in storage shed. Pan
> across fields. Men walking in centre of clipped hedge. Tree. Pans across
> seed fields, buildings, people walking by.

803. SEED REGISTRATION. (late 1920's)
p.c. B.C. Dept. of Agriculture
1. approx. 400'   g. 16mm   t. b+w   s. si.
d.   *
ph.   *
c.s. PABC

> Seeds being culled, cleaned, planted and nurtured on Experimental Farm prob-
> ably near Sidney. Later, men in suits examine various types of grain being
> grown on the farm, all named with signs: WESTERN, GARNET, MANCHURIAN, VICTORY,
> etc. Pan across farm and fields.

804. SEEKING STEELHEADS. (1929)
p.c. CGMPB (#152)
1. approx. 750'   g. 35mm   t. b+w & tinted   s. si. w/captions
d.   *
ph.   *
c.s. NFB (275' 16mm), BCPM (two 35mm prints)

> SEEKING STEELHEADS was first made for the Department of Trade and Commerce,
> Ottawa, but later, after reorganization, it was retitled to indicate the re-
> sponsibility being that of National Parks of Canada.
>
> "Fishing for steelheads - among the gamiest of the trout family - in the
> rivers of Vancouver Island, British Columbia."
>
> Qualicum Beach Hotel on Vancouver Island. Shot through the rose arbour to
> the beach. View over lawns to sea, people on a bench. People leaving in
> cars from the door of the Hotel. The road to Alberni through Cathedral Grove,
> a protected cluster of huge Douglas-firs that has never been logged. A man,
> one of a touring and fishing party in two cars, inspects one of the trees.
> The cars disappear along the road. The party halts at a stream where we see
> a sign reading: FISHING ARE NOT ALLOW IN THIS GARDEN by order of Sam Lee.
> Fishermen making their way through undergrowth past a cabin. The fishing
> begins - fly fishing with salmon rods. Shot of General Noel Money casting
> his fly. He nets a good sized trout and brings it out for the camera. Good
> CU's of techniques of pulling in another steelhead. Catching another; it is
> displayed. The fishermen walk out of the bush. Four good-sized trout strung
> up on a stick between two men. The two men are accompanied by two very low
> profile ladies who watch during the fishing.

805. SEVEN HUNDRED PETS DELIGHT JOYOUS KIDDIES, VANCOUVER,
B.C. (1936)
p.c. Universal Newsreel V.8 R.467
1. 68'   g. 35mm   t. b+w   s. si.
d.   *
ph.   ASN
c.s. USNA

> "Long shots and CU's parade. Bull dog, great dane, CU cat. Collies. Baby
> goat. White horse. Crowds. Scottie. White rat. Turtles, others."

806. SHAWNIGAN LAKE GALA DAYS & KOOTENAY LAKE CONSTRUCTION
SITE. (1930's)
p.c. private
1. 300'   g. 16mm   t. colour & b+w   s. si.
d.   *
ph.   Rev. George R.B. Kinney
c.s. NFA, Ottawa

*b+w: Shawnigan Lake Gala Day. A large group of people, at Shawnigan Lake,
Vancouver Island, parading through the main street. Good shots of buildings.
Parade consists of adults, kids pushing prams, pulling toy trucks, floats on
real trucks with kids dressed up, one group as Fijiians (1st Prize), someone
with a Mickey Mouse head, clowns, etc. Also a local band, a float with a
tiny queen aboard, decorated bicycles and cars. Float with a girl holding a
sign reading "3 Cheers for Gala Day."*

*colour: Shawnigan Lake Gala Day. Car towing a cart full of kids wearing
Seven Dwarfs masks. Kids dressed as pirates, scarecrows, darkies, pioneers,
etc. Float with a house, float with young girls dressed up. Mickey Mouse,
decorated bicycles, decorated cars, parade passing from many angles. CU's
of girls dressed up, Seven Dwarfs and many smiling spectators.*

*b+w: CPR construction site on Kootenay Lake. LS steam engines working across
the Lake LC. At site a steam shovel worries the rock while men work nearby
with shovels etc. Steam shovels dump soil and rock into barges at water's
edge. Very dramatic footage with steam blowing and silhouettes of shovels
grinding.*

807. SHE CLIMBS TO CONQUER. (1932)
    p.c. ASN/ASS (#B616)
    1. 1 reel   g. 35mm   t. b+w   s. sound & si. w/captions
    d.   Gordon Sparling
    ph. *
    c.s. NFB, United Artists, CFI

*CANADIAN CAMEO NO. 2. "Pretty Sally Sophomore decides to see the world –
from a mountain top! So she chooses towering eleven-thousand-foot Mount
Victoria in the Canadian Rockies. With her guide she scrambles over the
glaciers where one slip spells disaster. There is peril in the warm rays
of the sun slowly melting the ice, but Sally's eyes are set on the peak. Up
she climbs into a world of infinite sky with the giants of the Rockies at
her feet. Thrilling incidents mark Sally's progress as SHE CLIMBS TO CONQUER."
Both Alberta and British Columbia can be seen from the mountain peak.*

808. SHEEP DAY, SALTSPRING ISLAND. (1936)
    p.c. B.C. Dept. of Agriculture
    1. 100'   g. 16mm   t. b+w   s. si.
    d.   *
    ph. *
    c.s. PABC

*Sheep day was held to encourage interest in sheep farming and to demonstrate
and to allow competition in the various skills required of a sheep farmer.
Scenes show shearing with hand clippers and mechanical shears operated by
turning a hand crank. The large crowd of islanders in attendance watch
the shearing outside an unidentified building on community grounds. Sheep
being shown to crowd, more shearing. Brass band in uniform, playing. CU
sheep dog. Sheep dog demonstrations with sheep and one dog at a time. Two
gents chatting with a British Columbia Provincial Policeman. Band playing,
and crowd shots. This is the third item on a reel beginning with part of a
film about bee-keeping, the total length being 300' 16mm, ending with SHEEP
DAY, SALTSPRING IS., 1936.*

809. SHEEP DRIVEN TO HIGHER PASTURE – ROCKIES. (1939)
    p.c. Pathétone #494
    1. 63'   g. 35mm   t. b+w   s. sound
    d.   *
    ph. *
    c.s. EMI Pathé Film Library

*There is no indication that this film was shot in British Columbia or even
in Canada. It shows a man with a large flock of sheep driving them up into
spring pastures. Many shots of sheep. Sheep return again in the fall to
lowlands, all shorn, and pass through gates into a stockade.*

810. SHEEP TO WINTER PASTURES – ROCKIES. (1939)
    p.c. Pathétone #504
    1. 50'   g. 35mm   t. b+w   s. sound
    d.   *
    ph. *
    c.s. EMI Pathé Film Library

*We will probably never know where this film was shot; no location is given.
It shows various good shots of large flocks of sheep being herded along mountain roads, across a narrow bridge and through forests on their way to winter pasture in the valley. Sheep move under a log arch reading LAZY BAR DA.*

811. SHEEP SHEARING CONTEST, WILLOWS. VICTORIA, B.C. (late 1920's)
 p.c. B.C. Dept. of Agriculture
 l. approx. 100'   g. 16mm   t. b+w   s. si. w/captions
 d.   *
 ph. *
 c.s. PABC

This footage is #3 on a reel containing six items, beginning with the VARIOUS SHOTS OF BOUCHIE LAKE FAIR, 1948.

Scenes include men shearing sheep. Dr. A. Knight and A. Morton officiating. Many good shots of shearing. George Sangster, timekeeper. Fleeces being bundled. George Brown wins and poses for camera.

812. THE SHIP'S HUSBAND. (1910)
 p.c. Edison Mfg. Co. (Catalogue #6703)
 l. 1000'   g. 35mm   t. b+w   s. si. w/captions
 d.   Henry Cronjager
 ph. J. Searle Dawley
 c.s. Unknown

This is one of the Edison Mfg. Co. films made during a tour of the west for the CPR. It is a comedy about two couples living in Victoria. One of the wives discovers a telegram in her absent husband's pocket which reads CHARMER. She notifies her friend's husband and the two of them assume that their respective spouses have run off with each other. There is no end of confusion until finally everything is sorted out at sea between Victoria and Vancouver aboard the two CPR ferries PRINCESS VICTORIA and PRINCESS CHARLOTTE. The couples discover that the word CHARMER refers to a CPR ship newly berthed in Victoria, and the two couples are reconciled. There are good scenes at the E.B. McKay residence at 617 Douglas Street according to the Colonist newspaper. Unfortunately this film appears to be lost. It was begun on August 1, 1910 and completed on August 30 1910.

813. "SHOULD AULD ACQUAINTANCE BE FORGOT." OLD TIMERS RENEWING FORMER FRIENDSHIPS AT REUNION, VICTORIA, B.C. (1924)
 p.c. Fox Movietonews (Fox #007.4506-A179)
 l.   g. 35mm   t. b+w   s. si.
 d.   *
 ph. Len H. Roos
 c.s. Fox Movietonews, N.Y.; NFB (1920-FG-161)

Group of pioneers who arrived before 1850 gather near the first frame building and the first schoolhouse in the Province."

"Old men who worked Klondike, fought in Boer War, unite for "last fling". Shot of huge crowd of them. Two sourdoughs meet for the first time in 60 years. Seventy-five year old man visits his birthplace, a shack, and group visit Victoria's first frame house. Former teacher and pupil meet inside Victoria's first schoolhouse. Group photo pan of group, all pioneers from before 1850."

814. SHROPSHIRE SHEEP AND "KERRY HILL". (1931 ?)
 p.c. B.C. Dept. of Agriculture (Reel 56)
 l. approx. 400'   g. 16mm   t. b+w   s. si. w/captions
 d.   *
 ph. *
 c.s. PABC

Long wordy introduction and explanation of how sheep are bred and how breeds come into being. A flock of pure-bred Shropshire sheep on the run in a field. Flock with lambs. Men holding two rams back, side, and front to explain breed characteristics. Doing the same with two unshorn ewes and two lambs. The "Kerry Hill" (Wales) sheep - The Speckled-Faced Rent Payer! Map of England showing where Kerry Hills come from. Origin of Kerry Hill sheep explained. "Charles Eccleston of Vancouver Island is an old Shropshire sheep-

*man. With the assistance of the Provincial Department of Agriculture and the
Empire Marketing Board he imported the first Kerry Hills to America." Views
of Kerry Hill sheep while explaining salient features.*

815. THE SHUSWAP INDIANS OF BRITISH COLUMBIA. (1928)
    p.c. National Museum of Canada
    1. 1 reel   g. 35mm   t. b+w   s. si. w/captions
    d.   Harlan I. Smith
    ph. Harlan I. Smith
    c.s. NFA & National Museum of Man

> *"The Shuswap Indians of British Columbia live in the southern interior of the
> province in a large area most of which is dry, sage brush and cactus being
> the common forms of plant life. They may be seen from either the Canadian
> National or Canadian Pacific Railways at Kamloops.*
>
> *The film commences with views of the country. Elk, mountain goats, deer,
> beaver, and geese, used by them for food and clothing, are shown, as well as
> the old bark-covered summer lodge, the modern village, bark cradle, bow and
> arrow, costume, drying of roots, pounding of meat with a stone hammer, use
> of the bone awl in making baskets of rootlets and cherry bark, scraping of
> deer skin, and the methods of carrying burdens and infants. There are also
> pictures of the poor cottonwood dugout canoe of this land people, their
> drawings on the rocks, a woman smoking, the Indian "turkish bath", drumming
> and dancing."*
>
> *There are also good shots of the Kekuli pit houses, once used for winter
> housing, and good CU's of several Indians. The woman scraping the skin is
> at Salmon Arm. There are shots of an old woman carrying a basket and wood
> on her back into a house, and Indians in horse-drawn wagons, in carriages
> and in an auto. The "poor" canoes are fairly crude, but quite serviceable.
> One is shown on a lake being paddled. The pictograph shown is 2 ft. 8 in.
> in diameter and on the west side of Mara Lake. (Copy at NFA is 340' on 16mm)*

816. SILENT BARRIERS. (working titles: THE GREAT BARRIER and
    THE GREAT DIVIDE) (1937)
    p.c. Gaumont British Pictures Corporation
    1.   g. 35mm   t. b+w   s. sound
    d.   Milton Rosmer
    ph. Sidney R. Bonnett and Richard L. Deacon (?)
    c.s. NFA

> *Producer, Geoffrey Barkas; assistant
> associate producer, George R. Busby;
> script: Ralph Spruce w/Michael Barr-
> inger and Ian Dalrymple based on the
> novel THE GREAT DIVIDE by Alan Sullivan
> and the history STEEL OF EMPIRE by John
> Murray Gibbon.*

> *l.p. Richard Arlen as John Hickey,
> Lilli Palmer as Lou, Barry MacKay
> as Steve Carson, Antoinette Cellier
> as Mary Moody, J. Farrell MacDonald
> as Major "Hell's Bells" Rogers, Roy
> Emerton as Moody, and Jock Mackaye
> as Bates.*

> *Storyline: Hickey and Steve arrive in a Canadian construction town on the
> CPR. They do not come to work, but in search of adventure, and find it in
> the saloon where Hickey catches a man cheating at cards. A fight ensues and
> the law intervenes. The local gaol being full, Hickey and Steve are set to
> work on the railway, where Hickey injures his hand. Pretending the injury
> is serious, he is placed in the care of Mary, the construction boss's daughter,
> an amateur nurse.*
>
> *Meanwhile, Steve, who is drinking too much, falls under the spell of Lou,
> the town's "bad" woman. This leads to a breach between Hickey and Steve.
> Steve discovers Lou's real colours and decides to go with Hickey on a danger-
> ous blasting operation, but his nerve fails and he steals the truck on which
> the two were to have escaped, leaving Hickey to his fate. Hickey is buried
> under an avalanche, but is eventually saved by a rescue party.*
>
> *Work has stopped. The railroad cannot go further. The men are in an ugly
> mood. A pass must be found through the mountains. Steve persuades Hickey
> that he is not yellow and volunteers to go with him. One by one the party
> desert or lose their lives in swamps and forest fires until only Hickey,
> Steve, and another man, survive on the few remaining biscuits. At the last
> moment they spy an eagle disappearing into the mountains and, following it,*

264

discover the route the railway must take.

Back in camp the men have rioted and burned down Moody's house and are about to kill him. Suddenly Hickey returns with news of the pass, the railway is finished and Hickey and Mary are united.

SILENT BARRIERS opened in London, England in Feb., 1937, (with the title THE GREAT BARRIER) and in Vancouver on April 9, 1937.

817. SIR AUCKLAND GEDDES, BRITISH AMBASSADOR TO U.S.A., ARRIVING WITH WIFE, VICTORIA, B.C. (1922)
p.c. Fox Movietonews (Fox #201-B1470)
1. 35'   g. 35mm   t. b+w   s. si.
d.   *
ph. Young's Studio
c.s. Fox Movietonews, N.Y.

> *"PRINCESS VICTORIA arriving. The Geddes get off. At Goverment House as guest of Lt. Gov. and Mrs. Nichol. Walking down path."*

818. SIR HENRY THORNTON AND OTHER OFFICIALS OF CANADA'S OWN RAILWAY WELCOMED BY MAYOR TISDALL AND CITY COUNCIL, VANCOUVER, B.C./FIRST MOTION PICTURES OF SIR HENRY THORNTON, PRES. OF CNR, AND PARTY. (1923)
p.c. Fox Movietonews (Fox #095.3-B152)
1. 15'   g. 35mm   t. b+w   s. si.
d.   *
ph. Len H. Roos
c.s. Fox Movietonews, N.Y. and NFA

> *"First motion pictures of Sir Henry Thornton as he arrives after 7000 mile tour of Canada. He is greeted by Mayor Tisdall of Vancouver and other civic dignitaries. Pan of Sir Henry, Mayor & Council. CU of Sir Henry & Mayor. More of group - CNR officials."*

819. SIR WILLIAM HORNELL, GIVES INTERVIEW ON CHINESE EDUCATION SITUATION OF TODAY, VICTORIA, B.C. (1937)
p.c. Fox Movietonews (Fox #33-103)
1. 300'   g. 35mm   t. b+w   s. sound
d.   *
ph. ASN
c.s. Fox Movietonews, N.Y.

> *"CU of Sir William Hornell, Vice-Chancellor of the Hong Kong University, giving interview of the education situation in China today. He is retiring and returning to his home in England."*

820. SIXTY YEARS OF CANADIAN PROGRESS. (1927)
p.c. CGMPB
1. 1 reel   g. 35mm   t. b+w   s. si. w/captions
d.   *
ph.   *
c.s. Unknown

> *This film was made for the Department of Trade and Commerce, Ottawa. The description in the 1930 CGMPB catalogue does not indicate locations, but it is safe to assume that British Columbia is included: "A film depicting the growth of the Dominion of Canada since Confederation, commencing with a graphic illustration of its territorial growth and followed by comparative illustrations of its progress as exemplified in the growth of its cities and industrial centres."*

821. SKI CHAMPS MEET IN THRILLING CONTEST. SPECTATORS GASP AS JUMPERS ZOOM DOWN WORLD'S STEEPEST HILLSIDE IN REVELSTOKE, B.C. (1930)
p.c. Fox Movietonews (Fox #732.3-D3645)
1. 125'   g. 35mm   t. b+w   s. si.
d.   *
ph. Ross Beesley
c.s. Fox Movietonews, N.Y.

"Close shot made atop the jump, showing jumpers zooming down past camera. High shot landing at base of hill. Rear shot jumpers in air. High shot overlooking the town and valley, mountains in b.g. Tilt down to jump meet. Scenes at base of hill showing jumpers landing and some spilling."

822. SKI ENTHUSIASTS STAGE BIG MEET IN CITY LIMITS, VANCOUVER,
     B.C. (1938)
     p.c. Universal Newsreel V.10 R.639
     1. 97'   g. 35mm   t. b+w   s. si.
     d.   *
     ph. ASN
     c.s. USNA

"Mayor Miller does the honours on Sasamat Hill. Crowds skiing down the slope, lessons offered. Shots of different types in not-too-up-to-snuff outfits."

823. SKI JUMPING TRIALS FOR WESTERN CANADA IN REVELSTOKE, B.C.
     (1935)
     p.c. Fox Movietonews (Fox #24-931)
     1. 500'   g. 35mm   t. b+w   s. sound
     d.   *
     ph. ASN
     c.s. Fox Movietonews, N.Y.

"Various shots of ski-jumping for Olympics. Crowds. Gunner Gunnerson makes longest jump, 200feet. CU after jump. Hans Gunnerson, brother, wins meet. Spills, etc."

824. SKITIME IN THE ROCKIES. (1935-1938)
     p.c. ASN (A709 & B709)
     1.   g. 35mm & 16mm t. b+w s.
     d.   *
     ph. *
     c.s. Unknown

A promotional film made for the CPR. It is not known whether any of the scenes show British Columbia.

825. THE SKY SENTINEL. (1928-1930)
     p.c. Fox
     1. approx. 400'   g. 16mm   t. b+w   s. si.
     d.   *
     ph. *
     c.s. Unknown

A film about Mt. Robson. "Views of the mountain itself are given with shots of lakes, river, moose, geese swimming and flying, bear in the undergrowth, beaver swimming, mountain sheep, waterfall, glacier, and the snow-covered scenery near the summit. These scenes in the film are grouped round the figures of a rider and his pony as they climb the mountain." The description in an undated Kodascope Catalogue from the 1920's reads: "Following the lure of the great open places, we travel a horse through wild and beautiful country, passing the Emperor Falls, fording the cold Fraser River, crossing Moose Meadows till we reach our objective, Mt. Robson, one of the highest peaks in British Columbia, far from the haunts of man.

Glimpses of wild Canadian Gray Geese, Bears, Beavers, Moose, and Mountain Sheep furnish many interesting moments enroute."

826. SKYLINE MOTORING. (1935)
     p.c. ASN (A691)
     1. approx. 400'   g. 35mm & 16mm t. b+w s. si.
     d.   *
     ph. *
     c.s. Unknown

ASN made this film about the Rockies for the CPR. Whether it depicts British Columbia is not known.

827. SLASH, SNAGS AND SECOND GROWTH. (1939-40)
    p.c. B.C. Forest Service (Forestry reel 75)
    1. approx. 400'   g. 16mm   t. colour   s. si. w/captions
    d.   *
    ph. *
    c.s. B.C. Dept. of Forests

            *"Portraying the importance of proper snag and slash disposal after logging
            so as to give young second growth trees a chance to develop, and also to
            lessen the extreme fire hazard created by the presence of snags and slash."
            Scenes show workers removing snags & slash, etc.*

828. SLITHERING AND SKIDDING AROUND DIRT TRACK AT RECORD SPEED
    AUTOS RACE FOR PROVINCIAL HONOURS, VANCOUVER, B.C. (1928)
    p.c. Fox Movietonews (Fox #755.2-C4572)
    1. 100'   g. 35mm   t. b+w   s. si.
    d.   *
    ph. *
    c.s. Fox Movietonews, N.Y.

            "Shots of the race. Art Hines, champion."

829. SNOWPLOW BUCKING A 15 FOOT SNOWSLIDE. (1903)
    p.c. *
    1. 70'   g. 35mm   t. b+w   s. si.
    d.   *
    ph. *
    c.s. Unknown

            *"Taken on the wonderful White Pass and Yukon Railroad. This is the most
            expensively constructed railway of its length in the world. It is 114 miles
            in length, and contains more cuts and fills, trestles and bridges, tunnels
            and snowsheds, than any other 114 miles of continuous track in existence.
            The two miles shown in this subject give one an excellent idea of some of
            the difficulties of construction encountered." (Biograph Bulletins)*

830. SNOWSTORM, VICTORIA, B.C. (1916)
    p.c. *
    1. 150'   g. 35mm   t. b+w   s. si.
    d.   *
    ph. *
    c.s. NFA (Taylor reel 107)

            *Scenes of the aftermath of a heavy snowfall on Victoria. "Shot of two men
            in cutter moving toward & past camera. Service car trying to pull stuck ve-
            hicle, men shovelling snow, touring car almost completely covered with snow
            which is still falling throughout the city. Pedestrians walking in the mid-
            dle of the street. Horse-drawn plough trying to clear sidewalk. Streetcar
            sweeper firing snow as it passes camera. Streetcars moving along Government
            St. as men shovel snow in f.g. Slow pan & tilt over city as snow falls gently.
            More shots of streetcar and horse-drawn wagons, pedestrians ploughing through
            the snow." (NOTE: The famous BIG SNOW in Victoria occurred in 1916, when 76"
            of snow fell during January and February. This film was originally dated as
            1918, but since less than 6" fell that winter, I assume the film to have been
            shot in 1916.)*

831. SOCIETY THRONGS TO SEE POLO TEAMS BATTLE FOR POSSESSION
    OF B.C. SILVER CHALLENGE TROPHY, VANCOUVER, B.C. (1928)
    p.c. Fox Movietonews (Fox #700.8-C5055)
    1. 175'   g. 35mm   t. b+w   s. si.
    d.   *
    ph. Ross Beesley
    c.s. Fox Movietonews (Fox #700.8-C5055)

            Polo match, crowds.

832. "SOCKEYE", LION'S GATE BRIDGE, WHALING STATION ON QUEEN
    CHARLOTTE ISLANDS.
    p.c. private
    1. 300'   g. 8mm   t. b+w & colour   s. si.
    d.   *
    ph. H. Turner
    c.s. via Pacific Cinémathèque, Vancouver

"SOCKEYE" (1933): (Colour) Totems, graves, boardwalk at Alert Bay. Chinese man at Butedale Cannery. Conveyor from boat to cannery carrying fish, at Namu. Inside cannery at Namu, Indian woman packing salmon into cans. Halibut on a hoist at Butedale. Fisherman and boat, fish in hold. LS Klemtu cannery from sea. Indian, Norwegian and Japanese cannery girls at Namu. Feeding deer. Tongass Passage, northern Vancouver Island, going into Cee-Pee-Cee. Mail arriving in Namu. Indians. Long boats being towed out of Margaret Bay in Smith's Inlet for a week of fishing, manned by Indians. Scow load of pilchards at Nootka. Oil-burning retort used to dry the pilchards. Cases of salmon being loaded onto coastal freighter, a Union Steamship boat. Little Indian girl getting water. Indian woman mending nets at Tallheo near Bella Coola. Indian kids at Nootka. Indian kids at Tallheo swimming in glacial creek. Japanese fisherman's cottage at Namu. Scenic shots from American Can. Co. boat sailing thru inlets. Alaska Steamship Co. (?) ship MV ALASKA passing by. Union Steamship MV CARDENA in Rivers Inlet. Sea scenes on west cast, storm and tramp steamer. Union Steamship passing by. British warship in Grenville Channel. Sunsets at Namu. Porpoises diving near bow of boat. The weekly tub - - a bath on the cannery wharf. West coast scenes. Aboard PRINCESS MQUINNA. West coast shots.

LION'S GATE BRIDGE (1938-39): (Colour) Car crossing empty bridge with mountains on a clear day. CPR Princess ferry passing beneath the bridge. Excellent shot through floor of bridge of ferry passing under.

WHALING STATION: (b+w) Nadden Harbour on the Queen Charlottes. LS station. CU whale and gun on bow of whaling ship. (Colour) Lookout on mast of whaling ship. LS many shots of whales sounding. In a small boat, shooting at whales with a .303 rifle. CU of whale very near small boat.

833. Deleted.

834. SOCKEYE SALMON FISHING ON A B.C. RIVER BY A UNIQUE METHOD
BRINGS IN FINE CATCH. (1926)
p.c. Fox Movietonews (Fox #729.22-B3441)
1. 60' g. 35mm t. b+w s. si.
d. *
ph. *
c.s. Fox Movietonews, N.Y.

"Long shot across Broughton Strait. Indian preparing gear. Shots of the new seine. CU Indian grinning - he caught 580 fish. Shots of men and fish."

835. SOIL SURVEY OF A BLOCK BETWEEN CAMPBELL RIVER AND
MENZIES BAY, B.C. (1930's)
p.c. B.C. Dept. of Agriculture
1. approx. 200' g. 16mm t. colour & b+w s. si. w/captions
d. *
ph. *
c.s. PABC

Views of holes showing strata of soil which are identified by digger and by caption. A few shots of fields and swampy forest. There are no landmarks or identifiable scenes.

836. SOLDIERS (1). (1918-1925)
p.c. *
1. 800' g. 35mm t. b+w s. si.
d. *
ph. *
c.s. NFA (McMartin footage, reel 5)

"Man with horses. Men outside barracks. Barracks with old car parked near. Rows of early cars parked. Soldiers getting in or standing nearby, tinkering with one of the cars. Sandbags, bridge and an explosion (training?). Army camp. Various shots of officers in garden of a big house. Rows of Army vehicles. Numerous nurses sitting on steps. Man walking in large cultivated garden. Playing bowls, same large house in b.g. Operating theatre. Various shots of interior of Army hospital, equipment, wards, etc. Exterior shot of hospital (?) hut. New hut under construction. Officer sitting at desk." It is not known if the locations of any of these shots are in British Columbia.

837. SOLDIERS (2). (1918-1925)
    p.c. *
    1. 600'   g. 35mm   t. b+w   s. si. w/captions
    d.   *
    ph. *
    c.s. NFA (McMartin footage, reel 6)

                    "Soldiers doing PT. Audience watching, women in elaborate hats. Horse drawn
                    bus arriving at barracks, officers and soldiers getting out. Group outside
                    hut. Horse in stable. Officer looking at horse, leading horse away, man
                    examining horse's foot. Officers outside stables. At the blacksmith's.
                    Hill with houses at top. Practise field of some kind below. Smoke rising
                    from field (artillery practise?) Various shots of field with smoke rising.
                    Army manoeuvres. Gun carriages with large wheels in row to left of picture.
                    Artillery practice. CU of one of the field pieces. CU men standing behind
                    gun and firing. Officers supervising the digging of trenches. Soldiers
                    lined up by newly dug trenches. Officer inspecting an office, papers piled
                    up on desks. Men marching through streets. Banner reading RECRUITS WANTED -
                    ROLL UP - FOLLOW THE BAND. Man with stetson shouting. Numerous shots of
                    young men with boaters." No location given; assumed to be British Columbia.

838. SOLDIERS (3). (1918-1925)
    p.c. *
    1. 1000'   g. 35mm   t. b+w   s. si.
    d.   *
    ph. *
    c.s. NFA (McMartin footage, reel 7)

                    "Army officers on horseback standing in front of parading soldiers. Crowds
                    outside Canadian National Railway Station, liner in b.g. Soldiers marching.
                    Soldiers and crowds, officers on horseback. Same plus old cars in shot.
                    MCU's officers on horses. Horse-drawn heavy artillery. Cars and soldiers."
                    No indication given; assumed to be British Columbia.

839. THE SONG THAT REACHED HIS HEART. (1910)
    p.c. Edison Mfg. Co. (Catalogue #6690)
    1. 986'   g. 35mm   t. b+w   s. si.
    d.   J. Searle Dawley
    ph. Henry Conjager
    c.s. NFA

                    A dramatic short made by the Edison Co. during its tour of the Canadian west
                    during the summer of 1910, shooting promotional films for the CPR. It was
                    begun on June 7 and completed on July 18, with some additions made at Edison's
                    Bronx studio later. In the story, a Canadian lumberjack nostalgically recalls
                    his past as he listens to a record of the song Annie Laurie, his sweetheart
                    used to sing to him. The singer travels to western Canada for her health
                    and the lumberjack saves her from being robbed by two crooks. He then dis-
                    covers that she is his old sweetheart and she sits down to sing the old song
                    for him. The film was released on October 11, 1910. The locations were shot
                    in either Alberta or British Columbia.

840. SPA OF CANADA. (1938-40)
    p.c. B.C. Government Travel Bureau
    1. 1x400' reel   g. 16mm   t. colour s. si.
    d.   *
    ph. C.R.D. Ferris
    c.s. Unknown

                    "Harrison Lake and Springs in British Columbia."

841. SPANNING MIGHTY FRASER RIVER FOR 40 YEARS, THE OLD
    BUCKET CABLE IS STILL IN USE, YALE, B.C. (1927)
    p.c. Fox Movietonews (Fox #462.93-C1462)
    1. 35'   g. 35mm   t. b+w   s. si.
    d.   *
    ph. Mitford
    c.s. Fox Movietonews, N.Y.

                    Scenes of passengers coming across the river in bucket.

842. SPEARING SALMON. (1902)
p.c. Edison Mfg. Co.
1. 175'   g. 35mm   t. b+w   s. si.
d.   *
ph. *
c.s. Unknown

This film is probably lost for all time. It is not known whether the salmon spearing was done in British Columbia or on the west coast of the U.S.

843. SPECIAL INSPECTOR. (1938)
p.c. *
1.   g.   t.   s.
d.   *
ph. *
c.s. *

See ACROSS THE BORDER.

844. SPECTACULAR PARADE ON EMPIRE DAY, VICTORIA, B.C.
(1921)
p.c. Fox Movietonews (Fox #751.13-3895)
1. 90'   g. 35mm   t. b+w   s. si.
d.   *
ph. D.C. Davey
c.s. Fox Movietonews, N.Y.

"Street parade passing judges stand in front of Parliament Buildings and prize winners leaving. Parade at Beacon Hill Park. At Gorge, boat races and water sports."

845. SPLENDID PLAYGROUND FOR CHILDREN IS OPENED WITH HUNDREDS
OF YOUNGSTERS HAVING THE TIME OF THEIR LIVES, VANCOUVER,
B.C. (1925)
p.c. Fox Movietonews (Fox #750.1-B4670)
1. 70'   g. 35mm   t. b+w   s. si.
d.   *
ph. Film Title Service
c.s. Fox Movietonews, N.Y.

"Merry-go-round, slides, pool, sailing boats, wading, crowded grounds."

846. SPORTS MEET, VANCOUVER, B.C. (1920's)
p.c. CGMPB(?)
1.   g. 35mm   t. b+w   s. si.
d.   *
ph. *
c.s. NFB (#1920-P-21)

Male swimmers at poolside. Trick divers performing at slow and regular speed. Swimmer on diving board. Swimmers executing various swimming styles. Large number of beginners swimming under guidance of instructor. Large group of women bathers at pool, mixed groups, etc. Sculling regatta with people dressed up. Ladies tennis match. Golf game between men in plus fours with large gallery following. People relaxing at clubhouse after game. Shots of basketball game. Track and field events: running, jumping. Midget car racing in South America.

847. SS ADMIRAL FARRAGUT SLIPS FROM DRYDOCK WHILE UNDERGOING REPAIRS.
SCENES OF THE RESCUE. VICTORIA, B.C. (1922)
p.c. Fox Movietonews (Fox #090.1-C2578)
1. 20'   g. 35mm   t. b+w   s. si.
d.   *
ph. D.C. Davey
c.s. Fox Movietonews, N.Y.

Shots of damaged ship and rescue.

848. SS CANADIAN IMPORTER ARRIVES IN VICTORIA HARBOUR AFTER
CHEATING THE OCEAN OF ITS ANTICIPATED PREY, VICTORIA, B.C.
(1921)
p.c. Fox Movietonews (Fox #463.11-2715)
1. 16'   g. 35mm   t. b+w   s. si.
d.   *
ph. W.B. Young
c.s. Fox Movietonews, N.Y.

"SS CANADIAN IMPORTER being towed in by tugs."

849. SS DOMINIA, LARGEST OF CABLE SHIPS, STARTS LAYING 3600
MILES OF CABLE IN PACIFIC TO FANNING ISLAND, VANCOUVER,
B.C. (1926)
p.c. Fox Movietonews (Fox #463.19-B5391)
1. 55'   g. 35mm   t. b+w   s. si.
d.   *
ph. Herron
c.s. Fox Movietonews, N.Y.

"Various shots of ship laying cable."

850. SS EMPRESS OF ASIA LEAVES VANCOUVER FOR CHINA,
VANCOUVER, B.C. (1921)
p.c. Fox Movietonews (Fox #463.11-6103)
1. 7'   g. 35mm   t. b+w   s. si.
d.   *
ph. Singleow
c.s. Fox Movietonews, N.Y.

(John D. Rockefeller aboard?)

851. THE SS EMPRESS OF RUSSIA ARRIVES AT VANCOUVER WITH
100,000 CASES OF CHINESE EGGS, VANCOUVER, B.C. (1920)
p.c. Fox Movietonews (Fox #463.1-1534)
1. 33'   g. 35mm   t. b+w   s. si.
d.   *
ph. British-American Film Co.
c.s. Fox Movietonews, N.Y.

Shots of the EMPRESS OF RUSSIA arriving and eggs being unloaded.

852. SS ESTEVAN DELIVERING SUPPLIES TO THE PACHENA POINT
LIGHT. (1930's)
p.c. private
1. 302'   g. 16mm   t. colour & b+w s. si.
d.   *
ph. Rev. George R.B. Kinney
c.s. NFA, Ottawa

b+w: Scenes taken from the deck of the SS ESTEVAN on a windy day at Pachena
Light. Crewmen prepare a surf boat and lower it. The boat is filled with
supplies. The lifeboat from Bamfield approaches, and with its strong engine,
takes the surf boat in tow toward the surf smashing against the rocks. A
long boom extends out from a bluff above the sea and a hook is lowered to
the crew of the surf boat who attach a waterproofed bundle of supplies. The
supplies are carried up to land and the boom swung over when the bundle
reaches the block. Kinney has managed to get ashore, because the next shot
shows the crew of the surf boat rowing hard to keep the boat off the rocks
while the rest of the supplies are landed. Finally they row out to sea in
the swell.

Colour: Scenes shot from Pachena Point. Surf boat bobbing in a small bay,
delivering supplies to shore. Surf boat rowing back to SS ESTEVAN. LS
ESTEVAN. Motor surf boat cruising beneath bluff. Views of surf and shoreline. LS from high vantage point of supplies being unloaded from surf boat.
Shots of lighthouse crew disconnecting hook from supplies, making hamper
ready again. Lighthouse shots, lighthouse crew, keeper and his wife.

b+w: Pachena Point Light. Views around lighthouse; people on rocks waiting,
man coming ashore in small dinghy, sheds, houses, etc. CU Light. Life-rope
gun being loaded. Group posing, nurse McKinnon and keeper. Boat offshore.

Colour: View from Pachena. SS ESTEVAN lying offshore. Surf pounding in.
Man in dinghy being lowered into surf from boom, into the waiting surf boat.
Aboard ship again. Two large light buoys laid out on deck. CU Captain and
Mate of ESTEVAN. Mel Swartout on float at Bamfield.

853. STAMPEDE. (1936)
    p.c. Central Films, Ltd.
    1. 56 min. (5047') g. 35mm t. b+w   s. sound
    d.   Ford Beebe
    ph. George Meehan and William Beckway
    c.s. NFA

Canadian prod., Kenneth J. Bishop; script, Robert Watson; editor William Austin; Columbia overseer, Jack Fier.

l.p. Charles Starrett, Finis Barton, J.P. McGowan, LeStrange Millman, James McGrath, Reginald Hincks, Arthur Kerr, Jack Atkinson, and Michael Heppell.

Working title: GUN SMOKE. The third Quota Quickie begun by Columbia Pictures through Central Films in Victoria. A note in SCREEN FACTS mentions that: "The budget was so tight on ... STAMPEDE that Beebe couldn't afford the luxury of too many re-takes." Critics said it lacked dramatic appeal and suspense.

STAMPEDE was begun in February, 1936, but production had to be suspended because of rain. While waiting, the cast and crew began work on, and finished, an RCMP adventure called SECRET PATROL. Production recommenced immediately on STAMPEDE and the picture was completed by the second week of April. It was copyrighted in the United States by Columbia Pictures, Inc., on June 6, 1936.

The storyline is as follows: Larry Carson (Charles Starrett) and his brother, both horse buyers, find themselves prevented from reaching the Milford ranch in Montana. It turns out that the villain, Stevens (J.P. McGowan), hopes to impoverish Milford (LeStrange Millman) and force the sale of his ranch by making sure that potential buyers never reach their destination. When Carson's brother is killed Milford's own hands accuse him and he is jailed. Carson begins to realise that there is a plot against Milford and with the help of Milford's daughter Dale (Finis Barton), and an anonymous tip from one of Steven's men (James McGrath) who is getting cold feet, he sets about getting the necessary evidence against Stevens. His fate is sealed when carefully maintained records are found in his safe proving that Milford's men were in his pay. With Stevens and his men safely incarcerated and Milford free again, Carson and Dale announce their intention to marry immediately. (Storyline description courtesy of D. John Turner, NFA.)

854. STANLEY PARK & ENGLISH BAY, B.C. (1936)
    p.c. private
    1. approx. 25'   g. 8mm   t. b+w   s. si.
    d.   *
    ph. J.W. Bowdery
    c.s. via Pacific Cinémathèque, Vancouver

In Stanley Park: a girl walking under and posing beside Japanese Bridge. LS boat on lake. Throng of kids on roundabout. Costumed actress from Vancouver's 50th anniversary pageant. Charter yacht used for travelling about the harbour, etc., name not decipherable. Crowd on beach at English Bay, bath houses in b.g.

855. THE STOLEN CLAIM. (1910)
    p.c. Edison Mfg. Co. (Catalogue #6706)
    1. 1000'   g. 35mm t. b+w   s. si.
    d.   J. Searle Dawley
    ph. Henry Cronjager
    c.s. Unknown

This film was made during the Edison Co.'s tour of the Canadian west in the summer of 1910, shooting promotional pictures for the CPR. It was begun on July 16 and finished on August 12, with extra bits filmed at Edison's Bronx Studio upon the troupe's return. The location is not known but it appears to have been a mining story and so was likely shot in the mountains of British Columbia where the troupe mentioned have done extensive filming in mining districts. The story is not known.

856. THE STORY OF A CAN OF SALMON. (1923)
     p.c. CGMPB
     1. 1 reel   g. 35mm   t. b+w   s. si. w/captions
     d.   *
     ph. *
     c.s. NFB (1920-DN-46)

> *"An informative film depicting in an interesting and non-technical manner how salmon is canned in the great canneries of British Columbia. Every step in the process from delivering the catch to the cannery to completed product is graphically shown." The NFB footage contains the following scenes: LS pan along a cannery on a wharf. Fishermen unloading salmon catch. MS's & MCU's machine used to behead, scale, split and clean fish in one operation, of machine used for cutting fish into packageable pieces. (Iron Chink ?) Inside packing room, several women at work. MCU's of hands packing salmon into cans. Cans of salmon are moved onto a conveyor to the salter, then to a machine that puts lids on without sealing them. Cans go through a steamer for 8 minutes, then are sealed. MCU's intricate machine with cans moving at high speed. Men assemble several cans together and place them into a cooker. After cooking the cans are removed and tested for air leaks and washed. Interior of lacquering room. Thousands of cans piled one on top of the other. Lacquering operation. Final packing in interior of warehouse containing thousands of cases of salmon and cans being loaded aboard ship. Side view of piles of cases with address: LIVERPOOL.*

857. THE STORY OF TIMBER. (late 20's, early 30's)
     p.c. *
     1. approx. 335'   g. 16mm   t. b+w   s. si.
     d.   *
     ph. *
     c.s. NFA, BCPM Hist.

> *Logging operations of the Elk River Timber Company Ltd. on Vancouver Island. Steam donkeys and railroad hauling of logs - E.R.T. Co. Ltd. on side of locie and later spelled out entirely on a flat car. Logs are dumped into the ocean at the end of this print. The print is not complete but shows a logging camp, falling the trees, topping a spar tree, wooden houses and rooftops, high-lead logging, etc.*

858. STRANGE MACHINES HANDLE FOREST GIANTS AT WORLD'S LARGEST
     LUMBERING CAMP IN THE CANADIAN WEST, BRITISH COLUMBIA.
     (1933)
     p.c. British Movietonews (No. 6376)
     1. 261'   g. 35mm   t. b+w   s. sound
     d.   *
     ph. *
     c.s. British Movietonews

> *Big cat hauls limbed trees through the woods on a large A-frame on rollers. Logs are dragged behind inverted U by cable, then a steam crane loads logs onto railway flatcars marked TEELO. At the mill a giant steam crane dumps logs into a pond. CU log being rolled onto carriage, gripped, then run through great bandsaw, then back and forth, until plank is completely sawn. Actuality sound throughout: engines, steam whistles, saw screaming, etc. No location is given.*

859. STRAWBERRY GROWING, VANCOUVER ISLAND, KEATING, B.C.
     (1928)
     p.c. B.C. Dept. of Agriculture (reel 14)
     1. approx. 400'   g. 16mm   t. b+w   s. si. w/captions
     d.   *
     ph. *
     c.s. PABC

> *Illustrates the method of cultivating strawberries from clearing the land to planting, tending, harvesting, packing, crating and trucks driving away with fruit to the Saanich Fruit Growers Association shed at Keating, B.C. Scenes include: A visit of the District Horticulturist. Laying straw before fruiting. Good CU labels on crates: VICTORIA STRAWBERRIES. Pose by groups of pickers before tents - "tired and hungry." Good shot of fruit being del-*

ivered to Saanich Fruit Growers's Association shed at Keating. The manager of the Association helping to nail and sort crates of berries. Dominion Government inspectors at work opening crates and checking. Grower's book being signed. Berries leaving Association shed in trucks for pre-cooling shed and jam factory.

860. STRIPPING A FOREST IN WINTER. (1909)
    p.c. Urban-Eclipse
    1. 387'   g. 35mm   t. b+w & tinted s. si.
    d. *
    ph. *
    c.s. Unknown

"Few winter scenes can approach this picture for beauty, originality, picturesque effect, and realistic scenes of an important Canadian industry. This one phase of life in the great north west depicted with a thoroughness that leaves nothing to be desired ... We are first taken to the woodmen's camp of logs in the midst of snow-covered hills, and from there to groves of mammoth trees, where we watch the felling of the monarchs of the forest. The photography is so perfect one almost hears the crackling of the limbs and the rush of immense bodies as they crash to earth." The photographer also caught scenes of logs rolling down chutes, dog teams, traction engine sledges, and the piling and loading of logs preparatory to sliding them into a river for transport to the mill. It is difficult to say, from the descriptions available, where this film was made. The first half seems to be the west coast, and the second half Ontario or Quebec.

861. SUFFOLK SHEEP. (1931?)
    p.c. B.C. Dept. of Agriculture (Reel 64)
    1. approx. 250'   g. 16mm   t. b+w   s. si. w/captions
    d. *
    ph. *
    c.s. PABC

"Suffolk rams, showing massiveness and great strength, with strong hams." Two rams being shown on both sides, front and back, and their features being pointed out with captions and a man with a pointer. Flock of Suffolk sheep. CU features of ewes. Suffolk lambs and ewes.

862. SUMAS. (1929?)
    p.c. B.C. Dept. of Agriculture
    1. approx. 400'   g. 16mm   t. b+w   s. si. w/captions
    d. *
    ph. *
    c.s. PABC

Hop growing near Sumas in the Fraser Valley, sixty miles east of Vancouver. White and Indian workers. The film shows hop cultivation from early shoots until the hops, picked and threshed in a warehouse, are sacked and loaded onto a truck. Each step is thoroughly explained and depicted. A good film.

863. SUMMER CRUISE - PART II. (1939)
    p.c. private
    1. approx. 300'   g. 16mm   t. colour & b+w s. si. w/captions
    d. *
    ph. *
    c.s. PABC Agriculture Collection

Photographed during a private yachting holiday by one of the staff of the British Columbia Dept. of Agriculture. Part I appears to be missing and is probably lost. Almost all of the film is shot from the yacht. Colour: The Arran Rapids, raging waters, a 14' rise. Looking toward Bute Inlet from Dent Island. Yucultas. Estero Peak, from head of Frederick Arm. Looking into the Estero Basin; includes a shot of a small yacht, a building and a picnic on a beach. Phillips Arm, a Union Steamship bearing down on the camera, a wharf. Some yachts in a sheltered bay. Green Point Rapids, narrow channel. Indian painting near Green Point Rapids, red painting of two human figures. Indian painting on rock, Surge Narrows - two red figures, almost indecipherable. Store at Bodega Anchorage, Okisollo Channel, people posing. Long pontoon wharf with shed at the end. Union Steamships CARDENA and VENTURE in Discovery Passage. Seine boat, Discovery Passage, good shots of men hauling in nets. b+w: Totems - Karlukwees Village - excellent of house poles and welcome figure, seven poles shown. "Why we did not land at Tsatsichknukwomi" - a bull on the beach below Indian houses. Hauling hay at the Oiens, Village Island. Haying with oxen or bulls. Mr. Oien (?). Oxen eating hay as it is loaded into the wagon. Mr. Oien taking off his sweater. Totems at Mamalilaculla, Village Island - excellent of house pole totems and many different poles and posts shown including good shots of the village and, at the end, a long pan of the village from the water.

864. SUMMER SCHOOL OF THE UBC THEATRE. (1939)
    p.c. *
    l. approx. 100'   g. 16mm   t. b+w   s. si.
    d. *
    ph. *
    c.s. Special Collections Division, University of
            British Columbia, Library, Vancouver

            Theatre activities at University of British Columbia Summer School.

865. SUNKEN GARDENS MAKE FINE SETTING FOR SUMMER FETE,
    VANCOUVER, B.C. (1923)
    p.c. Fox Movietonews (Fox #050.456-B2087)
    l. 30'   g. 35mm   t. b+w   s. si.
    d. *
    ph. Len H. Roos
    c.s. Fox Movietonews, N.Y.

            "Folk dancing, ladies talking, Col. Rt. Rev. A.V. dePencier."

866. A SURE FOOT AND STEADY HANDS ARE ALL NECESSARY WHEN MOUN-
    TAINEERS CLIMB AMID CLOUDS ON ROCKIES PEAKS, WAPTA CAMP, B.C.
    (1929)
    p.c. Fox Movietonews (Fox #728-D2136)
    l. 180'   g. 35mm   t. b+w   s. si.
    d. *
    ph. *
    c.s. Fox Movietonews, N.Y.

            "Climbing scenes. Man atop mountain. Reflection of tall trees and mountain on still water."

867. SURVEY B.C. ROUTE FOR ALASKA HIGHWAY, VANCOUVER, B.C.
    (1939)
    p.c. Paramount (Lib. #8891)
    l. 63'   g. 35mm   t. b+w   s. sound
    d. *
    ph. ASN
    c.s. Lost

            "Group posing on steps of plane. Party inspects map. CU back view plane into water. SCU plane taking off. Airshot houses. Airshot winding road, or river, in b.g.: snowcapped mountains. CU Mr. Magnusson and Mr. Gruening reading map in plane. Snow capped mountains, water in f.g. Clouds, wing of plane in picture. Plane flying." See No. 868.

868. SURVEY OF B.C. - ALASKA HIGHWAY (AERIAL ROUTE). (1939)
    p.c. Universal Newsreel (#x3491, Roll 1)
    l. 776'   g. 35mm   t. b+w   s. si.
    d. *
    ph. ASN
    c.s. USNA

            "From Vancouver to Dawson City, Yukon - 4000 miles. Congressman W.G. Magnusson, Dr. E. Gruening, Jas. Carey and D. MacDonald in group. Take-off and return to Vancouver. Plane landing. Over mountains from air: Squamish Range, Coast Range, Mt. Murchison, Garibaldi Lake, Pemberton Meadows towards Kamloops B.C. At Williams Lake and Stewart Lake. Gassing and take-off for Whitehorse, Yukon. Inspect Indian map. Mt. Range. Arrival at Dawson. Junkers arriving. Checking planes. Aerial shot of mountains on Alaska Border. Return to Vancouver. Magnusson and Gruening talk into mikes."

869. SWIMMING STARS COMPETE IN 2½ MILE CONTEST ACROSS
     BURRARD INLET FOR MARPOLE TROPHY, VANCOUVER, B.C.
     (1928)
     p.c. Fox Movietonews (Fox #700.8-C5076)
     l. 100'   g. 35mm   t. b+w   s. si.
     d.   *
     ph. Ross Beesley
     c.s. Fox Movietonews, N.Y.

                    "Race, boats, CU Johnnie Bayley, the winner."

870. THE SWISS GUIDE. (1910)
     p.c. Edison Mfg. Co. (Catalogue #6696)
     l. 990'   g. 35mm   t. b+w   s. si.
     d.   J. Searle Dawley
     ph. Henry Cronjager
     c.s. Unknown

                    *One of the films made by Edison for the CPR during the summer of 1910. THE
                    SWISS GUIDE was probably filmed in both Banff, and Laggan, Alberta, and was
                    begun on July 10, finished on August 7. The description is as follows: "A
                    rough, married, mountain guide falls in love with a young girl staying at
                    the Chalet. He worships her from afar, even though he is helpless. His
                    wife knows but decides he'll get over his infatuation before long. On a
                    hike over the glacier the guide, suddenly overcome, reveals his love to the
                    young girl who slaps him soundly and starts over the icefield alone. She
                    slips and falls over a cliff and is only discovered after a long wait by
                    the guide's dog who carries the news back to his mistress, the guide's wife.
                    The wife follows the dog, finds her rival, and carries her back to her
                    friends. She will only accept as a gift the pair of gloves her husband gave
                    to the young girl. The guide realizes the "nobility" of his wife and the
                    two are warmly reunited." (Motion Picture World, Nov. 5 1910). Some of THE
                    SWISS GUIDE MAY HAVE BEEN FILMED IN B.C.*

871. A TALE OF THREE CITIES. (1920's)
     p.c. *
     l. 14 min.   g. 16mm   t. b+w   s. si.
     d.   *
     ph. *
     c.s. Unknown

                    *About Vancouver, Victoria and Seattle. In Vancouver, the main streets and
                    buildings are shown, the beach at English Bay, and the Harding and Burns mem-
                    orials. In Victoria, scenes include the Legislative Buildings and the Dom-
                    inion Astrophysical Observatory on Little Saanich Mountain. Described in
                    the BFI Educational Catalogue as "mildly interesting."*

872. TEA BUREAU PUPPET SHOW. (1937-38)
     p.c. Empire Tea Bureau
     l. approx. 300' g. 16mm   t. colour s. si.
     d.   Lilian Chambers
     ph. T.G.S. Chambers and Lilian Chambers
     c.s. NFA

                    *Made, by Mr. & Mrs. Chambers, to advertise tea and to stimulate tea-drinking
                    across Canada and accompanied by a narrative by Mrs. Chambers, in English
                    for English-speaking audiences and in French for French-speaking audiences.
                    The equipment to make the film was loaned by the Dunne and Rundle camera shop
                    in Vancouver, where the film was made.*

                    *The puppet story is about a Princess who mysteriously falls asleep with an
                    unknown disease and her father, the King, who sends far and wide to discover
                    a cure. Finally the Princess is revived with tea and the young man who
                    brings it to her is rewarded with her hand in marriage. The sponsor of the
                    film was the old Empire Tea Bureau, for whom the Chambers' worked during the
                    1930's.*

873. TEA PARTY AT BUTCHART'S GARDENS. (1923)
     p.c. *
     l.   g. 35mm   t. b+w   s. si.
     d.   *
     ph. *
     c.s. NFA (75-12-27)

Mr. & Mrs. R.P. Butchart entertain old ladies at a garden party in the Butchart Gardens. Various shots of Butchart Gardens, Butchart home, floral displays, tourists, artificial lake, touring automobile, etc. (There are three stories on this reel, totalling 420'. For further information contact NFA.)

874. TEACHER'S CONVENTION, VANCOUVER, B.C. (1933)
     p.c. Fox Movietonews (Fox #17-991)
     l. 450'   g. 35mm   t. b+w   s. sound
     d.   *
     ph. ASN
     c.s. Fox Movietonews, N.Y.

               "The B.C. Teacher's Convention. 1400 teachers on steps of the Court House. Closer shot on steps. Officials of the Convention. (Named l. to r. in dupe sheet). Short interview by C.G. Brown. Interview with Dean Buchman, Mr. C.G. McGeer, K.C."

875. TEN THOUSAND CHILDREN TAKE PART IN MAY DAY CELEBRATIONS
     AS NEW QUEEN IS CROWNED AMID ROUNDS OF APPLAUSE, NEW
     WESTMINSTER, B.C. (1926)
     p.c. Fox Movietonews (Fox #095.7-B2632)
     l. 40'   g. 35mm   t. b+w   s. si.
     d.   *
     ph. *
     c.s. Fox Movietonews, N.Y.

               "Shots of some children. LS crowning Queen of the May. Maypole dance."

876. THERE IS GREAT ACTIVITY NOW ALONG THE B.C. COAST FOR IT
     IS TIME TO CATCH THE SALMON AND EVERYBODY IS VERY BUSY.
     (1926)
     p.c. Fox Movietonews (Fox #410.02-B5566)
     l. 60'   g. 35mm   t. b+w   s. si.
     d.   *
     ph. Joseph Mandy
     c.s. Fox Movietonews, N.Y.

               "LS small fishing boat. Deck shot on boat. Motorboats operating purse seine. CU dipping fish out of seine. Fishing boats en route to cannery."

877. THEY MUST BE VERY SINCERE ENTHUSIASTS TO FOLLOW EVEN
     THE GOLFING ON SUCH A DAY AS THIS, VANCOUVER, B.C.
     (1925)
     p.c. Fox Movietonews (Fox #713-C7634)
     l. 60'   g. 35mm   t. b+w   s. si.
     d.   *
     ph. *
     c.s. Fox Movietonews, N.Y.

               "British Championship players in group: Monty Hill, Walter Hagen, Freddy Wood and Johnny Farrell. They drive off the tee." Shot in November.

878. THIRTY-FIFTH ANNUAL CALEDONIA GAMES, VANCOUVER, B.C.
     p.c. *
     l.   g. 35mm   t. b+w   s. si.
     d.   *
     ph. *
     c.s. NFB (1920-FG-206)

               "Shot of sack race. Shots of highland fling contest, of boy and girl in period costumes performing a dance in a garden, of awarding of prize. Games celebrate 35th Annual Day of Caledonia Society in Vancouver. Final view of three girls dancing on stage." See Fox Movietone story (Fox 751.13-A4834) - CALEDONIA SOCIETY'S ANNUAL DAY - #116.

879. THOUSANDS OF CHILDREN BENEFIT BY OPENING OF NEW PLAY-
     GROUND, THE GIFT OF GYRO CLUB, VANCOUVER, B.C.   (1923)
     p.c. Fox Movietonews (Fox #322.4-B1710)
     1. 150'   g. 35mm   t. b+w   s. si.
     d.   *
     ph. Len H. Roos
     c.s. Fox Movietonews, N.Y.

                    "Scenes of new park, and Jazz Band playing. Includes shots of R. Rowe Holland,
                    Mayor Tisdall and W.C. Shelly."

880. THOUSANDS THRONG TO SEE CHILDREN'S PAGEANT HELD AMIDST
     THE SPLENDOUR AND BEAUTY OF STANLEY PARK, VANCOUVER, B.C.
     (1920's)
     p.c. Fox Movietonews (Fox #751.13-C-1075)
     1. 50'   g. 35mm   t. b+w   s. si.
     d.   *
     ph. Jos T. Mandy
     c.s. Fox Movietonews, N.Y.

                    "Crowds. LS little pageant representing the old woman who lived in a shoe."

881. THRILLED KIDS GO FOR EXCITING RIDE ON SMALL TRAIN,
     VICTORIA, B.C.   (1939)
     p.c. Universal Newsreel (#11-757)
     1. 83'   g. 35mm   t. b+w   s. si.
     d.   *
     ph. ASN
     c.s. USNA

                    "People wait, get on train. CU engine. Engineer puts coal in. CU coal car.
                    CU steam engine, steam coming out stack, smoke. Engineer starts engine.
                    Four cars, moving away from camera. Travel shot of whole train, puffing
                    along, broadside shot, train steaming away." The cuts contain footage of
                    John W. Armstrong, the builder of the train; he may also be the engineer.

882. THRILLING FINISHES FEATURE ANNUAL BICYCLE RACE IN STANLEY
     PARK OVER 7½ MILE COURSE, VANCOUVER, B.C.   (1926)
     p.c. Fox Movietonews (Fox #755.4-B2799)
     1. 35'   g. 35mm   t. b+w   s. si.
     d.   *
     ph. Herron
     c.s. Fox Movietonews, N.Y.

                    "J.A. Davis wins in 15 minutes, 49.2/5 seconds."

883. THRILLING HILL CLIMBING COMPETITION IS STAGED ON UN-
     CONQUERABLE TRAIL BY DARING MOTORCYCLISTS, LADNER, B.C.
     (1929)
     p.c. Fox Movietonews (Fox #755.3-D0654)
     1. 50'   g. 35mm   t. b+w   s. si.
     d.   *
     ph. Ross Beesley
     c.s. Fox Movietonews, N.Y.

                    "Shot of the hill from base with cyclists starting the attempt. Groups of
                    spectators. Riders attempting the grade. Getting over the bumps. From the
                    top of the hill, riders coming up. LHS of the contest."

884. THROUGH CANADA FROM COAST TO COAST.   (1917)
     p.c. Dept. of Trade and Commerce
          Exhibits and Publicity Bureau, Ottawa
     1. 1 reel   g. 35mm   t. b+w   s. si. w/captions
     d.   *
     ph. *
     c.s. Unknown

                    One of the first tourist promotion films made by the Canadian Government.
                    The description in the first catalogue reads: "A film beginning at Cape Split,
                    N.S., and gradually a trip is made to Victoria. Many beauty spots are fea-
                    tured such as Nipigon Lake territory, the Valley of the Kicking Horse and

the Bow, as well as the most important cities of Canada including Montreal, Toronto, Winnipeg, Calgary, Vancouver and Victoria."

885. THROUGH CANADA'S ROCKIES. (n.d.)
p.c. *
l. approx. 400'   g. 16mm   t. b+w   s. si.
d.   *
ph. *
c.s. Unknown

886. THROUGH LION'S GATE TO PACIFIC PORT, VICE REGAL PARTY
COMMENCES RETURN JOURNEY FROM WEST COAST, VANCOUVER, B.C.
(1927)
p.c. Fox Movietonews (Fox #095.5-B8572)
l. 35'   g. 35mm   t. b+w   s. si.
d.   *
ph. Mitford
c.s. Fox Movietonews, N.Y.

> "Air shot of the SS PRINCESS ALICE arriving in harbour. Air shot of HMCS PATRICIAN, the escort ship, arriving in harbour. LS Lord & Lady Willingdon arriving at Stanley Park. BS Lord & Lady Willingdon greeting soldiers and other deputations including one Hindu."

887. THROUGH MOUNTAIN GATEWAYS. (1930)
p.c. CGMPB
l. 1 reel   g. 35mm   t. b+w   s. si. w/captions
d.   Bill Oliver
ph. Bill Oliver
c.s. Unknown

> This film, about a trip from Spokane, Washington, to the Canadian Rockies, likely contains scenes of British Columbia.

888. THROUGH SCENIC SEAS. (1930's)
p.c. CGMPB
l. approx. 750' g. 35mm   t. b+w   s. si. w/captions
d.   *
ph. *
c.s. NFB (1930-N-158)

> A trip through the Inside Passage from Vancouver to Prince Rupert on a ship of the Canadian Steamship Line. Scenes of ship preparing to leave: Captain telegraphing engine-room, horn blowing, ship leaving with Vancouver skyline in b.g. Passengers aboard ship relaxing and enjoying themselves. In Queen Charlotte Sound the ship meets another steamer. Steamer entering Dean Channel. Ship-to-shore shots of Ocean Falls. Interior and exterior shots of paper mill at Ocean Falls. Children playing on long stairs, studying in school - Japanese kids. Shots of passengers, shipboard activities and amusements. A lovely yacht sails by. Ship-to-shore shots of Prince Rupert. Shots of halibut fleet. Shots of tourists boarding the train for Jasper.

889. THROUGH THE CANADIAN ROCKIES. (1915)
p.c. Essanay Film Mfg. Company
l. about 100'   g. 35mm   t. b+w   s. si.
d.   *
ph. *
c.s. NFA

> This film consists of two 17.5mm bands on 35mm film. Presumably includes scenes in British Columbia.

890. THROUGH THE CLOUDS. (1910)
p.c. Edison Mfg. Co. (Catalogue #6709)
l. 1000'   g. 35mm   t. b+w   s. si.
d.   J. Searle Dawley (?)
ph. Henry Cronjager (?)
c.s. Unknown

> Copyrighted on Nov. 23, 1910, but was never logged in the Edison Mfg. Co.'s Production Log. It may have been photographed during the Edison Co.'s tour

through Western Canada during the summer of 1910 while making promotional films for the CPR. We have only the title to go on, however, which suggests the Rockies and possibly British Columbia.

891a. THROUGH THE NORWAY OF AMERICA. (1920)
    p.c. Dept. of Trade and Commerce
        Exhibits and Publicity Bureau, Ottawa
    l. 1 reel   g. 35mm   t. b+w   s. si. w/captions
    d.   *
    ph. *
    c.s. NFA (28mm), NFB outs (1920-L-39)

        The description in the CGMPB catalogue reads: "This film comprises a trip on the palatial Grand Trunk Pacific steamers from Vancouver to Prince Rupert. This is also a beautiful scenic film." The NFB outs include: The mountainous coast of British Columbia from the deck of the ship. Views of parts of the ship and the ship's wake. Pan of Seattle harbour. Travelling shot of the Victoria waterfront showing freighters, a jetty, etc. HA of the Vancouver skyline with the PRINCE GEORGE sailing into the harbour in the b.g. CU PRINCE GEORGE approaching. Excellent pan of city of Vancouver. Shots of mountains bordering Queen Charlotte Sound, from ship. Mountain with ship's smoke floating across screen. Shot of SS PRINCE RUPERT sailing by. Various shots of passengers. Prince Rupert waterfront. Waters teeming with salmon. Fishermen at work. Pan over Ocean Falls and its pulp mill. Travelling shot of Bella Coola village. Shot of Anyox and its copper smelter. Portland Channel. Various shots of shipboard games in progress.

891b. THE TIMBER INDUSTRY, BRITISH COLUMBIA (subtitled WOOD:
    FROM FOREST TO THE MILL). (1914)
    p.c. Kineto
    l. 89'   g. 35mm   t. b+w (Kinemacolor original) s. si.
    d.   *
    ph. H. Sintzenich
    c.s. BFI (Location #2606A)

        "Lumbermen hew down a large tree in the forest. The trunk is then hauled to the saw mill where it is sawn into planks. These are loaded onto a barge." This is an excerpt from a cinémagazine of a later date, possibly KINETO REVIEW.

        The Vancouver PROVINCE for Sept. 13, 1913, announced that the films made by Mr. Sintzenich while in British Columbia were at the instigation of the Provincial Government and that locations were to be Fraser River Mills, Hastings Saw Mill, and the Canadian Western Lumber Company's "flying machine" near Campbell River on Vancouver Island, an aerial railway that carried the logs across deep gorges in the forest. As well, he spent some time in the bush with the loggers, and filmed the operations there, all in Kinemacolor.

892. TIME HONOURED CORONATION CEREMONIES AND ANCIENT RITES OF MAY
    DAY VIEWED BY MANY LOYAL SUBJECTS, NEW WESTMINSTER, B.C. (1929)
    p.c. Fox Movietonews (Fox #756.6-D0167)
    l. 130'   g. 35mm   t. b+w   s. si.
    d.   *
    ph. *
    c.s. Fox Movietonews, N.Y.

        "Pan of crowd. May pole dance. Dainty Frances Schnoter - Queen of the May! Coronation ceremony."

893. TO THE PORTS OF THE WORLD THROUGH VANCOUVER. (1927-1929)
    p.c. National Harbours Board
    l. 3 reels   g. 35mm   t. b+w   s. si. w/captions
    d.   *
    ph. *
    c.s. NFB (N.H.B.-4-N-1,2&3)

        REEL ONE: Captain George Vancouver's monument. Entrance to Vancouver harbour. The Lions, mountains. LS ship approaching harbour. Siwash Rock. Boathouse at harbour entrance. LS freighter passing. Good pan of harbour filled with many different ships, piers and buildings. Excellent shot of HMS HOOD and HMS REPULSE in the harbour. Pan over downtown section of Van-

couver. *CU hemp rope being made in factory, being wound on drums. Woman operating a loom making woolen products. Pan of huge herd of cattle on a flat prairie, in stockyard pens. LS stockyards. MS tank car unloading oil. Mattresses being sewn and stitched in plant. LS plants along the waterfront. Apple trees in the Okanagan, apples being picked. Apples being packed and placed in warehouse. Good shots of cars driving along the Pacific Highway. Bathers on a very crowded beach. Crowds in Stanley Park. Autos and people entering the park. Pan of mine, ore cars, etc.; concentrators and milling of ore. Good shots of Trail smelter, ore cars and CU silver ingot. (960')*

REEL TWO: LS coal-carrying ore cars in freightyard. Waterfalls in British Columbia powerhouse. Sports fishermen holding up catch. Commercial fishermen hauling in seine nets filled with salmon. Herring being dumped into ship's hold. Man sitting astride giant tuna. Shots of mountain goat, white-tailed deer, mountain sheep and a giant brown bear (dead with hunter atop it). Trapper with dogteam in front of a cabin. Seals diving into the water, swimming away. Good shots of giant Douglas-firs being cut, felled, topped and yarded out of the forests. Logs being dumped from train at the mill. Raft being hauled by tug. Logs being sawn into lumber. Shots of furniture being made. Ships being loaded with lumber. Lovely old three-masted whaler moving through the harbour. New freighter tied up. Shot of original Vancouver wharf and new Ballantyne Pier. Cargo cranes for loading ships. Ships being loaded with cargo. Cars lined up on pier for shipping. More shots of ships loading, boxes, cargo, etc.

REEL THREE: Several shots of workers completing pier on Vancouver waterfront, of tug hauling a section. Canadian Pacific Pier being built. Passenger ship arriving in port, probably the EMPRESS OF ASIA. EMPRESS OF ASIA disembarking passengers and unloading cargo. CU nameplate on freighter's bow: CANADIAN INVENTOR. Excellent shot of 1920-model steam engine ploughing prairie, men seeding prairie with horses. Woman up to breasts in wheatfield. Horses haul binders through the fields of wheat. CU thresher in field threshing wheat, horses hauling wheat to elevators. Freight train crossing prairie. Freight train in Rockies, going through tunnel. Good waterfalls shots. Pan over Vancouver freightyards, grain elevators, one elevator being built. LS waterfront with ships tied up. Wheat in elevator being sampled. Wheat being loaded into ship's hold. Freighter and passenger ship moving out of harbour. CU members of Vancouver Harbour Commission posing: G.H. Kirkpatrick, Chairman; R.E. Beattie, Commissioner; and S.L. Prenter. (980')

894. TOBACCO GROWING IN BRITISH COLUMBIA (TOTEM TOBACCO
      PLANTATION). (1929)
      p.c. B.C. Dept. of Agriculture with the co-operation
            of the B.C. Tobacco Co. Ltd.
      l. 600' approx.   g. 16mm   t. b+w   s. si. w/captions
      d.   *
      ph.   *
      c.s. PABC (Agriculture reels 57 & 58)

            Depicts the growing, curing and processing of tobacco at the Totem Tobacco plantation owned by McKercher's Ltd. at Sumas Prairie. REEL ONE shows employees' dwellings, shack-like barracks, readying the field for the crop and fertilizing the soil. The seedlings are shown in the greenhouse, being transplanted and being planted out. Growth at stages of four to six weeks is shown. Workers top the plants and pinch out the suckers. 30-40 days after the topping the plants are picked by the split-stalk method and hung over wooden laths to dry. REEL TWO shows plants being loaded onto horse-drawn wagons and taken back to kilns where the curing begins. After curing, the leaves are taken to the processing plant, graded and sorted and steam processed. The leaves are then baled and driven off to the factory in a truck. The employees return to work after lunch.

            This very good film shows every step as it is carried out over a season, all the buildings, sheds and processing areas required, as well as interesting vignettes of the employees and their living conditions. Reel One contains 350'; Reel Two 250'.

895. TOLAN BEATS WYCKOFF IN RECORD RUN - MICHIGAN FLASH SETS
      NEW MARK - VANCOUVER, B.C. (1931)
      p.c. Universal Newsreel (V.3-R.71)
      l. 32'   g. 35mm   t. b+w   s. si.
      d.   *
      ph.   Motion Skreen Adz, Ltd.
      c.s. USNA

896. TOP O' THE WORLD. (1921)
     p.c. Dept. of Trade and Commerce
          Exhibits and Publicity Bureau, Ottawa
     1. 1 reel   g. 35mm   t. b+w   s. si. w/captions
     d. *
     ph. *
     c.s. Unknown

> "A film depicting the activities of a party of trail riders and alpinists in the Mount Robson section of Jasper National Park together with views of the outstanding scenic features of this picturesque mountain region." Although Jasper National Park is in Alberta, Mt. Robson is in British Columbia; therefore some of the scenes maybe in British Columbia.

897. TOP OF THE WORLD. (1937)
     p.c. ASN (#B707)
     1.   g. 35mm and 16mm t. b+w s.
     d. *
     ph. *
     c.s. Unknown

> Score by Horace Lapp.

> Produced for the CPR, about Banff. (The NFB Archives has a copy of a film about pulp making called TOP OF THE WORLD, but I suspect that there has been a cross-up in titling. See film titled PULP MAKING. C.B.)

898. TO REALIZE VICTORIA. (not actual title, which is lost)
     and PATHE NEWS, CANOE TRIP DOWN COWICHAN RIVER. (early
     1930's)
     p.c. Motion Skreen Adz for the Victoria and Island
          Publicity Bureau
     1. approx. 800'   g. 35mm   t. b+w on tinted stock s. si. w/captions
     d. *
     ph. Pathè News & Motion Screen Adz.
     c.s. BCPM

> The film begins with a quote from Rudyard Kipling: "To realize Victoria you must take all that the eye admires most, - in Bournemouth, Torquay, The Isle of Wight, The Happy Valley, Hong Kong, The Doon, Sorrento, and Camps Bay, add reminiscences of the Thousand Islands and arrange the whole. The Bay of Naples, with some Himalayas for the background."

> PRINCESS KATHLEEN, CPR ferry, sails into Victoria's Inner Harbour. Shots of Empress Hotel from bow of KATHLEEN with passengers in f.g. The ferry pulls alongside. Aerial shot of Empress Hotel from Belmont Building, pans out over Inner Harbour to Parliament Buildings and CPR ferries. Shot from veranda of Empress out onto Causeway and people and ferries. Looking up Government street along the Causeway from the corner of Belleville and Government, with cars and pedestrians going by. Shot of Butchart's house with a rose arbour in f.g. Pond with trellis in b.g. and Cupid on pedestal in pond. Two little kids in bathing suits play in a rock-built pond. LS bridge and swans in Beacon Hill Park, CU swans. Oak Bay golf course with CPR ferry in b.g. Man fishing in a river with creel and fly, pulling in a fish which he unhooks and places in his creel. Man fishing from clinker-built boat beside a man standing in hip-waders fishing as well. The boat ashore, the two men lift four salmon out and place them on the beach. A powerboat roars across a bay. Two men and a woman in a powerboat. One man and two women in powerboat. Man and woman examining petroglyphs on a rock face. Two small fawns feeding out of a bucket. Six people riding horses along a stone beach.

> PATHE NEWS, Pacific Northwest Edition. "Indian Canoemen pilot venturesome tourists through forty miles of thrills down the Cowichan River." Indian men ready two canoes at a dock, tourists getting ready to board. Canoe in white water - various shots of whites and Indians. The canoe is portaged over a log jam and past some falls. Canoes run the rapids, good CU's of both bowmen and sternmen of canoes; they seem to be fairly old. END PATHE. Sunset over Inner Harbour, ferries, Sooke Hills, etc.

899. TOTEM LAND. (1930)
    p.c. ASN
    1. 1 reel   g. 16mm and 35mm t. b+w and tinted s. si. w/captions
    d.   *
    ph. J.B. Scott
    c.s. BCPM Eth., NFA (82 (tinted), 3761 & 3762)

> *A B.E. Norrish Production. Edited and titled by Terry Ramsaye.
> Filmed on the west coast of Vancouver Island at Friendly Cove, Quatsino and
> Fort Rupert. Mr. & Mrs. George Hunt of Fort Rupert perform the dancing and
> exhibit masks, baskets, etc. The description in the Motion Picture Catalogue
> of the National Museum of Canada for 1933 reads: "Several Indian villages on
> Vancouver Island, and their people, are shown in this film. The first pic-
> tures show the rugged coastline and are followed by scenes in one of the
> Nootka villages. Here we see some of the totem poles that remain and one
> of the native graveyards. Other views included are: totem poles at Fort
> Rupert, and Indian carving a totem pole with the primitive tools of his an-
> cestors, dances in ceremonial costume, the art of basket-making, and digging
> clams along the shore." Presented to the National Museum by the CPR.*

> *The copies at the NFA and BCPM are about 350' long on 16mm. The NFA also
> possesses about 250' of out-footage. This film may have originally been
> titled LAND OF TOTEMS with ASN production Number B629.*

900. TOTEM POLE VILLAGES OF THE SKEENA. (1925-27)
    p.c. National Museums of Canada
    1. 1 reel   g. 35mm   t. b+w   s. si. w/captions
    d.   Harlan I. Smith
    ph. Harlan I. Smith
    c.s. Unknown

> *One of three films about the Skeena River Indians made by Harlan Smith for
> the National Museum of Canada. It likely contains scenes from both the upper
> and lower Skeena Valley, of towns and villages such as Hazelton, Kitwanga,
> Skeena Crossing, Gytsegucla, Kwinitsa, Skeena, etc. See THE TSIMSHIAN INDIANS
> OF THE SKEENA RIVER OF BRITISH COLUMBIA.*

901. TOTEM TOBACCO PLANTATION. (1929)
    p.c. B.C. Dept. of Agriculture with the co-operation
         of the B.C. Tobacco Co. Ltd.
    1. approx. 600' g. 16mm   t. b+w   s. si. w/captions
    d.   *
    ph. *
    c.s. PABC

> *Identical to TOBACCO GROWING IN BRITISH COLUMBIA, except that the opening
> shots present a picture of the McKercher Co. executives and give a plug for
> the company. Nowhere on this print is the British Columbia Dept. of Agricul-
> ture mentioned, although the government may have produced the film. Perhaps
> McKercher's put up the money, or some of it.*

902. TOUR OF B.C. INTERIOR. (1920's)
    p.c. *
    1. 175'   g. 16mm   t. b+w   s. si.
    d.   *
    ph. *
    c.s. NFA

903. A TOUR OF THE DOMINIONS BY THE RIGHT HON. L.S. AMERY,
    M.P. (SECRETARY OF STATE FOR DOMINION AFFAIRS). (1928)
    p.c. *
    1. 7,271'   g. 35mm   t. b+w & tinted s. si.
    d.   *
    ph. Captain W. Brass
    c.s. BFI (Location #498J)

> *See REEL 8: At Victoria, January 6, 1928. Visiting the Parliament Build-
> ings. Visit to the new dry dock. Scenes in Vancouver harbour and at the
> docks. Mr. Amery inspects a CPR locomotive. By train through snow-covered
> Rockies. Total British Columbia footage - 458'.*

904. TOURING AUSTRALIAN RUGBY TEAM BEATS REPS 9 - 6 IN
     RUGBY, VANCOUVER. (1925)
     p.c. Fox Movietonews (?)
     l.   g. 35mm   t. b+w   s. si.
     d.   *
     ph. ASN
     c.s. NFB (1920-FG-157)

               Section of CANADA CAPSULE NO. 10. "Shots of game underway, various angles
               and CU's showing roughness. Good group shot of Australian "Warahtahs"
               Rugby team. Good shot of old man playing violin at aftergame celebrations."

905. TRACTOR AT WORK. (late 20's/early 30's)
     p.c. *
     l. approx. 400'   g. 16mm   t. b+w   s. si.
     d.   *
     ph. *
     c.s. PABC (Forestry reel 74)

               This film shows the many uses of Caterpillar tractors, including supplying
               power for pneumatic drills and air hammers, ditching, excavation work, and
               hauling, both on clear ground and snow-covered terrain. Also includes shots
               of a portable crane loading steel onto a truck, and a railway car. Shots
               also of an old portable loader and a steam engine passing at speed. This
               film may not have been filmed in B.C.

906. TRAFALGAR CELEBRATION, VICTORIA, B.C.   (1932)
     p.c. Fox Movietonews (Fox #16-279)
     l. 700'   g. 35mm   t. b+w   s. sound
     d.   *
     ph. ASN
     c.s. Fox Movietonews, N.Y.

               "Inspection of the Guard of Honour by the Lt. Gov. of B.C. Address by Lt.
               Gov. Pan while talking. Bugle calls - taps. Drill by the Honour Guard.
               Sailors marching. Additional shots, same." (NOTE: Lt. Gov. at this time
               was J.W.F. Johnson)

907. TRAIL, B.C. - VARIOUS SCENES. (1920's-1930's)
     p.c. *
     l.   g. 16mm   t. b+w   s.
     d.   *
     ph. Various, including Jack Lorrie
     c.s. via Pacific Cinémathèque, Vancouver

               The Trail Historical Society has been active in collecting early motion pic-
               tures made in the Kootenays, and can be contacted for more information through
               Pacific Cinémathèque in Vancouver. The collection now includes about 3000'
               of film shot by former Trail police chief Jack Lorrie. One of these reels
               shows the arrival of Peter Veregin in Brilliant in 1924, and consists of
               200-300'. Information regarding the contents of the other reels can be ob-
               tained on request.

908. TRAIL, B.C. AND ENVIRONS. (1937)
     p.c. private
     l. 200'   g. 8mm   t. b+w   s. si.
     d.   *
     ph. *
     c.s. via Pacific Cinémathèque, Vancouver

               Paddlewheeler on Kootenay Lake, SS NASOOKIN. Bus driving onto Kootenay Lake
               ferry at Gray Creek. Scenes of the lake from the ferry. Train trip from
               Balfour to Nelson composed of shots taken through the window while speeding
               by; and likewise on from Nelson to Castlegar. Shots include bridges, river,
               town, Bonnington Falls Dam and Power station, Cora Lyn Dam and powerstation,
               and Brilliant Dam and powerstation, all passing very quickly. Town of Trail
               after a heavy snowstorm, showing city street, buildings, houses and trees.
               Trail Coronation Celebration of 1937, featuring Maple Leaf Band, floats,
               kids marching, other bands, all in a grand parade. Summer scenes of Trail,
               showing streets, theatres, buildings, various businessmen and friends. (1937)

909. TRAIL, B.C. - THE METALLURGICAL MECCA OF CANADA. (1919)
    p.c. *
    l. approx. 200'   g. 35mm   t. b+w   s. si.
    d.   *
    ph. *
    c.s. NFA (#4565)

        Shots of the Trail smelter and the Kimberley mine.

910. TRAIL BLAZING AND LOGGING (?). (1930's)
    p.c. Caterpillar Tractor Co. Ltd.
    l. approx. 400'   g. 16mm   t. b+w   s. si. w/captions
    d.   *
    ph. *
    c.s. PABC

        *"Showing the extensive use to which Caterpillar tractors and graders can be
        put in preparing an area for logging by putting in roads and fire trails.
        It also illustrates the wide variety of jobs performed by "cata" in actual
        logging work." A Caterpillar Tractor advertising film. It includes scenes
        in Australia and Carolina, and may or may not contain sequences filmed in
        British Columbia.*

911. TRAIL RIDERS OF THE CANADIAN ROCKIES HOLD FIRST POW-WOW
    IN HONOUR OF TOM WILSON, A PIONEER, NEAR FIELD, B.C. (1924)
    p.c. Fox Movietonews (Fox #728-A3882)
    l.   g. 35mm   t. b+w   s. si.
    d.   *
    ph. Len H. Roos
    c.s. Fox Movietonews, N.Y.

        *"Trail riders around tablet of Tom Wilson. Unveiling monument of Tom Wilson.
        Group around tablet. CU of Tom Wilson. Trail riders camp through trees,
        Yoho glacier in b.g. CU girls marking mileage on map. LS through trees of
        trail riders circling Indians during ceremonial dance. Closer view of
        Indians dancing with trail riders circling. Trail riders leaving camp. Jas.
        Brewster pinning Trail Rider button on Miss Marguerite Simpson. CU of Miss
        Simpson showing button. LS camp."*

912. TRAILS OF THE SOURDOUGH. (prob. 1921)
    p.c. Grant Trunk Pacific R.R. (later CNR)
    l. 2 reels   g. 35mm   t. b+w   s. si. w/captions
    d.   *
    ph. *
    c.s. NFB (1920-N-106-2)

        *"Northward, along Canada's Pacific coast, weaves a trail of romance and ad-
        venture where the sourdoughs of the "Trail of '98" struggled to reach the
        ElDorado of North America. In the footsteps of these men of iron journey
        latter day adventurers in their palatial steamers. Excellent shots of
        steamer PRINCE RUPERT moving slowly across screen. Pan over Vancouver and
        various shots of passengers amusing themselves aboard ship. Shot of halibut
        fishing fleet in Prince Rupert harbour, of freighter loading fish. Shots of
        Prince Rupert street scene. Customs official examining luggage on platform
        of station as train stands nearby. Good shot of ship sailing away, of sky,
        etc." The remainder of this reel, which is called PART ONE, is about Alaska.
        The whereabouts of PART TWO is not known.*

913. TRAILS TO THE WILDERNESS. (1930)
    p.c. CGMPB
    l. 1 reel   g. 35mm   t. b+w   s. si. w/captions
    d.   Bill Oliver
    ph. Bill Oliver
    c.s. NFA & NFB

        *Produced for the National Parks Bureau. "A saddle-pony trip through Jasper
        National Park, Alberta, visiting the famed Tonquin Valley and Amethyst Lakes
        and ending at Mount Robson in British Columbia." (NFA copy is approx. 400'
        on 16mm and NFB copy is approx. 350' on 16mm)*

914. TRAIN CLIMBING MOUNTAIN WITH THREE ENGINES. (1901?)
    p.c. Edison Mfg Co. (?)
    l. 85'   g. 35mm   t. b+w   s. si.
    d.   *
    ph. *
    c.s. Unknown

                    *This film sounds suspiciously like the Edison Co.'s ROYAL TRAIN WITH DUKE
                    AND DUCHESS OF YORK CLIMBING MOUNT HECTOR. There is no further information;
                    check ROYAL TRAIN... for possible details.*

915. TRAIN PLAY. (1930's)
    p.c. private
    l. approx. 25'   g. 8mm   t. b+w   s. si.
    d.   John W. Bowdery
    ph. John W. Bowdery
    c.s. via Pacific Cinémathèque, Vancouver

                    *Contains part of a story filmed by Mr. Bowdery about 2 boys who ride off in
                    a freight car. Includes good shots of a station, locomotives, box cars, and
                    a CPR train moving at high speed.*

916. TRAIN RIDE THROUGH CANADA. (1925)
    p.c. Fox Movietonews (Fox #462-A6542)
    l. 186'   g. 35mm   t. b+w   s. si.
    d.   *
    ph. *
    c.s. Fox Movietonews, N.Y.

                    *"Various shots of engine before start and forest and country through which
                    they passed."*

917. TRANS CANADA AIR LINES (TCA) INAUGURATES ITS FIRST PASSENGER
    TRANSCONTINENTAL SERVICE, VANCOUVER AND MONTREAL, CANADA. (1939)
    p.c. Hearst Metrotone News; Roll No. 7, Can No. 1002
    l.   g. 35mm   t. b+w   s. sound
    d.   *
    ph. ASN
    c.s. Hearst Metrotone News, N.Y.

                    Shots of TCA planes taking off and landing between Montreal and Vancouver.

918. TRANS CANADA AIR PAGEANT IN VANCOUVER (1930) AND
    MISCELLANEOUS AERIAL SHOTS.
    p.c. private
    l. approx. 450' g. 16mm   t. b+w   s. si.
    d.   *
    ph. W.M. Archibald
    c.s. NFA, Ottawa

                    *Trans Canada Air Pageant at Vancouver International Airport, 1930. CF-AQM,
                    a barnstorming plane (note bracing pyramid atop wings for extra strength)
                    performs aerobatics. Shots of observers. Note hangar with roof sign:
                    RUTLEDGE AIR SERVICE. CF-AGO, a Puss Moth, on runway. The three RCAF Siskin
                    fighters take off and, flying in formation, perform wonderful rolls, dives
                    and flypasts.*

                    *Aerial views of mountains below while flying, and another plane flying by.
                    Scene on the ground at Grand Forks, with a man signalling a plane, approach-
                    ing to land, with a handkerchief. Single biplane performing aerobatics at
                    Vancouver International Airport, CF-AOC. Man in uniform on runway and other
                    observers. U.S. plane flies over, NC 7212. Stunt flying and flypast by
                    Lockheed Vega with streamlined wheel pants. Aerobatics by monoplane CF-AGK,
                    also with pyramid brace. Three U.S. biplanes take off and fly in formation.
                    Man on runway in white: Pat Reid, Imperial Oil Company's Aviation Section
                    Sales Chief. Lineup of Cirrus Moths. Siskin flypast. Man in blazer walks
                    into camera: George Ross, General Secretary of the Air League of Canada.
                    Puss Moth CF-AGO and poseur on runway. Observers, old car, clowns - possibly
                    prelude to a barnstorming act. (Apparently stuntmen would often dress up as
                    backwoods hicks discovering aeroplanes for the first time. They would fiddle
                    around with the propeller and instruments and eventually get the planes off*

the ground, flying erratically all the while, with many near misses, before coming down again.)

An RCAF Ford Trimotor lands on the runway. Wonderful aerial shots of the mountains and of CF-AAM, a Fokker Super Universal, flying very close beside the plane containing the camera, moving in and out, forward and backward according to the air. Gives an exhilerating sense of flight. Aerial view of house. See No. 919.

919. TRANS CANADA AIR PAGEANT (1930) AND MISCELLANEOUS
     AEROPLANES.
     p.c. private
     l. approx. 450'   g. 16mm   t. colour and b+w   s. si.
     d.   *
     ph. W.M. Archibald
     c.s. NFA, Ottawa

> *(W.M. Archibald lived in Creston during the 30's and worked for Cominco. He was a keen pilot and was in charge of Cominco's fleet of aircraft.)*
>
> *b+w: Puss Moth, CF-AGT, owned by W.M. Archibald, at Creston. The plane lands on his private field and taxis to a good broadside stop. British consuls sponsored "Autogyro" flies overhead (at Grand Forks?) RCAF pilot Bill Riddell stands in front of his Siskin fighter at Vancouver International Airport during the 1930 Trans Canada Air Pageant. A second unidentified pilot poses, then walks toward the camera. MS officer walking on runway. Two civilians and man with a balloon. The three RCAF Siskin fighters fly in formation over Vancouver International Airport, including two good flypasts. This aerobatic team was famous and popular in its day, and performed across Canada during the 1930 Air Pageant. They arrived in Vancouver for the opening of the Airport on the last leg of their trip in 1930.*
> *colour: deHavilland Dragon Rapide, twin-engined biplane owned by Cominco, lands at airfield in Creston. Dept. of Transport Lockheed 10-A, CF-CCT, on the field at Creston, taking off and flying past.*
> *b+w: W.M. Archibald standing beside his Puss Moth CF-AGT in a field at Grand Forks. Two other planes are lined up: a Fairchaild 51, G-CAIH, and an unidentified plane, CF-AHH. A man named Bennett parachutes to earth. Planes take off. Family portrait beside Puss Moth CF-AGT - three generations: mother, grandmother and daughter, and Page McPhee, Cominco's flying instructor. Mother alone. Cirrus Moth owned by Cominco, on pontoons on the flooded Creston Flats in June or July, taxiing away from camera, then toward, then taking off. Archibald daughter posing beside two Cirrus Moths belonging to Cominco, and posing in cockpit. Pan across CF-AGO. Plane taxis away. Grand Forks. The planes in the Trans Canada Air Pageant stopped in Grand Forks after flying through the Rockies in 1930. These are scenes of people visiting the planes in a field outside town. Note Puss Moth, the three Siskins and the Autogyro. The planes take off and land. The Autogyro flies past. Formation flying by the three Siskins with some nice rolls, sun gleaming off wings. A single plane performs aerobatics. Autogyro flies overhead. Excellent aerobatics by a single plane at Vancouver International Airport in 1930. Various shots of Vancouver International Airport at 1930 opening: crowds, buildings, hangars, planes from the Pageant lined up as well as many visiting planes. A plane taxis away. Dragon Rapide taking off from airfield in Creston. Good shots of monoplane in flight*

920. TRANSCONTINENTAL PANORAMA OF THE POST OFFICE OF THE DOMINION OF
     CANADA. (before 1935)
     p.c. *
     l. 2 reels - 24 min.   g. 35mm   t. b+w   s. si.
     d.   *
     ph. *
     c.s. Unknown

> *"How the mail passes from East to West across Canada. Sorting process and modes of transport."*

921. TRAPPER AND DOGSLED IN SELKIRK MOUNTAINS. (1925?)
     p.c. Pathé News
     l.   g. 35mm   t. b+w   s. si.
     d.   probably Byron Harmon
     ph.   probably Byron Harmon
     c.s. NFB (1920-FG-175)

> *"Various shots of trapper and dogteam pulling sled through deep snow in Sel-*
> *kirk Mountains, taken from various angles, of trapper and dogs emerging from*
> *forest, moving through deep snow in valley, unloading fox furs from sled,*
> *entering cabin all but buried in snow." According to Byron Harmon's grand-*
> *daughter, the photographer went on a trip in 1925 through the Selkirk Range*
> *and photographed a trapper and his dogteam of Mackenzie River huskies in 13'*
> *of snow. Byron shot about 1000', including scenes of men specially employed*
> *by the CPR to shovel the snow off the roofs of its mountain hotels. See*
> *UNPRECEDENTED SNOWFALL IN THE CANADIAN ROCKIES BLANKETS THE FOREST WITH A*
> *DAZZLING MANTLE.*

922. TRAPPER IN SNOW IN THE SELKIRK MOUNTAINS OF B.C.
     (1926)
     p.c. Fox Movietonews (Fox #39-660)
     l. 75'   g. 35mm   t. b+w   s. si.
     d.   Byron Harmon (?)
     ph. Byron Harmon (?)
     c.s. Fox Movietonews, N.Y.

> *"Canadian North West trapper loading dog-sled with furs. LHS of dog team*
> *going through snow. Dog fight between huskies. Team arrives and trapper*
> *unloads at hut. Snow scenes with dog sled going through. Trapper and sled*
> *fall into a drift. This was taken from Silent Library 410.02/B-1195."*

923. TRAPPING SALMON ON THE FRASER RIVER, BRITISH COLUMBIA.
     (pre 1910)
     p.c. CPR (?)
     l. 75'   g. 35mm   t. b+w   s. si.
     d.   *
     ph. *
     c.s. Unknown

> *"Salmon being caught in their thousands by this method, being emptied from*
> *their nets by fishermen." George Kleine Catalogue, 1910, p.72.*

924. TRAVEL SCENES IN BRITISH COLUMBIA AND OTHER PROVINCES.
     (1939)
     p.c. private
     l. approx. 400'   g. 16mm   t. colour s. si.
     d.   *
     ph. Mr. & Mrs. T.G.S. Chambers
     c.s. NFA, Ottawa

> *1939 - The famous Mr. Charles Jones in Burnaby with his birds and family.*
> *(Mr. Jones had an uncanny relationship with local birds which did not fear*
> *either him or his family. Many amateur film buffs took their cameras to his*
> *backyard to watch him feeding birds from his mouth and letting them perch on*
> *his arms). Jericho Beach Golf Course. Theodore Phipps. T.G.S. Chambers.*
> *Patullo Bridge. Kamloops, looking up South Thompson. Kamloops, looking up*
> *North Thompson. Wild Sheep. Seven Sisters and lake near Lake Louise.*
> *Emerald Lake near Field.*

> *July and August 1939 - Sir Theodore Chambers KBE. Emerald Lake. CPR coming*
> *up from Field, drawn by Hudson locomotive. Kicking Horse Falls. Mount Mac-*
> *Donald. Looking down onto Field. Silver Falls near Winnipeg. T.G.S. Cham-*
> *bers fishing. Perch, pickerel and catfish. LaVerendrye monument. Fort*
> *Garry Gate, Winnipeg. Tame chipmunk. Golf course outside Winnipeg. Royal*
> *Train arriving. King standing behind Queen. Leaving Winnipeg at 20 mph into*
> *the sunset.*

925. TRAVELLERS SEE ODD SIGHTS IN INDIAN VILLAGES ALONG THE
     COAST ON WAY FROM VANCOUVER TO ALASKA, ALERT BAY, B.C.
     (1926)
     p.c. Fox Movietonews (Fox #007.434-B3602)
     l. 40'   g. 35mm   t. b+w   s. si.
     d.   *
     ph. Joseph T. Mandy
     c.s. Fox Movietonews, N.Y.

               "Semi CU and close shot of the coastline steamer PRINCESS CHARLOTTE. Indian
               totems of tree burial. Pathetic remains of child's toys in charred funeral
               pyre. LS of Indian totem pole."

926. TRAVELOGUE OF VICTORIA, B.C.
     p.c. Pathéscope
     l.   g. 28mm   t. b+w   s. si.
     d.   *
     ph. *
     c.s. Unknown

               "The climate of Victoria more nearly approaches that of England than any
               other part of the Dominion. We expect to see English rose gardens and Eng-
               lish hedges, and we are not disappointed. In this travelogue we also learn
               something of the architectural beauty of the city's public buildings and
               the activities of the downtown business sections." From the Province of
               Ontario Film Catalogue, May 1927.

927. TREATING SEED GRAIN - C.I.L.
     p.c. B.C. Dept. of Agriculture
     l. approx. 25'   g. 16mm   t. colour   s. si.
     d.   *
     ph. *
     c.s. PABC

               Part of a reel containing five other items, beginning with the Bouchie Lake
               Fair of 1948. TREATING SEED GRAIN is badly over exposed and faded, and shows
               Mr. T. Leach demonstrating how seed grain is treated chemically to prevent
               harm to it during germination.

928. TREBITCH LINCOLN (NOW CHAO KUNG), BUDDHIST MONK,
     ARRIVES IN CANADA WITH HIS DISCIPLES, VANCOUVER,
     B.C. (1934)
     p.c. Paramount (Lib. #3893) NL 1240
     l.   g. 35mm   t. b+w   s. sound
     d.   *
     ph. *
     c.s. Sherman Grinberg

               "General view and semi-pan of Lincoln on deck of ship with followers dressed
               in robes. CU Lincoln speaking. He tells of so many lies being written about
               him, that his disciples represent 5 nations who live in harmony and friend-
               ship with each other. He hopes to establish in the Western world the same
               happiness, and extends good wishes for the Canadian people's welfare, pros-
               perity and peace."

929. THE TRIANGLE TOUR. (before 1927)
     p.c. CNR (?)
     l. 921'   g. 35mm   t. b+w   s. si.
     d.   *
     ph. *
     c.s. NFB (#1930-N-159)

               "A pictorial jaunt through the wonder playground of Canada's alpine province."
               Vancouver scenery. Canadian Steamship Line steamer on way up the coast.
               Activities of passengers on board. Ocean Falls, and its paper mill, from
               the ship. Coastline from ship steaming north. Prince Rupert - pan from
               ship. Sailing into harbour. Train at Prince Rupert CN station. Travelling
               by train along the Skeena River. Totem poles and Indians at Kitwanga.
               Bulkley River and canyon. Indians fishing at Moricetown in traditional way.
               Train shots, tunnel. Rockies. Mt. Robson. Train enters Jasper station."

930. THE TRIANGULAR TOUR. (pre 1939)
    p.c. *
    1. 1 reel (15 min.) g. 35mm t. b+w s. si. w/captions
    d. *
    ph. *
    c.s. Unknown

> *This is apparently NOT the same film as THE TRIANGLE TOUR. It is not easy to sort out the confusion because the film listed as THE TRIANGLE TOUR in the NFB Archives is a travelogue about a trip from Vancouver to Prince Rupert to Edmonton via CNR ships and trains, although the famous "Triangle Tour" was a CPR run between Vancouver, Victoria and Seattle. THE TRIANGULAR TOUR might be about either of them, and since no known copy exists, it may never be known which "tour" is depicted. One thing is sure: the film was about British Columbia.*

931. A TRIP OVER THE ROCKIES AND SELKIRK MOUNTAINS.
    (1910)
    p.c. Edison Mfg. Co. Co. (Catalogue #6701)
    1. 150'   g. 35mm t. b+w   s. si.
    d.   J. Searle Dawley
    ph. Henry Cronjager
    c.s. NFA

> *This documentary-type film was made by Edison's troupe during their trip across Canada shooting promotional films for the CPR during the summer of 1910. All but one of the others are dramatic shorts but, alas, most are lost. This one shows a train approaching Field, the CPR's "Imperial Limited", and then presents various views of the Rockies. Unfortunately it is incomplete, the original having been 440' long. It was begun on July 10 and finished on August 12 and copyrighted on November 8, 1910.*

932. A TRIP THROUGH THE RANGELANDS IN BRITISH COLUMBIA. (1930?)
    p.c. B.C. Dept. of Agriculture (reel 29)
    1. approx. 350' g. 16mm t. b+w   s. si. w/captions
    d. *
    ph. *
    c.s. PABC

> *Mr. J.B. Munro, Deputy Minister of Agriculture, beside some beehives. Mr. Helmer, manager of Nicola Lake Ranching Co., shaking hands with visitor at a gate. Herd of purebred shorthorn bulls, cowboys working bulls. Steers in a field ready for shipping. Men look at Shorthorn bulls imported from England and a British Columbia bull. Clydesdale stallion. Pigs walking through a stream. Nicola Lake. At Guichon Ranch a cowboy in chaps plays at being a wild west gunman and fires his pistol off until arrested by a man with a car. Cars leaving Guichon Ranch bound for Douglas Lake. Chuckwagon hauled past camera by four horses. Pan Douglas Lake, quarter horses feeding on the range. Pan across Douglas Lake Ranch buildings from a hill. Meeting of the British Columbia Shorthorn Breeders' Association at Douglas Lake Ranch, posing. Mr. Ward, manager, and Alex Davie of Ladner parading past camera. Members proceed to lunch. Three cars drive through a swollen creek - "A cure for squeaky wheels." Members look over stock, including a Shorthorn bull imported from England. Group of members including Mr. and Mrs. Ward. Herd of purebred Shorthorn cows with calves. Shot of a roundup - a cowboy and a calf. Stray cattle. Chapperton Lake and surrounding country - pan.*

> *The film ends with the following admonitions: "The Provincial Department of Agriculture is organized for the benefit of the farmer and the welfare of the province. The department is yours. Make use of it." and "On behalf of the farming industry we welcome the new settler. It is your duty as a neighbour to help him."*

933. "TROTZKY", LARGEST BEAR IN CAPTIVITY, PERFORMS STUNTS FOR
    HIS KEEPER AT DINNER TIME, GETTING EXTRA TREAT. (1928)
    p.c. Fox Movietonews (Fox #411.34-C8342)
    1. 90'   g. 35mm t. b+w   s. si.
    d. *
    ph. Ross Beesley
    c.s. Fox Movietonews, N.Y.

> *Bear performs tricks.*

934. TRUMPETER SWANS. (1919)
    p.c. Dept. of Trade and Commerce
         Exhibits and Publicity Branch, Ottawa
    l. 1 reel   g. 35mm   t. b+w   s. si. w/captions
    d.   *
    ph. *
    c.s. Unknown

> *"The trumpeter swan is the greatest American bird in size and has long been
> considered to be verging on extinction. The flock shown in this picture
> winters in Canada and consists of about nineteen birds. One of the greatest
> and rarest wild fowl pictures ever taken. A print of this film was presented
> to the United States National Museum by the Government of the Dominion of
> Canada." This was the first motion picture made of these swans in the world,
> swimming, feeding and walking on the ice at a small mountain lake in British
> Columbia.*

935. THE TSIMSHIAN INDIANS OF BRITISH COLUMBIA/THE TSIMSHIAN
     INDIANS OF THE SKEENA RIVER OF BRITISH COLUMBIA. (1925-27)
    p.c. National Museum of Canada
    l. approx. 400'   g. 35mm (16mm available) t. b+w s. si. w/captions
    d.   Harlan I. Smith
    ph. Harlan I. Smith
    c.s. National Museum of Man & NFA (#3781)

> *"The beautiful Skeena valley of northern British Columbia, along the line of
> the Canadian National Railway, is the home of the Tsimshian Indians. They
> are shown gaffing salmon as they ascend the rapids and later drying them,
> picking and preserving berries, and gathering other plant food (wild cow
> parsnip). Supplies and various burdens are carried by women and dogs, and
> infants are carried by women in cradles hung on their backs. Among the handi-
> crafts shown are basket making and spinning of mountain goat wool. The totem
> poles, grave houses, and costumed dances of these Indians are great tourist
> attractions."*

> *There are also various views of the Skeena River near Hazelton and Hagwelgate.
> Villages shown are Kitwanga, Gytsegucla, Hazelton, Skeena Crossing. There
> are scenes of men working with cedar making a pole, a box, and a bowl, and
> women making baskets and spinning mountain goat wool with shots of final re-
> sults. Good shots of totem poles and dancers dancing, man drumming. Ref-
> erence at the end to the Dominion Government's actions in saving and re-
> erecting some of the totem poles, and reproducing one of them on a ten-cent
> postage stamp.*

936. TUGBOAT PRINCESS. (1935-36)
    p.c. Central Films, Ltd.
    l. 68 min. (6151') g. 35mm t. b+w   s. sound
    d.   David Selman
    ph. William C. Thompson & William Beckway
    c.s. NFA

> *Canadian producer, Kenneth J. Bishop;   l.p. Walter C. Kelly, Valerie
> script, Robert Watson, based on a story   Hobson, Edith Fellows, Clyde
> by Dalton Trumbo and Isador Bernstein;   Cook, Lester Matthews, Reginald
> editor, William Austin; Columbia over-   Hincks, Arthur Kerr, Arthur Legge-
> seer, Jack Fier.   Willis, and Ethel Reese-Burns.*

> *A Quota Quickie made for Columbia Pictures by Central Films in December, 1935,
> and January, 1936, and the second of 12 Central Films made in Victoria. Much
> of the film was photographed at Victoria's Outer Wharf and at an old tumble-
> down shack on Belleville Street close to the site of the Pendray Soap Works.
> Interiors were filmed at the Central Films studio barn in the Willows Exhib-
> ition grounds. Shooting took 16 days and was completed on January 6. TUG-
> BOAT PRINCESS was copyrighted in the United States by Columbia Pictures on
> October 2, 1936, and was first exhibited in British Columbia, at the Dominion
> Theatre in Victoria, from Feb. 2 to Feb 4, 1937. Before it was shown in
> British Columbia the Provincial Censor required that the following caption
> be inserted at the beginning of both the film and its trailer:*
> *SCENES DEPICTING WELFARE WORKERS AND COURTS IN THIS PICTURE ARE IMPOSSIBLE IN
> BRITISH COLUMBIA. THE LAW REQUIRES NOTIFICATION TO ALL PARTIES AND SWORN
> EVIDENCE PROVING NEGLECT BEFORE COMMITTAL OF ANY CHILD.*

The storyline is:

Captain Zack (Walter C. Kelly) lives with his trusty crew, engineer Steve (Clyde Cook) and first mate Bob (Lester Mathews) and a young orphan girl Judy (Edith Fellows), on a tugboat (PRINCESS JUDY) which has seen better days. Indeed, the old craft is so out of date that it is difficult for Zack to find work. Judy breaks a leg, and in order to pay the hospital bills Zack is forced to mortgage his boat to his arch rival Darling (Reginald Hincks).

Back in 1916 Zack once beat Darling in a race out to a crippled ship, winning $10,000 from him in the process, and they have been enemies ever since. Now Darling is a wealthy man, owning liners as well as tugs, while Zack still has only his old vessel of 1916 fame.

A romance meanwhile is blossoming between first mate Bob and Sally (Valerie Hobson), Judys's nurse at the hospital. Shortly after Judy's return from the hospital two do-gooders, armed with a court order, literally kidnap the child and haul her off to an orphanage.

Darling has driven a hard bargain. Zack must repay his $1,000 loan in 60 days or lose his boat. In a desperate attempt to get the last of the money, Zack agrees to go out in a heavy fog when everyone else has has refused. But the old tug is sunk when Zack deliberately crosses the path of a new liner, owned by Darling, to prevent it from going on the rocks. Next day Darling turns up with a cheque for $11,000. Zack's share of the salvage. So all ends happily as the old men are reconciled after 20 years of enmity. There is talk of a good education for Judy, who has escaped from the orphanage, and Bob and Sally are married in Darling's home. (courtesy of D. John Turner, NFA.)

937. TUUM EST (1915-1939)
    p.c. UBC
    l. approx. 400'   g. 16mm   t. b+w   s. si.
    d.   *
    ph.   *
    c.s. Special Collections Division, The Library, UBC

    TUUM EST is the motto of the University of British Columbia. This film is a tribute to the history of the University from 1915, when it was founded, to 1939. It contains several lengths of early footage, including shots of the first congregation. There are also scenes of the first Graduation Parade and "D" Company of the Western Universities Battalion.

938. TWELVE HUNDRED SCHOOL CHILDREN ACCLAIM A CHARMING
    DAUGHTER OF B.C. AS THE NEW "QUEEN OF THE MAY",
    KAMLOOPS, B.C.   (1920's)
    p.c. Fox Movietonews (Fox #751.13-C1514)
    l. 40'   g. 35mm   t. b+w   s. si.
    d.   *
    ph.   Len H. Roos
    c.s. Fox Movietonews, N.Y.

    "High shot parade, headed by band. Dissolve to SCU of children marching by. LS float car containing Queen and her attendants. CU Queen. Miss Chapman, former Queen, relinquishes crown in favour of new Queen Annie Lytle. SCU & CU-iris of Annie Lytle. LS Maypole Dance. LS calisthenic drill."

939. TWELVE THOUSAND AND THIRTY-SIX AUTO TOURISTS CROSS
    BORDER IN ONE DAY, DRIVING ON FAMOUS PACIFIC HIGHWAY.
    (1924)
    p.c. Fox Movietonews (Fox #633-A4054)
    l.   g. 35mm   t. b+w   s. si.
    d.   *
    ph.   Len H. Roos
    c.s. Fox Movietonews, N.Y. - Lost

    "Back shot of auto on highway, trees in background. Cars on highway. Lineup of cars at customs waiting entry to Canada. Customs inspector examining baggage. Girl filling out card. Getting cards stamped inside. Cars coming toward camera through green timber."

940. TWO MILLION DOLLAR FIRE RAZES BIG VANCOUVER PIER. RAGING
     FLAMES DESTROY STEAMER PIER AND QUANTITIES OF CARGO TOTAL-
     LING $2,000,000.00. FIREMEN SAVE OTHER WHARVES FROM DES-
     TRUCTION, VANCOUVER, B.C. (1938)
     p.c. Paramount (Lib. #7263)
     l. 70'   g. 35mm   t. b+w   s. sound
     d.   *
     ph. ASN
     c.s. Visnews (BPN Lib. #7718); Sherman Grinberg, N.Y.

                    "View of the fire. SCU pan crowds watching CPR pier burning. Elevated view
                    of fire. Pan of fire from boat. SCU girders collapse. Crowd on building.
                    SCU hose being played on fire. SCU fire, rowboat in f.g. SCU fireboats
                    spraying fire. Good waterfront shots. Fire lasted only 45 minutes."

941. UBC DEFEATS VETERANS 1-0 IN MAINLAND SOCCER CUP
     FINAL - THE PRIZE. (1923)
     p.c. Fox Movietonews (Fox #712.1-B1629)
     l. 65'   g. 35mm   t. b+w   s. si.
     d.   *
     ph. Len H. Roos
     c.s. Fox Movietonews, N.Y.

                    Shots of the game and players.

942. UBC ROWING CLUB HOLDS DAILY ROWING PRACTICE DURING
     WINTER, VANCOUVER, B.C. (1923)
     p.c. Fox Movietonews (Fox #718-B3023)
     l. 55'   g. 35mm   t. b+w   s. si.
     d.   *
     ph. Len H. Roos
     c.s. Fox Movietonews, N.Y.

                    Rowing team practising.

943. UBC TREK. (1922)
     p.c. UBC students
     l.   g. 16mm   t. b+w   s. si.
     d.   *
     ph.   *
     c.s. Special Collection Division, The Library, UBC

                    With the declaration of WW 1, construction of the first permanent campus of
                    the University of British Columbia at Point Grey ceased. Throughout the war,
                    and after, students continued to attend classes downtown, in temporary loca-
                    tions, looking forward to the day when they could move into their own build-
                    ings. By 1922, however, no motion had been made by the Provincial Government
                    to recommence work, so the students decided to move on their own.

                    During the summer, students gathered over 50,000 signatures on a petition
                    which was sent to the Government, and they planned a huge protest march. On
                    October 28, 1922, they paraded through downtown Vancouver, boarded streetcars,
                    reassembled at Tenth and Sasamat, and marched to the campus where they picked
                    up many sympathizers and made a dramatic appeal to the government. A fort-
                    night later Premier John Oliver announced an immediate grant of $1,500,000
                    to begin work on the Point Grey campus again. This film covers the march
                    through Vancouver and at the new campus. Original on 35mm film.

944. UNBLAZED TRAILS. (1919)
     p.c. Dept. of Trade and Commerce
          Exhibits and Publicity Bureau, Ottawa
     l. 1 reel   g. 35mm   t. b+w   s. si. w/captions
     d.   *
     ph.   *
     c.s. NFA

                    For many years this film was Number 1 in the CGMPB's SEEKING CANADA series.
                    It was released on Sept. 1, 1919, and described as follows: "This film is a
                    scenic, following the journeys of Alpinists on unblazed trails out from Lake
                    Louise, depicting the wonders of Bow Lake, and finally landing the traveller,
                    after many adventurous climbs into the Columbia ice area, back at Laggan
                    again." (The copy at the NFA is on 28mm film and is about 400' long.) Views

of British Columbia will be seen from the mountain tops.

945. UNDER CLOUDLESS SKIES, GAY, HAPPY THRONG WITH POMP AND
CEREMONY PAY HOMAGE TO THE NEW MAY QUEEN, NEW WESTMINSTER,
B.C.   (1927)
p.c. Fox Movietonews (Fox #751.15-B9746)
1. 60'   g. 35mm   t. b+w   s. si.
d.   *
ph. *
c.s. Fox Movietonews, N.Y.

> *"High shots of parade. SCU the parade and floats, SCU crowning of Mary Alice Graves as "Queen of the May". High shot of the fair grounds."*

946. UNDER SHADOW OF MT. STEPHEN, C.P.R.R. (1899)
p.c. American Mutoscope and Biograph Co.
1. 54'   g. 35mm   t. b+w   s. si.
d.   *
ph. G.W. (Billy) Bitzer
c.s. Unknown

> *Scenes shot from a stationary camera mounted on a CPR locomotive showing the station at Field, and views of the Rocky Mountains. Photographed by Billy Bitzer, on one of his first assignments.*

947. UNEMPLOYED USED FOR REFORESTATION, VANCOUVER ISLAND,
B.C. (1937)
p.c. Fox Movietonews (Fox #31-363)
1. 900'   g. 35mm   t. b+w   s. sound
d.   *
ph. ASN
c.s. Fox Movietonews, N.Y.

> *"Little Qualicum Falls where park is being made. Pavilion constructed for tourists. Lunch served in the woods. Falling a snag (a useless tree that is a fire hazard). Camp at Elk Falls, men going into dining hall for breakfast. Men leaving for woods, foreman giving instructions. Two unemployed interviewd. Shots of Elk Falls. Topping a spar tree. High rigger atop tree. Tree being felled."*

948. UNIDENTIFIED B.C. MISCELLANY AND STERNWHEELER ON
KOOTENAY LAKE (?). (1930's)
p.c. private
1. approx. 250'   g. 16mm   t. red & b+w s. si.
d.   *
ph. Rev. George R.B. Kinney
c.s. NFA, Ottawa

> *red: Mr. ?'s garden (overexposed). A beach with a village of huts built on poles off to the right. A speeder racing along railroad tracks into the village. Pilings in the water. An old locie backs into the camp with one freight car. Log boom. Good CU's men walking along log booms.*
>
> *b+w: Boats tied up at a wharf. Steam dredging up bottom of lake, dumping it into a barge. Tugboat pulling dredge across lake, scenery shots. Log cabin with men. CP sternwheeler, the MOYIE (?), sailing down lake toward camera. Sternwheeler comes alongside wharf, disgorges passengers, and sails away again. This is probably on Kootenay Lake. LS railway snaking along a valley floor. Deep gorge with river pounding through, bridge above, various views. Waterfalls, dam, hydroelectric installation. People gathered about looking and men working.*

949. UNPRECEDENTED SNOWFALL IN THE CANADIAN ROCKIES BLANKETS
THE FOREST WITH A DAZZLING ERMINE MANTLE, BRITISH COLUMBIA.
(1926)
p.c. Fox Movietonews (Fox #007.1364-B1784)
1. 83'   g. 35mm   t. b+w   s. si.
d.   W.J. Oliver, Byron Harmon
ph. W.J. Oliver, Byron Harmon.
c.s. Fox Movietonews, N.Y.

> *"LS Mt. Fairview, frozen-fog-covered trees in f.g. SCU tree bent over by*

snow. Several shots of snow covered trees. So heavy is the snowfall that
crews are kept busy clearing the hotel roofs to protect their collapse. LS
of men clearing snow from roof of CPR hotel." (Mountains include: Pope's
Peak, Cathedral, Fairview, Huber, Stephen, Hector & Napta.)

950. UNUSUAL SNOWSTORM CAUSED UNUSUAL SCENES IN THE BUSY
     SHOPPING DISTRICT OF VANCOUVER. (1923)
     p.c. Fox Movietonews (Fox #007.3621-3566)
     1. 60'   g. 35mm   t. b+w   s. si.
     d.   *
     ph. Len H. Roos
     c.s. Fox Movietonews, N.Y.

             "Pedestrians and traffic. Stop motion."

951. VACATION TRAILS AND VIMY RIDGE DAY IN VANCOUVER. (1932,
     1934).
     p.c. private
     1. 300'   g. 16mm   t. b+w   s. si. w/captions
     d.   *
     ph. I.J. Garrod
     c.s. via Pacific Cinematheque

             VACATION TRAILS (1932): Canadian destroyer at wharf in Vancouver harbour,
             LS, MS & CU. Pan across bush and lake, ending with two people on a little
             point reflected in still water. Shot of lake, forest and mountains. Hydro-
             electric dam and swiftly flowing river. Road with cars and buildings. Par-
             ade in a small unidentified town with a band, large crowds and floats on the
             Main Street. Shots of Nooksack River through front window of still and mov-
             ing car. Woman in passenger seat of an old Durant car. Three cars in the
             snow. Travelling cars in snow through windshield. Scenic views at foot of
             Mount Baker, patches of snow, trees, river. Shots from ferry moving through
             Gulf Islands. (All in U.S.A.). Dominion Astrophysical Observatory on Little
             Saanich Mountain on Vancouver Island. Butchart Gardens. Views on the Mala-
             hat. Chalet at Cameron Lake. Large boat on Alberni Canal. Vancouver water-
             front panned from moving ship entering harbour. HMCS SKEENA beside a CPR
             Empress liner, amid other ships tied up. Brockton Point from moving ship.
             Prospect Point from moving ship. PRINCESS KATHLEEN, CPR ferry, sails by.
             Sunset over Vancouver Island from ferry. Brunette Sawmills in New Westminster,
             burning down at night. Beach at White Rock. Chuckanut Bay and Chucknut
             Drive in Washington, U.S.A. (Total: 250').

             VIMY RIDGE DAY, 1933 or 1934: Cenotaph in Victory Square, Vancouver. Seaforth
             Highlanders' wreath on Cenotaph with Number 72 at base. Ranks of vets in
             civilian clothes, Seaforth Highlanders in uniform. Men outside Armouries
             door (a sign on the building reads THE VANCOUVER REGIMENT). Highlanders and
             vets march past, church parade with band, past Piggly Wiggly store down Georgia
             Street, with Pipes and Drums. (50')

952. VALLEY OF APPLES. (pre 1935)
     p.c. *
     1. 1 reel   g. 35mm   t. b+w   s. si.
     d.   *
     ph. *
     c.s. Unknown

             "Apple picking in the fertile valleys of British Columbia. Grading at local
             stations and distribution by lake and railroad."

953. THE VALLEY OF LAKELSE. (approx. 1939)
     p.c. B.C. Government Travel Bureau
     1. 1x400' reel   g. 16mm   t. colour s. si.
     d.   *
     ph. C.R.D. Ferris
     c.s. Unknown

             "Scenic beauty and sport-fishing near Terrace, B.C."

954. VANCOUVER AND DISTRICT ARE COVERED WITH SNOW, VANCOUVER,
     B.C. (1938)
     p.c. Hearst Metrotone News, Can no. 782; Roll no. 6
     1.   g. 35mm   t. b+w   s. sound
     d.   *
     ph. ASN
     c.s. Hearst Metrotone News, N.Y.

                    Huge blizzard strikes lower mainland. Scenes of digging out from under.

955. VANCOUVER AREA ROAD CONSTRUCTION: PORT HARDY: AND
     WATSON LAKE. (1920's and 1940)
     p.c. private
     1. 750½'   g. 16mm   t. b+w & colour s. si.
     d.   *
     ph. R.F. Mackenzie
     c.s. NFA

                    *Mr. Mackenzie worked for many years with the General Construction Co., Van-
                    couver.*

                    *VANCOUVER AREA ROAD CONSTRUCTION, 1920's: (b+w) Consists of many scenes of
                    bulldozers, graders, trucks, shovels and construction workers building a
                    road from scratch, possibly near UBC, according to Mr. Mackenzie's cousin.
                    Later in the film a group of men and equipment are paving a street in Van-
                    couver, smoothing asphalt, steam rolling it, building sidewalks, etc. In
                    this sequence a CN freight train grinds by as the men lay concrete forms
                    along a short stretch of the tracks, a Dunbar streetcar comes up the hill
                    barely missing a man sprinting across the road with two bottles of milk, and
                    two other streetcars pass by while construction work is in progress. A man
                    in a suit poses, takes off his hat, scratches his head, and puts his hat on
                    again. (252')*
                    colour: Both the PORT HARDY and the WATSON LAKE sequences were shot in 1940.

956. VANCOUVER - B.C.'S COASTAL PLAYGROUND. (about 1939)
     p.c. B.C.G.T.B. (?)
     1. 1x400' reel   g. 16mm   t. colour s. si.
     d.   *
     ph. *
     c.s. Unknown

                    "Vancouver to Chilliwack Lake."

957. VANCOUVER CELEBRATES BIRTHDAY. (1925)
     p.c. Fox Movietonews (?)
     1.   g. 35mm   t. b+w   s. si.
     d.   *
     ph. ASN (?)
     c.s. NFB (1920-FG-157-1)

                    Section of CANADA CAPSULE NO. 16.
                    *"Excellent shots of floats extolling virtues of the City. School children
                    lined up and good shot of Lord Byng, Governor General of Canada, with Mayor
                    G. McGeer. Girls doing dance and PT for Byng."*

958. VANCOUVER CELEBRATES 50TH ANNIVERSARY OF INCORPORATION,
     VANCOUVER, B.C. (1936)
     p.c. Paramount (Lib. #5647) NL 1622
     1.   g. 35mm   t. b+w   s. sound
     d.   *
     ph. *
     c.s. Sherman Grinberg, N.Y.

                    *"General view of city of Vancouver. Parade, officials arrive. Pan soldiers.
                    SCU listening to broadcast. Mayor McGeer talking. Prime Minister R.B.
                    Bennett posing and talking, CU. Pan Mackenzie King to parade. CU parade.
                    Crowd watching. Pan soldiers. Mayor G. McGeer talks and thanks the Lord
                    Mayor of London and members of his council for co-operation of London and
                    the people for words of good cheer. Prime Minister Bennett of Canada speaks:
                    'One has only to travel across the continent to realize what a joy it is to
                    be alive and to be a Canadian. I declare the celebration of the commemmoration*

*of the 50th anniversary of the incorporation of Vancouver officially opened.'
Off stage voice tells about celebration. Bagpipe music, band music and general noises."*

959. VANCOUVER CLUB WINS OVER VARSITY IN FIRST REGATTA WITH
     VERY CLOSE CONTEST BETWEEN EXCELLENT CREWS, VANCOUVER,
     B.C. (1929)
     p.c. Fox Movietonews (Fox #755.8-C9383)
     1. 120'   g. 35mm   t. b+w   s. si.
     d.   *
     ph. Ross Beesley
     c.s. Fox Movietonews, N.Y.

              *"Brentwood College and Varsity fours lose to Vancouver Club. Varsity eight
              loses to Vancouver Club in rowing competition."*

960. VANCOUVER 50TH ANNIVERSARY PAGEANT PLAYERS AND CCF
     SUMMER CAMP. (1936)
     p.c. private
     1. 50'   g. 8mm   t. colour s. si.
     d.   *
     ph. J.W. Bowdery
     c.s. via Pacific Cinematheque, Vancouver

              *Stanley Park: Players in the Vancouver 50th Anniversary Pageant pose for
              Bowdery. Shots include a group of pirates, Vancouver (?) and Quadra, and
              a group of women. CCF Summer Camp shows members enjoying an afternoon on
              the beach. Shots of the beach, bathers, bathing, life-saving techniques,
              and several CU's of various friends. The last two shots show J.W. Bowdery
              looking very dapper.*

961. VANCOUVER ISLAND. (1938-39)
     p.c. B.C. Bureau of Industrial and Tourist
             Development
     1. 871'   g. 35mm   t. colour s. sound
     d.   *
     ph. C.R.D. Ferris and R.L. Colby
     c.s. NFB

              *"A travelogue of Vancouver Island." This film was revised in 1951 and re-
              released under the same title.*

962. VANCOUVER ISLAND RELIEF CAMPS. (1930's)
     p.c. private
     1. 280'   g. 16mm   t. colour s. si.
     d.   *
     ph. Rev. George R.B. Kinney
     c.s. NFA, Ottawa

              *Unidentified relief camp (very dark). Man carving faces in logs. Mess hall;
              men coming in and eating. Cooks in the kitchen. Men sitting around the fire
              talking and smoking cigarettes. Kitchen; men with metal dishes. Men eating
              in mess hall.*

              *Elk Falls. Wooden huts. Men harvesting bracken with rakes and piling it
              into heaps. Huts. Vast fields of ferns with men raking and pitchforking
              them into many piles. Clearing land at Elk Falls, Chopping roots, long pan
              across bracken fields, burning stumps. Good CU cooks. Scenes around camp;
              truck pulls in, cooks, huts. Dumptruck deposits gravel along the road. Snow-
              fall at Elk Falls camp. Men dig out; camp scenery.*

              *Thetis Lake. Men in rowboat on lake; many scenic shots of rowboat from shore
              through arbutus. Bridge between lakes; boat is brought ashore and placed in
              second lake.*

              *Stamp Falls Park. Three trucks crossing newly constructed log bridge. Newly
              made rustic log bench. Base of Stamp Falls. LS bridge.*

963. VANCOUVER ISLAND RELIEF CAMPS. (1930's)
    p.c. private
    l. approx. 280'   g. 16mm   t. colour   s. si.
    d.   *
    ph. Rev. George R.B. Kinney
    c.s. NFA, Ottawa

> *Irrigation equipment working in a forest. Qualicum Beach, looking across
> sea to islands and mountains. Stamp Falls, Englishman's River. Men working
> and posing in front of Relief Camp huts. Scenic view falls. Men working on
> construction of pathways, bridges, handrails, etc. at Stamp Falls. View of
> tents in a row. Good view of falls.*
>
> *Reforestation at Elk Falls. Men planting trees with picks. Good CU tree
> planters. Rolling young trees in burlap, loading them into the back of a
> truck. Men clearing land, burning slash, stumps, digging a road. The camp.
> Cook rings guthammer, men come running to eat. Good CU man with cable around
> tree. Topping a tree at Stamp Falls. Good CU high rigger. Men working on
> park stairs and wedging logs open. Mount Arrowsmith in b.g. with snowy
> peak. Scenic pan down bank into Thetis Lake, man walking down to water's
> edge with a saw.*

964. VANCOUVER ISLAND WEST COAST. (1930's)
    p.c. private
    l. approx. 290'   g. 16mm   t. b+w   s. si.
    d.   *
    ph. Rev. George R.B. Kinney
    c.s. NFA, Ottawa

> *Ucluelet entrance; sunset. Sunset on Long Beach, a truck passing by. Ucluelet
> lighthouse. Clayoquot Sound, Tofino Harbour. Man riding bicycle past store.
> Road building above Tofino village. Many men clearing land by hand with
> axes and fire. Approach shot of mail boat DAWN. Good CU Captain. Rev.
> Gibson stepping into Mission boat.*
>
> *Seiner pulling in net and picking out salmon, chucking them into hold. Good
> CU Japanese crew, near Ahousat. Ahousat. LS boat. Small seiner passing by.
> Purse seining for crabs. Good CU's crew and crabs. Fishing inspector's
> boat. Good CU Inspector. Crab fishermen. Surf pounding in on Long Beach.
> Rev. Gibson on Ahousat School beach. A lathe structure (trellis?) and rail-
> ings at top of beach. Surf on Ahousat School beach.*
>
> *Matilda Creek. Reef Island near Kyuquot. LS seiner passing by. Surf break-
> ing on shoals off Kyuquot. Fish boats at Kyuquot, the WESTERN SPIRIT and
> the PORT ESSINGTON. Seiners leaving harbour. Good CU's fishermen, one with
> a pup. Daughter and child. Surf on shoals. Seiners at sea with nets laid
> out. Nets being laid out and hauled in by boom. One of the seiners is named:
> NO. 2 DEPARTURE BAY. Seiners tied up in Tofino - SNOW CLOUD, SNOW SLIDE.
> Fishermen on the boats. Good CU's fishermen. Views from the Mission boat
> passing through many islands with little coves and huts visible and a wreck
> near a reef. Buoy at Opitsat and Opitsat Village. Another village, and
> more islands passing by.*

965. VANCOUVER ISLAND WEST COAST - BARCLAY SOUND, ESTEVAN
    POINT. (1939)
    p.c. private
    l. approx. 300'   g. 16mm   t. b+w   s. si.
    d.   *
    ph. Rev. George R.B. Kinney
    c.s. NFA, Ottawa

> *Steam shovel dredging harbour at Port Alberni on Vancouver Island, town in
> b.g. Pan harbour and mud flats at low tide. Steam pile-driver operating.
> Very brief (9 sec.) killer whales sounding. Hand-logging operation. Mr.
> Fish in forest. Falling a huge cedar. Lumber mill. View across water to
> points of land from a bobbing boat, probably islands in Barclay Sound. Water
> grows choppy, white caps and surf on low islands. A quiet cove in Barclay
> Sound. Cannery, unidentified. Boat draws away from cannery wharf.*
>
> *Dark headlands. Small settlement in a protected cove. Scenery. An oil
> station in a little cove: sign on shed reads IMPERIAL OIL LIMITED. Scenery
> and ocean. Excellent shots of groups of men and women working and posing*

in a little coastal village. Excellent CU's, in front of their houses. Prob-ably fishermen and their wives. Large freighter, the SS MAQUINNA, sails by Rev. Kinney's little Mission boat.

Entrance to Nootka Sound. The GIVENCHY sails by. Lighthouse station. Har-bour with large freighter SOUTHHOLM, loading burlap sacks of fish meal. Good shots of men working boom, winches, lines, etc. Rows of fishboats. Group of kids, Japanese and white, on the dock. Masts of fishboats. Kids playing and running away.

Surf near Estevan Point. Rough weather. Mission boat takes a pounding. Estevan; the boom for loading supplies up to the light. Scenery. Mission boat passes through many islands. The LEO-PAT, a fishboat, passes by, family and crew come up top to look. Heavy surf inshore. A seiner following behind the Mission boat.

Calm water in a cove, probably in Barclay Sound. Fishermen mending nets. Wooden construction on end of wharf, possibly for unloading pilchards. Mil-lions of pilchards in fishboat being shovelled onto a conveyor belt. Nets being examined, ladies look on. Scenery. Loading fish meal aboard a freighter. Good CU Chinese cook. Small boat at sea. Sheds on wharves (Excellent reel).

966. VANCOUVER ISLAND WORK CAMPS. (1930's)
    p.c. private
    1. 386'   g. 16mm   t. b+w   s. si.
    d.   *
    ph. Rev. George R.B. Kinney
    c.s. NFA, Ottawa

Elk Falls, Vancouver Island. Men drilling into rock to lay charges. Stamp Falls, Vancouver Island; two men cutting down burnt trees with axes and swedish fiddle. Wooden A-frame and car lifting a cut log off the ground. Two more burnt or dead stubs being felled with axe, swedish fiddle and wedge. Elk Falls: men building a bridge over Englishman's River.

Oyster River, Vancouver Island, road building. Bulldozers, shovels and trucks working and filling. Large group of men sitting beside a fire eating sand-wiches and drinking from mugs. Another shot of the bridge scaffolding, and more road construction work at Oyster River.

John Dean Park, Vancouver Island. Men sawing fat logs into foot-thick slabs, chiselling out slate to make gate posts, burning slash beside a pond, walking across a bridge, and working on a log-framed gazebo. Glintz Lake, Vancouver Island. Rows of tents with slashfires burning along the lakeshore. Koksilah River, Vancouver Island. Bell ringing at Camp 17, men racing for the dining hall. Clearing the forest, river in b.g., peeling logs, carrying them away, burning slash. Building a road with a shovel and wheelbarrow. Cooks clown-ing around at the waterfalls. Pan of dead trees, burnt and black, in a swamp - quite striking.

967. VANCOUVER JUNIOR BOARD OF TRADE AIR SHOW. (approx. 1938)
    p.c. private
    1. approx. 30'   g. 8mm   t. b+w   s. si.
    d.   *
    ph. J.W. Bowdery
    c.s. via Pacific Cinémathèque

Small passenger plane on runway, CF-CCT. Aerobatics; planes flying over-head. United Airlines Mainliner on runway. Parachutist landing. Biplane taking off and landing. United Airlines Mainliner taxiing and taking off. Small monoplane flying by. Aerobatics above runway.

968. VANCOUVER POST OFFICE SIT-DOWN STRIKE. (1938)
    p.c. private
    1. 50'   g. 8mm   t. b+w   s. si.
    d.   *
    ph. John W. Bowdery
    c.s. via Pacific Cinémathèque, Vancouver

This is a film Mr. Bowdery shot and edited into a form of home newsreel called THE SECOND WORLD WAR - THE HAND OF TYRANNY. It is captioned with headlines from the People's Advocate newspaper. The footage contains scenes

*of the exterior of the Vancouver Post Office at Hastings and Granville.
Employees being checked at the entrance. Interior of building, protestors
in sit-down strike. CU trio of protestors, other good CU's. Protestors
singing THE RED FLAG, banjo and accordion accompaniment. Unemployed march.*

969. VANCOUVER SCENICS - I. (1939)
    p.c. *
    1. 1318'   g. 16mm t. colour s. si.
    d. *
    ph. Les Thatcher (?)
    c.s. Jack Chisholm, #C857, roll 1

> *Jack Chisholm suggested that VANCOUVER SCENICS I & II were probably shot by
> Les Thatcher for the CPR but never used. Scenes are not identified as to
> location, but appear to have been shot all through British Columbia, and
> include:"CU Indian outside a corral. Team of horses hitched behind him.
> Indian on wagon. Team of horses hitched to post. LS smokestacks on a moun-
> tain. Small creek overflowing. LS pine trees, and pine forest on a mountain-
> side. Very good shot of a train coming around a bend. LS snow covered moun-
> tains, Roger's pass. LS lights at night. Mountain stream. Buildings on
> shore. LS sandbags retaining mountain stream, houses in b.g. Fast-moving
> stream and sandbags around houses to protect them. Many shots of different
> totem poles from different angles, etc. Suspension bridge in the mountains.
> Pine trees. Dam. Pines again. Seagull, lighthouse, rocky sea shore on
> Pacific. Trees growing down to the water's edge. Large trees, probably in
> Stanley Park. Lion's Gate Bridge. CU mountain sheep."*

970. VANCOUVER SCENICS - II. (1939)
    p.c. *
    1. 1160'   g. 16mm t. colour s. si.
    d. *
    ph. Les Thatcher (?)
    c.s. Jack Chisholm, #C857, roll 2

> *See VANCOUVER SCENICS - I. Contains miscellaneous shots of Vancouver and
> the coast. Scenes include:"LS large fir, probably in Stanley Park. CU
> stump, camera pans up. People crossing small footbridge. Lion's Gate Bridge.
> Coal being unloaded at Vancouver dock. Large grain elevators, Vancouver.
> Grain being unloaded into hold of a ship, various shots. Man sampling grain.
> Grain elevators, Vancouver. Pulpwood coming down an incline and travelling
> into a mill. Huge pile of pulpwood. Snow on wood. Pulpwood being carried
> into the mill. Papers coming off press. Huge wreath of flowers on deck of
> ship. LS ship sailing up inland waterway. CU two Mounties. CU skipper of
> ship. CU two Eskimos aboard with their children. Eskimos coming down gang-
> way. CU's Eskimos and crew of ship. CU sending a telegram via old-fashioned
> telegraph key and operators. One of the instruments aboard ship. LS Saturn,
> LS earth with a telescope. CU very old map of South America and part of
> North America. CU apple blossoms. Boy standing on shore watching a pulp
> mill. CU old sailor. LS pulp mill and Vancouver harbour. Train ferry with
> several boxcars aboard moving under bridge at Vancouver. Cruise ship enter-
> ing harbour. LS fishing boats entering harbour. LS car ferry arriving from
> Victoria. CU car ferry in dry dock. LS ferry leaving Vancouver. Ships
> sailing in and out of Vancouver. Ferry sailing under bridge. CU old women
> reading books. CU nurse with four babies. Babies and nurses. CU girl at
> typewriter. Girl's desk. CU man at desk. CU boy being X-rayed. CU people
> waving at a departing ship. CU passenger steamship. CU engine room control
> levers (telegraph?). LS three-funnelled steamship. CU wake of ship."*

971. VANCOUVER VIGNETTE. (1936)
    p.c. ASN/ASS (#B-670)
    1. 1 reel   g. 35mm t. b+w   s. sound
    d. Gordon Sparling
    ph. *
    c.s. United Artists, NFA

> *CANADIAN CAMEO No. 34. "Vancouver, born from the wilderness little less
> than a hundred years ago, gazes proudly from Canada's western coast over the
> blue Pacific. Today, ships of every nationality drop anchor in her harbour.
> Cosmopolitan, bustling, the fast tempo of her commerce, her race-tracks and
> crowded beaches contrast with the cloistered quiet of her University. VAN-
> COUVER VIGNETTE highlights the vivid personality of Canada's third city."*

972. VANCOUVER'S WESTERNS MAKE CLEAN SWEEP ACROSS CANADA TO
SPORTSMAN'S CUP, EMBLEM FOR THE CANADIAN BASKETBALL
CHAMPIONS, VANCOUVER, B.C. (1938)
p.c. Hearst Metrotone; Can no. 847, Roll no. 4
1.   g. 35mm   t. b+w   s. sound
d.   *
ph. ASN
c.s. Hearst Metrotone News, N.Y.

> "Met at station by crowd and band who escort them through streets to Sports
> Centre where they line up on steps to be officially welcomed by Mayor G.E.
> Miller and Walter Hardwick. Wally Mayers, Captain of the team, receives the
> Sportsman Cup from Hardwick."

973. VENGEANCE. (1936)
p.c. Central Films, Ltd.
1. 57 mins. (5,140') g. 35mm   t. b+w s. sound
d.   Del Lord
ph. Harry Forbes and William Beckway
c.s. NFA

> Canadian producer, Kenneth J. Bishop; script, J.P. McGowan; editor, William Austin; sound, Herbert Eicke; and Columbia overseer, Jack Fier.
>
> l.p. Wendy Barrie, Lyle Talbot, Wally Albright, Marc Lawrence, Eddie Acuff, Lucille Lund, Robert Rideout, Reginald Hincks, Lois Albright and Arthur Kerr.

> Working title: WHY LET 'EM LIVE?. This was the sixth Quota Quickie made by
> Central Films and the fourth and final production of 1936. It was released
> in the United States by Rialto Productions, Corp., on April 2, 1937, under
> the title WHAT PRICE VENGEANCE.

> The storyline is: Tom Collins (Lyle Talbot), a Provincial Police officer,
> is a crack shot on the range, but during a bank hold-up demonstrates that
> he lacks the nerve to shoot at live persons, even in a situation where it
> is justified. The fleeing robbers, headed by Pete Brower (Marc Lawrence),
> take the young son (Wally Albright) of another officer as a hostage and
> when his usefulness is over throw him from their speeding car with near fatal
> results. Accused of cowardice, Collins resigns from the force, but immediately
> sets about infiltrating the gang. He first teams up with Tex McGirk (Eddie
> Acuff) and together they pull a series of jobs which bring them to the atten-
> tion of Brower. Collins is soon sent for by Brower and agrees to join his
> gang. When the gang plans an important warehouse robbery in Victoria's
> Chinatown, Collins is ready to call in his former colleagues. Despite a
> last minute change in the plans and Collins' exposure during the actual rob-
> bery the police arrive in time and it all ends in a rather improbable blaze
> of gunfire with Collins firing at everything that moves. He is subsequently
> reinstated in the force and, of course, his romance is seen to be headed for
> a successful conclusion. (courtesy of D. John Turner, NFA.)

974. VERY REALISTIC LIFESAVING DEMONSTRATION IS PUT ON BY
ROYAL SOCIETY FOR BENEFIT OF SWIMMERS, VANCOUVER, B.C.
(1925)
p.c. Fox Movietonews (Fox #090.131-B6643)
1. 45'   g. 35mm   t. b+w   s. si.
d.   *
ph. Herron
c.s. Fox Movietonews, N.Y.

> "People falling out of rowboat as it capsizes. Uniformed members of Royal
> Life Saving Society running to the rescue. The saving. The heroes them-
> selves afterwards."

975. VERY SHY FOX ARISTOCRAT IS NOT TOO SHY TO FLIRT WITH
MRS. BERT MORRISON ON B.C. SILVER FOX FARM, CLOVERDALE,
B.C. (1923)
p.c. Fox Movietonews (Fox #411.3334-C2881)
1. 50'   g. 35mm   t. b+w   s. si.
d.   *
ph. Jos. T. Mandy
c.s. Fox Movietonews, N.Y.

"SCU Mrs. Morrison with the fox. SCU of her picking up fox and holding it in her arms. CU of a fox alone on ground. Might be OK for a natural scene."

976. VETERANS BATTLE VARSITY FOR BOWSER CUP IN SOCCER. (1928)
    p.c. Fox Movietonews (?)
    1.   g. 35mm   t. b+w   s. si.
    d.   *
    ph. ASN(?)
    c.s. NFB (1920-FG-152)

            "VCU Bowser Trophy. CS UBC soccer team. Cs Veterans team. LS stadium. Good shots of the game underway. This excerpted from CANADA CAPSULE NO: 5."

977. VIC FOLEY, "CANADA'S PRIDE", AND TOD MORGAN, JUNIOR
LIGHTWEIGHT WORLD'S CHAMPION, TRAINING FOR TITLE
BOUT, VANCOUVER, B.C. (1927)
    p.c. Fox Movietonews (Fox #716-B8459)
    1. 100'   g. 35mm   t. b+w   s. si.
    d.   *
    ph. J.T. Mandy
    c.s. Fox Movietonews, N.Y., and NFB (1920-FG-153)

            "Foley training with trainer Jack Allen. Foley sparring with Harvey Holliday. Morgan at Capilano Canyon, and shadow boxing, sparring with another man."

            "Vic Foley and Tod Morgan train for Lightweight Championship fight. Shot of Foley and sparring partner leaving training camp with manager. Jack Allen drinking sulphur water from pump at Harrison Hot Springs. Foley playing tennis, skipping rope. Shot of Foley boxing fast round with Harvey Holliday, Canadian Flyweight Champ. Tod Morgan at Capilano Canyon. Morgan in ring. May 3, 1927."

978. VICTORIA - A KINOGRAM TRAVELOGUE. (1924)
    p.c. Associated Screen News
    1. 830'   g. 35mm (16mm available) t. b+w & tinted s. si. w/captions
    d.   *
    ph. W.G. King
    c.s. NFA (16mm & 35mm)

            B.E. Norrish ... presents
            A Kinogram Travelogue - "VICTORIA"
            Titled and Edited by Terry Ramsaye

            HS CPR wharf in Victoria, 2 small ferries in, one three-stacker sailing past. Empress Hotel with streetcars on causeway from same view point -- top of Parliament Buildings. PRINCESS CHARLOTTE coming alongside, sightseers and tourists on deck waving to wharf. Mobs of visitors throng the wharf and causeway, with a contingent of people with a U.S. flag passing by Belmont Building. Excellent shots of CPR's MOTOR PRINCESS ferry loading cars at Bellingham, Wash.; interior of ship with cars parking, shots of travellers en route, interior and exterior, and cars disembarking at Sidney.

            Various shots around the Empress Hotel: LS women going up front steps onto verandah, visitors in the Empress gardens, a group of women in white with pikestaves with pennants, one holding a large flag, lining the path to the front door. Visitors get into a large open limousine at the Empress and drive away, waving. Shots of Parliament Buildings. A ceremony on the front steps of the Parliament Buildings. Shots of grand homes and gardens about Victoria. Driftwood roots that look like an alligator and a swan. A three-stacker CPR ferry sails past through the Strait of Juan de Fuca. Two women playing golf. A horse is jumped twice over a car.

            Various shots of the Malahat Drive and road to Mill Bay Ferry. LS shots of Brentwood Bay, Senanus Island, Pat Bay from Malahat. Shots of the Sunken Garden at Butchart Gardens, and of the little gnome fishing. Little Saanich Mountain LS, and man operating telescope inside Dominion Astrophysical Observatory on top of Mountain. Sun goes down over Victoria Inner Harbour, boats in f.g. (317' on 16mm)

979. VICTORIA AND VANCOUVER IN CHAMPIONSHIP ENGLISH RUGBY
     GAME AT BROCKTON POINT, VANCOUVER, B.C. (1923)
     p.c. Fox Movietonews (Fox #712.1-9106)
     l. 80'   g. 35mm   t. b+w   s. si.
     d.   *
     ph. Len H. Roos
     c.s. Fox Movietonews, N.Y.

              Shots of the game and the teams.

980. VICTORIA AND WEST COAST, V.I. (1930's)
     p.c. private
     l. approx. 150'   g. 16mm   t. b+w & red   s. si.
     d.   *
     ph. Rev. George R.B. Kinney
     c.s. NFA, Ottawa

              *b+w: A lighthouse on a point. LS fishing boat. LS tugboat. Wake churning
              out astern of a moving shop. The PRINCESS NORAH approaches and sails by.
              Coastal scenery. Shot from a moving boat: a CPR Princess ferry enters Vic-
              toria Harbour from breakwater to Parliament Buildings. Pan over to Parlia-
              ment Buildings, Customs House, etc. LS fishing boat with sail up. Views
              from Mission boat travelling through islands in Barclay Sound: villages,
              houses, etc. on shore. Mission boat arrives at a specific, unidentified
              house, perhaps in Bamfield. Mother and kids gather on wharf, walkway. A
              sleek water cruiser glides by.*

              *red: Rev. Kinney's son Bliss on a brief tour around Bamfield. Good shots of
              harbour and shore line with houses. Kids in rowboats. Old coastal freighter,
              GIVENCHY, steaming out of Bamfield. Scenes in Bamfield: floats, boats, etc.*

981. VICTORIA. (pre 1939)
     p.c. *
     l. approx. 400'   g. 16mm   t. b+w   s. sound
     d.   *
     ph. *
     c.s. Unknown

              A film about the capital of British Columbia.

982. VICTORIA. (approx. 1939)
     p.c. BCGTB (?)
     l. 1x400' reel   g. 16mm   t. colour s. si.
     d.   *
     ph. *
     c.s. Unknown

              "The capital city of British Columbia and its environs."

983. VICTORIA - 1919.
     p.c. *
     l. approx. 750'   g. 35mm   t. b+w   s. si.
     d.   *
     ph. *
     c.s. NFA (#1098, 1093)

              *City of Victoria 1919. No further information is known, but it may be
              wise to refer to THE CITY OF SUNSHINE made by the Dept. of Trade and
              Commerce in Victoria in 1919, of which this film might be a duplicate.*

984. VICTORIA, B.C., NEWS ITEMS - 1913.
     p.c. *
     l.   g. 35mm   t. b+w   s. si.
     d.   *
     ph. *
     c.s. NFA (Taylor reel 114)

              *"SHRINERS ARRIVE: Liner (ferry?) approaches Victoria dock returning from USA
              and passengers disembark. Among the passengers are a delegation of Shriners
              from Tacoma, Washington. Shots of Shriners in hats and spangles parading
              downtown to dinner. Next day, automobiles and Shriners parade down Govern-*

ment St. as crowds line the sidewalk and cheer.

GOATS - GOATS: Just outside Victoria, Major Unisock cavorts and plays, enjoying the freedom of the pasture. He is a goat, one of several rare pedigree ones owned by Mrs. Frederick Crawford. Shots of goats, little kids being fed by Mrs. Crawford. Shots of goats feeding, being milked by Mrs. Crawford and Mrs. Crawford cutting one's toe nails."

985. VICTORIA, B.C., TRAVELOGUE. (n.d.)
 p.c. *
 l. approx. 260' g. 16mm t. b+w s. si.
 d. *
 ph. *
 c.s. NFA (#70)

    A film about Victoria; incomplete.

986. VICTORIA, CANADA'S GARDEN CITY, HOLDS "GARDEN WEEK"
    WHEN INTERNATIONAL VISITORS INSPECT OUTSTANDING DIS-
    PLAYS. (1938)
 p.c. Hearst Metrotone News; Can no. 846, Roll no. 1
 l.   g. 35mm t. b+w s. sound
 d. *
 ph. ASN
 c.s. Hearst Metrotone News, N.Y.

987. VICTORIA CARNIVAL. (1912)
 p.c. *
 l.   g. 35mm t. b+w s. si.
 d. *
 ph. *
 c.s. NFA (75-12-27)

    Several views of parade, Cartercar Gearless Automobile. Kids' foot races.
    Bicycle races. Sulky races. Livestock competitions. Agricultural exhib-
    ition, etc. in Victoria park (Willows?). (Three stories are on this reel,
    totalling about 420'. Further details available from NFA.)

988. VICTORIA-CITY OF SUNSHINE AND FLOWERS. (n.d.)
 p.c. *
 l. approx. 2000' g. 35mm t. b+w s. si.
 d. *
 ph. *
 c.s. NFA (three prints: #'s 344, 345 & 346)

    Tourist-type descriptive film about Victoria. Almost every film made about
    Victoria in the early days contained something about "City of Sunshine",
    either as a title or subtitle, giving rise to speculation about a rather
    fundamental climactic shift. See also the two CGMPB films, CITY OF SUNSHINE.

989. VICTORIA HIGH SCHOOL AGRICULTURAL CLASS FIELD DAY AT
    SIDNEY EXPERIMENTAL FARM, SIDNEY, B.C. & VANCOUVER
    ISLAND HORTICULTURAL ASSOCIATION LUNCHEON. (late 1920's)
 p.c. B.C. Dept. of Agriculture
 l. approx. 400' g. 16mm t. b+w s. si. w/captions
 d. *
 ph. *
 c.s. PABC

    Students are shown field crops, fall-sown oats, Jersey cows, poultry incu-
    bator, tulips. An "Alfresco Lunch" is provided by the farm at long tables
    outside. Minister of Agriculture W. Atkinson and Deputy Minister J.B. Munro
    and their wives join them for lunch. Minister makes a speech. The VIP's
    size up the crops and pose with their wives. They inspect the bees and the
    grapes in the greenhouses. Mr. Toomer, the gardner, in greenhouse. Pan of
    the Dominion Experimental Station. Vancouver Island Horticultural Associa-
    tion is entertained by the superintendant at outdoor tables for lunch and
    speeches at Sidney. The advantages of paper mulch demonstrated. Various
    shots of Horticultural Association group.

990. VICTORIA IN SUMMER, VICTORIA, B.C.   (1912)
    p.c. *
    l.   g. 35mm   t. b+w   s. si.
    d.   *
    ph.   *
    c.s. NFA (Taylor reel 112)

> "PARADE: *Excellent shots of men carrying flowers, parading solemnly through
> the streets of downtown Victoria. One car in procession is decorated with
> flowers.*
>
> U-DRIVE: *DRIVE YOURSELF AUTO SERVICE opens in downtown Victoria. Shots of
> signs all over building announcing service. Cars pulling up to and leaving
> front of shop. Woman and family load into U-Drive and drive off.*
>
> TENNIS: *Outdoor tennis match in Victoria park. Shots of men and women arri-
> ving; one auto appears briefly. Tennis match with men and women playing as
> crowd looks on."*

991. VICTORIA NEWS ITEMS, 1919. VICTORIA, B.C.
    p.c. *
    l.   g. 35mm   t. b+w   s. si.
    d.   *
    ph.   *
    c.s. NFA (Taylor reel 120)

> "MAY 24TH CELEBRATIONS: *Shots of parade which was held on Queen Victoria's
> Birthday. Automobiles, floats, militia units including men of the RCN, Cdn.
> Army Infantry and Artillery in parade with horse-drawn pieces. Float repre-
> senting Anacortes - Victoria ferry.*
>
> MOTORCYCLE RACES: *Cyclists speed around track at Victoria Raceway and raise
> clouds of dust as they round turn and pass camera. CU happy winner & bevy
> of friends around him.*
>
> PHILLIPINE DELEGATION: *Brief pan of delegation of Government officials from
> the Phillipines, in Victoria to study Government methods.*
>
> MERVILLE FIRE: *Disastrous fire destroys home and surrounding forest, leaving
> ashes and scars. Pan across scarred remains of forest, ruins & brick chim-
> ney. Forlorn looking dog sitting in ruins. Pan across rubble, burned ani-
> mals.*
>
> DE-RAILED TRAIN: *Workmen digging area between twisted rails; short shot of
> freight train moving slowly and CU engineer in cab of locomotive.*

992. VICTORIA PAGEANT PARADE, VICTORIA, B.C.   (1914)
    p.c. *
    l.   g. 35mm   t. b+w   s. si.
    d.   *
    ph. Capital Films
    c.s. NFA (Taylor reel 129)

> *With ravages of hate and war brewing in Europe, a huge pageant is held in
> Victoria and men of the Canadian Militia, veterans, lumbermen's organisations,
> Wallace Shipyards, Orangemen, and various other groups parade through the
> city. Floats represent City of Victoria, firemen, police and public utili-
> ties, E.H. Heaps & Co., RNWMP, and many others*

993. VICTORIA SCENES.   (1929-1932)
    p.c. private
    l. 100'   g. 16mm   t. b+w   s. si.
    d.   *
    ph. Mr. Barney Olson
    c.s. Barry Casson Film Productions, Victoria

> *Brentwood Bay ferry wharf. Bus driving off Brentwood ferry, up ramp. Barney
> Olson and friend. Lansdowne Airfield near Willows Exhibition Grounds, Vic-
> toria. Inner Harbour, Victoria: pan across CPR ships from Parliament Build-
> ings, from Empress corner to upper Government Street, Belmont Building and
> old Post Office, cars and pedestrians on causeway. Empress Hotel: pan back
> to beginning. Pan across Inner Harbour. PRINCESS KATHLEEN. Mock fight*

between Tally-ho drivers. Policeman in early uniform with bobby-type helmet. Tourists disembarking from PRINCESS KATHLEEN. Tourists buying tickets for tour buses parked outside Empress - shot from Empress.

994. VICTORIA - THE SUNSHINE CITY. (1936)
```
p.c. CGMPB
1. 818'          g. 35mm   t. b+w      s. sound
d.   *
ph.  *
c.s. NFA
```

A tour of the capital of British Columbia, including views of the Butchart Gardens, Marine Drive, and Beacon Hill Park.

995. VICTORIA TO CRESTON. (1934)
```
p.c. private
1. 350'          g. 16mm   t. b+w      s. si.
d.   *
ph.  *
c.s. NFA (#4262)
```

Footage taken on a trip from Victoria to Creston in the Kootenays.

996. VICTORIA VIEWS - 1907.
```
p.c. *
1.               g. 35mm   t. b+w      s. si.
d.   *
ph.  *
c.s. NFA (Taylor reel 124)
```

THE COLONIST DELIVERY BOYS: The Victoria Daily Colonist, established in 1858, today honours its staff of delivery boys who line up in front of the newspaper office carrying commemorative editions. Later they enter the building for a feast as a reward for faithful service.

POLITICAL RALLY HELD: Politicians on platform moving nervously about. One is peering through binoculars. Shots of a huge crowd with streetcars moving slowly in b.g. Men and women mingle after rally.

VISITORS ARRIVING IN VICTOIRA: Passengers come down gangplank, are met by waiting officials to be driven to hotel. Two tourists stop a policeman in front of VISITORS BUREAU INFORMATION sign. They are given directions to hotel. Tourists entering and leaving bureau office, being given advice. Scenes of Victoria across harbour. Two men at site of OAK BAY SWIMMING AND BATHS, a proposed recreational site.

997. VICTORIA WARTIME - 1915, VICTORIA, B.C. (1915)
```
p.c. *
1.               g. 35mm   t. b+w      s. si.
d.   *
ph.  *
c.s. NFA (Taylor reel 127)
```

VICTORIA SOLDIERS HONOUR GUARD: Soldiers line up outside Parliament Buildings for ceremonial inspection. Shot of an 18-pounder gun range. Soldiers lined up for camp inspection.

CONTINGENT LEAVING FOR OVERSEAS: Huge crowds at CP Wharf. Large group of soldiers on their way to ship for embarkation overseas.

NAVY LEAGUE VETS PARADE: Men of Navy League parade to parliament buildings to aid Canadian Bond Drive and help win the war.

998. VICTORIA WATERFRONT, 1909. VICTORIA, B.C. (1909)
```
p.c. *
1.               g. 35mm   t. b+w      s. si.
d.   *
ph.  *
c.s. NFA (Taylor reel 119)
```

"Excellent pan across Victoria's Inner Harbour from Grand Trunk Pacific Railway building, past marine sheds with various business establishments in down-

town Victoria in b.g. (PITHER & LEADER WINES & LIQUORS) - Pier D - EVANS -
COLEMAN - EVANS, and others. Good shot of Empress Hotel, Parliament Build-
ings, docks, piers and waterfront in general."

999. VIRGIN FIELDS FOR EXPLORERS (CANADIAN ROCKIES). (1917-18)
    p.c. Dept. of Trade and Commerce
          Exhibits and Publicity Bureau, Ottawa
    1. 1 reel   g. 35mm t. b+w   s. si. w/captions
    d. *
    ph. Byron Harmon
    c.s. Unknown

> *Byron Harmon was a freelance photographer based in Banff, Alberta. Although*
> *no details are known, he probably sold this film to the Exhibits and Pub-*
> *licity Bureau for their new series of promotional films. While it was prob-*
> *ably photographed in Alberta, the film no doubt shows mountain ranges in*
> *British Columbia. The description in the first Exhibits and Publicity Bureau*
> *Catalogue reads: "This film has created great interest in the unexplored*
> *territories of the Canadian Rockies. Mr. Byron Harmon, the photographer,*
> *exhibited this film in New York, and during the week that it ran in one of*
> *the most famous New York Motion Picture Houses, it created quite a sensation,*
> *and drew forth much newspaper and magazine comment."*

1000. VIRGINIA BEAUTY BREAKS LANSDOWNE TRACK RECORD BY WINNING
     FEATURE EVENT ON OPENING DAY OF MEET, VICTORIA, B.C. (1929)
     p.c. Fox Movietonews (Fox #755.1-D1048)
     1. 80'   g. 35mm t. b+w   s. si.
     d. *
     ph. *
     c.s. Fox Movietonews, N.Y.

> *Shots of horse and racetracks.*

1001. VISCOUNT ADMIRAL JELLICOE VISITS CANADA. (1919)
     p.c. Government of Canada
     1.   g. 35mm t. b+w   s. si.
     d. *
     ph. *
     c.s. NFB (1910-P-122)

> *"The H.M.S. NEW ZEALAND, the battle cruiser that brought Jellicoe from the*
> *Antipodes, anchors in Esquimalt Harbour as the Viscount stops in Canada during*
> *his world tour. Shots of Esquimalt Harbour. Shots of Jellicoe, with Vice*
> *Admiral Kingsmill of the RCN and Captain Martin of the RN, inspecting the*
> *Naval station and dockyards at Esquimalt. Shots of Premier Oliver of B.C.*
> *and party being transported to the flagship for a reception. Shots of them*
> *on board. CU Capt. Leggett, skipper of the NEW ZEALAND, and Cdr. Calvery,*
> *XO. Shots of ship leaving the Harbour, of rating on board, of an automatic*
> *semaphore signaller sending a message from shore. MLS of the NEW ZEALAND*
> *as she sails through the narrows of Vancouver Harbour. MS from the front of*
> *of the warship moored at the dock. Low angle MS of crest commemorating the*
> *Battle of Jutland. Tilt down MS to Jellicoe standing by one of the gun tur-*
> *rets. Closer shot of Jellicoe standing beside a hole in the armour plating*
> *made by the only enemy shell to hit the ship. CU of hole, high angle shot*
> *of one of the fore main gun mounts."*

1002. VISIT OF HIS MAJESTY KING GEORGE VI AND HER MAJESTY QUEEN
     ELIZABETH TO VANCOUVER AND NEW WESTMINSTER - MAY 1939.
     p.c. *
     1. 422'   g. 16mm t. colour s. si. w/captions
     d. *
     ph. *
     c.s. Christ Church Cathedral Archives, Victoria, B.C.

> *Good long MS Royal Hudson locomotive, 2850, from side. Good CU front of*
> *2850 with scarlet-jacketed, bearskinned guards on either side. Pipe band*
> *marching down street lined with people, followed by veterans with red arm*
> *bands.*

> *"Inspection of Guard of Honour at Pier C and Procession up Burrard Street*
> *through the Welcome Arch." The inspection is missing, but there are good*
> *shots from various angles of the royal car passing through the Welcome Arch.*

Royal couple en route to and arriving at City Hall, Vancouver, through crowds of people with flags, etc. King and Queen leave City Hall to tumultuous goodbye from crowds.

Scenes in Vancouver Harbour as the King and Queen depart for Victoria aboard the CPR ferry PRINCESS MARGUERITE. The harbour is thronged with small boats waiting for them to pass. Three biplanes fly overhead, low over the Lion's Gate Bridge. The PRINCESS MARGUERITE sails out under the bridge.

King and Queen drive through mobs of people in New Westminster. Veterans and pipe band. Children, dressed up in May Day costumes are waiting in Queen's Park. The royal couple arrive to a tumultuous welcome. A huge maypole display. Kids perform calesthenics. Crowds at Patullo Bridge. The King and Queen arrive alongside the CN train and reviewing stand. King and Queen leave car, board train and train leaves, everyone waving frantically.

1003. THE VISIT OF KING GEORGE VI AND QUEEN ELIZABETH TO
CANADA AND THE UNITED STATES. (1939)
p.c. Castle Films and B.C. Dept. of Agriculture
l. approx. 500' g. 16mm t. b+w & colour s. si. w/captions
d. *
ph. *
c.s. PABC Agricultural Collection; NFA has a copy of the
Castle Films reel.

The Castle Films production of the entire visit is b+w and is about 360' long. The sections filmed in British Columbia show the Royal Hudson pulling into Vancouver with a good shot of the engine and tender; the Guard of Honour in Vancouver; the arrival and departure of the King and Queen; the arrival and departure of the King and Queen at Vancouver City Hall; and the arrival of the King and Queen at the Parliament Buildings, Victoria, and the inspection of the Honour Guard by King George.

The B.C. Dept. of Agriculture footage is on colour stock and is 140' long. Scenes include: the yellow convertible and the King and Queen's limousine driving through the crowds on Government Street in Victoria. Victoria City Hall. Crowds at the Parliament Buildings. Three nurses beneath a sign reading FIRST AID POST. Highlanders and veterans marching down the street. Tumultuous crowds massed at parliament buildings, soldiers, etc.

1004. VISIT TO BRITTANIA MINES, BRITTANIA BEACH, B.C. (1932)
p.c. National Harbours Board
l. 220' g. 35mm t. b+w s. si.
d. *
ph. *
c.s. NFB (N.H.B.-N-3)

"On Sept. 8 1932, Lord, Earl of Bessborough, and Lady, Countess of Bessborough, visited Brittania Mine, north of Vancouver. They arrived aboard the RVY VENCEDOR. CU Mr. & Mrs. E.W. Hamber posing on pier, Commodore J.B. Thomson & R.D. Williams of Vancouver Harbour Commission posing. Governor General & Lady Bessborough arrive by 1932 Packard and are greeted. Good shot of yacht VENCEDOR steaming into Vancouver Harbour and band playing upon Bessborough's arrival. Gov. Gen. & Lady Bessborough are met by Mine Manager C.P. Browning and various shots show them visiting main concentrator and machine rooms of mine. LS VENCEDOR steaming up harbour with mountains in b.g. and good shot of the crew of the yacht posing along the railing of the ship for camera." This story appears to be a little confused. Perhaps the VENCEDOR is arriving at Brittania Beach, and steaming up Howe Sound, not Vancouver Harbour; Brittania Mines is 30 miles north of Vancouver.

1005. VISITORS ARRIVING VICTORIA, B.C. - 1907.
p.c. *
l. g. 35mm t. b+w s. si.
d. *
ph. *
c.s. NFA (Taylor reel 125)

TOURISTS ARRIVE FROM THE USA; Two CPR ferries move toward dock laden with American visitors to Victoria. Shots of passengers disembarking and drivers waiting for them (See Taylor reel 124). One shot, through porthole, of two

ships   Cameraman with huge camera set up on a hill to photograph people at
Oak Bay picnic.   Various races being run, followed by friendly game of tug-
o-war and address being given by local minister who awards prizes in the
form of diplomas and ribbons.

AUTOMBILE RACES: Brief shot of autos being prepared, racing on dust track.
More scenes of Oak Bay picnic, of ships in harbour with Victoria in b.g.
Crowds along the Causeway and children parading past signs on Douglas Street.

1006. VOLLEYBALL AT FORT RODD HILL, NEAR ESQUIMALT, B.C.
      (1937-1939)
      p.c. private
      l. 300'   g. 8mm   t. b+w   s. si.
      d.   *
      ph. G.A. York
      c.s. via Pacific Cinémathèque, Vancouver

              Gunners of the 5th Heavy Battery, R.C.A., summer camp at Fort Rodd Hill
              near Esquimalt, B.C.   Much of the film is taken up with a game of volleyball,
              but there are scenes of tents, and one pan of the lower battery.

1007. VOYAGEUR TRAILS.   (1930's)
      p.c. CGMPB (?)
      l. approx. 800' g. 35mm   t. b+w   s. sound
      d.   *
      ph. *
      c.s. Unknown

              Canoe trip through the Canadian Rockies, fishing in the rivers.   It is not
              known if any of the film was shot in B.C.

1008. WAGON RACES FOR BOYS IN PLAYGROUND MAKE NOVEL COMPETITION,
      VANCOUVER, B.C.   (1928)
      p.c. Fox Movietonews (Fox #700.8-C5035)
      l. 125'   g. 35mm   t. b+w   s. si.
      d.   *
      ph. Ross Beesley
      c.s. Fox Movietonews, N.Y.

              Races, winner with trophy.

1009. WARM WELCOME TO PRESIDENT HARDING, FIRST U.S. CHIEF
      EXECUTIVE TO VISIT CANADA DURING TERM OF OFFICE.
      ENTHUSIASM RUNS HIGH, VANCOUVER, B.C.   (1923)
      p.c. Fox Movietonews (Fox #201-B1964)
      l. 100'   g. 35mm   t. b+w   s. si.
      d.   *
      ph. *
      c.s. Fox Movietonews, N.Y.

              "Ship HENDERSON coming in.   Party landing, coming down gangplank.   Pres.
              coming down, after some of the party.   Pres. coming down wharf.   Group on
              wharf.   Pres. inspecting guard of honour.   Parade entering park.   Coming up
              to stand.   Pres. on speaking platform, microphone.   CU of him reading speech."
              (Personalities include: Dr. Sawyer; Admiral Rodman; Hubert S. Work, Secretary;
              Secretary Wallace; Herbert Hoover; Speaker Gillett; & Mrs. Warren G. Harding.)

1010. WAR COMES TO VICTORIA, B.C.   (1914)
      p.c. *
      l.   g. 35mm   t. b+w   s. si.
      d.   *
      ph. *
      c.s. NFA (Taylor reel 126)

              ANTI-GERMAN FEELINGS: (Aug. 1914) - Mobs gather in front of German-owned
              stores, wreck clubs such as the German-Canadian Club and the Kaiserhoff Hotel.
              Mob can be seen in second story of building, firing books and records into
              crowds below.   Excellent shots of mob, two cars passing in f.g.

              YUKON REGIMENT TRAINING: (Oct. 1914) - Yukon Regiment training at a camp
              outside Victoria.   Shots of men performing P.T. in civilian dress, at roll
              call, lining up to eat, inspection and general camp life.   Later they start

on a 25-mile route march. The men top off the day with a vigorous bayonet drill.

UNLOADING HORSES FOR WAR: (1914) - Horses that were working on farms a short time ago arrive on a local train, are unloaded and line up for inspection. They will be sent overseas after brief training with a local cavalry regiment.

1011. WAR PLANES RUSHED FOR CANADA'S DEFENSE, VANCOUVER, B.C.
(1939)
p.c. Paramount (Lib #7855)
l. 94'   g. 35mm   t. b+w   s. sound
d.   *
ph. ASN
c.s. Lost

"Machine shop. Man at work, SCU, in machine shop. CU of plaster pattern of one of the machines. Side view of man dipping one of the parts into Anodic tank. Man testing metal for hardness. CU metal being tested. SCU stamping parts from sheet metal. Man removing part of stamp metal. General & CU views of men at wheeling machine. Man at work on wings of plane. CU man drilling holes in nose of ship. Top view showing parts of plane."

1012. WARTIME PARADE, VANCOUVER. (1939)
p.c. private
l. 55'   g. 8mm   t. b+w   s. si.
d.   *
ph. J.W. Bowdery
c.s. via Pacific Cinémathèque, Vancouver

The first five feet show a train driven by a steam locomotive entering a snowy station in the Rockies. (colour, c. 1940). The footage is on two reels. It shows a parade, mounted in the early days of World War II marching down Granville Street, shot from a window high up in the original Eaton's building. All the while a Union Jack flutters back and forth across the window. Scenes include a float with a world globe and Union Jack, soldiers marching, clowns with batons, floats with sailors and a plane, a fighter plane, and various trucks, marching men, soldiers and bands. At the end there is a shot of Granville Street and pedestrians from street level.

1013. WARTIME VICTORIA, B.C. - 1914.
p.c. *
l.   g. 35mm   t. b+w   s. si.
d.   *
ph. *
c.s. NFA (Taylor reel 128)

"CANADIAN INFANTRY MARCH PAST: Troops of Canadian Infantry Expeditionary Force march smartly past camera and reviewing stand on Yates Street.

CANADIAN CONTINGENT PARADE: Men of the Canadian Army line up for inspection & parade to Parliament Buildings prior to marching to CPR wharf for embarkation overseas. Troops on deck of ship, cheering wildly as the ship glides away from the dock. Men & Cavalry Reg't. assemble outside Victoria, prior to embarkation parade to ferries. Excellent shots of assembled parade leaving stadium for route march & embarkation. High angle shot of long line of soldiers marching through Victoria to ships, final inspection & more parade."

1014. WASHING GOLD ON 20 ABOVE HUNKER, KLONDIKE. (1899-1900)
p.c. Edison Mfg. Co.
l. 24'   g. 35mm (16mm available) t. b+w s. si.
d.   *
ph. Robert Bonine
c.s. (L.O.C.) Paper Print Collection & NFB

"This picture shows the miners washing out gold by what is known as the sluice box method. Here we see the miners shovelling from both sides the soil containing the gold into the sluice boxes, where the water, rushing at a rapid rate, carries away the dirt and stones, leaving the precious metal, which settles to the bottom of the box, to be recovered in the clean up at the end of the day's work. This is a very good subject, full of action and detail." Also shown is a horse-drawn sled which moves the soil to be washed to a crusher. (The original 35mm print was 65' and was copyrighted in May, 1901

1015. WASHINGTON CREW BEATS U.B.C., VANCOUVER, B.C. (1939)
    p.c. Fox Movietonews (Fox #37-249)
    1. 750'   g. 35mm   t. b+w   s. sound
    d.   *
    ph. ASN
    c.s. Fox Movietonews, N.Y.

            "Elevation B.C. crew take boat to water. Same for Washington. Shots from
            float. Pull away from clubhouse to starting line. Crowd. Race shots.
            Finish line. Washington crew wins. Takes cox and throws him in the water.
            Boat shots. Starting line. Race."

1016. WATER POWERS OF CANADA, TRIBUTARY TO VANCOUVER. (1916-
    1917)
    p.c. Dept. of Trade and Commerce, Ottawa
    1. 2 reels   g. 35mm   t. b+w   s. si. w/captions
    d.   *
    ph. Essanay Film Mfg. Co.
    c.s. Unknown

            This film marks the beginning of the Federal Government's involvement in
            making promotional films. The U.S. Bureau of Commercial Economics in Wash-
            ington, D.C., asked the Canadian Government for cinematic information about
            Canadian water power, and during 1916 and early 1917 six films were made,
            five concerned with hydroelectric power and one with the harvesting, inspec-
            ting and transporting of Canadian wheat.

            WATER POWERS OF CANADA, TRIBUTARY TO VANCOUVER has long been lost and for-
            gotten, but the description in the Canadian Trade and Publicity Bureau's
            first Catalogue, typed out on 14" sheets of paper, reads: "A technical film
            featuring the Water Power developments at Lake Buntzen and Stave Lake where
            electrical energy for the Fraser River Valley is obtained, also industrial
            and residential views of Vancouver and New Westminster."

1017. WATER TESTS AND GOLD PANNING. (1909)
    p.c. *
    1.   g. 35mm   t. b+w   s. si.
    d.   *
    ph. *
    c.s. NFA (75-12-27)

            High-pressure water hose being tested, men directing stream against building.
            Couple of shots of 'sourdough' panning for gold in a gold field in British
            Columbia. (Three stories are on this reel, totalling about 420'. For further
            details contact NFA.)

1018. WE TAKE YOU TO THE FAMOUS FIVE FINGERS IN CANADA,
    ONE OF THE HAZARDS IN GOLD RUSH TO DAWSON, YUKON.
    (1932)
    p.c. British Movietonews (No. 6600)
    1. 105'   g. 35mm   t. b+w   s. sound
    d.   *
    ph. *
    c.s. British Movietonews

            Small steamboat beating upriver. Shot of rapids. CU aerial view of steam-
            boat churning through water. Shot of rapids. Steamboat, named LOON, approach-
            ing shore. LS, 2 caribou swimming river. CU caribou. The pair swims along
            the bank until they find a place to get out, then, scrambling with great diffi-
            culty, they claw up the bank away from the cameraman. LOON being washed
            backward by rapid water, despite valiant forward efforts. Excellent.

1019. A WEDDING TRIP FROM MONTREAL THROUGH CANADA TO HONG KONG
    (1910)
    p.c. Edison Mfg. Co. (Catalogue #6694)
    1. 1000'   g. 35mm   t. b+w   s. si.
    d.   J. Searle Dawley
    ph. Henry Conjager
    c.s. Unknown

            One of the dramatic shorts made by the Edison Co. during the journey by its
            troupe through Western Canada shooting promotional films for the CPR. This

one was begun on June 27 when they left Montreal aboard their own private
car, and was finished on July 28, in the Gulf of Georgia, with additions
filmed at the Bronx Studio on their return. It is the story of Algernon
and his wife to be, who meet on a CPR train in Montreal, get engaged in Van-
couver, and who sail away as newlyweds on the EMPRESS OF CHINA. One of the
scenes has been described as follows: "They are hardly on board before "Loveys"
curiosity overpowers him and he tries to find out, perhaps for the purpose of
impressing "Dearie" with his knowledge, the purpose of the great air funnels
on the deck of the ship. He finds out after he makes a "shoot-the-chute"
drop into the coal bunkers in the hold of the ship, from which he is rudely
hoisted, a mass of dirt, soot and coal dust, into the waiting arms of his
terrified bride. We leave them on board, confident that if a poor beginning
guarantees a good ending we may safely wave them a hearty bon voyage as the
ship fades in the distance." (Motion Picture World, Oct. 29 1910). A
WEDDING TRIP... was released on October 21, 1910.

1020. WEST AND EAST KOOTENAYS. (1939-1940)
    p.c. private
    1. 158'   g. 16mm   t. colour s. si.
    d.   *
    ph. R.F. Mackenzie
    c.s. NFA

        Sign: THE MEADOWS. TEA ROOM, MILK, LOG CABINS, CAMP. A bear in the bush.
        Purple morning glories. A squirrel. Columbia River. "The Meadows" gardens.
        Sheep at Skookumchuck in snow. The Hoodoos at Dutch Creek. A parade in a
        small unidentified town. Sea-cadets and their band march past. Rainbow.
        Cotton Creek Bridge with steam train passing over Cotton Creek. Pan of
        Wyndel, Creston Flats. Wharf at Gray Creek. Bonnington Dam. South Slocan
        Dam. Taghum Bridge. Cora Lynn Dam. Ferry at Nelson. Doukhobor women and
        young boy at Valican (more likely Winlaw, from name painted on railroad hut).

1021. WEST COAST GUN DEFENCES. (1939)
    p.c. ASN
    1.   g. 35mm   t. b+w   s.
    d.   *
    ph. ASN
    c.s. NFB (1940-WW II-143-DN)

        "Various shots of gun crews running to their posts, going through the motions
        of loading huge coastal guns, aiming, firing, etc. Shots through huge barrel.
        Men on look-out, peering through instruments, code sending, sounding alert,
        gun crew runs into action. Side view of gun, no firing." No indication of
        location, but probably Esquimalt.

1022. WEST COAST INDIANS. (1930's)
    p.c. private
    1. approx. 450'   g. 16mm   t. b+w & red s. si.
    d.   *
    ph. Rev. George R.B. Kinney
    c.s. Nfa, Ottawa

        red: Indistinct views of the sea.

        b+w: Coastal freighter in Bamfield. Kids in rowboats. Entrance to Creek.
        Fish boat putting to sea; seagulls. Scenery - mountains and islands of Bar-
        clay Sound. Indian fisherman on wharf at Dodger Cove (?). Jellyfish. CU
        fisherman.
        red: Old Indian man making a dugout canoe with an axe. Two white men, inclu-
        ding Rev. Kinney, give it a try. Indian fishermen with salmon.
        b+w: Family visits lighthouse, pan from top over houses, sea. CU light,
        either Tofino or Ahousat. LS fish packer at sea. Entering an unidentified
        harbour. Fishing boat sailing by, the ROSE. Large seiner passing by. Storm
        at sea from deck of Mission boat. Visit to the Gibsons at Ahousat. Birds
        on the sand at Long Beach. Truck driver, truck drives along sand on Long
        Beach. Surf rolling in. Fishing boats tied up in Tofino. (?)
        red: fishing huts on piles. Silhouettes of heads. Calm glassy bay. Sea-
        lions on rocks, sea-lions in sea, leaping off rocks, perhaps near Tofino.
        Scenery, islands.
        b+w: Lighthouse, kids outside in sun. Pan up lighthouse to top. Keeper and
        wife pose with kids and dog. The CPR ship PRINCESS NORAH sails by. Indian
        women readying baskets to sell, women sitting about with baskets on wharf at

*Nootka. Unloading salmon at Nootka onto a conveyor belt. Stern portside
of PRINCESS MAQUINNA tied up in Nootka. Unloading supplies. White woman
buying baskets from Indian women. Salmon being unloaded from boat, moving
up conveyor belt. Salmon in hold. White tourists with baskets. Unloading
oil drums from ship. White girls disembark. People coming out in boats to
greet the ship. Totem poles at Friendly Cove, some standing, some fallen
down. One is a figure of a man, leaning over on an angle.*
*b+w: Mountains and scenery, on west coast. Logging camp on floats, from
water. Indian village with totems, Indians come out to meet Melvin Swartout.
Seiners working at sea. Seiners tied up at small floats. A rock, weathered
and watered, sticks out of the sea in a crusty column, acting as a marker.
CU rock. Kyuquot Indian lodges with totems, lodge poles/house posts, very
beautiful. Woman in shawl. Many, many shots of poles, all painted, quite
excellent. Well-loaded seiner hauling in net after net of salmon. CU Indian
fishermen. Indian school at Ahousat. Kids and Rev. Gibson, singing, in
classroom, playing basketball with all their families watching. Sunset at
Ahousat.*

1023. WEST COAST INDIANS. (1930's)
    p.c. *
    l. approx. 450' g. 16mm t. colour s. si.
    d.   *
    ph. *
    c.s. NFA (#4496)

1024. WEST COAST LOGGING & KOOTENAY LAKE. (1930's)
    p.c. private
    l. approx. 300' g. 16mm t. b+w s. si.
    d.   *
    ph. Rev. George R.B. Kinney
    c.s. NFA, Ottawa

*Shovel dredging in Kootenay Lake. Old logging locie hauling logs through
the snow near a logging show. CU's engineer and other loggers. LS landing
with railway flatcars passing in f.g., steam from donkey in b.g. CU spar
tree. Pile of logs. Steam donkey hard at work yarding logs and loading them
on rail cars. Man riding tongs up into air. A jetty on the sea with a
freighter and sheds. Loggers moving logs around inside a boom, some excellent log burling. Logs being dumped off railcars into booming ground.*

*Kootenay Lake. Bulldozer working on railway construction, men and wheel-
barrows. Work camp with men milling about. Camera pans across camp. Bathing beauties: girls in bathing suits diving and jumping into Kootenay Lake.
Bulldozer at Procter, pulling a grader along a dirt road. Men working on
road with machines and by hand. A car drives by a house on the Lake. A
girl dives into the Lake. 1931.*

*Men repairing tractors and equipment in a garage at Procter. Visitors leave
Procter by a small boat. Others watch, walk away. Train arrives, conductor
disembarks, passengers disembark. Views of station at Procter. Cabin cruiser
on Lake. Men who disembarked from train board Cabin cruiser and leave wharf,
speeding out onto the Lake. Freight piled up at the siding. Men working at
siding moving freight. A train moves through backwards, box cars etc. Men
appear to be building a platform. Pans of freight. CU old carpenter.*

1025. WEST COAST LOGGING, VANCOUVER ISLAND - 1939.
    p.c. History Division, BCPM
    l. approx. 325' g. 16mm t. b+w s. sound
    d. Colin Browne & Karl Spreitz
    ph. Jerry Wellburn & Phil LeMare
    c.s. History Division, BCPM

*The footage for this film was shot originally on 8mm stock, 200' by Mr. Well-
burn and 200' by Mr. LeMare. It was enlarged to 16mm and edited to its
present length, and a sound track consisting of steam engine, internal com-
bustion, and saw-mill noises as well as some fiddle music added to simulate
the sound of the logging activities, under the guidance of and with the help
of Mr. Wellburn. Mr. Wellburn, who owned the logging operation depicted in
much of the film, contributed the commentary, which is as vital and authentic
as one might expect from a man who has spent much of his life in the woods.*

The scenes include a few brief views of Duncan, on Vancouver Island, in the early days, falling giant Douglas-Fir with new chainsaws, bucking them into portable lengths, and the transportation of the logs by truck and railway. Good scenes at the base of the spar tree where the logs are being yarded out of the bush, tongs thrown about them with great skill, and the massive trunks lifted onto the rail cars by a steam donkey. Logs are loaded onto trucks by a gasoline donkey. There are scenes around the mill showing the arrival of the logs, the endless chain up onto the deck, the carriage which carries the logs through the circular saw, the edger, and all mill operations including sorting in the lumber yard. A steam crane is shown working in the yard lifting and piling huge loads of lumber. A truck drives under the sawdust hopper and is loaded with sawdust which will be delivered to houses for stove fuel. And trucks leave the mill loaded with cut lumber. Also shown is an excellent tree-topping sequence by the high-rigger.

1026. WEST COAST NEAR BAMFIELD and NEAR DUNCAN, V.I. (1930's)
    p.c. private
    1. approx. 260'   g. 16mm   t. colour & b+w s. si.
    d.   *
    ph. Rev. George R.B. Kinney
    c.s. NFA, Ottawa

    colour: The Creek, Bamfield. A Nootka canoe with six people, two of them paddling, moves toward the sea. Construction on the Malahat Drive, near Duncan. Shovels and trucks working, blasting, bulldozer, etc. Views up and down Findlayson Arm. Car speeding around corner of the Malahat.
    b+w: Sunset on West Coast, surf at Pachena.
    colour: Two petroglyphs of Big Foot. West coast scenery, islands, from Mission boat. Fishing boat. Man in uniform under a plaque on a ship which reads: S.O.B.C. No. 4. Views of ships from wharf at Bamfield (?). Party at lifesaving station (Bamfield?). Men digging, picking, in a field, gently, as if looking for something small.
    b+w: Plowing at Koksilah, near Duncan, with a two-horse team. Plowing with a tractor. CU men driving horse team. Construction on the Malahat. Shovel and truck. Truck dumping fill. Bulbs drying in racks at Koksilah. Combining at Koksilah. Good CU's threshing crew. Leaves falling on lawns and roofs in Koksilah.
    b+w: Indian kids carding wool at Koksilah, all in a row and hard at it. Older boys are carving spindles with jackknives, girls are pulling wool apart and carding it - a large active group, including two white women. Three men with an old farm truck picking up baskets of something (potatoes?) from a field.
    colour: - Scenery - sea and rocks. (No good - faded).

1027. WEST COAST VANCOUVER ISLAND. (1930's)
    p.c. private
    1. 170'   g. 16mm   t. colour & b+w s. si.
    d.   *
    ph. Rev. George R.B. Kinney
    c.s. NFA, Ottawa

    b+w: Two old Indian fellows sitting on the beach at Hesquiat with a pile of dogfish. Man and boy walking along trail from Hesquiat to Estevan Light. Various shots of light when they arrive.
    colour (faded): PRINCESS MAQUINNA visits tiny west coast settlement - good shots of ship, shore. Fishboat sailing alongside ship, bobbing in sea. Views of many islands. Many good shots of PRINCESS MAQUINNA, first in Bamfield (?) then on open sea.
    b+w: Freighter loading lumber in Port Alberni (?). Good pans of wharf area, loading crane, piles of lumber, etc. Old Indian couple and white boy in rowboat beneath Friendly Cove or Ahousat Light. Good shots of Light. Surf roaring in on beach. What appears to be a forest fire across the water is overexposed very quickly. Logging operations on the west coast. Yarding around the spar tree. Good CU's loggers. Camera attached to something moving very erratically. Donkey engine being skidded through the forest.

1028. WEST VANCOUVER MAY QUEEN CEREMONY. (1939)
    p.c. private
    1. 50'   g. 8mm   t. b+w   s. si.
    d.   *
    ph. J.W. Bowdery
    c.s. via Pacific Cinémathèque, Vancouver

May Queen in leaf-covered wagon. Various shots of children in costumes on parade. Snow White and Seven Dwarfs (kids). St. Bernard dog pulling a little girl in a buggy. May Queen contestants in convertible. Highland cadets escorting queen and princesses. Horse drawn coach with queen and two princesses. CU queen. Decorated convertible. Floats, decorated bicycles in parade. Costumed kids again, and St. Bernard. Kitsalino Boys' Band. Cameraman Harold Turner. Children watching parade of pipers and adults. Children dancing to a large crowd. CU children dancing in a circle. Maypole Dance. Enthroned May Queen and princesses. Highlanders.

1029. WESTERN CANADA. (1926)
    p.c. Regent Studies, London/British Instructional Films
    1. 907'   g. 35mm   t. b+w   s. si. w/captions
    d.   *
    ph. *
    c.s. BFI (Location #7662A)

> *This film, part of THE EMPIRE SERIES, contains 410' of British Columbia material. Scenes include: Mt. Robson. Kamloops, an old Hudson Bay post. Thompson River from above. The pine and spruce forests in British Columbia. Stripping the trees of their branches and felling them. Sawing them into logs. A team of horses pulling the logs to the river. Piloting a raft of logs downstream. Sawing the logs into planks in a mill in Vancouver. Ships in Vancouver harbour.*

1030. WESTERN CANADA AIR SHOW, VANCOUVER, B.C. (1937)
    p.c. Fox Movietonews (Fox #32-261)
    1. 1100'   g. 35mm   t. b+w   s. sound
    d.   *
    ph. ASN
    c.s. Fox Movietonews, N.Y.

> *"Miss Rollie Moore doing aerobatics. Shots during dogfight. Crowd shots. Formation flying. Tex Rankin in aerobatic display."*

1031. WESTERN CANADA SKI CHAMPIONS IN PRINCETON, B.C. (1938)
    p.c. Fox Movietonews (Fox #33-618)
    1. 812'   g. 35mm   t. b+w   s. sound
    d.   *
    ph. ASN
    c.s. Fox Movietonews, N.Y.

> *"Ladies Slalom race. Men's jump. Waxing skiis. Crowd shot. Group shot of winners. Tom Morbraaten, Peggy Mobraaten, Gertie Wepsale, Johnny Leed. Men's Jumping event. Crowd."*

1032. WESTERN CANADA SKI-MEET SLALOM EVENTS, PRINCETON, B.C. (1939)
    p.c. Fox Movietonews (Fox #36-821)
    1. 400'   g. 35mm   t. b+w   s. sound
    d.   *
    ph. ASN
    c.s. Fox Movietonews, N.Y.

> *"Skiers leaving train. Leaving station in sleighs. Train arriving from Vancouver. CU of Bert Irwin of Princeton, B.C. who won slalom event. Surrounding country. CU starter with flag. Skiers climbing. Skier doing turn. Contestants come down."*

1033. WESTERN HOLIDAY. (1937)
    p.c. private, then CNR
    1. 2500'   g. 16mm   t. colour s. si.
    d.   Hamilton W. Jones
    ph. Hamilton W. Jones
    c.s. Unknown

> *WESTERN HOLIDAY won first prize in a contest held by the Amateur Cinema League of New York in 1937. It was made by Hamilton W. Jones, an amateur from either Buffalo, N.Y., or Toronto. The film was purchased by the CNR and shown as a travelogue of Alberta and British Columbia. Scenes included Victoria, Vancouver, Mt. Robson Park, and Jasper.*

1034. WESTERN INTER-COLLEGIATE FOOTBALL, VANCOUVER, B.C.   (1938)
        p.c. Fox Movietonews (Fox #35-937)
        l. 666'   g. 35mm   t. b+w   s. sound
        d.   *
        ph. ASN
        c.s. Fox Movietonews, N.Y.

                *"University of British Columbia VS University of Saskatchewan for the Hardy
                Trophy. UBC wins by score of 2 - 1. Various shots of game and crowd."*

1035. WESTERN UNIVERSITIES BATTALION, 1916-1917.
        p.c. *
        l.   g. 16mm   t. b+w   s. si.
        d.   *
        ph. *
        c.s. Special Collections Division, The Library, UBC

                *A compilation of early footage showing members of the Western Universities
                Battalion from UBC. Originally filmed on 35 mm.*

                *A partial description reads: "General Alarm - all fall in. University
                Beach. Off for the training camp. 196th Battalion entrains for Camp Hughes."
                There also appears to be a section containing footage shot in 1923 during a
                protest by UBC students to call attention to their need for a new university.
                The description reads: "The grounds now temporarily occupied have proven
                totally inadequate to accomodate the rapidly increasing attendance. Students
                stage huge demonstration during Varsity Week to impress upon the public the
                need for a new University. 1200 Boosters."*

1036. WESTERNERS CELEBRATE THE DOMINION'S BIRTHDAY WITH A MONSTER
        PARADE HAVING A NUMBER OF BEAUTIFUL FLOATS, VANCOUVER, B.C.
        (1926)
        p.c. Fox Movietonews (Fox #751.15-B3601)
        l. 50'   g. 35mm   t. b+w   s. si.
        d.   *
        ph. Herron
        c.s. Fox Movietonews, N.Y.

                "Long shots of the parade. Semi-CU of some of the floats."

1037. WHERE COHOES PLAY.   (1938)
        p.c. CGMPB
        l. 811'   g. 35mm   t. b+w   s. si. w/captions
        d.   *
        ph. *
        c.s. NFB (330'16mm), BCPM (35mm print)

                Produced for the National Parks Bureau, Ottawa.

                *"A picture of particular interest to anglers, depicting the fighting quali-
                ties of the coho or silver salmon, found in the coastal waters of British
                Columbia."*

                *This film contains no identifiable landmarks. It shows various shots of
                coho sporting in the water, then a boy with a large salmon coming in after
                an early-morning fishing trip. He gives a few hints to two men on a foggy
                beach. The two men leave in a small clinker-built boat and begin trolling
                for coho with salmon flies. They eventually display ten salmon on the wharf
                at the end of their fishing trip. As well, a fisherman in hip-waders demon-
                strates coho fishing in a river and comes ashore with a salmon. Two fisher-
                men at the end compare their catch.*

1038. WHERE FIGHTING BEAUTIES RISE.   (1935)
        p.c. CGMPB
        1 approx. 800'   g. 35mm   t. b+w   s. si. w/captions
        d.   Bill Oliver
        ph. Bill Oliver
        c.s. NFA (380' 16mm), BCPM (35mm), NFB (378' 16mm)

                "Fly-fishing for the famous Kamloops trout at Knouff Lake, British Columbia."

                A party of apparently well-known Vancouver fishing enthusiasts arrives by

316

*car at a small fishing cabin on the shores of Knouff Lake. They unload their
gear. The men leave the dock in two boats to go fishing. The first fish is
hooked and, after a fight, netted. The other boat catches a 15-pounder. The
men put ashore and fry their fish for lunch. They set off again and another
fish is landed and held up for the camera. Another fish, a long fight, and
the trout is displayed in a net. The men row ashore with their catch and
spill the fish out of their creels onto the lawn. A tableau of 11 Kamloops
trout, one creel, and two rods on the lawn. At sunset a fisherman is still
out on the water trying to catch the one that got away. (NOTE: No disting-
uishing landmarks). Produced for the National Parks of Canada, Ottawa.*

1039. WHERE THE COLUMBIA RIVER RISES. (1921)
    p.c. Ford Motion Picture Laboratories
    1. 569'   g. 35mm   t. b+w   s. si. w/captions
    d.   *
    ph. *
    c.s. USNA Ford Film Collection (200FC-2409)

        *Part of the Ford Educational Library, a series of educational films shot in
        many parts of the world. Its category: Regional Geography, Volume V.
        British Columbia. The film begins with a map showing Washington State, part
        of Oregon, and a corner of British Columbia. The captions are charged with
        poetic spirit and explain that the various scenes represent the headwater
        of the Columbia. Shots include:"Tourists looking at river from high over-
        look point, passing automobile. View of mountains and valleys in the Rockies,
        large glassy lakes, and autos on the road. The varies and spectacular
        scenery of the Rockies is well represented by snow-capped peaks, crystal
        clear lakes, forests, cliffs, and rugged mountain roads traversed by auto-
        mobiles in almost every sequence. At the end a man lingers, looking out
        over a lake as the Columbia gathers strength "for its journey through Nature's
        wonders to the sea."*

1040. WHILE EAST PREPARES FOR WINTER THESE KIDDIES CONTINUE TO
     ENJOY FAVOURITE CONFECTIONS OF SUMMER, VANCOUVER, B.C. (1923)
    p.c. Fox Movietonews (Fox #427.44-B3019)
    1. 35'   g. 35mm   t. b+w   s. si.
    d.   *
    ph. Len H. Roos
    c.s. Fox Movietonews, N.Y.

        "Chinese, Jewish & Negro kids eating ice cream cones."

1041. WHITE WINGS. (1933)
    p.c. CGMPB
    1. 1 reel   g. 35mm   t. b+w   s. si. w/captions
    d. Bill Oliver
    ph. Bill Oliver
    c.s. NFA

        *"Remarkable shots of glaucous-winged gulls along the coast of Vancouver
        Island, British Columbia, during the herring fishing season." (The copy at
        the NFA is 290' long on 16mm). Produced for the National Parks Bureau,
        Ottawa.*

1042. WHOOPEE! AND A COUPLE OF POW WOWS!! HERE IS RIDING IN
     CIRCLES AND IN EVERY WAY AT FAMOUS CARIBOO RODEO, WILLIAMS
     LAKE, B.C. (1929)
    p.c. Fox Movietonews (Fox #751.11-D0834)
    1. 150'   g. 35mm   t. b+w   s. si.
    d.   *
    ph. Ross Beesley
    c.s. Fox Movietonews, N.Y.

        *"Bucking broncos, men riding 2 horses, "Modern version of Roman race", and
        other rodeo events at Williams Lake Stampede."*

1043. WILD FLOWERS OF BRITISH COLUMBIA. (1930's)
    p.c. B.C. Dept. of Agriculture
    1. approx. 300' g. 16mm   t. colour s. si. w/captions
    d.   *
    ph. *
    c.s. PABC

Includes shots of Easter lilies (dogtooth-violets), peacocks, dogwood, daisies, trilliums, periwinkle, Indian paintbrush, honeysuckle, yellow daisies, broom, oregon grape, yarrow, fireweed, and many others. It appears as if most of this film was shot on Vancouver Island.

1044. WILD LIFE WAYS. (1936)
    p.c. CGMPB
    l. 1 reel   g. 35mm   t. b+w   s. si. w/captions
    d.   Bill Oliver
    ph. Bill Oliver
    c.s. NFA

"Various species of Canadian animals and birds in their native habitat." Produced for the National Parks Bureau, Ottawa. It is safe to assume that some of the animals are inhabitants of the Rocky Mountains and that therefore they were photographed during Bill Oliver's many trips through Alberta and British Columbia.

1045. THE WILDERNESS PATROL. (1928)
    p.c. British Canadian Pictures, Ltd.
    l.   g. 35mm   t. b+w   s. si.
    d.   J.P. McGowan
    ph. *
    c.s. Unknown

*Producer; Samuel Bischoff; script, Ford   l.p. Bill Cody
Beebe.*

British Canadian Pictures Ltd. was a Canadian front for American producer Samuel Bischoff who made a contract with The Gaumont Company in England to supply them with action pictures starring the German Police dog SILVERSTREAK at $12,000 a film, a neat arrangement which enabled Gaumont to circumvent the new quota legislation in Britain. The Company never tendered an annual report and seems to have disappeared without making one SILVERSTREAK picture.

Bischoff may have produced a western entitled THE WILDERNESS PATROL, however, starring Bill Cody. If so, it may have been filmed on location in North Vancouver.

1046. THE WINDS OF CHANCE. (1925)
    p.c. First National Pictures
    l. 9554'   g. 35mm   t. b+w   s. si.
    d.   Frank Lloyd
    ph. *
    c.s. Unknown

*Script, G. Hawks, based on the novel   l.p. Ben Lyon, Anna Q. Nilsson, Viola
The Winds of Chance by Rex Beach.   Dana, Hobart Bosworth, and Dorothy
                                      Sebastion.*

THE WINDS OF CHANCE was produced on location in Capilano Canyon, North Vancouver, near Lytton, B.C., and in Pendleton, Oregon. The story is as follows: "Pierce Phillips joins the Alaska gold rush and is trimmed clean by the operator of a shell game. He gets a job packing luggage for the Countess Corteau, and a mutual love develops. When she finally admits that she is still entangled in the bonds of matrimony, Pierce brokenheartedly returns to Dawson and gets a job as a gold-weigher in a dance hall. He is framed for robbery by the Count Corteau and a piqued vamp called Laura, but the Countess obtains evidence to clear him. Count Corteau is killed, and Pierce is blamed unjustly for his death. The Mounties find the real killer, and Pierce is free to find happiness with the Countess." (Synopsis courtesy AFI)

1047. WINGS OF A CONTINENT. (1930's)
    p.c. *
    l.   g. 16mm   t. b+w   s.
    d.   *
    ph. *
    c.s. NFB (1930-DN-328)

Shows several types of aircraft flying, landing and taking off all over Canada. In British Columbia, there are scenes of aircraft on the runway at the

Vancouver Airport, mail planes being loaded, and a TCA Lodestar taking off.

1048. WINTER GOLF TOURNAMENT ATTRACTS LARGE FIELD OF ENTHUSIASTS AS
      WEATHER CONDITIONS PROVE IDEAL, VICTORIA, B.C. (1929)
      p.c. Fox Movietonews (Fox #713-C9144)
      1. 200'   g. 35mm   t. b+w   s. si.
      d.   *
      ph. Ross Beesley
      c.s. Fox Movietonews, N.Y.

              *"Lt. Gov. Randolph Bruce presents W.E. Beatty Cup to T.L. Swan, the winner.
              Shots of golfers playing."*

1055. WINTER'S GRAND FINALE IS OBSERVED BY STARS OF SKIIS AND BY
      WATCHING CROWDS ON THE SLOPES OF GROUSE MOUNTAIN, VANCOUVER,
      B.C. (1929)
      p.c. Fox Movietonews (Fox #732.3-C9685)
      1. 50'   g. 35mm   t. b+w   s. si.
      d.   *
      ph. Ross Beesley
      c.s. Fox Movietonews, N.Y.

              "Nels Nelson receiving trophy, skis with Mr. Snersrud. Skiing."

1050. WITH DUE CEREMONY THE SECOND NARROWS BRIDGE IS OPENED FOR TRAFFIC
      BY HON. W.H. SUTHERLAND, VANCOUVER, B.C. (1925)
      p.c. Fox Movietonews (Fox #353-B7488)
      1. 30'   g. 35mm   t. b+w   s. si.
      d.   *
      ph. Herron
      c.s. Fox Movietonews, N.Y. & NFA

              "Autos drive over, boat passes under."

1051. WITH POMP AND GLITTER OF PRE-WAR DAYS, LT. GOV.
      OFFICIATES AT OPENING OF LEGISLATURE, VICTORIA,.
      B.C. (1929)
      p.c. Fox Movietonews (Fox #095.63-C8584)
      1. 120'   g. 35mm   t. b+w   s. si.
      d.   *
      ph. Ross Beesley
      c.s. Fox Movietonews, N.Y.

              "Lt. Gov. Bruce, Premier Tolmie, soldiers parade and inspection."

1052. WITH THE INTERNATIONAL CARAVAN TO THE LAND OF THE
      GOLDEN TWILIGHT. (1930)
      p.c. Automobile Club of Southern California
      1. 2,400'   g. 35mm   t. b+w   s. si.
      d.   Douglas C. Mitchell
      ph. Douglas C. Mitchell
      c.s. Automobile Club of Southern California

              *A film covering a motor journey made by members of the Automobile Club of
              Southern California during the summer of 1930. According to the Vancouver
              Province of Dec. 21, 1930, the trip was participated in by "prominent visit-
              ors" from the U.S. and by British Columbians headed by Lt. Gov. R.R. Bruce and
              Premier Tolmie. The Land of the Golden Twilight was northern British Columbia,
              and the tour left from Seattle, travelling through the Cariboo to Hazelton
              and Kispiox. Scenes included the Stampede at Williams Lake, a dance by
              medicine men, and many scenic views of northern British Columbia along the
              highway. The film was shown in British Columbia in December, 1930, and a
              copy was deposited with the Provincial Bureau of Information.*

              *Other scenes included were the Parliament Buildings, Victoria, views at the
              Canada-U.S. boundary (Blaine?), Hazelton and New Hazelton with views of the
              Skeena River, Indian cemeteries showing "dead houses", Indian dances, totems
              at Kispiox Village, mountain ranges and glaciers, views of Smithers and the
              Nautley River, Summit Lake, gathering at Vanderhoof and Indians there, Lillooet,
              Pavillion Mountains, the Fraser River and small towns nearby.*

1053. WITH THEIR MAJESTIES IN WESTERN CANADA, VANCOUVER
      AND VICTORIA, B.C. (INCLUDES SHOTS IN CALGARY,
      BANFF, AND EDMONTON, ALBERTA). ROYAL VISIT OF
      KING GEORGE VI & QUEEN ELIZABETH.
      p.c. Paramount (Lib. #8277)
      1. total 560'   g. 35mm   t. b+w   s. sound
      d.   *
      ph. ASN
      c.s. Sherman Grinberg, N.Y. — Lost

                    VANCOUVER: "Crowd of singers at City Hall. Tilt up from singers to King and
                    Queen on platform. King and Queen leave City Hall. Railway Station. "Welcome"
                    sign. CU Japanese sign. Japanese kids lined up in street. Royal car pass-
                    ing Japanese children. EN ROUTE VICTORIA: CPR ferry PRINCESS MARGUERITE
                    leaving with King and Queen for Victoira. Shoreline. Flotillas of small
                    boats. King and Queen on deck. Union Jack. Bridge overhead. Night shot
                    of Victoria Harbour. Beacon light on shore. Fireworks.
                    VICTORIA: Elevated view of King and Queen riding through the streets. Car
                    arrives. King and Queen through crowd. King walks onto parade ground at
                    Beacon Hill Park, presents Colours, and walks back to the reviewing stand.
                    Salute of flag lifted from ground. CU King and Queen. People shouting: WE
                    WANT OUR KING! Sailors passing in review."

                    ADDED SCENES: "Royal car arrives Vancouver City Hall. King and Queen and
                    activity in, about City Hall. Singers, crowds. Japanese sign, crowd. Riding
                    shot through street. CU pan Japanese children. Crowd along riverbank waving.
                    EN ROUTE VICTORIA: King and Queen walk to platform. CU King and Queen at
                    salute. King and Queen on reviewing stand. Queen with parasol. CU King and
                    Queen on deck of ship. Side view of escorting destroyer. Empress Hotel."
                    The two escorting destroyers were HMCS FRASER and HMCS ST. LAURENT.

1054. WITHOUT TITLE: AN AUTO TRIP FROM VANCOUVER THROUGH
      KAMLOOPS TO PENTICTON. (1931)
      p.c. Motion Skreen Adz Ltd.
      1. 30 minutes   g.   t. b+w   s. si.
      d.   J. Howard Boothe
      ph. J. Howard Boothe
      c.s. Unknown

                    A provincially supported travelogue showing an auto trip from Vancouver to
                    Penticton via Kamloops, destined for the Provincial Bureau of Information.

1055. WOMAN AGAINST THE WORLD. (1937)
      p.c. Central Films Ltd.
      1. 66 minutes (5907') g. 35mm t. b+w s. sound
      d.   David Selman
      ph. Harry Forbes and William Beckway
      c.s. NFA

                    Canadian prod., Kenneth J. Bishop;   l.p. Ralph Forbes, Alice Moore,
                    script, Edgar Edwards; editor, William   Sylvia Welsh, Edgar Edwards,
                    Austin; asst. d., William Brown; sound,   James McGrath, Reginald Hincks,
                    Herbert Eicke; Columbia overseer, Jack   Collette Lyons, Ethel Reese-
                    Fier.   Burns, George Hallet, Grant Mac-
                                                                 Donald, Fred Bass, Harry Hay,
                                                                 and Enid Cole.

                    Working title: WOMEN AGAINST THE WORLD. This was the seventh Quota Quickie
                    made for Columbia Pictures by Central Films in Victoria and the first pro-
                    duction of 1937. According to Martin Kroeger, who wrote continuity for all
                    the Central Films, the movie reviewer Jimmy Fiddler gave WOMAN AGAINST THE
                    WORLD "three bells", a sign of high praise, and cited particularly the court-
                    room scene, shot in Victoria's courthouse, as being excellent. WOMAN AGAINST
                    THE WORLD was copyrighted in the United States by Columbia Pictures, Inc.,
                    on March 15, 1938.

                    The story is as follows: Anna (Alice Moore) falls in love with Johnny Masters
                    (Edgar Edwards), a hired hand on her father's farm. They are married secretly
                    but her father discovers the deception and sends the young man away at gun-
                    point. Johnny, working in the city as a watchman, is about to send for Anna
                    when he is killed by robbers. Anna is pregnant and moves to the city to live
                    with her Aunt Frieda (Ethel Reese-Burns), an unsympathetic and uncharitable

woman. *Anna has the baby, Betty Jane, and seeks work to support herself and her baby. She returns home one evening to find the baby gone. The Aunt claims to have given it up for adoption. A struggle ensues in which Anna accidentally kills her aunt as she attempts to extract from her the whereabouts of her baby. Anna is sentenced to five years in prison but her lawyer, Larry Steele (Ralph Forbes), soon has her out on parole. Now she engages Flavin (James McGrath), a seedy private detective, to search for her child. Flavin's price is high and Anna's friend Patsy (Collette Lyons) gets her a job in a clip joint. Meanwhile Flavin locates Betty Jane (Sylvia Welsh), now five years old, living happily with her wealthy adoptive parents, Mr. & Mrs. Martin (Harry Hay and Enid Cole) but does not tell Anna. Instead he accepts $2,000 from Martin, supposedly a pay-off to Anna, which he keeps and continues to take his fee from Anna. Eventually becoming suspicious, under the prodding of the cynical Patsy, Anna accepts a date with Jimmy (Grant MacDonald), Flavin's assistant, and after plying him with liquor at the club where she works she learns the truth. Anna now visits the select district where the Martins live and gets a glimpse of Betty Jane. Later she abducts the child, keeps her for a few days, then returns her. Now everyone appears in court and Anna is accused of abducting the child as well as breaking parole. Larry now plays out the big melodramatic court room scene and of course, as the baby had not been adopted legally, Anna is cleared of the abduction charge. Flavin's duplicity is also exposed. But little Betty Jane does not recognize Anna as her mother and Anna eventually agrees to leave the child with the Martins. At the fade-out she is in Larry's arms.*

Though effective as a tear-jerker, the plot is hopelessly implausible. At her trial for murder Anna refuses to reveal the reason for the struggle and it is only afterwards that she tells the story to Larry who can thus secure her parole. Then she goes to Flavin without approaching the police to find her baby, something Larry would surely have advised her to do. Larry for his part continues to express a romantic interest in Anna even though she never sees him - she's working day and night - and never even tells him what she's doing. (Courtesy D. John Turner, NFA.)

1056. WOMEN DECORATE GRAVES OF WAR DEAD. (early 1920's)
p.c. *
l.   g.   t.   s.
d.   *
ph.   *
c.s. *

See *B.C. WOMEN'S ASSOCIATION DECORATES GRAVES OF FALLEN HEROES.*

1057. WOMEN'S MILITARY UNIT, VANCOUVER, B.C. (1939)
p.c. Fox Movietonews (Fox #36-820)
l. 350'   g. 35mm   t. b+w   s. sound
d.   *
ph.   *
c.s. Fox Movietonews, N.Y.

"*Group who enrolled first in organization, CU's of women. Officers of unit. Sound interview with Mrs. Hugo Rayment, adjutant - L - R bottom row & top row on dupe sheets.*"

1058. "WONDERS OF CANADA". (1909. Filmed 1900-1902.)
p.c. Charles Urban Trading Company, London
l. 735'   g. 35mm   t. b+w   s. si.
d.   Joseph Rosenthal
ph.   Joseph Rosenthal
c.s. Unknown

"*A grand selection of special pictures arranged for the purposes of this display, comprising the most wonderful and awe-inspiring of the many wonders which the Bioscope has been the means of introducing to public notice; marvels of Nature, of human handiwork and country such as the world has never before seen. No pains or expenses have been spared in the preparation of these subjects, which are selected from miles of film and represent absolutely the finest photographic quality. ... (3) Fraser River Falls - a glorious panorama. (4) The "Imperial Limited" Express (C.P.R.R.) on its 3,000 mile run across the Continent. (5) The Great Loop at Glacier House, Kicking Horse Pass, taken from the front of the express engine. A snow shed in process of*

*construction is also shown. (6) Kicking Horse Pass, from the Fraser River
Canyon. A monument of engineering skill, and a sublime panorama of mountain
and river scenery. (7) Beavermouth Canyon, as seen from the Observation car.
(8) Tree felling in the Forests. Axemen supported on platforms eight feet
from the base first attack the gigantic tree, then expert sawyers cut through
the trunk: finally a wedge is driven into the cut and the giant falls with a
crash. (9) Method of transporting logs through a gully. Hauled by means of
a block and tackle to the vicinity of the corduroy roads. (10) Hauling logs
through Forest to Sea. "Snigged" by teams of ten horses. This "train" is
composed of ten logs, each averaging 40 feet in length and weighing from one
to one and a half tons. (11) Corduroy Roads through the Forest. Made by
placing timbers across the road. The man in front greases the grooves to
prevent friction and facilitate draught. (12) Sliding Logs into the River.
As the log train reaches the chute, the team is hitched to the back, the
connecting "dogs" are removed, and each log, as it arrives at the end of the
chute, falls into the water with a splash. (13) Hoisting logs to the Mills.
Drawn from the water by means of an endless chain gear. (14) Panoramic view
of Steveston, B.C. The water front of this important fishing village. (15)
Hauling in the salmon nets. Fraser River during the salmon season. This
picture shows thousands of fish struggling in the nets as the latter are
drawn to the surface and finally emptied of their contents. (16) Transfer-
ring salmon to Scows. Each scow holds from 6,000 to 10,000 salmon, and the
fish are delivered at the factories within a few hours of being lifted. (17)
Filling Scows by Steam Hoist. The lifting of the catch from the salmon traps.
By means of "steam brailing", 15,000 fish may be lifted in half an hour. (18)
Specimen salmon, weight 32 pounds." George Kleine Catalogue, 1910. p.132,
and Urban Catalogue, 1909. (Description courtesy CPR.)*

1059. WOOD: FROM FOREST TO THE MILL. (1914)
   p.c. *
   l.   g.   t.   s.
   d.   *
   ph. *
   c.s. *

   See: THE TIMBER INDUSTRY, BRITISH COLUMBIA.

1060. WOOD INDUSTRY IN CANADA. (pre 1910)
   p.c. *
   l. 541'   g. 35mm   t. b+w   s. si.
   d.   *
   ph. *
   c.s. Unknown

   *"We see the evolution of that product from the felling of the huge trunks;
   they are taken to a saw mill where powerful saws pass through the massive
   trunks as they would through butter; several kinds of saws are shown and
   worked. Then the wood is passed through several different stages, until in
   large, new planks it is hoisted on board a steamer for distribution, several
   views being given of the work at the quay." George Kleine Catalogue, 1910.
   p. 226.*

1061. WOODEN SHIPBUILDING IN CANADA. (1918)
   p.c. Dept. of Trade and Commerce
        Exhibits and Publicity Bureau, Ottawa
   l. 1 reel   g. 35mm   t. b+w   s. si.
   d.   *
   ph. *
   c.s. Unknown

   *It is a shame that this film has been lost, for we are the poorer thereby.
   The Catalogue of the Exhibits and Publicity Bureau, Ottawa, gives the following description: "An educational and industrial film produced in co-
   operation with the Imperial Munitions Board. A journey is made to Vancouver
   Island and, in the forest of the Island lumbermen are shown at work. A log
   is obtained in its native birthplace which, after journeying down the skidway
   to the lumber mill enters a British Columbia shipyard as the keel-stick of
   the ship upon which is built up a magnificent wooden ship." Released March
   10, 1919.*

1062. A WORLD OF SCENIC WONDERS. (1918)
　　　p.c. Dept. of Trade and Commerce
　　　　　Exhibits and Publicity Bureau, Ottawa
　　　1. 1 reel　　　　g. 35mm　t. b+w　　s. si.
　　　d.　*
　　　ph.　*
　　　c.s. Unknown

　　　　　　　　　　*The description in the original catalogue of the EPB reads: "This film has
　　　　　　　　　　been produced in co-operation with the Dominion Parks Branch of the Depart-
　　　　　　　　　　ment of the Interior, and is the first film that has been produced that has
　　　　　　　　　　brought Jasper Park before the public. It takes one into the heart of Jasper
　　　　　　　　　　Park and shows the wonders of the Athabaska Valley and the Maligne, it shows
　　　　　　　　　　the woodland caribou and the mountain goat, and ends with a journey to the
　　　　　　　　　　top of Mount Robson, and on the same is disclosed as never before the workings
　　　　　　　　　　of a glacier's machinery. This film is a rare educational film as well as
　　　　　　　　　　a scenic beauty film." Released March 24, 1919.*

1063. WORLD RECORD FLIGHT, VANCOUVER, B.C. (pre 1920)
　　　p.c. *
　　　1.　　　　　　　g. 35mm　t. b+w　　s. si.
　　　d.　*
　　　ph.　W.B. Young
　　　c.s. NFA (Taylor reel 131)

　　　　　　　　　　*"Two American pilots, Evans and Wells, set a world record by circling the
　　　　　　　　　　globe in 28 days in a U.S. Mail plane, equipped with landing floats. Shots
　　　　　　　　　　of crowd around. Evans & Wells in cockpit, taxiing out to take off position."*

1064. WORLD'S HIGHEST SINGLE PIECE FLAGPOLE GETS ITS ANNUAL COAT OF
　　　PAINT, VANCOUVER, B.C. (1924)
　　　p.c. Fox Movietonews (Fox #440.9292-A3623)
　　　1.　　　　　　　g. 35mm　t. b+w　　s. si.
　　　d.　*
　　　ph.　Len H. Roos
　　　c.s. Fox Movietonews, N.Y.

　　　　　　　　　　*"Shot through archway of Hotel Vancouver roof garden. Painter is Charles
　　　　　　　　　　Wren."*

1065. THE WORST BLIZZARD IN THE HISTORY OF VICTORIA, B.C.
　　　(1923)
　　　p.c. Fox Movietonews (Fox #007.3621-3535)
　　　1. 31'　　　　　g. 35mm　t. b+w　　s. si.
　　　d.　*
　　　ph.　Young's Studios
　　　c.s. Fox Movietonews, N.Y.

　　　　　　　　　　*"Various shots of the snow blocked streets." The _heaviest_ snowfall in
　　　　　　　　　　Victoria's history actually occured in 1916.*

1066. W.S. BOWEN THRILLS SPECTATORS WITH UNUSUAL CLIMBING
　　　STUNTS, VICTORIA, B.C. (1922)
　　　p.c. Fox Movietonews (Fox #703.1-4516)
　　　1. 24'　　　　　g. 35mm　t. b+w　　s. si.
　　　d.　*
　　　ph.　W.B. Young
　　　c.s. Fox Movietonews, N.Y.

　　　　　　　　　　Bowen performs tricks on a flagpole.

1067. YACHT RACING IN DISTANCE, YACHTS PASSING, STAR BOATS ON
　　　THE COURSE. "SIR THOMAS" DEFEATS "PATRICIA". (early 1920's)
　　　p.c. Fox Movietonews (Fox #731.51-7461)
　　　1. 40'　　　　　g. 35mm　t. b+w　　s. si.
　　　d.　*
　　　ph.　Len H. Roos
　　　c.s. Fox Movietonews, N.Y.

1068. YACHT REGATTA, VANCOUVER, B.C.   (1933)
    p.c. Fox Movietonews (Fox #18-883)
    l. 800'   g. 35mm   t. b+w   s. sound
    d. *
    ph. ASN
    c.s. Fox Movietonews, N.Y.

> *"Various shots of the annual International Yachting regatta as seen from boat. Commodore Roy W. Corbett speaks for USA. Commodore E.W. Hamber speaks for Canada. Additional scenes of the yachts racing in the regatta."*

1069. YOHO!   (1928?)
    p.c. CGMPB
    l. 1 reel   g. 35mm   t. b+w   s. si. w/captions
    d. *
    ph. *
    c.s. NFA

> *"'YOHO!' is the word the Indians used to express surprise and wonder. What more suitable name could have been chosen for that little valley in the Canadian Rockies? A dozen waterfalls - Takakkaw, Point Lace, Twin Falls and the rest of them - are tumbling all over themselves to get into it. And we, as we climb the High Line Trail, and look down from the top of the world, are lost in the natural beauty of it all. When at last we find our voice it is to echo the old Indian cry of 'YOHO!'"* The copy at the NFA, Ottawa, is 640' long.

1070. YOHO, WONDER VALLEY.   (late 1930's)
    p.c. CGMBP?
    l. 385'   g. 16mm   t. b+w   s. si. & sound
    d. *
    ph. *
    c.s. NFB

1071. YOUNG PEOPLE'S CAMP AT KOOTENAY LAKE.   (1928-1931)
    p.c. private
    l. approx. 400' g. 16mm   t. b+w   s. si.
    d. *
    ph. Rev. George R.B. Kinney
    c.s. via Pacific Cinémathèque, Vancouver

> *Group of campers, including Rev. Beverley Oaten. Flag-raising ceremony, kids saluting. Running to breakfast. Pan of tents. Group of campers. Dodgeball. Hike. Meal in roofed shelter. Swimming in Kootenay Lake, water polo. Dodge-ball with net. Swimming at the lake, Kinney's boat, the BROADCASTER. (1928-30) Campers going into chapel. Old cars at Molly Gibson mine during 1931 climb to Kokanee Glacier, with climbers sitting about. Old unused skyline and buckets at Molly Gibson. Several pans and shots of mine sites and mountains. Kokanee Lake. Wild flowers. Climbers and climbing glacier.*

> *Shots from Rev. Kinney's boat cruising down the Lake. Mess hall at Camp Kokanee, canvas roof over the tables. Boat at float. Campers and boat. Dr. Daley's swimming lessons. CGIT camp. Girls running, folk dancing. Rev. Kinney's boat at Camp Kokanee wharf. Water sports with campers. Campers on beach, in woods, playing sports. Blanket-toss in front of tent. Kids and boat. CU kids.*

1072. YUKON.   (1928)
    p.c. ASN (A Kinogram Travelogue)
    l. 900'   g. 35mm   t. b+w   s. si. w/captions
    d. *
    ph. *
    c.s. NFA

> *A scenic travelogue of the Yukon gold fields. Scenes include: A train travelling from Skagway over the White Pass. Dead Horse Gulch. The boundary between Alaska and the Yukon. Bennett, a former gold-rush city. Miles Canyon. Whitehorse station and scenes in town. By steamer down the Yukon River. Five Finger Rapids. Selkirk. Moosehide. Dawson City. Jimmy Oglow selling apples as he did in 1898. The gambling casinos, now closed. The*

dog taxi system. Dredgers searching for gold in the river bottoms. YUKON was very likely edited by Terry Raymsaye.

ADDENDA

A 1   THE CARIBOO ROAD. (1926-27)
p.c. Provincial Bureau of Information
1. 1 reel   g. 35mm   t. b+w   s. si.
d.   *
ph.   *
c.s. Unknown

The only information about this film comes from a series of questions and answers in the Journal of the Legislative Assembly for March 27, 1931. The Attorney-General revealed that in 1926 he had asked Dr. A.R. Baker, formerly head of the British Columbia Patriotic and Educational Picture Service and a seemingly irrascible public relations man for the Liberal Government, to oversee the production of a publicity film about the Cariboo Road. The film cost $2,699.25, and was only shown once, at the World's Poultry Conference in Ottawa in 1927. Only one positive print was made, and the Attorney-General gave, as reason for its failure to be exhibited more widely, that "the film was not in shape for advantageous distribution." Apparently he had required that the film be on non-flammable stock and Baker had provided it on flammable stock. This was no particular reason to hide the film, however, for another print could have been made on non-flammable stock. The real reason was probably that the film was just not competent enough or good enough to make the impression the department sought.

A 2   THE FILMS OF ALFRED BOOTH. (1929-1930's)
p.c. Alfred Booth
1. over fifteen thousand feet g. 16mm   t. b+w & colour s. si.
d.   *
ph. Alfred Booth
c.s. Alfred Booth, c/o Hawthorne Lodge, Port Coquitlam, B.C.

Beginning in 1929, Mr. Booth toured British Columbia with his camera dozens of times, shooting many reels of 16mm film and exhibiting them in the little towns and relief camps as he went. From 1935-1939 he was employed by the Columbia Coast Mission to film their activities during the summer, and some of these reels still exist (See #191, 192). The films have not been sorted for several years, but in an interview Mr. Booth gave the following partial list of their contents: Fraser Canyon during the 1930's, including CU Hell's Gate, Indians drying salmon, old highway, Yale, North Bend, Lytton, Lillooet, Spences Bridge, Ashcroft, Cache Creek, Kamloops. The Big Bend Country - Revelstoke to Golden during the 30's. Columbia Coast Mission footage, from Pender Harbour to Alert Bay. Vancouver Island during the 1930's, including Great Central Lake, Della Falls, Della Lake, Big Interior Mountain (1932), Herbert Island, Barclay Sound, Ahousat, Flores Island, Indian villages on the west coast, Alert Bay, Sointula, Malcolm Island, Etc. Totem poles at the head of Kingcome Inlet. Chilcotin/Cariboo during the 1930's, including placer gold mining operations, Barkerville, Wells, Antler Creek, monitor operations on Lougheed and Ketch Creeks, Dragon Creek and Willow River, Jack Of Clubs Lake, and the Antler Hotel. The following areas in the province: Prince George, Summit Lake, Salmon Arm and district, Kamloops and district, Merritt and district, Princeton and district, Keremeos and district, Okanagan Fruit Growers, Trial, Nelson, Castlegar, Bonnington Falls, Kaslo, Nakusp, and New Denver, all during the 1930's. Also Ashcroft, William's Lake, stampedes at the Flying U Ranch, Harrison Lake, Fraser Valley including Frasea Farms. Vancouver harbour, including the traffic of ships, particularly CPR EMPRESS liners and the CPR Pier D fire of 1938. (See also A5.)

A 3   A FISHING TRIP IN TWEEDSMUIR PARK, B.C. (1938)
p.c. private
1. 200'   g. 16mm   t. colour s. si.
d.   *
ph. Edward Gillespie
c.s. via Pacific Cinémathèque, Vancouver

The film opens with a rainbow. A sequence follows in which a group of ladies

*pose for the camera before boarding a small float plane, CF-BJR. They climb
into the plane and it begins to taxi across the lake. It flies overhead in
the opposite direction. The same ladies and others, seemingly a family group,
pose outside a large ivy-covered, half-timbered building.*

*A group of seven professional men in suits pose in front of two late-model
cars outside a large wooden building, preparatory to leaving on their fishing
trip. They appear to have hired two guides for the trip through what was
once a chain of lakes, including Ootsa Lake. Much of the region they fished
is now entirely flooded, forming one huge lake. The men leave on their
trip; they have hired two long wooden boats driven by outboard motors, perhaps with a guide in each boat. There are many shots of the boats travelling
across the lakes, scenery along the shore and snow-capped mountains, several
good CU shots of various men reclining in the boats as they glide across the
lake, scenes of the fishermen eating and making camp and, most fascinating,
several views of the men hauling the heavy wooden boats through the forest on
the numerous portages between lakes. There are shots of waterfalls, the men
having a wee nip in their boats as the sky clouds up, and two interesting
sequences where one man alone poles one boat at a time through a very shallow
creek while the others carry the supplies and gear across by land, loading
everything again when they reach deep water. Scenes follow of fishing, more
portaging, some white water, waterfalls, and the men posing with a display
of trout at their camp. At the end of the trip, the seven fishermen and two
guides pose in front of a huge log barn in their fishing clothes, and the
seven are seen again by their cars on the way home.*

*The final two shots are an excellent pan of Kamloops from the lookout above
the city, and a view of the lookout itself. The colour in this Kodachrome
print is still as good as the day it was exposed and the film itself is in
very good shape.*

A 4   REVELSTOKE MISCELLANY. (mid 1930's-1940)
       p.c. private
       l.   g. 16mm & 8mm   t. b+w & colour s. si.
       d.   *
       ph. C. Rutherford
       c.s. via Pacific Cinémathèque, Vancouver

              *Unfortunately, little data is available about this excellent collection, but
              more information may be gained by writing to the Pacific Cinémathèque.*

A 5   COLUMBIA COAST MISSION OUTFOOTAGE. (late 1930's-
       early 1940's)
       p.c. *
       l. approx. 60 minutes g. 16mm t. colour s. si.
       d.   Alfred Booth
       ph. Alfred Booth
       c.s. Discovery Passage Video Project, Campbell River

              *According to the Discovery Passage Video Project in Campbell River, the foot-
              age contained in these out-takes consists of the following: The three boats
              used by the Columbia Coast Mission, COLUMBIA, RENDEZVOUS and JOHN ANTLE;
              assorted sequences of hospitals on the coast; Union steamships; mission per-
              sonnel; logging; fishing; canneries; sequences of Cortes Island; and four
              minutes of Kingcome village.*

              *This material has been transferred to 3/4" video tape. More information can
              be obtained from Campbell River Television, 594-11th Avenue, Campbell River,
              (604) 287-8829.*

A 6   LOGGING SCENES IN BRITISH COLUMBIA. (1930's)
       p.c. private
       l. approx. 275' g. 16mm   t. b+w   s. si. w/captions
       d.   *
       ph. Ernest Johnson
       c.s. NFA

              *The lid of the can is marked "Very Good - Cats. Train. (High Rigger)".
              The head of the film is missing and parts of the film appear to be contained
              in the Ernest Johnson reel titled OLD LOGGING MILLS. In fact, OLD LOGGING
              MILLS appears to be a continuation of this reel with the addition of*

extra logging material

LOGGING SCENES IN BRITISH COLUMBIA *begins with an excellent high-rigging sequence at Cowichan Lake on Vancouver Island. A high-rigger buckles his belt, climbs a tall fir, tops it, holds on while the tree sways fiercely, then climbs down again. A rigger is hauled up on a little seat called a "jack ladder" to the conjunction of guy wires on a spar tree. Good scenes of high-lead logging with donkey engine. Trees crashing up to the landing. A log scaler measures the logs, good CU's. He poses and smiles embarrassedly. Logs piled on rail cars. Good shots of a logging train loaded with red cedar and Douglas-fir rolling past a landing, three men riding on the front of the locomotive. The train arrives at a wharf (Cowichan Bay) and the logs are dumped into the sea with a great splash. Good HA shot of the locomotive. Men sorting logs in the booming ground.*

The next sequence is unusual because it shows high-lead logging carried out with a donkey engine and an A-frame on a raft offshore. There are good shots of the donkey and the A-frame working as well as good long sequences showing logs being hauled into the water by the cables. The logging show is the J.R. Morgan camp on the Queen Charlotte Islands.

Scenes of a landing in the forest with good CU's of a donkey engine operating, logs being yarded to the base of a spar tree, a logging train passing by carrying huge logs, and the train moving out onto a wharf where the logs are released into the sea.

The final sequence appears to be a demonstration before a group of men in suits of the uses of a Caterpillar tractor in the woods. A Cat hauls a great turn of logs through the woods by means of an elaborate A-frame mounted on tracks. The logs are loaded onto trucks by means of a spar-tree. The Cat performs some particularly difficult jobs with heavy and cumbersome logs. On one of the Caterpillar tractors is written the words: TANSKEY LOGGING COMPANY.

A 7. OLD LOGGING MILLS. (1930's)
   p.c. private
   1. approx. 375' g. 16mm t. b+w s. si. w/captions
   d. *
   ph. Ernest Johnson
   c.s. NFA

   Initial captions read: British Columbia's Largest Industry
   Employing Over 20,000 Men
   Average Yearly Production - $60,000,000-$70,000,000
   See Ernest Johnson reel LOGGING SCENES IN BRITISH COLUMBIA.

   Fallers at work in the forest with axes and swedish fiddle. A high-rigger rides up a spar tree on a "jack-ladder".

   A booming ground in a bay. Pan of a huge sawmill near Vancouver, possibly Fraser Mills. Men piking logs from pond onto the end of the endless chain running into the mill. Logs being sprayed to wash off mud and grit as they run up endless chain. Saw carriage and turning device demonstrated. Sawing a log 74' long, 5'4" in diameter, containing 4418 board feet of lumber, with a double-cut head saw which cuts a board both coming and going. Good CU's of log going through saw. Edger sawing boards into various widths. Resawing process splits wood further. Gang or riff-saw slices huge timbers into boards of precise width and thickness. Automatic trimmer trims boards to various lengths. CU trimmer operating "keyboard". Preliminary sorting by workers in the plant as boards leave the sawing area on an endless chain. Lumber stacked for seasoning in the yard - pan. Motorized lumber carrier working in the yard, picking up stacks of lumber and moving them about. Mechanized lumber piler with men working on a stack. Timber dock and loading the lumber for export. Freighter being loaded with lumber. 4-masted sailing vessel tied up at wharf in b.g. The freighter sails away with its lumber for the ports of the seven seas. (See No. A6)

A 8 PIONEER GOLD MINE IN BRALORNE, B.C. (1930's)
   p.c. private
   1. 100' g. 16mm t. b+w s. si.
   d. *
   ph. Ernest Johnson
   c.s. NFA

A 9   LOGGING AT MORGAN CAMP AND ON VANCOUVER ISLAND.
      (late 1930's)
      p.c. private
      l. approx. 400'   g. 16mm   t. colour   s. si. w/captions
      d.   *
      ph. Ernest Johnson
      c.s. NFA

*Logging scenes on Vancouver Island begin this reel. A Caterpillar tractor
is being towed out of a harbour on a barge. The barge arrives in an inlet.
The camera lingers at a landing while large spools of cable are lifted off
the barge onto the landing area. In the background a donkey engine and A-
frame can be seen mounted on a raft. In the forest, two men are falling
trees with axe and swedish fiddle. CU of the butt end of a log with writing
on it. Views of the spar-tree landing with the donkey engine working and
trees being yarded up to the spar. Steam shovel working. Spar tree. Pan
across landing with steam donkey working, etc., with snow-capped mountains
in the b.g. Logs being yarded into the landing by spar tree and steam donkey, many shots. MS donkey working with steam locomotive approaching in the
distance. Various shots of piles of logs at the landing, men throwing tongs
onto the logs and logs being lifted onto rail cars for transport out of the
woods. Excellent sequence.*

*The second part of this film shows the J.R. Morgan Logging Company camp on
the Queen Charlotte Islands. LS of the camp situated on floats along the
shore. Freighter J.R. MORGAN (formerly the C.N.S.S. PRINCE CHARLES) comes
alongside. Kids waving and posing on the wharf, two alone and then with a
woman. A second coastal freighter approaches and then is seen in LS. View
of donkey engine on a raft. J.R. MORGAN tied up alongside. Floating boom-
raft of logs. Donkey on raft with a great saw that reaches out and saws
logs into more manageable lengths in the water. A massive boom-raft of logs
is being readied for towing to a mill. The caption reads: "400 feet long,
75 feet wide and 25 feet deep.". Donkey and A-frame on raft in b.g.*

*The last part of the film shows a "modern electrically operated saw mill".
Pan across mill showing buildings and sheds and piles of stacked lumber. A
huge crane lifts lumber off wharf and places it beside a ship already well-
loaded with lumber. Good pans across wharf area showing activities and
loading of stacks of lumber onto the ship. Good shot of lumber piling machine and motorized lumber carrier. This is likely Hastings Mill near Vancouver,
identified by "The Lions" in b.g. of some of the shots.*

A10   ROYAL VISIT TO VANCOUVER AND VICTORIA.   (1939)
      p.c. private and commercial (commercial may be Castle
           Films footage of Royal Visit)
      l. approx. 775'   g. 16mm   t. colour & b+w   s. si. w/some captions
      d.   *
      ph. Ernest Johnson and others
      c.s. NFA

*Mr. Johnson's two-reel account of the Royal Visit in 1939 is a composite.
About 375' are part of a commercial film in b+w with captions, probably by
Castle Films. Mr. Johnson photographed the sequence in Vancouver and an un-
identified friend in Victoria filmed the King and Queen in that city.*

*Reel 1 begins with the b+w commercial material and shows the King and Queen
in London, embarking for Canada, arriving in Quebec City, visiting Ottawa
and Toronto and Banff, Alberta. (225') Mr. Johnson's footage in colour
begins with a pan across the decorations on the buildings at the corner of
Granville and Georgia Street in Vancouver. Bunting and flags are draped
everywhere. People are milling about waiting for the parade and streetcars
to pass to and fro. From a vantage point high in the Birk's Building, Mr.
Johnson photographed the parade, crowds lining the sidewalks, bands passing
by, streetcars. The atmosphere is festive, with many marching bands going
down Georgia Street, highlanders, sailors and all manner of uniformed troops.
At last the royal car passes with the King and Queen waving. People throng
the streets. More bands and soldiers march by. Highland cadets line the
street waiting for the arrival of the King and Queen. Brief shot of people
running through Stanley Park to catch a glimpse of the King and Queen. LS
Lion's Gate Bridge and pan back into Vancouver harbour revealing thousands
of little boats waiting for the PRINCESS MARGUERITE which is carrying the
King and Queen to Vancouver Island and which is a small speck just departing*

from the CPR wharves at the end of the pan. Two groups of three planes fly over in formation. LS PRINCESS MARGUERITE sailing past on her way to Vancouver Island surrounded by little craft. LS PRINCESS MARGUERITE sailing west under the Lion's Gate Bridge, from Vancouver. (175')
Reel 2 begins with Johnson's footage recording the arrival of the King and Queen at the CPR station in Vancouver. A parade of highlanders and sailors marches down toward the station under a great WELCOME banner stretched across the street. LS marching troops. LS Royal Hudson locomotive, tender, and train in CPR railyard with steam up, perhaps having just arrived. CPR station decorated with bunting and flags. King and Queen drive up street under banner into the city. Crowds of people watching. Marine Building in b.g. Three RCN destroyers (HMCS FRASER, SKEENA & ST. LAURENT) tied up at CPR wharf, all dressed. Good MS Royal Hudson locomotive. Band marches by. CU Royal Hudson locomotive (#2850) with CPR employees and crowds around it. Group of high-landers and other soldiers waiting for King and Queen to arrive. King and Queen walk through crowds waving and smiling, saying goodbye.

The remaining colour sequence takes place in Victoria. It begins with huge crowds thronging the Causeway in front of the Empress Hotel, waiting to catch a glimpse of the King and Queen. Pan across crowded Causeway to Post Office and Belmont Building showing ferries in b.g. and crowds in f.g. MS Empress Hotel detail. King and Queen disembark from their auto at Beacon Hill Park; the crowds are very thick. King and Queen arrive on the saluting stand with other dignitaries.

After the presentation of colours to the RCN, the King and Queen walk down the ramp of the saluting stand and mix with dignitaries on the lawn prepara-tory to leaving. Good shots of Queen Elizabeth strolling with British Colum-bia Premier Duff Patullo and chatting with him. The King and Queen get back into their car and begin to drive away. LS decorated Empress Hotel. Good shot of decorated Victoria City Hall with crowds lining Douglas Street in anticipation. King and Queen drive past corner of Yates and Douglas Street, crowds waving and cheering as cavalcade rolls by. King and Queen arrive at Causeway entrance to the Empress Hotel, thousands of people crushing in for a look, harbour and ferries in b.g. King and Queen mingling with guests at Beacon Hill Park. Good shots of the corner of Yates and Douglas Street in Victoria, all decorated, with soldiers standing by waiting for cavalcade. A military band and soldiers march by, people waiting for King and Queen to arrive. (225') The remaining 150' is b+w with captions, from the same source as the footage at the beginning of Reel 1, and shows the Royal Visit to the United States in June, 1939, after the King and Queen completed their Royal Tour of Canada.

A11   EMPRESS OF JAPAN AND CONSTRUCTION OF LION'S GATE BRIDGE.
    (1937-1938)
    p.c. private
    1. approx. 450'   g. 16mm   t. colour   s. si.
    d.   *
    ph. Ernest Johnson
    c.s. NFA

Excellent shot of the EMPRESS OF JAPAN at CPR pier in Vancouver. Pan of wharf area with scows in f.g. EMPRESS OF JAPAN leaves wharf, moving astern then sailing out to sea. Various shots with Vancouver harbour in b.g. as EMPRESS OF JAPAN sails west, through the Lion's Gate before the bridge was built.

The rest of the film deals with the construction of the Lion's Gate Bridge. LS foundations on either side, Capilano River running out into the sea. Bridge with catwalks, LS with EMPRESS ship sailing under. Pan of tower of bridge, catwalks in place. Pan along catwalks to North Vancouver. Tugs in the harbour; an EMPRESS ship leaves. Good shot of catwalks from Vancouver side as they leave the ground and rise up to the towers. At this point the vertical cables which will hold the deck superstructures are hanging from the horizontal cables. The next scene shows the first section of steel deck superstructure in place. A CPR PRINCESS boat sails off to Vancouver Island, passing under the bridge. S. shots of the brightly painted original figure-head of the EMPRESS OF JAPAN in Stanley Park with the bridge in b.g. Small boats at the base of a tower. Deck superstructures almost completed, LS. Men proceeding up catwalks to the top. Tug boat. North Vancouver shoreline. Bridge under construction shot from beneath, men walking along catwalks and

cables. Officials walking up catwalks. Pan of bridge from top to tower.
Students watching ships passing below. Men in suits high up on top of one
of the towers. Pan of Vancouver from top of tower. Freighter sailing under
the bridge. Direct view down onto a PRINCESS boat sailing under the bridge,
filmed from the deck. Men in suits on top of the bridge, grinning. Same
men returning down catwalks slowly, looking about them nervously. Man paint-
ing clustered cables. Cables being wound with wire. Sunset from high on
the bridge. Freighter sailing under the bridge at sunset. Ships passing in
Vancouver harbour at dusk. Freighter in reflection of sunset in water. Pan
across bridge from water, deck finished. Sailing under the bridge, looking
up. Cars crossing the finished bridge from the Vancouver side. A ship sails
under the bridge. A freighter sails under the bridge. Ships in the harbour:
small lighter and freighter steaming by in b.g. Lady in black fur coat walk-
ing on the bridge.

A12   CONSTRUCTION OF THE LION'S GATE BRIDGE - OUTS.   (1938-39)
       p.c. private
       l. approx. 200'   g. 16mm   t. colour   s. si.
       d.   *
       ph. Ernest Johnson
       c.s. NFA

Most of this reel consists of out-takes deleted by Mr. Johnson while he was
putting together the reel titled EMPRESS OF JAPAN AND CONSTRUCTION OF LION'S
GATE BRIDGE (ADDENDUM 11). Good MS with original figurehead of EMPRESS OF
JAPAN in f.g. with uncompleted Lion's Gate Bridge in b.g. Pan across un-
completed bridge with North Shore in b.g. LS Capilano River spilling into
the harbour then pan up along bridge cable to northern tower and down lower
to water. LS bridge tower and North Shore from Vancouver side. Choppy sea,
small tug buffeting up harbour, from Vancouver side with North Vancouver in
b.g. MS views of bridge construction from Vancouver side. Rivetted steel
sections of bridge being lifted and fastened into place. Work boat sails under
unfinished bridge, pan across bridge. MS men working on steel trusses. Pan
down tower showing catwalks and roadbed. Men working on truss, pan out across
to southern tower. Men working on trusses. LS bridge across harbour, prob-
ably from the vicinity of CPR pier. Men working on catwalks, pan down to
wire cables and blocks.
The location on the last sequence is not identified: a huge log is carried
through a city street and past camera, on a logging truck. MS two girls in
bathing suits sitting atop the log. A sign on the hood of the truck reads:
SEASIDE HERE WE COME! People watching. Truck moves away from camera, girls
hold up a large V (for Victory) sign between them and wave as they pass the
camera. CU large red, spools of Canada Wire and Cable steel wire rope on
the back of a flat bed truck.

A13   FISHING CAMP AT CAMPBELL RIVER, CANNERY AT STEVESTON
       AND TUGBOATS IN VANCOUVER. (approx. 1938-39)
       p.c. private
       l. 300'   g. 16mm   t. colour   s. si.
       d.   *
       ph. Ernest Johnson
       c.s. NFA

A fishing camp on the beach near Campbell River, Vancouver Island. Various
scenes of tents, where families stay, and people posing in the tents. Three
pans of a huge rainbow stretching across Discovery Passage with boats and
white houses occasionally in the f.g. Man weighing a good-sized Tyee salmon.
Family posing in their tent. Two sporty fellows posing and clowning in front
of the Johnson car. Two boys posing and playing with a Tyee on the scales.
Two men and a woman posing with a Tyee on the scales. LS tents and campers
at the top of the beach, various miscellaneous shots. Various shots of a
dog chasing something in the water. Pan of tents and houses at the top of
the beach. LS a floatplane taking off out in the bay. Pan tents, houses
and beach. MS packing up the trailer behind the black car preparatory to
leaving for home. CU boy posing on trailer. Shots of what is either Elk
Falls near Campbell River or Englishman's River Falls near Parksville, and
a bridge across the river.

At Steveston Cannery: A Japanese fisherman and his family hanging their nets
to dry, Home Oil tank in b.g. Pan of nets drying and Japanese fishermen
working on them, houses on stilts in b.g. White man sawing through a huge

driftwood log on the beach with a Swedish fiddle. Two Japanese kids on wharf between nets, Japanese woman mending net, pan down long rack of drying nets. Japanese woman walking down wharf. Good shots of houses on wharves with flowers in window boxes, vegetables in a rowboat, kids playing, laundry flapping, pan across homes and wharves, nets and fishermen. Two men mending nets on wharf. Japanese kids playing. East Indian kids posing in a line.

Various shots of snow-covered mountains and clouds from a small plane.

Good pan and various shots of crowded tugboat wharves in Vancouver. Steam and smoke and fog all about - may be early morning, or late evening. Men working with steel-wire rope winch, others standing nearby talking. Pan of tugboat ARMOCO. CU Canada Wire and Cable Co. bright red spools of wire rope. Bow shot of large tugboat SNOHOMISH. Broadside shot of ship at wharf, man walking ashore across gangplank, steel wire cable feeding out of winch. Pan up to lifeboat and hold.

.A14   "NOR' BY WEST THROUGH THE INSIDE PASSAGE ON THE B.C. COAST" and
        "MOTOR TRIP FROM VANCOUVER TO NELSON VIA THE BEAUTIFUL FRASER,
        COLUMBIA, AND KOOTENAY ROUTE".
        p.c. private
        l. 450'   g. 16mm   t. colour s. si.
        d.   *
        ph. Ernest Johnson
        c.s. NFA

NOR' BY WEST THROUGH THE INSIDE PASSAGE ON THE B.C. COAST: Various shots and pans over the bow of a large coastal freight and passenger ship during a westerly blow; the water is blue and bits of spray are gusting off the crest of each wave, dappling the sea. The ship may be a Canadian Steamship coastal vessel. Shot astern showing port side of ship with three funnels and lifeboats, wake streaming astern. Engine telegraph and compass on open bridge. Pan astern, showing funnels. Gulls float above the after flagstaff. Three pans of tree-covered mountains rising out of the sea in a narrow part of the Inside Passage between Vancouver Island and the mainland. Pan of shore from moving ship and reflection of mountains in calm water slightly rippled by passage of steamer. Several good pans of Ocean Falls from the ship, showing the Pacific Mills pulp and paper mill briefly and the wharves and buildings on the wharves, hotel-like buildings, houses scattered back on the hill above the harbour. Shot under wharf showing buildings, etc., and what appears to be a streetcar on rails. LS Union steamship entering Hardy Bay (could this be Hartley Bay?). LS tug with barge and, in next two shots, two whalers heading for the Bering Sea.

MOTOR TRIP FROM VANCOUVER TO NELSON VIA THE BEAUTIFUL FRASER, COLUMBIA AND KOOTENAY ROUTE: Pan of Vancouver waterfront from harbour, showing a CPR EMPRESS at berth. Pan totempoles in Stanley Park. "Burrard and Georgia Streets, showing British Columbia Electric Railway underground crew installing 12 KV lead-covered cable" - various shots and angles with Marine Building in b.g. LS Alexandra suspension bridge with car driving across. LS rain moving on tracks on other side of Fraser Canyon pan over to river. Pan across Nicola Lake near Merritt. Trail, showing Consolidated Mining and Smelting smelter at Tadanac, - pan back and forth across Trail, smelter in b.g. Man walking over to and standing beside large spools of steel wire rope and cable. Columbia River cable ferry at Castlegar - pan river, LS ferry moving toward camera and shot of cable in water. Junction of the Kootenay and Columbia Rivers. Tomb of Peter Verigin, assassinated Doukhobor leader. Pan along river and tracks. South Slocan, Lower Bonnington and Upper Bonnington, all West Kootenay Power and Light Company plants on the Kootenay River - LS of each in respective order. LS power plant owned and controlled by the City of Nelson. Cora Lynn, the most recent West Kootenay power plant. Kootenay River several months later during high water. Pan across raging water to South Slocan power house with sign WEST KOOTENAY POWER AND LIGHT. Staff houses of West Kootenay Power and Light Company's South Slocan powerhouse. Pan across residences, people posing, to raging river. Man walking along path outside staff residence. Mr. Wid Bennett, engineer at South Slocan and Mr. T.A. Gass of Canada Wire and Cable Company, Ltd. posing. LS's power house at South Slocan. Various shots of South Slocan dam. LS city of Nelson on Kootenay Lake. Five pans across construction of Grand Coulee Dam in U.S. on the way back to Vancouver through the States. Sunset on English Bay in Vancouver with a LS steamship sailing away.

A15 EMPRESS OF RUSSIA IN DRYDOCK AND VANCOUVER WATERFRONT
SCENES. (1937-45)
p.c. private
l. approx. 250' g. 16mm   t. colour s. si.
d. *
ph. Ernest Johnson
c.s. NFA

*Coastal freighter in Vancouver pulling into wharf. View of clouds from an
airplane. Good aerial shots of coastal freighter sailing up inside passage,
perhaps between Vancouver Island and the mainland. Aerial shots of snowy,
coniferous, hillsides on an inlet. Harmac pulpmill near Crofton (?) from
the air, an Island Tug and Barge company barge at jetty.*

*Many excellent shots from bow to stern, CU and MS of the SS EMPRESS OF RUSSIA
in drydock at Yarrows shipyards in Esquimalt. Good sequences of men painting
the hull, shots along the hull, good CU's of the propeller, etc. Johnson
family posing on the bridge of the EMPRESS OF RUSSIA. Chinese steward posing
on the deck of the drydocked ship. (1937 or 1939).*

*Excellent shots of HMS IMPLACABLE, a British aircraft carrier, arriving in
Vancouver in 1945.*

*Shots along length of Canadian Steamship PRINCE CHARLES at wharf in Vancouver
harbour. Fourmasted sailing vessel FANTOME all dressed and at anchor in
Vancouver harbour. Canadian Steamship ferry sails by. Surf rolling in on
unidentified beach. Shots of CPR PRINCESS ferry sailing under Lion's Gate
Bridge on a blustery day. A little tugboat buffets against the choppy sea
sailing toward Vancouver Island. Good pan over the North Shore and Vancouver
Island to PRINCESS ship in the distance on her way to Victoria. Surf pounding on a beach.*

A16 THE THOUSAND DAYS, (1942)
p.c. ASN/ASS (#B-760)
l. 2 reels   g. 35mm   t. b+w   s. sound
d. Gordon Sparling
ph. *
c.s. NFA

*CANADIAN CAMEO NO. 51. A review of the first thousand days of World War II.
This was the only two-reel CANADIAN CAMEO and contained scenes of the 72nd
Regiment and Seaforth Highlanders being recruited in Vancouver in 1939. "A
dramatic, impressionistic Canadian Cameo dealing with perhaps the most important three years in all Canada's history. The story opens on September
3rd, 1939, and tells, by means of the vivid, fast moving Rhapsodic Technique,
of a people transformed ... from the complacent days of the phoney war, through
the black days of disillusion, to the days of expansion and finally the days
of high gear in the desperate race for victory. Here is the proud and authentic record of Canada's first THOUSAND DAYS of war."*

A17 HOT AND HAPPY. (1935)
p.c. ASN/ASS (#B-652)
l. 1 reel   g. 35mm   t. b+w   s. sound
d. Gordon Sparling
ph. *
c.s. NFA (?)

*CANADIAN CAMEO NO. 31. "When summer comes and Old Sol smiles benignly, there
are any number of things to do. There's aquaplaning with its thrills and
spills. There is dinghy-racing and motor-cycling, and the scientific art
of archery. And if you like to fish, then let's go and get a big one. We
can have a swim on the way or perhaps a spot of summer skiing. All these
and more add to the fun on torrid days, when everyone is HOT AND HAPPY."
The summer skiing sequences were filmed on the mountains near Vancouver.*

A18 MOUNTAIN SUMMER. (1938)
p.c. ASN (A&B-750)
l. 1 reel   g. 35mm   t. Cinécolor s. sound
d. John Alexander
ph. *
c.s. Unknown

Promotional film for the CPR showing scenes in British Columbia.

A19 THE DEPARTURE OF THE BANTAMS (143rd REGIMENT) AND THE YUKON
     REGIMENT FROM VICTORIA, AND THE LAUNCHING OF THE MARGARET
     HANEY, VICTORIA, B.C. (1917)
     p.c. Superfluities Motion Pictures, Ltd.
     l.   g. 35mm   t. b+w   s. si.
     d.   Reginald Hincks
     ph. Richard Rosedale
     c.s. lost

            *Superfluities Motion Pictures, Ltd., was registered in Victoria on January
            25, 1917, with Hincks and Rosedale listed as two of its four shareholders.
            Their ambition was to begin small, hoping to build into a large, capable
            concern.*

            *The company presented a programme of war films at the Royal Victoria Theatre
            during the week commencing February 26, 1917. At the same time, they ex-
            hibited some of their films, depicting the departure of the Bantams (143rd
            Regiment) from Victoria on February 10, 1917, the departure of the Yukon
            Regiment at the end of January, and the launching of the MARGARET HANEY in
            late January. The MARGARET HANEY was a five-masted wooden ship that was to
            be the prototype of a new fleet of lumber ships working out of British Col-
            umbia ports.*

            *At the same time as this programme was playing at the Royal, Hincks and Rose-
            dale hoped, barring inclement weather, to film patrons entering the theatre,
            showing the films later in the week to what they hoped would be a returning
            crowd. There is no record of the success of this venture, or whether the film
            was even exposed.*

A20 WINTER LOGGING AT ROCK BAY. (approx. 1935)
     p.c. private
     l. 100'   g. 16mm   t. b+w   s. si.
     d.   *
     ph. *
     c.s. BCPM History

            *This reel was photographed by a crewman of the COLUMBIA, the flagship of the
            Columbia Coast Mission boats, under the command of John Antle, founder and
            Superintendent of the Mission. The location is likely the Hastings Mill
            Logging Company's operation at Rock Bay, 50 miles north of Campbell River
            on Vancouver Island.*

            *The film opens with an aerial shot of an inlet. There is snow on the hills
            and the clouds hang low above the sea. Various panning shots filmed from
            the water of a small village or logging camp at the foot of a hill just above
            the beach. There are log booms in the water and a log-dumping wharf protrudes
            from the camp. A logging locomotive moves toward the camera. Snow between
            three sets of railway tracks. Steam locomotive is followed by several flat-
            cars loaded with logs. Men pull off chains fastening logs to cars and the
            logs clatter into the sea. Watertank in b.g. Shot of locomotive. Group
            shot of two women and a child and a man with a tripod. Two men outside door
            of infirmary, one on crutches. Sequence of two logs being yarded into land-
            ing by high-lead method, many other cut logs lying on the ground, snow all
            about. Two steam donkeys operating, one each side of the railroad tracks
            in the middle of the forest, one loading logs onto railway flatcars. Pan
            up spar tree and down again. LS high rigger up spar tree working on rigging.
            Pan down tree to men working at the landing and the steam donkey puffing
            away. Good MS steam donkey, man sawing wood in b.g. with Swedish fiddle.
            CU men chopping at a log with double-bladed axes. Turn of logs coming in
            and being dumped on a pile. Chokerman walks down from setting chokeer around
            a pile of logs and waves to the donkey operator. Pan donkey operator,
            Chinese man sawing up log with Swedish fiddle, and loggers on their break.
            LS steam donkey at base of spar tree. Pan of logs on rail cars, steam donkey
            billowing in distance, logs being loaded onto cars. Two loggers outside shed
            pointing.*

A21   VANCOUVER ISLAND PICNIC AND COLUMBIA COAST MISSION
       BOAT DEDICATION.   (1935)
       p.c. private
       1. 100'   g. 16mm   t. b+w   s. si.
       d.   *
       ph. *
       c.s. BCPM History

          This reel was likely photographed by a crewman of the COLUMBIA, the flagship of the Columbia Coast Mission boats, under the command of John Antle, founder and superintendent of the Mission. No location is known for either the picnic or for what looks to be a dedication, but both events likely occurred on Vancouver Island.

          Pan across what is probably a church picnic outside a hall. Cooking pits, people eating and talking, etc., ends on CU of a car with a 1935 licence plate with men gathered about talking. Meat roasting on fire. Pan across smoking cooking pit. Pan across picnickers. Men tossing horseshoes. Mother with baby, other picnickers.

          Group shot on what is probably the Columbia Coast Mission boat COLUMBIA. Two women, two men and a boy. Wharf in b.g. with car. CU's of each of the women laughing into the camera.

          Three Anglican ministers on the stern of what is probably a Columbia Coast Mission boat, performing what appears to be a dedication service. Windy. A small crowd listens as the boat rocks in the sea. Boat appears to be tied up alongside another, from which vantage point this film is being shot. MS, LS, then CU of the three ministers performing ceremony. Various other shots of service.

A22   NOVA SCOTIA TO BRITISH COLUMBIA – PART IV. (approx.
       1910–11)
       p.c. Natural Color Kinematograph Company
       1. 1 reel (approx. 1,250') g. 35mm   t. Kinemacolor s. si w/captions
       d.   *
       ph. H. Sintzenich (?)
       c.s. Unknown

   1. *"LAKES AND PEAKS of the Rocky Mountains. The first lake shown is that known as Emerald, which contains the greenest water in the world. This curious phenomenon is caused by the fact that ice-cold glacial water enters the lake, whose mountainous slopes are covered by vast pine forests.*

   2. *"A TYPICAL CANADIAN ROADWAY. A pony party leaving for Emerald Lake. The trail through the woods, affording many beautiful vistas amongst the pine trees. A first glimpse of the lake.*

   3. *"REFLECTIONS OF MOUNTAINS in the waters of Emerald Lake. At the bridge, Emerald Lake. A Western boatman.*

   4. *"THE PEAKS OF THE ROCKY MOUNTAINS. In this section are included all the most famous peaks in the Canadian Rockies, viz., Emerald Peak, Mount Wapta, Mount Burgess, Mount Lefroy, Castle Crags, Mount Aberdeen, Mount beehive and Mount Victoria. Many beautiful examples of scenic photography are to be seen here.*

   5. *"A SUMMER CAMP at the foot of the Rockies. "The Faithful Friend." A log fire at camp. The exact hue of the flames is perfectly reproduced.*

   6. *"KICKING HORSE RIVER. In the section are shown Mount Stephen, the Whirlpool and the Natural Arch where the rocks form a natural bridge from which it is possible to step from one side of the river to the other. Close views of the Natural Arch and the tumbling waters are very effective.*

   7. *"LAKE LOUISE, the gem of the Rockies. This lake is 4,500 feet above sea level. A view of the Canadian Pacific Railway chateau is given in the opening section. This is a magnificent structure provided for the accommodation of the numerous tourists who spend some months every year amid the beautiful scenery of the Rockies. Of the lake itself a number of views are given showing the reflections of Mount Victoria and the forests of pines."*

   The above descriptions are reproduced from the Kinemacolor Catalogue of Films,

*1912-13, and are prefaced by the following: "In the photographing of this
series of KINEMACOLOR films we have pleasure in acknowledging invaluable
assistance from the Canadian Pacific Railway Company, which operates over
11,000 miles of railway throughout Canada.   This system is the longest continuous railway under one management in the world. ... The series in its
completeness conveys a never-to-be-forgotten impression of the extent and
importance of the vast Dominion of Canada."   The series consists of 4 reels.*

A23   SCENIC CANADA: RAILWAY PANORAMAS, ROCKY MOUNTAINS, ETC.
       (1913)
       p.c. Kinemacolor Ltd.
       1. 1190'   g. 35mm   t. Kinemacolor s. si.
       d.   *
       ph. H. Sintzenich
       c.s. Unknown

              *Probably photographed by Mr. Sintzenich during his tour of western Canada in
              September-October 1913.   No information about locations is available. (Infor-
              mation from Kinemacolor Films catalogue, 1915-16.) Production no. 1108.)*

              *The Victoria Daily Colonist, October 21, 1913, p.7, quotes Mr. Sintzenich as
              saying that he filmed the Rockies from the cowcatcher of a train.   This was
              probably in September on his way through to British Columbia.*

A24   INDUSTRIAL CANADA: FRUIT-GROWING, CATTLE AND HORSE-
       RANCHING, WHEAT HARVESTING, ETC. (1913)
       p.c. Kinemacolor Ltd.
       1. 1255'   g. 35mm   t. Kinemacolor s. si.
       d.   *
       ph. H. Sintzenich
       c.s. Unknown

              Kinemacolor production no. 1109.

              *According to a report in the Victoria Daily Colonist, October 21, 1913, p.7,
              Mr. Sintzenich arrived in Victoria on October 20 from a trip through the Okan-
              agan Valley.   It appears that the B.C. Department of Lands had an agreement
              with the Kinemacolor company to make promotional films in this area, and the
              results became part of this reel.*

              *According to the newspaper, shots included a general view of Goldstream or-
              chards; views showing how trees are budded; men pruning trees; sixty horse-
              power plow in action breaking orchard land; nursery stock; the growth of
              trees and the stages of their growth; and a demonstration of how nursery and
              orchard workers grow their crop, showing all the phases the fruit passes
              through on its way from producer to consumer, from planting to packing and
              loading onto railroad cars for transit.   Of the ranching, or harvesting,
              nothing more is known.*

A25   VICTORIA, BRITISH COLUMBIA: GENERAL VIEWS. (1913)
       p.c. Kinemacolor Ltd.
       1. 1135'   g. 35mm   t. Kinemacolor s. si.
       d.   *
       ph. Harold Sintzenich
       c.s. Unknown

              *Shot during Mr. Sintzenich's tour of British Columbia in September-October
              1913.   This reel may have been filmed at the behest of the provincial gov-
              ernment as a promotional film, but no record of such an arrangement re-
              mains. (Kinemacolor No. 1111)*

A26   PICTURESQUE BRITISH COLUMBIA: BEACON HILL, VANCOUVER,
       ETC. (1913)
       p.c. Kinemacolor Ltd.
       1. 1040'   g. 35mm   t. Kinemacolor s. si.
       d.   *
       ph. Harold Sintzenich
       c.s. Unknown

              *Photographed during Mr. Sintzenich's tour of British Columbia in September-
              October 1913.   Since he was making industrial films for the provincial gov-*

ernment at the time, he may also have been commissioned to make tourist pro-
motion reels at the same time, such as PICTURESQUE BRITISH COLUMBIA.
(Kinemacolor No. 1112)

A27   CATCHING FIFTY-THOUSAND SALMON IN TWO HOURS; ON THE
       FRASER RIVER, CANADA. (1900-1902)
       p.c. Charles Urban Trading Company, London
       1. 500'   g. 35mm   t. b+w   s. si.
       d.   Joseph Rosenthal
       ph. Joseph Rosenthal
       c.s. Unknown

                    Description reads: "By courtesy of The Anglo British Columbia Packing Com-
                    pany."

                    "The first Section of this highly interesting series depicts a panorama view
                    of the river front of Steveston, B.C., the prosperous town, practically, com-
                    posed of scores of vast "Canneries" of the salmon which are caught in hun-
                    dreds of thousands annually. These huge structures are built on piles driven
                    into the bed of the river. Scores of fishing boats of the salmon catching
                    fleet are moored to the wharfs and landing stages, and these, with the build-
                    ings, form in the background a constant change of panorama as the tugboat
                    (from which this view was photographed), glides rapidly past.

                    "The next Section shows a tugboat towing a fleet of fishing craft down the
                    river, "dropping" one after the other as the salmon "grounds" are reached;
                    after each small boat casts loose, the crew of same hoist sail and begin op-
                    erations.

                    "The third Section gives a splendid view of one of the many salmon traps in
                    the Fraser River, being emptied of its catch.

                    "These salmon traps are a series of nets strung between piles driven into
                    the bed of the river. The fishermen are seen hauling in these nets and
                    emptying their contents into a scow by various methods: viz., pole or catch
                    net, fork, hoisting nets by hand and steam, &c., until the scow is filled
                    with a squirming, slashing mass of salmon, wonderful to behold.

                    "As soon as scow is filled, it is towed to one of the Canneries at Steveston
                    by tugboat, and the next Section depicts such scene.

                    "The fish are finally landed by "Chuting" same from the scows into the clean-
                    ing sheds of the Canneries. Here hundreds of Indians are at work, opening,
                    gutting and cutting the salmon into sections, when these latter are put into
                    tin cans, sealed, steamed, labelled, crated and are then ready for transpor-
                    tation to the World's Markets for tinned salmon, England drawing her main
                    supply from Steveston, B.C." (Charles Urban No. 1092 Special. Information
                    from Urban Catalogue of 1903.)

A28   SALMON FISHING ON THE FRASER RIVER. (1904)
       p.c. Charles Urban Trading Company, London
       1. 400'   g. 35mm   t. b+w   s. si.
       d.   Joseph Rosenthal
       ph. Joseph Rosenthal
       c.s. Unknown

                    Description reads: "By courtesy of the Anglo British Columbia Packing Com-
                    pany, Limited."

                    Part of the Charles Urban "LIVING CANADA" series. This appears to be a con-
                    densation of the material used by Urban for CATCHING FIFTY-THOUSAND SALMON
                    IN TWO HOURS. (Addendum 27).

                    "The first picture shows the waterfront at Steveston, which is a fishing
                    village at the mouth of the Fraser River, and is situated about 12 miles
                    south of Vancouver. To this place the fishing population - a mixed lot of
                    Indians, Japanese, Chinese, and whites of all nationalities - flock during
                    the fishing season; the busiest time being from July 15th to August 20th,
                    when some 2,000 to 3,000 boats are employed.

                    "Towing out of Fleet. - There is a weekly close time from 6pm on Saturday

night till 6pm Sunday night, at which hour a gun is fired to notify fisher-
men that they may begin. The picture depicts boats being towed out and
casting off to take up their positions ready to begin; and it is a fine sight
to see hundreds of boats all casting their nets simultaneously at gun fire.
The boats deliver their catches at the canneries in the river, or at receiv-
ing camps placed at convenient points outside, and a number of tugboats are
employed in gathering up and distributing the fish. In a big season, which
occurs every fourth year, 500,000 to 600,000 salmon, of an average weight
of 7½ pounds, will be caught and canned in one day on Fraser River.

"Fish Traps. - This picture shows the lifting of salmon traps, belonging to
the Anglo-British Columbia Packing Company, Limited, at Point Roberts. These
traps are substantial and costly structures, consisting of piles with netting
attached, which extend to the bottom - and comprise "Pot" and "Spiller", from
which the fish are taken - also "Heart", "Jigger", and "Lead", - the latter
being often nearly half a mile in length. The "Pot" is emptied by means of
"Handrailer" and "Steambrailer" - (both of which are shown) - the latter
being a small net worked from a boom by a steam winch on the attendent tug-
boat. By means of "Steam brailing" 15,000 fish may be lifted in half-an-hour. In
a big run 70,000 fish have been caught in one trap in a day, where they may
be held for several days without injury; but in poor years the catches are
often very small, while the cost of operation remains the same. The "Pot"
and "Spiller" are frequently placed in 60 feet of water.

"Towing Barges or "Fish Scows". - Each trap requires two fish-scows, in which
the fish are loaded and towed to destination - they hold from 6,000 to 10,000
salmon, which are delivered ready for canning at the factories within a few
hours of being lifted. The principal salmon canned is the "Sockeye" of
about 7.1/2 pounds weight which has a deep red colour.

"Interior Work. - This picture shows the first process after delivery of fish
at the factory, when the heads, fins and tails are taken off, and they are
carefully cleaned, scraped, brushed and washed several times. The later
work of cutting up into sizes and nearly all subsequent processing is done
by machinery - except the actual filling of the tins. The tin containing
the raw fish is hermetically sealed: and is cooked by steam for thirty min-
utes; pricked to allow steam and any air inside to blow off; sealed up again
at once and cooked a second time in a steam retort, under pressure for one
hour. During processing various tests are applied to eliminate defects.
The skilled labour inside the canneries is all Chinese under the supervision
of white men - the unskilled consist largely of Indian women. The fishing
industry is a very important one in British Columbia. From 15,000 to 20,000
people are employed during the season, and the catch is valued at four to
five million dollars; about three-quarters of the catch being shipped to
London and Liverpool." (Charles Urban No. 1092 Special. Information from
Supplement 1 to Urban Catalogue of 1903, 1904.)

A29   TRAPPING SALMON ON THE FRASER RIVER.   (1900-1902)
      p.c. Charles Urban Trading Company, London
      l. 75'   g. 35mm   t. b+w   s. si.
      d.   Joseph Rosenthal
      ph. Joseph Rosenthal
      c.s. Unknown

          "Another view of a salmon trap showing the fishermen emptying the nets. The
          salmon are caught in thousands by this method of trapping, and the sight
          fairly turns the head of a fisher after salmon who traverses a stream for
          two hours and finally lands a sprat." (Charles Urban No. 1093. Information·
          from Urban Catalogue of 1903).

A30   THE ROCKY MOUNTAINS, CANADA.   (1900-1902)
      p.c. Charles Urban Trading Company, London
      l. 725'   g. 35mm   t. b+w   s. si.
      d.   Joseph Rosenthal
      ph. Joseph Rosenthal
      c.s. Unknown

          "A series of Panorama Views taken from the front of the Express Train pass-
          ing through the most gorgeous scenery of the Kicking Horse Canyon. By
          courtesy of the Canadian Pacific Railway." (Charles Urban No.'s 1098, 1099,
          1100. Information from Urban Catalogue of 1903.)

For the three sections see PANORAMA OF THE KICKING HORSE CANYON (A31), THE KICKING HORSE CANYON AND THE GREAT LOOP AT GLACIER HOUSE (A32), and WITH THE IMPERIAL LIMITED THROUGH THE KICKING HORSE CANYON (A33). The three reels were available separately or in one continuous reel.

A31　PANORAMA OF THE KICKING HORSE CANYON.　(1900-1902)
　　　p.c. Charles Urban Trading Company, London
　　　1. 150'　　　　　g. 35mm　t. b+w　　s. si.
　　　d.　Joseph Rosenthal
　　　ph.　Joseph Rosenthal
　　　c.s. Unknown

　　　　　　　Part of Charles Urban's THE ROCKY MOUNTAINS, CANADA series. See A30.

　　　　　　　"A wonderful picture of majestic scenery as the train (from the front of which these photos were secured), speeds over the rails, around curves, over bridges and ledges cut into the rocky sides of the mountain, with the torrent below and the towering mountain peaks above, ever in view, and of constant changing aspect. This is the shortest Section of one of the most wonderful railway pictures ever biscoped." (Charles Urban No. 1098. Information from Urban Catalogue of 1903.)

A32　THE KICKING HORSE CANYON AND THE GREAT LOOP AT GLACIER HOUSE.
　　　(1900-1902)
　　　p.c. Charles Urban Trading Company, London
　　　1. 250'　　　　　g. 35mm　t. b+w　　s. si.
　　　d.　Joseph Rosenthal
　　　ph.　Joseph Rosenthal
　　　c.s. Unknown

　　　　　　　Part of the Charles Urban THE ROCKY MOUNTAINS, CANADA series. See A30.

　　　　　　　"The line, which has gradually curved towards the south since crossing the summit at Stephen, runs due south from here to Leanchoil, where the Beaverfoot River comes in from the south and joins the Kicking Horse. At the left, the lofty peaks of the Ottertail Mountains, walled, massive and castellated, rise abruptly to an immense height; and looking south, a magnificent range of peaks extends in orderly array towards the south-east as far as the eye can reach. These are the Beaverfoot Mountains appearing to slope away from the railway. At the right Mt. Hunter, a long gradual slope, pushes its huge mass forward like a wedge between the Ottertail and Beaverfoot ranges. The river turns abruptly against its base and plunges into the Lower Kicking Horse Canyon, down which it disputes the passage with the railway. The next Section shows the great curve at Glacier House, which the train negotiates by passing through numerous snow-sheds, over bridges, through tunnels, &c. The railroad forms a complete loop or circle at this point, and by a gradual ascent, passes over itself at the higher altitude. A complete circular panorama is thus obtained which for grandeur, is difficult to equal." (Charles Urban No. 1099. Information from Urban catalogue of 1903.)

A33　WITH THE IMPERIAL LIMITED THROUGH THE KICKING HORSE CANYON.
　　　(1900-1902)
　　　p.c. Charles Urban Trading Company, London
　　　1. 325'　　　　　g. 35mm　t. b+w　　s. si.
　　　d.　Joseph Rosenthal
　　　ph.　Joseph Rosenthal
　　　c.s. Unknown

　　　　　　　Part of the Charles Urban THE ROCKY MOUNTAINS, CANADA series. See A30.

　　　　　　　"This is <u>perhaps</u> the most varied Section of the "Kicking Horse Canyon" Series, the scenery, however, being of a more rugged character than in the preceding films. Bridges, curves and tunnels are more numerous. The canyon at this point rapidly deepens, until beyond Palliser, the mountain sides become vertical, rising straight up thousands of feet, in a bronze wall crested by a long line of nameless peaks, and within an easy stone's throw from wall to wall. Down this vast chasm go the railway and the river together, the former crossing from side to side to ledges cut out of the solid rock, and twisting and turning in every direction, and every minute or two plunging through projecting angles of rock which seem to close the way. With the towering cliffs almost shutting out the sunlight, and the roar of the river and the train increased a hundredfold by the echoing walls, the passage of this terrible gorge

will never be forgotten." (Charles Urban No. 1100. Information from the Urban Catalogue of 1903.)

A34   THE "EMPRESS OF CHINA" LEAVING VANCOUVER FOR THE FAR EAST.
       (1900-1902)
       p.c. Charles Urban Trading COmpany, London
       1. 50'   g. 35mm   t. b+w   s. si.
       d.   Joseph Rosenthal
       ph.   Joseph Rosenthal
       c.s. Unknown

               "The Pride of the Pacific Fleet of the Canadian Pacific Railway is seen approaching the camera at full speed, the progress of this liner being followed by means of our rotary tripod, thus giving a splendid view of the steamship ploughing the waters until it passes out of the picture. Excellent quality." (Charles Urban No. 1101. Information from Urban Catalogue of 1903.)

A35   HAULING IN SALMON NETS AT VANCOUVER.   (1900-1902)
       p.c. Charles Urban Trading Company, London
       1. 75'   g. 35mm   t. b+w   s. si.
       d.   Joseph Rosenthal
       ph.   Joseph Rosenthal
       c.s. Unknown

               "A lively scene among the fishing fleet on the Fraser River during the salmon season, showing hundreds of salmon struggling in the nets as these are drawn to the surface and finally emptied of their contents." (Charles Urban No. 1102. Information from Urban Catalogue of 1903.)

A36   FELLING PINES IN NORTH WEST TERRITORY.   (1900-1902)
       p.c. Charles Urban Trading Company, London
       1. 60'   g. 35mm   t. b+w   s. si.
       d.   Joseph Rosenthal
       ph.   Joseph Rosenthal
       c.s. Unknown

               "The gigantic pines of the North-West Territory are the envy of the Lumbering world. This picture shows the axemen and sawyers attacking one of these trees, which, after cutting and sawing through its trunk, upset its perpendicular by driving a wedge. The giant falls with a crash, carrying with it many branches of surrounding trees in its descent." (Charles Urban No. 1106. Information from Urban Catalogue of 1903.) Filmed in British Columbia.

A37   DRAGGING LOGS OVER CORDOROY ROADS THROUGH THE PINE FORESTS.
       (1900-1902)
       p.c. Charles Urban Trading Company, London
       1. 75'   g. 35mm   t. b+w   s. si.
       d.   Joseph Rosenthal
       ph.   Joseph Rosenthal
       c.s. Unknown

               "Lumbering in many of the Canadian forests is conducted during the summer months. There being no snow or ice to aid in the transportation of logs to the river, these latter are chained in long rows and dragged through the forests over cordoroy roads by teams of ten or a dozen horses. The scene is one not likely to be soon forgotten." (Charles Urban No. 1107. Information from Urban Catalogue of 1903.)

               Although this description would suggest that the logging scenes depicted take place in Ontario or Quebec, it occurs with a selection of reels photographed in British Columbia and appears to contain the same material. The description writer, living in England, was likely confused or, in trying to be helpful, made a mistake. See LUMBERING IN THE CANADIAN PINE FORESTS, A38.

A38   LUMBERING IN THE CANADIAN PINE FORESTS.   (1900-1902)
       p.c. Charles Urban Trading Company, London
       1. 300'   g. 35mm   t. b+w   s. si.
       d.   Joseph Rosenthal
       ph.   Joseph Rosenthal
       c.s. Unknown

"A splendid picture series of Logging in the North-West Territory (differing
in many respects to that placed on the market last year). The first section
shows the felling of a monster tree, which is transported over gullies by
means of cable and pulley. The trunks are then chained together and dragged
through the forest by teams of ten horses. The last section shows the "log
rolls" by the sea, where, one after the other, these massive logs are hurled
into the water with great splashes. A grand subject, of best photographic
quality." (Charles Urban No. 1108. Information from Urban Catalogue of
1903.) A still photograph in the catalogue shows a ten-horse team "near
Welcome, B.C."*

A39   LOGGING IN CANADIAN FOREST. (1904)
      p.c. Charles Urban Trading Company, London
      l. 300'   g. 35mm   t. b+w   s. si.
      d.   Joseph Rosenthal
      ph. Joseph Rosenthal
      c.s. Unknown

           *This reel appears to be a condensation of the Charles Urban pictures listed
           in the 1903 Catalogue under the titles FELLING PINES IN NORTH WEST TERRITORY
           (A36); DRAGGING LOGS OVER CORDOROY ROADS THROUGH THE PINE FORESTS (A37);
           LUMBERING IN THE CANADIAN PINE FORESTS (A38); MILLING LOGS ON PACIFIC COAST
           (NORTH WEST TERRITORY), CANADA (A40).*

           "This series of pictures depicts the method employed in felling and trans-
           porting pine logs during the summer months in British Columbia.

           "The first shows the Axmen supported on platforms 8 feet from the base of
           the tree, attacking same from the side in the direction it is intended the
           tree should fall. Expert sawyers now cut through the trunk. After which
           a wedge is driven into the "cut" from the opposite direction in which the
           tree falls. The logs are then hauled through the forest over gullies and
           irregular places by means of block and tackle to the vicinity of cordoroy
           roads, where they are transported to the sea, being "snigged" by a train
           of ten horses. The cordoroy road is built by placing smaller timbers across
           the road, as sleepers are laid for a railroad bed. At regular intervals are
           placed grooved timbers, which act as guides to obviate the side-rolling of
           the logs during their progress over this road. You will note the occupation
           of the man preceding the team - he greases the grooves to prevent friction
           and facilitate the draught. These logs average 40 feet in length, weighing
           from one to one-and-a-half tons each, and are coupled by means of chains
           attached to "dogs" driven into the ends. As each train of logs reaches the
           chute, the teams are hitched to the back of the log train, and as the "dogs"
           have been removed, the result is that, as each log reaches the edge of the
           chute, it falls into the water with a splash. After being towed in rafts
           to the sawmills, the logs are guided into a race, where the grips of an end-
           less chain carry them up the incline to be sawn.

           "The last picture shows the refuse heaps outside a sawmill, where the super-
           fluous cuttings and slabs are burnt, as in British Columbia it costs more to
           transport these cuttings than their value." (Charles Urban No. 1108. Infor-
           mation from the Supplement to the Urban Catalogue of 1903, 1904.)

A40   MILLING LOGS ON PACIFIC COAST (NORTH WEST TERRITORY),
      CANADA. (1900-1902)
      p.c. Charles Urban Trading Company, London
      l. 150'   g. 35mm   t. b+w   s. si.
      d.   Joseph Rosenthal
      ph. Joseph Rosenthal
      c.s. Unknown

           "This subject would form an appropriate continuation of the preceding film
           (LUMBERING IN THE CANADIAN PINE FORESTS A38), showing further progress of the
           log. Here we give an excellent panoramic view of the log rafts, having been
           floated down the river and caught by chained "booms", are held in tow until
           required to be milled into lumber, when they are drawn from the water over
           a log-way by means of an endless chain gear. Arriving at the mill, they are
           sawed into boards and proper lengths, these again being loaded into the hold
           of a ship lying alongside the mill dock, while the refuse (sawdust and cuttings)
           is chuted into a heap in the mill yard and consumed by fire. Many of these
           burning heaps are shown in this picture." (Charles Urban No. 1109. Informa-

A41   LABOUR DAY PARADE IN VANCOUVER, BRITISH COLUMBIA. (1904-
1908)
p.c. Charles Urban Trading Company, London
1. 250'   g. 35mm   t. b+w   s. si.
d.   *
ph. *
c.s. Unknown

> *"A procession of marching members of Labour Societies in uniforms character-*
> *istic of their trades, headed by bands and banners. Many floats of elaborate*
> *display, bearing machinery in motion, manufacturing processes in operation,*
> *and others representing various trades, are drawn past the camera by teams*
> *of four, six, and eight horses each." (Charles Urban No. 1128. Information*
> *from Urban Catalogue, 1909.)*

A42   RACE BETWEEN THE "CITY OF SEATTLE" AND THE C.P.R.
STEAMER "PRINCESS VICTORIA". (1900-1903)
p.c. Charles Urban Trading Company, London
1. 60'   g. 35mm   t. b+w   s. si.
d.   Joseph Rosenthal
ph. Joseph Rosenthal
c.s. Unknown

> *Part of the Charles Urban LIVING CANADA series.*
>
> *"A fine picture of an exciting race between these two crack steamers of rival*
> *navigation companies on their way to Vancouver, up the Straits of Georgia,*
> *British Columbia." (Charles Urban No. 1147. Information from Supplement 1*
> *to Urban Catalogue of 1903, 1904.)*

A43   SPEARING FISH IN BRITISH COLUMBIA. (1900-1903)
p.c. Charles Urban Trading Company, London
1. 100'   g. 35mm   t. b+w   s. si.
d.   Joseph Rosenthal
ph. Joseph Rosenthal
c.s. Unknown

> *Part of the Charles Urban LIVING CANADA series.*
>
> *"This picture shows a party of five men spearing salmon in a Canadian river.*
> *As each fish is taken from the spear it is handed to the dog, who carries*
> *the prize ashore. A laughable incident occurs when one of the fishermen,*
> *forgetting the dog, flings the fish on the banks. The dog, taking exception*
> *to this slight, hurries to the bank, picks up the fish in his teeth, and*
> *carries it to the party in the river who had committed the breech of faith."*
> *(Charles Urban No. 1148. Information from Supplement 1 to Urban Catalogue*
> *of 1903, 1904.)*

A44   THREE C.P.R. TRAINS CROSSING THE SELKIRKS. (1900-1903)
p.c. Charles Urban Trading Company, London
1. 100'   g. 35mm   t. b+w   s. si.
d.   Joseph Rosenthal
ph. Joseph Rosenthal
c.s. Unknown

> *Part of the Charles Urban LIVING CANADA series.*
>
> *"This picture was obtained in three localities in the Rocky Mountains, each*
> *amidst most picturesque surroundings. First we note a C.P.R. passenger train*
> *rounding a curve and proceeding towards the camera at a high rate of speed -*
> *then follows a view of the "Imperial Express" thundering by, while the last*
> *section shows a heavy train drawn by two gigantic engines coming up a heavy*
> *grade of the Kicking Horse Pass. An excellent picture with fine smoke and*
> *steam effects." (Charles Urban No. 1152. Information from Supplement 1 of*
> *Urban Catalogue of 1903, 1904.)*

A45   ALONG THE WATER FRONT OF STEVESTON, B.C. (1900-1902)
       p.c. Charles Urban Trading Company, London
       l. 75'   g. 35mm   t. b+w   s. si.
       d.   Joseph Rosenthal
       ph. Joseph Rosenthal
       c.s. Unknown

                   Part of the Charles Urban LIVING CANADA series sponsored by the CPR.

                   *"Steveston is a fishing village at the mouth of the Fraser River, and is
                   situated about 12 miles south of Vancouver, B.C. To this place a mixed lot
                   of Indians, Japanese, Chinese, and Whites flock during the fishing season,
                   when some 2,000 to 3,000 boats are employed. This shows a panoramic view
                   of the Canneries and whole water front of the village." (Charles Urban No.
                   1215. Information from Urban's Catalogue of 1903.)*

A46   THROUGH THE BEAVERMOUTH CANYON, SELKIRK MOUNTAINS,
       DURING A BLIZZARD. (1900-1902)
       p.c. Charles Urban Trading Company, London
       l. 200'   g. 35mm   t. b+w   s. si.
       d.   Joseph Rosenthal
       ph. Joseph Rosenthal
       c.s. Unknown

                   Part of the Charles Urban LIVING CANADA series sponsored by the CPR.

                   *"Here the Rockies and Selkirks crowding together force the river through a
                   deep, narrow gorge, the railway clinging to the slopes high above it. Emerg-
                   ing from the gorge at Beavermouth, the most northly station on the transcon-
                   tinental route, the line soon turns abruptly to the left and enters the Sel-
                   kirks through the Gate of the Beaver River - a passage so narrow that a felled
                   tree serves as a footbridge over it - just where the river makes its final
                   and mad plunge down to the level of the Columbia. Here a natural bridge is
                   seen across the boiling torrent.*

                   *"NOTE. - This picture and the following one (WITH THE IMPERIAL EXPRESS ALONG
                   THE COLUMBIA RIVER - ROCKY MOUNTAINS IN WINTER) differ from all other railway
                   panoramas ever photographed, as it does not only show the approaching and
                   passing scenery, but shows the entire train with the puffing engine drawing
                   the coaches constantly in view." (Charles Urban No. 1217. Information from
                   Urban's Catalogue of 1903.)*

A47   WITH THE IMPERIAL EXPRESS ALONG THE COLUMBIA RIVER -
       ROCKY MOUNTAINS IN WINTER. (1900-1902)
       p.c. Charles Urban Trading Company, London
       l. 300'   g. 35mm   t. b+w   s. si.
       d.   Joseph Rosenthal
       ph. Joseph Rosenthal
       c.s. Unknown

                   Part of the Charles Urban LIVING CANADA series sponsored by the CPR.

                   *"A sublime panorama of the Rocky Mountains in winter, snow covering the road-
                   bed mountain slopes and pines. A raging torrent runs parallel with the rail-
                   way, and as at each curve another aspect of the panorama opens into view, the
                   picture is one of the most interesting ever taken. The entire train in view
                   each time it curves to the left as the picture was photographed from a special
                   platform constructed, overhanging the side of the last coach of the train.
                   The last portion shows the descent from the Glacier House, and following
                   around the mountain-side. The Loop is soon reached, where the line makes
                   several startling turns and twists, first crossing a valley over a high trestle
                   leading down from the Mount Bonney glacier, touching for a moment on the base
                   of Ross Peak, then doubling back to the right a mile or more upon itself to
                   within a biscuit's toss; then sweeping around to the right, touching Cougar
                   Mount, on the other side of the Illecillewaet, crossing again to the left,
                   and at last shooting down the valley parallel with its former course. Look-
                   ing back, the railway is seen cutting two long gashes, one above the other,
                   on the mountain-slope, and farther to the left, and high above the long snow-
                   shed the summit range, near Roger's Pass, is yet visible, with Sir Donald
                   overlooking all. A wonderful picture - new sensation! (Charles Urban No.
                   1218. Information from the Urban Catalogue of 1903.)*

A48   THE GLORIOUS FRASER CANYON, B.C. – Encountering
       Eight Tunnels, Forty-eight Curves, and crossing
       a very high Trestle. (1900–1902)
       p.c. Charles Urban Trading Company, London
       l. 300'   g. 35mm   t. b+w   s. si.
       d.   Joseph Rosenthal
       ph. Joseph Rosenthal
       c.s. Unknown

                   Part of the Charles Urban LIVING CANADA series sponsored by the CPR.

                   "*The train runs suddenly along the very brink of several remarkably deep
                   fissures in the solid rock, whose walls rise straight up, hundreds of feet
                   on both sides, to wooded craigs, above which sharp distant peaks cut the sky.
                   The most striking of these canyons is the Fraser, where the river is seen
                   nearly 300 feet below the railway, compressed into a boiling flume scarcely
                   20 feet wide.*

                   "*One of the most picturesque Railroad Panoramas ever taken.*

                   "*NOTE. – This film is in various sections, and comprises the choicest por-
                   tions of panorama of glorious Mountain Scenery selected from over 1500 feet
                   of film exposed.)*" *(Charles Urban No. 1219. Information from Urban Catalogue
                   of 1903.)*

A49   CROSSING THE GOLD RANGE, B.C. (1900–1902)
       p.c. Charles Urban Trading Company, London
       l. 225'   g. 35mm   t. b+w   s. si.
       d.   Joseph Rosenthal
       ph. Joseph Rosenthal
       c.s. Unknown

                   Part of the Charles Urban LIVING CANADA series sponsored by the CPR.

                   "*The train suddenly emerges into daylight as Golden is reached. The broad
                   river ahead is the Columbia moving northward. The supremely beautiful moun-
                   tains beyond to the left and the south are the Selkirks, rising from their
                   forest-clad bases and lifting their ice-crowned heads far into the sky. They
                   extend in an apparently unbroken line from the southwest to the northeast,
                   gradually melting into the remote distance. Parallel with them, and rising
                   eastward, to the right and the north from the Columbia, range upon range,
                   are the Rockies, only the loftiest peaks to be seen just now over the massive
                   benches upon which they rest. Golden is a mining town upon the bank of the
                   Columbia, at the mouth of the Kicking Horse. During the summer steamers
                   make trips from here up the Columbia to Windermere on the lakes at the head
                   of the river, 100 miles distant. About Golden, and at various places above,
                   especially at the base of the Spillimichene Mts., gold and silver mines are
                   being developed.*" *(Charles Urban No. 1220. Information from the Urban Cata-
                   logue, 1903.)*

A50   THROUGH THE GLENOGLE GULCH, ROCKY MOUNTAINS. (1900–
       1902)
       p.c. Charles Urban Trading Company, London
       l. 175'   g. 35mm   t. b+w   s. si.
       d.   Joseph Rosenthal
       ph. Joseph Rosenthal
       c.s. Unknown

                   Part of the Charles Urban LIVING CANADA series sponsored by the CPR.

                   "*The line now follows the right-hand side of the canyon, with river surging
                   and swirling far below. The old Government road, built in the early 60's
                   and abandoned since the opening of the railway. Usually twisting and turning
                   about the cliffs, it sometimes ventures down to the river side, whence it is
                   quickly driven by angry turn of the waters. Six miles below Kanaka, where
                   it follows the cliffs opposite to the railway, it is forced to the height
                   of a thousand feet above the river, and is pinned by seemingly slender sticks
                   to the face of a gigantic precipice.*" *(Charles Urban No. 1221. Information
                   from the Urban Catalogue of 1903.)*

A51   CROSSING THE ROCKIES VIA C.P.R.   (1900-1902)
p.c. Charles Urban Trading Company, London
1. 150'   g. 35mm   t. b+w   s. si.
d.   Joseph Rosenthal
ph.   Joseph Rosenthal
c.s. Unknown

Part of the Charles Urban LIVING CANADA series sponsored by the CPR.

"The strange forms and gaudy hues of the rocks and scantily herbaged terraces impress themselves most strongly on the memory. Five miles beyond Drynoch, Nicomen, a little mining town is seen and on the opposite bank of the river gold was first discovered in British Columbia, in 1857. The mountains now draw together again, and the railway winds along their face hundreds of feet above the struggling river. This is the Thompson Canyon. The gorge rapidly narrows and deepens, and the scenery becomes wild beyond description. The crowning cliffs opposite are mottled and streaked in many striking colours, and now and then through breaks in the high escarpment, snowy peaks are seen glistening above the clouds." (Charles Urban No. 1222. Information from Urban Catalogue of 1903.)

A52   OVER THE COAST RANGE B.C.   (1900-1902)
p.c. Charles Urban Trading Company, London
1. 100'   g. 35mm   t. b+w   s. si.
d.   Joseph Rosenthal
ph.   Joseph Rosenthal
c.s. Unknown

Part of the Charles Urban LIVING CANADA series sponsored by the CPR.

"The river makes an abrupt turn to the left, and the railway, turning to the right, disappears into a long tunnel, emerging into daylight and rejoining the river at Yale. Yale is the head of navigation, and was formerly an outfitting point for miners and ranchmen northward. It occupies a bench above the river in a deep "cul de sac" in the mountains, which rise abruptly and to a great height on all sides. Indian huts are seen on the opposite bank, and in the village a conspicuous Joss-house indicates the presence of Chinamen, who are seen washing gold on the river bars for a long way below Yale." (Charles Urban No. 1224. Information from Urban Catalogue of 1903.)

A53   PASSING NORTHBEND STATION, FRASER CANYON.   (1900-1902)
p.c. Charles Urban Trading Company, London
1. 75'   g. 35mm   t. b+w   s. si.
d.   Joseph Rosenthal
ph.   Joseph Rosenthal
c.s. Unknown

Part of the Charles Urban LIVING CANADA series sponsored by the CPR.

"A charming chalet hotel makes North Bend (a divisional point) a desirable and delightful stopping-place for tourists who wish to see more of the Fraser Canyon than is possible from the trains. At Boston Bar, a few miles below, where mining operations are carried on, the principal canyon of the Fraser commences, and from here to Yale, 23 miles, the scenery is not only intensely interesting but startling. It has been well described as "matchless". The great river is forced between vertical walls of black rocks where, reportedly thrown back upon itself by opposing cliffs, or broken by ponderous masses of fallen rocks, it madly foams and roars." (Charles Urban No. 1225. Information from Urban Catalogue of 1903.)

A54   THE SELKIRKS FROM FRONT OF A TRAIN.   (1900-1902)
p.c. Charles Urban Trading Company, London
1. 75'   g. 35mm   t. b+w   s. si.
d.   Joseph Rosenthal
ph.   Joseph Rosenthal
c.s. Unknown

Part of the Charles Urban LIVING CANADA series sponsored by the CPR.

"Nature has worked here on so gigantic a scale that many travellers fail to notice the extraordinary height of the spruce, Douglas fir and cedar trees,

which seem to be engaged in a vain competition with the mountains themselves. From Six Mile Creek Station one sees ahead, up the Beaver Valley, a long line of the higher peaks of the Selkirks, "en echelon", culminating in an exceedingly lofty pinnacle, named Sir Donald, (10,600 feet), with which a more intimate acquaintance will be made at Glacier House. Again, from Mountain Creek Bridge, a few miles beyond, where a powerful torrent comes down from the mountains northward, the same view is obtained, nearer and larger, and eight peaks can be counted in a grand array, the last of which is Sir Donald, leading the line." (Charles Urban No. 1226. Information from Urban Catalogue of 1903.)

A55   LAKE OF THE HANGING GLACIERS. (1920)
p.c. Byron Harmon
l.   g. 35mm   t. b+w   s. si.
d.   Byron Harmon
ph.   Byron Harmon
c.s. Unknown

In his remarkable book, Down the Columbia, Lewis R. Freeman mentions an encounter with Byron Harmon in September, 1920. Freeman and cameraman Len H. Roos were engaged in making a travelogue at the Lake of the Hanging Glaciers for Chester-Outing Pictures Ltd. of Los Angeles, and believed that they were the first to do so. When they discovered that Harmon was a day ahead of them, their competitive urge drove them to catch up with him. Roos and Harmon eventually collaborated with each other, both using Freeman as the subject of their sporting travelogues. See No. 412.

It is not known whether Harmon made one or several films at the Lake of the Hanging Glaciers. He may have sold footage to the large film distribution companies for inclusion in one of their own reels. Freeman's candid book explains how Harmon set up some of his more spectacular shots, and how both cameramen resorted to dynamite at the Lake of the Hanging Glaciers to get footage of avalanches and what they called "the birth of an iceberg."

Freeman's reminiscences of Harmon are revealing: "'Stills,' it appeared, were the main thing with him; his movie work was carried on merely as a side-line to pay the expenses of trips he could not otherwise afford. He had been photographing in the Selkirks and Rockies for a dozen years, and he would not be content until the sets of negatives - as nearly perfect as they could be made - of every notable peak and valley of western Canada (sic). Then he was going to hold a grand exhibition of mountain photographs at Banff and retire. The Lake of the Hanging Glaciers was one of the very few great scenic features he had never photographed, and he only hoped he would be able to do it justice. The fine reverence of Harmon's attitude was completely beyond Roos' ken. "I never worries about not doing 'em justice - not for a minute. What does worry me is whether or not these cracked up lakes and glaciers are going to turn out worth my coming in to do justice to. Get me?" "Yes, I think so," replied the veteran with a very patient smile." (Lewis R. Freeman, Down the Columbia. pp. 46-7.)

A56   DOWN THE COLUMBIA: THE CHESTER-OUTING TRAVELOGUES. (1920)
p.c. Chester-Outing Pictures
l.   g. 35mm   t. b+w   s. si.
d.   Len H. Roos
ph.   Len H. Roos
c.s. Unknown

Scenic travelogues were in great demand during the summer of 1920 when C.L. Chester of Los Angeles, owner of Chester-Outing Pictures, decided to send a cameraman along with his friend Lewis R. Freeman to film the descent of the Columbia River from its source near Windermere, British Columbia to the Pacific Ocean. Freeman describes in his book, Down the Columbia, how Len H. Roos joined him in September, 1920, and lavishes much entertaining detail on their cinematic and personal relationship over the next two months.

Roos was a Canadian-born, hot-shot news photographer, and in each of the five films Chester requested of him he used Freeman alternately as a gentleman sportsman, a hunter, or an actor portraying a fictionalized hero travelling downriver in search of the ocean and adventure. Their guide was Bob Blackmore of Revelstoke, and all came close to losing their lives several times in the perilous rapids. Roos joined Freeman in Invermere early in September

*and left him at the foot of Priest Rapids, about 250 miles from Portland,
Oregon, in late October or early November, 1920. The exposed film was processed and edited in Los Angeles, Roos sending off numerous reels when they
reached Nelson and taking the rest with him when he left Freeman at Priest
Rapids.*

*What happened to the films is not known. Freeman suggests that he and Roos
were the first men to take a camera through the Big Bend country, which would
make theirs the first films ever shot there.*

According the Freeman, the five films to be made were as follows:

1. *A "Windermere Picture", showing the scenic, camping, fishing, and hunting
   life of that region. Freeman himself played the part of the camper, hunter
   and fisherman.*

2. *A "Lake of the Hanging Glaciers Picture" about a gentleman sportsman
   (Freeman) travelling up into the Lake of the Hanging Glaciers to view the
   scenery and wildlife. It was here that Roos dynamited the glacier to
   create the illusion of "the birth of an iceberg". (See LAKE OF THE HANGING
   GLACIERS, A55)*

3. *A "goat hunting picture". See No. 412.*

4. *A travelogue of the dangerous white-water journey journeying dwon the Big
   Bend of the Columbia River in British Columbia by a sportsman gentleman
   (Freeman). There were to be many camping, fishing and hunting scenes, with
   views of the rapids and the excitement of the boiling river.*

5. *A story of a "young rancher (Freeman) who was farming his hard won clearing
   on the banks of the Columbia near its source. With the last of his crops
   in he is assailed one day with a great longing to see the ocean. Suddenly
   it occurs to him that the river flowing right by his door runs all the way
   to the sea, and the sight of a prospector friend, about to push off with
   a sack of samples for the smelter many hundreds of miles below, suggests
   a means of making the journey. And so the two of them start off down the
   Columbia. What happened to them on their way was to be told in the picture.'
   (Lewis R. Freeman, Down the Columbia. p. 77.)*

*Although the working title of the film was "The Farmer Who Would See the Sea",
it was never completed because Roos left Freeman to finish the journey alone.*

*An amusing incident is related by Freeman about filming the guides and packers
and himself on their way through the bush with pack horses: "The next shot
was a quarter of a mile further up the trail. Here Roos found a natural sylvan
frame through which to shoot the whole outfit as it came stringing along. Unfortunately, the 'Director' failed to tell the actors not to look at the camera - that, once and for all, the clicking box must be reckoned as a thing
non-existent - and it all had to be done over again. The next time it was
better, but the actors still had a wooden expression on their faces. They
didn't look at the camera, but the expression on their faces showed they they
were conscious of it. Roos then instructed me to talk to my companions, or
sing, or do anything that would take their minds off the camera and make them
appear relaxed and natural. That time we did it famously. As each, in turn,
cantered by the sylvan bower with its clicking camera he was up to his neck
"doing something." Nixon was declaiming Lincoln's Gettysburg speech as he
had learned it from his phonograph, Gordon was calling his dog, Jim was larrup-
ing a straggling pinto and cursing it in fluent local idiom, and I was singing
"Onward Christian Soldiers!" We never had any trouble about "being natural"
after that; but I hope no lip reader ever sees the pictures." (Lewis, p.33.)*

A57   LA VISITE DE NOS SOUVERAINS. (1939)
       p.c. CGMPB
       l. 7,700'   g. 35mm   t. b+w   s. sound
       d.   *
       ph. CGMPB
       c.s. Direction Générale du Cinéma et de l'Audiovisuel,
            Quebec, and NFA.

            *French-language version of THE ROYAL VISIT, with narration by Jacques Des-
            baillets. See No. 758.*

A58   TRAVEL TOUR OF THE WEST COAST OF VANCOUVER ISLE. (early 1920's)
       p.c. Pathéscope of Canada
       1. 1 reel   g. 35mm   t. b+w   s. si. w/captions
       d.   *
       ph. A. D. Kean (?)
       c.s. NFA (Belton collection)

                    *May have been made for the British Columbia Patriotic and Educational Motion
                    Picture Service which would date it between 1920 and 1923.*

A59   WHALING - B. C.'s LEAST KNOWN AND MOST ROMANTIC INDUSTRY. (1916)
       p.c. Pathéscope of Canada (?)
       1. 1 reel   g. 35mm   t. b+w   s. si. w/captions
       d. A. D. Kean
       ph. A. D. Kean
       c.s. NFA

                    *This film was likely shot in September, 1916, under the auspices of the
                    Publicity and Industries Department of the City of Vancouver. Kean was
                    apparently interested in filming scenes of the whaling industry and with
                    the assistance of the Industrial Commissioner secured a berth on one of the
                    Victoria Whaling Company's whalers. Kean later wrote an account of his
                    filming of the whale hunt in the Vancouver business journal INDUSTRIAL
                    PROGRESS AND COMMERCIAL RECORD (Vol. IV, No. 6, November 1916, pp. 125-128.).*

                    *Kean sailed up the west coast of Vancouver Island from Victoria aboard the
                    Victoria Whaling Company's whaler S.S. GREY to the company's Kyuquot
                    station, where he filmed "water scenes" and a giant fin-back whale being
                    hauled onto the slips. He also filmed Japanese flensers cutting blubber and
                    a steam winch tearing strips of blubber off the whale.*

                    *Kean went to sea the next day aboard the whaler S.S. BLACK where he lashed
                    his two heavy cameras to the bridge in preparation for shooting. His first
                    shots at sea were of a pod of fin-back whales being pursued by another
                    whaler owned by the Victoria Whaling Company, the S.S. ST. LAWRENCE. Two
                    days later the BLACK sighted its own whale, and Kean was able to record the
                    harpoon gunner's shot and the whale's struggle. The whaler was towed by the
                    whale for three hours, by which time it had tired sufficiently for the
                    gunner to dispatch it with another harpoon fired into its heart. Kean
                    describes the whale's death in these words: "A few lurches after the
                    shot and the biggest game the world affords lay helpless upon the water, a
                    victim to the cunning of man."*

                    *The following July, Kean was able to secure a commission from the B. C.
                    Provincial Game Department to film sea-lions at the Cape St. James rookery
                    off the southern tip of the Queen Charlotte Islands. Here Kean and his
                    party also killed a number of sea-lions and Kean lassoed one with his lariat
                    from the front of their rowboat. See Kean's account of this hunt in
                    INDUSTRIAL PROGRESS AND COMMERCIAL RECORD, Vol. V, No. 7, December 1917,
                    pp. 467-471. It is not known whether any copies of Kean's sea-lion footage
                    still exist or, in fact, whether a finished film was produced.*

                    *For further information about both these trips see Capt. Kettle (James H.
                    Hamilton), WESTERN SHORES, Narratives of the Pacific Coast, Vancouver:
                    Progress Publishing Company Limited, 1933, pp. 87-115.*

A cross-index is regrettably only as comprehensive as the material it represents, and although I have attempted to make the task of looking for specific information as easy as possible, I have been restricted by the many cases in which I was not able to view the film in question. In some instances I have extrapolated, although this can be a dangerous and misleading practice. Be fore-warned: there is more meat on these bones yet.

The numbers after each entry in the index refer to the film number, not the page number. To collate information more efficiently, subjects falling under the general headings of AGRICULTURE and SPORTS are gathered under those headings. Specific locations in the cities of Vancouver and Victoria will be found under the general headings VANCOUVER and VICTORIA. Films listed in the ADDENDA section are also indexed, but information arrived too late to include them in the alphabetical listings.

Numbers preceded by the letter A indicate addendum entries.

Aberdeen, Mount - A22

Accetti, Angelo (cinematographer) - 144

accidents & catastrophes - 219, 228

acrobats - 1, 76, 178, 1066

Acuff, Eddie - 973

Adams, J. (Acting Mayor of Victoria) - 23

ADMIRAL FARRAGUT, S.S. - 847

Adorée, Renée - 307

aerial surveys - 867, 868

aerial tramways - 529, 530, 590, 608, 841, 891b

aerial views -
  Campbell River - 89
  Gulf Islands - 52
  Kootenay River & dams - 7
  Kootenays - 7,918
  Saanich - 52
  Trail - 7
  Vancouver - 8, 12, 13, 14, 126, 153, 337,
    726b, 917
  Victoria - 52, 177, 337
  general - 87, 89, 111, 136, 214, 392, 408,
    503, 615, 726b, 867, 868, 918

Agassiz, B.C. - 100, 165, 439

agricultural workers - 112, 395, 399, 543,
  859, 862, 894, 901

agriculture -
  alfalfa - 19, 383
  apples - cultivation - 55, 128, 337, 370,
    383, 543, 567, 648, 893, A24
    - grading & packing - 358, 543, 648, 893,
    952, A24
  beans - 801, 802
  bees - 932, 989
  bulbs - 19, 109, 447, 989, 1026
  cabbage - 43, 439
  cattle & dairy - 43, 79, 80, 92, 112, 158,
    190, 226, 439, 454, 507, 597, 657, 893, 932,
    A24
  celery - 43, 128, 439
  cherries - cultivation - 55, 128, 341, 383,

  567
  combining - 43, 215, 216, 275, 378, 447,
    893, 1026
  Dominion Government Experimental Farms -
    Sidney, B.C. - 19, 92, 803, 989
    Summerland, B.C. - 665
  family farm - 93
  foxes - 11, 617, 975
  goats - 714, 984
  grain - 43, 64, 112, 142, 215, 216, 275,
    339, 378, 447, 535, 803, 893, 989
  grapes - 383, 989
  greenhouses - 383, 989
  holly - 395
  honey - 597
  hops - 112, 399, 862
  horse-drawn farm machinery - 11, 43, 112,
    370, 597, 657, 801, 893, 1026
  horses - 80, 439, 597, A24
  lettuce - 439, 801
  model farming - 40, 164
  onions - 439, 801
  peaches - cultivation - 128, 341, 567
  pears - cultivation - 55, 128, 383, 567
  peas - 379, 657, 801, 802
  plums - cultivation - 383
  potatoes - 11, 79
  poultry - 79, 80, 158, 164, 165, 187, 204,
    233, 279, 350, 674, 989
  rabbits - 11
  raspberries - 128
  seed farming - 447, 535, 801, 802, 803, 927
  sheep - 80, 597, 792, 808, 809, 810, 811,
    814, 861
  strawberries - 128, 341, 859
  swine - 80, 597, 932
  tobacco - 112, 894, 901
  trees - 181, 368

agricultural demonstration train - 187

agricultural exhibitions - 11, 43, 79, 80,
  134, 187, 190, 209, 272, 439, 808

Ahousat, B.C. - 95, 964, 1022, 1027, A2

Ahousat Indian School - 1022

aircraft -
  Autogyro - 919
  Avro 504 Lynx trainers - 726b
  Avro 626 - 728

bush planes - 111, 462, 918, 919, A3
  DeHavilland Dragon Rapide - 919
  Fairchild - 111, 919
  Fokker Super Universal - 918
  Ford Trimotor - 918
  HS - 2 - L Flying Boat - 87, 89, 136
  Lockheed Electra - 10A, 232, 420, 919
  Lockheed Lodestar - 917, 1047
  Lockheed Vega - 918
  model airplanes - 42
  Moths - 727, 728, 918, 919
  Schreck Flying Boat - 136
  Siskins - 728, 918, 919
  stunt planes - 111, 918, 919, 967, 1030
  Trans Canada Air Pageant - 918, 919
  general - 52, 87, 89, 108, 111, 125, 136,
    147, 193, 206, 216, 232, 293, 310, 311,
    314, 323, 420, 427, 443, 459, 462, 469,
    607, 657, 726b, 727, 728, 759, 760, 790,
    867, 868, 917, 918, 919, 967, 1002
    1011, 1030, 1047, 1063, A3, A10, A13,
    A15

aircraft construction - 108, 1011

airshows - 111, 216, 918, 919, 967, 1030

Alaska, State of - 195, 392, 925, 1072

ALASKA, M.V. - 832

Alaska Highway - 867, 868

Alberni, B.C. - 604, 804

Alberni Canal - 951

Albert Canyon - 641

Albert Head, V.I. - 774

Albreda Summit, B.C. - 187

Albright, Lois - 973

Albright, Wally - 973

Aldworth, T. (Mayor of Armstrong, B.C.) - 610

Alert Bay, B.C. - 191, 192, 216, 832, 834,
  925, A2

Alexander, John (d.) - A18

Alexandra Lodge - 97

Alexandra Suspension Bridge - 97, A14

ALEXANDRIA, S.S. - 65

Alfonso, Prince of Spain - 712

All Sooke Day - 21

Allen, Jack - 977

Allison, (cinematographer) - 440

Alpine Club of Canada - 200, 317, 428

Alrem, Bill - 403

American Mutoscope and Biograph Company -
  252, 332, 333, 585, 946

American Alpine Club - 200

Amery, Hon. L.S. (M.P.) - 903

Anacortes, Wash. - 26, 991

Anarchist Mountain - 100

Anderson, Erna - 751

Andros, (Victoria Alderman) - 545

Anglican Church of Canada - 72, 85, 191, 192,
  193, A2, A5, A21

angling - see fishing

Anglo British Columbia Packing Company - A27,
  A28

animals, general - 71, 194, 1044

anti-German feelings - 1010

anti-war protestors - 550

Antle, John - A20, A21

Antler Creek, B.C. - A2

Anyox, B.C. - 891a

AORANGI, S.S. - 269

APOLLO, H.M.S. - 101, 519

aquaplaning - 39, 679, 680, 682, 687, 690,
  692

archaeology - 31, 32, 33

Archibald, W.M. (cinematographer) - 7, 213,
  214, 215, 216, 918, 919

Arlen, Richard - 816

ARMOCO (tugboat) - A13

Armstrong, B.C. - 43, 80, 187, 439, 610

Armstrong, John W. - 881

Arnaut Brothers - 670

Arran Rapids - 863

Arrowsmith, Mount - 963

artillery - 600, 837, 838, 991, 997, 1006,
  1021

Ashcroft, B.C. - 187, A2

Assiniboine, Mount - 371, 425, 574

Associated Screen News, Ltd. - 4, 20, 45, 82

240, 241, 246, 247, 248, 298, 318, 338,
346, 399, 497, 652, 747, 756, 778, 785,
796, 807, 824, 826, 897, 899, 971, 978,
1021, 1072, A16, A17, A18

Asulkan Glacier - 422

Asulkan River - 422

athletics - See sports

Atkinson, Jack - 853

Atkinson, William (Minister of Agriculture) -
226, 610, 788, 989

Atlin, B.C. - 419, 498

AURORA, H.M.C.S. - 133, 614

Austin, Edward (sc.) - 235

Austin, William (ed.) - 5a, 202, 235, 307,
527, 540, 586, 798, 799, 853, 936, 1055

Australia - 41, 127, 277, 340, 635, 792,
904

automobiles - 97, 155, 176, 214, 295, 315,
386, 449, 538, 701, 987, 990, 991, 1005,
1052, A20

Automobile Club of Southern California -
1052

automobile rentals - 990

AVIANGE, A.R.M.S. - 635

Avola Station, B.C. - 187

Ayrshire cattle - 43, 597, 610

babies - 603, 670

Baden-Powell, Lady - 47

Baden-Powell, Lord - 47, 166

Badgley, Frank - 758

Bahr, Andy - 27

Baidukoff, (Russian flyer) - 607

Baker, Dr. A.R. - A1

Baker, Mount - 149

Baldy, Mount - 57

Balfour, B.C. - 908

Ball, (cinematographer) - 162

Ballantyne Pier, Vancouver - 347

Balts, (cinematographer) - 460

Bamfield, B.C. - 77, 315, 449, 980, 1022,

1026, 1027

Banff, Alberta - 48, 49, 381, 572, 573, 620,
652, 678, 679, 682, 686, 697, 699, 724,
870, 897, A25

Banks, Lionel - 5a

Barbeau, C. Marius - 588, 785

Barclay, (pilot) - 293

Barclay Sound, V.I. - 50, 965, 980, 1022,
1026, A2

Barker, Reginald (d.) - 307

Barkerville, B.C. - 51, 259, A2

Barlow, Ben - 260

Barnard, John - 799

Barnes, Jim - 456

Barrie, Wendy - 973

Barringer, Michael (sc.) - 816

Barsha, Leon (d.) - 5a, 202, 540, 586

Barton, Finis - 798, 853

Bass, Fred - 5a, 586, 1055

Baxter, Lloyd - 750

Bayley, Joe - 161

Bayley, Johnnie - 189, 869

Beach, Cdr. W.J.R. - 140

bears - 54, 61, 74, 337, 410, 413, 479, 679,
686, 688, 693, 783, 825, 893, 933, 1020

Beatrice, Princess Dona of Spain - 712

Beattie, R.E. - 893

Beatty Cup (golf) - 1048

beaver - 815, 825

Beaver Harbour - 486

Beaverfoot Mountains - A32

Beaverfoot River - A32, A46, A54

Beavermouth Canyon - 1058, A46

Beckway, William (cinematographer) - 217, 235,
527, 528, 798, 799, 853, 936, 973, 1055

Beebe, Ford (d.) - 798, 853, 1045

Becher Bay, B.C. - 188

Beehive, Mount - A22

beer & ale - 613

Beesley, Ross (cinematographer) - 3, 37, 42,
115, 134, 135, 189, 239, 268, 393, 409, 450,
459, 467, 470, 524, 591, 622, 673, 712, 774,
821, 828, 831, 869, 877, 883, 933, 959, 1008,
1042, 1048, 1049, 1051

Beliakof, (Russian flyer) - 607

Bell-Irving, Major A.D. - 443

Bell-Irving, Miss - 772

Bella Bella - 57

Bella Coola - 31, 32, 61, 62, 313, 677, 832,
891a

Bellingham, Wash. - 978

Bennett, Prime Minister R.B. - 958

Bennett, Yukon - 1072

Bennett, Wid - A14

Beregi, Oscar - 307

Berg Lake - 24, 634

Bergdahl, Chris - 160

Bernstein, Isador - 936

Berry, J.W. (M.L.A.) - 226

Bessborough, Governor General & Lady - 1004

BESSIE DOLLAR, S.S. - 9, 732

betting & wagering - 403

Betts, Corporal (RCMP) - 498

Bevan, William - 587

bicycles - 225

Big Bend, The - A56

Big Interior Mountain , V.I. - A2

Birch Island - 187

bird sanctuary - 729

birds - 53, 69, 70, 71, 147, 257, 284, 321,
388, 409, 729, 731, 783, 794, 924, 934,
1041

Birdstone, Aloysius - 689

Bischoff, Samuel (p.) - 1045

Bishop, Kenneth J. (p.) - 5a, 202, 217, 235,
527, 528, 540, 586, 587, 798, 799, 853,
936, 973, 1055

Bishop of London - 72, 85

bison - 137, 254

Bitzer, G.W. (Billy) (cinematographer) - 252,
332, 333, 585, 946

Black, Dave - 135, 456

Black, Ken - 630

Blackmore, Bob - A56

Blaine, Washington, & Peace Arch - 545, 655,
1052

Blaisdell, Margot (narr.) - 338

Bloedel Logging Co. - 510

Boas, Franz - 486

Bodega Anchorage - 863

Bolton, David - 524

BONANZA KING (sternwheeler) - 17

Bones Bay Cannery - 192

Bonine, Robert (cinematographer) - 110, 559,
633, 638, 741, 1014

Bonney, Mount - A47

Bonnington Falls - 99, 908, A2

Booth, Alfred (cinematographer) - 191, 192,
A2, A5

Boothe, J. Howard (cinematographer) - 1054

Borden, Sir Robert (Prime Minister of Canada)
- 437

borders & boundaries - 247, 655, 1052

Boston Bar, B.C. - A53

Bosustow, R. - 81

Bosworth, Hobart - 1046

Boundary Bay - 759

Bourne, Clifford (cinematographer) - 217

Bourne, R.E. (cinematographer) - 159

Boving, Professor (UBC) - 226

Bow Lake, Alta. - 944

Bow River Valley, Alta. - 49

Bowdery, J.W. (cinematographer) - 208, 446,
550, 854, 915, 960, 967, 1012, 1028

Bowen Island, B.C. - 113, 374, 375

Bowen, W.S. - 1066

Bowman, H. (CNR Agricultural Rep.) - 187

Bowser, Mrs. (wife of Premier) - 600

Bowser Cup - 976

Boy Scouts - 47, 78, 166, 206, 216, 261, 516, 517

Boys and Girls Clubs - 79, 80, 233, 610

Boyd, Jack - 672

Brace Bay, B.C. - 261

Bradshaw, Dorothy - 235

Brady's Beach (near Bamfield) - 449

Bralorne Mine - 81, A8

Brandywine Falls - 460, 736

Brass, Capt. W. - 903

Brazill, (cinematographer) - 36, 105, 415

Brenon, Herbert (d.) - 16

Brent, Evelyn - 587

Brentwood Bay, B.C. - 52, 176, 234, 978, 993

Brentwood Bay - Mill Bay ferry - 52, 176, 454, 993

Brentwood College rowing team - 959

Brentwood Hotel - 176

Brethertin, James (cinematographer) - 217, 799

Brewster, Jack (cinematographer) - 410

Brewster, Jas. - 911

Bridal Veil Falls - 57

Bridge River District, B.C. - 83, 101

bridges - 82, 96, 99, 100, 140, 193, 201, 228, 491, 726a, 734, 739, 759, 969, 1002, 1050, 1053

Brilliant, B.C. - 721

Brilliant Dam - 908

Brittania Beach - 186, 1004

Brittania Mines - 1004

British-American Film Company - 342, 551, 715, 851

British-Canadian Pictures, Ltd. - 1045

British Columbia Bureau of Industrial and

Tourist Development - See British Columbia Government Travel Bureau

British Columbia Department of Agriculture - 11, 19, 40, 43, 79, 80, 92, 109, 112, 163, 187, 190, 226, 233, 279, 358, 379, 383, 439, 454, 455, 597, 610, 657, 788, 790, 792, 801, 802, 803, 808, 811, 814, 835, 859, 861, 894, 901, 926, 932, 989, 1003, 1043

British Columbia Electric Railway Company - A14

British Columbia Forest Service - 46, 87, 89, 104, 147, 181, 207, 210, 288, 326, 363, 368, 458, 513, 762, 763, 764, 765, 767, 790, 827,

British Columbia Government Travel Bureau - 21, 234, 244, 270, 319, 382, 606, 761, 794, 840, 862, 953, 961

British Columbia Legislature, opening of - 106, 650, 717, 788, 1051

British Columbia Patriotic and Educational Picture Service - 57, A2

British Columbia Provincial Bureau of Information - 107, A1

British Columbia Provincial Fisheries Department - 768, 790

British Columbia Provincial Police - 764, 766, 790, 808

British Columbia Shorthorn Breeder's Association - 932

British Columbia Silver Challenge Trophy - 831

British Columbia Teacher's Association convention - 874

British Columbia Women's Association - 105

British Properties - 201

BROADCASTER (U.C.C. mission boat) - 1071

Brodeur, Capt. V.G. - 140, 141

Brodie, Mr. - 792

Bromley, Sheila - 235

Brooks, Rocky - 321

Broughton Strait - 834

Brown, Bill (asst.-d.) - 1055

Brown, C.G. - 874

Brown, George - 811

Browne, Colin (co-d.) - 1025

Browne, Lucille - 217, 799

Bruce, C.D. - 472

Bruce, Nigel - 396

Bruce, Hon. Randolph R., Lt. Gov. of B.C. – 209, 357, 441, 610, 666, 712, 1048, 1051, 1052

Brunette Sawmills – 951

Buchan, John (Lord Tweedsmuir) – 272, 519, 520, 521, 522

Buchman, Dean – 874

bucking broncos – 38, 43, 230, 273, 336, 430, 553, 680, 684, 1042

Buddhism – 928

Bulkley River – 929

Bull River, B.C. – 198

Buntzen Lake – 1016

Burgess, Mount – A22

Burke Channel – 57

Burnett, Dr. – 472

Burrard Bridge – 726a

Burrard Inlet – 869

burros – 110

buses & coaches – 52, 151, 216, 993

Butchart, Mr. & Mrs. R.P. – 873

Butchart Gardens – 52, 101, 113, 176, 177, 445, 587, 873, 898, 951, 978, 994

Bute Inlet – 863

Butedale, B.C. – 832

Byng, Lord (Gov. General of Canada) – 29, 417, 515, 516, 517, 518, 957

Byron, Walter – 235

Cache Creek, B.C. – A2

cadets – 220, 449, 793

Cadwallader Creek – 81

Caledonia Games – 114, 115, 116, 287, 878

calesthenics – 107, 129, 547, 664, 760, 938, 957, 1002

Caley, Dorothy & Hazel – 751

Calgary, Alberta – 386

Calvery, Cdr. (R.N.) – 1001

cameras & cameramen – 66, 69, 117, 284, 311, 410, 413, 530, 659, 1005

Cameron Lake – 701, 951

CAMOSUN, S.S. – 385

Camp Kokanee – 482, 1071

Camp Skookumchuck-in-the-Rockies – 678 to 699 incl.

Campbell River, B.C. – 31, 89, 101, 195, 304, 326, 363, 835, A13, A20

camping – 305, 482, 574, 793, 960, 1071, A22

Canada Wire and Cable Company steel wire rope – A9, A12, A13, A14

Canadian Alpine Club – 24

Canadian Army – 106, 121, 123, 131, 138, 144, 145, 146, 148, 175, 319, 342, 417, 436, 437, 452, 517, 519, 522, 523, 537, 600, 627, 650, 702, 703, 704, 707, 708, 717, 728, 735, 758, 759, 760, 762, 763, 764, 765, 766, 767, 768, 769, 770, 771, 788, 790, 836, 837, 838, 991, 992, 997, 1002, 1003, 1006, 1009, 1010, 1012, 1013, 1021, 1035, 1051, 1053

Canadian Army Militia – 214, 992

Canadian British Empire Games team – 127

Canadian Broadcasting Corporation – 349

Canadian Cameos (ASN) – 45, 82, 240, 241, 246, 247, 248, 346, 652, 796, 807, 971, A16, A17

Canadian Girls in Training (CGIT) – 1071

Canadian Government Motion Picture Bureau (see also Exhibits and Publicity Bureau, Dept. of Trade and Commerce) – 2, 8, 24, 30, 48, 63, 73, 119, 122, 149, 151, 177, 182, 184, 204, 285, 304, 306, 323, 335, 338, 341, 345, 351, 370, 372, 381, 388, 410, 413, 425, 434, 445, 463, 494, 531, 535, 543, 572, 573, 595, 614, 620, 623, 651, 674, 737, 758, 776, 783, 795, 797, 804, 820, 846, 856, 887, 888, 913, 994, 1007, 1037, 1038, 1041, 1044, 1069, 1070 A57

Canadian Historic Features, Ltd. – 672

CANADIAN IMPORTER, S.S. – 848

Canadian Industries Limited (C.I.L.) – 927

Candian Infantry Expeditionary Force – 1013

CANADIAN INVENTOR, S.S. – 893

Canadian National Railway trains (see also Grand Trunk Pacific R.R.) – 17, 187, 335, 740, 759, 818, 888, 929, 935, 1002

Canadian Pacific Exhibition – 134

Canadian Pacific Railway Company – 418, A22, A55

Canadian Pacific Railway Company dramatic promotional films – 211, 231, 499, 506, 570, 579, 625, 812, 839, 855, 870, 890, 1019

13

Canadian Pacific Railway Company's Pier
   "D", Vancouver - 100, 667, 759, 940, A2

Canadian Pacific Railway trains - 4, 20, 97,
   132, 199, 211, 252, 286, 320, 332, 333, 386,
   483, 506, 585, 619, 636, 637, 639, 641,
   642, 643, 644, 645, 646, 661, 662, 757,
   787, 790, 791, 816, 903, 908, 915, 924,
   931, 946, 1024, 1058, A22, A23, A30-33,
   A44, A46-55

Canadian Pacific Steamships - 4, 8, 10, 17,
   44, 52, 95, 100, 101, 123, 149, 151, 176,
   177, 220, 222, 263, 264, 265, 315, 337,
   387, 396, 445, 446, 459, 495, 497, 517,
   599, 613, 615, 705, 713, 736, 758, 759,
   761, 762, 763, 767, 770, 771, 774, 790,
   812, 832, 850, 851, 886, 893, 898, 925,
   951, 970, 978, 980, 993, 1002, 1005,
   1019, 1053, A2, A10, A11, A14, A15, A34,
   A42

Canadian Press - 94

CANADIAN RANGER, S.S. - 591

Canadian Red Cross Society - A19

Canadian Steamship Lines - 17, 30, 61, 94,
   176, 337, 765, 758, 765, 768, 769, 790,
   888, 891a, 912, 929, A14, A15

Canadian Wheat Board - 64

canneries & canning (fish) - 50, 95, 499,
   510, 588, 593, 628, 776, 777, 780, 781,
   782, 832, 856, 965, 1058, A5, A27, A28,
   A45

cannibals - 387

canoes - 3, 95, 111, 185, 357, 445, 483,
   499, 548, 581, 660, 680, 690, 779, 784,
   785, 815, 844, 898, 1007, 1022, 1026

Canyon Falls - 57

CAPILANO, M.V. (ferry to Bowen Island) -
   374, 375

Capilano Canyon & suspension bridge - 8,
   151, 211, 394, 723, 749, 969, 1046

Capilano River - A11, A12

Capilano Valley - 94, 394

Capital Film Company, Victoria - 161, 992

Caplan, Rupert - 776

Carcross, Yukon - 392

CARDENA, M.V. - 832, 863

Carey, Jas. - 868

Cariboo District, B.C. - 83, 91, 156, 187,
   230, 259, 336, 672, 1042, 1052, A1, A2

caribou - 364, 410, 413, 1018, 1062

Carpe, Allan - 200

carrier pigeons - 147

cars - see Automobiles

Cartercar Gearless automobile - 987

casinos - 1072

Cassiar Creek, B.C. - 475

Castle Crags - A22

Castle Films - 1003, A10

Castle Mountain - 49, 686

Castlegar, B.C. - 908, A2, A14

Caterpillar tractors - 905, 910, A6, A9

Cathedral Grove - 315, 804

Cathedral Mountain - 949

cats - 194, 805

Cedarvale, B.C. - 187

Cee-Pee-Cee, B.C. - 832

Cellier, Antionette - 816

cemetaries - 516, 517

Central Films, Ltd. - 5a, 202, 235, 527,
   528, 540, 586, 798, 853, 936, 973, 1055

Challenger, Mr. - 792

Chambers, Lilian (sc. & cinematographer) -
   99, 100, 101, 872, 924

Chambers, T.G.S. (cinematographer) - 99, 100,
   101, 872, 924

Chamberlain, Sir Austen - 712

Chao Kung (see Lincoln, Trebitch)

Charles Urban Trading Company, Ltd. - A27-54

CHARMER, S.S. - 812

Chautard, Emile - 307

Cheakamus River & Canyon, Wash. - 460, 736

Chekaloff (Russian flyer) - 607

Chemainus, B.C. - 560

Chester, C.L. - A56

Chester-Outing Pictures - A55, A56

Chichibou, Prince & Princess (of Japan) -
   558, 706

Chilcoot Pass - 110

Chilcotin region, B.C. - A2

children - 8, 50, 55, 104, 116, 134,
    148, 162, 167, 168, 169, 173, 178,
    187, 188, 192, 194, 203, 206, 212, 214,
    215, 216, 224, 254, 261, 298, 304, 320,
    321, 328, 343, 352, 373, 431, 464, 465,
    466, 467, 473, 487, 514, 542, 600, 603
    610, 622, 665, 666, 700, 706, 720, 722,
    762, 765, 788, 790, 793, 805, 806, 845,
    875, 879, 880, 881, 915, 938, 945, 957,
    996, 1002, 1005, 1008, 1028, 1040

Children's Aid Society, Vancouver - 669

Chilliwack, B.C. - 112, 187, 188, 226

Chilliwack Lake - 58, 956

China - 819, 851

Chinese & Chinatowns in B.C. - 91, 171,
    172, 206, 272, 398, 639, 642, 644, 799, 832,
    965, 1040, A15, A20, A27, A28, A45, A52

Chinese junk - 154

CHOYU MARU, S.S. - 450

Christ Church Cathedral, Victoria - 72,
    85

Christine Lake, B.C. - 99

Christmas - 541, 720

chrysanthemums - 541

circuses - 178

CITY OF NEW YORK (globe-circling aeroplane) -
    459

CITY OF SEATTLE, S. S. - A42

Clare, Phyllis - 202, 540

Clark, G.H. - 293

Clark, General R.P. - 516, 517

Clay, Gwen - 189

Clayoquot town & Sound - 95, 964

Clear Brook, B.C. - 91

Clearwater District, B.C. - 461

Cloverdale, B.C. - 366, 617, 975

"Cloverdale", home of B.C. Premier Dr. S.
    F. Tolmie - 40

Clyde, David - 527

Coast Range of British Columbia - 218,
    421, A52

Cody, Bill - 1045

Colby, R.L. (cinematographer) - 21, 761, 961

Coldstream Ranch - 226, A23,

Cole, Enid - 1055

Collins, Lewis D. (d.) - 527

Collyer, Charles G.D. - 459

Collyer, R. - 758

COLOMBO, H.M.S. - 393

Columbia Coast Mission - 191, 192, 193, A2,
    A5, A20, A21

Columbia Glacier & Icefields - 73, 944

Columbia Lake - 257

COLUMBIA, M.V. (mission boat) - 191, 192,
    193, A5, A20, A21

Columbia River - 100, 257, 1020, 1039, A14,
    A46, A47, A49, A55, A56

Columbia River Valley - 620

Combe, Vivian - 217, 235, 1055

Cominco smelter, Trail, B.C. - 7, 893, 907,
    909

Commonwealth Productions, Ltd. - 217, 587,
    799

Communist Party of Canada - 550, 968

Connaught, Duke and Duchess of - 191, 253,
    254, 255

Connelly, Edward - 198

Connolly, Factor - 666

Conway, Philip (sc.) - 527

Cook, Captain James - 274, 427

Cook, Clyde - 936

cooks - 962, 963, 966

Coombe, Virginia - 5a

Cooperative Commonwealth Federation (C.C.F.)
    summer camp - 960

Cora Lynn Dam - 205, 908, 1020, A14

Corbett, Commodore Roy W. (yachting) - 1068

"cordoroy" roads - A37-40

cormorants - 794

Cornett, Acting-Mayor of Vancouver - 140, 141

Coronation Festival - 206, 212

Cortes Island, B.C. - A5

Cosmopolitan Productions - 307

Cotton Creek & Cotton Creek Bridge - 1020

Cougar Mount - A47

cougars - 365

Courtenay, B.C. - 31, 320, 321, 324, 325, 326, 363

Courtesy Week - 471

Cow Testing Association - 226

cowboys - 38, 209, 336, 430, 502, 553, 577, 853, 932, 1042, 1052, A2

Cowichan Lake - 527

Cowichan River - 445

Cowichan sweaters (made by Cowichan Indians) - 46, 1026

Cowichan Valley - 46, 210, 279, 326, 445, 454, 966, 1025, 1026

Cox, E.C. - 671

coyotes - 539

Cranbrook, B.C. - 198, 212, 430, 493, 578

Crane, Fred - 180

Crawford, Capt. - 635

Crawford, Mrs. Frederick - 984

Crawley, Daniel C. - 27

Creston, B.C. - 213, 214, 215, 216, 919, 995

Creston Flats - 1020

Cronjager, Henry (cinematographer) - 211, 231, 499, 506, 570, 579, 625, 787, 812, 839, 855, 870, 890, 931, 1019

Cross, Lt. Col. Lorne - 517

Crow's Nest Pass - 580

crows - 729

Crowsnest Mountain - 257

Croydon, B.C. - 187

Crusaders, Most Noble Order of - 518

Curtis, Edward S. - 424

Curwood, James Oliver - 16, 307

Cusack, Noel - 202

customs inspection - 939

Czar, Paul - 721

Dad Quick - 224

Daley, Dr. - 1071

Dalrymple, Ian (sc.) - 816

DALVEEN, S.S. - 535

Dana, Viola - 1046

Daniels, William H. (cinematographer) - 749

Darling, (cinematographer) - 754

Davey, D.C. (cinematographer) - 35, 76, 133, 186, 400, 465, 545, 844, 847

Davie, Mr. - 792

Davis, J.A. - 882

Davis, John K. - 125

Dawley, J. Searle (d.) - 211, 231, 499, 506, 570, 579, 625, 812, 839, 855, 870, 890, 931, 1019

Dawson, Yukon - 754, 868, 1072

Deacon, Richard (cinematographer) - 816

Dead Horse Gulch - 1072

Dean Channel - 57, 888

Dean, Priscilla - 198

Deaville, Clifford - 587

deer - 344, 445, 510, 659, 815, 832, 893, 898

Della Falls, B.C. - A2

Della River, B.C. - A2

Delta, B.C. - 79

Dent Island - 863

Denver "Safeways" basketball team - 23

dePencier, Chaplain Bishop A.V. - 518, 865

Depression - 91, 98, 107, 260, 481, 550, 947, 962, 963, 968

DesBrisay, A.C. - 99

Devonshire, Duke of - 256

Dewey, Bernard O. (cinematographer) - 343

Diamond Jubilee, Canada - 148

Dill, Mr. & Mrs. John - 584

Discovery Passage - 863

diving, stunt - 726a

dockyards - 1001

Dodger Cove - 1022

dog sleds - 344, 633, 921, 922

dogs - 90, 194, 235, 344, 386, 633, 660,
  805, 808, 893, 920, 921, 1072, A43

dolls - 245

Dome, Mount - 422

DOMINIA, S.S. - 77, 849

Dominion Astrophysical Observatory, Saanich,
  B.C. - 52, 176, 177, 316, 871, 951, 978

Dominion Bridge Company - 201

Dominion Day - 1036

Dominion Experimental Farms - see agriculture

Dominion Government Emergency Radio
  Station - 192

Donald, B.C. - 386

Douglas Channel - 17

Douglas, Donald - 5a, 202, 540

Douglas Fir trees - 4, 67, 276, 315, 327,
  368, 531, 538, 591, 804, 893, 1025, A6

Douglas Lake - 932

Douglas Lake Ranch - 932

Douglas, Mount - 100

Doukhobors - 91, 250, 251, 721, 907, 1020,
  A14

Doyle, Maxine - 528

Dragon Creek, B.C. - A2

dredge, steam - 948, 965, 1024, 1072

drill squads - 384

drydocks & graving docks - 130, 385, 397,
  405, 416, 445, 846, 903, 1001, A15

Drynoch, B.C. - A51

ducks - 411

Dun-Waters, Capt. J.C. - 439

Duncan, B.C. - 46, 326, 1025, 1026

Dunsmuir, (Vice president of Canadian
  Pacific Exhibition) - 507

Dunsmuir, Kathleen (Mrs. Seldon Humphries)
  - 217, 587, 799

Dunstan, Eric (narr.) - 558

Dutch Creek "hoodoos" - 1020

Dwyer, (cinematographer) - 123

Eagle's Nest Pass - 410

earthquakes - 296

East Indians in British Columbia - 91, 510,
  523, 886, A13

Easter - 362

eating - 1

Eccleston, Charles - 814

Eddy, Nelson - 749

Edison Mfg. Company - 54, 211, 231, 476, 489,
  499, 506, 559, 561, 570, 575, 579, 619, 625,
  633, 637, 638, 641, 642, 643, 644, 645, 646,
  661, 662, 748, 757, 787, 812, 839, 842, 855,
  870, 890, 914, 931, 1014, 1019

Edwards, C.P. - 232

Edwards, Edgar (sc.) - 52, 202, 235, 540, 586,
  1055

eggs - 851

Eicke, Herbert (sd.) - 235, 527, 528, 540, 973,
  1055

Eisenhardt, Ian - 547

El Bar Ranch - 714

elections - 124, 139

ELECTRA (yacht) - 223

elk - 686, 688, 815

Elk Falls - 101, 481, 947, 962, 963, 966

Elk Lake (near Victoria) - 321

Elk River Falls - 701

Elk River Timber Company Ltd. - 857

Elk's Club - 466, 551

Emerald Lake, B.C. 48, 428, 620, 924, A22

Emerald Peak - A22

emergency measures for aircraft in distress
  - 147

emergency measures for wounded hiker on
  isolated West Coast - 192

Emerton, Roy - 816

Emory Creek, B.C. - 260

Emory Creek Placer Mining School - 260

Emperor Falls - 634

Empire Day celebrations - 261, 844

EMPRESS OF ASIA - 290, 296, 850, 893

EMPRESS OF CANADA - 10, 263, 264, 265, 396, 446, 600

EMPRESS OF CANADA - aground at Homer Bay - 52, 68, 408, 503, 615, 774

EMPRESS OF CHINA (original) - 1019, A34

EMPRESS OF FRANCE - 774

EMPRESS OF JAPAN - original - 144 (?), A11

EMPRESS OF JAPAN - succeeding - 101, 142, 149, 201, 269, 290, 316, 505, A11

EMPRESS OF RUSSIA - 266, 459, 851, A15

EMPRESS ships (Canadian Pacific steamships) - 8, 44, 101, 142, 149, 151, 201, 263, 264, 265, 266, 290, 296, 316, 387, 396, 408, 446, 459, 497, 503, 505, 599, 600, 615, 705, 774, 850, 851, 893, 951, 970, 1019, A11, A14, A34

Englishman's River - 481, 963, 966

Errington, R.J. (cinematographer) - 418, 444, 549, 569, 635

Eskimos - 970

Esquimalt, B.C. - 9, 100, 130, 149, 281, 282, 283, 299, 302, 312, 316, 405, 438, 445, 450, 495, 561, 613, 623, 730, 732, 765, 766, 847, 903, 1001, 1021, A15

Essanay Film Mfg. Company - 367, 1016

Estero Basin - 863

Estero Peak - 863

Estevan Point - 965, 1027

ESTEVAN, S.S. - 852

Eucharistic pilgrims - 269

Evans, (pilot) - 1063

Evans, John Newell (ex-MLA) - 210

exhibitions - 43, 209, 272, 273, 279, 358, 439, 597, 610, 700, 987

Exhibits and Publicity Bureau, Dept. of Trade and Commerce - 48, 108, 118, 176, 267, 367, 378, 404, 427, 428, 536, 574, 616, 648, 709, 723, 740, 782, 884, 891a, 896, 934, 944, 999, 1016, 1061, 1062

factories - 893

Fair, David - 587

Fairchild, Mount - 59

Fairmont Hot Springs, B.C. - 686, 687, 691

Fairview, Mount - 949

Falkland Station, B.C. - 187

FANTOME (sailing ship) - A15

farm loans - 163

farming - see Agrilculture

Farrell, Johnny - 877

Farrington, R.J. (cinematographer) - 263

Federal Soldier's Housing Scheme - 402

Fellows, Edith - 936

Fernie, B.C. - 257

Ferris, Clarence (cinematographer) - 234, 244, 292, 319, 382, 461, 761, 840, 953, 961

Feuz, Eduard - 184

Field, B.C. - 590, 637, 644, 911, 924, 931, 946

Field, Mount - 644

Fier, Jack (p.) - 5a, 202, 235, 527, 528, 540, 586, 798, 853, 936, 973, 1055

Fifth British Columbia Coast Brigade - 34, 452 (?), 758, 762, 764, 766, 767, 768

Film Title Service (cinematographers) - 845

Finlayson Arm - 149, 1026

Finlayson, Colin - 753

Fintry, Laird of - 43, 439

Fire Warden's badges - 391

fireboats - 290, 940

firemen, firetrucks & firehalls - 74, 243, 363, 452

fires - forest - 87, 89, 210, 267, 288, 311, 323, 324, 325, 363, 391, 458, 513, 827, 1027; urban - 360, 667, 759, 786, 925, 940, 951, 991, A2

first aid - 292

First Narrows Bridge, Vancouver - 99

First National Pictures - 1046

fish packers - 335

fishermen - 964, 965

fishing - crab - 964
             - dogfish - 1027
        - halibut - 35, 335, 337, 377, 832, 888, 912
        - herring - 893, 1041
        - pilchards - 604, 832, 965
        - salmon, commercial - 50, 61, 95, 157,

188, 191, 192, 193, 214, 234, 298, 299,
300, 302, 303, 316, 318, 337, 380, 404,
434, 445, 449, 462, 489, 499, 510, 536,
588, 593, 616, 628, 658, 701, 776, 777,
779, 780, 781, 782, 832, 834, 842, 856,
863, 876, 891a, 893, 923, 964, 965, 1022,
1026, 1058, A5, A13, A27, A28, A29, A35,
A45
- salmon, sport - 234, 301, 304, 778, 898,
953, 1037, A13, A43
- spear - A43
- trout - 28, 97, 301, 306, 337, 410, 775,
804, 1007, 1038, A3
- tuna - 893

Fitzpatrick Traveltalk films - 742

Five Finger Rapids, Yukon - 1018, 1072

flagpoles - 591, 1064, 1066

Flavin, James - 799

floods - 153, 186, 313, 331, 969

Flores Island, B.C. - A2

flowers - 52, 101, 113, 176, 177, 445, 447,
541, 587, 788, 873, 898, 951, 978, 994,
1043, 1071

flumes - 493, 554, 568

Flying U Ranch - A2

Flynn, Errol - 396

Fogg, Howard - 758

Foley, Vic - 977

Forbes, Harry (cinematographer) - 235,
527, 973, 1055

Forbes Landing Hotel - 363

Forbes, Ralph - 1055

Forbes, Rt. Honourable G.W. (Prime
Minister of New Zealand) - 738

Forbidden Plateau - 315, 320

Ford, Henry - 386

Ford Motion Picture Laboratories - 576,
577, 589, 593, 745, 746

Foreman, (cinematographer) - 224, 592

Forin, Doug - 609

Forman, Harrison - 6

Fort Fraser, B.C. - 187

Fort Rodd Hill - 1006

Fort Rupert, B.C. - 486, 899

Fort St. James, B.C. - 666

Fort Steele - 212, 307

Fortes, Joe - 102, 343

Foster, Col. J. - 140

Foster, John - 391

Foster Station, B.C. - 187

France - 334

Frank Slide - 257

Franklin River - 510

Franzka, Dale - 227

Frasea Farms - 455, 657, A2

Fraser Canyon - 52, 97, 101, 332, 333, 1058,
A2, A14, A48, A52-53

FRASER, H.M.C.S. (H-48) - 138, 140, 193,
238, 324, 325, 468, 469, 770, 1053, A10

Fraser Lake - 726

Fraser Mills - A7

Fraser River - 268, 380, 499, 628, 776,
781, 791, 841, 923, 1016, 1052, 1058, A27,
A28, A29, A35, A45
- flooded - 153, 331, 734, 739
- frozen - 37

Fraser Valley - 58, 100, 112, 165, 187, 188,
226, 399, 409, 439, 455, 657, 663, 862,
894, 901, 956, 1016, 1052, A2

Frederick Arm - 863

Freeman, Lewis R. - A55, A56

French, Percy - 43, 439

Friendly Cove - 899, 1022, 1027

Friml, Rudolph - 749

funerals - 40, 102, 125, 171, 192, 343, 721,
990

furs - 5a

Gale, Mrs. Margaret - 391

Garden parties - 600, 647, 865, 873

"Garden Week" in Victoria - 986

Gardener Canal - 17

Gargan, William - 527

Garibaldi Lake - 868

Garibaldi Station - 736

Garrett, Charles "Hoop" - 374, 508

Garrod, I.J. (cinematographer) - 759, 951

Gass, T.A. - A14

Gatten, Harper - 474

Gaullaudet, John - 540, 586

Geddes, Sir Auckland - 817

geese - 411, 815, 825

Germans in British Columbia - 1010

Germany - 347

ghost towns - 240

Gibbon, John Murray - 816

Gibson Brothers sawmill, Victoria - 510

Gibson, Mount - 411

Gibson, Rev. (U.C.C.) - 964, 980

Gillett, (speaker of U.S. House of Representatives) - 1009

Girl Guides - 47, 166

GIVENCHY, S.S. - 965, 980

Glacier House (C.P.R. Hotel) - 1058, A32, A47, A54

Glacier National Park - 184

glaciers - 48, 61, 73, 278, 348, 392, 421, 422, 425, 428, 447, 574, 576, 583, 634, 807, 825, 911, 944, 1052, 1062, 1071

Glass, H.R. - 669

Glenochle, B.C. - 646, A50

Glintz Lake, V.I. - 966

goats, mountain - 410, 412, 413, 783, 815, 893, 1062

Godfrey, Major - 443

Gold Range, B.C. - A49

gold rush, gold panning & gold mining - 15, 51, 81, 110, 215, 216, 259, 260, 419, 435, 475, 476, 534, 559, 563, 633, 741, 792, 1014, 1017, 1046, 1072, A2, A8, A51, A52

Goldbeck, Willis (sc.) - 16

Golden, B.C. - 463, 620, 646, A2, A49

Golden, Mount - 639

Gomley Dyke - 331

Goodenough, M.E. (sc.) - 744

Goodrich, Frances - 749

Goulding, George - 671

Government House, Victoria - 78, 526, 712, 768, 817

Governor of Bombay - 523

Graham, Donald (veteran of the first Riel Rebellion) - 43

Grand Forks, B.C. - 216, 250, 918, 919

Grand Trunk Pacific R.R. - 912

Grand Trunk Pacific steamships - 891, 912

Granite Skating Club - 751

Granstrom, Ethel - 280

graves - 40, 61, 105, 899, 1052

Gray Creek, B.C. - 1020

Gray, Hon. Arthur Wellsley (Wells Gray) (Minister of Lands) - 722

Great Central Lake, V.I. - A2

Great Divide - 59, 311, 463

Greely, B.C. - 386

Green Lake - 97

Green Point Rapids - 863

Green Timbers Forest Nursery - 181, 368

GREGALIA, S.S. - 142

Grenfell Mission - 369

Grierson, John - 199

Grindrod, B.C. - 233

Gruening, Dr. E. - 867, 868

Guichon Ranch - 932

Guilavoff, Vera (composer) - 45

Gulf Islands - 52, 808

gun defences - 1006, 1021

Gunnerson, Gunner - 823

Gunnerson, Hans - 823

Gwydyr, David (sc.) - 776

gymkhana - 294

gypsum mine - 187

Gyro Club, Vancouver - 18, 373, 374, 375, 508, 669, 879

Gytsegucla, B.C. - 900, 935

Hackett, Albert - 749

Hagen, Walter - 135, 877

Hager, Al - 377

Hager, Kolin - 587

Hague, (cinematographer) - 442

Hagwelgate, B.C. - 935

Halcyon, Mount - 101

Halfway Falls - 57

Hallet, George - 1055

Hamber, Lt. Governor E.W. - 106, 120, 236,
  281, 282, 283, 526, 650, 702, 703, 704,
  722, 1004, 1068

Hamilton, John - 586

Hamilton, Wally (sd.) - 217, 799

Harding, President Warren G. (U.S.A.) & Mrs.
  Harding - 1009

Hardwick, Walter - 972

Hardy Trophy - 1034

Harmac pulpmill, near Crofton, V.I. - A15

Harmon, Byron (cinematographer) - 24, 344,
  412, 921, 922, 949, 999, A55, A56

Harrison Hot Springs, B.C. - 227, 784, 840

Harrison Lake - 100, 227, 840, A2

Hartley Bay - A14

Hassen, Mat - 43, 163, 439,

Hastings, Harry - 527, 799

Hastings Saw Mill - 531, A9, A20

hatcheries - salmon - 300, 536, 628
  - whitebait - 300

Hatley Park - 445, 587

Hawks, Eagle - 621

Hay, Harry - 1055

Haynes, Jack - 528, 540

Hayward, Mayor of Victoria - 561

Hayworth, Rita - 5a, 202

Hazelton, B.C. - 187, 726b, 900, 935, 1052

Heaps, E.H. & Company - 992

Hector, Mount - 639, 644, 757, 949

Hector Station - 757

Hedley, B.C. - 792

Heeny, Tom - 599

HEIAN MARU, S.S. - 706

Heisy, Paul (cinematographer) - 613

Hell's Gate, Fraser Canyon - 97, A2

Helmcken Island - 330, 789

Helmer, Mr. - 792

HENDERSON, U.S.S. - 1009

Henry, Prince - 405

Heppell, Michael - 202, 217, 528, 540,
  853

Herbert Island - A2

Herron, (cinematographer) - 29, 55, 209,
  242, 264, 273, 397, 417, 431, 472,
  493, 557, 731, 849, 882, 974, 1036, 1050

Hershell Island - 407

Hesquiat, B.C. - 1027

Heyd, Alan - 160

Hicks, Judge - 439

high school bands - 207, 751, 1028

highway and road construction - 257, 366,
  390, 580, 905, 955, 966, 1024, 1026

hiking - 173, 391, 394, 447, 1071

Hill, Monty - 877

Hill, Robert (d.) - 217

Hill, Samuel - 545

Hillburn, Percy (cinematographer) - 307

Hilton, Arthur - 587

Hincks, Reginald - 217, 235, 528, 540,
  587, 798, 799, 853, 936, 973, 1055, A19

Hines, Art - 828

Hobson, Valerie - 936

Hoch, Winston C. (cinematographer) - 742

Hodge, George - 773

Hoerl, Arthur (sc.) - 217, 587

Holdsworth, Mrs. - 635

Holland, R. Rowe - 879

Holliday, Harvey - 977

Holmes, Lt. Cdr. W. - 238

Home Oil Company - 201

Homer Bay, B.C. - 52, 68, 408, 503, 615, 774

homesteading - 93

HOOD, H.M.S. - 893

Hoover, President Herbert (U.S.A.) - 1009

Hope, Lt. Cdr. A.M. - 138, 140, 238

Hornby Island - 449, 480

Hornell, Sir William - 819

horse-drawn wagons & sleighs - 93, 254, 370,
    A41

horses - 38, 55, 80, 131, 144, 400, 401, 439,
    452, 490, 502, 597, 632, 755, 805, 836, 837,
    838, 853, 898, 932, 969, 978, 1010, 1058, A24,
    A37-39. See also - bucking broncos.

hospitals - 101, 178, 187, 720, 836, A5, A20

hot springs - 381, 686, 687, 691

housing - 402

Houston, B.C. - 187

Howe, C.D. - 232

Howe, James (cinematographer) - 16

Howe Sound - 736, 1004

howitzer, giant - 600

Huber, Mount - 949

Hudson's Bay Company - 159, 406, 407, 612, 666

Hudson locomotive (later "Royal Hudson") - 924
    1002, 1003

Hughes, Sir Sam - 436, 437

Hull, George C. (sc.) - 198

Hume, Mayor of New Westminster - 722

Hunt, Mr. & Mrs. George - 486, 899

Hunter, (co-pilot) - 232

Hunter, (Superintendant of Dominion Experi-
    mental Farm, Summerland, B.C.) - 665

Hunter, Mt. - A32

hunting & shooting - 90, 337, 409, 410, 411,
    412, 413, 419

Hutchison, Jock - 456

Hutton, Barbara - 705

hydroelectric dams & power stations - 7,
    57, 99, 205, 893, 908, 948, 951, 1016

ice carnivals - 750, 751

Illecillewaet River - A47

Imhof, Roger - 403

immigrants, non English-speaking - see
    specific cultural group

Imperial Economic Conference - 122

Imperial Munitions Board - 108, 1061

Imperial Press Conference - 740

Impett, Ernie - 527

IMPLACABLE H.M.S. - A15

Independent Club - 566

Indians - see East Indians, Native Indians.

Inside Passage between Vancouver Island
    and Mainland - A14

Interior of British Columbia - 33, 97, 187,
    254, 439, 902 and specific locations

International Caravan to the Land of the
    Golden Twilight - 1052

International Yachting Regatta - 1068

Invermere - A56

irrigation - 370, 383, 792

Irving, Bill - 5a, 202

Irwin, Bert - 1032

Island Tug and Barge Company - A15

Italian Veterans Association in B.C. -
    34, 468

IWATE, S.S. - 448

J.R. MORGAN S.S. - A9

Jack Of Clubs Lake - A2

jacks (game) - 542

Jacob France Trophy - 23

Jacobson, Captain - 613

James, Gardener - 307

James Seed Farm - 447

Janes, Harold (cinematogaapher) - 198

Japan - 296, 405, 441, 447, 450, 451, 452,
    558

Japanese in B.C. - 34, 434, 449, 451, 452, 468, 469, 558, 706, 832, 888, 965, 1053, A13, A28, A45

Jasper National Park - 351, 381, 740, 896, 913, 929, 1062

JEANNE D'ARC (French cruiser) - 334

Jellicoe, Viscount Admiral - 1001

Jericho Beach, near Vancouver - 179

Jersey cattle & breeders - 92, 226, 454, 455, 597, 610, 657, 989

Jewett, Robert - 384

Jewish children - 1040

Joffre, Marshall - 545, 546

JOHN ANTLE, M.V. (mission boat) - A5

John Dean Park - 966

Johnson Canyon - 620

Johnson, Captain - 613

Johnson, Ernest (cinematographer) - A6-14 incl.

Johnson, Lt. Gov. John William Fordham - 552, 906

Johnson, Pauline - 569

Johnston, J.J. (Mayor of New Westminster) - 473

Jones, Charles & family (bird man) - 69, 70, 284, 924

Jones, Hamilton (cinematographer) - 1033

KAIKYU MARU S.S. - 330, 789

Kalamalka Lake - 101

Kamloops - 43, 187, 254, 267, 461, 618, 673, 868, 924, 938, 1029, 1054, A2

Kanaka, B.C. - A50

KARLSRUHE (German warship) - 347

Karlukwees village, B.C. - 863

Kaslo, B.C. - 660, A2

Kean, A.D. "Cowboy" (cinematographer) - 88, 672

Keating, B.C. - 859

Keith, Rosalind - 540

Kelly, Rev. - 565

Kelly, Walter C. - 936

Kelowna, B.C. - 100, 383

Kennedy Lake - 462

Kennedy, W.F. (M.L.A.) - 226

Kenny, Colin - 586

Keremeos, B.C. - 792, A2

Kermode, Douglas (cinematographer) - 206

Kerr, Arthur - 235, 527, 798, 853, 973

Ketch Creek, B.C. - A2

Kicking Horse Canyon - 372, 620, 642, 643, 644, 645, 1058, A30-33

Kicking Horse Falls - 924

Kicking Horse Pass - 252, 339, 463, 590, 644, 1058, A44

Kicking Horse River - A22, A30-33

Kildonan, B.C. - 50

killer whales - 965

Kimberley Mines - 257, 909

Kincolith, B.C. - 298

Kinemacolor - 891b, A22-26

KING CLOSING, S.S. - 397

King, Hon. J.H. (B.C. Minister of Public Works) - 397

King, Mackenzie (later Prime Minister of Canada) - 711, 958

King, W.G. (cinematographer) - 978

Kingcome Inlet - A2, A5, 191

Kingcome village - A5

Kingsmill, Vice Admiral - 1001

Kinney, John - 750

Kinney, Rev. G.R.B. (cinematographer) - 50, 95, 113, 173, 183, 447, 449, 462, 478, 479, 480, 481, 482, 483, 484, 510, 660, 806, 852, 948, 962, 963, 964, 965, 966, 980, 1022, 1024, 1026, 1027, 1071

Kipling, Rudyard - 898

Kirkpatrick, G.H. - 893

Kispiox, B.C. - 1052

kite flying - 467

Kitsilano Boy's Band - 751, 1028

Kitwanga, B.C. - 900, 929, 935

Kiwanis International – 440, 467, 471, 472, 473, 474

Klayoquot, B.C. – See Clayoquot

Klemtu, B.C. – 832

Klinck, Dr. L.S. – 706

Klondike – 15, 17, 401, 475, 476, 559, 633, 640, 741, 813, 1014, 1018

Knight, Dr. (Livestock Commissioner) – 665, 792, 811

Knight's Inlet – 411

Knights of Columbus – 254

Knouff Lake – 1038

Kokanee, Mount & glacier – 173, 183, 447, 1071

Koksilah, B.C. – 46, 966, 1026

Koksilah River – 966

Kootenay Lake – 95, 99, 173, 215, 216, 478, 479, 480, 481, 482, 483, 484, 510, 806, 908, 948, 1024, 1071, A14

Kootenay National Park – 49, 150, 372, 381, 386

Kootenay River – 7, 99, 581, 1020, A14

Kootenays – 7, 49, 91, 95, 99, 101, 150, 173, 183, 212, 213, 214, 215, 216, 250, 251, 257, 307, 372, 381, 386, 447, 449, 477, 478, 479, 480, 481, 482, 483, 484, 510, 581, 678-699 incl., 721, 806, 893, 907, 908, 909, 918, 919, 948, 995, 1020, 1024, 1071

Kroeger, Martin A. (sc.) – 587

Kwinitsa, B.C. – 900

Kyne, Peter B. – 798, 853

Kyuquot, B.C. – 964, 1022

Labour Day – A41

Labour Societies – A41

Ladner, B.C. – 883

LADY ALEXANDER (ferry to Bowen Island) – 113

LADY CYNTHIA (ferry to Bowen Island) – 113

LADY KINDERSLEY (H.B.C. schooner) – 407

LADY NELSON (Canadian Steamships cruise ship) – 337

Laemmle, Carl – (prod.) – 198

Laggan, Alberta – 944

Laing, H.M. (cinematographer) – 200

Lake Kaslo – 449

Lake Louise, Aleerta – 48, 49, 73, 371, 372, 463, 620, 652, 678, 679, 686, 697, 699, 944, A22

Lake O'Hara, B.C. – 96, 372, 595

Lake of the Hanging Glaciers – 412, A55, A56

Lakelse, B.C. – 536, 953

Lamont, Molly – 527

landslides – 186

Langford, B.C. – 528

Lansdowne Racetrack – 214, 490

Lapointe, Ernest – 627

Lapointe Pier, Vancouver – 276

Laughton, Eddie – 5a, 202

Lawrence, Marc – 202, 973

Lawrence, Raymond – 799

Lawton, Frank – 396

Layritz Nurseries – 11

Leach, T. – 927

lead mining – 590

Leanchoil, B.C. – 645, A32

Leed, Johnny – 1031

Leek, Mr. & Mrs. (President of Canadian Pacific Exhibition) – 507, 665

Lefroy, Mount – A22

Legge-Willis, Arthur – 217, 587, 799, 936

Leggett, Capt. (R.N.) – 1001

Legion, American – 213

Legion, Canadian – 236

Legislature of British Columbia – see British Columbia Legislature

LeMare, Phil (cinematographer) – 1025

Lendegren, Rene – 587

LEO-PAT (fish boat) – 965

Lessage, Dick – 3

Leslie, Colonel – 735

Lewis, Ben (ed.) – 307

lifeguards - 102, 343, 384, 557, 974

lighthouses - 193, 356, 852, 980, 1022, 1027

Lillooet, B.C. - 501, 502, 1052, A2

Lincoln, Trebitch - 928

Link Falls - 57

Lion's Gate Bridge - 138, 193, 201, 504, 505,
   758, 759, 765, 770, 790, 832, 969, 970, 1002,
   1053, A10, A11, A12, A15

Lipton Cup (yacht racing) - 143

Little Qualicum Falls - 947

livestock exhibitions - 507, 597, 610, 665,
   808, 811, 987

Lloyd, Doris - 586

Lo Chong (Chinese Consul) - 398

Logan, Mount - 200, 583

logger's games - 21, 160, 239, 393

logging - 50, 67, 87, 89, 93, 94, 101, 108,
   160, 180, 191, 192, 210, 237, 308, 316,
   326, 337, 367, 399, 432, 433, 462, 493,
   510, 511, 529, 530, 531, 532, 554, 560,
   568, 601, 827, 857, 858, 860, 891b, 893,
   947, 1024, 1025, 1027, 1029, 1058, 1060,
   1061, A5, A6, A7, A9, A12, A20, A36-40

logging camps - 50, 57, 93, 101, 217, 235, 510,
   527, 798, 839, 947, 1022, A9, A20

logging machinery - 242, 529, 910, A6, A7,
   A9, A20

Lomens, Rolf - 27

Lone Butte Hotel - 97

Long Beach, B.C. - 964, 1022

Long, Chief - 443

longevity - 224

LOON, M.V. (Yukon steamboat) - 1018

The Great Loop (at Glacier House) - A32, A47

Lord, Del (d.) - 973

Lord Mayor of London - 959

Lorrie, Jack (cinematographer) - 907

Lougheed, Miss - 672

Lougheed Creek, B.C. - A2

Lougheed, Sir James - 353

Lovington, B.C. - 187

Lower Skeena River Valley - 525

Lowery, (cinematographer) - 282

LOYAL BRITON, S.S. - 199

Lucas, Rupert - 758

Lulu Island - 492

lumber mills - See sawmilling

lumbermen's organizations - 992

Lumby, B.C. - 43

Lund, Lucille - 973

Lundequist, Britta - 751

Lynn Creek, North Vancouver - 394

Lyon, Ben - 1046

Lyons, Collette - 1055

Lyons, Teddy - 8

Lytton, B.C. - 1046, A2

MacBeth, Rev. R.G. - 672

MacBrien, Mayor General Sir James (K.C.B.,
   C.M.G., DSO.), R.C.M.P. - 235

MacDonald, D. - 868

MacDonald, Grant - 5a, 202, 540, 1055

MacDonald, J. Farrell - 816

MacDonald, Jeanette - 749

MacDonald, Dr. K.C. (Minister of Agriculture)
   - 439

MacDonald, Mount - 924

MacGregor, Doreen - 202

Mack, Connie - 44

MacKay, Barry - 816

Mackenzie, Miss (companion of Lt. Gov. Randolph
   R. Bruce) - 357, 712

Mackenzie Park - 533

Mackenzie, R.F. (cinematographer) - 205, 257,
   390, 760, 955, 1020

MacLaren, Major D.R. - 42

MacLaren, Squadron Leader - 443

MacLean, Dr. J.D. - 669

MacMillan, Dr. Ernest - 588, 785

MacPherson, Hon. F.M. (Minister of Public
   Works) - 439

MacRae, Mrs. J.R. - 635

Magnusson, U.S. Congressman Warren G. - 867, 868

mail & air mail - 293, 314, 420, 832, 920, 964, 1047, 1063

MAKURA, S.S. - 126

Malahat Drive, V.I. - 52, 101, 149, 538, 701 951, 978, 1026

MALAHAT, S.S. - 510

Malcolm Island, B.C. - A2

Malkin, William Harold (Mayor of Vancouver) - 3

Mamalilaculla, B.C. - 863

Mandy, Jos. T. (cinematographer) - 131, 164, 277, 308, 309, 330, 336, 357, 514, 568, 617, 789, 876, 880, 925, 975

Manguall, Ken - 602

Manners, David - 528

manufacturing - 244

MAPLE LEAF (fish boat) - 510

Maple Ridge, B.C. - 766, 790

Maquinna, Chief - 274

MAQUINNA, S.S. - 965

Mara Lake - 815

marathon walk - 524, 584

Marble Canyon - 49, 97

marbles (kid's game) - 542

Margaret Bay - 832

MARGARET HANEY - A19

Marpole Trophy - 869

Martin, Capt. (R.N.) - 1001

Massey, Rt. Hon. R.F. (Premier of New Zealand) - 772

Matheson, Mr. & Mrs. (Manager & Secretary of Vancouver Exhibitions Association) - 665

Mathews, Lester - 936

Matilda Creek - 964

Mattox, Martha - 198

May Day parade - 550

Maypole dancing & coronation of May Queens - 104, 162, 167, 168, 206, 207, 215, 216, 514, 549, 571, 596, 598, 722, 765, 788, 790, 875, 892, 938, 945, 1002, 1028

Mayell, Eric (cinematographer) - 224, 592, 613, 729, 754

Mayers, Wally - 972

McBride, B.C. - 187

McBride, Sir Richard (Premier of B.C.) - 352, 436, 437

McCarthy, Red - 751

McCauley Plains, near Victoria - 123, 600

McClay, S. (Pres. of Vancouver Harbour Commission) - 276, 290

McCleave, Doris O. - 564

McCrae, Henry - 387

McDonald, Frank (d.) - 235

McDougall, John (d.) - 338

McGeer, Gerald (Mayor of Vancouver) - 125, 726a, 874, 957, 958

McGowan, H. (Inspector, Vancouver Police) - 335

McGowan, J.P. (d. & sc.) - 527, 798, 853, 973, 1045

McGrath, James - 217, 235, 527, 528, 587, 798, 799, 853, 1055

McIntosh, Captain - 613

McIntyre, William - 586

McKay, George - 5a, 202, 540, 586

McKay, "Mickey" - 374

McKechnie, H.E. - 522

McKechnie, R.E. - 773

McKeen, Stanley (M.L.A.) - 125

McKenna, Vincent - 5a

McKercher's Ltd. - 894, 901

McLarnin, Jimmy - 457

McLeod, Earl - 42

McMillan, Marcus - 391

McNaughton, Major General A.G.L. - 537

McNeil, A. - 217

Mdivani, Prince - 705

Mears, John Henry - 459

Meehan, George (cinematographer) - 5a, 202, 540, 586, 798, 853

Meighan, Thomas - 16

Meilicke, Hugo - 718

Melrose, George (cinematographer) - 46, 210, 326, 363

Menzies Bay, B.C. - 89, 835

Meredith, Iris - 586

Merritt, B.C. - 792, A2, A14

Merville, B.C. - 991

Metis - 307

Michel, B.C. - 257

Middleton, (pilot) - 293

Miles Canyon, Yukon - 559, 1072

militia - 214, 992

Mill Bay, V.I. - 978

Miller, G.E. (Mayor of Vancouver) - 232, 293 464, 722, 822, 972

Millman, LeStrange - 798, 853

Mikado (of Japan) - 558

Minaret Lake - 775

mining - 81, 110, 183, 187, 214, 215, 216, 257, 259, 260, 292, 414, 432, 435, 483, 534, 559, 562, 563, 590, 633, 741, 792, 855, 893, 909, 1014, 1017, 1071, 1072, A2, A8, A51, A52, A53

Mission, B.C. - 663

MISSISSIPPI, U.S.S. - 393

Mitchell, Douglas C. (cinematographer) - 1052

Mitchell, Leslie (narr.) - 770

Mitford, (cinematographer) - 841, 886

Mitlenatch Island, B.C. - 729

Mobraaten, Peggy - 1031

Mobraaten, Tom - 1031

Mollison, Henry - 798

Molly Gibson Mine - 183, 1071

Money, General Noel - 804

monuments & memorials - 8, 105, 175, 274, 285, 417, 418, 440, 448, 496, 516, 517, 518, 519, 523, 545, 569, 706, 770, 788, 871, 893, 951

Moody Park, New Westminster - 467

Moore, Alice - 1055

Moore, Miss Rollie - 1030

Moore Theatre, Seattle - 424

moose - 137, 410, 413, 620, 783, 825

Moosehide, Yukon - 1072

More, Pete - 507

Morel, Leon (sculptor) - 496

Moreno, Antonio - 307

Morgan, J.R., Logging Company - A6, A9

Morgan, Tod - 977

Moricetown, B.C. - 929

Morton, A. - 811

Morton, Guy - 799

Moscow, U.S.S.R. - 607

Moss, (President of Kiwanis International) - 440

Motion Skreen Adz Ltd. - 315, 316, 895, 898, 1054

MOTOR PRINCESS, M.V. - 978

mountain climbing - 24, 73, 96, 118, 173, 182, 183, 184, 200, 218, 278, 306, 315, 317, 320, 346, 351, 371, 372, 392, 425, 428, 447, 574, 576, 577, 583, 595, 807, 866, 870, 896, 897, 944, 1071

Mountain Creek Bridge (C.P.R. line) - A54

mountain goats - A56

mountains - See specific mountain ranges.

Moyie Lake, B.C. - 257

MOYIE, S.S. - 173, 215, 216, 478, 483, 484, 948

Mud Creek - 257

Munday, Edith - 731

Munro, J.B. (Deputy Minister of Agriculture) - 226, 792, 932, 989

Murchison, Mount - 868

Murray, Gladstone - 349

Musquiam, B.C. - 188

Nadden Harbour - 832

Nakusp, B.C. - A2

Namu, B.C. - 832

Nanaimo, B.C. - 52, 236, 292, 701

Napta, Mount - 949

NASOOKIN, S.S. - 908

Nass River - 298, 588

NASUTLIN, S.S. (sternwheeler) - 17

National Harbours Board - 276, 290, 893

National Museum of Man, Ottawa - 31, 32, 33,
    61, 62, 188, 200, 229, 313, 320, 421, 429,
    477, 485, 501, 525, 533, 588, 604, 611, 677,
    785, 815, 899, 900, 935

Native Indians - 25, 43, 46, 61, 95, 157,
    188, 191, 192, 193, 206, 214, 229, 230,
    254, 274, 298, 313, 336, 337, 357, 399,
    424, 427, 429, 430, 431 (costumed kids),
    432, 434, 445, 462, 468, 469, 477, 483,
    485, 486, 499, 500, 501, 525, 553, 578, 588,
    604, 611, 616, 620, 621, 666, 677, 680,
    684, 688, 689, 696, 698, 776, 782, 784,
    785, 815, 832, 834, 862, 898, 899, 900,
    911, 925, 929, 935, 964, 969, 1022, 1023,
    1026, 1027, 1042, 1052, A2, A27, A28, A45,
    A52
    - Athapaskans - 157
    - Coast Salish - 46, 61, 188, 357, 445,
      499, 898
    - Kootenay - 477, 483, 680, 684, 688, 689,
      696, 698
    - Kwakiutl - 424, 485, 486
    - Lillooet - 501
    - Nass River - 298, 588, 785
    - Nootka - 427, 462, 486, 604, 899
    - Okanagan - 611
    - Shuswap - 815
    - Tsimshian - 525, 900, 929

Nautley River - 1052

Navy League Vets - 997

Needham, Arthur - 280

Negroes in B.C. - 1040

Nelson, B.C. - 251, 449, 908, 1020, A2, A14,
    A56

Nelson, Lord - 552, 906

Nelson, M. (cinematographer) - 414, 430, 578

New Denver, B.C. - A2

New Westminster, B.C. - 37, 100, 104, 162,
    167, 168, 181, 207, 209, 239, 273, 368,
    467, 473, 514, 549, 596, 597, 598, 654,
    714, 722, 759, 765, 875, 892, 924, 945,
    951, 1002, 1016

New York City - 457, 603

New Zealand - 444, 603

NEW ZEALAND, H.M.S. - 1001

Newmeyer, Fred (d.) - 799

newspapers & journalists - 60, 92, 179, 225,
    374, 375, 460, 542, 550, 996

NIAGARA, S.S. - 41, 340

Nichol, (golfer) - 600

Nichol, Arthur (cinematographer) - 212

Nichol, Lt. Governor W.C. - 78, 274, 418,
    571, 817

Nichols, Cicele - 587

Nicola Lake - 932, A14

Nicola Lake Ranching Company - 932

Nicomen, B.C. - A51

Nicomen Island, B.C. - 331

Nielson, Nels - 100, 376, 1049

Nilsson, Anna Q. - 1046

Nitobe, Inazo (memorial to...) - 706

Niven, David - 749

NO. 2 DEPARTURE BAY (fish boat) - 964

Noel, Mrs. D.C. - 81

Nootka, B.C. - 95, 274, 427, 832, 965, 1022,
    1027

Nootka Packers Co. Ltd. - 95

Nootka Sound - 965

Nor'West Farmer (newspaper) - 92

Norquay, Mount - 605

Norrish, B.E. (prod.) - 45, 298, 785, 899,
    978, 1072

North Bend, B.C. - A2, A53

North Pole - 607

North Vancouver, B.C. - 8, 100, 151, 188, 201,
    211, 394, 491, 591, 723, 749, 969, 1045,
    1046, A11, A12, A15

Northern Films, Ltd. - 799

Northwest Territories - 498

Norwegians - 421, 832

Number Three Coast Artillery Co-op Squadron,
    R.C.A.F. - 727

Oak Bay (municipality, near Victoria) - 561,
    766, 996, 1005

Oak Bay Golf Course - 149, 337, 898

Oak Bay Swimming & Baths - 996

Oakalla, B.C. - 766

Oaten, Rev. Beverley - 183, 1071

O'Brien, Miss Kathleen - 192

Ocean Falls, B.C. - 15, 17, 57, 888, 891, 929,
    A14

Odlum, General Victor W. - 537

Oglow, Jimmy - 1072

Oingg, Barbara Ann - 750

Okanagan Lake - 100, 383, 791

Okanagan Valley - 43, 55, 80, 99, 100, 101, 128,
187, 206, 226, 233, 337, 341, 383, 439, 567,
610, 611, 648, 665, 791, 792, 891a, 893,
952, 1054, A2, A24

Okisollo Channel - 863

Olag, Mrs. - 600

Old Timer's Picnic - 483

Oldfield, (cinematographer) - 716

O'Leary, Johnnyie - 161

Oliver, B.C. - 101

Oliver, John (Premier of British Columbia) -
366, 1001

Oliver, W.J. (cinematographer) - 96, 149, 184,
304, 306, 311, 351, 388, 410, 413, 422, 425,
445, 580, 595, 620, 666, 783, 795, 796, 887,
913, 949, 1038, 1041, 1044

Olson, Barney (cinematographer) - 52, 495,
993

Olympic Games - 626, 823

Olympic Mountains - 149

OLYMPIC, S.S. - 149

O'Malley, Henry - 195

Opitsat, B.C. - 964

Orangemen in B.C. - 992

ORION (fireboat) - 290

Osoyoos Lake - 99, 100

Osterhaut, Rev. - 565

Ostman, Ernest - 217

OTTAWA, H.M.C.S. - 238

Ottertail Group (mountain range) - 644, 646,
A32

Owen, William Reid (Mayor of Vancouver) -
175, 487, 584

oxen - 863

Oyster River, B.C. - 481, 966

Pachena Bay - 1026

Pachena Point - 193, 852

Pacific Great Eastern Railway (Galloping
Goose) - 97, 101, 736

Pacific Mills (Ocean Falls) - 57, A14

pack trains - 110, 183, 631, 632, 633, 678-699
incl.

pageants - New Westminster - 104 and see Maypole dancing
- Port Moody - 286
- Vancouver - 159, 431, 464, 550, 854, 880,
960
- Victoria - 85, 571, 992
- elsewhere - 578, 806

Palliser, Alberta - 637

Palmer, Lilli - 816

Pan-Pacific Women's Association - 647

Paquin, Paul - 3

parachutists - 216, 919, 967

parades - Coronation festivals - 206, 212, 908
- King's Birthday - 214
- New Westminster - 104, 209, 597
- Royal Visit - 758-771 incl.
- Vancouver - 29, 88, 90, 102, 144, 148, 159,
166, 175, 254, 272, 285, 343, 464, 507,
550, 943, 951, 957, 958, 1012, 1036, A10,
A41
- Victoria - 26, 106, 123, 145, 255, 261, 319,
436, 437, 452, 468, 540, 571, 650, 844, 987,
990, 991, 992, 1013, A10
- miscellaneous - 216, 236, 254, 321, 578,
618, 908, 951, 1020, 1028

park rangers - 513, 634, 649

Pasternack, Mrs. Mike - 391

Paton, Stuart (d.) - 198

PATRICIA (yacht) - 1067

Patricia Bay, B.C. - 149, 978

PATRICIAN, H.M.C.S. - 133, 523, 886

PATRIOT, H.M.C.S. - 133

Patterson, Mr. - 792

Patullo Bridge - 100, 654, 759, 765, 924, 1002

Patullo, T.D. (Premier of British Columbia) -
469, 547, 650, 654, 758, 766, 768, 770, A10

Pavillion Mountains - 1052

peanuts - 403

Pearson, Norman - 391

Pemberton Meadows - 868

Pendray, J.C. (Mayor of Victoria) - 147, 177,
453

PENNSYLVANIA, U.S.S. - 221

Penticton, B.C. - 100, 792, 1054

People's Advocate (newspaper) - 550

pet shows - 660, 805

Peters, W.F. (Superintendent of the C.P.R.) -
265, 353

petroglyphs - 449, 480, 898, 1026

Pheasants - 409

PHELPS, U.S.S. - 120, 281, 282, 283, 702, 703,
704

Phillipines - 991

Phillipinos in B.C. - 289

Phillips Arm - 863

photograph contest - 659

picnics - 113, 173, 179, 192, 214, 216, 226,
352, 374, 375, 452, 454, 466, 483, 665,
1005, A20

pictographs - 815, 863

pile driver, steam - 965

pioneers - 81, 159, 199, 210, 421, 483, 652,
665, 813, 911

Piper, (cinematographer) - 408

Point Grey, near Vancouver - 100, 135, 166,
305, 361, 521, 522, 608, 656, 706, 773,
793, 800, 864, 937, 941, 942, 943, 971, 976,
1015, 1034, 1035

Point-No-Point - 193

political rallies - 91, 550, 968, 996

polling booth - 139

Pope's Peak - 59, 949

porpoises - 832

Port Alberni, B.C. - 510, 538, 965, 1027

Port Coquitlam, B.C. - 409, 766, 790

PORT ESSINGTON (fishboat) - 964

Port Moody, B.C. - 286

Portland Canal - 891a

Post Office sit-down & protest, Vancouver -
91, 968

Post, Wiley - 125

Powley, W.R. (President of Cow Testing Association)
- 226

Prajadhipok, King of Siam - 470

Premier Lake, B.C. - 678-699 incl.

Premier Lake Ranch Camp - 678-699 incl.

Prenter, S.L. - 893

President, Mount - 317

Priest Rapids, U.S.A. - A56

PRINCE CHARLES, C.N.S.S. - A9, A15

Prince George, B.C. - 91, 187, A2

PRINCE GEORGE, C.N.S.S. - 94, 891a

Prince of Wales - See Royal Visits

PRINCE ROBERT, C.N.S.S. - 17, 758, 765, 768,
769, 790

Prince Rupert, B.C. - 15, 17, 61, 214, 310, 335,
404, 421, 494, 616, 740, 782, 888, 891a, 912,
929

PRINCE RUPERT, C.N.S.S. - 891a, 912

PRINCESS ships (Canadian Pacific Steamships)
- 26, 34, 52, 100, 123, 149, 176, 177, 193,
220, 222, 315, 337, 353, 355, 445, 468, 469,
495, 517, 523, 612, 713, 736, 758, 759, 762,
763, 767, 769, 770, 790, 812, 832, 886, 893,
925, 951, 965, 978, 980, 993, 1002, 1005,
1022, 1027, 1053, A10, A11, A15, A42
- PRINCESS ALICE - 220, 523, 886
- PRINCESS CHARLOTTE - 812, 925, 978
- PRINCESS ELAINE - 445, 495
- PRINCESS KATHLEEN - 149, 445, 898, 951,
993
- PRINCESS LOUISE - 26, 353, 713
- PRINCESS MAQUINNA - 222, 832, 1022, 1027
- PRINCESS MARGUERITE - 34, 193, 468, 469,
713, 736, 758, 759, 762, 763, 767, 769,
770, 790, 1002, 1053, A10
- PRINCESS MARY - 123
- PRINCESS NORAH - 980, 1022
- PRINCESS PATRICIA - 355
- PRINCESS VICTORIA - 812, A42

Princess Patricia's Canadian Light Infantry -
319, 650

Princeton, B.C. - 792, 1031, 1032, A2

prison - 451

"The Private Secretary" (comedy film, 1913) -
716

Procter, B.C. - 447, 482, 1024

Prospect Point Signal Station, Vancouver - 355

protests - 91, 251, 550, 943, 968, 1035

Provincial Recreation (Pro-Rec) - 107, 547,
718

pulp mills - 17, 57, 719, 888, 891a, 929, 970,
A14, A15

Punch & Judy Show - 116

puppets - 720, 872

Quadra, Bodega y - 960

Qualicum Beach, B.C. - 99, 315, 804, 963

Qualicum Beach Hotel & Golf Course - 315, 804

Quatsino, B.C. - 899

Queen Charlotte Islands - 108, 796, 963, A6, A9

Queen Charlotte Sound - 888, 891a

Quesnel, B.C. - 131

Quigley, Charles - 5a, 202

Quota Quickies - 202, 217, 235, 527, 528,
   586, 587, 798, 799, 843, 853, 936, 973,
   1045, 1055

radio - 349

Radium Hot Springs - 381

railway construction - 50, 478, 479, 480,
   481, 482, 484, 510, 791, 806, 816, 1024

railways - see Trains; CNR; CPR.

Rambaibami, Queen of Siam - 470

Ramsaye, Terry (ed.) - 899, 978

ranching - 158, 932, A24

Range, Mount - 868

Rankin, Tex - 1030

Rayment, Mrs. Hugo - 1057

Reconstruction Party - 124

Red Cross - 88, 266

Red Pass, B.C. - 187

Reese-Burns, Ethel - 1055

Reeves, A.E. (cinematographer) - 267

reforestation - 481, 947, 962, 963, 966

regattas - 143, 185, 223, 499, 566, 629, 660,
   844, 959, 1067, 1068

Reid, Lt. Cdr. H.E. - 140, 141

Reid, Pat - 918

reindeer - 27

relief camps - 481, 947, 962, 963, 966

religious matters - 61, 72, 85, 95, 269, 324,
   362, 369, 449, 565, 785, 928, 1071, A21

See also entries under Anglican Church of
Canada; United Church Young People's Association; United Church Waterways Missions;
and Rev. G.R.B. Kinney.

RENDEZVOUS, M.V. (mission boat) - A5

RENOWN, H.M.S. - 312

REPULSE, H.M.S. - 893

RESTIGOUCHE, H.M.C.S. - 238

Revelstoke, B.C. - 100, 280, 376, 556, 715,
   821, 823, A2, A4, A56

Rhein, George (asst.-d.) - 5a, 202, 540

Richmond, B.C. - 79

Riddell, Bill - 919

Rideout, Bob - 5a, 202, 527, 540, 973

Riel, Louis - 307

Rin Tin Tin the Third - 235

RIO BONITA, M.V. - 411

Riondel Mine - 483

riots - 1010

Rivers Inlet, B.C. - 832

Robinson, Captain of the EMPRESS OF ASIA -
   296

Robson, Mount - 24, 187, 351, 634, 740, 775,
   825, 896, 913, 929, 1029, 1033, 1062

Rock Bay, V.I. - A20

Rocky Mountains - 2, 4, 5, 20, 24, 25, 48, 49,
   54, 59, 73, 84, 96, 118, 132, 137, 150, 182,
   197, 216, 252, 278, 306, 311, 318, 338, 339,
   344, 346, 348, 372, 381, 386, 410, 412, 414,
   422, 494, 572, 573, 574, 575, 576, 577, 580,
   581, 589, 590, 595, 605, 619, 620, 625, 632,
   634, 636, 637, 639, 640, 641, 642, 643, 644,
   645, 646, 652, 653, 668, 678-699 incl., 724,
   741, 742, 743, 744, 745, 746, 747, 748, 752,
   758, 775, 787, 791, 807, 809, 810, 824, 825,
   826, 866, 885, 887, 889, 890, 896, 897, 903,
   911, 913, 929, 931, 944, 946, 969, 999, 1007,
   1039, 1044, 1062, 1069, 1070, A2, A4, A18,
   A22, A23, A30-33, A46, A47, A49, A50, A51,
   A55, A56

rodeos - 38, 209, 230, 273, 336, 430, 553, 680,
   684, 688, 696, 698, 1042, 1052, A2

Roger's Pass - A47

Roman Catholics - 269

Roos, Len (cinematographer) - 1, 10, 18, 22,
   39, 65, 74, 87, 89, 94, 147, 169, 174, 175,
   185, 194, 203, 219, 237, 243, 245, 256,
   265, 266, 274, 280, 296, 327, 353, 354, 355,
   361, 362, 365, 366, 373, 374, 375, 376, 384,

385, 387, 394, 398, 399, 402, 403, 407, 411,
416, 433, 443, 451, 453, 473, 487, 508, 509,
539, 541, 548, 566, 571, 590, 594, 608, 626,
659, 663, 669, 671, 714, 725, 729, 733, 753,
772, 813, 818, 865, 879, 911, 938, 939, 941,
942, 950, 979, 1040, 1064, 1067

Roosevelt, F.D. (President of U.S.A.) - 120,
281, 282, 283, 702, 703, 704

rope making factory - 893

Rosedale, Richard (cinematographer) - A19

Rosenbaum, Harry - 217

Rosenthal, Joseph (cinematographer) - 1058,
A27-A40, A42-A54

Rosmer, Milton (d.) - 816

Ross, George - 918

Ross Peak - A47

Rotary Club - 272, 750, 751

rotary snowplows for railway tracks - 137,
187, 752, 829

Routledge, P.H. - 663

Rowe, H. (Dairy Commissioner) - 226

Roy, Lucien (cinematographer) - 172, 442, 664

Royal Canadian Air Force - 136, 726b, 727,
728, 918, 919

Royal Canadian Mounted Police (incl. RNWMP) -
5a, 99, 196, 214, 216, 235, 307, 451, 672,
729, 749, 754, 755, 798, 992, 1046

Royal Canadian Navy - 34, 63, 101, 133, 138,
140, 141, 193, 216, 221, 223, 238, 299, 302,
324, 325, 438, 443, 448, 468, 469, 623, 730,
758, 762, 763, 766, 767, 768, 769, 770, 951,
991, 1001, 1003, 1053, A10

"Royal Hudson" locomotive (#2850) - A10

Royal Lifesaving Society - 557, 974

Royal Navy - 101, 312, 519, 893, 1001

Royal Oak Burial Park, near Victoria, B.C.
- 40

Royal Visits - King George VI & Queen
Elizabeth (1939) - 34, 193, 201, 468, 469,
526, 756, 758-770, incl., 790, 1002, 1003,
1053, A10, A57
- Prince Henry - 405, 673
- Edward, Prince of Wales (1919) - 86,
220, 312, 709, 710, 711
- Edward, Prince of Wales (1927) - 678,
686, 707, 708

Russian expedition by Canadian & Allied
troops, 1918-1919 - 131, 144

Ruth, Babe - 44

Saanich, B.C. - 19, 40, 52, 79, 92, 109, 149,
176, 188, 316, 321, 765, 801, 859, 871, 951,
978, 1026

Saanich Fruit Growers Association - 859

Saanich Inlet - 149, 978, 1026

Saanich Mountain - 52, 176, 316, 871, 951,
978

Saanichton, B.C. - 188

saddle-making - 224

Sailor's Home contribution box - 355

sailors - 34, 116, 133, 138, 140, 141, 238,
299, 302, 324, 325, 334, 347, 393, 407,
438, 448, 452, 468, 469, 613, 730, 758,
762, 763, 766, 767, 768, 769, 770, 906,
1053, A10

St. Andrew's Society, Vancouver - 287

St. Elias Range, Yukon - 392, 583

ST. LAURENT, H.M.C.S. (H-83) - 138, 140, 238,
468, 469, 770, 1053, A10

Salmon Arm, B.C. - 43, 390, 439, 610, 815, A2

salmon canning - See Canning & canneries

salmon fishing - See Fishing - salmon

Salt Spring Island, B.C. - 808

SALVAGE KING (tug) - 330

SALVAGE QUEEN (tug) - 612

Sangster, George - 163, 811

Sankey, Gerald - 718

Sapperton, B.C. - 786

Sardis, B.C. - 399

Sarno, Hector - 198

Sasquatch - 784, 1026

sawmilling - 67, 81, 93, 220, 382, 510, 531,
532, 560, 719, 786, 858, 860, 891b, 893,
951, 965, 1025, 1029, 1058, 1060, 1061,
A7, A9, A39-40

Sawyer, Dr. - 1009

Schofield, J.H. (veteran M.L.A. for Trail,
B.C.) - 43

Scott-Burritt, Edith - 587

Scott Cove, B.C. - 568

Scott, Edward - 258

Scott Island Group - 795

Scott, J.B. (cinematographer) - 758, 899

Scottish games and costumes - 114, 115, 116, 287, 352, 878

Scottish regiments in British Columbia - 106, 121, 145, 146, 236, 253, 254, 436, 437, 517, 519, 537, 703, 707, 717, 735, 758, 759, 764, 765, 788, 951, 1002, A10, A16

sculpture - 496

Sea Cadets - 95, 206

Sea Island - 79

sea-lions - 329, 795, 796, 1022

Seachart, B.C. - 510

SEADOG, U.S.S. - 223

Seaforth Highlanders, 72nd Regiment - 519, 537, 707, 735, 758, 759, 951, A16

seagulls - 729, 794, 969, 1041

seals - 893

Seattle, Washington - 891a, 1052

Seattle Mountaineers - 372

Seattle skating Club - 751

Sebastian, Dorothy - 1046

self-dumping scows - 268

Selkirk, Yukon - 1072

Selkirk Range - 184, 412, 620, 921, 922, 931, A44, A46, A49, A54, A55

Selman, David (d.) - 798, 936, 1055

Selwyn, B.C. - 364

Senanus Island - 978

Seton Lake & Lodge - 97, 101

Seven Sisters waterfalls - 96, 924,

70 Mile House, B.C. - 97

Sexton, Bishop - 236

Seymour Canyon - 394

Shannon, Sam - 439

Shawnigan Lake, B.C. - 99, 806

Shawnigan Lake Gala Days - 806

Shaughnessy (Vancouver Residential district) - 100, 456

sheep, mountain - 410, 413, 686, 688, 783, 825, 893, 924, 969

Shelly Films, Ltd. - 56, 270, 606

Shelly, W.C. (Vancouver alderman) - 18, 879

Shilkret, Jack & Nathaniel (mus.) - 742

ship-building - 1061

ships - See Canadian Pacific Steamships; Canadian Steamship Line; PRINCESS ships; Union Steamships; Vancouver Harbour and Victoria Inner and Outer Harbours.
  - freighters - 9, 36, 142, 152, 199, 327, 330, 339, 353, 362, 397, 450, 509, 535, 591, 706, 732, 733, 789, 893, 1024, 1027, A7, A9, A11
  - coastal service - 9, 17, 50, 65, 94, 113, 176, 192, 353, 356, 510, 732, 758, 765, 768, 769, 790, 832, 863, 891a, 912, 965, A9, A13, A14, A15, A42
  - sailing ships - A7 see - Sternwheelers

shipwrecks - 52, 68, 330, 408, 450, 503, 615, 713, 732, 774, 789

Shriners - 550, 984

Siam - 387, 470

Siberian Expedition by Canadian & Allied troops, 1918-1919 - 131, 144

Sidney, B.C. - 19, 92, 978, 989

Sikhs - 91, 510

Silver Spring Brewery, Victoria - 613

SILVER STATE, S.S. - 545

Silverstreak (German Shepherd dog) - 1045

Simpson, Bobby (the human fly) - 76

Simpson, Dorothy - 245

Simpson, George - 159, 592

Simpson, Sir George - 666

Simpson, Miss Marguerite - 911

Sinclair Canyon - 678, 686

Singelow, (cinematographer) - 496, 564, 850

Sinkey, (cinematographer) - 69

Sintzenich, H. (cinematographer) - 891b, A22-26

Sir Donald, Mount - A47, A54

SIR THOMAS (yacht) - 1067

Six Mile Creek Station (C.P.R.) - A54

Skagway, Alaska - 1072

Skaha Lake - 100

Skeena Crossing, B.C. - 900, 935

SKEENA, H.M.C.S. - 140, 141, 951, A10

Skeena River – 187, 525, 593, 616, 740, 776, 782, 900, 929, 935, 1052

Skeena Valley – 187, 525, 593, 616, 740, 726b, 776, 782, 900, 935, 953, 1052

Skookumchuck, B.C. – 212, 678-699 incl., 1020

Sky Blue Water, Lake & Camp – 97

skyscrapers – 1, 8, 13, 76, 142, 285, 354, 595

smelting – 7, 81, 259, 891a, 893, 907, 909, A14

Smith, C. Aubrey – 396

Smith, Clifford S. (d.) – 587

Smith, Fyfe – 772

Smith, Harlan I. (cinematographer) – 31, 32, 33, 61, 62, 157, 188, 229, 313, 320, 421, 429, 477, 485, 501, 525, 533, 604, 611, 677, 815, 900, 935

Smith, Horton – 135

Smith, Irving – 587

Smith, J.H. (d.) – 742

Smith, Jack – 295

Smith, Jacob – 725

Smith's Inlet – 832

Smithers, B.C. – 187, 1052

Snersrud, Mr. (skiier) – 1049

SNOHOMISH (tugboat) – A13

SNOW CLOUD (fishboat) – 964

SNOW SLIDE – (fishboat) – 964

snowfall, heavy – 328, 478, 830, 908, 949, 950, 954, 962, 1065

Society for Visual Education – 744

soil surveys – 835

Sointula, B.C. – A2

soldiers – 106, 121, 123, 139, 144, 145, 146, 148, 175, 214, 236, 253, 254, 319, 417, 436, 437, 452, 517, 519, 522, 523, 537, 600, 627, 650, 702, 703, 704, 707, 708, 717, 735, 758, 759, 760, 762, 764, 765, 766, 767, 768, 769, 770, 771, 788, 790, 800, 836, 837, 838, 886, 951, 958, 991, 992, 997, 1002, 1003, 1006, 1009, 1010, 1012, 1013, 1021, 1035, 1051, 1057, A10, A16, A19

Sooke, B.C. – 21, 79

South Slocan Dam – 1020, A14

SOUTHHOLM, S.S. – 965

Sovereign, Rev. Art – 375

Spacey, John G. – 586

Spanish Civil War veterans – 550

Sparling, Gordon (d.) – 45, 82, 240, 241, 246, 247, 248, 346, 389, 652, 747, 796, 807, 971, A16, A17

Spences Bridge, B.C. – A2

Spokane, Washington – 887

sports – general – 270, 548, 578
  – angling – See Fishing
  – baseball – 44, 309, 403
  – basketball – 23, 846, 972, 1022
  – bicycle racing – 225, 602, 882, 987
  – boxing – 127, 161, 457, 599, 977
  – broad jump (long jump) – 127, 213, 215, 846
  – calesthenics – 107, 129, 547, 664, 760, 938, 957, 1002
  – canoe racing – 185, 499, 548, 660, 784, 844
  – car racing – 155, 295, 725, 828, 1005
  – cricket – 396
  – discus – 127
  – football – 1034
  – golf – 135, 149, 176, 201, 456, 600, 630, 665, 711, 846, 877, 978, 1048
  – grass hockey – 41, 361
  – hammer throw – 127
  – high jumping – 215, 846
  – hockey – 321, 415
  – horse jumping – 439
  – horse racing – 214, 400, 452, 490, 502, 971, 987, 1000
  – hurdles – 127, 564, 592
  – javelin – 127
  – lawn bowling – 149, 479, 624
  – motorcycle racing – 883, 991
  – pole vault – 213
  – polo – 294, 673, 831
  – relay races – 127
  – riding (horses) – 294, 400, 439
  – rowing – 393, 609, 626, 753, 844, 846, 942, 959, 1015
  – rugby – 277, 444, 773, 904, 979
  – running races – 127, 213, 214, 352, 555, 592, 671, 718, 846, 895, 987, 1005
  – skating – 321, 415, 750, 751
  – ski jumping – 100, 280, 376, 556, 715, 821, 823, 1031, 1049
  – skiing – 170, 297, 321, 419, 605, 649, 822, 824, 1031, 1032, 1049, A16
  – soccer – 701, 941, 976
  – speedboat racing – 227
  – swimming – competition – 127, 189, 844, 869
    – pleasure – 8, 22, 45, 50, 203, 337, 381, 557, 660, 678, 679-683 incl., 685, 686, 687, 689, 690, 691, 692, 693, 694, 697, 698, 699, 846, 960, 971, 974, 1024, 1071
    – New Year's Day in English Bay, Vancouver – 22, 557
  – tennis – 687, 689, 690, 695, 699, 846, 977, 990
  – trap shooting – 624

- tug of war - 1005
- volleyball - 1006
- walking races - 524, 671
- water skiing & aquaplaning - 39, 660, 679, 680, 682, 687, 690, 692
- yacht racing - 143, 223, 566

Sportsman's Cup (basketball trophy) - 972

Spreitz, Karl (cinematographer, co-d.) - 1025

Spring Brook, B.C. - 257

Spruce, Ralph (sc.) - 816

Squamish, B.C. - 188, 736

Squamish Range - 868

Stamp Falls - 962, 963, 966

Stanley Park Lawn Bowling Club - 624

Staples, Charles - 225

Staples, Claire & Elmore - 678, 679, 682, 686, 690, 692, 696

Staples, J. - 472

Starrett, Charles - 798, 853

Stave Lake - 1016

steam donkeys - 50, 192, 316, 462, 510, 531, 857, 1024, 1025, 1027, A20 - see also logging

steelhead trout - 804

steers, wild - 38, 273, 336, 553, 680, 684, 688, 696, 698, 1042

Steger, C.W. - 237

Stenuf, Huddy - 750

Stephen, Mount - 585, 590, 644, 946, 949, A22

Stephens, H.H. - 124

sternwheelers - 17, 173, 215, 216, 419, 478, 483, 484, 791, 908, 948, 1018

Stevens, H.H. (Minister of Trade & Commerce) - 290

Stevens, Paul - 688, 689

Steveston, B.C. - 268, 1058, A13, A27, A28, A45

Stewart, Brigadier General J.C. - 727

Stewart, James - 749

Stewart Lake - 868

Stewart, Miss Margaret - 443

stockyards - 893

Stoloff, Morris - 5a, 202

Stork, Billy - 681, 683, 696, 698

storms - 450, 732, 830

Strait of Georgia - A42

Strathcona Park, V.I. - 701

strikes - 152, 303

strongmen - 321

Stuart, Nick - 217, 799

students - 943, 989

submarines - 63

Sullivan, Allan - 816

Sumas Prairie, B.C. - 862, 894

Summerland, B.C. - 100, 665

Summit Lake - 1052, A2

Superfluities Motion Pictures, Ltd. - A19

Surge Narrows - 863

Surratt, (cinematographer) - 583

Sutherland, Duke and Duchess of - 287

Sutherland, Duncan - 135

Sutherland, Dr. W.H. (Minister of Public Works) - 366, 1050

Swan Lake (near Victoria) - 321

Swan, T.L. - 1048

Swans - 53, 321, 388

swans, trumpeter - 934

Swanzy, Mount - 422

Swartout, Melvin - 852, 1022

Symington, H.J. - 232

SYRENE (yacht) - 223

Tadanac, B.C. - A14

Taghum Bridge - 1020

Takakkaw Falls - 48, 372, 428, 686, 1069

Talbot, Lyle - 973

Tallheo, B.C. - 832

Taylor, A.J.T. - 201

Taylor, D.F. (ed.) - 797

Taylor, Estelle - 16

Taylor, Libby - 527

Taylor, Louis Denison (Mayor of Vancouver) -
   386, 635

Taylor, Phil - 456

tea - 100, 272, 613, 873

Technocracy - 258

telegraphs & telegraph cables - 77, 315, 849

telephones - 435

Telford, Dr. Lyle (Mayor of Vancouver) - 34,
   468, 469, 522, 758, 770, 771, 1053

Telkwa, B.C. - 187

Temple Mountain - 57

Terminal City Gun Club - 624

Terrace, B.C. - 187, 953

Terry, Dr. Kingsley - 101

Thatcher, Les (cinematographer) - 969, 970

theatrical events - 208, 656, 864

Thetis Lake, V.I. - 481, 962, 963

THIEPVAL, H.M.C.S. - 443

THOMAS CROSBY 3RD - 565

THOMAS CROSBY 4TH - 565

Thomas, Jameson - 235, 587

Thomson, Corey (narr.) - 45, 338

Thomson, (cinematographer) - 167

Thomson, F.D. - 772

Thompson Canyon - A51

Thompson, Commodore J.B. - 1004

Thompson, Phyllis - 751

Thompson River - 101, 924, 1029, A51

Thompson, William (cinematographer) - 936

Thompson, William (sheep farmer) - 792

Thornton, Sir Henry - 397, 818

TILLICUMS (tour boat, Ocean Falls) - 57

Tinsley, Theodore - 540, 586

Tisdall, Charles Edward (Mayor of Vancouver)
   - 818, 879

Tofino, B.C. - 462, 964, 1022

Tolan, Eddie - 555, 592, 895

Tolmie, Mount - 362

Tolmie, Dr. Simon Fraser (Premier of B.C.) -
   11, 40, 98, 134, 226, 442, 700, 717, 788,
   1051, 1052

Tondra, (cinematographer) - 704

Tongass Passage - 832

topiary - 147, 177, 453

totem poles - 61, 274, 315, 337, 369, 427,
   588, 604, 785, 832, 863, 899, 900, 925, 929,
   935, 969, 1022, 1052, A2

Totem Tobacco Plantation - 894, 901

tourists - 176, 315, 316, 372, 589, 723, 804,
   939, 978, 984, 990, 996, 1005, 1022, 1039, A22

TOYOOKA MARU, S.S. - 509

tractors - 19, 43, 112, 215, 905, 910, 1024,
   1026

Trafalgar Day celebrations - 552, 906

Trail, B.C. - 7, 99, 101, 893, 907, 908, 909,
   A2, A14

trail riding - 315, 320, 422, 678-699 incl.,
   775, 825, 896, 911, 913, A22

trains - logging - 50, 67, 237, 433, 462, 510,
   531, 554, 560, 857, 893, 948, 1024, 1025, A6,
   A9, A20
   - locomotives - 52, 187, 286, 320, 335, 337,
   663, 701, 759, 903, 915, 916, 991, A6, A10,
   A20, A44
   - model - 881
   - passenger - 2, 4, 5, 17, 20, 34, 101, 132,
   197, 241, 286, 320, 337, 881, 912, 916,
   1024, 1032
   - wrecked - 991
   - freight - See Canadian National Railway
   trains; Canadian Pacific Railway trains;
   Grand Truck Pacific Railway trains & Pacific
   Great Eastern Railway trains.

Tranquille, B.C. - 101, 187

Trans Canada Air Lines - 232, 293, 420, 917,
   1047

Trans Canada Air Pageant - 918, 919

trapping - 344, 407, 893, 921, 922

travelogues - 2, 4, 5, 48, 49, 56, 58, 66, 91,
   97, 99, 100, 101, 103, 117, 119, 122, 149,
   151, 176, 177, 197, 271, 285, 315, 316, 337,
   338, 371, 372, 445, 461, 463, 494, 572, 573,
   589, 606, 620, 653, 724, 792, 826, 871, 884,
   902, 924, 926, 929, 930, 956, 961, 971, 978,
   985, 994, 1020, 1033, 1039, 1054, 1063

Treffry, John - 665

"Trotzky" (bear) - 933

trout fishing - See Fishing

Trumbo, Dalton - 936

Tsatsichknukwomi, B.C. - 863

tuberculosis sanitorium - 101, 187

Tudhope, (pilot) - 232

tugboats - 52, 68, 193, 199, 228, 276, 601,
    612, 848, 893, 936, 948, A11, A12, A13, A15,
    A27, A28

Tupper, Mount - 184, 346

turkeys - 350

Turner, Eugene - 751

Turner, Harold (cinematographer) - 97

Turner, Jim - 439

turtles - 492

Tweedsmuir, Lady - 520, 521, 522

Tweedsmuir Lord - 272, 519, 520, 521, 522

Tweedsmuir Park - A3

Twin Falls - 428, 1069

Twin Sister Mountains - 57

Tyee Club - 304, 776

Tyee Salmon - 304, A13

Uchucklesit Inlet (Barclay Sound) - 50

Ucluelet, B.C. - 604, 964

unemployed - 481, 947, 962, 963, 966, 968

Union Steamship Lines - 192, 832, 863, A5, A14

United Air Lines - 967

United Church of Canada Waterways Missions -
    50, 95, 478, 479, 480, 481, 482, 483, 484,
    565, 964, 965, 980, 1022, 1024, 1026, 1027,
    1071

United Church of Canada Young People's
    Association - 113, 173, 183, 447, 449, 482,
    1071

United States Coast Guard - 223

United States Consul to Vancouver - 125

United States Marines - 285

United States Navy - 116, 120, 221, 223, 281,
    282, 283, 393, 702, 703, 704

Universal Film Mfg. Company - 198

University of British Columbia - 100, 361,
    521, 522, 608, 656, 706, 773, 800, 864,
    937, 941, 942, 943, 971, 976, 1015, 1034,
    1035

University of British Columbia students in
    the militia or the Army - 522, 800, 937, 1035

University of California - 773

University Hill Church, Vancouver - 449

University of Saskatchewan - 1034

University School for Boys, Victoria - 216

Upper Arrow Lake - 101

Urban, Charles - See Charles Urban Trading
    Company, Ltd.

Valican, B.C. - 1020

Van Dyke, S.S. (d.) - 749

Van Horne Range - 636

Vancouver, B. C. - aerial views - 8, 12, 13,
    14, 126, 153, 337, 726b, 917
  - Albany Hotel - 360
  - Armoury - 519, 951
  - Big House Arena - 161
  - Birks Building - 8, A10
  - Brighouse Park Racetrack - 400, 971
  - Brockton Point - 100, 107, 951, 979
  - Burrard Inlet - 151, 189, 726a, 869
  - Burrard Street - 759, 1002
  - Burrard Street Bridge - 726a, 759, A14
  - Cambie Street Bridge - 100
  - Canadian National Railway Station - 34,
    337, 469, 723, 770, 838, 1053
  - CPR Pier "D" fire - 100, 667, 759, 940, A2
  - Canadian Pacific Railway Station - A10
  - Cenotaph on Hastings Street - 8, 175, 417
    518, 519, 951
  - Chinatown - 91
  - churches - 95, 449
  - City Hall - 34, 468, 469, 522, 584, 758,
    759, 770, 1002, 1003, 1053
  - Coal Harbour - 8
  - Confederation Arch - 148
  - Courthouse - 99, 254, 723, 874
  - Devonshire Hotel - 8
  - downtown - 8, 99, 100, 151, 174, 285, 337,
    386, 723, 758, 759, 760, 770, 871, 893, A10
  - Dunbar Street - 955
  - Eaton's - 1012
  - Empire Stadium - 760
  - EMPRESS OF JAPAN original figurehead - A11,
    A12
  - English Bay - 8, 22, 45, 102, 143, 151, 285,
    343, 386, 557, 723, 854, 871, 893, 971, A14
  - exhibitions - 38, 134, 272, 358, 507, 700
  - 50th Anniversary Celebrations - 208, 854,
    957, 958, 960
  - Gastown - 8
  - general views - A26
  - George Vancouver (statue) - 770, 893
  - Georgia Hotel - 8
  - Georgia Street - 8, 100, 151, 174, 759,
    951, A10, A14
  - giant checkers in Stanley Park - 285, 479,
    594, 670
  - grain elevators & grain shipping facilities
    - 13, 64, 142, 152, 199, 275, 339, 353, 359,
    378, 509, 535, 893, 970
  - Granville Street - 8, 99, 151, 174, 254,

360, 723, 968, 1012, A10
- Grouse Mountain - 297, 391, 731, 1049
- Grouse Mountain Chalet - 391
- Harding Memorial - 8, 285, 440, 871
- Hastings Park - 148, 466
- Hastings Street - 8, 151, 550, 723, 968
- hollow tree, Stanley Park - 285
- Hotel Vancouver - 8, 100, 706, 759, 1064
- Hudson's Bay Company store - 8, A10
- Jericho golf course - 711, 924
- Kingsway - 759
- Knight Street - 759
- Lions Gate Bridge - see separate entry
- Lumberman's Arch - 723
- Main Street - 343
- Malkin Bowl - 8
- Marine Building - 8, 100, A10, A14
- Medical Arts Building - 108
- Metropolitan Building - 100
- Orpheum Theatre - 8, 99
- pageants - 159, 431, 464, 550, 854, 880,
  960
- parades - 29, 88, 90, 102, 144, 148, 159,
  166, 175, 254, 272, 285, 343, 464, 507,
  550, 943, 951, 957, 958, 1012, 1036, A10, A41
- Pauline Johnson Memorial - 285, 569
- personalities - 69
- playgrounds - 169, 272, 337, 373, 473, 487,
  622, 669, 845, 879, 1008
- police - 140, 347, 355, 361, 464, 671, 1002
- Post Office - 8, 91, 723, 968
- Post Office sit-down & protest - 91, 968
- Prospect Point - 303, 355, 951
- residential - 8, 446, 723, 760, 1016
- Robert Burns Memorial - 871
- Royal Bank Building - 100
- Sasamat Hill - 822
- Second Beach - 8, 45
- Second Narrows Bridge - 1050
- Siwash Rock - 285, 893
- Stanley Park - 8, 95, 99, 100, 129, 148,
  151, 180, 208, 248, 285, 337, 431, 440,
  465, 479, 523, 524, 550, 569, 594, 624,
  670, 718, 723, 758, 854, 880, 882, 886,
  893, 960, 969, 970, 971, A10
- Stanley Park Zoo - 8, 285, 365, 396, 492,
  539
- streetcars - 8, 144, 151, 201, 219, 285,
  386, 723, 955, A10
- Vancouver Building - 8, 174
- waterfront & docks - 8, 13, 15, 17, 35,
  36, 41, 44, 65, 100, 113, 126, 138, 140,
  141, 142, 151, 152, 193, 199, 221, 264,
  265, 266, 269, 275, 276, 290, 303, 327,
  334, 337, 339, 340, 345, 347, 353, 355,
  359, 374, 375, 377, 385, 387, 393, 396,
  397, 401, 407, 416, 443, 446, 448, 470,
  504, 505, 509, 545, 599, 635, 660, 705,
  706, 733, 758, 759, 770, 771, 838, 849,
  886, 888, 891a, 893, 903, 912, 928, 929,
  940, 951, 970, 971, 1001, 1002, 1009, 1029,
  A2, A10, A11, A12, A13 & 14, A34
- Winch Building - 76
- Windsor United Church - 95

Vancouver, Captain George - 274, 770, 893, 960

Vancouver Club rowing team - 959

Vancouver International Airport - 111, 232,
  726b, 917, 918, 919, 967, 1047

Vancouver Island Horticultural Association - 989

Vancouver Junior Board of Trade - 967

Vancouver Motion Pictures, Ltd. - 60

Vancouver Post Office sit-down & protest -
  91, 968

Vancouver Province (newspaper) - 92

Vancouver "Rips" (rugby team) - 277

Vancouver Skating Club - 751

Vancouver Sun (newspaper) - 542

Vancouver "Westerns" (basketball team) - 972

Vanderhoof, B.C. - 187, 1052

Vannan, Wilson - 602

VENCEDOR, R.V.Y. - 1004

VENTURE, S.S. - 192, 863

Veregin, Peter Dasilivich - 721, 907, A14

Vermillion Range - 581

Vernon, B.C. - 187, 206, 226, 383

veterans - 342, 417, 518, 765, 766, 768, 790,
  976, 992, 997

viaducts - 561

Vice President, Mount - 428

Victoria, B.C. - aerial view - 52, 177, 337
  - Beacon Hill Park - 34, 53, 176, 177, 255,
    261, 337, 445, 468, 469, 758, 762, 763,
    764, 766, 768, 770, 790, 844, 898, 994,
    1053, A10, A26
  - Belleville Street - 764, 898
  - Belmont Building - 149, 176, 177, 763,
    898, 978, 993, A10
  - breakwater - 176, 765, 980
  - buses - 52, 993
  - Camosun College - 52
  - Canadian Pacific Railway docks - 52, 95,
    145, 176, 177, 315, 337, 398, 612, 627,
    978, 984, 993, 996, 997, 998, 1013
  - Capitol Theatre - 716, 799
  - Christ Church Cathedral - 72, 85
  - City Hall - 766, 1003, A10
  - Crystal Gardens - 149, 528
  - Customs House - 149, 545, 980
  - Douglas Street - 177, 812, 1005, A10
  - downtown - 177, 812, 926, 1005, 1013, A10
  - Empire Theatre - 799
  - Empress Hotel - 34, 40, 100, 149, 176,
    177, 193, 315, 443, 468, 469, 762, 763, 764,
    768, 770, 788, 790, 871, 893, 926, 978, 993,
    994, 998, 1053, A10
  - firemen - 452, 922
  - general views - A25, A26
  - German-Canadian Club - 1010
  - the Gorge - 176, 185, 499, 844
  - Gorge Vale Golf Club - 600
  - Government House - 78, 526, 768
  - Government Street - 34, 40, 100, 123, 149,
    176, 177, 762, 763, 764, 768, 770, 830, 898,
    978, 984, 993, 1003, 1053, A10

- Hatley Park - 149
- Hibben Building - 452
- Hudson Bay Company building - 612
- Inner Harbour - 4, 95, 100, 149, 154, 176,
  177, 193, 281, 289, 315, 319, 337, 443,
  468, 510, 517, 612, 627, 758, 762, 763,
  764, 765, 766, 768, 770, 790, 871, 891,
  898, 926, 978, 980, 984, 993, 994, 996,
  997, 998, 1005, A10

- Kaiserhoff Hotel - 1010
- Lansdowne airfield - 52, 993
- Lansdowne racetrack - 145, 146, 987, 991,
  1000
- MacKenzie Avenue - 321
- Marine drive - 994
- Mayor Pendray's topiary garden - 149, 177,
  453
- Moss Street - 149
- Oak Bay - 561, 766, 996, 1005
- Oak Bay Golf Course - 149, 337, 898
- outer wharf - 452, 600, 848
- pageants - 85, 571, 992
- parades - 26, 106, 123, 145, 255, 261,
  319, 436, 437, 452, 468, 540, 571, 650,
  844, 987, 990, 991, 992, 1013, A10
- Parliament Buildings - 34, 40, 92, 106,
  149, 176, 177, 289, 337, 436, 437, 443,
  468, 469, 650, 717, 758, 762, 763, 764,
  765, 768, 770, 788, 790, 844, 871, 898,
  903, 926, 978, 980, 991, 997, 998, 1003,
  1051, 1052
- picnics - 352, 452, 1005
- police - 671, 702, 703, 704, 799, 992, 993,
  996
- Post Office - 149, 176, 764, 993, A10
- Public Library - 52
- Quadra Street - 40
- residential - 149, 176, 177, 926, 978
- Spencer's store - 452
- Strathcona Hotel - 52
- streetcars - 149, 337, 830, 978
- War Memorial - 515, 788
- the willows - 52, 811, 987
- Yates Street - 177, 1013, A10

Victoria, Mount - 807, A22

Victoria and Island Publicity Bureau - 315,
316, 898

Victoria Colonist - 996
- delivery boys - 996

Victoria "Dominoes" (basketball team) - 23

Victoria Golf Club - 176

Victoria High School - 989

Victoria Lumber & Mfg. Company, Ltd. - 560

Victoria Park Jockey Club - 452

Victoria Visitor's Bureau - 996

VICTORY, S.S. - 327

Village Island, B.C. - 191, 192, 863

Vladivostok - 144

VOREDA, S.S. - 733

Waarde, Captain - 154

WAIRUMA, S.S. - 36

Wallace Shipyards, Victoria - 992

Walsh, Sylvia - 1055

Wapta Camp, B.C. - 866

Wapta Falls - 463, 620

Wapta, Mount - A22

Wapta Pass - 48, 463

war memorials - 8, 105, 175, 417, 418, 448,
  496, 515, 516, 517, 518, 519, 523, 545,
  788, 951

Warren, George I. - 315

warships - 63, 101, 116, 120, 133, 138, 140,
  141, 193, 216, 221, 223, 238, 281, 282, 283,
  299, 302, 312, 334, 347, 438, 448, 452, 468,
  469, 510, 702, 703, 704, 730, 758, 770, 790,
  832, 893, 951, 1001, 1009, 1053

WASHINGTON, S.S. - 269

Waterton Lakes National Park, Alberta - 311

Watson, Dr. J.S. (cinematographer) - 298, 588,
  785

Watson, Robert (sc.) - 798, 853, 936

Watson, Sir Norman - 218

weaving - 893

Webb, Barrett - 217

Webb, Bob - 217

Webster, Miss Marilyn - 70

Wedgewood, Mount - 425

weight-lifters - 321

Welcome, B.C. - A38

Wellburn, Gerry (cinematographer) - 1025

Wells, (pilot) - 1063

Wells, B.C. - A2

Wells, E.P.H. - 293

Wells Gray Park - 461

Welsh, Sylvia - 1055

Wepsale, Gertie - 1031

West Coast of Vancouver Island - 50, 77, 95,
  191, 192, 222, 274, 315, 424, 427, 429, 449,
  462, 510, 604, 832, 899, 964, 965, 980, 1022,
  1023, 1024, 1025, 1026, 1027, A2, A5

West Kootenay Power and Light Company - A14

West Vancouver - 1028

Westbank (Okanagan Lake) - 100

Western Canada Air Show - 1030

Western Lumbermen's Convention - 237

WESTERN SPIRIT (fishboat) - 964

Westholme, B.C. - 164

Westland, Jack - 630

whaling - 832, 893, A14, A59

White Pass and Yukon Railroad - 392, 638,
    829, 1072

White Rock, B.C. - 951

White Swan Lake - 212, 679, 681, 683, 685

Whitefoot Studio (cinematographers) - 201

Whitehorse, Yukon - 1072

Whiteman, Cy (cinematographer) - 761

Wyte, Mount - 576

widows - 402

Wilcox Pass - 118

wild cow milking - 680, 684, 688, 696, 698

Wilkinson, Charles - 391

Wilkinson, T. (Vancouver alderman) - 125

Williams Lake, B.C. - 230, 336, 1042, 1052,
    A2

Williams, R.D. - 1004

Willingdon, Lord and Lady (Governor General
    of Canada) - 357, 514, 523, 524, 627, 711,
    886

Willow River, B.C. - A2

Wilson, Blake - 772

Wilson, Frank C. - 586

Wilson, Tom (pioneer) - 652, 911

Windermere, B.C. - 572, 573, 581, A49, A56

Winlaw, B.C. - 1020

Winnington - Ingram, D.D., Rt. Rev. & Rt. Hon. A.F.
    (Bishop of London) - 72, 85

Winnipeg, Manitoba - 293

Withers, Sergeant Walter, R.C.M.P. - 235

Wolf Cubs - 78

Wong, Anna May - 16

Wood, Freddy - 877

Woods, Lotta - 307

Woods, Ray - 726a

Woodstock, B.C. - 187

Woodward, Reggie - 773

Woolrich, Cornell - 202

work camps (during Depression) - 481, 947
    962, 963, 966

Work, Hubert S. - 1009

World War One - aftermath - 105, 175, 342,
    402, 417, 418
    - mobilization - 88, 123, 145, 146, 436,
        437, 800, 836, 837, 838, 997, 1010, 1013,
        1035, A19
    - overseas - 139, 144, 437
    - parades - 88, 123, 145, 146, 436, 437,
        992, 997, 1010, 1013, 1035, A19
    - Siberian intervention - 131, 144

World War Two - mobilization - 121, 138, 299,
    302, 319, 730, 735, 1011, 1012, 1021, 1057,
    A16
    - training - 121, 299, 728, 730, 735, 1021,
        A16

Worthington, G.H. (Vancouver alderman) - 18

Wren, Charles - 1064

Wright, Basil (asst.-d.) - 199

Wright, Mrs. F. - 391

Wright, Padre J.H. - 236

Wyckoff, Tom (?) (sprinter) - 895

Wyndel, B.C. - 1020

yachts - 143, 223, 566, 629, 654, 863, 1004,
    1067, 1068

Yale, B.C. - 333, 841, A2, A52, A53

Yarrows Shipyard - 495, A15

Yoho National Park - 48, 96, 118, 150, 182,
    317, 372, 428, 595, 911, 1069, 1070

Yoho Valley - 317, 428, 1069, 1070

York, Duke and Duchess of - 757

York, G.A. (cinematographer) - 1006

Young Men's-Young Women's Christian Association
    (YM-YWCA) - 129

Young's Studio, Victoria - 9, 78, 130, 154,
    456, 517, 817, 848, 1063, 1065, 1066

Young, W.B. (cinematographer) - 9, 78, 130,
    154, 456, 515, 516, 517, 817, 848, 1063,
    1065, 1066

Yuculta Rapids - 411, 863

Yukon Regiment - A19

Yukon River - 364, 1072

Yukon Territory - 110, 200, 212, 392, 419,
  498, 562, 583, 638, 741, 754, 829, 868,
  1010, 1014, 1018, 1072

ADDENDA

Bonnington Dam - 1020, A14

Desbaillets, Jacques - A57

Lloyd, Frank (d) - 1046

PAT, M.V. (U.C.C. Mission Boat) - 483, 484